Philosophy:
Paradox and Discovery

Philosophy: Paradox and Discovery

THIRD EDITION

Arthur J. Minton

Thomas A. Shipka
Youngstown State University

McGraw-Hill Publishing Company
New York St. Louis San Francisco Auckland Bogotá Caracas
Hamburg Lisbon London Madrid Mexico Milan Montreal New Delhi
Oklahoma City Paris San Juan São Paulo Singapore Sydney Tokyo Toronto

Philosophy: Paradox and Discovery

234567890 HALHAL 99876543210

ISBN 0-07-042432-2

This book was set in Palatino by the College Composition Unit in cooperation with Black Dot, Inc.
The editors were Judith R. Cornwell and Susan Gamer;
the production supervisor was Janelle S. Travers.
The cover was designed by Carla Bauer.
Arcata Graphics/Halliday was printer and binder.

Library of Congress Cataloging-in-Publication Data

Philosophy: paradox and discovery/[edited by] Arthur J. Minton,
    Thomas A. Shipka.—3rd ed.
        p.   cm.
    Bibliography: p.
    Includes index.
    ISBN 0-07-042432-2
    1. Philosophy.   2. Ethics.   3. Political science—Philosophy.
    I. Minton, Arthur J., (date).   II. Shipka, Thomas A.
    B29.P5256   1990
    100—dc20   89-36093

To Chris and Scott

To Kate, Anne Louise, and Andrew

To the students of
Youngstown State University—
past, present, and future

CONTENTS

CHAPTER 6
Truth

PART THREE
FREE WILL AND DETERMINISM

CHAPTER 7
Choice: From Chance to Compulsion

CHAPTER 8
Moral Responsibility in a Determined World

PART FOUR
MORALITY

CHAPTER 9
Sources of Morality:
God, Society, and the Individual

CHAPTER 10
The Search for Objectivity:
Classicial Ethical Theories

PART FIVE
POLITICAL PHILOSOPHY

CHAPTER 11
The State and the Individual

CHAPTER 12
Classical Political Theories:
Dictatorship, Democracy, and Communism

PREFACE

This collection of readings in philosophy was assembled after an extensive survey of teachers across the country indicated a widespread dissatisfaction with traditional texts, as well as with more recent texts which emphasize "relevance." A great many instructors indicated the need for a text that speaks to the beginning student without sacrificing the hard-won insights of the past. The fundamental questions of philosophy are "relevant" in the highest sense of that much-abused word, for the simple fact is that most great philosophers theorized to solve some pressing moral and intellectual concern. From Plato to Marx, the history of the world has moved from the pressure of their pens.

Since the task of philosophy is to examine life, to tear down the comfortable barriers of dogma which prevent us from growth, the teacher of philosophy must always keep a finger on the pulse of immediate experience. But, at the same time, philosophy builds where it destroys, and this constructive task demands that the connection between first principles and the world of the here and now be made explicit. It is not enough to mix a few of the classics with articles dealing with contemporary concerns, praying that the connection will be made. In this text a different approach has been tried. First, every effort has been made to ensure that the readings deal with issues of fundamental concern. Selections that supplement one another, building together to create complexity and rigor, were chosen over more extensive, but technical, writing. Whenever possible, thinkers of unusual clarity and style were selected. Second, selections which make a clear connection between theory and practice are included in every part. In addition, the readings are integrated so that selections in one part supplement those in another. Robert Paul Wolff's defense of anarchism, for example, is founded on Kant's ethics, and the two may be read together. Mark Twain's devastating attack on traditional religion can be productively read with Clarence Darrow's defense of Leopold and Loeb, and John Hick's rebuttal to Twain is nicely supplemented by Peter Bertocci's defense of free will. There are many interesting combinations that allow the instructor to show how different areas of experience fit together to form a unified system of thought.

ORGANIZATION

As the table of contents illustrates,

- The text is divided into five major parts, each beginning with a short essay designed to confront the student with the paradoxes inherent in this general area of experience.
- Within each part, every chapter takes up a specific problem area, introduced by an essay that furnishes the unifying historical and conceptual thread between the readings. These problem introductions avoid technical language as much as possible, for two reasons: (1) many instructors have individual classification systems; and (2) an abundance of technical terms in introductory material can be counterproductive pedagogically.
- Each reading within a chapter is preceded by a critical headnote providing a brief biography of its author as well as a hint of the major ideas presented in the selection. The headnotes are designed to arouse the reader's interest and to suggest questions for reflection, so that reading the selection will be undertaken more critically.
- Each reading is followed by a series of study questions designed both to aid the student in locating and understanding the main ideas of the reading, and to stimulate reflection on these ideas and their implications. The questions do more than force the student to review the reading—they also focus attention on new avenues of inquiry.

NEW TO THIS EDITION

We believe that this third edition is improved as well as revised. We have applied the same criteria that governed selection of materials in the previous two editions. However, we have made a special effort to select readings that are likely to stimulate discussion of basic philosophical issues both in and out of class. "Doing philosophy" requires dialogue and active participation, not merely careful listening. Not surprisingly, a recent study of students' evaluation of philosophy courses and instructors shows that students want and expect an opportunity for class discussion.*

David Stewart's ingenious essay "The Philosopher as Detective," which appears in print for the first time, will help students better answer the Introduction's question: What is philosophy? In Part One, **Philosophy of Religion,** this edition has a new third chapter, "Faith and Reason." In addition to the essays by Stace and Scriven, retained from the second edition, you will find the pragmatic justification for believing in God by William James, the great American pragmatist; and an overview of humanism, an alternative to theism, by Corliss Lamont, a long-time spokesperson for American humanism. There is also a new selection in the second chapter: J. L. Mackie's "Evil and Omnipotence."

* Lee C. Rice, "Student Evaluation of Teaching: Problems and Prospects," *Teaching Philosophy,* Volume II, Number 4, December 1988, pp. 329–344.)

In Part Two, **Knowledge**, a chapter from George Johnson's *Machinery of the Mind* gives the mind-body debate new currency.

In this edition, **Free Will and Determinism** appears as Part Three, and **Morality** appears as Part Four—the reverse of the previous edition. The reason for this is that if human choice is not free, then discussion of morality, in the view of many, is pointless. If I cannot avoid doing what I do, why consider me blameworthy or praiseworthy? Except for this transposition, however, Free Will and Determinism is unchanged.

In Part Four, **Morality**, there are two exceptional additions. One is a feminist essay by Jane Caputi, an award-winning author from the University of New Mexico, that delivers a powerful indictment of modern mass communication as a preserver of sexism. The other is an elegant, balanced critique of cultural relativism by James Rachels.

In Part Five, **Political Philosophy**, there are two new articles. Martin Luther King's "Letter from Birmingham Jail" gives a justification of morally grounded resistance to law, and Carl Cohen's essay from his *Four Systems* argues, against philosophical anarchism, that autonomy and authority are compatible.

You will find new study questions for some readings, and increased bibliographic material in every section. For the first time, an Instructor's Manual is available to aid instructors with developing teaching strategies, presenting material in class, selecting the right mix of readings, preparing examinations and assignments, using films and videotapes to increase students' interest and learning, and fostering class discussion.

ACKNOWLEDGMENTS

Over the years this book has profited from the help of many persons. They include users of the book and the publisher's reviewers, who have once again given solid advice to make the book more useful to instructors and students. For their help with this edition, we would like to thank Jeffrey Barker, Albright College; Richard Glidewell, Fitchburg State College; John McKenney, Community College of Philadelphia; Gunnulf Myrbo, Pacific Lutheran University; James Treanor, Southwest Texas State University; Paul de Vries, Wheaton College; and Edward Walter, University of Missouri, Kansas City. Thanks also to the faculty members in the Department of Philosophy and Religious Studies at Youngstown State University, especially Christopher Bache, James Dale, Brendan Minogue, Charles Reid, J-C. Smith, L. J. Tessier, and Victor Wan-Tatah. As in the past, the staff at McGraw-Hill proved to be highly competent, thorough, and cooperative. Special thanks are due to Phillip Butcher, Judith Cornwell, and Susan Gamer for their important roles in producing the third edition. Publishers and authors, as in the past, have been most cooperative in granting permissions for reprinting copyright material. To all these persons, we express our gratitude. Finally, we acknowledge the valuable support which the University Research Council of Youngstown State University has provided for preparation of this edition.

Arthur J. Minton

Thomas A. Shipka

Philosophy:
Paradox and Discovery

Introduction

WHAT IS PHILOSOPHY?

Philosophy, like other studies, aims at knowledge. But philosophers seek a special sort of knowledge that eludes exact definition. The word "philosophy" comes from the Greek *philein*, "to love or desire," and *sophia*, "wisdom." The philosopher, then, is a "lover of wisdom." Wisdom is knowledge in its broadest sense. It does not concern things that huddle on the periphery of life. It is knowledge directed to the fundamental and pervasive concerns of existence. To desire wisdom is to seek principles that cut through the superficial and trivial facts that clutter our intellectual landscape, revealing the basic shape of things beneath. Philosophy, as a quest for wisdom, is an attempt to provide a vision of the world that is systematic and clear, in which the connections between significant facts are made manifest. It is the search for first things and last things—for first principles and their ultimate implications.

We all become philosophers at crucial points in life. We go at the painful task of living with a set of beliefs—faiths, if you will—that organize the helter-skelter of experience into a more or less systematic and coherent whole. From culture, class, religion, and family we are provided with a general framework, a world view, that filters out the unimportant and impregnates experience with meaning. This framework of beliefs and values is largely unconscious and inarticulate; and when it smashes against the hard rock of reality, the dilemma we feel, but do not yet understand, kindles philosophical reflection. As our personal relationships become more complicated, youthful optimism about human nature is tempered by disappointment and hurt. As more and more is demanded of us and we begin to see flaws in ourselves, the infinite horizon of opportunity shrinks in the face of our limitations. As we see ourselves and others repeating the same errors, playing out the same roles, we begin to wonder whether society and nature have conspired to lock us into a mechanical mode of reaction impossible to resist. As we grow conscious of the enormous

1

amount of suffering and anguish in the world, seeing at first hand the vast waste of human life, the old easy answers about a good and loving God are shattered. As we face wholesale changes in the behavior of society, each decade overthrowing the values of the last, we cannot help wondering whether our own commitments will stand the test of time or even whether such commitments are more than subjective whims that we have elevated to first principles. At such times we lose our way in the world and we ask, "What am I about?" This is philosophical territory.

Traditionally, philosophy has been partitioned into three areas: epistemology, metaphysics, and value theory. *Epistemology* is the theory of knowledge. The following are typical epistemological questions: What is scientific method? What is the role of observation in knowing? Can there be absolute certainty about anything? What is an explanation? What is a proof? *Metaphysics* is concerned with the description of the fundamental aspects of reality. These are typical metaphysical questions: What is mind? Is it different from matter? Is there necessity in nature? Is there necessity in human decision? Does God exist? Are numbers real? Which is basic—force or matter? *Value theory* consists in resolving a number of problems about the nature of value in art, ethics, and politics: What makes something beautiful? Is it taste or an objective property? What makes something good? Again, is personal morality subjective or can it be assessed by an absolute standard? When should I disregard my own interests, if at all? What makes one political system better than another? Should I always obey the law? What makes someone into a moral authority? As you can see, sometimes philosophical inquiry becomes lofty and abstract; but even the most abstract theorizing is generated in a practical dilemma and will eventually come back to illuminate its beginnings. The philosophical perspective is ever the human perspective.

But the human perspective is limited. No one can scan the entire horizon of human concern with the eye of a god. We see the world from where we stand, and partial vision yields only partial truth. To recognize this fact, however, is not to counsel inaction, indecision, or despair. Nor is it to fall back on the comfortable but wholly fallacious assumption that since no one has all the answers, everyone's opinion is equally valid. The recognition of fallibility is simply an acknowledgment of our humanity. We have to get on in this world, and either we entrust our course to intellect and whatever insight we can muster or we flounder and take our chances with fate. There are no other alternatives. The basic assumption of philosophical inquiry is that the most intractable puzzles of life—no matter how large— will ultimately give way to rational analysis. But before this can happen, we must develop, as carefully as we can, our own vision of things. Lived experience is the testing ground for these partial insights. The experience of one individual or even of a generation may not be sufficient; but eventually what is true in our outlook will enlarge our understanding of the world and open it up to our command, while what is false will lead us to confusion and frustration.

THE SEARCH FOR BEDROCK: PARADOX

Philosophical thought usually begins when the world does not behave as we thought it must. In frustration, the wise person takes stock. "Know thyself" is the first injunction of philosophy, for until we appreciate the extent to which self colors experience with its own loyalties, infuses it with its inarticulate commitments, we cannot enjoy the flexibility of action and purpose that is the mark of true freedom. Many people believe that the mind is like a sponge, soaking up facts which then present themselves on the stage of consciousness in all their pristine reality. The mind, according to this view, is simply a receptacle which does not alter or transform what flows into it. This conception of the "passivity" of intellect is perhaps the greatest barrier to philosophical thinking. Philosophers are constantly reminding us that we are the active shapers of experience, investing it with meaning from a hidden fund of presuppositions, mostly submerged beneath consciousness like the great mass of an iceberg beneath the water. The first task of philosophy is to bring these presuppositions to consciousness—to remind us that the sense of obviousness accompanying certain facts has been contributed by ourselves. An example will make this clearer.

When surgical techniques allowed for the safe removal of cataracts, people who had been afflicted with this condition since birth were able to see for the first time. It is tempting to think that upon opening their eyes, they experienced the beautiful and familiar world of vision—a world of form and color, of public objects in a public space. But this does not occur. The patient is immediately confronted with a wall of brightness containing color patches that blend indistinguishably into one another. The flood of sensations is absolutely meaningless. There is no awareness of shape or size, nor any idea of distance. In fact, some patients report the impression that the swirl of color is touching their eyes. Familiar shapes, such as squares and triangles, which are easily identified by touch, are unrecognized in the visual array. One investigator writes:

> The newly-operated patients do not localize their visual impressions; they do not relate them to any point, either to the eye or to any surface, even a spherical one; they see colors much as we smell an odor of peat or varnish, which enfolds and intrudes upon us, but without occupying any specific form of extension in a more exactly definable way.*

* This quotation and all following quotations are taken from Marius Von Senden, *Space and Sight* (New York: Free Press, 1960). This remarkable book is a collection of case histories of persons who acquired sight for the first time through surgery or by spontaneous remission.

Gradually, the newly sighted learn that the color patches represent objects at a distance. They discover that they can move through the field of color, that the colors move to the edge of the visual field as they walk, and that no matter how they turn their bodies, the visual swirl surrounds them. Slowly, they begin to apprehend that there are things behind them and in front of them, but their conception of the spatial world is woefully inadequate. About his patient, one doctor wrote:

> I have found in her no notion of size, for example, not even within the narrow limits she might have encompassed with the aid of touch. Thus when I asked her to show me how big her mother was, she did not stretch out her hands, but set her two index fingers apart.

Another physician reported similar effects in his patients:

> Those who are blind from birth have no real conception of distance. A house that is a mile away is thought of as nearby, but requiring the taking of a lot of steps.

Only after long and painful experience do the patients come to have an idea of objective space. At first, only things extremely close are seen in depth, while objects at a distance remain parts of a flat wall of sensation where everything ends. Here one object moving in front of another is seen as two color patches melding into one another. When a newly sighted girl first saw photographs and paintings, she asked: "Why do they put those dark marks all over them?" "Those aren't dark marks," her mother responded, "those are shadows;...if it were not for shadows, many things would look flat." The girl answered: "Well, that's how things do look. Everything looks flat with dark patches." With time, however, the world begins to assume depth and the flat curtain of color recedes into the background.

   The mental effort involved in learning to see is enormous. Without mental exertion, experimentation, and training, the bright wall of sensation remains a dazzling, incoherent barrier. Sometimes the task proves too much for adults who have spent their lifetime relying on other senses, and they relapse into their old habits. A doctor writes about his twenty-one-year-old patient:

> Her unfortunate father, who had hoped for so much from this operation, wrote that his daughter carefully shuts her eyes whenever she wishes to go about the house, especially when she comes to a staircase, and that she is never happier and more at ease than when, by closing her eyelids, she relapses into her former state of total blindness.

For the first time these people are struck by the tremendous size of the world, and they are oppressed by their own insignificance. They become aware of the fact that they have been visible to others all along, and they feel it as an intrusion into their privacy. Their emotional and mental lives are shaken to the very core.

The newly sighted undergo experiences which those of us born with vision toiled through in infancy and have long since forgotten. Long ago the flat wall of sensation fragmented into objects that zoomed away into space, and now it is almost impossible for us to regard our visual field as a blur of color patches. Our perceptual skills have become so routine and automatic that they give the illusion of naturalness, like the technique of an accomplished musician. We tend to forget that what is now easy was once painfully difficult. The experience of the blind in coping with their newfound sense of vision illustrates that even in the most elementary perception, reason and judgment are at work, albeit in dim and forgotten ways. The world that presents itself to our eyes—the world of three-dimensional objects in a public space—is as much a result of thought as of pure sensation. How much more thought and assumption, then, must lie half-hidden beneath our explicit beliefs about morality, science, politics, religion, and the other great topics of human concern. Philosophy is an attempt to ferret out the most significant of these, to bring them into the bright light of awareness, and, if possible, to submit them to critical appraisal.

Socrates was the greatest practitioner of this analytical search for fundamental assumptions. Walking through the streets of ancient Athens, he would buttonhole the powerful men of his time, asking them irreverent questions about their opinions. To those who pretended to know about justice, he quietly asked, *tò tí*—what is it? What do you mean by justice and right and goodness? Don't just give me a list of those things which possess these qualities, but tell me the essence of the idea. Define your terms. What is virtue, morality, knowledge? What do you mean by *yourself*, your soul, your mind? By skillful questioning, Socrates would pry into depths of one's system of beliefs, dragging out cherished certainties and displaying their ragged clothing. This demand for clarity of thought and exactness of definition left his victims confused and reeling. After being questioned, poor Euthyphro confesses: "I do not know, Socrates, how to express what I mean. For somehow or other our arguments, on whatever ground we rest them, seem to turn around and walk away from us."

Socrates had asked Euthyphro to define piety, and then showed, through a series of deductions, that his definition was in serious conflict with other things he believed. He was trying to make him feel a paradox in those beliefs and values which, on their face, were so familiar and obvious. Piety, Euthyphro says, is whatever is pleasing to the gods. "Do the gods love piety in and of itself?" Socrates asks. "Of course," his victim replies. If this is so, Socrates retorts, then the gods must love piety because it is pleasing to them—an absurd conclusion. Euthyphro is staggered: "Come again...how was that?" This sort of procedure is analytic in nature. By bringing out the paradoxical in the familiar, our attention is forced inward, to our system of definitions, to the conceptual paths we have made for ourselves in the world. The confusion we feel is that of a traveler who has used a road daily in one direction and now for the first time must travel the opposite way. The old landmarks are alien, the curves and hills are not where they are supposed to be, the terrain is confusing. Philosophy is an adventure into the commonplace. It is the human mind become conscious of itself and its contribution to what is known.

THE SEARCH FOR SYSTEM: DISCOVERY

The search for hidden assumptions and fundamental premises is actually part of a larger enterprise. In the end, a philosophy should present us with a unified vision of the world and of our place in it. It is impossible, however, to identify and evaluate the bedrock of our belief system without uncovering the relations, however vague, among basic beliefs. Perhaps another analogy from the study of vision will illustrate this point. Ordinary perceptual experience leads us to believe that our visual image is sharp and clear at any one time, like the image on a photograph. In fact, however, the greatest part of the visual field is a blur. Only about a one-thousandth part of the visual field—the part isolated by a focal area of 4 degrees out of a total of 180 degrees—is presented to consciousness with real clarity. The rest seems sharp and clear because the eye is constantly moving, summing up these focal areas in a fraction of a second to create a larger area of clarity. Stop the motion of the eye and concentrate on one word. You will notice how this small circle of clarity recedes into an expanse of vagueness and haze. Experiments have shown that when the eye is completely immobilized (it takes a machine to do it), the visual image fragments and disappears. Exploration is the *sine qua non*, the indispensable condition, of clear vision.

Mental clarity is not unlike visual clarity. When we try to fasten onto a concept, to hold it fixed in the light of awareness, it tends to disintegrate into meaninglessness. "Every definite image in the mind," wrote William James, "is steeped and dyed in the free water that flows around it. With it goes the sense of its relations, near and remote, the dying echo of whence it came to us, the dawning sense of whither it is to lead. The significance, the value of the image, is all in this halo or penumbra that surrounds and escorts it." To see our beliefs clearly, we must scan our mental field to discover the ways an idea interacts with its surroundings. What a person does with a concept in his or her total intellectual framework is a better clue to understanding what it means than the most exacting definition.

Paradox and discovery are two sides of the same coin. Things seem paradoxical when two firmly established beliefs which have been kept apart and allowed to function in their own domains are brought side by side and seen to be inconsistent. Until then we really do not know what we believe, for usually our assumptions are nebulous and vague. We sharpen them by experimentation—by examining the effect they have on other areas of experience. What are your religious beliefs? How do you reconcile God's goodness with the creation of people who God knows will be responsible for the suffering of millions of innocents? How do you justify Hitler, Stalin, Genghis Khan, Nero, etc.? You say that they have free will and are therefore responsible for what they do. But, then, how can free will exist in light of the findings of science? Physical processes flow inevitably from their antecedent conditions. There are no alternatives. But we are not physical, you say. We possess a soul, a nonmaterial essence that escapes the rigid fatalism of matter. What is your evidence for this? And so it goes. We shall not find systematic answers to such questions lying within us, ready to spring to light when we need them. Instead, we will have a vague feeling of where we are, and we may discover that there are cracks in our belief system that cannot be repaired. Philosophical discovery is not merely clarifying what was already fully there but hidden; it is also growth.

PHILOSOPHY AND SCIENCE

Philosophy, it seems, is speculation about matters that can have no final answers. Religion, morality, the existence of the soul, free will, the ultimate structure of the world—such issues cannot be treated with precision. Science, on the other hand, presents us with a definite method, a down-to-earth approach to things. We may have to settle for less, but at least we shall know what we have got.

Is there a yawning gap between science and philosophy? In order to answer this question, we should look briefly at the dawn of modern science.

In the thirteenth century, Christian Europe rediscovered the learning of antiquity which had been lost during the Middle Ages. This vast wealth of information had to be merged with the Christian tradition, for as a system of knowledge it was far superior to anything then known. The greatest name in Greek science was that of Aristotle, whose work systematized physics, astronomy, biology, and psychology.

Things in nature, Aristotle held, are a composite of two factors—form and matter. Matter is the raw material, form the structure. To know what a thing is, one must know both of these aspects: What is it made of? What is its form? The key to understanding the form of a thing is its *telos*—the goal or end toward which it moves. Everything in nature is directed by an inner force to a specific fulfillment. To know what an acorn is, for example, is to know that it will grow into a certain sort of tree. From common observation, Aristotle reasoned that the *telos* of matter is rest. Roll a ball, throw a stone, shoot an arrow, row a boat—all these experiences confirm it: matter naturally seeks a state of rest. Pick up a stone and feel it resist being moved. The pressure you feel against your hand, its weight, is a manifestation of an inner drive to move back to earth, its natural place of rest.

This reasoning, however, produces a problem. Matter, if left alone, should seek out its place of rest and remain there. The world should be static and dead. Why hasn't this occurred? Something must be actively interfering with the elements, Aristotle thought, to keep them in motion. Looking to the heavens, he saw the stars moving in circular paths around the earth. Here was the force needed to account for activity and change in dead matter. The heavenly spheres must communicate some of their motion by friction to the world below. But this explanation meant that if the stars continued to move forever, they were not made of ordinary matter. Indeed, they were perfect, incorruptible bodies. Eternal circular motion was perfect motion, and the stars, following the urging of their special *telos*, were striving for perfection.

Aristotle's physics and astronomy merged with Christianity in the thirteenth century to produce a world view that was at once commonsensical and profound. Although Christian thinkers continued to regard the stars and planets as perfect, the suggestion that they moved themselves in a celestial struggle for perfection smacked too much of ancient polytheism. The heavenly bodies, like ordinary matter, required an external force to keep them in motion. Whatever such a force was, it could not be material, for then it would need a further force to move it, *ad infinitum*. God was the logical solution. God was the wind in the sails of the universe, actively moving the heavenly spheres around the center of creation. This was the element that the Christian tradition needed for intellectual completion. Here was physical proof for the existence of God. Henceforth no scientific person could doubt the religious vision of the world. Astronomy, physics, and religion were molded into a unified system of explanation.

By the sixteenth century, however, this world view had become ungainly. In order to account for the erratic movements of the planets—called "wandering stars"—the original system of eight concentric spheres had evolved into an enormously complicated and cumbersome tangle of movements. The orbits of the planets were practically unimaginable. Each planet moved in a small circle, like a horse on a merry-go-round, the center of which was attached to the periphery of a larger circle with the earth in the middle. Yet the planets did not move in their little circles around the earth, but about a point slightly off center. To the mathematical minds of the period, such a loping cosmic circus seemed unworthy of the divine intellect. But in spite of these inelegant complications, Aristotle's astronomy remained the preferred view because it rested on concepts that were in agreement with observation and common sense. Observation suggests that the earth is a steady platform around which the heavens move in large arcing paths. Common sense tells us a thousand times a day that a moving object will come to rest unless a continuous force is applied to it. These commonplaces were the cornerstones of Aristotle's science, and before a new vision of the world could hope to stand, they would have to be destroyed.

The year 1543 marked the publication by Nicholas Copernicus of *On the Revolutions of the Celestial Spheres.* In this book he theorized that the earth and the rest of the planets moved in circular orbits around the sun. In order to account for the apparent movement of the sun across the sky each day, he suggested that the earth rotates on its axis once each twenty-four hours. The simplicity of this account appealed to many scientists, but it faced what appeared to be insurmountable obstacles. If the earth were rotating on its axis at the required rate, its surface at the equator would be moving at great speeds. An object thrown high into the air would not land in the same spot. Birds would not be able to fly in the direction of rotation, for they would be constantly falling behind the speeding ground beneath them. Besides, at such velocities, objects would be thrown away from the surface of the earth like stones flung from a sling. These objections strike us today as absurd, but only because we have become accustomed to the concept of inertia. In the sixteenth century, they were irrefutable.

At the beginning of the seventeenth century, Galileo Galilei was a professor of mathematics at the University of Padua. Early in his career he had realized that Aristotle's science could not explain the flight of a cannonball. The cannonball continues to fly through space when there are no apparent forces acting on it to keep it in motion. Most scientists, unable to surmount their theoretical assumptions, invented invisible forces to account for this kind of case. Some said that the air behind the ball continued to push it along, and as this force died, the ball fell to earth. But to Galileo, such explanations seemed to be born of desperation. Besides, God was a mathematician, he believed, and could not have made the universe as inelegant as depicted in Aristotle's astronomy. And so Galileo became a Copernican, while continuing to teach the old astronomy. Later, in 1632, he would publish *Dialogues on the Two Chief World Systems,* which would ring the death knell for Aristotle's system.

The experiments in 1604 which led to this dramatic outcome seemed innocuous enough at first glance. Galileo had already proven that the velocity acquired by a freely falling body was not proportional to its weight. Now he was seeking to establish a lawful relation between velocity and time. Lacking an accurate timepiece, he had to "slow down" a falling object in order to measure the relation between distance traversed and time elapsed. To accomplish this, he rolled smooth brass balls down an inclined plane on the assumption that the velocity achieved is due to the vertical factor alone. In this way he discovered that the distance traversed is proportional to the square of the elapsed time. No matter what the degree of the slope, this relation remained constant. Since the final velocity of a ball rolled down an inclined plane is due to the vertical factor alone, it can be assumed that it will acquire enough force to roll up a similar plane to its original height, no matter what the slope of the plane. Of course, Galileo's brass balls rolling down grooves lined with polished parchment did not roll back to exactly the height from which they began. He surmised that this was due to the friction of the plane. He then imagined a ball rolling down the grooved incline onto a plane tilted by the minutest fraction of a degree. What would happen? All of his experiments implied that the ball would roll up the plane until it had achieved its original height, even if this meant that it had to traverse a vast distance to do so. But what if it rolled onto a horizontal *frictionless* plane? Here Galileo made a dramatic intellectual leap: the horizontal plane is simply an incline of 0 degrees. The ball should roll over an infinite distance. A moving object, then, does not come to rest because its *telos* demands it. It comes to rest because a force, such as friction, impedes its continued motion. This is the principle of inertia.

The principle of inertia turns Aristotle's common sense on its head. A body in motion will continue in motion—a rock thrown up from the surface of the moving earth will retain whatever velocity the earth imparts to it, falling back to exactly the same spot. The centuries-old arguments against a moving earth were now shown to be bankrupt. The active, moving universe no longer required God as the force to sustain its motion. With the publication of these new ideas, the Church saw Galileo and his new science as dangerous enemies of religion. Six months after its printing, *Dialogues* was banned. Galileo was called to Rome and threatened with torture. At almost seventy years of age, he recanted, in abject terms, his defense of Copernicus. Legend has it that at the end of his recantation he muttered beneath his breath *Eppur si muove* ("it still moves"). But this is mere legend. Galileo had been broken, and he died in 1642, blind and under house arrest.

This episode from the history of science shows clearly that science and philosophy do not tread different paths.

In its fundamental aspect, Galileo's defense of Copernicus was a philosophical enterprise. Aristotle's system had reigned for so long that what had originally begun as speculation had hardened into intuition. The concepts of *weight, force,* and *motion* rested on assumptions so deeply ingrained in habits of mind that they seemed to define the limits of thought itself. To see the world afresh, Galileo had to turn his attention to the concepts which organized experience. Every major advance in science reiterates this theme. Faraday had to think of the magnetic field as an object just as real as the gross visible magnet. In so doing he revised our conception of matter. Einstein had to imagine that clocks are not equivalent in different frames of reference. Our idea of time as flowing uniformly throughout the universe was the victim. At the frontiers of knowledge, there is no authority, no tested method, no formula to apply which will churn out the answers. Instead there is a breakdown in the usual ways of thinking. This too is philosophical territory.

The scientific image of the world affects every corner of human experience. Galileo's work began a revolution in thinking which spread out from physics to the entire conception of human knowledge. Here was a new way of explaining things—a way which ignored tradition and authority, which made no reference to purposes and goals in nature, which represented the physical world as a mechanism moving according to its own law, not enmeshed with a spiritual force that guides it. It gave rise to a new temperament, a new faith in the power of reason to reveal the structure of things. It placed new demands on political thought, ethics, religion, and psychology to establish their credentials on a similar empirical basis.

In the end, there is no hard-and-fast distinction between philosophy and science. A philosophy worth its salt will find a place within itself for the successes of science. Conversely, science, as we know it, rests on unchallenged assumptions which deserve philosophical analysis. If there is a conflict between science and philosophy, it is not between two bodies of truth; it is an internal conflict within human experience as the mind struggles to form a comprehensive picture of the whole while the pieces in the puzzle continue to change.

VALUE OF PHILOSOPHY

Philosophy is valuable in itself. This is not to say that philosophical reflection is the whole end of living, but merely that such activity is an essential part of happiness. Happiness is growth. It is the expansion and refinement of those powers and drives that make us distinctly human. Since curiosity is one expression of those essential human capabilities, philosophical reflection is an important part of self-fulfillment. Imagine, if you can, a society in which philosophical thought is prohibited. You are not permitted to wonder about the foundations of morality, or to discuss theology. You cannot question the fundamental assumptions of the sciences, and you are not allowed to connect the scientific image of humanity with the usual questions about the meaning of life, the existence of the soul, the possibility of human freedom, etc. Can you imagine that every important need of the human personality has been met in such a world? Hasn't something fundamental been left out? If we acknowledge that human beings have a drive to know, to explore, to connect and analyze, then by refusing to allow philosophical reflection, we would be refusing an intelligent nature its highest logical outcome. It is like saying to an athlete: "You may run, but you may not strain." Strain, however, is the only way to growth, and philosophical thought is the mind straining to understand itself and its place in the scheme of things.

The value of philosophy does not lie exclusively in the answers it gives. There is no systematic body of knowledge called "philosophy." There are, instead, people trying to think systematically about the fundamental questions of life. The great thinkers of the past differed in their conclusions, and those of today are no better off. But this is to be expected in an undertaking so grand, so final, and so audacious. The most enduring value of philosophy lies in the habit of mind it breeds in those who have discovered its pleasures. It produces a vision of things large enough to generate a life plan, a direction, tempered by the nagging suspicion that the vision may be an illusion. Philosophic thought, the exhilarating experience of paradox and discovery, is the first step toward a civilized faith.

The Philosopher as Detective
David Stewart

David Stewart (1938-   ) is professor of philosophy at Ohio University,
author of several successful philosophy textbooks, and a specialist in the
philosophy of religion.

In this essay, published here for the first time, Professor Stewart finds
important parallels between what detectives do and what philosophers do.
Like the detective, the philosopher is a seeker of truth. In the quest for truth,
detectives and philosophers think logically about the facts of their experience.
They try to solve mysteries, to find meaning in what first appears to be
meaningless, to make sense out of the world. Both construct hypotheses—
trial solutions, explanations, or theories—which fit the known facts. Further,
Stewart tells us, they should abandon a hypothesis when the facts no longer
support it, but not before.

As you read this essay, pay special attention to important assumptions
which detectives make: that it is possible to learn the truth; that human
beings are responsible for their actions and deserve punishment for
wrongdoing; and that there is a clear and uniform distinction between right
(good) and wrong (evil). In the pages which follow, you will find that these
assumptions are highly controversial and a source of dispute among
philosophers.

What attracts me to detective fiction is also what attracts me to philosophy:
dependence on reason, the search for moral order, the development of analytical skills, the desire to find things out. In no other kind of literature does
reason and reason's tool—logical analysis—figure as prominently as it does in
detective fiction. John Cawelti, a noted authority on popular culture, in a well-
turned phrase, observes that "the classical detective formula is perhaps the
most effective fictional structure yet devised for creating the illusion of rational
control over the mysteries of life."

Those of us who teach courses involving detective fiction have to face the
fact that most academic courses deal mainly with "serious" literature and that
most people are ambivalent toward mystery stories. Nevertheless, I want to
make the case for viewing mysteries as dealing with serious themes, and to
argue that detective fiction provides an entrée into important philosophical
issues.

Scholarly opinion is virtually united, to the extent that scholarly opinion
is ever united, on the view that, in spite of the fact that it flourished in Britain
(especially between the two world wars, the golden age of detective fiction),
detective fiction as a literary form was invented by an American—Edgar Allan
Poe. Whether Poe wrote five detective stories or only three depends on whether
you agree with Howard Haycraft's rejection of "The Gold Bug" and "Thou Art

the Man" as qualifying for the reason that "every shred of the evidence on which Legrand's brilliant deductions are based is withheld from the reader until *after* the solution is disclosed." That leaves as unquestioned examples of the form "The Murders in the Rue Morgue," "The Purloined Letter," and "The Mystery of Marie Roget."

Haycraft's comment brings up the essential feature of detective fiction: playing fair with the reader and giving the reader all the information the fictional detective has. Equally abhorrent are explanations that fly in the face of common sense or reason. Poisons unknown to science, supernatural interventions (the *deus ex machina*), and secret passageways are all beneath the dignity of serious practitioners of the art. Poe's pioneering of the form was true to these later canons, except for the two examples already mentioned.

But something else is involved, too. Detective fiction can emerge only when there are detectives. And this requirement sets apart the true form of the mystery from its competitors and spurious antecedents. A detective *detects*. Whether the detective is professional or amateur is not important. What is important is that the means of detection be logical and rational. Not emotion, romance, action, brute force, luck, or supernatural intervention can lead to the solution of the difficulty in a detective story. Guesswork won't do at all. Whether it is Poe's process of ratiocination, Poirot's "little grey cells," or Sherlock Holmes's search for data, the detective's only weapon is reason. At base the detective story is a match of wits between the detective and the adversary, and the detective succeeds by out thinking the criminal.

All else is irrelevant: background color, manners, locales, character development, historical settings, romance—especially romance and that *sine qua non* of current popular fiction, sex. Dorothy Sayers rails against "the heroes who insist on fooling about after young women when they ought to be putting their minds on the job of detection," though she wrote this comment in 1929, before Lord Peter Wimsey fell in love with Harriet Vane in *Gaudy Night* (1935) and married her in *Busman's Honeymoon* (1937). Sayer's reasons? "Just at the critical moment when the trap is set to catch the villain, the sleuth learns that his best girl has been spirited away. Heedlessly he drops everything, and rushes off to Chinatown or to the lonely house on the marshes or wherever it is without even leaving a note to say where he is going. Here he is promptly sandbagged or entrapped or otherwise made a fool of, and the whole story is impeded and its logical development ruined."

Detective fiction is enjoyed most by those who love puzzles and the challenge to reason correctly, and here is a major point of contact with philosophy. In a well-crafted mystery the detective confronts us, the readers, with a contest of reason as surely as the detective challenges the wrongdoer. Ellery Queen serves notice at the beginning of his first novel, *The Roman Hat Mystery* (subtitled "A Problem in Deduction"), that he intends to play fair with the reader by providing a "lexicon of persons connected with the investigation" to which Ellery Queen urges the reader to return often "if toward no other end than to ward off the inevitable cry of 'Unfair!'—the consolation of those who read and do not reason." What makes a mystery fun is matching our wits against those of the detective, and so the author must give us all the data that are available to the detective. Hence Ellery Queen's challenge to his reader at the end of the novel:

> ... The alert student of mystery tales, now being in possession of all the pertinent facts, should at this stage of the story have reached definite conclusions on the questions propounded. The solution—or enough of it to point unerringly to the guilty character—may be reached by a series of logical deductions and psychological observations.

But having all the facts is not enough. What conclusion you draw from these facts is as important. Someone among the ancient Greeks, probably Aristotle, first discovered that there are two ways our reasoning can go wrong: we can reason on the basis of incorrect data, or we can have correct data and reason incorrectly from them. There is actually a third way, too: we can both have erroneous information *and* reason incorrectly. What we hope for is correct information and correct reasoning, and this is what the detective must have. Three ways to go wrong and only one to go right; no wonder the fictional detective can usually outwit us!

The kind of reasoning used is also important, depending on the nature of the case. Arthur Upfield's detective Napoleon Bonaparte (Bony to his friends) observed that "crime investigators are trained minds. I have been trained to think along lines of deduction and induction. These are two separate processes of thinking..." (*The Bushman Who Came Back*). The two processes of reasoning are not really as separate as Bony says, for in the real world we alternate constantly between them. *Deduction* (all horses have hearts, and so this horse has one) and *induction* (each horse I have ever seen has had a heart, and so all horses must have them) are both important in science, though deduction is more closely associated with mathematics and induction with laboratory science.

Observational skills, often more than inductive reasoning, characterize the successful detective, who sees a problem where the surrounding dullards see only the commonplace. Watson came upon Sherlock Holmes in the act of examining a hat which Watson describes as "a very seedy and disreputable hard-felt hat, much the worse for wear." Holmes urges Watson to "look upon it not as a battered billycock but as an intellectual problem" ("The Adventure of the Blue Carbunkle").

Many think that deduction is the privileged mode of detection, but it is not. More important even than deduction is the detective's ability to form a *hypothesis* after amassing a collection of observational detail. How this comes about is something of a mystery in its own right and has been a perennial puzzle for philosophers concerned with the logic of scientific discovery, but the detective has the ability. One requirement for successful hypothesis formation is sufficient factual detail. Watson recounts Holmes's self-condemning comment: "'I had,' said he 'come to an entirely erroneous conclusion which shows, my dear Watson, how dangerous it always is to reason from insufficient data'" ("The Adventure of the Speckled Band").

As philosophers of science know, there are no rules for hypothesis formulation as there are for deductive reasoning, but one principle that is close to being a rule is that the detective should abandon a hypothesis when the facts no longer support it. Refusing to do this is the downfall of many a detective, but philosophers are of no particular help here in telling when to abandon a hypothesis. Nicholas Blake's Superintendent Armstrong had committed himself to a theory that his sergeant was convinced was wrong. "The sergeant felt that this reasoning, though specious, had been rather flimsily constructed by Armstrong as a defence against a possibility which he had not explored with his usual thoroughness" (A Question of Proof).

A second near-rule for hypothesis formation, rather the inverse of the first, is that one should not abandon a theory that fits the facts no matter how improbable the theory may be. Holmes reminded Watson, "It is an old maxim of mine that when you have excluded the impossible, whatever remains, however improbable, must be the truth" ("The Adventure of the Beryl Coronet").

The process of hypothesis formulation and testing is the logic of scientific discovery, and as anyone who has tried to do science knows, it escapes precise formulation. It certainly is not produced by a rigid approach that sees hypothesis formulation as a step-by-step process which can be taught and perfected by practice. We should therefore forgive detectives who are unable to say precisely how they arrived at the correct conclusion; and we should not blame the author or accuse the author of foul play if the process of correct hypothesis formulation itself seems to be a little mysterious.

When to make what philosophers call the inductive leap from observational detail to causal antecedents is the critical decision. Reflecting on this difficult aspect of reasoning, Napoleon Bonaparte observed that "inductive reasoning must keep to specified rules, and often to indulge in such reasoning is unwise until all the available facts and probable assumptions are marshalled" (The Bushman Who Came Back). Holmes describes inductive logic as the process of analytical reasoning, or reasoning backward. "In the everyday affairs of life," he notes, "it is more useful to reason forward." He then explains to Watson what he means. "Most people, if you describe a train of events to them, will tell you what the result would be. They can put those events together in their minds, and argue from them that something will come to pass. There are few people, however, who, if you told them a result, would be able to evolve from their own inner consciousness what the steps were which led up to that result. This power is what I mean when I talk of reasoning backward, or analytically" (A Study in Scarlet).

If inductive reasoning can be described as reasoning backward (from effects to causes), deductive reasoning can be characterized as reasoning forward (from premises to conclusion). Deduction can be valid even if the detective does not know whether the premises reasoned from are true or false.

The detective can therefore proceed with many what-if chains of reasoning: "If Lord Melbourne lied when he told me he saw the gardener in the garden, then he wasn't in the library at the time and could *not* have seen you enter the conservatory." Harry Kemelman in "The Nine Mile Walk" used this distinction between the *process* of deductive reasoning and the *content* of deductive reasoning. Overhearing someone remark that "a nine-mile walk is no joke, especially in the rain," Nicky Welt showed what could be deduced from this statement. The story has a surprise ending, and I will not give it away here.

The rationality that I have been describing holds true of British detective fiction and its imitators in the so-called British drawing room style of murder mystery. The fundamental assumption behind English detective fiction is that there is always a logical explanation. The contrasting assumption of American detective fiction of the hard-boiled type is that crimes are not always committed for logical reasons. The detective who emerges in the writings of Raymond Chandler and Dashiell Hammett does not confront a crime as a puzzle to be solved but is someone who earns a living by stalking criminals down "mean streets." Raymond Chandler, in a dedication accompanying a collection of *Black Mask* stories, reflected that these stories come from "The time when we were trying to get murder away from the upper classes, the weekend house party and the vicar's rose-garden, and back to the people who are really good at it."

If the hard-boiled detective's weapons are not so much deductive reasoning as quick wits and a strong right cross, the detective hero in American mystery fiction confronts a world gone wrong. Rather than trying to restore a lost rationality, the hard-boiled detective, like Albert Camus's absurd hero, struggles to find meaning in what appear to be meaningless encounters. The hard-boiled detective is presented as something like a moral man in an immoral society, an absurd hero who confronts life as a series of existential crises. Hammett's Sam Spade is a very moral man, probably the only moral man in *The Maltese Falcon,* where he is surrounded by liars, murderers, and cheats.

While considerably more violent, American detective fiction nonetheless continues the tradition of detective fiction that presents us with a moral world in which the distinctions between right and wrong are clear and vivid. Criminals are caught and punished. There is little moral ambiguity. Crime does not pay, and it is clear that the detective thinks it *should* not pay either. Detective fiction rarely deals with the actual punishment of the criminal; but there is the demand that the guilty person be caught and punished. I think this is a partial explanation for the popularity of detective fiction. The world of detective fiction is a moral world ruled by reason. Criminals are caught and punished. It is as Lamont Cranston's Shadow observed, "The weed of crime bears bitter fruit. Crime does not pay."

But the real world does not strike us as moral. Terrorists kill children in crowded air terminals. Murderers go free on technicalities. Dealers in illegal drugs amass huge fortunes. Crime pays, and pays very well.

The morally tidy world of detective fiction appeals to our rationality in another sense. The philosopher Immanuel Kant argued that a rational world would be a world where virtue is rewarded and vice punished, or more specifically, where the virtuous are happy and deserve to be and the wicked are unhappy. Certainly our world is not like that, and so one can only conclude that our world is not rational. Kant disagreed with many of his contemporaries who thought that we have a special moral sense, arguing instead that we use reason to make moral judgments just as surely as we use reason to gain knowledge about the world. Any rational person, he thought, has to acknowledge the demands of moral duty. Failure to do so is a breakdown in our moral reason just as surely as an inability to do geometry would indicate an irrationality of a different kind.

No wonder detective fiction appeals to us. As moral and rational beings, we crave a world that makes sense, a world where villains are easily identified and the good guys finally win. Detective fiction presents us with all this and more: a world where there is respect for law and order, and justice triumphs. No wonder mystery stories were banned in Nazi Germany and do not flourish in countries with tyrannical regimes. The great corpus of detective fiction has come from the world's democracies.

One might think that the renewed popularity of detective fiction, with its emphasis on law and order, is just another reflection of the increasing conservatism of our age. That may be partially correct, but more is involved than that. The structure of detective fiction has pretty much remained unchanged since its beginnings. There are exceptions, but the mainstream of the genre has adhered to certain definite structural constants. Among these are concern for plot development, the buildup of dramatic tension, and the final resolution of that tension. Or to use Aristotle's words, detective stories have a beginning, a middle, and an end.

To quote Aristotle in this context is not beside the point. In her 1935 essay, "Aristotle on Detective Fiction," Dorothy Sayers convincingly showed that detective fiction fulfills many of the demands for dramatic literature which Aristotle described in his *Poetics*. She points out that Aristotle said that the characters in a dramatic story should be good. That is, "Even the wickedest of them (should) be not merely monsters and caricatures...but endued with some sort of human dignity, so that we are enabled to take them seriously." The detective should be cleverer than we are, and the villain should be bad. But how bad is *bad?* A general rule Aristotle lays down is that the character should be worse than most other people not in every respect but only regarding one particular thing; the "plot ought not to turn on the detection and punishment of a hopelessly bad man who is villainous in all directions at once— forger, murderer, adulterer, thief." Mystery stories are filled with examples of crimes committed by intelligent, even moral, people who had a single fatal flaw. Inspector Appleby of Scotland Yard describes a murderer as not an entirely evil man, certainly not stupid, a scoundrel but also "a very, very able man" (*Hamlet, Revenge*).

Then there is Aristotle's well-known view that drama imitates life and thereby arouses emotions of fear and pity. To accomplish this, the action of the story must be complete in itself. Sayers says about this Aristotelian principle that "a detective story that leaves any loose ends is no proper detective story at all—with incidents arousing pity and fear, wherewith to accomplish its catharsis of such emotions." But Aristotle says that the really violent action must be committed offstage out of sight of the audience. In detective fiction proper, the punishment of the criminal takes place later—and elsewhere. Aristotle's principles can help us understand better why the English country house is such an ideal setting as the scene of the crime. A close second is a deserted island, as Agatha Christie favored in *Ten Little Indians;* or a hotel, the closest believable modern alternative to a weekend in a manor house.

Then there is the matter of plot. Detective fiction offers the essential element for a good read: a *story.* The plot, Aristotle thought, should be believable. The puzzle that dominates mystery fiction seems to serve up just the right amount of complexity. In addition to believability, an acceptable plot faces moral restraints as well. A plot is unacceptable if it shows a good person passing from happiness to misery, or a bad person from misery to happiness. Why? Because Aristotle knew that we will not feel pity if one of the characters suffers undeserved misfortune. And the characters must be like ourselves, forcing us to face the possibility that maybe we could commit a crime similar to the one which we confront in the story. Holmes says at the conclusion of "The Boscombe Valley Mystery," "There but for the grace of God goes Sherlock Holmes."

Holmes's remark points up another aspect of Aristotle's theory of tragedy. The effect of having emotions of fear and pity aroused in us is that we are somehow purged of them—Aristotle's well-known theory of catharsis. Sayers noted in her article that Aristotle used the contemporary Greek theater for his examples "because it was, at that time, the most readily available, widespread and democratic form of entertainment presented for his attention. But what, in his heart of hearts, he desired was a good detective story; and it was not his fault, poor man, that he lived some twenty centuries too early." What Aristotle really craved, though he did not know it, was nothing less than a good detective story.

A final point of contact between philosophy and detective fiction is the task detective fiction places before the reader. The predominance of the puzzle and the presence of a detective are necessary conditions for a mystery story. Certainly the detective is necessary to the story, for the role of the detective (and whether the detective is called that or not is irrelevant) is to help us understand the events narrated in the story. In an adventure story the reader is borne along by the sequence of events to the ending of the story which resolves the dramatic tension. But in a detective story, we can be brought along to the end of the story and still feel a sense of dissatisfaction. The narrative is ended, the action has stopped, but the mystery is not dispelled. Until the events of the story have been *interpreted* to us, we do not understand what the story is about. This feature of detective fiction can be best described by invoking Robert Champigny's descriptive phrase, a *hermeneutic tale.*

Hermeneutics, or interpretation theory, is almost as old as Western philosophy itself, going back to Aristotle's treatise *On Interpretation,* known to us usually under its Latin title *De interpretatione,* a Latin form of the original Greek title *Peri hermeneias.* Here Aristotle defined interpretation, or hermeneutics, as "the operation of the mind in making statements which have to do with the truth or falsity of a thing." Interpretations, in Aristotle's sense, are statements about something that are true or false. Rhetoric, or persuasive discourse, and dramatic discourse, do not deal with truth or falsity but have as their aim moving the hearer. The aim of rhetoric is to persuade, that of poetry to arouse and purge the emotions. Certainly, if on no other grounds than this, detective fiction deserves to be called hermeneutical because of its emphasis on discovering the truth of what happened.

Until recently, *hermeneutics* was used to refer to the theory for interpreting religious texts, reflecting the origin of the term from the Greek word *hermeios,* associated with the oracle of Delphi and derived from the wing-footed messenger-god Hermes. The utterances of the oracle of Delphi were notoriously obscure (sufficiently so to protect the oracle from charges of error) and therefore demanded interpretation. The Greeks associated Hermes with the origins of language and writing, the mechanisms for communicating in human terms what is beyond human understanding. Although the messages of the gods may be beyond human understanding, the task of hermeneutics is to interpret those messages into terms that can be understood. The term *hermeneutics* was by and large dormant until the seventeenth century, when it was used by the German theologian J. C. Danhauer to describe the difference between exegesis (finding out what a sacred text *says*) and hermeneutics (interpreting what it *means*). Perhaps because of the origins of the term, and because of its use in a work dealing with the interpretation of religious texts, the religious association of hermeneutics was dominant for the next two centuries, until William Dilthey used the term to characterize the method which he felt was appropriate to the social sciences.

What is a detective, anyway? A scientist? Sherlock Holmes certainly showed a smattering of scientific interests (though in selective fields), but he could scarcely be said to be a scientist in terms of what we now think of as characterizing the natural sciences. But if we characterize Holmes (and his imitators) as social scientists, we mean more than merely that they use the methods of observation and analysis that are present in the natural sciences. We can turn to Dilthey, whose view was that human society should be investigated as a kind of *text* consisting of human actions, cultural creations, and so forth that stand in need of being interpreted.

Detective stories present us with precisely such a text: the events of the crime itself, the activities of all the participants in the dramatic events, the motives of all the suspects. From this seemingly unstructured text the detective provides an interpretation of events into a coherent story. Whereas an adventure story leads us along to a culminating event, the detective story leads us back (through interpretation) to an understanding of an event that occurred rather early in the story. But now the event is understood, whereas when we witnessed the event (through the eyes of the narrator) we did not understand it, because we did not have the proper interpretation of the event. This feature of the detective story can be used by clever authors to set up several interpretations, all of which are false, until the detective gives the final and correct interpretation.

But as Aristotle says frequently in his writings, "Enough of these things." And to paraphrase the twentieth-century philosopher Ludwig Wittgenstein, don't think but look. While you read detective stories or see them unfold on television or the stage, look for philosophical themes yourself. Not only might you discover that you are a closet philosopher; you will also have enormous fun.

STUDY QUESTIONS

1. The essay refers to two types of reasoning. What are they? Give examples of each.
2. Stewart opines that the real world is not as "rational" as the world of detective fiction. What does he mean by this? What reasons does he give to support his view? Do you agree with him?
3. What is a hypothesis? What are some of the hypotheses which you have formed in recent days or weeks? Why do you embrace one hypothesis instead of another to explain a set of facts or to solve a problem?
4. What is hermeneutics? Why is a detective, or a philosopher, necessarily involved in hermeneutics?

PART ONE

Philosophy of Religion

THE PARADOXES OF RELIGION

Religion is not just a belief that some mysterious being exists. It is, on the contrary, a complex network of beliefs concerning morality, the purpose of life, the nature of the individual, and the ultimate explanation of things. Our rational, scientific experience of the world is fragmented and incomplete, and religion attempts to bring these fragments together to form a coherent, meaningful image of the whole. Philosophers have always concerned themselves with religious issues because the philosophical enterprise itself is just such an attempt to bring together the strands of experience and discover the hidden connections between every area of human concern. This is why the philosophy of religion is an excellent place to begin the study of philosophy. In examining the religious vision of the world, we are forced to lay bare our fundamental assumptions concerning knowledge, morality, and the possibility of a meaningful existence. Once our assumptions have been critically examined, whatever of worth that remains will have to be put back together again to form a coherent system.

The Judaic-Christian religious tradition, for example, claims to be relevant to life in many ways. First, it offers an ultimate explanation of things by claiming that the world is the creation of an all-powerful, all-knowing, benevolent being. The universe, then, is a rational system, not merely an arrangement of blind accidents. Ultimately, this means that important features of the world must be explained in terms of the plan and goals of the creator. Closely allied with this belief is the claim that the life of each individual is significant in the divine scheme of things. Many people believe that without God, life becomes a meaningless charade, traced out briefly on the surface of an insignificant planet. But if God exists, even our most bitter disappointments serve some ultimate purpose. In addition, religion offers an explanation of morality. In Dostoyevsky's famous novel *The Brothers Karamazov*, one of the characters proclaims that if God does not exist, anything is permitted. In other words, God is needed

23

to transform moral sentiment from a subjective feeling into an objective requirement.

But the religious picture of the world must deal with several crucial questions. First and foremost is the question of knowledge. Can the existence of God be established by the usual patterns of reasoning and observation, or is a special source of knowledge required? If religious claims must ultimately rest on faith or mystical insight, what is the best way to understanding these states? Second, does religion actually provide a sense of purpose and significance to life which cannot be gained without God? Does it help, for example, to know that our suffering was planned and carried out in order to serve some higher ideal? Third, why should God's commandments be morally authoritative? The proponents of a religious moral theory must be able to deal with the claims of those who maintain that adequate ethics can be formulated by human beings for human needs. Finally, the religious view of life must face what appears to be an agonizing paradox. If God is all-good and all-knowing, why did God create a world full of suffering and injustice? Why, for example, must millions of innocents suffer the ravages of disease and other natural disasters? Could any purpose, no matter how noble, justify this enormous tragedy?

1

Does God Exist?

PROBLEM INTRODUCTION

"The unexamined life is not worth living." These were the words of the Greek philosopher, Socrates, as he faced a jury in Athens on charges of corruption of the youth and blasphemy. He was found guilty and sentenced to death by poisoning. Socrates might have escaped punishment by promising to stop teaching his students to question the basic beliefs of his culture. He chose death instead. Socrates understood that if we never reflect upon ourselves, our actions, or our beliefs, the life we lead is not really ours at all, but simply the mechanical expression of the prevailing ideas of our times. Further, some of these ideas may be true, but by refusing to challenge them we do them a great disservice—we treat them as dogmas.

In Western culture today one of the most pervasive beliefs is belief in the existence of God. Recent surveys indicate that in America, for instance, well over 90 percent of the people, including every age group, claim to believe in God. Over the centuries philosophers have examined this belief to determine whether there is a rational justification for believing in God. The readings in this section include some of the most important writings in this historic inquiry.

For many individuals an examination of God's existence is a unique challenge. They have been taught that God exists since they were children, and this belief is important in giving meaning and direction to their lives. They find it very difficult, therefore, to call God's existence into question. On the other hand, we must remember that we are rational beings, and that we should not accept beliefs blindly. The fact that a particular belief is widespread, or old, or personally important, does not in itself mean that it is true. Many students recognize this, and sense the need to examine the question of God's existence, but are nevertheless ill at ease about doing so. In these mixed feelings they are confronting the philosopher's dilemma—a philosopher is frequently required to examine those very beliefs, such as belief in God, whose examination is unsettling, and at times even anguishing. Thus, philosophical inquiry takes

courage—perhaps not as much as Socrates showed—but courage nevertheless.

The first argument for God's existence which you will find in the readings is called the ontological argument. It is called the ontological argument
because the Greek word *on* means "being," and this argument asks you to
reflect on the being of God. If only you reflect on the nature of God's being,
it says, you must conclude that God exists. St. Anselm and Descartes have
given us separate versions of this argument, and St. Anselm's is reprinted
here.

Actually, there are two lines of reasoning in Anselm. First, after defining
God as "a being than which none greater can be thought"—substitute "the
greatest conceivable being" if you like—he observes that when you hear these
words spoken, you grasp their meaning; you understand what is said. In other
words, at that point you have an *idea* of "a being than which none greater can
be thought." (Anselm's use of the term "greater," by the way, refers not to
physical size but to superiority as a being. Thus, God is the perfect being.)
Now, if such a thing is truly that than which none greater can be thought,
would it exist merely as an idea in your mind, or would it exist also as a being
apart from your mind? Anselm reasons that it would exist apart from your
mind as well, since such a being would be greater than one that existed only
in your mind. Therefore, to have an idea of "a being than which none greater
can be thought" is to imply that such a being actually exists. Next, putting the
argument in slightly different terms, Anselm challenges you to try to think of
"a being than which none greater can be thought" as nonexistent. He suggests
that this is impossible—you simply cannot think of God as nonexistent. Why?
Because, again, if you were to think of a nonexistent being, you could yet
think of one which is greater, namely, an existent being. Thus, you could not
possibly think of "a being than which none greater can be thought" as nonexistent. The very idea is contradictory. You might be able to *say* that there is
no God, Anselm observes, but you are merely saying something that you cannot possibly think.

The ontological argument came under attack from believers and nonbelievers alike. St. Thomas Aquinas and Immanuel Kant are two believers who
found it flawed. You will find Kant's rejoinder summarized in Nagel's article.
As for Aquinas, he argued that man cannot know God's essence—what God
is—directly. A physical, imperfect being—man—cannot directly comprehend
a spiritual, perfect being—God. Instead, we can know God only *indirectly*,
through God's effects in the world. Aquinas therefore proceeded to formulate
a set of arguments for God's existence which point to features of the universe—
the cosmos—as clues to God's existence, and so they are called cosmological
arguments. God, he tells us, is necessary to account for motion, causality,
contingency, gradation, and design in nature. In his second of the "Five Ways,"
for instance, he claims that nature could not contain causes and effects unless
there were a first cause. An infinite series of causes, according to him, is an
absurdity.

Aquinas's fifth argument, from "the governance of the world," is an early rendition of an argument which became popular several centuries later. This is called the *teleological* argument, from the Greek word *telos*, which means "goal" or "end." It asserts, briefly, that the universe reflects design—its parts are arranged to achieve identifiable goals or ends—and this, in turn, requires a designer. The teleological argument compares natural objects to those produced by human beings, such as clocks or engines. Since the former have many of the same features as the latter, they too must have been designed by an intelligence. Further, since natural objects, such as a human eye, exhibit an organization far surpassing the most complex human products, such as a computer, the designer of the universe is far superior to man.

This argument is the subject of debate in David Hume's *Dialogues Concerning Natural Religion*. Philo is the speaker who levels criticism at the argument. Among his points are these: (1) We have so little reliable information about the universe that it is precipitous of us to say that it reflects order and design; (2) Even if we grant, for the sake of the debate, that the universe reflects order and design, these features could be the result of the activity of finite designers; (3) Presuming once again that the universe reflects order and design, this could be the outcome of nature's spontaneous development; matter may develop—today we might say "evolve"—according to inherent laws or propensities; and (4) The analogy between human products and nature does not hold. We can *observe* the clockmaker producing the clock; the same is not true of a supposed cosmic designer and nature.

The final reading in this section features a contemporary philosopher who is an atheist. Ernest Nagel provides us with criticisms of the three classical arguments debated thus far in the readings, as well as two other arguments advanced by believers—the moral argument and the argument from religious or mystical experience.

Once you have studied these readings, you will have a good start on the complex question whether belief in God withstands the test of intelligent criticism. But your own position should remain open until you have taken time to reflect on perhaps the most serious obstacle to belief in the God of the three major monotheistic religions in the world—Islam, Judaism, and Christianity. This obstacle is the problem of evil: how can an all-good, all-loving, and all-powerful God allow so much suffering in the world? That is the topic of Chapter 2.

The Ontological Argument for the Existence of God

St. Anselm

St. Anselm (1033–1103) was Archbishop of Canterbury. He is often called the father of Scholasticism and is known primarily for his version of the ontological argument. Anselm attempts to prove the existence of God by reflecting on the idea or concept of God. He believes that God is the only being which can be proved to exist by this method. Although deeply committed to rationalism, he characterized his position as "faith seeking understanding." In other words, the belief in God comes from faith, and faith is then illuminated by reason.

Anselm argues that the concept of God is that of "the greatest being that can be thought of." If you think of something having all the attributes of God, such as omnipotence, omniscience, etc., but you can also imagine that this thing does not exist, then you are not thinking of God, for surely a being which is thought of as existing is greater than one which is thought of as not existing. Therefore, Anselm concludes, since it is impossible to even frame the idea of a nonexistent God, it is impossible to doubt that God exists.

A monk by the name of Gaunilo wrote a reply to Anselm in which he claimed that he could use Anselm's method to prove the existence of a perfect island. After all, if I can think of an island as not existing, then I am not thinking of the perfect island, for I can certainly conceive of a better one, namely, one that exists. It is impossible, then, to doubt the existence of the perfect island. Our selection contains Anselm's response to Gaunilo.

PREFACE

Some time ago, at the urgent request of some of my brethren, I published a brief work,[1] as an example of meditation on the grounds of faith. I wrote it in the role of one who seeks, by silent reasoning with himself, to learn what he does not know. But when I reflected on this little book, and saw that it was put together as a long chain of arguments, I began to ask myself whether *one* argument might possibly be found, resting on no other argument for its proof, but sufficient in itself to prove that God truly exists and that he is the supreme good, needing nothing outside himself, but needful for the being and well-being of all things. I often turned my earnest attention to this problem, and at times I believed that I could put my finger on what I was looking for, but

Reprinted from *A Scholastic Miscellany*, edited and translated by Eugene R. Fairweather (Volume X, The Library of Christian Classics). First published MCMLV by SCM Press, Ltd., London, and the Westminster Press, Philadelphia, Pennsylvania. Used by permission.

[1] The *Monologion*, probably Anselm's first work, was written at Bec in the second half of 1076 (cf. Landgraf, *Einführung*, 53). Text in Schmitt, I, 7–87. (Translator's note.)

at other times it completely escaped my mind's eye, until finally, in despair, I decided to give up searching for something that seemed impossible to find. But when I tried to put the whole question out of my mind, so as to avoid crowding out other matters, with which I might make some progress, by this useless preoccupation, then, despite my unwillingness and resistance, it began to force itself on me more persistently than ever. Then, one day, when I was worn out by my vigorous resistance to the obsession, the solution I had ceased to hope for presented itself to me, in the very turmoil of my thoughts, so that I enthusiastically embraced the idea which, in my disquiet, I had spurned.

I thought that the proof I was so glad to find would please some readers if it were written down. Consequently, I have written the little work that follows, dealing with this and one or two other matters, in the role of one who strives to raise his mind to the contemplation of God and seeks to understand what he believes. Neither this essay nor the other one I have already mentioned really seemed to me to deserve to be called a book or to bear an author's name; at the same time, I felt that they could not be published without some title that might encourage anyone into whose hands they fell to read them, and so I gave each of them a title. The first I called *An Example of Meditation on the Grounds of Faith,* and the second *Faith Seeking Understanding.*

But when both of them had been copied under these titles by a number of people, I was urged by many people—and especially by Hugh, the reverend archbishop of Lyons, apostolic legate in Gaul, who ordered this with apostolic authority—to attach my name to them. In order to do this more fittingly, I have named the first *Monologion* (or *Soliloquy*), and the second *Proslogion* (or *Address*).

GOD TRULY IS *arg. begins here*

And so, O Lord, since thou givest understanding to faith, give me to understand—as far as thou knowest it to be good for me—that thou dost exist, as we believe, and that thou art what we believe thee to be. Now we believe that thou art a being than which none greater can be thought. Or can it be that there is no such being, since "the fool hath said in his heart, 'There is no God'"? But when this same fool hears what I am saying—"A being than which none greater can be thought"—he understands what he hears, and what he understands is in his understanding, even if he does not understand that it exists. For it is one thing for an object to be in the understanding, and another thing to understand that it exists. When a painter considers beforehand what he is going to paint, he has it in his understanding, but he does not suppose that what he has not yet painted already exists. But when he has painted it, he both has it in his understanding and understands that what he has now produced exists. Even the fool, then, must be convinced that a being than which none greater can be thought exists at least in his understanding, since when he hears this he understands it, and whatever is understood is in the understanding. But clearly that than which a greater cannot be thought cannot exist in the understanding alone. For if it is actually in the understanding alone, it can be thought of as existing also in reality, and this is greater. Therefore, if that than which a greater cannot be thought is in the understanding alone, this same thing than which a greater cannot be thought is that than which a greater can be thought. But obviously this is impossible. Without doubt, therefore, there exists, both in the understanding and in reality, something than which a greater cannot be thought.

GOD CANNOT BE THOUGHT OF AS NONEXISTENT

And certainly it exists so truly that it cannot be thought of as nonexistent. For something can be thought of as existing, which cannot be thought of as not existing, and this is greater than that which *can* be thought of as not existing. Thus, if that than which a greater cannot be thought can be thought of as not existing, this very thing than which a greater cannot be thought is *not* that than which a greater cannot be thought. But this is contradictory. So, then, there truly is a being than which a greater cannot be thought—so truly that it cannot even be thought of as not existing.

And *thou* art this being, O Lord our God. Thou so truly art, then, O Lord my God, that thou canst not even be thought of as not existing. And this is right. For if some mind could think of something better than thou, the creature would rise above the Creator and judge its Creator; but this is altogether absurd. And indeed, whatever is, except thyself alone, can be thought of as not existing. Thou alone, therefore, of all beings, hast being in the truest and highest sense, since no other being so truly exists, and thus every other being has less being. Why, then, has "the fool said in his heart, 'There is no God,'" when it is so obvious to the rational mind that, of all beings, thou dost exist supremely? Why indeed, unless it is that he is a stupid fool?

HOW THE FOOL HAS SAID IN HIS HEART
WHAT CANNOT BE THOUGHT

But how did he manage to say in his heart what he could not think? Or how is it that he was unable to think what he said in his heart? After all, to say in one's heart and to think are the same thing. Now if it is true—or, rather, since it is true—that he thought it, because he said it in his heart, but did not say it in his heart, since he could not think it, it is clear that something can be said in one's heart or thought in more than one way. For we think of a thing, in one sense, when we think of the word that signifies it, and in another sense, when we understand the very thing itself. Thus, in the first sense God can be thought of as nonexistent, but in the second sense this is quite impossible. For no one who understands what God is can think that God does not exist, even though he says these words in his heart—perhaps without any meaning, perhaps with some quite extraneous meaning. For God is that than which a greater cannot be thought, and whoever understands this rightly must understand that he exists in such a way that he cannot be nonexistent even in thought. He, therefore, who understands that God thus exists cannot think of him as nonexistent.

Thanks be to thee, good Lord, thanks be to thee, because I now understand by thy light what I formerly believed by thy gift, so that even if I were to refuse to believe in thy existence, I could not fail to understand its truth.

AN EXCERPT FROM THE AUTHOR'S REPLY TO THE CRITICISMS OF GAUNILO

But, you say, suppose that someone imagined an island in the ocean, surpassing all lands in its fertility. Because of the difficulty, or rather the impossibility, of finding something that does not exist, it might well be called "Lost Island." By reasoning like yours, he might then say that we cannot doubt that it truly exists in reality, because anyone can easily conceive it from a verbal description.[2] I state confidently that if anyone discovers something for me, other than that "than which is greater cannot be thought," existing either in reality or in thought alone, to which the logic of my argument can be applied, I shall find his lost island and give it to him, never to be lost again. But it now seems obvious that this being than which a greater cannot be thought cannot be thought of as nonexistent, because it exists by such a sure reason of truth. For otherwise it would not exist at all. In short, if anyone says that he thinks it does not exist, I say that when he thinks this, he either thinks of something than which a greater cannot be thought or he does not think. If he does not think, he does not think of what he is not thinking of as nonexistent. But if he does think, then he thinks of something which cannot be thought of as nonexistent. For if it could be thought of as nonexistent, it could be thought of as having a beginning and an end. But this is impossible. Therefore, if anyone thinks of it, he thinks of something that cannot even be thought of as nonexistent. But he who thinks of this does not think that it does not exist; if he did, he would think what cannot be thought. Therefore, that than which a greater cannot be thought cannot be thought of as nonexistent.

You say, moreover, that when it is said that the highest reality cannot be *thought of* as nonexistent, it would perhaps be better to say that it cannot be *understood* as nonexistent, or even as possibly nonexistent.[3] But it is more correct to say, as I said, that it cannot be thought. For if I had said that the reality itself cannot be understood not to exist, perhaps you yourself, who say that

[2] Cf. Gaunilo, *Pro insipiente*, 6 (Schmitt, I, 128).
[3] *Ibid.*, 7 (I, 129).

according to the very definition of the term what is false cannot be understood,[4] would object that nothing that is can be understood as nonexistent. For it is false to say that what exists does not exist. Therefore it would not be peculiar to God to be unable to be understood as nonexistent.[5] But if some one of the things that most certainly are can be understood as nonexistent, other certain things can similarly be understood as nonexistent. But this objection cannot be applied to "thinking," if it is rightly considered. For although none of the things that exist can be understood not to exist, still they can all be thought of as nonexistent, except that which most fully is. For all those things—and only those—which have a beginning or end or are composed of parts can be thought of as nonexistent, along with anything that does not exist as a whole anywhere or at any time (as I have already said).[6] But the only being that cannot be thought of as nonexistent is that in which no thought finds beginning or end or composition of parts, but which any thought finds as a whole, always and everywhere.

   You must realize, then, that you can think of yourself as nonexistent, even while you know most certainly that you exist. I am surprised that you said you did not know this.[7] For we think of many things as nonexistent when we know that they exist, and of many things as existent when we know that they do not exist—all this not by a real judgment, but by imagining that what we think is so. And indeed, we can think of something as nonexistent, even while we know that it exists, because we are able at the same time to think the one and know the other. And yet we cannot think of it as nonexistent, while we know that it exists, because we cannot think of something as at once existent and nonexistent. Therefore, if anyone distinguishes these two senses of the statement in this way, he will understand that nothing, as long as it is known to exist, can be thought of as nonexistent, and that whatever exists, except that than which a greater cannot be thought, can be thought of as nonexistent, even when it is known to exist. So, then, it is peculiar to God to be unable to be thought of as nonexistent, and nevertheless many things, as long as they exist, cannot be thought of as nonexistent. I think that the way in which it can still be said that God is thought of as nonexistent is stated adequately in the little book itself.[8]

STUDY QUESTIONS

1. Suppose that someone said "I can imagine a universe which does not contain God." Does Anselm believe this is possible? Do you?
2. "Anselm has merely proven that when we define the word 'God,' we must

[4] *Ibid.*
[5] *Ibid.*
[6] *Responsio,* 1 (I, 131 f.).
[7] Gaunilo, *loc. cit.*
[8] Cf. *Proslogion,* Chapter IV. (See p. 9 above.)

include existence in the definition. But this is just 'definitional' existence, not 'real' existence." How do you think Anselm would reply to this?

3. Could there be an ontological argument for the "devil"?

4. Can you prove that something *does not* exist just by looking at its definition? What about a "circular triangle"?

5. A "squircle" is a square circle. A "super-squircle" is an existing squircle. Do super-squircles exist?

6. Gaunilo criticized Anselm's argument by claiming that it could be used to prove the greatest conceivable "anything"—unicorn, island, etc. Do you think that Anselm adequately defends himself against this criticism?

The Five Ways   *Cosmological*
St. Thomas Aquinas

St. Thomas Aquinas (1226–1274) was one of the greatest philosophers of all time. His systematic marriage of Aristotle's philosophy and Christianity forms much of the basis of Catholic theology. Aquinas's "Five Ways" are among the most important and controversial of the arguments for God's existence. Each of the arguments is designed to show that the existence of God is required to explain certain features of the world.

Some of Aquinas's arguments are difficult to understand because they were written within a special philosophical framework. When Aquinas talks about a "cause," for example, there are two ways of interpreting what he means. The most common interpretation is that a cause brings about the existence of something else, but it is not required to maintain that thing in existence. For example, the cause of a table is the builder, but the table continues to exist even when the builder does not. The second sense of "cause," and the one which concerns Aquinas, is quite different. In this sense, the continued existence of the cause is necessary for the continued existence of the effect. For example, atmospheric pressure is the cause of water rising in a vacuum pump, and the condition of atmospheric pressure must be maintained if water is to continue to be pumped. Similarly, the presence of gravity is the cause of atmospheric pressure, since the continued existence of atmospheric pressure depends upon the continued existence of gravity. In his second argument, then, Aquinas is asking whether there can be an infinite series of such causes. If there cannot be such a series, he has shown that there is a *presently existing* first cause.

From Thomas Aquinas, *Summa Theologica*, Part 1, Question 2, Article 3, pp. 22–23, in Anton C. Pegis, Editor, *The Basic Writings of St. Thomas Aquinas*. Reprinted by permission of Richard J. Pegis.

The existence of God can be proved in five ways.

The first and more manifest way is the argument from motion. It is certain, and evident to our senses, that in the world some things are in motion. Now whatever is moved is moved by another, for nothing can be moved except it is in potentiality to that towards which it is moved; whereas a thing moves inasmuch as it is in act. For motion is nothing else than the reduction of something from potentiality to actuality. But nothing can be reduced from potentiality to actuality, except by something in a state of actuality. Thus that which is actually hot, as fire, makes wood, which is potentially hot, to be actually hot, and thereby moves and changes it. Now it is not possible that the same thing should be at once in actuality and potentiality in the same respect, but only in different respects. For what is actually hot cannot simultaneously be potentially hot; but it is simultaneously potentially cold. It is therefore impossible that in the same respect and in the same way a thing should be both mover and moved, i.e., that it should move itself. Therefore, whatever is moved must be moved by another. If that by which it is moved be itself moved, then this also must needs be moved by another, and that by another again. But this cannot go on to infinity, because then there would be no first mover, and, consequently, no other mover, seeing that subsequent movers move only inasmuch as they are moved by the first mover; as the staff moves only because it is moved by the hand. Therefore it is necessary to arrive at a first mover, moved by no other; and this everyone understands to be God.

The second way is from the nature of efficient cause. In the world of sensible things we find there is an order of efficient causes. There is no case known (neither is it, indeed, possible) in which a thing is found to be the efficient cause of itself; for so it would be prior to itself, which is impossible. Now in efficient causes it is not possible to go on to infinity, because in all efficient causes following in order, the first is the cause of the intermediate cause, and the intermediate is the cause of the ultimate cause, whether the intermediate cause be several, or one only. Now to take away the cause is to take away the effect. Therefore, if there be no first cause among efficient causes, there will be no ultimate nor any intermediate, cause. But if in efficient causes it is possible to go on to infinity, there will be no first efficient cause, neither will there be an ultimate effect, nor any intermediate efficient causes; all of which is plainly false. Therefore it is necessary to admit a first efficient cause, to which everyone gives the name of God.

The third way is taken from possibility and necessity, and runs thus. We find in nature things that are possible to be and not to be, since they are found to be generated, and to be corrupted, and consequently, it is possible for them to be and not to be. But it is impossible for these always to exist, for that which can not-be at some time is not. Therefore, if everything can not-be, then at one time there was nothing in existence. Now if this were true, even now there would be nothing in existence, because that which does not exist begins to exist only through something already existing. Therefore, if at one time nothing was in existence, it would have been impossible for anything to have begun to exist; and thus even now nothing would be in existence—which is absurd. Therefore, not all beings are merely possible, but there must exist something the existence of which is necessary. But every necessary thing either has its necessity caused by another, or not. Now it is impossible to go on to infinity in necessary things which have their necessity caused by another, as has been already proved in regard to efficient causes. Therefore we cannot but admit the existence of some being having of itself its own necessity, and not receiving it from another, but rather causing in others their necessity. This all men speak of as God.

The fourth way is taken from the gradation to be found in things. Among beings there are some more and some less good, true, noble, and the like. But *more* and *less* are predicated of different things according as they resemble in their different ways something which is the maximum, as a thing is said to be hotter according as it more nearly resembles that which is hottest; so that there is something which is truest, something best, something noblest, and, consequently, something which is most being, for those things that are greatest in truth are greatest in being, as it is written in *Metaph.* ii. Now the maximum in any genus is the cause of all in that genus, as fire, which is the maximum of heat, is the cause of all hot things, as is said in the same book. Therefore there must also be something which is to all beings the cause of their being, goodness, and every other perfection; and this we call God.

The fifth way is taken from the governance of the world. We see that things which lack knowledge, such as natural bodies, act for an end, and this is evident from their acting always, or nearly always, in the same way, so as to obtain the best result. Hence it is plain that they achieve their end, not fortuitously, but designedly. Now whatever lacks knowledge cannot move towards an end, unless it be directed by some being endowed with knowledge and intelligence; as the arrow is directed by the archer. Therefore some intelligent being exists by whom all natural things are directed to their end; and this being we call God.

STUDY QUESTIONS

1. Suppose Aquinas's "Five Ways" are all sound arguments. Are they sufficient to prove that God exists?
2. In his first proof, Aquinas uses the analogy of the hand pushing the stick to show that change must come from something which is not itself changed. Do you think that this is a fair analogy?
3. In his second proof, Aquinas claims that an infinite series of causes cannot exist. Apparently he thinks that if you believe there is such a series of causes, you cannot believe that the world exists right now. What are the crucial assumptions in his argument? Do you see any unstated assumptions?
4. "If everything has a cause, then God must have a cause. The First Cause Argument is just that easy to refute." What do you think?

5. Aquinas's third proof is based on a distinction between two alleged types of beings—*contingent* and *necessary*. What do these terms mean? Do you agree with Aquinas that there must be a necessary being, for if all beings were contingent, there would be nothing in existence now or ever? Explain.
6. In his fourth argument, Aquinas claims that we must have an idea of the "best" before we can say that something is "better" than another thing. Do you agree? Can you give illustrations as evidence for your belief?

Design and God
David Hume

David Hume (1711–1776), one of the great skeptics of all time, was a central figure in the development of British empiricism. This school of thought maintains that all ideas arise from perceptual experience and, consequently, that all knowledge must be based on observation. His distrust of abstract reasoning and his failure to discover any empirical evidence for the existence of God made Hume unsympathetic to religion. In the following selection from *Dialogues Concerning Natural Religion*, Philo, who represents Hume's position, is pitted against Cleanthes, who symbolizes all theologians who think that the existence of God can be proved by scientific reasoning. Hume would not allow the *Dialogues* to be published during his lifetime, for he was unsure what the public reaction would be.

Cleanthes believes that the universe exhibits traces of design. If we were to discover a clock, for example, we would be justified in inferring that it was created by an intelligent being because we have observed things like clocks being created by such beings. Since the universe itself is like a clock, we can infer that it, too, was created by an intelligent being. Philo, however, thinks that such an argument is too weak to justify belief. Arguing in the empiricist tradition, Philo maintains that since we have not observed universes in the making, we cannot be justified in believing that the present universe came about by an intelligent cause. He suggests that perhaps matter has within itself the power to produce complex organizations similar to those created by humans. It is on this point that Hume's thought displays the scientific limitations of his era. A century later, Darwin would add a new dimension to this debate, ensuring that it would rage into the twentieth century.

Not to lose any time in circumlocutions, said CLEANTHES, addressing himself to DEMEA, much less in replying to the pious declamations of PHILO; I shall briefly explain how I conceive this matter. Look round the world: Contemplate the whole and every part of it: You will find it to be nothing but one great machine, subdivided into an infinite number of lesser machines, which again

From *Dialogues Concerning Natural Religion* by David Hume, first published in 1779.

admit of subdivisions, to a degree beyond what human senses and faculties can trace and explain. All these various machines, and even their most minute parts, are adjusted to each other with an accuracy, which ravishes into admiration all men, who have ever contemplated them. The curious adapting of means to ends, throughout all nature, resembles exactly, though it much exceeds, the productions of human contrivance; of human design, thought, wisdom, and intelligence. Since therefore the effects resemble each other, we are led to infer, by all the rules of analogy, that the causes also resemble; and that the Author of nature is somewhat similar to the mind of man; though possessed of much larger faculties, proportioned to the grandeur of the work, which he has executed. By this argument *a posteriori*, and by this argument alone, we do prove at once the existence of a Deity, and his similarity to human mind and intelligence.

I shall be so free, CLEANTHES, said DEMEA, as to tell you, that from the beginning, I could not approve of your conclusion concerning the similarity of the Deity to men; still less can I approve of the mediums, by which you endeavour to establish it. What! No demonstration of the being of a God! No abstract arguments! No proofs *a priori!* Are these, which have hitherto been so much insisted on by philosophers, all fallacy, all sophism? Can we reach no farther in this subject than experience and probability? I will not say, that this is betraying the cause of a Deity: But surely, by this affected candour, you give advantage to atheists, which they never could obtain, by the mere dent of argument and reasoning.

What I chiefly scruple in this subject, said PHILO, is not so much, that all religious arguments are by CLEANTHES reduced to experience, as that they appear not to be even the most certain and irrefragable of that inferior kind. That a stone will fall, that fire will burn, that the earth has solidity, we have observed a thousand and a thousand times; and when any new instance of this nature is presented, we draw without hesitation the accustomed inference. The exact similarity of the cases gives us a perfect assurance of a similar event; and a stronger evidence is never desired nor sought after. But wherever you depart, in the least, from the similarity of the cases, you diminish proportionably the evidence; and may at last bring it to a very weak *analogy*, which is confessedly liable to error and uncertainty. After having experienced the circulation of the blood in human creatures, we make no doubt that it takes place in Titius and Maevius: But from its circulation in frogs and fishes, it is only a presumption, though a strong one, from analogy, that it takes place in men and other animals. The analogical reasoning is much weaker, when we infer the circulation of the sap in vegetables from our experience that the blood circulates in animals; and those, who hastily followed that imperfect analogy, are found, by more accurate experiments, to have been mistaken.

If we see a house, CLEANTHES, we conclude, with the greatest certainty, that it had an architect or builder; because this is precisely that species of effect, which we have experienced to proceed from that species of cause. But surely you will not affirm, that the universe bears such a resemblance to a house, that we can with the same certainty infer a similar cause, or that the analogy is here entire and perfect. The dissimilitude is so striking, that the utmost you can here pretend to is a guess, a conjecture, a presumption concerning a similar cause; and how that pretension will be received in the world, I leave you to consider.

It would surely be very ill received, replied CLEANTHES; and I should be deservedly blamed and detested, did I allow that the proofs of a Deity amounted to no more than a guess or conjecture. But is the whole adjustment of means to ends in a house and in the universe so slight a resemblance? The economy of final causes? The order, proportion, and arrangement of every part? Steps of a stair are plainly contrived, that human legs may use them in mounting; and this inference is certain and infallible. Human legs are also contrived for walking and mounting; and this inference, I allow, is not altogether so certain, because of the dissimilarity which you remark; but does it, therefore, deserve the name only of presumption or conjecture?

Good God! cried DEMEA, interrupting him, where are we? Zealous defenders of religion allow, that the proofs of a Deity fall short of perfect evidence! And you, PHILO, on whose assistance I depended, in proving the adorable mysteriousness of the divine nature, do you assent to all these extravagant opinions of CLEANTHES? For what other name can I give them? Or why spare my censure, when such principles are advanced, supported by such an authority, before so young a man as PAMPHILUS?

You seem not to apprehend, replied PHILO, that I argue with CLEANTHES in his own way; and by showing him the dangerous consequences of his tenets, hope at least to reduce him to our opinion. But what sticks most with you, I observe, is the representation which CLEANTHES has made of the argument *a posteriori*; and finding that that argument is likely to escape your hold and vanish into air, you think it so disguised that you can scarcely believe it to be set in its true light. Now, however much I may dissent, in other respects, from the dangerous principles of CLEANTHES, I must allow, that he has fairly represented that argument; and I shall endeavor so to state the matter to you, that you will entertain no farther scruples with regard to it.

Were a man to abstract from every thing which he knows or has seen, he would be altogether incapable, merely from his own ideas, to determine what kind of scene the universe must be, or to give the preference to one state or situation of things about another. For as nothing, which he clearly conceives, could be esteemed impossible or implying a contradiction, every chimera of his fancy would be upon an equal footing; nor could he assign any just reason, why he adheres to one idea or system, and rejects the others, which are equally possible.

Again; after he opens his eyes, and contemplates the world, as it really is, it would be impossible for him, at first, to assign the cause of any one event; much less, of the whole of things or of the universe. He might set his fancy a rambling; and she might bring him in an infinite variety of reports and representations. These would all be possible; but being all equally possible, he would never, of himself, give a satisfactory account for his preferring one of them to the rest. Experience alone can point out to him the true cause of any phenomenon.

Now according to this method of reasoning, DEMEA, it follows (and is, indeed, tacitly allowed by CLEANTHES himself) that order, arrangement, or the adjustment of final causes is not, of itself, any proof of design; but only so far as it has been experienced to proceed from that principle. For aught we can know *a priori*, matter may contain the source or spring of order originally, within itself, as well as mind does; and there is no more difficulty in conceiving, that the several elements, from an internal unknown cause, may fall into the most exquisite arrangement, than to conceive that their ideas, in the great, universal mind, from a like internal, unknown cause, fall into that arrangement. The equal possibility of both these suppositions is allowed. By experience we find (according to CLEANTHES), that there is a difference between them. Throw several pieces of steel together, without shape or form; they will never arrange themselves so as to compose a watch: Stone, and mortar, and wood, without an architect, never erect a house. But the ideas in a human mind, we see, by an unknown, inexplicable economy, arrange themselves so as to form the plan of a watch or house. Experience, therefore, proves, that there is an original principle of order in mind, not in matter. From similar effects we infer similar causes. The adjustment of means to ends is alike in the universe, as in a machine of human contrivance. The causes, therefore, must be resembling.

I was from the beginning scandalised, I must own, with this resemblance, which is asserted, between the Deity and human creatures; and must conceive it to imply such a degradation of the supreme Being as no sound theist could endure. With your assistance, therefore, DEMEA, I shall endeavour to defend what you justly call the adorable mysteriousness of the divine nature, and shall refute this reasoning of CLEANTHES; provided he allows, that I have made a fair representation of it.

When CLEANTHES had assented, PHILO, after a short pause, proceeded in the following manner.

where he starts to refute

That all inferences, CLEANTHES, concerning fact, are founded on experience, and that all experimental reasonings are founded on the supposition, that similar causes prove similar effects, and similar effects similar causes; I shall not, at present, much dispute with you. But observe, I entreat you, with what extreme caution all just reasoners proceed in the transferring of experiments to similar cases. Unless the cases be exactly similar, they repose no perfect confidence in applying their past observation to any particular phenomenon. Every alteration of circumstances occasions a doubt concerning the event; and it requires new experiments to prove certainly, that the new circumstances are of no moment or importance. A change in bulk, situation, arrangement, age, disposition of the air, or surrounding bodies; any of these particulars may be attended with the most unexpected consequences: And unless the objects be quite familiar to us, it is the highest temerity to expect with assurance, after any of these changes, an event similar to that which before fell under our observation. The slow and deliberate steps of philosophers, here, if any where, are distinguished from the precipitate march of the vulgar, who, hurried on by the smallest similitude, are incapable of all discernment or consideration.

But can you think, CLEANTHES, that your usual phlegm and philosophy have been preserved in so wide a step as you have taken, when you compared to the universe houses, ships, furniture, machines; and from their similarity in some circumstances inferred a similarity in their causes? Thought, design, intelligence, such as we discover in men and other animals, is no more than one of the springs and principles of the universe, as well as heat or cold, attraction or repulsion, and a hundred others, which fall under daily observation. It is an active cause, by which some particular parts of nature, we find, produce alterations on other parts. But can a conclusion, with any propriety, be transferred from parts to the whole? Does not the great disproportion bar all comparison and inference? From observing the growth of a hair, can we learn any thing concerning the generation of a man? Would the manner of a leaf's blowing, even though perfectly known, afford us any instruction concerning the vegetation of a tree?

But allowing that we were to take the *operations* of one part of nature upon another for the foundation of our judgment concerning the *origin* of the whole (which never can be admitted) yet why select so minute, so weak, so bounded a principle as the reason and design of animals as found to be upon this planet? What peculiar privilege has this little agitation of the brain which we call thought, that we must thus make it the model of the whole universe? Our partiality in our own favour does indeed present it on all occasions: But sound philosophy ought carefully to guard against so natural an illusion.

So far from admitting, continued PHILO, that the operations of a part can afford us any just conclusion concerning the origin of the whole, I will not allow any one part to form a rule for another part, if the latter be very remote from the former. Is there any reasonable ground to conclude, that the inhabitants of other planets possess thought, intelligence, reason, or any thing similar to these faculties in men? When nature has so extremely diversified her manner of operation in this small globe; can we imagine, that she incessantly copies herself throughout so immense a universe? And if thought, as we may well suppose, be confined merely to this narrow corner, and has even there so limited a sphere of action; with what propriety can we assign it for the original cause of all things? The narrow views of a peasant, who makes his domestic economy the rule for the government of kingdoms, is in comparison a pardonable sophism.

But were we ever so much assured, that a thought and reason, resembling the human, were to be found throughout the whole universe, and were its activity elsewhere vastly greater and more commanding than it appears in this globe: Yet I cannot see, why the operations of a world, constituted, arranged, adjusted, can with any propriety be extended to a world, which is in its embryo-state, and is advancing towards that constitution and arrangement. By observation, we know somewhat of the economy, action, and nourishment of a finished animal; but we must transfer with great caution that observation to the growth of a foetus in womb, and still more, to the formation of a an-imalcule in the loins of its male parent. Nature, we find, even from our limited experience, possesses an infinite number of springs and principles, which in-cessantly discover themselves on every change of her position and situation. And what new and unknown principles would actuate her in so new and unknown a situation as that of the formation of a universe, we cannot, with-out the utmost temerity, pretend to determine.

A very small part of this great system, during a very short time, is very imperfectly discovered to us: And do we thence pronounce decisively con-cerning the origin of the whole?

Admirable conclusion! Stone, wood, brick, iron, brass have not, at this time, in this minute globe of earth, an order of arrangement without human art and contrivance: Therefore the universe could not originally attain its order and arrangement, without something similar to human art. But is a part of nature a rule for another part very wide of the former? Is it a rule for the whole? Is a very small part a rule for the universe? Is nature in one situation, a certain rule for nature in another situation, vastly different from the former?

And can you blame me, CLEANTHES, if I here imitate the prudent reserve of SIMONIDES, who, according to the noted story, being asked by HIERO, *What God was?* desired a day to think of it, and then two days more; and after that manner continually prolonged the term, without ever bringing in his defini-tion or description? Could you even blame me, if I had answered at first, *that I did not know*, and was sensible that this subject lay vastly beyond the reach of my faculties? You might cry out sceptic and raillier as much as you pleased: But having found, in so many other subjects, much more familiar, the im-perfections and even contradictions of human reason, I never should expect any success from its feeble conjectures, in a subject, so sublime, and so remote from the sphere of our observation. When two *species* of objects have always been observed, to be conjoined together, I can *infer*, by custom, the existence of one whenever I *see* the existence of the other: And this I call an argument from experience. But how this argument can have place, where the objects, as in the present case, are single, individual, without parallel, or specific resem-blance, may be difficult to explain. And will any man tell me with a serious countenance, that an orderly universe must arise from some thought and art, like the human; because we have experience of it? To ascertain this reasoning, it were requisite, that we had experience of the origin of worlds; and it is not sufficient surely, that we have seen ships and cities arise from human art and contrivance....

But because I know you are not much swayed by names and authorities, I shall endeavour to show you, a little more distinctly, the inconveniences of that anthropomorphism, which you have embraced; and shall prove, that there is no ground to suppose a plan of the world to be formed in the divine mind, consisting of distinct ideas, differently arranged; in the same manner as an architect forms in his head the plan of a house which he intends to execute.

It is not easy, I own, to see what is gained by this supposition, whether we judge of the matter by *reason* or by *experience*. We are still obliged to mount higher, in order to find the cause of this cause, which you had assigned as satisfactory and conclusive.

If *reason* (I mean abstract reason, derived from enquiries *a priori*) be not alike mute with regard to all questions concerning cause and effect; this sentence at least it will venture to pronounce. That a mental world or universe of ideas requires a cause as much as does a material world or universe of objects; and if similar in its arrangement must require a similar cause. For what is there in this subject, which should occasion a different conclusion or inference? In an abstract view, they are entirely alike; and no difficulty attends the one supposition, which is not common to both of them.

Again, when we will needs force *experience* to pronounce some sentence, even on these subjects, which lie beyond her sphere; neither can she perceive any material difference in this particular, between these two kinds of worlds, but finds them to be governed by similar principles, and to depend upon an equal variety of causes in their operations. We have specimens in miniature of both of them. Our own mind resembles the one: A vegetable or animal body the other. Let experience, therefore, judge from these samples. Nothing seems more delicate with regard to its causes than thought; and as these causes never operate in two persons after the same manner, so we never find two persons, who think exactly alike. Nor indeed does the same person think exactly alike at any two different periods of time. A difference of age, of the disposition of his body, of weather, of food, of company, of books, of passions; any of these particulars or others more minute, are sufficient to alter the curious machinery of thought, and communicate to it very different movements and operations. As far as we can judge, vegetables and animal bodies are not more delicate in their motions, nor depend upon a greater variety or more curious adjustment of springs and principles.

How therefore shall we satisfy ourselves concerning the cause of that Being, whom you suppose the Author of nature, or, according to your system of anthropomorphism, the ideal world, into which you trace the material? Have we not the same reason to trace that ideal world into another ideal world, or new intelligent principle? But if we stop, and go no farther; why go so far? Why not stop at the material world? How can we satisfy ourselves without going on *in infinitum?* And after all, what satisfaction is there in that infinite progression? Let us remember the story of the INDIAN philosopher and his elephant. It was never more applicable than to the present subject. If the material world rests upon a similar ideal world, this ideal world must rest upon some other; and so on, without end. It were better, therefore, never to look beyond the present material world. By supposing it to contain the principle of its order within itself, we really assert it to be God: and the sooner we arrive at that divine Being so much the better. When you go one step beyond the mundane system you only excite an inquisitive humour, which it is impossible ever to satisfy.

To say, that the different ideas, which compose the reason of the supreme Being, fall into order, of themselves, and by their own nature, is really to talk without any precise meaning. If it has a meaning, I would fain know, why it is not as good sense to say, that the parts of the material world fall into order, of themselves, and by their own nature? Can the one opinion be intelligible, while the other is not so?

We have, indeed, experience of ideas, which fall into order, of themselves, and without any *known* cause: But, I am sure, we have a much larger experience of matter, which does the same; as in all instances of generation and vegetation, where the accurate analysis of the cause exceeds all human comprehension. We have also experience of particular systems of thought and of matter, which have no order; of the first, in madness, of the second, in corruption. Why then should we think, that order is more essential to one than the other? And if it requires a cause in both, what do we gain by your system, in tracing the universe of objects into a similar universe of ideas? The first step, which we make, leads us on forever. It were, therefore, wise in us, to limit all our enquiries to the present world, without looking farther. No satisfaction can ever be attained by these speculations, which so far exceed the narrow bounds of human understanding.

In like manner, when it is asked, what cause produces order in the ideas of the supreme Being, can any other reason be assigned by you, anthropomorphites, than that it is a *rational* faculty, and that such is the nature of the Deity? But why a similar answer will not be equally satisfactory in accounting for the order of the world, without having recourse to any such intelligent Creator as you insist on, may be difficult to determine. It is only to say, that *such* is the nature of material objects, and that they are all originally possessed of a *faculty* of order and proportion. These are only more learned and elaborate ways of confessing our ignorance; nor has the one hypothesis any real advantage above the other, except in its greater conformity to vulgar prejudices.

You have displayed this argument with great emphasis, replied CLEANTHES: You seem not sensible, how easy it is to answer it. Even in common life, if I assign a cause for any event; is it any objection, PHILO, that I cannot assign the cause of that cause, and answer every new question, which may incessantly be started? And what philosophers could possibly submit to so rigid a rule? philosophers, who confess ultimate causes to be totally unknown, and are sensible, that the most refined principles, into which they trace the phenomena, are still to them as inexplicable as these phenomena themselves are to the vulgar. The order and arrangement of nature, the curious adjustment of final causes, the plain use and intention of every part and organ; all these bespeak in the clearest language an intelligent cause or Author. The heavens and the earth join in the same testimony: The whole chorus of nature raises one hymn to the praises of its Creator: You alone, or almost alone, disturb this general harmony. You start abstruse doubts, cavils, and objections: you ask me, what is the cause of this cause? I know not; I care not; that concerns not me. I have found a Deity; and here I stop my enquiry. Let those go farther, who are wiser or more enterprising.

I pretend to be neither, replied PHILO: And for that very reason, I should never perhaps have attempted to go so far; especially when I am sensible, that I must at last be contented to sit down with the same answer, which, without farther trouble, might have satisfied me from the beginning.

But to show you still more inconveniences, continued PHILO, in your anthropomorphism; please to take a new survey of your principles. *Like effects prove like causes.* This is the experimental argument; and this, you say too, is the sole theological argument. Now it is certain, that the liker the effects are, which are seen, and the liker the causes, which are inferred, the stronger is the argument. Every departure on either side diminishes the probability, and renders the experiment less conclusive. You cannot doubt of this principle: Neither ought you to reject its consequences.

Now, CLEANTHES, said PHILO, with an air of alacrity and triumph, mark the consequences. *First*, By this method of reasoning, you renounce all claim to infinity in any of the attributes of the Deity. For as the cause ought only to be proportioned to the effect, and the effect, so far as it falls under our cognisance, is not infinite; what pretensions have we, upon your suppositions, to ascribe that attribute to the divine Being? You will still insist, that, by removing him so much from all similarity to human creatures, we give into the most arbitrary hypothesis, and at the same time weaken all proofs of his existence.

Secondly, You have no reason, on your theory, for ascribing perfection to the Deity, even in his finite capacity; or for supposing him free from every error, mistake, or incoherence in his undertakings. There are many inexplicable difficulties in the works of nature, which, if we allow a perfect Author to be proved *a priori,* are easily solved, and become only seeming difficulties, from the narrow capacity of man, who cannot trace infinite relations. But according to your method of reasoning, these difficulties become all real; and perhaps will be insisted on, as new instances of likeness to human art and contrivance. At least, you must acknowledge, that it is impossible for us to tell, from our limited views, whether this system contains any great faults, or deserves any considerable praise, if compared to other possible, and even real systems. Could a peasant, if the AENEID were read to him, pronounce that poem to be absolutely faultless, or even assign to it its proper rank among the productions of human wit; he, who had never seen any other production?

But were this world ever so perfect a production, it must still remain uncertain, whether all the excellencies of the work can justly be ascribed to the workman. If we survey a ship, what an exalted idea must we form of the ingenuity of the carpenter, who framed so complicated, useful, and beautiful a machine? And what surprise must we entertain, when we find him a stupid mechanic, who imitated others, and copied an art, which, through a long succession of ages, after multiplied trials, mistakes, corrections, deliberations, and controversies, had been gradually improving? Many worlds might have been botched and bungled, throughout an eternity, ere this system was struck out: Much labour lost: Many fruitless trials made: And a slow, but continued improvement carried on during infinite ages in the art of world-making. In such subjects, who can determine, where the truth; nay, who can conjecture where the probability, lies; amidst a great number of hypotheses which may be proposed, and a still greater number which may be imagined?

And what shadow of an argument, continued PHILO, can you produce, from your hypothesis, to prove the unity of the Deity? A great number of men join in building a house or ship, in rearing a city, in framing a Commonwealth: Why may not several Deities combine in contriving and framing a world? This is only so much greater similarity to human affairs. By sharing the work among several, we may so much farther limit the attributes of each, and get rid of that extensive power and knowledge, which must be supposed in one Deity, and which, according to you, can only serve to weaken the proof of his existence. And if such foolish, such vicious creatures as man can yet often unite in framing and executing one plan; how much more those Deities or Daemons, whom we may suppose several degrees more perfect?

It must be a slight fabric, indeed, said DEMEA, which can be erected on so tottering a foundation. While we are uncertain, whether there is one Deity or many; whether the Deity or Deities, to whom we owe our existence, be perfect or imperfect, subordinate or supreme, dead or alive; what trust or confidence can we repose in them? What devotion or worship address to them? What veneration or obedience pay them? To all the purposes of life, the theory of religion becomes altogether useless: And even with regard to speculative consequences, its uncertainty, according to you, must render it totally precarious and unsatisfactory.

I must confess, PHILO, replied CLEANTHES, that of all men living, the task which you have undertaken, of raising doubts and objections, suits you best, and seems, in a manner, natural and unavoidable to you. So great is your fertility of invention, that I am not ashamed to acknowledge myself unable, in a sudden, to solve regularly such out-of-the-way difficulties as you incessantly start upon me: Though I clearly see, in general, their fallacy and error. And I question not, but you are yourself, at present, in the same case, and have not the solution so ready as the objection; while you must be sensible, that common sense and reason is entirely against you, and that such whimsies, as you have delivered, may puzzle, but never can convince us.

What you ascribe to the fertility of my invention, replied PHILO, is entirely owing to the nature of the subject. In subjects, adapted to the narrow compass of human reason, there is commonly but one determination, which carries probability or conviction with it; and to a man of sound judgment, all other suppositions, but that one, appear entirely absurd and chimerical. But in such questions as the present, a hundred contradictory views may preserve a kind of imperfect analogy; and invention has here full scope to exert itself. Without any great effort of thought, I believe that I could, in an instant, propose other systems of cosmogony, which would have some faint appearance of truth; though it is a thousand, a million to one, if either yours or any one of mine be the true system.

For instance; what if I should revive the old EPICUREAN hypothesis? This is commonly, and I believe, justly, esteemed the most absurd system, that has yet been proposed; yet, I know not, whether, with a few alterations, it might not be brought to bear a faint appearance of probability. Instead of supposing matter infinite, as EPICURUS did; let us suppose it finite. A finite number of particles is only susceptible of finite transpositions: And it must happen, in an eternal duration, that every possible order or position must be tried an infinite number of times. This world, therefore, with all its events, even the most minute, has before been produced and destroyed, and will again be produced and destroyed, without any bounds and limitations. No one, who has a conception of the powers of infinite, in comparison of finite, will ever scruple this determination.

But this supposes, said DEMEA, that matter can acquire motion, without any voluntary agent or first mover.

And where is the difficulty, replied PHILO, of that supposition? Every event, before experience, is equally difficult and incomprehensible; and every event, after experience, is equally easy and intelligible. Motion, in many instances, from gravity, from elasticity, from electricity, begins in matter, without any known voluntary agent; and to suppose always, in these cases, an unknown voluntary agent, is mere hypothesis; and hypothesis attended with no advantages. The beginning of motion in matter itself is as conceivable a priori as its communication from mind and intelligence.

Besides, why may not motion have been propagated by impulse through all eternity, and the same stock of it, or nearly the same, be still upheld in the universe? As much as is lost by the composition of motion, as much is gained by its resolution. And whatever the causes are, the fact is certain, that matter is, and always has been in continual agitation, as far as human experience or tradition reaches. There is not probably, at present, in the whole universe, one particle of matter at absolute rest.

And this very consideration too, continued PHILO, which we have stumbled on in the course of the argument, suggests a new hypothesis of cosmogony, that is not absolutely absurd and improbable. Is there a system, an order, an economy of things, by which matter can preserve that perpetual agitation, which seems essential to it, and yet maintain a constancy in the forms, which it produces? There certainly is such an economy: For this is actually the case with the present world. The continual motion of matter, therefore, in less than infinite transpositions, must produce this economy or order; and by its very nature, that order, when once established, supports itself, for many ages, if not to eternity. But wherever matter is so poised, arranged, and adjusted as to continue in perpetual motion, and yet preserve a constancy in the forms, its situation must, of necessity, have all the same appearance of art and contrivance which we observe at present. All the parts of each form must have a relation to each other, and to the whole: And the whole itself must have a relation to the other parts of the universe; to the element, in which the form subsists; to the materials, with which it repairs its waste and decay; and to every other form, which is hostile or friendly. A defect in any of these particulars destroys the form; and the matter, of which it is composed, is again set loose, and is thrown into irregular motions and fermentations, till it unite itself to some other regular form. If no such form be prepared to receive it, and if there be a great quantity of this corrupted matter in the universe, the universe itself is entirely disordered; whether it be the feeble embryo of a world in its first beginnings, that is thus destroyed, or the rotten carcass of one, languishing in old age and infirmity. In either case, a chaos ensues; till finite, though innumerable revolutions produce at last some forms, whose parts and organs are so adjusted as to support the forms amidst a continued succession of matter.

Suppose (for we shall endeavour to vary the expression), that matter were thrown into any position, by a blind, unguided force; it is evident that this first position must in all probability be the most confused and most disorderly imaginable, without any resemblance to those works of human contrivance, which, along with a symmetry of parts, discover an adjustment of means to ends and a tendency to self-preservation. If the actuating force cease after this operation, matter must remain for ever in disorder, and continue an immense chaos, without any proportion or activity. But suppose, that the actuating force, whatever it be, still continues in matter, this first position will immediately give place to a second, which will likewise in all probability be as disorderly as the first, and so on, through many successions of changes and revolutions. No particular order or position ever continues a moment unaltered. The original force, still remaining in activity, gives a perpetual restlessness to matter. Every possible situation is produced, and instantly destroyed. If a glimpse or dawn of order appears for a moment, it is instantly hurried away, and confounded, by that never-ceasing force, which actuates every part of matter.

Thus the universe goes on for many ages in a continued succession of chaos and disorder. But it is not possible that it may settle at last, so as not to lose its motion and active force (for that we have supposed inherent in it), yet so as to preserve a uniformity of appearance, amidst the continual motion and fluctuation of its parts? This we find to be the case with the universe at present. Every individual is perpetually changing, and every part of every individual, and yet the whole remains, in appearance, the same. May we not hope for such a position, or rather be assured of it, from the eternal revolutions of unguided matter, and may not this account for all the appearing wisdom and contrivance which is in the universe? Let us contemplate the subject a little, and we shall find, that this adjustment, if attained by matter, of a seeming stability in the forms, with a real and perpetual revolution or motion of parts, affords a plausible, if not a true solution of the difficulty.

STUDY QUESTIONS

1. Philo says that "order, arrangement, or the adjustment of final causes is not, of itself, any proof of design." When are such features good evidence for design, according to Philo? Do you agree with Philo?
2. Philo points out that thought, as well as natural objects, has an organized structure. What is the significance of this for his argument?
3. Philo claims that Cleanthes's argument cannot establish any of the usual properties of God. Why is this? Can you think of any additional arguments which might get Cleanthes out of his difficulties?
4. What is the modified Epicurean hypothesis which Philo wishes to revive? Would you say it is a plausible explanation of the universe?
5. Suppose you discovered a complicated machine that made other machines just like itself. Would your curiosity be satisfied if you were told that these machines had been creating themselves for an infinitely long time? If not, what sort of facts would you wish explained?
6. According to Voltaire, accepting the teleological argument is like believing that the nose was designed to fit spectacles. What is the point of this remark? Do you agree with Voltaire?

An Atheist's Critique of Belief in God

Ernest Nagel

Ernest Nagel (1901–1985) was a philosopher of science who was born in Czechoslovakia and came to America as a child. For most of his career he taught at Columbia University. His major works include *An Introduction to Logic and Scientific Method* (1934), with his teacher, Morris R. Cohen; *The Structure of Science* (1961); *Principles of the Theory of Probability* (1939); and *Gödel's Proof* (1958), with James R. Newman. He was not only a gifted thinker, but one who wrote and spoke on technical subjects with great clarity and simplicity.

After explaining his criticisms of the ontological, cosmological, and teleological arguments for God's existence, he comments on Kant's idea of God as a postulate for the moral life. He evaluates this as nothing more than wishful thinking. He also replies to mystics who claim to encounter God in religious or mystical experience. In this connection he raises the specter of hallucination and cautions that feeling strongly that God exists hardly establishes that God exists.

From "Philosophical Concepts of Atheism," in Basic Beliefs—*The Religious Philosophies of Mankind,* edited by Johnson E. Fairchild (New York: Sheridan House Publishers, 1959). Reprinted by permission of the publisher.

... Before turning to the philosophical examination of the major classical arguments for theism, it is well to note that such philosophical attitudes do not quite convey the passion with which atheists have often carried on their analysis of theistic views. For historically, atheism has been and indeed continues to be, a form of social and political protest, directed as much against institutionalized religion as against theistic doctrine. Atheism has been, in effect, a moral revulsion against the undoubted abuses of the secular power exercised by religious leaders and religious institutions.

Religious authorities have opposed the correction of glaring injustices, and encouraged politically and socially reactionary policies. Religious institutions have been havens of obscurantist thought and centers for the dissemination of intolerance. Religious creeds have been used to set limits to free inquiry, to perpetuate inhumane treatment of the ill and the underprivileged, and to support moral doctrines insensitive to human suffering.

These indictments may not tell the whole story about the historical significance of religion; but they are at least an important part of the story. The refutation of theism has thus seemed to many as an indispensable step not only towards liberating men's minds from superstition, but also towards achieving a more equitable reordering of society. And no account of even the more philosophical aspects of atheistic thought is adequate, which does not give proper recognition to the powerful social motives that actuate many atheistic arguments.

But however this may be, I want now to discuss three classical arguments for the existence of God, arguments which have constituted at least a partial basis for theistic commitments. As long as theism is defended simply as dogma, asserted as a matter of direct revelation or as the deliverance of authority, belief in the dogma is impregnable to rational argument. In fact, however, reasons are frequently advanced in support of the theistic creed, and these reasons have been the subject of acute philosophical critiques.

One of the oldest intellectual defenses of theism is the cosmological argument, also known as the argument from first cause. Briefly put, the argument runs as follows. Every event must have a cause. Hence an event A must have as cause some event B, which in turn must have a cause C, and so on. But if there is no end to this backward progression of causes, the progression will be infinite; and in the opinion of those who use this argument, an infinite series of actual events is unintelligible and absurd. Hence there must be a first cause, and this first cause is God, the initiator of all change in the universe.

The argument is an ancient one, and is especially effective when stated within the framework of assumptions of Aristotelian physics; and it has impressed many generations of exceptionally keen minds. The argument is nonetheless a weak reed on which to rest the theistic thesis. Let us waive any questions concerning the validity of the principle that every event has a cause, for though the question is important its discussion would lead us far afield. However, if the principle is assumed, it is surely incongruous to postulate a first cause as a way of escaping from the coils of an infinite series. For if everything must have a cause, why does not God require one for His own existence? The standard answer is that He does not need any, because He is self-caused. But if God can be self-caused, why cannot the world be self-caused? Why do we require a God transcending the world to bring the world into existence and to initiate changes in it? On the other hand, the supposed inconceivability and absurdity of an infinite series of regressive causes will be admitted by no one who has competent familiarity with the modern mathematical analysis of infinity. The cosmological argument does not stand up under scrutiny.

The second "proof" of God's existence is usually called the ontological argument. It too has a long history going back to early Christian days, though it acquired great prominence only in medieval times. The argument can be stated in several ways, one of which is the following. Since God is conceived to be omnipotent, He is a perfect being. A perfect being is defined as one whose essence or nature lacks no attributes (or properties) whatsoever, one whose nature is complete in every respect. But it is evident that we have an idea of a perfect being, for we have just defined the idea; and since this is so, the argument continues, God who is the perfect being must exist. Why must He? Because his existence follows from his defined nature. For if God lacked the attribute of existence, He would be lacking at least one attribute, and would therefore not be perfect. To sum up, since we have an idea of God as a perfect being, God must exist.

There are several ways of approaching this argument, but I shall consider only one. The argument was exploded by the 18th century philosopher Immanuel Kant. The substance of Kant's criticism is that it is just a confusion to say that existence is an attribute, and that though the word "existence" may occur as the grammatical predicate in a sentence, no attribute is being predicated of a thing when we say that the thing exists or has existence. Thus, to use Kant's example, when we think of $100 we are thinking of the nature of this sum of money; but the nature of $100 remains the same whether we have $100 in our pockets or not. Accordingly, we are confounding grammar with logic if we suppose that some characteristic is being attributed to the nature of $100 when we say that a hundred dollar bill exists in someone's pocket.

To make the point clearer, consider another example. When we say that a lion has a tawny color, we are predicating a certain attribute of the animal, and similarly when we say that the lion is fierce or is hungry. But when we say the lion exists, all that we are saying is that something is (or has the nature of) a lion; we are not specifying an attribute which belongs to the nature of anything that is a lion. In short, the word "existence" does not signify any attribute, and in consequence no attribute that belongs to the nature of anything. Accordingly, it does not follow from the assumption that we have an idea of a perfect being that such a being exists. For the idea of a perfect being does not involve the attribute of existence as a constituent of that idea, since there is no such attribute. The ontological argument thus has a serious leak, and it can hold no water.

The two arguments discussed thus far are purely dialectical, and attempt

teleological

False statement

[to establish God's existence without any appeal to empirical data] The next argument, called the argument from design, is different in character, for it is based on what purports to be empirical evidence. I wish to examine two forms of this argument.

One variant of it calls attention to the remarkable way in which different things and processes in the world are integrated with each other, and concludes that this mutual "fitness" of things can be explained only by the assumption of a divine architect who planned the world and everything in it. For example, living organisms can maintain themselves in a variety of environments, and do so in virtue of their delicate mechanisms which adapt the organisms to all sorts of environmental changes. There is thus an intricate pattern of means and ends throughout the animate world. But the existence of this pattern is unintelligible, so the argument runs, except on the hypothesis that the pattern has been deliberately instituted by a Supreme Designer. If we find a watch in some deserted spot, we do not think it came into existence by chance, and we do not hesitate to conclude that an intelligent creature designed and made it. But the world and all its contents exhibit mechanisms and mutual adjustments that are far more complicated and subtle than are those of a watch. Must we not therefore conclude that these things too have a Creator?

The conclusion of this argument is based on an inference from analogy: the watch and the world are alike in possessing a congruence of parts and an adjustment of means to ends; the watch has a watch-maker; hence the world has a world-maker. But is the analogy a good one? Let us once more waive some important issues, in particular the issue whether the universe is the unified system such as the watch admittedly is. And let us concentrate on the question, what is the ground for our assurance that watches do not come into existence except through the operations of intelligent manufacturers. The answer is plain. We have never run across a watch which has not been deliberately made by someone. But the situation is nothing like this in the case of the innumerable animate and inanimate systems with which we are familiar. Even in the case of living organisms, the parents do not "make" their progeny in the same sense in which watchmakers make watches. And once this point is clear, the inference from the existence of living organisms to the existence of a supreme designer no longer appears credible.

Moreover, the argument loses all its force if the facts which the hypothesis of a divine designer is supposed to explain can be understood on the basis of a better supported assumption. And indeed, such an alternative explanation is one of the achievements of Darwinian biology. For Darwin showed that one can account for a variety of biological species, as well as for their adaptations to their environments, without invoking a divine creator and acts of special creation. The Darwinian theory explains the diversity of biological species in terms of chance variations in the structure of organisms, and of a mechanism of selection which retains those variant forms that possess some advantages for survival. The evidence for these assumptions is considerable; and developments subsequent to Darwin have only strengthened the case for a thoroughly naturalistic explanation of the facts of biological adaptation. In any event, this version of the argument from design has nothing to recommend it.

A second form of this argument has been recently revived in the speculations of some modern physicists. No one who is familiar with the facts, can fail to be impressed by the success with which the use of mathematical methods has enabled us to obtain intellectual mastery of many parts of nature. But some thinkers have therefore concluded that since the book of nature is ostensibly written in mathematical language, nature must be the creation of a divine mathematician. However, the argument is most dubious. For it rests, among other things, on the assumption that mathematical tools can be successfully used only if the events of nature exhibit some *special* kind of order, and on the further assumption that if the structure of things were different from what they are, mathematical language would be inadequate for describing such structure. But it can be shown that no matter what the world were like—even if it impressed us as being utterly chaotic—it would still possess some order, and would in principle be amenable to a mathematical description. In point of fact, it makes no sense to say that there is absolutely *no* pattern in any conceivable subject matter. To be sure, there are differences in complexities of structure, and if the patterns of events were sufficiently complex we might not be able to unravel them. But however that may be, the success of mathematical physics in giving us some understanding of the world around us does not yield the conclusion that only a mathematician could have devised the patterns of order we have discovered in nature.

The inconclusiveness of the three classical arguments for the existence of God was already made evident by Kant, in a manner substantially not different from the above discussion. There are, however, other types of arguments for theism that have been influential in the history of thought, two of which I wish to consider, even if only briefly.

Indeed, though Kant destroyed the classical intellectual foundations for theism, he himself invented a fresh argument for it. Kant's attempted proof is not intended to be a purely theoretical demonstration, and is based on the supposed facts of our moral nature. It has exerted an enormous influence on subsequent theological speculation. In barest outline the argument is as follows. According to Kant, we are subject not only to physical laws like the rest of nature, but also to moral ones. These moral laws are categorical imperatives, which we must heed not because of their utilitarian consequences, but simply because as autonomous moral agents it is our duty to accept them as binding. However, Kant was keenly aware that though virtue may be its reward, the virtuous man (that is, the man who acts out of a sense of duty and in conformity with the moral law) does not always receive his just desserts in this world; nor did he shut his eyes to the fact that evil men frequently enjoy the best things this world has to offer. In short, virtue does not always reap happiness. Nevertheless, the highest human good is the realization of happiness commensurate with one's virtues; and Kant believed that it is a practical postulate of the moral life to promote this good. But what can guarantee that the highest good is realizable? Such a guarantee can be found only in God, who must therefore exist if the highest good is not to be a fatuous ideal. The existence of an omnipotent, omniscient, and omnibenevolent God is thus postulated as a necessary condition for the possibility of a moral life.

Despite the prestige this argument has acquired, it is difficult to grant it any force. It is easy enough to postulate God's existence. But as Bertrand Russell observed in another connection, postulation has all the advantages of theft over honest toil. No postulation carries with it any assurance that what is postulated is actually the case. And though we may postulate God's existence as a means to guaranteeing the possibility of realizing happiness together with virtue, the postulation establishes neither the actual realizability of this ideal nor the fact of his existence. Moreover, the argument is not made more cogent when we recognize that it is based squarely on the highly dubious conception that considerations of utility and human happiness must not enter into the determination of what is morally obligatory. Having built his moral theory on a radical separation of means from ends, Kant was driven to the desperate postulation of God's existence in order to relate them again. The argument is thus at best a *tour de force,* contrived to remedy a fatal flaw in Kant's initial moral assumptions. It carries no conviction to anyone who does not commit Kant's initial blunder.

One further type of argument, pervasive in much Protestant theological literature, deserves brief mention. Arguments of this type take their point of departure from the psychology of religious and mystical experience. Those who have undergone such experiences, often report that during the experience they feel themselves to be in the presence of the divine and holy, that they lose their sense of self-identity and become merged with some fundamental reality, or that they enjoy a feeling of total dependence upon some ultimate power. The overwhelming sense of transcending one's finitude which characterizes such vivid periods of life, and of coalescing with some ultimate source of all existence, is then taken to be compelling evidence for the existence of a supreme being. In a variant form of this argument, other theologians have identified God as the object which satisfies the commonly experienced need for integrating one's scattered and conflicting impulses into a coherent unity, or as the subject which is of ultimate concern to us. In short, a proof of God's existence is found in the occurrence of certain distinctive experiences.

It would be flying in the face of well-attested facts were one to deny that such experiences frequently occur. But do these facts constitute evidence for the conclusion based on them? Does the fact, for example, that an individual experiences a profound sense of direct contact with an alleged transcendent ground of all reality, constitute competent evidence for the claim that there is such a ground and that it is the immediate cause of the experience? If well-established canons for evaluating evidence are accepted, the answer is surely negative. No one will dispute that many men do have vivid experiences in which such things as ghosts or pink elephants appear before them; but only the hopelessly credulous will without further ado count such experiences as establishing the existence of ghosts and pink elephants. To establish the existence of such things, evidence is required that is obtained under controlled conditions and that can be confirmed by independent inquirers. Again, though a man's report that he is suffering pain may be taken at face value, one cannot take at face value the claim, were he to make it, that it is the food he ate which is the cause (or a contributory cause) of his felt pain—not even if the man were to report a vivid feeling of abdominal disturbance. And similarly, an overwhelming feeling of being in the presence of the Divine is evidence enough for admitting the genuineness of such feeling; it is no evidence for the claim that a supreme being with a substantial existence independent of the experience is the cause of the experience.

STUDY QUESTIONS

1. In the early part of his article, Nagel is less than complimentary about religion. What does he say? Can you cite historical evidence which supports, or refutes, his accusations?
2. Nagel cites Kant as an authority in declaring that existence is not a predicate. What does it mean to say that existence is not a predicate? What force does this assertion have in rebutting the ontological argument?
3. What does Nagel say about the analogy between a watch and the world in his discussion of the "design" proof? Do you find his criticisms of the analogy sound?
4. "Let the skeptics go to war. When their life is on the line and people are falling like flies, they will swallow their misplaced pride and reach out for God." How would Nagel respond to this claim?
5. "I was dying. The doctors gave up hope. All of a sudden, without explanation, I was fit as a fiddle. It was a miracle! Thank God, my prayers were answered!" What would Nagel say to this?

2

The Problem of Evil

PROBLEM INTRODUCTION

Probably the most perplexing issue for theists is how to reconcile the existence of God with the fact of evil in the world. Christianity, for example, views God as all-good, all-loving, all-knowing, and all-powerful. The prefix "all" carries the implication that God has such traits without limit, far surpassing the extent to which humans have them. Presuming that God possesses these traits, how do we explain the fact that God's creation is filled with so much suffering and pain? If God is all-good and all-loving, God would want to spare creatures this burden. If God is all-knowing and all-powerful, God could in fact do so. Why, then, do suffering and pain persist? This, in a nutshell, is the problem of evil.

The arguments for God's existence which you have studied contribute very little to the solution of this problem. Indeed, ironically, they may worsen it. For instance, the teleological argument tells us that the universe is a system whose parts are arranged by a Divine Architect in a deliberate, careful fashion, so that each part has a goal, end, or purpose. This seems to imply, logically, that every bit of suffering and pain is also planned, for surely God would not allow pointless suffering.

Mark Twain seizes on this very point. In *Letters from the Earth* he reflects critically and irreverently on the misery which pervades our existence and concludes that this world could only have been created by a merciless villain. He argues that God has the responsibility of a parent to protect and nourish the weak creatures God has created, but instead allows the human race to suffer the ravages of disease and disaster. Moreover, Twain maintains, God has created us with a disposition to sin. To hold us responsible for our sins is as ludicrous as a clockmaker blaming the clock for failing to tell time.

One theistic reply to such charges is that evil is not real—it is an *illusion* which we suffer due to our limited, flawed perspective as humans. If we were to observe the flow of events in history as God does, then what seems to be a tragedy would turn out to be a blessing in disguise. But is this reply sound? Our status as humans is a given; it seems absurd to expect us to deal with reality as if we were not human. Moreover, if human beings are so prone to skew reality, to distort it, perhaps what they take to be "good" is really evil. Further, individuals who confront suffering and pain firsthand are unlikely to be impressed by the claim that evil is only an illusion. The woman who has been brutally raped, the soldier whose war experience has made him a paraplegic, and the parent whose child has contracted an incurable disease are likely to dismiss the illusion argument as cruel and insulting.

A related defense is that humans should not criticize God for permitting evil in the world because God is so different from us. What is morally appropriate for God may be quite different from what is morally appropriate for us. The difficulty with this position is that if we are not allowed to condemn God's actions, we cannot praise them either. Therefore, unless we are willing to treat the existence of God as a morally neutral fact, thereby depriving religion of any moral connection with life, the problem of evil must be met head on.

A third theistic stance holds that evil is indeed real, and not merely an illusion, but that God lacks the power to remove it. The American philosopher William James is one who held this position. James saw this dilemma before him: either God is able to remove evil but chooses not to, or God wishes to remove evil but lacks the power to do so. The first option, he felt, undermined God's goodness, a charge which he found unthinkable. He therefore chose the second one. Seeing history as a struggle of good against evil, James had the confidence, based on precedent, that the persistent cooperation of God and humanity is likely to produce a better world. He described his approach as *meliorism*, from the Latin word for "better." Yet James's line of reasoning has precious few supporters. Believers are typically anxious to retain their traditional perspective to the effect that God is all-powerful; the prospect that God is really not in charge of nature is singularly repugnant to them.

The much more common attempt to explain and justify the presence of evil is stated in the selection by John Hick. Hick's assessment of the problem of evil bears two important assumptions: human beings are free, and suffering is necessary for moral development. Human beings possess free will, Hick argues, and are therefore morally responsible agents. But God could have made us otherwise. He could have made us so that we automatically choose the right thing all the time, but the price is very high indeed—the price is our freedom. Thus, humanity is responsible for a great deal of its own suffering and pain. Being free, and facing genuine options of good and evil, humans often choose the latter. Sometimes we cause evil directly, as in stealing or murder; on other occasions we cause it indirectly because of ignorance for which we can be blamed. Hick calls this "culpable incompetence." For instance, diseases and storms are the cause of enormous human suffering. Yet if we had been more dedicated and aggressive in studying humans and nature, we could have learned enough to avoid much of this suffering. Further, Hick tells us, evil enables humans to grow in virtue, and to merit their salvation. This is done by choosing good over evil, and coping with problems and challenges.

J. L. Mackie finds arguments such as Hick's unconvincing. In a rigorous critique of such arguments, Mackie argues that it is futile for theists to attempt to justify evil while maintaining the core beliefs of "ordinary theism"—God is omnipotent, God is wholly good, evil exists—because these beliefs are contradictory. If any two of them were true, he says, the third would be false. Mackie attempts to show that justifications of evil by theists which purport to affirm these three beliefs *explicitly* actually deny one or more of them *implicitly*. The central dilemma which defeats theism, according to Mackie, is the "paradox of omnipotence." If God has created humans with freedom, such that God cannot control them, then it would seem that God is really not omnipotent.

Letters from the Earth
Mark Twain

The writings of Samuel Clemens (1835–1910) are well known and much loved. Everyone in America is familiar with *The Adventures of Tom Sawyer* and *Huckleberry Finn,* his most popular works. But there is another side to his writing which has received little attention—his role as a caustic social philosopher and critic of traditional religious belief. The following selection displays this side of Twain at its best.

The setting itself shows Twain's ingenuity. Satan has been banished from heaven for making sarcastic comments about God's creation. He decides to visit the earth and he writes back home to his friends. In the course of the correspondence, Satan argues convincingly that only mad beings would adopt the religious beliefs of humans. He bases his argument on what has been called the *problem of evil*. A perfectly good, powerful, and all-knowing God would not allow unnecessary evil to exist in creation. But Satan points out that many of the conventional religious beliefs of humans seem to make God into a barbaric deity who tortures humanity for the sheer joy of it. What is especially amazing, Satan contends, is that humanity then blames itself for all these woes, instead of the guilty one. In his own inimitable way, Twain puts the problem of evil before us with such force and skill that we are not likely to forget that this is no mere intellectual game, but a deadly serious challenge to conventional religious belief.

Satan had been making admiring remarks about certain of the Creator's sparkling industries—remarks which, being read between the lines, were sarcasms. He had made them confidentially to his safe friends the other archangels, but they had been overheard by some ordinary angels and reported at Headquarters.

He was ordered into banishment for a day—the celestial day. It was a punishment he was used to, on account of his too flexible tongue. Formerly he had been deported into Space, there being nowhither else to send him, and had flapped tediously around there in the eternal night and the Arctic chill; but now it occurred to him to push on and hunt up the earth and see how the Human-Race experiment was coming along.

By and by he wrote home—very privately—to St. Michael and St. Gabriel about it.

SATAN'S LETTER

This is a strange place, an extraordinary place, and interesting. There is nothing resembling it at home. The people are all insane, the other animals are all insane, the earth is insane. Nature itself is insane. Man is a marvelous curiosity. When he is at his very very best he is a sort of low grade nickel-plated angel; at his worst he is unspeakable, unimaginable; and first and last and all the time he is a sarcasm. Yet he blandly and in all sincerity calls himself the "noblest work of God." This is the truth I am telling you. And this is not a new idea with him, he has talked it through all the ages, and believed it. Believed it, and found nobody among all his race to laugh at it.

Moreover—if I may put another strain upon you—he thinks he is the Creator's pet. He believes the Creator is proud of him; he even believes the Creator loves him; has a passion for him; sits up nights to admire him; yes, and watch over him and keep him out of trouble. He prays to Him, and thinks He listens. Isn't it a quaint idea? Fills his prayers with crude and bald and florid flatteries of Him, and thinks He sits and purrs over these extravagancies and enjoys them. He prays for help, and favor, and protection, every day; and does it with hopefulness and confidence, too, although no prayer of his has ever been answered. The daily affront, the daily defeat, do not discourage him, he goes on praying just the same. There is something almost fine about this perseverance. I must put one more strain upon you: he thinks he is going to heaven!

He has salaried teachers who tell him that. They also tell him there is a hell, of everlasting fire, and that he will go to it if he doesn't keep the Commandments. What are the Commandments? They are a curiosity. I will tell you about them by and by.

LETTER III

You have noticed that the human being is a curiosity. In times past he has had (and worn out and flung away) hundreds and hundreds of religions; today he has hundreds and hundreds of religions, and launches not fewer than three new ones every year. I could enlarge that number and still be within the facts.

One of his principal religions is called the Christian. A sketch of it will interest you. It is set forth in detail in a book containing two million words, called the Old and New Testaments. Also it has another name—The Word of God. For the Christian thinks every word of it was dictated by God—the one I have been speaking of.

It is full of interest. It has noble poetry in it; and some clever fables; and some blood-drenched history; and some good morals; and a wealth of obscenity; and upwards of a thousand lies.

This Bible is built mainly out of the fragments of older Bibles that had their day and crumbled to ruin. So it noticeably lacks in originality, necessarily. Its three or four most imposing and impressive events all happened in earlier Bibles; all its best precepts and rules of conduct came also from those Bibles; there are only two new things in it: hell, for one, and that singular heaven I have told you about.

What shall we do? If we believe, with these people, that their God invented these cruel things, we slander him; if we believe that these people invented them themselves, we slander them. It is an unpleasant dilemma in either case, for neither of these parties has done *us* any harm.

For the sake of tranquillity, let us take a side. Let us join forces with the people and put the whole ungracious burden upon *him*—heaven, hell, Bible and all. It does not seem right, it does not seem fair; and yet when you consider that heaven, and how crushingly charged it is with everything that is repulsive to a human being, how can we believe a human being invented it? And when I come to tell you about hell, the strain will be greater still, and you will be likely to say, No, a man would not provide that place, for either himself or anybody else; he simply couldn't.

That innocent Bible tells about the Creation. Of what—the universe? Yes, the universe. In six days!

God did it. He did not call it the universe—that name is modern. His whole attention was upon this world. He constructed it in five days—and then? It took him only one day to make twenty million suns and eighty million planets!

What were they for—according to his idea? To furnish light for this little toy-world. That was his whole purpose; he had no other. One of the twenty million suns (the smallest one) was to light it in the daytime, the rest were to help one of the universe's countless moons modify the darkness of its nights.

It is quite manifest that he believed his fresh-made skies were diamond-sown with those myriads of twinkling stars the moment his first-day's sun sank below the horizon; whereas, in fact, not a single star winked in that black vault until three years and a half after that memorable week's formidable industries had been completed.[1] Then one star appeared, all solitary and alone, and began to blink. Three years later another one appeared. The two blinked together for more than four years before a third joined them. At the end of the first hundred years there were not yet twenty-five stars twinkling in the wide wastes of those gloomy skies. At the end of a thousand years not enough stars were yet visible to make a show. At the end of a million years only half of the present array had sent their light over the telescopic frontiers, and it took another million for the rest to follow suit, as the vulgar phrase goes. There being at that time no telescope, their advent was not observed.

For three hundred years, now, the Christian astronomer has known that his Deity didn't make the stars in those tremendous six days; but the Christian astronomer does not enlarge upon that detail. Neither does the priest.

In his Book, God is eloquent in his praises of his mighty work, and calls them by the largest names he can find—thus indicating that he has a strong

---

[1] It takes the light of the nearest star (61 Cygni) three and a half years to come to the earth, traveling at the rate of 186,000 miles per second. Arcturus had been shining 200 years before it was visible from the earth. Remoter stars gradually became visible after thousands and thousands of years.—*The Editor* [M. T.]

and just admiration of magnitudes; yet he made those millions of prodigious suns to light this wee little orb, instead of appointing this orb's little sun to dance attendance upon them. He mentions Arcturus in his Book—you remember Arcturus; we went there once. It is one of this earth's night lamps!—that giant globe which is fifty thousand times as large as this earth's sun, and compared with it as a melon compares with a cathedral.

However, the Sunday school still teaches the child that Arcturus was created to help light this earth, and the child grows up and continues to believe it long after he has found out that the probabilities are against its being so.

According to the Book and its servants the universe is only six thousand years old. It is only within the last hundred years that studious, inquiring minds have found out that it is nearer a hundred million.

During the Six Days, God created man and the other animals.

He made a man and a woman and placed them in a pleasant garden, along with the other creatures. They all lived together there in harmony and contentment and blooming youth for some time; then trouble came. God had warned the man and the woman that they must not eat of the fruit of a certain tree. And he added a most strange remark: he said that if they ate of it they should surely die. Strange, for the reason that inasmuch as they had never seen a sample of death they could not possibly know what he meant. Neither would he nor any other god have been able to make those ignorant children understand what was meant, without furnishing a sample. The mere word could have no meaning for them, any more than it would have for an infant of days.

Presently a serpent sought them out privately, and came to them walking upright, which was the way of serpents in those days. The serpent said the forbidden fruit would store their vacant minds with knowledge. So they ate it, which was quite natural, for man is so made that he eagerly wants to know; whereas the priest, like God, whose imitator and representative he is, has made it his business from the beginning to keep him *from* knowing any useful thing.

Adam and Eve ate the forbidden fruit, and at once a great light streamed into their dim heads. They had acquired knowledge. What knowledge—useful knowledge? No—merely knowledge that there was such a thing as good, and such a thing as evil, and how to do evil. They couldn't do it before. Therefore all their acts up to this time had been without stain, without blame, without offense.

But now they could do evil—and suffer for it; now they had acquired what the Church calls an invaluable possession, the Moral Sense; that sense which differentiates man from the beast and sets him above the beast. Instead of below the beast—where one would suppose his proper place would be, since he is always foul-minded and guilty and the beast always clean-minded and innocent. It is like valuing a watch that must go wrong, above a watch that can't.

The Church still prizes the Moral Sense as man's noblest asset today, although the Church knows God had a distinctly poor opinion of it and did what he could in his clumsy way to keep his happy Children of the Garden from acquiring it.

Very well, Adam and Eve now knew what evil was, and how to do it. They knew how to do various kinds of wrong things, and among them one principal one—the one God had his mind on principally. That one was the art and mystery of sexual intercourse. To them it was a magnificent discovery, and they stopped idling around and turned their entire attention to it, poor exultant young things!

To proceed with the Biblical curiosities. Naturally you will think the threat to punish Adam and Eve for disobeying was of course not carried out, since they did not create themselves, nor their natures nor their impulses nor their weaknesses, and hence were not properly subject to anyone's commands, and not responsible to anybody for their acts. It will surprise you to know that the threat *was* carried out. Adam and Eve were punished, and that crime finds apologists unto this day. The sentence of death was executed.

As you perceive, the only person responsible for the couple's offense escaped; and not only escaped but became the executioner of the innocent.

In your country and mine we should have the privilege of making fun of this kind of morality, but it would be unkind to do it here. Many of these people have the reasoning faculty, but no one uses it in religious matters.

The best minds will tell you that when a man has begotten a child he is morally bound to tenderly care for it, protect it from hurt, shield it from disease, clothe it, feed it, bear with its waywardness, lay no hand upon it save in kindness and for its own good, and never in any case inflict upon it a wanton cruelty. God's treatment of his earthly children, every day and every night, is the exact opposite of all that, yet those best minds warmly justify these crimes, condone them, excuse them, and indignantly refuse to regard them as crimes at all, when *he* commits them. Your country and mine is an interesting one, but there is nothing there that is half so interesting as the human mind.

Very well, God banished Adam and Eve from the Garden, and eventually assassinated them. All for disobeying a command which he had no right to utter. But he did not stop there, as you will see. He has one code of morals for himself, and quite another for his children. He requires his children to deal justly—and gently—with offenders, and forgive them seventy-and-seven times; whereas he deals neither justly nor gently with anyone, and he did not forgive the ignorant and thoughtless first pair of juveniles even their first small offense and say, "You may go free this time, I will give you another chance."

On the contrary! He elected to punish *their* children, all through the ages to the end of time, for a trifling offense committed by others before they were born. He is punishing them yet. In mild ways? No, in atrocious ones.

You would not suppose that this kind of a Being gets many compliments. Undeceive yourself: the world calls him the All-Just, the All-Righteous, the All-Good, the All-Merciful, the All-Forgiving, the All-Truthful, the All-Loving, the Source of All Morality. These Sarcasms are uttered daily, all over the world. But not as conscious sarcasms. No, they are meant seriously: they are uttered without a smile. . . .

LETTER V

Noah began to collect animals. There was to be one couple of each and every sort of creature that walked or crawled, or swam or flew, in the world of animated nature. We have to guess at how long it took to collect the creatures and how much it cost, for there is no record of these details. When Symmachus made preparation to introduce his young son to grown-up life in imperial Rome, he sent men to Asia, Africa and everywhere to collect wild animals for the arena-fights. It took the men three years to accumulate the animals and fetch them to Rome. Merely quadrupeds and alligators, you understand—no birds, no snakes, no frogs, no worms, no lice, no rats, no fleas, no ticks, no caterpillars, no spiders, no houseflies, no mosquitoes—nothing but just plain simple quadrupeds and alligators: and no quadrupeds except fighting ones. Yet it was as I have said: it took three years to collect them, and the cost of animals and transportation and the men's wages footed up $4,500,000.

How many animals? We do not know. But it was under five thousand, for that was the largest number *ever* gathered for those Roman shows, and it was Titus, not Symmachus, who made that collection. Those were mere baby museums, compared to Noah's contract. Of birds and beasts and fresh-water creatures he had to collect 146,000 kinds; and of insects upwards of two million species.

Thousands and thousands of those things are very difficult to catch, and if Noah had not given up and resigned, he would be on the job yet, as Leviticus used to say. However, I do not mean that he withdrew. No, he did not do that. He gathered as many creatures as he had room for, and then stopped.

If he had known all the requirements in the beginning, he would have been aware that what was needed was a fleet of Arks. But he did not know how many kinds of creatures there were, neither did his Chief. So he had no kangaroo, and no 'possum, and no Gila monster, and no ornithorhychus, and lacked a multitude of other indispensable blessings which a loving Creator had provided for man and forgotten about, they having long ago wandered to a side of this world which he had never seen and with whose affairs he was not acquainted. And so everyone of them came within a hair of getting drowned.

They only escaped by an accident. There was not water enough to go around. Only enough was provided to flood one small corner of the globe—the rest of the globe was not then known, and was supposed to be nonexistent.

However, the thing that really and finally and definitely determined Noah to stop with enough species for purely business purposes and let the rest become extinct, was an incident of the last days: an excited stranger arrived with some most alarming news. He said he had been camping among some mountains and valleys about six hundred miles away, and he had seen a wonderful thing there: he stood upon a precipice overlooking a wide valley, and up the valley he saw a billowy black sea of strange animal life coming. Presently the creatures passed by, struggling, fighting, scrambling, screeching, snorting— horrible vast masses of tumultuous flesh! Sloths as big as an elephant; frogs as big as a cow; a megatherium and his harem huge beyond belief; saurians and saurians and saurians, group after group, family after family, species after species—a hundred feet long, thirty feet high, and twice as quarrelsome; one of them hit a perfectly blameless Durham bull a thump with its tail and sent it whizzing three hundred feet into the air and it fell at the man's feet with a sigh and was no more. The man said that these prodigious animals had heard about the Ark and were coming. Coming to get saved from the flood. And not coming in pairs, they were *all* coming: they did not know the passengers were restricted to pairs, the man said, and wouldn't care a rap for the regulations, anyway—they would sail in that Ark or know the reason why. The man said the Ark would not hold the half of them; and moreover they were coming hungry, and would eat up everything there was, including the menagerie and the family.

All these facts were suppressed, in the Biblical account. You find not a hint of them there. The whole thing is hushed up. Not even the names of those vast creatures are mentioned. It shows you that when people have left a reproachful vacancy in a contract they can be as shady about it in Bibles as elsewhere. Those powerful animals would be of inestimable value to man now, when transportation is so hard pressed and expensive, but they are all lost to him. All lost, and by Noah's fault. They all got drowned. Some of them as much as eight million years ago.

Very well, the stranger told his tale, and Noah saw that he must get away before the monsters arrived. He would have sailed at once, but the upholsterers and decorators of the housefly's drawing room still had some finishing touches to put on, and that lost him a day. Another day was lost in getting the flies aboard, there being sixty-eight billions of them and the Deity still afraid there might not be enough. Another day was lost in stowing forty tons of selected filth for the flies' sustenance.

Then at last, Noah sailed; and none too soon, for the Ark was only just sinking out of sight on the horizon when the monsters arrived, and added their lamentations to those of the multitude of weeping fathers and mothers and frightened little children who were clinging to the wave-washed rocks in the pouring rain and lifting imploring prayers to an All-Just and All-Forgiving and All-Pitying Being who had never answered a prayer since those crags were builded, grain by grain out of the sands, and would still not have answered one when the ages should have crumbled them to sand again.

LETTER VI

On the third day, about noon, it was found that a fly had been left behind. The return voyage turned out to be long and difficult, on account of the lack of chart and compass, and because of the changed aspects of all coasts, the steadily rising water having submerged some of the lower landmarks and given to higher ones an unfamiliar look; but after sixteen days of earnest and faithful seeking, the fly was found at last, and received on board with hymns of praise and gratitude, the Family standing meanwhile uncovered, out of reverence for its divine origin. It was weary and worn, and had suffered somewhat from the weather, but was otherwise in good estate. Men and their families had died of hunger on barren mountain tops, but it had not lacked for food, the multitudinous corpses furnishing it in rank and rotten richness. Thus was the sacred bird providentially preserved.

Providentially. That is the word. For the fly had not been left behind by accident. No, the hand of Providence was in it. There are no accidents. All things that happen, happen for a purpose. They are foreseen from the beginning of time, they are ordained from the beginning of time. From the dawn of Creation the Lord had foreseen that Noah, being alarmed and confused by the invasion of the prodigious brevet fossils, would prematurely fly to sea unprovided with a certain invaluable disease. He would have all the other diseases, and could distribute them among the new races of men as they appeared in the world, but he would lack one of the very best—typhoid fever; a malady which, when the circumstances are especially favorable, is able to utterly wreck a patient without killing him; for it can restore him to his feet with a long life in him, and yet deaf, dumb, blind, crippled, and idiotic. The housefly is its main disseminator, and is more competent and more calamitously effective than all the other distributors of the dreaded scourge put together. And so, by foreordination from the beginning of time, this fly was left behind to seek out a typhoid corpse and feed upon its corruptions and gaum its legs with the germs and transmit them to the re-peopled world for permanent business. From that one housefly, in the ages that have since elapsed, billions of sickbeds have been stocked, billions of wrecked bodies sent tottering about the earth, and billions of cemeteries recruited with the dead.

The human being is a machine. An automatic machine. It is composed of thousands of complex and delicate mechanisms, which perform their functions harmoniously and perfectly, in accordance with laws devised for their governance, and over which the man himself has no authority, no mastership, no control. For each one of these thousands of mechanisms the Creator has planned an enemy, whose office is to harass it, pester it, persecute it, damage it, afflict it with pains, and miseries, and ultimate destruction. Not one has been overlooked.

From cradle to grave these enemies are always at work; they know no rest, night or day. They are an army: an organized army; a besieging army; an assaulting army; an army that is alert, watchful, eager, merciless; an army that never relents, never grants a truce.

It moves by squad, by company, by battalion, by regiment, by brigade, by division, by army corps; upon occasion it masses its parts and moves upon mankind with its whole strength. It is the Creator's Grand Army, and he is the Commander-in-Chief. Along its battlefront its grisly banners wave their legends in the face of the sun: Disaster, Disease, and the rest.

Disease! That is the main force, the diligent force, the devastating force! It attacks the infant the moment it is born; it furnishes it one malady after another: croup, measles, mumps, bowel troubles, teething pains, scarlet fever, and other childhood specialties. It chases the child into youth and furnishes it some specialties for that time of life. It chases the youth into maturity, maturity into age, and age into the grave.

With these facts before you, you will now try to guess man's chiefest pet name for this ferocious Commander-in-Chief? I will save you the trouble—but you must not laugh. It is Our Father in Heaven!

It is curious—the way the human mind works. The Christian begins with this straight proposition, this definite proposition, this inflexible and uncompromising proposition: *God is all-knowing, and all-powerful.*

This being the case, nothing can happen without his knowing beforehand that it is going to happen; nothing happens without his permission; nothing can happen that he chooses to prevent.

That is definite enough, isn't it? It makes the Creator distinctly responsible for everything that happens, doesn't it?

The Christian concedes it in that italicized sentence. Concedes it with feeling, with enthusiasm.

Then, having thus made the Creator responsible for all those pains and diseases and miseries above enumerated, and which he could have prevented, the gifted Christian blandly calls him Our Father!

It is as I tell you. He equips the Creator with every trait that goes to the making of a fiend, and then arrives at the conclusion that a fiend and a father are the same thing! Yet he would deny that a malevolent lunatic and a Sunday school superintendent are essentially the same. What do you think of the human mind? I mean, in case you think there is a human mind.

LETTER IX

The Ark continued its voyage, drifting around here and there and yonder, compassless and uncontrolled, the sport of the random winds and the swirling currents. And the rain, the rain, the rain! It kept on falling, pouring, drenching, flooding. No such rain had ever been seen before. Sixteen inches a day had been heard of, but that was nothing to this. This was a hundred and twenty inches a day—ten feet! At this incredible rate it rained forty days and forty nights, and submerged every hill that was four hundred feet high. Then the heavens and even the angels went dry; no more water was to be had.

As a Universal Flood it was a disappointment, but there had been heaps of Universal Floods before, as is witnessed by all the Bibles of all the nations, and this was as good as the best one.

At last the Ark soared aloft and came to a rest on the top of Mount Ararat, seventeen thousand feet above the valley, and its living freight got out and went down the mountain.

Noah planted a vineyard, and drank of the wine and was overcome.

This person had been selected from all the populations because he was the best sample there was. He was to start the human race on a new basis. This was the new basis. The promise was bad. To go further with the experiment was to run a great and most unwise risk. Now was the time to do with these people what had been so judiciously done with the others—drown them. Anybody but the Creator would have seen this. But he didn't see it. That is, maybe he didn't.

It is claimed that from the beginning of time he foresaw everything that would happen in the world. If that is true, he foresaw that Adam and Eve would eat the apple; that their posterity would be unendurable and have to be drowned; that Noah's posterity would in their turn be unendurable, and that by and by he would have to leave his throne in heaven and come down and be crucified to save that same tiresome human race again. The whole of it? No! A part of it? Yes. How much of it? In each generation, for hundreds and hundreds of generations, a billion would die and all go to perdition except perhaps ten thousand out of the billion. The ten thousand would have to come from the little body of Christians, and only one in the hundred of that little body would stand any chance. None of them at all except such Roman Catholics as should have the luck to have a priest handy to sandpaper their souls at the last gasp, and here and there a Presbyterian. No others savable. All the others damned. By the million.

Shall you grant that he foresaw all this? The pulpit grants it. It is the same as granting that in the matter of intellect the Deity is the Head Pauper of the Universe, and that in the matter of morals and character he is away down on the level of David.

STUDY QUESTIONS

1. Some people argue that evil is due to the sin of Adam and Eve. How does Twain respond to this argument?
2. Some people claim that since humans are finite beings and God is infinite, we cannot comprehend God and God's ways. They conclude that there is no problem of evil. Are they right?
3. Why does Twain believe that God's foreknowledge of events is inconsistent with God's goodness? What do you think?

4. Twain claims that humanity works with a double standard of morality—people excuse God for acts which would convict an ordinary person of being a moral fiend. Do you agree with this?
5. Someone might respond to Twain by claiming that the evil in the world was necessary for a greater good. Would you accept such a reply? Under what conditions do the ends justify the means?

Free Will, Moral Growth, and Evil
John Hick

John Hick (1922–   ) began his career as a Presbyterian minister in England. His many writings on religion have gained him wide recognition as a philosopher. He has taught at Cornell University, Princeton Theological Seminary, Cambridge University, the University of Birmingham, and most recently the Claremont Graduate School. Elaborating the position of Irenaeus, an early Christian theologian, Hick believes that the presence of evil—evil caused by human beings and evil caused by natural phenomena—is compatible with the existence of an infinitely merciful and good God.

The evil caused by human beings is a result of free will. Of course, God could have made beings which always made the right decision; but, then, such beings would be mere mechanisms, passively acting out God's will. Hick claims that God cannot make free beings who always choose the right course of action. The fact that people possess free will makes it possible for them to construct their own characters—for good or for ill. But a necessary condition for becoming a morally superior person is that pain and suffering exist. Without a world containing such evils, moral traits such as courage, patience, and sympathy could not develop. The world, with all its shocks, is a place where we are given the opportunity to develop into moral beings. This greater good outweighs the evil.

Hick's argument depends upon several complex assumptions. Although his conception of "free will" is not spelled out carefully in this selection, perhaps the readings by James and Bertocci in Part Three will help you understand his position. Hick's argument assumes that the ends sometimes justify the means. It may prove helpful to consider when this is not true and why. His argument may require some supplementation on this point.

To many, the most powerful positive objection to belief in God is the fact of evil. Probably for most agnostics it is the appalling depth and extent of human suffering, more than anything else, that makes the idea of a loving Creator seem so implausible and disposes them toward one or another of the various naturalistic theories of religion.

From John Hick, *Philosophy of Religion* © 1963, pp. 40–47. Reprinted by permission of Prentice-Hall, Inc., Englewood Cliffs, N. J.

As a challenge to theism, the problem of evil has traditionally been posed in the form of a dilemma: if God is perfectly loving, he must wish to abolish evil; and if he is all-powerful, he must be able to abolish evil. But evil exists; therefore God cannot be both omnipotent and perfectly loving.

Certain solutions, which at once suggest themselves, have to be ruled out so far as the Judaic-Christian faith is concerned.

To say, for example (with contemporary Christian Science), that evil is an illusion of the human mind, is impossible within a religion based upon the stark realism of the Bible. Its pages faithfully reflect the characteristic mixture of good and evil in human experience. They record every kind of sorrow and suffering, every mode of man's inhumanity to man and of his painfully insecure existence in the world. There is no attempt to regard evil as anything but dark, menacingly ugly, heart-rending, and crushing. In the Christian scriptures, the climax of this history of evil is the crucifixion of Jesus, which is presented not only as a case of utterly unjust suffering, but as the violent and murderous rejection of God's Messiah. There can be no doubt, then, that for biblical faith, evil is unambiguously evil, and stands in direct opposition to God's will.

Again, to solve the problem of evil by means of the theory (sponsored, for example, by the Boston "Personalist" School)[1] of a finite deity who does the best he can with a material, intractable and co-eternal with himself, is to have abandoned the basic premise of Hebrew-Christian monotheism; for the theory amounts to rejecting belief in the infinity and sovereignty of God.

Indeed, any theory which would avoid the problem of the origin of evil by depicting it as an ultimate constituent of the universe, coordinate with good, has been repudiated in advance by the classic Christian teaching, first developed by Augustine, that evil represents the going wrong of something which in itself is good.[2] Augustine holds firmly to the Hebrew-Christian conviction that the universe is *good*—that is to say, it is the creation of a good God for a good purpose. He completely rejects the ancient prejudice, widespread in his day, that matter is evil. There are, according to Augustine, higher and lower, greater and lesser goods in immense abundance and variety; but everything which has being is good in its own way and degree, except in so far as it may have become spoiled or corrupted. Evil—whether it be an evil will, an instance of pain, or some disorder or decay in nature—has not been set there by God, but represents the distortion of something that is inherently valuable. Whatever exists is, as such, and in its proper place, good; evil is essentially parasitic upon good, being disorder and perversion in a fundamentally good creation. This understanding of evil as something negative means that it is not willed and created by God; but it does not mean (as some have supposed) that evil

---

[1] Edgar Brightman's *A Philosophy of Religion* (Englewood Cliffs, N.J.: Prentice-Hall, Inc., 1940), Chaps. 8–10, is a classic exposition of one form of this view.
[2] See Augustine's *Confessions*, Book VII, Chap. 12; *City of God*, Book XII, Chap. 3; *Enchiridion*, Chap. 4.

is unreal and can be disregarded. Clearly, the first effect of this doctrine is to accentuate even more the question of the origin of evil.

Theodicy,[3] as many modern Christian thinkers see it, is a modest enterprise, negative rather than positive in its conclusions. It does not claim to explain, nor to explain away, every instance of evil in human experience, but only to point to certain considerations which prevent the fact of evil (largely incomprehensible though it remains) from constituting a final and insuperable bar to rational belief in God.

In indicating these considerations it will be useful to follow the traditional division of the subject. There is the problem of _moral evil_ or wickedness: why does an all-good and all-powerful God permit this? And there is the problem of the _non-moral evil_ suffering or pain, both physical and mental: why has an all-good and all-powerful God created a world in which this occurs?

Christian thought has always considered moral evil in its relation to human freedom and responsibility. To be a person is to be a finite center of freedom, a (relatively) free and self-directing agent responsible for one's own decisions. This involves being free to act wrongly as well as to act rightly. The idea of a person who can be infallibly guaranteed always to act rightly is self-contradictory. There can be no guarantee in advance that a genuinely free moral agent will never choose amiss. Consequently, the possibility of wrongdoing or sin is logically inseparable from the creation of finite persons, and to say that God should not have created beings who might sin amounts to saying that he should not have created people.

This thesis has been challenged in some recent philosophical discussions of the problem of evil, in which it is claimed that no contradiction is involved in saying that God might have made people who would be genuinely free and who could yet be guaranteed always to act rightly. A quotation from one of these discussions follows:

> If there is no logical impossibility in a man's freely choosing the good on one, or on several occasions, there cannot be a logical impossibility in his freely choosing the good on every occasion. God was not, then, faced with a choice between making innocent automata and making beings who, in acting freely, would sometimes go wrong: there was open to him the obviously better possibility of making beings who would act freely but always go right. Clearly, his failure to avail himself of this possibility is inconsistent with his being both omnipotent and wholly good.[4]

[3] The word "theodicy" from the Greek _theos_ (God) and _dike_ (righteous) means the justification of God's goodness in the face of the fact of evil.

[4] J. L. Mackie, "Evil and Omnipotence," _Mind_ (April, 1955), p. 209. A similar point is made by Antony Flew in "Divine Omnipotence and Human Freedom," _New Essays in Philosophical Theology._ An important critical comment on these arguments is offered by Ninian Smart in "Omnipotence, Evil and Supermen," _Philosophy_ (April, 1961), with replies by Flew (January, 1962) and Mackie (April, 1962).

Hick's to reply to mackie

A reply to this argument is suggested in another recent contribution to the discussion.[5] If by a free action we mean an action which is not externally compelled but which flows from the nature of the agent as he reacts to the circumstances in which he finds himself, there is, indeed, no contradiction between our being free and our actions being "caused" (by our own nature) and therefore being in principle predictable. There is a contradiction, however, in saying that God is the cause of our acting as we do but that we are free beings in relation to God. There is, in other words, a contradiction in saying that God has made us so that we shall of necessity act in a certain way, and that we are genuinely independent persons in relation to him. If all our thoughts and actions are divinely predestined, however free and morally responsible we may seem to be to ourselves, we cannot be free and morally responsible in the sight of God, but must instead be his helpless puppets. Such "freedom" is like that of a patient acting out a series of posthypnotic suggestions; he appears, even to himself, to be free, but his volitions have actually been predetermined by another will, that of the hypnotist, in relation to whom the patient is not a free agent.

A different objector might raise the question of whether or not we deny God's omnipotence if we admit that he is unable to create persons who are free from the risks inherent in personal freedom. The answer that has always been given is that to create such beings is logically impossible, since there is nothing here to accomplish, but only a meaningless conjunction of words[6]—in this case "person who is not a person." God is able to create beings of any and every conceivable kind; but creatures who lack moral freedom, however superior they might be to human beings in other respects, would not be what we mean by persons. They would constitute a different form of life which God might have brought into existence instead of persons. When we ask why God did not create such beings in place of persons, the traditional answer is that only persons could, in any meaningful sense, become "children of God," capable of entering into a personal relationship with their Creator by a free and uncompelled response to his love.

When we turn from the possibility of moral evil as a correlate of man's personal freedom to its actuality, we face something which must remain inexplicable even when it can be seen to be possible. For we can never provide a complete causal explanation of a free act; if we could, it would not be a free act. The origin of moral evil lies forever concealed within the mystery of human freedom.

The necessary connection between moral freedom and the possibility, now actualized, of sin throws light upon a great deal of the suffering which afflicts mankind. For an enormous amount of human pain arises either from the inhumanity or the culpable incompetence of mankind. This includes such

---

[5] Flew, in *New Essays in Philosophical Theology.*
[6] As Aquinas said, "...nothing that implies a contradiction falls under the scope of God's omnipotence," *Summa Theologica,* Part I, Question 25, article 4.

major scourges as poverty, oppression and persecution, war, and all the injustice, indignity, and inequity which occur even in the most advanced societies. These evils are manifestations of human sin. Even disease is fostered to
an extent, the limits of which have not yet been determined by psychosomatic
medicine, by moral and emotional factors seated both in the individual and in
his social environment. To the extent that all of these evils stem from human
failures and wrong decisions, their possibility is inherent in the creation of free
persons inhabiting a world which presents them with real choices which are
followed by real consequences.

We may now turn more directly to the problem of suffering. Even though
the major bulk of actual human pain is traceable to man's misused freedom as
a sole or part cause, there remain other sources of pain which are entirely
independent of the human will, for example, earthquake, hurricane, storm,
flood, drought, and blight. In practice, it is often impossible to trace a bound-
ary between the suffering which results from human wickedness and folly
and that which falls upon mankind from without. Both kinds of suffering are
inextricably mingled together in human experience. For our present purpose,
however, it is important to note that the latter category does exist and that it
seems to be built into the very structure of our world. In response to it, theodicy,
if it is wisely conducted, follows a negative path. It is not possible to show
positively that each item of human pain serves the divine purpose of good;
but, on the other hand, it does seem possible to show that the divine purpose
as it is understood in Judaism and Christianity could not be forwarded in a
world which was designed as a permanent hedonistic paradise.   perfect

An essential premise of this argument concerns the nature of the divine
purpose in creating the world. The skeptic's assumption is that man is to be
viewed as a completed creation and that God's purpose in making the world
was to provide a suitable dwelling-place for this fully-formed creature. Since
God is good and loving, the environment which he has created for human life
to inhabit is naturally as pleasant and comfortable as possible. The problem is
essentially similar to that of a man who builds a cage for some pet animal.
Since our world, in fact, contains sources of hardship, inconvenience, and
danger of innumerable kinds, the conclusion follows that this world cannot
have been created by a perfectly benevolent and all-powerful deity.[7]

Christianity, however, has never supposed that God's purpose in the
creation of the world was to construct a paradise whose inhabitants would
experience a maximum of pleasure and a minimum of pain. The world is seen,
instead, as a place of "soul-making" in which free beings grappling with the
tasks and challenges of their existence in a common environment, may become "children of God" and "heirs of eternal life." A way of thinking theo-
logically of God's continuing creative purpose for man was suggested by some
of the early Hellenistic Fathers of the Christian Church, especially Irenaeus.

---

[7] This is the nature of David Hume's argument in his discussion of the problem of evil in his
Dialogues, Part XI.

Following hints from St. Paul, Irenaeus taught that man has been made as a person in the image of God but has not yet been brought as a free and responsible agent into the finite likeness of God, which is revealed in Christ.[8] Our world, with all its rough edges, is the sphere in which this second and harder stage of the creative process is taking place.

This conception of the world (whether or not set in Irenaeus' theological framework) can be supported by the method of negative theodicy. Suppose, contrary to fact, that this world were a paradise from which all possibility of pain and suffering were excluded. The consequences would be very far-reaching. For example, no one could ever injure anyone else: the murderer's knife would turn to paper or his bullets to thin air; the bank safe, robbed of a million dollars, would miraculously become filled with another million dollars (without this device, on however large a scale, proving inflationary); fraud, deceit, conspiracy, and treason would somehow always leave the fabric of society undamaged. Again, no one would ever be injured by accident; the mountain-climber, steeplejack, or playing child falling from a height would float unharmed to the ground; the reckless driver would never meet with disaster. There would be no need to work, since no harm could result from avoiding work; there would be no call to be concerned for others in time of need or danger, for in such a world there could be no real needs or dangers.

To make possible this continual series of individual adjustments, nature would have to work by "special providences" instead of running according to general laws which men must learn to respect on penalty of pain or death. The laws of nature would have to be extremely flexible: sometimes gravity would operate, sometimes not; sometimes an object would be hard and solid, sometimes soft. There could be no sciences, for there would be no enduring world structure to investigate. In eliminating the problems and hardships of an objective environment, with its own laws, life would become like a dream in which, delightfully but aimlessly, we would float and drift at ease.

One can at least begin to imagine such a world. It is evident that our present ethical concepts would have no meaning in it. If, for example, the notion of harming someone is an essential element in the concept of a wrong action, in our hedonistic paradise there could be no wrong actions nor any right actions in distinction from wrong. Courage and fortitude would have no point in an environment in which there is, by definition, no danger or difficulty. Generosity, kindness, the *agape* aspect of love, prudence, unselfishness, and all other ethical notions which presuppose life in a stable environment, could not even be formed. Consequently, such a world, however well it might promote pleasure, would be very ill adapted for the development of the moral qualities of human personality. In relation to this purpose it would be the worst of all possible worlds.

It would seem, then, that an environment intended to make possible the growth in free beings of the finest characteristics of personal life, must have

[8] See Irenaeus' *Against Heresies,* Book IV, Chaps. 37 and 38.

a good deal in common with our present world. It must operate according to general and dependable laws; and it must involve real dangers, difficulties, problems, obstacles, and possibilities of pain, failure, sorrow, frustration, and defeat. If it did not contain the particular trials and perils which—subtracting man's own very considerable contribution—our world contains, it would have to contain others instead.

To realize this is not, by any means, to be in possession of a detailed theodicy. It is to understand that this world, with all its "heartaches and the thousand natural shocks that flesh is heir to," an environment so manifestly not designed for the maximization of human pleasure and the minimization of human pain, may be rather well adapted to the quite different purpose of "soul-making."[9]

These considerations are related to theism as such. Specifically, Christian theism goes further in the light of the death of Christ, which is seen paradoxically both (as the murder of the divine Son) as the worst thing that has ever happened and (as the occasion of Man's salvation) as the best thing that has ever happened. As the supreme evil turned to supreme good, it provides the paradigm for the distinctively Christian reaction to evil. Viewed from the standpoint of Christian faith, evils do not cease to be evils; and certainly, in view of Christ's healing work, they cannot be said to have been sent by God. Yet, it has been the persistent claim of those seriously and wholeheartedly committed to Christian discipleship that tragedy, though truly tragic, may nevertheless be turned, through a man's reaction to it, from a cause of despair and alienation from God to a stage in the fulfillment of God's loving purpose for that individual. As the greatest of all evils, the crucifixion of Christ, was made the occasion of man's redemption, so good can be won from other evils. As Jesus saw his execution by the Romans as an experience which God desired him to accept, an experience which was to be brought within the sphere of the divine purpose and made to serve the divine ends, so the Christian response to calamity is to accept the adversities, pains, and afflictions which life brings, in order that they can be turned to a positive spiritual use.[10]

At this point, theodicy points forward in two ways to the subject of life after death.

First, although there are many striking instances of good being triumphantly brought out of evil through a man's or a woman's reaction to it, there are many other cases in which the opposite has happened. Sometimes ob-

---

[9] This brief discussion has been confined to the problem of human suffering. The large and intractable problem of animal pain is not taken up here. For a discussion of it, see, for example, Nels Ferré, *Evil and the Christian Faith* (New York: Harper & Row, Publishers, Inc., 1947), Chap. 7; and Austin Farrer, *Love Almighty and Ills Unlimited* (New York: Doubleday & Company, Inc., 1961), Chap. 5.

[10] This conception of providence is stated more fully in John Hick, *Faith and Knowledge* (Ithaca: Cornell University Press, 1957), Chap. 7, from which some sentences are incorporated in this paragraph.

stacles breed strength of character, dangers evoke courage and unselfishness, *evil not always constructive.* and calamities produce patience and moral steadfastness. But sometimes they lead, instead, to resentment, fear, grasping selfishness, and disintegration of character. Therefore, it would seem that any divine purpose of soul-making which is at work in earthly history must continue beyond this life if it is ever to achieve more than a very partial and fragmentary success.

Second, if we ask whether the business of soul-making is worth all the toil and sorrow of human life, the Christian answer must be in terms of a future good which is great enough to justify all that has happened on the way to it.

STUDY QUESTIONS

1. What does Hick mean by "free will"? Do you think that he defines it correctly? What if you did not believe that this sort of free will existed: how would this affect Hick's argument?
2. Is Hick committed to the view that God could not have made human beings better than they are? Do you think that this is true?
3. Why does Hick say that God could not create people who always choose the right thing? Do you think that his is a sound argument here?
4. "Hick says that pain and suffering are necessary to develop virtues such as courage, sympathy, etc. But if God is really all-powerful, God should be able to give us these virtues without putting us through the suffering." How would Hick respond to this criticism? What do you think?
5. A brilliant young researcher is on the verge of discovering a cure for all diseases. Would Hick advise the person to go ahead?
6. Hick says that courage, patience, and sympathy are virtues. Why are they virtues? Are they good in and of themselves, or are they means to a further end?
7. Suppose you had a chance to painlessly eliminate Adolf Hitler before 1940, knowing that if you did not, he would be responsible for millions of deaths. What would you do? What would Hick recommend?
8. "Hick believes that God is all-powerful *and* that humans are free. But to be all-powerful is to be the direct and immediate cause of all events in the universe. This forecloses the possibility of any other power, including humans. Therefore, Hick may believe *either* that God is all-powerful *or* that humans are free, but not both." Do you agree with this assessment? How do you think Hick would respond?

Evil and Omnipotence

J. L. Mackie

J. L. Mackie (1917–1981), who taught philosophy in Australia and England, addresses attempts by theists to solve the problem of evil in the article below. Though published in 1955, it is still recognized as probably the most powerful critique of such attempts written in this century. Mackie was convinced that theists who strive to reconcile evil with belief in a good, omnipotent being succeed only by implicitly (if not explicitly) rejecting one of the core beliefs of ordinary theism—God is omnipotent, God is good, Evil exists. Mackie gives a subtle analysis of four major theistic arguments. To the claim that evil is necessary as a counterpart to good, Mackie observes that this claim, if true, compromises the omnipotence of God because it sets a limit to what God can do, and it fails to account for superfluous (excessive) evil. To the claim that evil is necessary as a means to good, Mackie again says that this implies a severe restriction of God's power. To the claim that the universe is better with some evil in it than it could be if there were no evil, he counters that such a claim compromises God's benevolence for it assumes that God is not concerned to eliminate evil. And to the claim that evil is due to human freedom, Mackie gives two replies: (1) God could have made humans always to freely choose the good; and (2) genuine human freedom is at odds with divine omnipotence. This last point highlights what Mackie calls the "Paradox of Omnipotence"—for humans to be free means that God can make beings which God cannot subsequently control and this seems to mean that God's power is therefore limited.

   As you read Mackie's analysis, pay special attention to how he defines the terms omnipotence and omnibenevolence (all-good). Also, make sure that you understand what he means by "adequate," "half-hearted," and "fallacious" solutions to the problem of evil.

The traditional arguments for the existence of God have been fairly thoroughly criticised by philosophers. But the theologian can, if he wishes, accept this criticism. He can admit that no rational proof of God's existence is possible. And he can still retain all that is essential to his position, by holding that God's existence is known in some other, non-rational way. I think, however, that a more telling criticism can be made by way of the traditional problem of evil. Here it can be shown, not that religious beliefs lack rational support, but that they are positively irrational, that the several parts of the essential theological doctrine are inconsistent with one another, so that the theologian can maintain his position as a whole only by a much more extreme rejection of reason than in the former case. He must now be prepared to believe, not merely what cannot be proved, but what can be *disproved* from other beliefs that he also holds.

   The problem of evil, in the sense in which I shall be using the phrase, is

Reprinted from *Mind*, vol. 64 (1955), pp. 200–212, by permission of Oxford University Press.

a problem only for someone who believes that there is a God who is both omnipotent and wholly good. And it is a logical problem, the problem of clarifying and reconciling a number of beliefs: it is not a scientific problem that might be solved by further observations, or a practical problem that might be solved by a decision or an action. These points are obvious; I mention them only because they are sometimes ignored by theologians, who sometimes parry a statement of the problem with such remarks as "Well, can you solve the problem yourself?" or "This is a mystery which may be revealed to us later" or "Evil is something to be faced and overcome, not to be merely discussed."

In its simplest form the problem is this: God is omnipotent; God is wholly good; and yet evil exists. There seems to be some contradiction between these three propositions, so that if any two of them were true the third would be false. But at the same time all three are essential parts of most theological positions: the theologian, it seems, at once *must* adhere and *cannot consistently* adhere to all three. (The problem does not arise only for theists, but I shall discuss it in the form in which it presents itself for ordinary theism.)

However, the contradiction does not arise immediately; to show it we need some additional premises, or perhaps some quasi-logical rules connecting the terms 'good,' 'evil,' and 'omnipotent.' These additional principles are that good is opposed to evil, in such a way that a good thing always eliminates evil as far as it can, and that there are no limits to what an omnipotent thing can do. From these it follows that a good omnipotent thing eliminates evil completely, and then the propositions that a good omnipotent thing exists, and that evil exists, are incompatible.

A. ADEQUATE SOLUTIONS

Now once the problem is fully stated it is clear that it can be solved, in the sense that the problem will not arise if one gives up at least one of the propositions that constitute it. If you are prepared to say that God is not wholly good, or not quite omnipotent, or that evil does not exist, or that good is not opposed to the kind of evil that exists, or that there are limits to what an omnipotent thing can do, then the problem of evil will not arise for you.

There are, then, quite a number of adequate solutions of the problem of evil, and some of these have been adopted, or almost adopted, by various thinkers. For example, a few have been prepared to deny God's omnipotence, and rather more have been prepared to keep the term 'omnipotence' but severely to restrict its meaning, recording quite a number of things that an omnipotent being cannot do. Some have said that evil is an illusion, perhaps because they held that the whole world of temporal, changing things is an illusion, and that what we call evil belongs only to this world, or perhaps because they held that although temporal things *are* much as we see them, those that we call evil are not really evil. Some have said that what we call evil is merely the privation of good, that evil in a positive sense, evil that would really be opposed to good, does not exist. Many have agreed with Pope that disorder is harmony not understood, and that partial evil is universal good. Whether any of these views is *true* is, of course, another question. But each of them gives an adequate solution of the problem of evil in the sense that if you accept it this problem does not arise for you, though you may, of course, have *other* problems to face.

But often enough these adequate solutions are only *almost* adopted. The thinkers who restrict God's power, but keep the term 'omnipotence,' may reasonably be suspected of thinking, in other contexts, that his power is really unlimited. Those who say that evil is an illusion may also be thinking, inconsistently, that this illusion is itself an evil. Those who say that "evil" is merely privation of good may also be thinking, inconsistently, that privation of good is an evil. (The fallacy here is akin to some forms of the "naturalistic fallacy" in ethics, where some think, for example, that "good" is just what contributes to evolutionary progress, and that evolutionary progress is itself good.) If Pope meant what he said in the first line of his couplet, that "disorder" is only harmony not understood, the "partial evil" of the second line must, for consistency, mean "that which, taken in isolation, falsely appears to be evil," but it would more naturally mean "that which, in isolation, really is evil." The second line, in fact, hesitates between two views, that "partial evil" isn't really evil, since only the universal quality is real, and that "partial evil" is really an evil, but only a little one.

In addition, therefore, to adequate solutions, we must recognise unsatisfactory inconsistent solutions, in which there is only a half-hearted or temporary rejection of one of the propositions which together constitute the problem. In these, one of the constituent propositions is explicitly rejected, but it is covertly re-asserted or assumed elsewhere in the system.

B. FALLACIOUS SOLUTIONS

Besides these half-hearted solutions, which explicitly reject but implicitly assert one of the constituent propositions, there are definitely fallacious solutions which explicitly maintain all the constituent propositions, but implicitly reject at least one of them in the course of the argument that explains away the problem of evil.

There are, in fact, many so-called solutions which purport to remove the contradiction without abandoning any of its constituent propositions. These must be fallacious, as we can see from the very statement of the problem, but it is not so easy to see in each case precisely where the fallacy lies. I suggest that in all cases the fallacy has the general form suggested above: in order to solve the problem one (or perhaps more) of its constituent propositions is given up, but in such a way that it appears to have been retained, and can therefore be asserted without qualification in other contexts. Sometimes there is a further complication: the supposed solution moves to and fro between, say, two of the constituent propositions, at one point asserting the first of these but covertly abandoning the second, at another point asserting the second but covertly abandoning the first. These fallacious solutions often turn upon some equivocation with the words 'good' and 'evil,' or upon some vagueness about the way in which good and evil are opposed to one another, or about how much is meant by 'omnipotence.' I propose to examine some of these so-called solutions, and to exhibit their fallacies in detail. Incidentally, I shall also be considering whether an adequate solution could be reached by a minor modification of one or more of the constituent propositions, which would, however, still satisfy all the essential requirements of ordinary theism.

> 1. "Good cannot exist without evil" or "Evil is necessary as a counterpart to good."

It is sometimes suggested that evil is necessary as a counterpart to good, that if there were no evil there could be no good either, and that this solves the problem of evil. It is true that it points to an answer to the question "Why should there be evil?" But it does so only by qualifying some of the propositions that constitute the problem.

First, it sets a limit to what God can do, saying that God *cannot* create good without simultaneously creating evil, and this means either that God is not omnipotent or that there are *some* limits to what an omnipotent thing can do. It may be replied that these limits are always presupposed, that omnipotence has never meant the power to do what is logically impossible, and on the present view the existence of good without evil would be a logical impossibility. This interpretation of omnipotence may, indeed, be accepted as a modification of our original account which does not reject anything that is essential to theism, and I shall in general assume it in the subsequent discussion. It is, perhaps, the most common theistic view, but I think that some theists at least have maintained that God can do what is logically impossible. Many theists, at any rate, have held that logic itself is created or laid down by God, that logic is the way in which God arbitrarily chooses to think. (This is, of course, parallel to the ethical view that morally right actions are those which God arbitrarily chooses to command, and the two views encounter similar difficulties.) And *this* account of logic is clearly inconsistent with the view that God is bound by logical necessities—unless it is possible for an omnipotent being to bind himself, an issue which we shall consider later, when we come to the Paradox of Omnipotence. This solution of the problem of evil cannot, therefore, be consistently adopted along with the view that logic is itself created by God.

But, secondly, this solution denies that evil is opposed to good in our original sense. If good and evil are counterparts, a good thing will not "eliminate evil as far as it can." Indeed, this view suggests that good and evil are not strictly qualities of things at all. Perhaps the suggestion is that good and evil are related in much the same way as great and small. Certainly, when the term 'great' is used relatively as a condensation of greater than so-and-so,' and 'small' is used correspondingly, greatness and smallness are counterparts and cannot exist without each other. But in this sense greatness is not a quality, not an intrinsic feature of anything; and it would be absurd to think of a movement in favor of greatness and against smallness in this sense. Such a movement would be self-defeating, since relative greatness can be promoted only by a simultaneous promotion of relative smallness. I feel sure that no theists would be content to regard God's goodness as analogous to this—as if what he supports were not the *good* but the *better,* and as if he had the paradoxical aim that all things should be better than other things.

This point is obscured by the fact that 'great' and 'small' seem to have an absolute as well as a relative sense. I cannot discuss here whether there is absolute magnitude or not, but if there is, there could be an absolute sense for 'great,' it could mean of at least a certain size, and it would make sense to speak of all things getting bigger, of a universe that was expanding all over, and therefore it would make sense to speak of promoting greatness. But in *this* sense great and small are not logically necessary counterparts: either quality could exist without the other. There would be no logical impossibility in everything's being small or in everything's being great.

Neither in the absolute nor in the relative sense, then, of 'great' and 'small' do these terms provide an analogy of the sort that would be needed to support this solution of the problem of evil. In neither case are greatness and smallness *both* necessary counterparts *and* mutually opposed forces or possible objects for support and attack.

It may be replied that good and evil are necessary counterparts in the same way as any quality and its logical opposite: redness can occur, it is suggested, only if non-redness also occurs. But unless evil is merely the privation of good, they are not logical opposites, and some further argument would be needed to show that they are counterparts in the same way as genuine logical opposites. Let us assume that this could be given. There is still doubt of the correctness of the metaphysical principle that a quality must have a real opposite: I suggest that it is not really impossible that everything should be, say, red, that the truth is merely that if everything were red we should not notice redness, and so we should have no word 'red'; we observe and give names to qualities only if they have real opposites. If so, the principle that a term must have an opposite would belong only to our language or to our thought, and would not be an ontological principle, and, correspondingly, the rule that good cannot exist without evil would not state a logical necessity of a sort that God would just have to put up with. God might have made everything good, though *we* should not have noticed it if he had.

But, finally, even if we concede that this *is* an ontological principle, it will provide a solution for the problem of evil only if one is prepared to say, "Evil exists, but only just enough evil to serve as the counterpart of good." I doubt whether any theist will accept this. After all, the *ontological* requirement that non-redness should occur would be satisfied even if all the universe, except for a minute speck, were red, and, if there were a corresponding requirement for evil as a counterpart to good, a minute dose of evil would presumably do. But theists are not usually willing to say, in all contexts, that all the evil that occurs is a minute and necessary dose.

2. "Evil is necessary as a means to good."

It is sometimes suggested that evil is necessary for good not as a counterpart but as a _means_. In its simple form this has little plausibility as a solution of the problem of evil, since it obviously implies a severe restriction of God's power. It would be a _causal_ law that you cannot have a certain end without a certain means, so that if God has to introduce evil as a means to good, he must be subject to at least some causal laws. This certainly conflicts with what a theist normally means by omnipotence. This view of God as limited by causal laws also conflicts with the view that causal laws are themselves made by God, which is more widely held than the corresponding view about the laws of logic. This conflict would, indeed, be resolved if it were possible for an omnipotent being to bind himself, and this possibility has still to be considered. Unless a favorable answer can be given to this question, the suggestion that evil is necessary as a means to good solves the problem of evil only by denying one of its constituent propositions, either that God is omnipotent or that 'omnipotent' means what it says.

3. "The universe is better with some evil in it than it could be if there were no evil."

Much more important is a solution which at first seems to be a mere variant of the previous one, that evil may contribute to the goodness of a whole in which it is found, so that the universe as a whole is better as it is, with some evil in it, than it would be if there were no evil. This solution may be developed in either of two ways. It may be supported by an aesthetic analogy, by the fact that contrasts heighten beauty, that in a musical work, for example, there may occur discords which somehow add to the beauty of the work as a whole. Alternatively, it may be worked out in connection with the notion of progress, that the best possible organisation of the universe will not be static, but progressive, that the gradual overcoming of evil by good is really a finer thing than would be the eternal unchallenged supremacy of good.

In either case, this solution usually starts from the assumption that the evil whose existence gives rise to the problem of evil is primarily what is called physical evil, that is to say, pain. In Hume's rather half-hearted presentation of the problem of evil, the evils that he stresses are pain and disease, and those who reply to him argue that the existence of pain and disease makes possible the existence of sympathy, benevolence, heroism, and the gradually successful struggle of doctors and reformers to overcome these evils. In fact, theists often seize the opportunity to accuse those who stress the problem of evil of taking a low, materialistic view of good and evil, equating these with pleasure and pain, and of ignoring the more spiritual goods which can arise in the struggle against evils.

But let us see exactly what is being done here. Let us call <u>pain</u> and <u>misery</u> '<u>first order evil</u>' or 'evil (1).' What contrasts with this, namely, <u>pleasure</u> and <u>happiness</u>, will be called '<u>first order good</u>' or 'good (1).' Distinct from this is '<u>second order good</u>' or '<u>good (2)</u>' which somehow emerges in a complex situation in which evil (1) is a necessary component—logically, not merely causally, necessary. (Exactly *how* it emerges does not matter: in the crudest version of this solution good (2) is simply the heightening of happiness by the contrast with misery, in other versions it includes sympathy with suffering, heroism in facing danger, and the gradual decrease of first order evil and increase of first order good.) It is also being assumed that second order good is more important than first order good or evil, in particular that it more than outweighs the first order evil it involves.

Now this is a particularly subtle attempt to solve the problem of evil. It defends God's goodness and omnipotence on the ground that (on a sufficiently long view) this is the best of all logically possible worlds, because it includes the important second order goods, and yet it admits that real evils, namely first order evils, exist. But does it still hold that good and evil are opposed? Not, clearly, in the sense that we set out originally: good does not tend to eliminate evil in general. Instead, we have a modified, a more complex pattern. First order good (*e.g.* happiness) *contrasts with* first order evil (*e.g.* misery): these two are opposed in a fairly mechanical way; some second order goods (*e.g.* benevolence) try to maximize first order good and minimise first order evil; but God's goodness is not this, it is rather the will to maximise *second* order good. We might, therefore, call God's goodness an example of a third order goodness, or good (3). While this account is different from our original one, it might well be held to be an improvement on it, to give a more accurate description of the way in which good is opposed to evil, and to be consistent with the essential theist position.

There might, however, be several objections to this solution.

First, some might argue that such qualities as benevolence—and *a fortiori* the third order goodness which promotes benevolence—have a merely derivative value, that they are not higher sorts of good, but merely means to good (1), that is, to happiness, so that it would be absurd for God to keep misery in existence in order to make possible the virtues of benevolence, heroism, etc. The theist who adopts the present solution must, of course, deny this, but he can do so with some plausibility, so I should not press this objection.

Secondly, it follows from this solution that God is not in our sense benevolent or sympathetic: he is not concerned to minimise evil (1), but only to promote good (2); and this might be a disturbing conclusion for some theists.

But, thirdly, the fatal objection is this. Our analysis shows clearly the possibility of the existence of a second order evil, an evil (2) contrasting with good (2) as evil (1) contrasts with good (1). This would include malevolence, cruelty, callousness, cowardice, and states in which good (1) is decreasing and evil (1) increasing. And just as good (2) is held to be the important kind of good, the kind that God is concerned to promote, so evil (2) will, by analogy, be the important kind of evil, the kind which God, if he were wholly good and omnipotent, would eliminate. And yet evil (2) plainly exists, and indeed most theists (in other contexts) stress its existence more than that of evil (1). We should, therefore, state the problem of evil in terms of second order evil, and against this form of the problem the present solution is useless.

An attempt might be made to use this solution again, at a higher level, to explain the occurrence of evil (2): indeed the next main solution that we shall examine does just this, with the help of some new notions. Without any fresh notions, such a solution would have little plausibility: for example, we could hardly say that the really important good was a good (3), such as the increase of benevolence in proportion to cruelty, which logically required for its occurrence the occurrence of some second order evil. But even if evil (2) could be explained in this way, it is fairly clear that there would be third order evils contrasting with this third order good: and we should be well on the way to an infinite regress, where the solution of a problem of evil, stated in terms of evil (n), indicated the existence of an evil ($n + 1$), and a further problem to be solved.

4. "Evil is due to human freewill."

Perhaps the most important proposed solution of the problem of evil is that evil is not to be ascribed to God at all, but to the independent actions of human beings, supposed to have been endowed by God with freedom of the will. This solution may be combined with the preceding one: first order evil (*e.g.* pain) may be justified as a logically necessary component in second order good (*e.g.* sympathy) while second order evil (*e.g.* cruelty) is not *justified*, but is so ascribed to human beings that God cannot be held responsible for it. This combination evades my third criticism of the preceding solution.

The freewill solution also involves the preceding solution at a higher level. To explain why a wholly good God gave men freewill although it would lead to some important evils, it must be argued that it is better on the whole that men should act freely, and sometimes err, than that they should be innocent automata, acting rightly in a wholly determined way. Freedom, that is to say, is now treated as a third order good, and as being more valuable than second order goods (such as sympathy and heroism) would be if they were deterministically produced, and it is being assumed that second order evils, such as cruelty, are logically necessary accompaniments of freedom, just as pain is a logically necessary pre-condition of sympathy.

I think that this solution is unsatisfactory primarily because of the incoherence of the notion of freedom of the will: but I cannot discuss this topic adequately here, although some of my criticisms will touch upon it.

First I should query the assumption that second order evils are logically necessary accompaniments of freedom. I should ask this: if God has made men such that in their free choices they sometimes prefer what is good and sometimes what is evil, why could he not have made men such that they always freely choose the good? If there is no logical impossibility in a man's freely choosing the good on one, or on several, occasions, there cannot be a logical impossibility in his freely choosing the good on every occasion. God was not, then, faced with a choice between making innocent automata and making beings who, in acting freely, would sometimes go wrong: there was open to him the obviously better possibility of making beings who would act freely but always go right. Clearly, his failure to avail himself of this possibility is inconsistent with his being both omnipotent and wholly good.

If it is replied that this objection is absurd, that the making of some wrong choices is logically necessary for freedom, it would seem that 'freedom' must here mean complete randomness or indeterminacy, including randomness with regard to the alternatives good and evil, in other words that men's choices and consequent actions can be "free" only if they are not determined by their characters. Only on this assumption can God escape the responsibility for men's actions; for if he made them as they are, but did not determine their wrong choices, this can only be because the wrong choices are not determined by men as they are. But then if freedom is randomness, how can it be a characteristic of *will?* And, still more, how can it be the most important good? What value or merit would there be in free choices if these were random actions which were not determined by the nature of the agent?

I conclude that to make this solution plausible two different senses of 'freedom' must be confused, one sense which will justify the view that freedom is a third order good, more valuable than other goods would be without it, and another sense, sheer randomness, to prevent us from ascribing to God a decision to make men such that they sometimes go wrong when he might have made them such that they would always freely go right.

This criticism is sufficient to dispose of this solution. But besides this there is a fundamental difficulty in the notion of an omnipotent God creating men with free will, for if men's wills are really free this must mean that even God cannot control them, that is, that God is no longer omnipotent. It may be objected that God's gift of freedom to men does not mean that he *cannot* control their wills, but that he always *refrains* from controlling their wills. But why, we may ask, should God refrain from controlling evil wills? Why should he not leave men free to will rightly, but intervene when he sees them beginning to will wrongly? If God could do this, but does not, and if he is wholly good, the only explanation could be that even a wrong free act of will is not really evil, that its freedom is a value which outweighs its wrongness, so that there would be a loss of value if God took away the wrongness and the freedom together. But this is utterly opposed to what theists say about sin in other contexts. The present solution of the problem of evil, then, can be maintained only in the form that God has made men so free that he *cannot* control their wills.

This leads us to what I call the Paradox of Omnipotence: can an omnipotent being make things which he cannot subsequently control? Or, what is practically equivalent to this, can an omnipotent being make rules which then bind himself? (These are practically equivalent because any such rules could be regarded as setting certain things beyond his control, and *vice versa.*) The second of these formulations is relevant to the suggestions that we have already met, that an omnipotent God creates the rules of logic or causal laws, and is then bound by them.

It is clear that this is a paradox: the questions cannot be answered satisfactorily either in the affirmative or in the negative. If we answer "Yes," it follows that if God actually makes things which he cannot control, or makes rules which bind himself, he is not omnipotent once he has made them: there are *then* things which he cannot do. But if we answer "No," we are immediately asserting that there are things which he cannot do, that is to say that he is already not omnipotent.

It cannot be replied that the question which sets this paradox is not a proper question. It would make perfectly good sense to say that a human mechanic has made a machine which he cannot control: if there is any difficulty about the question it lies in the notion of omnipotence itself.

This, incidentally, shows that although we have approached this paradox from the free will theory, it is equally a problem for a theological determinist. No one thinks that machines have free will, yet they may well be beyond the control of their makers. The determinist might reply that anyone who makes anything determines its ways of acting, and so determines its subsequent behavior: even the human mechanic does this by his *choice* of materials and structure for his machine, though he does not know all about either of these: the mechanic thus determines, though he may not foresee, his machine's actions. And since God is omniscient, and since his creation of things is total, he both determines and foresees the ways in which his creatures will act. We may grant this, but it is beside the point. The question is not whether God *originally* determined the future actions of his creatures, but whether he can *subsequently* control their actions, or whether he was able in his original creation to put things beyond his subsequent control. Even on determinist principles the answers "Yes" and "No" are equally irreconcilable with God's omnipotence.

Before suggesting a solution of this paradox, I would point out that there is a parallel Paradox of Sovereignty. Can a legal sovereign make a law restricting its own future legislative power? For example, could the British parliament make a law forbidding any future parliament to socialise banking, and also forbidding the future repeal of this law itself? Or could the British parliament, which was legally sovereign in Australia in, say, 1899, pass a valid law, or series of laws, which made it no longer sovereign in 1933? Again, neither the affirmative nor the negative answer is really satisfactory. If we were to answer "Yes," we should be admitting the validity of a law which, if it were actually made, would mean that parliament was no longer sovereign. If we were to answer "No," we should be admitting that there is a law, not logically absurd, which parliament cannot validly make, that is, that parliament is not now a legal sovereign. This paradox can be solved in the following way. We should distinguish between first order laws, that is laws governing the actions of individuals and bodies other than the legislature, and second order laws, that is laws about laws, laws governing the actions of the legislature itself. Correspondingly, we should distinguish two orders of sovereignty, first order sovereignty (sovereignty (1)) which is unlimited authority to make first order laws, and second order sovereignty (sovereignty (2)) which is unlimited authority to make second order laws. If we say that parliament is sovereign we might mean that any parliament at any time has sovereignty (1), or we might mean that parliament has both sovereignty (1) and sovereignty (2) at present, but we cannot without contradiction mean both that the present parliament has sovereignty (2) and that every parliament at every time has sovereignty (1), for if the present parliament has sovereignty (2) it may use it to take away the sovereignty (1) of later parliaments. What the paradox shows is that we cannot ascribe to any continuing institution legal sovereignty in an inclusive sense.

The analogy between omnipotence and sovereignty shows that the paradox of omnipotence can be solved in a similar way. We must distinguish between first order omnipotence (omnipotence (1)), that is unlimited power to act, and second order omnipotence (omnipotence (2)), that is unlimited power to determine what powers to act things shall have. Then we could consistently say that God all the time has omnipotence (1), but if so, no beings at any time have powers to act independently of God. Or we could say that God at one time had omnipotence (2), and used it to assign independent powers to act to certain things, so that God thereafter did not have omnipotence (1). But what the paradox shows is that we cannot consistently ascribe to any continuing being omnipotence in an inclusive sense.

An alternative solution of this paradox would be simply to deny that God is a continuing being, that any times can be assigned to his actions at all. But on this assumption (which also has difficulties of its own) no meaning can be given to the assertion that God made men with wills so free that he could not control them. The paradox of omnipotence can be avoided by putting God outside time, but the freewill solution of the problem of evil cannot be saved in this way, and equally it remains impossible to hold that an omnipotent God *binds himself* by causal or logical laws.

CONCLUSION

Of the proposed solutions of the problem of evil which we have examined, none has stood up to criticism. There may be other solutions which require examination, but this study strongly suggests that there is no valid solution of the problem which does not modify at least one of the constituent propositions in a way which would seriously affect the essential core of the theistic position.

Quite apart from the problem of evil, the paradox of omnipotence has shown that God's omnipotence must in any case be restricted in one way or another, that unqualified omnipotence cannot be ascribed to any being that

<u>continues through time</u>. And if God and his actions are not in time, can omnipotence, or power of any sort, be meaningfully ascribed to him?

STUDY QUESTIONS

1. Mackie says that the problem of evil offers a "more telling criticism" of belief in God than the criticisms of the traditional arguments for the existence of God. Why? Do you agree?
2. What, according to Mackie, are the core beliefs of "ordinary theism"?
3. How does Mackie define the terms "good" and "omnipotent"? Are these the only acceptable definitions?
4. If Mackie were to characterize John Hick's attempt to solve the problem of evil, would he call it *adequate, half-hearted,* or *fallacious?* Why?
5. What is Mackie's "paradox of omnipotence"?
6. Mackie says that even if evil is needed as a counterpart to good, "a minute dose of evil would presumably do." Do you agree?
7. Mackie contends that there is no contradiction in asserting that God could have made humans so that they would always *freely* choose the good. Do you agree?

3

Faith and Reason

PROBLEM INTRODUCTION

What if the arguments for the existence of God fail? What if the problem of evil defies a fully satisfactory solution? Has every avenue to belief in God been blocked to an intelligent person? If so, what kind of world do we face? These are not idle questions. A world without God is a world without direction, a world in which humanity is alone, a world which moves on uncaringly and has, at best, an uncertain future, and at worst, a bleak one. With the death of God, the face of the universe becomes "It" instead of "Thou." It is no surprise that many people find the prospect of a godless world frightening beyond description, since, for better or worse, our values are seriously shaken by this picture of reality.

Reason must give out somewhere in the search for the truth about God, for a major part of that truth, according to believers, is that the infinite nature of God transcends the reach of the human mind. Consequently, believers turn to faith in religious matters. Exactly what *faith* means, however, is subject to considerable interpretation. Martin Luther suggested that the essence of faith is "to believe that God, who saves so few and condemns so many, is merciful; that He is just, who, at his own pleasure, has made us necessarily doomed to damnation, so that He seems to delight in the torture of the wretched and to be more deserving of hate than of love" (*De servo arbitrio*). Luther imples that faith is simply blind belief in spite of overwhelming evidence to the contrary. In effect, the believer is saying, "I find this comforting, and so I will believe it no matter what the facts are." This, of course, is rampant irrationalism.

Fortunately, religious faith need not be interpreted in this way. There are at least two other alternatives. The first is to show that reason is not the only way in which human beings can encounter reality. This is the path of the mystic. The other alternative is to show that religious faith is reasonable. The proponents of such a view usually maintain that our ordinary lives are full of examples of rational faith, and that religious belief need not be any different. Let us look more closely at these two positions.

For many philosophers and theologians, the essence of religious belief lies in the nature of religious experience. Religious attitudes do not originate in an empirical investigation of the world, but rather result from a special insight into the nature of things. This insight, however, is extremely difficult—if not impossible—to express in the language of ordinary experience. In our readings, W. T. Stace maintains that there are two distinct ways of coming to know the nature of reality. The method of the "rational intellect" must be contrasted with "mystical intuition." Persons who have experienced a mystical insight into the nature of things describe their vision in terms which strike the rational mind as absurd. In all religious traditions, the experience of God is "ineffable"; that is, all attempts to describe God are doomed to failure because the nature of God cannot be grasped by reason or logic. As Meister Eckhart, the famous Christian mystic, put it: "Why dost thou prate about God? Whatever thou sayest of Him is untrue."

In the following reading, Michael Scriven, unwilling to discard reason or to denigrate its importance, counters that a God which cannot be comprehended by reason cannot be an object of worship. If we take Eckhart literally, then when we say that God is loving, good, and kind, we must be saying things which are untrue. Scriven claims that when the truths of religion are emptied of rational content, religion ceases to have any bearing on the conduct of our lives. Mystics, of course, may simply refuse to argue, for logic and reason, according to them, are incapable of settling the issue.

But perhaps the contrast between faith and reason has been overstated, for it seems as if much of ordinary living involves an element of faith. To have faith in a friend, for example, is to believe that the friend will continue to act in familiar ways. Faith, in this context, means a willingness to act, even though the evidence is incomplete and less than perfect. A gamble is being taken, it is true, but not every gamble is irrational. Life does not always wait while we gather conclusive evidence to back up our decisions. Reason is a tool which helps us move into an uncertain future, but it can never remove all uncertainty. Indeed, we have faith in reason just as we have faith in our friends—we act as though reason will continue to guide us successfully *even though we cannot know this with absolute certainty*. Faith, then, is an essential part of reasonable living.

In our readings, William James attempts to set forth the conditions under which religious faith is a reasonable gamble for guidance in an uncertain life. What is especially interesting in James's position is his claim that acting on the basis of a belief sometimes creates the conditions which make the belief true. Believing that someone will be your friend may be a necessary condition for establishing a friendship with that person, or believing that you will succeed in college may be a necessary condition for doing so. James maintains that believing that there is a God may be the necessary condition for discovering the evidence which substantiates the belief.

Now, if you adopt the belief—take the gamble—that you have the talent and drive to cope with the challenges of college as a necessary condition to prove that your belief is justified, then you will know what evidence to look for. As you enroll in courses, write papers, perform experiments, take tests, and carry out other assignments, you will look for passing grades as a sign that your belief is well-founded, and failing grades that it is not. Such a gamble therefore seems quite reasonable.

On the other hand, this does not seem to be the case with James's *pragmatic* line of reasoning. Basically, James tells us that if we act on the assumption that there is a God, then we may enable ourselves to uncover the evidence substantiating our assumption. When critics attempted to pin James down as to what facts or experiences would be a sign that there is or is not a God, however, he was vague or evasive. To many critics, James was saying that one is entitled to believe that there is a God if one finds such a belief satisfying. They charged him with conducting an exercise in wish fulfillment and rationalization. The fact is, they said, James was a victim of his religious upbringing; psychologically, he was simply incapable of seriously entertaining the prospect of a life without God. For James, as for many religious people, there seems to be "no event or series of events the occurrence of which would be admitted...to be a sufficient reason for conceding 'There wasn't a God after all' or 'God does not really love us then'" (Antony Flew, *New Essays in Philosophical Theology*). If a person stubbornly refused to admit even the possibility that his or her beliefs about sports, television shows, or automobiles could be in error, whatever the facts, then we would write off such a person as foolish, if not demented. Yet, according to critics of James, this is exactly what James asks us to permit on the question of the existence of God. If this is true, then James has really undertaken no gamble. He has simply asserted that there is a God—period.

If James is in fact vulnerable to these charges, then perhaps all rational routes to religious belief are closed. If this is so, many of the most profound issues of life are affected. The universe is not the manifestation of a divine plan, and, accordingly, is indifferent to our hopes and fears. There are no values, no ideals, beyond those shaped by human beings. All opportunities for a meaningful existence must be seized within the short period given to us or forever lost. To many people such thoughts are a source of despair. But in every era, there have been those who believe that a world without God is livable, challenging, and even exhilarating. One such group is *humanists*. The final reading in this section features one of the best contemporary statements of humanism by Corliss Lamont. Humanists paint a picture of traditional religious beliefs—God, an afterlife, the efficacy of prayer, miracles, and revelation—as antiquated, unsubstantiated, and downright harmful to humankind. They call for a renewed commitment throughout the world to the solution of pressing problems and the full development of every person. They believe that their secular, realistic, and action-oriented world view can inspire great progress in the years ahead. The first indispensable step in that direction, for humanists, is summoning the courage to dispatch belief in a deity to the trash bin of history, along with the flat earth and phlebotomies.

To humanists, the finality of death need not mean that our ideals are empty illusions. Immortality, they observe, is no blessing, for it provides for the possibility of unending pain as well as infinite bliss. Existence is made meaningful, they say, by its ethical quality, not its duration; and there is no apparent reason why a short existence cannot possess such qualities.

All this echoes the sentiments of the Roman poet Lucretius about sixty years before the birth of Jesus—a fitting counterpoint to the promise of eternal life:

> What is your grievance, mortal, that you give yourself up to this whining and repining? Why do you weep and wail over death? If the life you have lived till now has been a pleasant thing—if all its blessings have not leaked away like water poured into a cracked pot and run to waste unrelished—why then, you silly creature, do you not retire as a guest who has had his fill of life and take your care-free rest with a quiet mind.*

* Lucretius, *The Nature of the Universe*, translated by Robert Latham (Baltimore: Penguin, 1951).

Mysticism and the Limits of Reason

W. T. Stace

W. T. Stace (1886–1967) was a district judge in Ceylon, later became mayor of Colombo, and subsequently joined the philosophy department of Princeton University. This many-faceted individual devoted the last years of his life to defending the view that mysticism and science are not opposed to one another. In this essay, Stace claims that the mystical traditions of the world have a common thread of paradox running through them. He argues that the sort of vision of reality which mystics have cannot be accurately reproduced by the ordinary concepts of the understanding.

The theme of Stace's essay is a familiar one in all religious traditions. Reason is said to be incapable of understanding the nature of God. Instead, God can be known only by direct experience or intuition. As soon as we try to express, in logical terms, what intuition has revealed, paradoxes appear. These paradoxes, Stace claims, are not signs of the inadequacy of the religious vision, but indications that the logical intellect has reached its limits. Religion is not essentially an intellectual affair—it is an immediate experience which lies forever beyond the grasp of logic.

Stace's interpretation of the mystical vision, however, is not the only possible one. Perhaps the paradoxes which he cites are not strictly contradictions, but unusual metaphors which have a profound, but logical, significance. In Shakespeare's plays, for example, usually the clearest vision of reality is expressed by a character who appears to be insane. So too with the mystics—there may be method in their madness.

Anyone who is acquainted with the mystical literature of the world will know that great mystics invariably express themselves in the language of paradox and contradiction; and it is to this aspect of mysticism that I especially want to draw your attention tonight. But before I do so I would like to make a few introductory remarks about mysticism in general. Mysticism is not a regional or local phenomenon. It is universal. By this I mean that it is found in every country, in every age, in every culture, and in association with every one of the great world-religions. I do not speak here of primitive cultures and primitive religions. No doubt mysticism expresses itself in them in primitive ways. But I am only speaking about advanced cultures and advanced religions. For instance, those ancient inspired documents, the Upanishads, which go back in time from 2,500 to 3,000 years, and which are the fountainheads both of the Hindu religion and of the Vedanta philosophy, are a direct report of mystical experience. Buddhism, too, is a mystical religion throughout. It is founded upon the mystical experience of Gautama Buddha. In the East, in India, the word "mysticism" or any word corresponding to it is not generally used. It is

From W. T. Stace, "Mysticism and Human Reason," University of Arizona Bulletin Series, vol. 26, no. 3, published in 1955. Reprinted by permission of the University of Arizona Press.

called "enlightenment" or "illumination." But the enlightenment experience of the East is basically the same as what is called the mystical experience in the West. In the Mohammedan religion the Sufis were the great representatives of mysticism. Mysticism appears in China in connection with Taoism. The Tao is a mystical conception. Judaism produced notable mystics. The history of Christianity is rich with the names of great mystics and some of these names are household words: Meister Eckhart, Saint Teresa, St. John of the Cross, and many others. Even outside the boundaries of any institutional religion, in the ancient Greco-Roman pagan world, not attached, perhaps, to any particular religion, Plotinus was one of the supremely great mystics.

Now, of course, as between these mysticisms in the various cultures, there are certain differences. For instance, Hindu mysticism is not quite the same as Christian mysticism. But I believe that the resemblances, the common elements, the elements which are universally found in all these mysticisms, are far more striking than the differences. I should say that the differences are superficial, while the common, basic, universal elements in all mysticism are fundamental. Should you ask me: "What are those common elements which appear in mysticism in all these different cultures and religions?" I can, perhaps, very briefly, summarize them.

In the first place, the absolutely basic, fundamental characteristic of all mystical experience is that it is called "the unitary consciousness," or, as it is sometimes called, "the unifying vision." We may contrast the mystical consciousness with our ordinary, everyday, rational consciousness. Our ordinary, everyday consciousness is characterized by multiplicity. I mean that both the senses and the intellect, which constitute our everyday consciousness, are in contact with and are aware of a vast number, a plurality, a multiplicity of different things. In our ordinary consciousness we discriminate between one thing and another. But the mystical consciousness transcends all differences and all multiplicity. In it there is no multiplicity and no division of difference. "Here," says Eckhart "all is one, and one is all." He goes on to say that in that supreme vision there are "no contrasts." "Contrast" is Eckhart's word for the difference between one thing and another, for instance between yellow and green. He even goes so far as to say that in that experience there are no contrasts, i.e. differences, between grass, wood, and stone, but that all these "are one."

Closely connected with, and perhaps as a result of this characteristic of transcending all multiplicity, discrimination, and division are other characteristics common to mystical experience in all religions. It is non-sensuous, non-intellectual, and non-conceptual. And since all words except proper names stand for concepts, this means mystical experience is beyond all words, incapable of being expressed in any language; "ineffable" is the usual word. Another characteristic is that what is experienced is beyond space and beyond time. It is timeless; and timelessness is eternity. And therefore the mystical consciousness, even though it lasts only for a very short while, perhaps only a moment, is nevertheless eternal. For that moment gathers into itself all eternity. It is an eternal moment.

Another universal characteristic is that mystical consciousness is bless-edness—it is the peace which passeth all understanding. One might quote at length from the utterances of great mystics in all religions to prove that these are the common characteristics. I have time for only one quotation which I choose because it happens to include most of them in a few sentences. In the Mandukya Upanishad it is written:

> It is neither inward experience nor outward experience. It is neither
> intellectual knowledge nor inferential knowledge. It is beyond the
> senses, beyond the understanding, beyond all expression. It is the pure
> unitary consciousness wherein awareness of the world and of
> multiplicity is completely obliterated. It is ineffable peace. It is the
> supreme good. It is the One without a second.

One other common element I must mention. The mystic everywhere, except perhaps in Buddhism, which is a rather doubtful case here, invariably feels an absolute certainty that he is in direct touch with, and not only in direct touch with, but has entered into actual union with, the Divine Being. Plotinus expressed this by saying that "the man"—the mystic, that is—"is merged with the Supreme, sunken into it, one with it." And William James in his famous book, *Varieties of Religious Experience*, has an excellent brief chapter on mysticism, and in that he uses these words:

> This overcoming of all barriers between the individual and the Absolute
> is the great mystic achievement. In mystic states we become one with
> the Absolute. This is the everlasting and triumphant mystic tradition,
> hardly altered by differences of climate, culture, or creed. In Hinduism,
> in Neo-Platonism, in Sufism, in Christian mysticism, we find the same
> recurring note, so that there is about mystic utterances an eternal
> unanimity which ought to make the critic stop and think.

Now, of course, this mystical experience, basically the same in all cultures as it is, might nevertheless be nothing but a beautiful dream. It is possible that it is a purely subjective state of the mystic's own mind, and that he is under an illusion when he thinks that he is in contact with some great being objective and outside himself. The only logical argument, the only piece of evidence which can be used to show that it is more than a beautiful dream, that it does actually reveal contact with an objective, divine being is this remarkable agreement, as regards basic features, of the different mysticisms in all the cultures of the world. Of course one may be convinced by faith, or intuition, or feeling. But I am speaking here of logical argument or evidence....

I turn now to what is the essential subject of my lecture, the paradoxes of mysticism. There are many such paradoxes. Their general character is this: that whatever is affirmed of God must be at the same time and in one and the same breath categorically denied. Whatever is said of the Divine Being, the opposite, the contradictory, must also be said. There are many such paradoxes, but I am going to speak tonight only about one, which is perhaps the most startling of them. This may be expressed by saying that God is both being and non-being. If you like, you can say it means that God both exists and does not exist; or again that God is beyond both existence and non-existence. There is thus both a positive and negative aspect. There is the positive divine and the negative divine. As to the positive divine, it is hardly necessary for me to say much about it because it is well known to everyone. It is the content of popular religion everywhere. We begin, I suppose, by saying that God exists. "Exist" is a positive word. We go on to say that he is a mind, a spirit, a person. These, too, are positive conceptions. Finally, we say that God is love, justice, mercy, power, knowledge, wisdom, and so on. All these are positive terms. And you will recognize that statements of this kind about the Divine Being are the content of ordinary, everyday, popular religious thought. This is true not only of Christianity but, I think, of all the great religions of the world, with the possible exception of Buddhism which is often called an atheistic religion. I don't think that there is really very much disagreement between the great world religions in regard to these basic attributes of God. There may be some difference of emphasis. No doubt it is the case that in Christianity the emphasis is upon God as love. In Hinduism the emphasis is on God as bliss. In Islam perhaps the emphasis is on God as power, and so on.

If we turn now to the negative divine, we pass into a region which is not so well known. This is usually especially associated with mystical religion. It may be expressed by saying that, just as for the positive divine God is being, here God is non-being. Even more striking words than this are used by the great mystics. God is "Nothing." He is "empty." He is "the Void." He is "the bottomless abyss of nothingness." And sometimes metaphors are used. Darkness as the absence of light, and silence as the absence of sound, are negative. Therefore God is spoken of as the great darkness, the great silence.

I am going to document these statements by referring very briefly (I cannot give very much of the evidence in a short lecture) to some of the great mystic utterances in the different religions of the world. I want to show that this is universal.

To begin with Christianity: Meister Eckhart, as you know, was a great Roman Catholic mystic of the 13th century. In one place he says: "God is as void as if he were not." Elsewhere he says: "Thou shalt worship God as he is, a non-God, a non-form, a non-person." One of his followers wrote this of him: "Wise Meister Eckhart speaks to us about Nothingness. He who does not understand this, in him has never shone the divine light." Using the metaphor of darkness, Eckhart says: "The end of all things is the hidden darkness of the eternal Godhead." He also refers on many occasions to God as "the nameless nothing." Another well-known Christian mystic, Tauler, uses the same kind of language. He, too, refers to God as "the nameless nothing." Albertus Magnus writes this: "We first deny of God all bodily and sensible attributes, and then all intelligible attributes, and lastly, that being which would place him among created things." Notice that being, existence, is here said to be the mark of created things.

Turning to Judaism we find that Jewish mystics often referred to Jehovah as "the mystical Nothing." And again, "in depths of His nothingness" is a common phrase. One of the Hassidic mystics wrote: "There are those who worship God with their human intellects, and others whose gaze is fixed on Nothing. He who is granted this supreme experience loses the reality of his intellect, but when he returns from such contemplation to the intellect, he finds it full of divine and inflowing splendor."

Turning to Buddhism we find a rather difficult case for our expression because it is often said that Buddhism is an atheistic religion. This is true with some reservations. It is true that you do not find the Western concept of God in Buddhism. And it therefore might be said that it is obvious that Buddhism can have neither a positive nor a negative conception of God. This, however, is really not a justifiable conclusion. I can't go into the matter in any great detail here. On the whole, the concept of Nirvana is what corresponds in Buddhism to the Christian and Jewish concept of God. Nirvana, the experience of Nirvana, is, I think, what we would recognize as the divine experience, the experience of the divine element in the world. It is not important that the word God is not used. If Nirvana corresponds to the concept of the divine, then one can say that the concept of Nirvana has both the positive and negative aspects. Positively, it is bliss unspeakable. Negatively, it is the Void. This conception of the Void which you see that Eckhart also uses, is basic to Buddhism. Ultimate reality is the Void.

I find that in Hinduism this positive-negative paradox is more fully developed, more clear than it is in Christianity, Judaism, or Buddhism. In Hinduism it may be said that this paradox has three aspects. Brahman is the name used in the Upanishads and generally in Hindu thought for the ultimate, supreme God. The first aspect of the paradox is that Brahman both has qualities and yet is without any qualities at all. On the positive side the qualities of Brahman are the usual divine qualities to which I have already referred. On the negative side he is "unqualified." This is often expressed in the Upanishads by using a string of negative terms. For example, it is said that Brahman "is soundless, formless, shapeless, intangible, tasteless, odorless, mindless." Notice this last word, "mindless." This quotation is similar in meaning to the one which I read from Albertus Magnus. First we deny all physical qualities. He is "soundless, formless, shapeless, intangible, odorless, and tasteless." Next we deny all "intelligible," i.e., psychological or spiritual attributes. He is "mindless." But the negative of the paradox, the denial of all qualities, is summed up in a very famous verse in the Upanishads. Brahman is here, as often, referred to as the Self. The verse says: "That Self is to be described as not this, not that." One of the earlier translators worded it thus: "That Self is to be described by 'No! No!'" The force of this "No! No!" is clear. Whatever attribute you suggest, whatever predicate you suggest, whatever quality you suggest, of Brahman, the answer always is "No." Is he matter? No. Is he mind? No. Is he good? No. Is he evil? No. And so throughout every word that you can possibly choose.

The second aspect of the paradox in Hinduism is that Brahman is both

personal and impersonal. His personality is carried by the very word "Self."
He is the Self. He is personal and as such is wise, just, good, and so on. But
he is also wholly impersonal. The word "mindless" contains this implication.
For a person must necessarily be a mind. Also he is specifically referred to as
"the impersonal Brahman." And sometimes the word "he" and sometimes
the word "it" is used of Brahman. "He" conveys the notion of personality,
"it" the notion of impersonality.

The third and final aspect of the paradox in Hinduism is that Brahman
is both dynamic and static. Dynamic means he is active, static means he is
actionless. On the positive side God is dynamic. He is the creative energy of
the world, the creator. Also he acts in the world, guides and controls the world.
On the static side it is specifically stated in the Upanishads that he is wholly
actionless.[1] And the entire paradox is summed up in the following verse from
the Upanishads:

> That One, though never stirring, is swifter than thought; though
> standing still, it overtakes those who run. It moves and it moves not.

In this phrase, "It moves and it moves not," you have the whole paradox of
the dynamic and static character of God summed up in five words.

Perhaps you will say, "Well, this is just poetic language. Everybody knows
that poets like pleasant sounding phrases. And they like a balance of clauses.
'It moves and it moves not' sounds very well but it is mere words." I think you
are quite mistaken if you take that interpretation. This is a literal statement of
the paradox of the dynamic and the static.

Now I am persuaded that this entire paradox, and particularly that of the
dynamic and the static character of the divine being, is not peculiar to Hinduism
but is a universal characteristic of the religious consciousness everywhere, although in Hinduism it is more explicit, more baldly stated, than in other religions. In other religions it is present but tends to be veiled. Let us look at
Christianity, for example. No one will deny that the Christian God is active.
He is the creator of the world; he guides and controls it. But where, you will
ask me, do you find evidence that the Christian God is static, inactive? It is
true that you must look under the surface to find this. It is implied, implicit
rather than explicit, in the concept of God as *unchangeable and immutable.* The
changelessness, the immutability of God, is not only a Christian idea. It is a
universal intuition of the religious consciousness found in all religions. "In
him is no shadow of turning," and there is a well-known hymn which begins
with the words:

> O strength and stay upholding all creation
> Who ever dost thyself *unmoved abide.*

---

[1] Rudolph Otto in his *Mysticism East and West* claims it as a superiority of the Christian God over
the Hindu, that the latter is merely static, the former dynamic. He has missed the paradox and
been misled by the frequent statements that Brahman is inactive.

The last two words convey the idea of the motionless, actionless character of God. We hardly realize when we speak of God as "immutable" and yet as the Creator of the world that we are uttering a paradox. There is, in fact, a contradiction between God as active and God as unchanging, because that which acts necessarily changes—changes from that state in which the action is not done to that state in which the action is done. Therefore, that which is wholly unchanging is also wholly inactive. The same idea also appears in poetry. T. S. Eliot twice to my knowledge in his poems uses the phrase, "The still point of the turning world." The literal meaning of this is obvious. It refers to the planet, the periphery and the outer parts of which are turning, while the axis in the middle is motionless. But the mystical meaning is also clear. It means that this world is a world of flux and change and becoming, but at the center of it, in the heart of things, there is silence, stillness, motionlessness.

So much, then, for the exposition of this paradox. But the human intellect, when it comes to a logical contradiction, necessarily attempts to get rid of it, attempts to explain away the contradiction. It tries to show that although there is an apparent contradiction, there is not really one. To get rid of a contradiction is essential to the very nature of our logical and rationalistic intellect....

My own belief is that all attempts to rationalize the paradox, to make it logically acceptable, are futile because the paradoxes of religion and of mysticism are irresoluble by the human intellect. My view is that they never have been, they never can be, and they never will be resolved, or made logical. That is to say, these paradoxes and contradictions are inherent in the mystical experience and cannot be got rid of by any human logic or ingenuity. This, in my opinion, is an aspect of what is sometimes called the mystery of God or the incomprehensibility of God. This mystery of God is not something which we can get rid of, something which we could understand by being a little more clever or a little more learned. It is ultimate, it is an ultimate and irremovable character of the divine. When you say that God is incomprehensible, one thing you mean is just that these contradictions break out in our intellect and cannot be resolved, no matter how clever or how good a logician you may be. And I think that this view is in the end the view of the mystics themselves, including Eckhart, in spite of his apparent attempt to explain the paradox.

In order to show that this is in fact the view of the mystics themselves in all religions, I will read to you from a Christian mystic, a Hindu, and a Buddhist. The Christian example again is Eckhart. Rudolph Otto writes that "Eckhart establishes a polar unity between rest and motion within the Godhead itself. The eternally resting Godhead is also the wheel rolling out of itself." And in Eckhart's own words: "This divine ground is a unified stillness, immovable in itself. Yet from this immobility all things are moved and receive life."

The Hindu from whom I wish to quote is Aurobindo, who died only a few years ago. There is no doubt in my mind that he himself experienced the mystical vision in full measure. He says:

> Those who have thus possessed the calm within can perceive always
> welling out from its silence the perennial supply of the energies which
> work in the world.

I wish to comment on this sentence. "Those who have thus possessed the
calm within" means those who have possessed mystical vision. "Can perceive
always welling out from its silence"—"silence" is the motionlessness, the stillness, the inactivity of the divine. "The perennial supply of the energies which
work in the world" refers to the creative activity of the divine. These creative
energies are said to "well out from the silence." In other words, they issue out
of the empty void. Finally, we see the paradox of the static and the dynamic
directly stated as an *experience*. The word "perceive" is used. This is not an
intellectual proposition, a theory, an intellectual construction, a philosophical
opinion. It is a direct perception or vision of reality.

My last example is Suzuki, the well-known Zen Buddhist mystic, now
teaching in New York. He writes:

> It is not the nature of "prajna" to remain in the state of "sunyata,"
> absolutely motionless.

("Prajna" is the word for mystical intuition, while "sunyata" means the void.)
So he is saying it is not the nature of mystical consciousness to remain in a
state of void, absolutely motionless.

> It demands of itself that it differentiate itself unlimitedly and, at the
> same time, it deserves to remain in itself undifferentiated. This is why
> "sunyata" is said to be a reservoir of infinite possibility, and not just a
> state of mere emptiness. Differentiating itself and yet remaining in itself
> undifferentiated, it goes on eternally in the work of creation. We can
> say of it that it is creation out of nothing. "Sunyata" is not to be
> conceived statically but dynamically, or better, as at once static and
> dynamic.

David Hume asked ironically, "Have you ever seen a world created under your eyes—have you ever observed an act of creation of the world?" The
answer is: Yes, there are men who have seen this.

I conclude that these contradictions and paradoxes are impossible of logical adjustment or resolution. What, then, should we think about the matter?
Should we say that there is contradiction in the nature of God himself, in the
ultimate being? Well, if we were to say that, I think that we shouldn't be saying anything very unusual or very shocking. Many people have said this or at
any rate implied it. Does not the Christian doctrine of the Trinity itself imply
this? What could be a greater paradox than that? And it is not to be believed
that the three-in-one, the three which is one and the one which is three, could
be understood or explained by a super-Einstein, or by a higher mathematics
than has yet been invented. It is irremovable and an absolute paradox. Also
one might quote the words of Jacob Boëhme suggesting that there is contradiction in the heart of things, in the ultimate itself. Schwegler, a distinguished
German historian of philosophy, writes this:

> The main thought of Boëhme's philosophizing is this: that self-distinction, inner diremption is the essential characteristic of spirit, and, consequently of God. God is the living spirit only if and insofar as he comprehends within himself difference from himself.

One might also perhaps quote Boëhme's well-known statement that God is both "the Eternal Yea" and "the Eternal Nay," but this perhaps might also be taken simply as a brief expression of the negative-positive paradox.

Although I do not think it would be anything seriously erroneous if we would say that there is contradiction in the Ultimate, yet I would prefer myself to use other language. I should say that the contradiction is in us, in our intellect, and not in God. This means that God is utterly and forever beyond the reach of the logical intellect or of any intellectual comprehension, and that in consequence when we try to comprehend his nature intellectually, contradictions appear in our thinking. Let me use a metaphor to express this. We speak of God as the "Infinite" and of ourselves as "finite" minds. As a matter of fact what the word "infinite" means in this connection is itself a difficult problem in the philosophy of religion. It is certain that the word "infinite," when applied to God, is not used in the same sense as when we speak of infinite time or infinite space or the infinite number series. What it does mean is a problem. I believe that it can be solved, that is to say, it is possible to give a clear meaning to the word "infinite"—different from the infinity of space and time—as the word is applied to God. However, if I am allowed to use this language of finite and infinite, my metaphor is that if you try to pour the infinite into the finite vessels which are human minds, these finite vessels split and crack, and these cracks and splits are the contradictions and paradoxes of which I have been talking. Therefore this amounts to saying that God is utterly incomprehensible, incapable of being intellectually understood. In order to make my final point I will use the word "unknowable." It means that God is, in a sense, unknowable. But we must be very careful of this. If God were absolutely unknowable, and in no sense knowable, then there could be no such thing as religion, because in some sense or other religion is the knowledge of God.

The explanation of this is that he is unknowable to *the logical intellect*, but that he can be known in direct religious or mystical experience. Perhaps this is much the same as saying that he can be known by "faith" but not by "reason." Any attempt to reach God through logic, through the conceptual, logical intellect, is doomed, comes up against an absolute barrier; but this does not mean the death of religion—it does not mean that there is no possibility of that knowledge and communion with God which religion requires. It means that the knowledge of God which is the essence of religion is not of an intellectual kind. It is rather the direct experience of the mystic himself. Or if we are not mystics, then it is whatever it is that you would call religious experience. And this experience of God—in the heart, shall we say, not any intellectual understanding or explanation—this experience of God is the essence of religion.

STUDY QUESTIONS

1. List some of the similarities which Stace finds in the different mystical traditions of the world.
2. What are some of the "paradoxes" in the mystical vision of God?
3. How does Stace account for these paradoxes? In what sense is God unknowable?
4. Can you think of ordinary experiences which might be used to back up Stace's position? For example, are some aspects of ordinary experience indescribable?
5. Is it possible to view the poet as a mystic?
6. In light of Stace's comments on the mystical traditions of the world, interpret these sayings of some famous mystics:

I went from God to God, until they cried out from me in me, "O thou I!" (Bayadzid of Bistun).

The philosophers are clever enough, but wanting in wisdom; As to the others, they are either ignorant or puerile! They take an empty fist as containing something real and the pointing finger as the object pointed at. Because the finger is adhered to as though it were the moon, all their efforts are lost (Yoka Daishi).

How shall I grasp it? Do not grasp it. That which remains when there is no more grasping is the Self (Panchadasi).

No Alternative to Reason
Michael Scriven

Michael Scriven (1928–   ) is a distinguished philosopher who is well known for his lucid and comprehensive treatment of many classic philosophical questions. As you will soon discover, Scriven is an uncompromising defender of reason as the best tool for discovering truth. His central claim is that if God transcends the human intellect, then religious belief can have no relevant connection with life. Faith is not enough.

In general, Scriven argues that religious knowledge must always be tied to the usual forms of experience. Faith, he claims, cannot be considered an alternative to reason unless it is first shown that faith leads to consistently reliable predictions. If this could be done, then faith, as a way of knowing, would have been validated by reason. But Scriven thinks that the lack of agreement in the religious community shows that faith cannot be "proved out" in the way that the techniques of ordinary reason can be, and thus it cannot serve as an alternative to ordinary reason.

The issues raised in this essay are extremely important, and the arguments may be difficult to appreciate. As you read Scriven you might adopt Stace's position in order to locate sources of disagreement between them. It may be possible, for example, that Scriven bases his argument on assumptions which the mystic would say are just the points in question.

What kind of God, if any, exists? This is the primary problem about God, and it is simply stated. Nothing else about the issue is simple. And the problem's complexity is matched by its profundity. No other problem has such important consequences for our lives and our thinking about other issues, and to no other problem does the answer at first seem so obvious. There *must* be a God, for how else could the Universe have come to exist, or life and morality have any point? So one feels. The informal versions of the arguments for the existence of God are probably the oldest and the most widely known of all philosophical arguments. But the centuries have not been entirely kind to them, and many contemporary theologians have wholly abandoned the attempt to prove that God exists, the original task of natural theology....

Does it matter whether the arguments are sound? Indeed, should we be trying to reason about God at all? It is often said that such an attempt is hopelessly inappropriate, and indeed it is sometimes said to be sacrilegious. By His very nature God transcends merely human categories of thought, and to attempt to imprison Him in them is a simple fallacy. The attempt, in fact, demonstrates that some other, limited being is under discussion, not God Himself. Our enterprise and, indeed, our very definition of "God" in terms of human concepts are thus doomed from the start.

But a mountain that is infinitely tall does not thereby cease to be a mountain; those who lived in its shadow would not lack good reason for saying that there was a mountain near them just because none could determine where the end of the shadow was to be found. A God that exists everywhere is nonetheless present here and now. A God that is perfectly loving is at least as loving as a human being who loves with all his human heart. An omnipotent God is at least as powerful as you and I; indeed He is certainly more powerful than any human being. So we *can* legitimately begin by looking into the question whether there is any reason for thinking that this world is inhabited (or permeated) by a Being who is superhuman in respect of His knowledge, power, and love to the extent set out in our definition.

If such a Being exists, then we might or might not be able to go on to argue that It is *infinitely* powerful, etc., or the grounds we uncover may immediately lead to that conclusion. Despite a common belief to the contrary, this task is obviously possible in principle. We have already learned, from the fossils and footprints of the dinosaurs, that there were once beings on the Earth's surface with greater physical power than human beings. There is nothing in the least self-contradictory about a human being reasoning to the conclusion that there are beings with *more-than-human* power, just as the big-game hunter frequently reasons to the presence of elephants. One might as well argue that it is impossible to reason about the existence of beings with *less-than-human* power—after all, they are just as different from us. Indeed we can go further; the whole of modern particle physics involves reasoning about the existence of beings with properties that are so fundamentally different from the ones with which we are familiar that comprehension in the sense of simple analogy with the familiar is almost completely lacking, but the success of applied physics shows that such inferences are not only possible but very effective. And mathematics readily demonstrates the possibility of reasoning to the existence of infinite entities and properties....

In a somewhat desperate move, some theologians have argued that the words we use to describe God do not have their ordinary use at all. All religious language is symbolic and not to be taken literally, they say. This move throws out the baby of belief with the bath water of mythology; it is too sophisticated for its own good. In the first place, almost all believers and potential believers, past and present, take the usual claims about God's nature to be something like the truth, even if not quite literally true; and it is to them we are addressing these discussions. The points made will not be vulnerable to the possibility that analogical or symbolic reference is the best we can do (in any comprehensible sense of "analogical" or "symbolic"). In the second place, if we try to take the sophisticated position seriously and ask what it is about religious belief, interpreted in this way, that distinguishes it from the beliefs of a pagan or an avowed atheist, we find that either there is no agreement on the answer or the answer is that no such distinction exists. The latter comment has been taken to be the profound discovery that everyone is "really" religious or even theistic (for example, because everyone has some "ultimate concern" about something or believes in the existence of substance). But, of course, it equally well proves that everyone is "really" irreligious or atheistic; if there is no difference between chalk and cheese, you can just as well call the stuff on the supermarket's cold shelves chalk as call the stuff on the blackboard cheese. There is a real difference between almost everyone who believes in the existence of God and everyone who does not; the difference is that the two groups disagree about what a thorough census of all existing entities would show and only one of them thinks it would include an intelligent Being with supernatural powers, concerned with our welfare. Attempts to eliminate this residual content in theism, common in recent "liberal" Protestant theology, are the survival attempts of a system of belief that sees its only salvation in camouflage but fails to see that what is indistinguishable cannot be indispensable.

Someone who wanted to adopt a really disproof-proof position here (many have been tempted, and at least one Indian philosopher has succumbed) could *define* God as the Unknowable; or he could say that whatever else God is, He is certainly unknowable. The only trouble with this position is that you really cannot eat your cake and worship it too; there cannot be any reason for worshiping, or respecting, or loving, or praying to, or believing in such a God. The

Unknowable may be evil, stupid, inanimate, or nonexistent; a religion dedicated to such a pig in a poke would be for the feebleminded. If religious belief means anything at all, it means belief in something whose properties may not be entirely clear but which are at least worthy of respect (most have said, humble adoration). Such a Being is not wholly unknowable, since we know some very important things about Him, such as His goodness. We may certainly say that He is not fully knowable, and the ensuing discussion does not assume that God is fully knowable. The theist's claim is that there is a good supernatural force, perhaps with many mysterious properties. And the atheist's claim is simply that the God of the great religions has quite enough properties to make him, on the one hand, worthy of respect and, on the other, nonexistent.

The extreme form of the defense against the relevance of reason is therefore itself indefensible. There are no obvious mistakes in the attempt to reason about God. One can all too easily get carried away by catchy little slogans like "The finite cannot comprehend the infinite," "Man cannot presume to judge God," "God takes up where Reason gives out," and so on. Their merits, if any, lie in their potential use as tricky titles for sermons in fashionable suburban churches. They have no force as a defense against skepticism or as a support for belief. We can be quite sure there *is* an infinite sequence of digits after 1, 2, and 3, and we can be quite sure there *is not* an infinitely long ribbon in our typewriter or an infinitely heavy nuthatch sitting on the bird feeder; so the preacher just has to get down from the pulpit and do some hard, logical work to show that there is some special reason why an infinite God cannot be reasoned about in the same way. Why should the human mind be incapable of dealing with the infinite in theology but not in mathematics or cosmology, where it is a commonplace and well-defined part of the subject?

Yet, a more profound point is involved behind the scenes here. There is a nagging nervousness about talking as if there were no limitations on the power of the human reason. After all, there *must* be a certain parochialism about our present views and a certain poverty about our capacity for analyzing the evidence. We have only been thinking systematically for a few millenniums (some would say, centuries), and in that short span we have constantly found ourselves abandoning the absolute convictions of previous generations. How then can one have any degree of certainty about the existence or nonexistence of a Being so different from the beings of our immediate experience and so vastly superior to ourselves in thought?

The point is very weighty, but it is not decisive here. In the first place, the very nature of the Being we are now undertaking to discuss makes Him approachable by reason. For God, Who is often said to be ever present, is at the very least *able* to be present almost anywhere at almost any time—He is ever accessible. If He lacked this power, He would be of little concern to us. We cannot be certain about the existence of beings on other planets just because they are on other planets and not here, and thus far we have not been close enough to see if they do, in fact, exist. But a Being that is here, indeed often said to have been here since Creation—such a Being, with the opportunity and the power and the interest in doing something that would prevent or improve an imperfect work, would surely have to leave some traces in *this* world. Indeed, whether He created the world or merely had the chance to change it, the world itself must to some extent be a reflection of His character. If we can show that the world is best explicable in terms of a Divine Plan, we have the best reasons for theism. If the world is simply a natural phenomenon, whose natural properties are grossly imperfect for our needs and not improved by any unseen force, it seems at first sight as if we would have some kind of reason for thinking Him less than good, powerful, and wise. So reason can in principle both prove and disprove the existence of God....

We must now contend with the suggestion that reason is irrelevant to the commitment to theism because this territory is the domain of another faculty: the faculty of faith. It is sometimes even hinted that it is morally wrong and certainly foolish to suggest we should be reasoning about God. For this is the domain of faith or of the "venture of faith," of the "knowledge that passeth understanding," of religious experience and mystic insight.

Now the normal meaning of *faith* is simply "confidence"; we say that we have great faith in someone or in some claim or product, meaning that we believe and act as if they were very reliable. Of such faith we can properly say that it is well founded or not, depending on the evidence for whatever it is in which we have faith.[1] So there is no incompatibility between this kind of faith and reason; the two are from different families and can make a very good marriage. Indeed if they do not join forces, then the resulting ill-based or inadequate confidence will probably lead to disaster. So faith, in this sense, means only a high degree of belief and may be reasonable or unreasonable.

But the term is sometimes used to mean an <u>*alternative to reason* instead of something that should be founded on reason</u>. Unfortunately, the mere use of the term in this way does not demonstrate that faith is a possible route to truth. It is like using the term "winning" as a synonym for "playing" instead of one possible outcome of playing. This is quaint, but it could hardly be called a satisfactory way of proving that we are winning; any time we "win" by changing the meaning of winning, the victory is merely illusory. And so it proves in this case. T<u>o use "faith" *as if* it were an alternative way to the truth cannot by-pass the crucial question whether such results really have any like</u>lihood of being true. A rose by any other name will smell the same, and the inescapable facts about "faith" in the new sense are that it is still *applied to* a belief and is still supposed to imply *confidence in* that belief: the belief in the existence and goodness of God. So we can still ask the same old question about that belief: Is the confidence justified or misplaced? To say we "take it on faith" does not get it off parole.

Suppose someone replies that theism is a kind of belief that does not

---

[1] For faith to be well founded, especially faith in a person, it is not required that the evidence available at a particular moment justify exactly the degree of confidence one exhibits. There may be overriding reasons for retaining trust beyond the first point of rationally defensible doubt.... But this minor divergence does not seriously affect the discussion here.

need justification by evidence. This means either that no one cares whether it is correct or not or that there is some other way of checking that it is correct besides looking at the evidence for it, i.e., giving reasons for believing it. But the first alternative is false since very many people care whether there is a God or not; and the second alternative is false because any method of showing that belief is likely to be true is, by definition, a justification of that belief, i.e., an appeal to reason. You certainly cannot show that a belief in God is likely to be true just by having confidence in it and by saying this is a case of knowledge "based on" faith, any more than you can win a game just by playing it and by calling that winning.

It is psychologically possible to have faith in something without any basis in fact, and once in a while you will turn out to be lucky and to have backed the right belief. This does not show you "really knew all along"; it only shows you cannot be unlucky all the time....But, in general, beliefs without foundations lead to an early grave or to an accumulation of superstitions, which are usually troublesome and always false beliefs. It is hardly possible to defend this approach just by *saying* that you have decided that in this area confidence is its own justification.

Of course, you might try to *prove* that a feeling of great confidence about certain types of propositions is a reliable indication of their truth. If you succeeded, you would indeed have shown that the belief was justified; you would have done this by justifying it. To do this you would have to show what the real facts were and show that when someone had the kind of faith we are now talking about, it usually turned out that the facts were as he believed; just as we might justify the claims of a telepath. The catch in all this is simply that you have got to show what the real facts are in some way *other* than by appealing to faith, since that would simply be assuming what you are trying to prove. And if you can show what the facts are in this other way, you do not need faith in any new sense at all; you are already perfectly entitled to confidence in any belief that you have shown to be well supported.

How are you going to show what the real facts are? You show this by any method of investigation that has itself been tested, the testing being done by still another tested method, etc., through a series of tested connections that eventually terminates in our ordinary everyday reasoning and testing procedures of logic and observation.

Is it not prejudiced to require that the validation of beliefs always involve ultimate reference to our ordinary logic and everyday-plus-scientific knowledge? May not faith (religious experience, mystic insight) give us access to some new domain of truth? It is certainly possible that it does this. But, of course it is also possible that it lies. One can hardly accept the reports of those with faith or, indeed, the apparent revelations of one's own religious experiences on the ground that they *might* be right. So *might* be a fervent materialist who saw his interpretation as a revelation. Possibility is not veracity. Is it not of the very greatest importance that we should try to find out whether we really can justify the use of the term "truth" or "knowledge" in describing the content of faith? If it is, then we must find something in that content that is known to be true in some other way, because to get off the ground we must first push off against the ground—we cannot lift ourselves by our shoelaces. If the new realm of knowledge is to be a realm of knowledge and not mythology, then it must tell us something which relates it to the kind of case that gives meaning to the term "truth." If you want to use the old word for the new events, you must show that it is applicable.

Could not the validating experience, which religious experience must have if it is to be called true, be the experience of others who also have or have had religious experiences? The religious community could, surely, provide a basis of agreement analogous to that which ultimately underlies scientific truth. Unfortunately, agreement is not the only requirement for avoiding error, for all may be in error. The difficulty for the religious community is to show that its agreement is not simply agreement about a shared mistake. If agreement were the only criterion of truth, there could never be a shared mistake; but clearly either the atheist group or the theist group shares a mistake. To decide which is wrong must involve appeal to something other than mere agreement. And, of course, it is clear that particular religious beliefs are mistaken, since religious groups do not all agree and they cannot all be right.

Might not some or all scientific beliefs be wrong, too? This is conceivable, but there are crucial differences between the two kinds of belief. In the first place, any commonly agreed religious beliefs concern only one or a few entities and their properties and histories. What for convenience we are here calling "scientific belief" is actually the sum total of all conventionally founded human knowledge, much of it not part of any science, and it embraces billions upon billions of facts, each of them perpetually or frequently subject to checking by independent means, each connected with a million others. The success of *this* system of knowledge shows up every day in everything that we do; we eat, and the food is not poison; we read, and the pages do not turn to dust; we slip, and gravity does not fail to pull us down. We are not just relying on the existence of agreement about the interpretation of a certain experience among a small part of the population. We are relying directly on our extremely reliable, nearly universal, and independently tested senses, and each of us is constantly obtaining independent confirmation for claims based on these, many of these confirmations being obtained for many claims, independently of each other. It is the wildest flight of fancy to suppose that there is a body of common religious beliefs which can be set out to exhibit this degree of repeated checking by religious experiences. In fact, there is not only gross disagreement on even the most fundamental claims in the creeds of different churches, each of which is supported by appeal to religious experience or faith, but where there is agreement by many people, it is all too easily open to the criticism that it arises from the common cultural exposure of the child or the adult convert and hence is not independent in the required way.

This claim that the agreement between judges is spurious in a particular case because it only reflects previous common indoctrination of those in agreement is a serious one. It must always be met by direct disproof whenever agreement is appealed to in science, and it is. The claim that the food is not poison cannot be explained away as a myth of some subculture, for anyone, even if told nothing about the eaters in advance, will judge that the people who ate it are still well. The whole methodology of testing is committed to the doctrine that any judges who could have learned what they are expected to say about the matter they are judging are completely valueless.[2] Now anyone exposed to religious teaching, whether a believer or not, has long known the standard for such experiences, the usual symbols, the appropriate circumstances, and so on. These suggestions are usually very deeply implanted, so that they cannot be avoided by good intentions, and consequently members of our culture are rendered entirely incapable of being independent observers. Whenever observers are not free from previous contamination in this manner, the only way to support their claims is to examine independently testable *consequences* of the novel claims, such as predictions about the future. In the absence of these, the religious-experience gambit, whether involving literal or analogical claims, is wholly abortive.

A still more fundamental point counts against the idea that agreement among the religious can help support the idea of faith as an alternative path to truth. It is that every sane theist also believes in the claims of ordinary experience, while the reverse is not the case. Hence, the burden of proof is on the theist to show that the *further step* he wishes to take will not take him beyond the realm of truth. The two positions, of science and religion, are not symmetrical; the adherent of one of them suggests that we extend the range of allowable beliefs and yet is unable to produce the same degree of acceptance or "proving out" in the ordinary field of human activities that he insists on before believing in a new instrument or source of information. The atheist obviously cannot be shown his error in the way someone who thinks that there are no electrons can be shown his, *unless some of the arguments for the existence of God are sound.* Once again, we come back to these. If some of them work, the position of religious knowledge is secure; if they do not, nothing else will make it secure.

In sum, the idea of separating religious from scientific knowledge and making each an independent realm with its own basis in experience of quite different kinds is a counsel of despair and not a product of true sophistication, for one cannot break the connection between everyday experience and religious claims, for purposes of defending the latter, without eliminating the consequences of religion for everyday life. There is no way out of this inexorable contract: if you want to support your beliefs, you must produce some experience which can be shown to be a reliable indicator of truth, and that can

---

[2] More precisely, a judge is said to be "contaminated" if he could know which way his judgment will count insofar as the issue at stake is concerned. The famous double-blind experimental design, keystone of drug research, achieves reliability by making it impossible for either patient or nurse to know when the real drug, rather than the dummy drug or placebo, is being judged.

be done only by showing a connection between the experience and what we know to be true in a previously established way.

So, if the criteria of religious truth are not connected with the criteria of everyday truth, then they are not criteria of truth at all and the beliefs they "establish" have no essential bearing on our lives, constitute no explanation of what we see around us, and provide no guidance for our course through time.

STUDY QUESTIONS

1. Why does Scriven believe that the claim that we cannot reason about the infinite is untrue?
2. Scriven says that it is impossible to remain religious and think that God is unknowable. Why does he maintain this position?
3. "Human thought categories may be quite limited. We may be nothing more than the egotistic infants of the universe, so impressed by our limited faculties that we cannot see their limitations." How would Scriven reply to this suggestion? What do you think?
4. "Super-rationalists like Scriven simply replace one faith with another. Instead of faith in God, they place their faith in Science, that god above God. But for all their cool, rational protests, they are still gambling that their faith is the true one." Do you agree? How would Scriven respond to this argument?
5. Why does Scriven think it significant that theists believe in the procedures of ordinary experience for testing ordinary beliefs? Do you agree with his conclusion?

The Will to Believe
William James

William James (1842–1910) taught anatomy and physiology at Harvard before moving to psychology, a field in which he acquired an international reputation. His interests, however, turned to philosophy and he soon became one of America's foremost philosophers. James defended a theory called *pragmatism*—a view which held that the truth of an idea is determined by the consequences it has on experience. In his own words: "Ideas (which themselves are but parts of our experience) become true just insofar as they help us to get into satisfactory relation with other parts of our experience." If

An Address to the Philosophical Clubs of Yale and Brown Universities. Published in the *New World*, June, 1896.

two theories do not have different consequences for experience, then there can be no real difference between them.

In this essay, James applies his pragmatism to religious belief and argues that what poses as a healthy, rational skepticism is actually no different from the most committed form of atheism. In fact, James maintains that when we consider the consequences of religious belief, faith in God is actually a more rational attitude than skepticism. Both faith and skepticism, he claims, are emotional commitments, but the emotions which guide faith are logically superior to those behind the skeptical position.

James has had his passionate critics as well as devoted defenders. His critics usually accuse him of licensing wishful thinking, whereas his defenders point out that he has focused on an important insight into the way we make decisions in the real world. Undoubtedly, you will join this debate. As you read this classic statement, however, try to keep in mind the qualifications which James attaches to his defense of faith.

In the recently published Life by Leslie Stephen of his brother, Fitz-James, there is an account of a school to which the latter went when he was a boy. The teacher, a certain Mr. Guest, used to converse with his pupils in this wise: "Gurney, what is the difference between justification and sanctification?—Stephen, prove the omnipotence of God!" etc. In the midst of our Harvard freethinking and indifference we are prone to imagine that here at your good old orthodox College conversation continues to be somewhat upon this order; and to show you that we at Harvard have not lost all interest in these vital subjects, I have brought with me to-night something like a sermon on justification by faith to read to you,—I mean an essay in justification *of* faith, a defence of our right to adopt a believing attitude in religious matters, in spite of the fact that our merely logical intellect may not have been coerced. "The Will to Believe," accordingly, is the title of my paper.

I have long defended to my own students the lawfulness of voluntarily adopted faith; but as soon as they have got well imbued with the logical spirit, they have as a rule refused to admit my contention to be lawful philosophically, even though in point of fact they were personally all the time chock-full of some faith or other themselves. I am all the while, however, so profoundly convinced that my own position is correct, that your invitation has seemed to me a good occasion to make my statements more clear. Perhaps your minds will be more open than those with which I have hitherto had to deal. I will be as little technical as I can, though I must begin by setting up some technical distinctions that will help us in the end.

Let us give the name of *hypothesis* to anything that may be proposed to our belief; and just as the electricians speak of live and dead wires, let us speak of any hypothesis as either *live* or *dead*. A live hypothesis is one which appeals as a real possibility to him to whom it is proposed. If I ask you to believe in the Mahdi, the notion makes no electric connection with your nature,—it refuses to scintillate with any credibility at all. As an hypothesis it is completely dead. To an Arab, however (even if he be not one of the Mahdi's followers), the hypothesis is among the mind's possibilities: it is alive. This shows that deadness and liveness in an hypothesis are not intrinsic properties, but relations to the individual thinker. They are measured by his willingness to act. The maximum of liveness in an hypothesis means willingness to act irrevocably. Practically, that means belief; but there is some believing tendency wherever there is willingness to act at all.

Next, let us call the decision between two hypotheses an _option_. Options may be of several kinds. They may be—1, _living_ or _dead;_ 2, _forced or avoidable;_ 3, _momentous_ or _trivial;_ and for our purposes we may call an option a _genuine_ option when it is of the forced, living, and momentous kind.

1. A living option is one in which both hypotheses are live ones. If I say to you: "Be a theosophist or be a Mohammedan," it is probably a dead option, because for you neither hypothesis is likely to be alive. But if I say: "Be an agnostic or be a Christian," it is otherwise: trained as you are, each hypothesis makes some appeal, however small, to your belief.
2. Next, if I say to you: "Choose between going out with your umbrella or without it," I do not offer you a genuine option, for it is not forced. You can easily avoid it by not going out at all. Similarly, if I say, "Either love me or hate me," "Either call my theory true or call it false," your option is avoidable. You may remain indifferent to me, neither loving nor hating, and you may decline to offer any judgment as to my theory. But if I say, "Either accept this truth or go without it," I put on you a forced option, for there is no standing place outside of the alternative. Every dilemma based on a complete logical disjunction, with no possibility of not choosing, is an option of this forced kind.
3. Finally, if I were Dr. Nansen and proposed to you to join my North Pole expedition, your option would be momentous; for this would probably be your only similar opportunity, and your choice now would either exclude you from the North Pole sort of immortality altogether or put at least the chance of it into your hands. He who refuses to embrace a unique opportunity loses the prize as surely as if he tried and failed. _Per contra_, the option is trivial when the opportunity is not unique, when the stake is insignificant, or when the decision is reversible if it later prove unwise. Such trivial options abound in the scientific life. A chemist finds an hypothesis live enough to spend a year in its verification: he believes in it to that extent. But if his experiments prove inconclusive either way, he is quit for his loss of time, no vital harm being done.

The thesis I defend is, briefly stated, this: _Our passional nature not only lawfully may, but must, decide an option between propositions, whenever it is a genuine option that cannot by its nature be decided on intellectual grounds; for to say, under such circumstances, "Do not decide, but leave the question open," is itself a passional decision,—just like deciding yes or no,—and is attended with the same risk_ *of losing the truth.* The thesis thus abstractly expressed will, I trust, soon become quite clear....

One more point, small but important, and our preliminaries are done. There are two ways of looking at our duty in the matter of opinion,—ways entirely different, and yet ways about whose difference the theory of knowledge seems hitherto to have shown very little concern. *We must know the truth;* and *we must avoid error,*—these are our first and great commandments as would-be knowers; but they are not two ways of stating an identical commandment, they are two separable laws. Although it may indeed happen that when we believe the truth A, we escape as an incidental consequence from believing the falsehood B, it hardly ever happens that by merely disbelieving B we necessarily believe A. We may in escaping B fall into believing other falsehoods, C or D, just as bad as B; or we may escape B by not believing anything at all, not even A.

Believe truth! Shun error!—these, we see, are two materially different laws; and by choosing between them we may end by coloring differently our whole intellectual life. We may regard the chase for truth as paramount, and the avoidance of error as secondary; or we may, on the other hand, treat the avoidance of error as more imperative, and let truth take its chance. Clifford, in the instructive passage which I have quoted, exhorts us to the latter course. Believe nothing, he tells us, keep your mind in suspense forever, rather than by closing it on insufficient evidence incur the awful risk of believing lies. You, on the other hand, may think that the risk of being in error is a very small matter when compared with the blessings of real knowledge, and be ready to be duped many times in your investigation rather than postpone indefinitely the chance of guessing true. I myself find it impossible to go with Clifford. We must remember that these feelings of our duty about either truth or error are in any case only expressions of our passional life. Biologically considered, our minds are as ready to grind out falsehood as veracity, and he who says, "Better go without belief forever than believe a lie!" merely shows his own preponderant private horror of becoming a dupe. He may be critical of many of his desires and fears, but this fear he slavishly obeys. He cannot imagine any one questioning its blinding force. For my own part, I have also a horror of being duped; but I can believe that worse things than being duped may happen to a man in this world: so Clifford's exhortation has to my ears a thoroughly fantastic sound. It is like a general informing his soldiers that it is better to keep out of battle forever than to risk a single wound. Not so are victories either over enemies or over nature gained. Our errors are surely not such awfully solemn things. In a world where we are so certain to incur them in spite of all our caution, a certain lightness of heart seems healthier than this excessive nervousness on their behalf. At any rate, it seems the fittest thing for the empiricist philosopher.

And now, after all this introduction, let us go straight at our question. I have said, and now repeat it, that not only as a matter of fact do we find our passional nature influencing us in our opinions, but that there are some options between opinions in which this influence must be regarded both as an inevitable and as a lawful determinant of our choice.

I fear here that some of you my hearers will begin to scent danger, and lend an inhospitable ear. Two first steps of passion you have indeed had to admit as necessary,—we must think so as to avoid dupery, and we must think so as to gain truth; but the surest path to those ideal consummations, you will probably consider, is from now onwards to take no further passional step.

Well, of course, I agree as far as the facts will allow. Wherever the option between losing truth and gaining it is not momentous, we can throw the chance of *gaining truth* away, and at any rate save ourselves from any chance of *believing falsehood*, by not making up our minds at all till objective evidence has come. In scientific questions, this is almost always the case; and even in human affairs in general, the need of acting is seldom so urgent that a false belief to act on is better than no belief at all. Law courts, indeed, have to decide on the best evidence attainable for the moment, because a judge's duty is to make law as well as to ascertain it, and (as a learned judge once said to me) few cases are worth spending much time over; the great thing is to have them decided on *any* acceptable principle, and got out of the way. But in our dealings with objective nature we obviously are recorders, not makers, of the truth; and decisions for the mere sake of deciding promptly and getting on to the next business would be wholly out of place. Throughout the breadth of physical nature facts are what they are quite independently of us, and seldom is there any such hurry about them that the risks of being duped by believing a premature theory need be faced. The questions here are always trivial options, the hypotheses are hardly living (at any rate not living for us spectators), the choice between believing truth or falsehood is seldom forced. The attitude of skeptical balance is therefore the absolutely wise one if we would escape mistakes. What difference, indeed, does it make to most of us whether we have or have not a theory of the Röntgen rays, whether we believe or not in mind-stuff, or have a conviction about the causality of conscious states? It makes no difference. Such options are not forced on us. On every account it is better not to make them, but still keep weighing reasons *pro et contra* with an indifferent hand.

I speak, of course, here of the purely judging mind. For purposes of discovery such indifference is to be less highly recommended, and science would be far less advanced than she is if the passionate desires of individuals to get their own faiths confirmed had been kept out of the game. See for example the sagacity which Spencer and Weismann now display. On the other hand, if you want an absolute duffer in an investigation, you must, after all, take the man who has no interest whatever in its results; he is the warranted incapable, the positive fool. The most useful investigator, because the most sensitive observer, is always he whose eager interest in one side of the question is balanced by an equally keen nervousness lest he become deceived. Science has organized this nervousness into a regular *technique*, her so-called method of verification; and she has fallen so deeply in love with the method that one may even say she has ceased to care for truth by itself at all. It is only truth as technically verified that interests her. The truth of truths might come in merely affirmative form, and she would decline to touch it. Such truth as that, she might repeat with Clifford, would be stolen in defiance of her duty to mankind. Human passions, however, are stronger than technical rules. "Le coeur a ses raisons," as Pascal says, "que la raison ne connaît pas";[1] and however indifferent to all but the bare rules of the game the umpire, the abstract intellect, may be, the concrete players who furnish him the materials to judge of are usually, each one of them, in love with some pet 'live hypothesis' of his own. Let us agree, however, that wherever there is no forced option, the dispassionately judicial intellect with no pet hypothesis, saving us, as it does, from dupery at any rate, ought to be our ideal.

The question next arises: Are there not somewhere forced options in our speculative questions, and can we (as men who may be interested at least as much in positively gaining truth as in merely escaping dupery) always wait with impunity till the coercive evidence shall have arrived? It seems *a priori* improbable that the truth should be so nicely adjusted to our needs and powers as that. In the great boardinghouse of nature, the cakes and the butter and the syrup seldom come out so even and leave the plates so clean. Indeed, we should view them with scientific suspicion if they did.

Moral questions immediately present themselves as questions whose solution cannot wait for sensible proof. A moral question is a question not of what sensibly exists, but of what is good, or would be good if it did exist. Science can tell us what exists; but to compare the *worths,* both of what exists and of what does not exist, we must consult not science, but what Pascal calls our heart. Science herself consults her heart when she lays it down that the infinite ascertainment of fact and correction of false belief are the supreme goods for man. Challenge the statement, and science can only repeat it oracularly, or else prove it by showing that such ascertainment and correction bring man all sorts of other goods which man's heart in turn declares. The question of having moral beliefs at all or not having them is decided by our will. Are our moral preferences true or false, or are they only odd biological phenomena, making things good or bad for *us,* but in themselves indifferent? How can your pure intellect decide? If your heart does not *want* a world of moral reality, your head will assuredly never make you believe in one. Mephistophelian scepticism, indeed, will satisfy the head's play-instincts much better than any rigorous idealism can. Some men (even at the student age) are so naturally cool-hearted that the moralistic hypothesis never has for them any pungent life, and in their supercilious presence the hot young moralist always feels strangely ill at ease. The appearance of knowingness is on their side, of naïveté and gullibility on his. Yet, in the inarticulate heart of him, he clings to it that he is not a dupe, and that there is a realm in which (as Emerson says) all their wit and intellectual superiority is no better than the cunning of

---

[1] "The heart has its reasons, which reason cannot know."

a fox. Moral scepticism can no more be refuted or proved by logic than intellectual scepticism can. When we stick to it that there *is* truth (be it of either kind), we do so with our whole nature, and resolve to stand or fall by the results. The sceptic with his whole nature adopts the doubting attitude; but which of us is the wiser, Omniscience only knows.

Turn now from these wide questions of good to a certain class of questions of fact, questions concerning personal relations, states of mind between one man and another. *Do you like me or not?*—for example. Whether you do or not depends, in countless instances, on whether I meet you half-way, am willing to assume that you must like me, and show you trust and expectation. The previous faith on my part in your liking's existence is in such cases what makes your liking come. But if I stand aloof, and refuse to budge an inch until I have objective evidence, until you shall have done something apt, as the absolutists say, *ad extorquendum assensum meum,*[2] ten to one your liking never comes. How many women's hearts are vanquished by the mere sanguine insistence of some man that they *must* love him! he will not consent to the hypothesis that they cannot. The desire for a certain kind of truth here brings about that special truth's existence; and so it is in innumerable cases of other sorts. Who gains promotions, boons, appointments, but the man in whose life they are seen to play the part of live hypotheses, who discounts them, sacrifices other things for their sake before they have come, and takes risks for them in advance? His faith acts on the powers above him as a claim, and creates its own verification.

A social organism of any sort whatever, large or small, is what it is because each member proceeds to his own duty with a trust that the other members will simultaneously do theirs. Wherever a desired result is achieved by the co-operation of many independent persons, its existence as a fact is a pure consequence of the precursive faith in one another of those immediately concerned. A government, an army, a commercial system, a ship, a college, an athletic team, all exist on this condition, without which not only is nothing achieved, but nothing is even attempted. A whole train of passengers (individually brave enough) will be looted by a few highwaymen, simply because the latter can count on one another, while each passenger fears that if he makes a movement of resistance, he will be shot before any one else backs him up. If we believed that the whole car-full would rise at once with us, we should each severally rise, and train-robbing would never even be attempted. There are, then, cases where a fact cannot come at all unless a preliminary faith exists in its coming. *And where faith in a fact can help create the fact,* that would be an insane logic which should say that faith running ahead of scientific evidence is the "lowest kind of immorality" into which a thinking being can fall. Yet such is the logic by which our scientific absolutists pretend to regulate our lives! In truths dependent on our personal action, then, faith based on desire is certainly a lawful and possibly an indispensable thing.

But now, it will be said, these are all childish human cases, and have nothing to do with great cosmical matters, like the question of religious faith.

---

[2] "Coercing my assent."

Let us then pass on to that. Religions differ so much in their accidents that in discussing the religious question we must make it very generic and broad. What then do we now mean by the religious hypothesis? Science says things are; morality says some things are better than other things; and religion says essentially two things.

First, she says that the best things are the more eternal things, the overlapping things, the things in the universe that throw the last stone, so to speak, and say the final word. "Perfection is eternal,"—this phrase of Charles Secrétan seems a good way of putting this first affirmation of religion, an affirmation which obviously cannot yet be verified scientifically at all.

The second affirmation of religion is that we are better off even now if we believe her first affirmation to be true.

Now, let us consider what the logical elements of this situation are *in case the religious hypothesis in both its branches be really true.* (Of course, we must admit that possibility at the outset. If we are to discuss the question at all, it must involve a living option. If for any of you religion be a hypothesis that cannot, by any living possibility be true, then you need go no farther. I speak to the "saving remnant" alone.) So proceeding, we see, first, that religion offers itself as a *momentous* option. We are supposed to gain, even now, by our belief, and to lose by our non-belief, a certain vital good. Secondly, religion is a *forced* option, so far as that good goes. We cannot escape the issue by remaining sceptical and waiting for more light, because, although we do avoid error in that way *if religion be untrue,* we lose the good, *if it be true,* just as certainly as if we positively chose to disbelieve. It is as if a man should hesitate indefinitely to ask a certain woman to marry him because he was not perfectly sure that she would prove an angel after he brought her home. Would he not cut himself off from that particular angel-possibility as decisively as if he went and married some one else? Scepticism, then, is not avoidance of option; it is option of a certain particular kind of risk. *Better risk loss of truth than chance of error,*—that is your faith-vetoer's exact position. He is actively playing his stake as much as the believer is; he is backing the field against the religious hypothesis, just as the believer is backing the religious hypothesis against the field. To preach scepticism to us as a duty until "sufficient evidence" for religion be found, is tantamount therefore to telling us, when in presence of the religious hypothesis, that to yield to our fear of its being error is wiser and better than to yield to our hope that it may be true. It is not intellect against all passions, then; it is only intellect with one passion laying down its law. And by what, forsooth, is the supreme wisdom of this passion warranted? Dupery for dupery, what proof is there that dupery through hope is so much worse than dupery through fear? I, for one, can see no proof; and I simply refuse obedience to the scientist's command to imitate his kind of option, in a case where my own stake is important enough to give me the right to choose my own form of risk. If religion be true and the evidence for it be still insufficient, I do not wish, by putting your extinguisher upon my nature (which feels to me as if it had after all some business in this matter), to forfeit my sole chance in life of getting upon the winning side,—that chance depending, of course, on my willingness to run the risk of acting as if my passional need of taking the world religiously might be prophetic and right.

All this is on the supposition that it really may be prophetic and right, and that, even to us who are discussing the matter, religion is a live hypothesis which may be true. Now, to most of us religion comes in a still further way that makes a veto on our active faith even more illogical. The more perfect and more eternal aspect of the universe is represented in our religions as having personal form. The universe is no longer a mere *It* to us, but a *Thou*, if we are religious; and any relation that may be possible from person to person might be possible here. For instance, although in one sense we are passive portions of the universe, in another we show a curious autonomy, as if we were small active centres on our own account. We feel, too, as if the appeal of religion to us were made to our own active good-will, as if evidence might be forever withheld from us unless we met the hypothesis halfway. To take a trivial illustration: just as a man who in a company of gentlemen made no advances, asked a warrant for every concession, and believed no one's word without proof, would cut himself off by such churlishness from all the social rewards that a more trusting spirit would earn,—so here, one who should shut himself up in snarling logicality and try to make the gods extort his recognition willy-nilly, or not get it at all, might cut himself off forever from his only opportunity of making the gods' acquaintance. This feeling, forced on us we know not whence, that by obstinately believing that there are gods (although not to do so would be so easy both for our logic and our life) we are doing the universe the deepest service we can, seems part of the living essence of the religious hypothesis. If the hypothesis *were* true in all its parts, including this one, then pure intellectualism, with its veto on our making willing advances, would be an absurdity; and some participation of our sympathetic nature would be logically required. I, therefore, for one, cannot see my way to accepting the agnostic rules for truth-seeking, or wilfully agree to keep my willing nature out of the game. I cannot do so for this plain reason, that *a rule of thinking which would absolutely prevent me from acknowledging certain kinds of truth if those kinds of truth were really there, would be an irrational rule.* That for me is the long and short of the formal logic of the situation, no matter what the kinds of truth might materially be.

I confess I do not see how this logic can be escaped. But sad experience makes me fear that some of you may still shrink from radically saying with me, *in abstracto,* that we have the right to believe at our own risk any hypothesis that is live enough to tempt our will. I suspect, however, that if this is so, it is because you have got away from the abstract logical point of view altogether, and are thinking (perhaps without realizing it) of some particular religious hypothesis which for you is dead. The freedom to "believe what we will" you apply to the case of some patent superstition; and the faith you think of is the faith defined by the schoolboy when he said, "Faith is when you believe something that you know ain't true." I can only repeat that this is misapprehension. *In concreto,* the freedom to believe can only cover living options which the intellect of the individual cannot by itself resolve; and living options never seem absurdities to him who has them to consider. When I look at the religious question as it really puts itself to concrete men, and when I think of all the possibilities which both practically and theoretically it involves, then this command that we shall put a stopper on our heart, instincts, and courage, and *wait*—acting of course meanwhile more or less as if religion were *not* true—till doomsday, or till such time as our intellect and senses working together may have raked in evidence enough,—this command, I say, seems to me the queerest idol ever manufactured in the philosophic cave. Were we scholastic absolutists, there might be more excuse. If we had an infallible intellect with its objective certitudes, we might feel ourselves disloyal to such a perfect organ of knowledge in not trusting to it exclusively, in not waiting for its releasing word. But if we are empiricists, if we believe that no bell in us tolls to let us know for certain when truth is in our grasp, then it seems a piece of idle fantasticality to preach so solemnly our duty of waiting for the bell. Indeed we *may* wait if we will,—I hope you do not think that I am denying that,—but if we do so, we do so at our peril as much as if we believed. In either case we *act,* taking our life in our hands. No one of us ought to issue vetoes to the other, nor should we bandy words of abuse. We ought, on the contrary, delicately and profoundly to respect one another's mental freedom: then only shall we bring about the intellectual republic; then only shall we have that spirit of inner tolerance without which all our outer tolerance is soulless, and which is empiricism's glory; then only shall we live and let live, in speculative as well as in practical things.

I began by a reference to Fitz-James Stephen; let me end by a quotation from him. "What do you think of yourself: What do you think of the world?...These are questions with which all must deal as it seems good to them. They are riddles of the Sphinx, and in some way or other we must deal with them....In all important transactions of life we have to take a leap in the dark....If we decide to leave the riddles unanswered, that is a choice; if we waver in our answer, that, too, is a choice: but whatever choice we make, we make it at our peril. If a man chooses to turn his back altogether on God and the future no one can prevent him; no one can show beyond reasonable doubt that he is mistaken. If a man thinks otherwise and acts as he thinks, I do not see that any one can prove that *he* is mistaken. Each must act as he thinks best; and if he is wrong, so much the worse for him. We stand on a mountain pass in the midst of whirling snow and blinding mist, through which we get glimpses now and then of paths which may be deceptive. If we stand still we shall be frozen to death. If we take the wrong road we shall be dashed to pieces. We do not certainly know whether there is any right one. What must we do? 'Be strong and of a good courage.' Act for the best, hope for the best, and take what comes....If death ends all, we cannot meet death better."

STUDY QUESTIONS

1. James believes that faith is justified only under special conditions. What are those special conditions?
2. James compares religious questions with moral questions. Why are they similar? Do you agree with his thesis about morality?
3. Why does James say that the skeptic is betting against the religious hypothesis? Why does he believe that the skeptic has no better claim to rationality than the believer?
4. James mentions a train of passengers who allow themselves to be robbed by a few bandits. What point is he trying to make? How does it fit into his defense of faith?
5. "James is simply allowing anyone to indulge in wishful thinking. In effect, he is saying that if something strikes your fancy and you do not know of any reason why it should not be believed, then you are justified in believing it." Do you think this is a fair way of representing James's position?
6. Suppose you are an atheist who believes that the religious life is degrading to humanity. What would happen if you and James were trying to convert a skeptic?

Humanism Defined

Corliss Lamont

Corliss Lamont (1902–   ) has spent his long and productive life clarifying the principles of humanism in a variety of forums. Lamont celebrates a world view which treats God as a residue of a prescientific era that stands in the way of human progress. To humanists, religion is a distraction, deflecting attention from urgent personal and social needs, and cultivating apathy and resignation. For the humanist, if God is in charge of the universe, why need humans worry? We are merely God's tools, acting out a script which we cannot alter, anxious for the eternal bliss reserved for those whom God elects to save. Lamont challenges us to cast aside this fiction, and address the problems which beset the human race—poverty, hunger, disease, illiteracy, racial and ethnic intolerance, the threat of nuclear war, and suppression of human and civil rights. The traditional functions of God—hope, compassion, forgiveness, problem solving, security—are to be carried out by individuals and groups guided by high ethical standards. That belief in God and an afterlife would prosper in the age of science, to humanists, is testimony to the stranglehold which tradition can have us in. Lamont calls for an initiative of

From *Philosophy and Humanism*, by Corliss Lamont, © 1949, 1957, 1962, 1982, by Corliss Lamont. Reprinted by permission of the Ungar Publishing Company.

realism and courage wherein humans, as world citizens, unleash the potential
of science and technology to assure that every human being reaches his or
her full potential. Traditional believers frequently say to humanists, "But you
have to believe in *something!*" In what follows, Lamont clarifies just what that
something is.

Humanism has had a long and notable career, with roots reaching far back
into the past and deep into the life of civilizations supreme in their day. It has
had eminent representatives in all the great nations of the world. As the
American historian Professor Edward P. Cheyney says, Humanism has meant
many things: "It may be the reasonable balance of life that the early Humanists discovered in the Greeks; it may be merely the study of the humanities or
polite letters; it may be the freedom from religiosity and the vivid interest in
all sides of life of a Queen Elizabeth or a Benjamin Franklin; it may be the
responsiveness to all human passions of a Shakespeare or a Goethe; or it may
be a philosophy of which man is the center and sanction. It is in the last sense,
elusive as it is, that Humanism has had perhaps its greatest significance since
the sixteenth century."

It is with this last sense of Humanism that this book is mainly concerned.
And I shall endeavor to the best of my ability to remove any elusiveness or
ambiguity from this meaning of the word. The philosophy of Humanism represents a specific and forthright view of the universe, the nature of man, and
the treatment of human problems. The term *Humanist* first came into use in
the early sixteenth century to designate the writers and scholars of the European
Renaissance. Contemporary Humanism includes the most enduring values of
Renaissance Humanism, but in philosophic scope and significance goes far
beyond it.

To define twentieth-century humanism briefly, I would say that it is a
philosophy of joyous service for the greater good of all humanity in this natural world and advocating the methods of reason, science, and democracy.
While this statement has many profound implications, it is not difficult to grasp.
Humanism in general is not a way of thinking merely for professional philosophers, but is also a credo for average men and women seeking to lead
happy and useful lives. It does not try to appeal to intellectuals by laying claim
to great originality, or to the multitude by promising the easy fulfillment of
human desires either upon this earth or in some supernatural dream world.
But Humanism does make room for the various aspects of human nature.
Though it looks upon reason as the final arbiter of what is true and good and
beautiful, it insists that reason should fully recognize the emotional side of
man. Indeed, one of Humanism's main functions is to set free the emotions
from cramping and irrational restrictions.

Humanism is a many-faceted philosophy, congenial to this modern age,
yet fully aware of the lessons of history and the richness of the philosophic
tradition. Its task is to organize into a consistent and intelligible whole the

chief elements of philosophic truth and to make that synthesis a powerful force and reality in the minds and actions of living men. What, then, are the basic principles of Humanism that define its position and distinguish it from other philosophic viewpoints? There are, as I see it, ten central propositions in the Humanist philosophy:

First, Humanism believes in a naturalistic metaphysics or attitude toward the universe that considers all forms of the supernatural as myth; and that regards Nature as the totality of being and as a constantly changing system of matter and energy which exists independently of any mind or consciousness.

Second, Humanism, drawing especially upon the laws and facts of science, believes that man is an evolutionary product of the Nature of which he is part; that his mind is indivisibly conjoined with the functioning of his brain; and that as an inseparable unity of body and personality he can have no conscious survival after death.

Third, Humanism, having its ultimate faith in man, believes that human beings possess the power or potentiality of solving their own problems, through reliance primarily upon reason and scientific method applied with courage and vision.

Fourth, Humanism, in opposition to all theories of universal determinism, fatalism, or predestination, believes that human beings, while conditioned by the past, possess genuine freedom of creative choice and action, and are, within certain objective limits, the masters of their own destiny.

Fifth, Humanism believes in an ethics or morality that grounds all human values in this-earthly experiences and relationships and that holds as its highest goal the this-worldly happiness, freedom, and progress—economic, cultural, and ethical—of all mankind, irrespective of nation, race, or religion.

Sixth, Humanism believes that the individual attains the good life by harmoniously combining personal satisfactions and continuous self-development with significant work and other activities that contribute to the welfare of the community.

Seventh, Humanism believes in the widest possible development of art and the awareness of beauty, including the appreciation of Nature's loveliness and splendor, so that the aesthetic experience may become a pervasive reality in the life of men.

Eighth, Humanism believes in a far-reaching social program that stands for the establishment throughout the world of democracy, peace, and a high standard of living on the foundations of a flourishing economic order, both national and international.

Ninth, Humanism believes in the complete social implementation of reason and scientific method; and thereby in the use of democratic procedures, including full freedom of expression and civil liberties, throughout all areas of economic, political, and cultural life.

Tenth, Humanism, in accordance with scientific method, believes in the unending questioning of basic assumptions and convictions, including its own. Humanism is not a new dogma, but is a developing philosophy ever open to experimental testing, newly discovered facts, and more rigorous reasoning.

I think that these ten points embody Humanism in its most acceptable modern form. This philosophy can be more explicitly characterized as scientific Humanism, secular Humanism, naturalistic Humanism, or democratic Humanism, depending on the emphasis that one wishes to give. Whatever it be called, Humanism is the viewpoint that men have but one life to lead and should make the most of it in terms of creative work and happiness; that human happiness is its own justification and requires no sanction or support from supernatural sources; that in any case the supernatural, usually conceived of in the form of heavenly gods or immortal heavens, does not exist; and that human beings, using their own intelligence and cooperating liberally with one another, can build an enduring citadel of peace and beauty upon this earth.

It is true that no people has yet come near to establishing the ideal society. Yet Humanism asserts that man's own reason and efforts are man's best and, indeed, only hope; and that man's refusal to recognize this point is one of the chief causes of his failures throughout history. The Christian West has been confused and corrupted for almost 2,000 years by the idea so succinctly expressed by St. Augustine, "Cursed is everyone who places his hope in man."

In an era of continuing crisis and disintegration like that of the twentieth century, men face the temptation of fleeing to some compensatory realm of make-believe or supernatural solace. Humanism stands uncompromisingly against this tendency, which both expresses and encourages defeatism. The Humanist philosophy persistently strives to remind men that their only home is in this mundane world. There is no use in our searching elsewhere for happiness and fulfillment, for there is no place else to go. We human beings must find our destiny and our promised land in the here and now, or not at all. And Humanism is interested in a future life, not in the sense of some fabulous paradise in the skies, but as the on-going enjoyment of earthly existence by generation after generation through eternities of time.

On the ethical and social side Humanism sets up service to one's fellowmen as the ultimate moral ideal. It holds that the individual can find his own highest good in working for the good of all, which of course includes himself and his family. In this sophisticated and disillusioned era Humanism emphatically rejects, as psychologically naïve and scientifically unsound, the widespread notion that human beings are moved merely by self-interest. It repudiates the constant rationalization of brute egoism into pretentious schemes on behalf of individuals or groups bent on self-aggrandizement. It refuses to accept the reduction of human motivation to economic terms, to sexual terms, to pleasure-seeking terms, or to *any* one limited set of human desires. It insists on the reality of genuine altruism as one of the moving forces in the affairs of men.

Since we live during a time of nationalism run wild, of terrible world wars, of hate and misunderstanding between peoples and governments, I want to underscore at the start Humanism's goal of the welfare of *all* mankind. In its primary connotation Humanism means simply human-being-ism, that is, devotion to the interests of human beings, wherever they live and whatever their status. Though certain groups in certain countries have in the past put themselves beyond the pale of human decency, and though this could happen again, Humanism cannot tolerate discrimination against any people or nation as such. And it reaffirms the spirit of cosmopolitanism, of international friendship, and of the essential brotherhood of man. Humanists feel *compassionate concern* for their fellowmen throughout the globe.

An English bishop recently asserted that "50 per cent of the intelligent people of the modern world are Humanists." Most of the individuals to whom he refers probably do not call themselves Humanists and may never have taken the trouble to find out to what precise school of philosophy they belong. It is important, however, that all those who actually are Humanists should come to recognize in the word *Humanism* the symbol of their central purpose in life, their community of interests and their sense of fellowship. As Walter Lippmann has written in his Humanist book, *A Preface to Morals*, "If civilization is to be coherent and confident it must be *known* in that civilization what its ideals are." This implies that those ideals shall be given a habitation and a name in some philosophy.

Now much that is essentially Humanist in twentieth-century civilization is not openly acknowledged to be so. In the United States, where there is so much confusion of spirit and intellect, lip service to outworn religious concepts or their mere ceremonial use has steadily increased among those who profess some form of supernatural faith. No nation in the world is more secular and this-worldly in its predominant interests than America. These secular trends have extended to the Sabbath. Automobiles, the massive Sunday newspapers, golf and baseball, radio, television, and motion pictures have all made tremendous inroads on the day of worship.

In order to keep their following, the churches themselves have turned more and more to philanthropic activities and the Social Gospel, that is, away from concern with the future joys and punishments of the next world to a concern with the present needs of their parishioners and humanity in this world. Modern secularization has penetrated deep into the great organized religious bodies. In Protestant circles the Young Men's Christian Association and the Young Women's Christian Association have sought to attract youth into religious paths by providing facilities for social life, lodging, sports, and vocational training. Even the Catholic Church, which has retained with little compromise its traditional theology, has bowed to secular pressures by instituting organizations with a lay purpose and program, such as the Knights of Columbus and the National Catholic Welfare Conference.

America's belief in democracy and progress, its buoyant optimism and idealism, its reliance on science and invention, all fit into the Humanist pattern. Our increasing dependence on the machine and on scientific techniques tends to do away with old-time appeals to the supernatural. The stronghold of supernatural religion has always been in the country rather than in the city. But today the spread of urban culture generally and of scientific methods in agriculture has radically altered the outlook of the rural population. Modern farmers turn more and more to tractors, irrigation, flood control, and the rotation of crops to solve their problems, in place of last-minute prayers to supernatural forces.

There is a great deal in the American tradition that is fundamentally Humanist in character. In fact, our Declaration of Independence gave resounding affirmation to the social aims of Humanism when it proclaimed that "all men" have the inalienable right to "life, liberty and the pursuit of happiness." This generalization was clearly meant to apply to human beings everywhere and not just to the inhabitants of the thirteen colonies. Accordingly, the famous document that launched the United States on its career as an independent nation makes a close approach to the cardinal Humanist doctrine that holds out the welfare of humanity at large as the final goal.

The author of the Declaration himself, Thomas Jefferson, described by Charles and Mary Beard as "the natural leader of a humanistic democracy," alluded to the Declaration in these words: "May it be to the world, what I believe it will be (to some parts sooner, to others later, but finally to all), the signal of arousing men to burst the chains under which monkish ignorance and superstition had persuaded them to bind themselves, and to assume the blessings and security of self-government."

Abraham Lincoln expanded on these Humanist sentiments in his Independence Hall speech of 1861 in which he defined the "great principle" that had held the United States together for so long: "It was not the mere matter of separation of the colonies from the motherland, but that sentiment in the Declaration of Independence which gave liberty not alone to the people of this country, but hope to all the world, for all future time. It was that which gave promise that in due time the weights would be lifted from the shoulders of all men, and that all should have an equal chance."

The Preamble to the American Constitution gives a significant summary of Humanist purposes limited to a national scale. Thus: "We, the people of the United States, in order to form a more perfect Union, establish justice, insure domestic tranquility, provide for the common defence, promote the general welfare and secure the blessings of liberty to ourselves and our posterity, do ordain and establish this Constitution for the United States of America." The specific concern here for future generations is unusual and is definitely an advanced Humanist idea. It is worthy of note, too, that both the Preamble and the Constitution itself omit all reference to Deity. The Bill of Rights further clears the way for secular interests by guaranteeing separation between the state and religion.

While the American people today do not yet recognize clearly the direction in which they are moving, their highest aims and much in their everyday pattern of existence implicitly embody the viewpoint of Humanism. As for the large social-economic programs of the contemporary world centering around such terms as capitalism, free enterprise, collectivism, socialism, and communism, Humanism should be able to illumine them to a considerable degree. But no matter what happens to these programs in the light of human events and the march of history, no matter which ones succeed or do not succeed, the philosophy of Humanism will always remain pertinent.

If this philosophy approximates the truth in its underlying generalizations, then it is a philosophy which, with some changes in phraseology, was appropriate to ancient times and which in the main will hold good for the shape of things to come. Economic and political systems will come and go, nations and empires and civilizations rise and fall, but Humanism, as a philosophic system in which mankind's interests upon this earth are the first word and the last word, is unlikely to become obsolete. Naturally, however, any particular expression of Humanism will eventually be superseded.

The humanistic spirit, then, while finding wider and more conscious formulation in the modern era and in the more developed nations, has been inherent and struggling for expression in the race of man since first he appeared upon this planet. So Humanism sums up not only the current tendencies of mankind to construct a more truly human world, but also the best in men's aspirations throughout the age-long history of human thought and endeavor.

STUDY QUESTIONS

1. What is Lamont's definition of humanism?
2. Which of Lamont's ten principles of humanism, if any, could a traditional theist embrace?
3. Why, according to Lamont, do people continue believing in God and an afterlife?
4. What, according to Lamont, is the ultimate moral ideal which ought to guide our lives?
5. What conception of human nature underlies humanism?
6. In what ways are modern churches and other religious organizations secular?
7. Lamont mentions Thomas Jefferson as holding humanist ideals and values. What, specifically, were his views about religion—God, afterlife, miracles, revelation, the divinity of Jesus, and prayer? You might consult Adrienne Koch and William Peden (eds.), *The Life and Selected Writings of Thomas Jefferson,* (New York: Modern Library, 1944); their listings under "God" and "Religion" in the index will guide you to the places where you can discover his opinions.

SELECTED READINGS FOR PART ONE

The following are good general anthologies: John Hick (ed.), *Classical and Contemporary Readings in the Philosophy of Religion* (Englewood Cliffs, N.J.: Prentice-

Hall, 1970); Rowe and Wainwright (eds.), *Philosophy of Religion* (New York: Harcourt Brace Jovanovich, 1973); Steven M. Cahn (ed.), *Philosophy of Religion* (New York: Harper & Row, 1970); Stuart C. Brown (ed.), *Reason and Religion* (Ithaca, N.Y.: Cornell University Press, 1977); and David Stewart (ed.), 2d edition, *Exploring the Philosophy of Religion* (Englewood Cliffs, N.J.: Prentice-Hall, 1980).

A balanced, accessible treatment of the issues dealt with in Part One will be found in Roger Schmidt, 2d edition, *Exploring Religion* (Belmont, Calif.: Wadsworth, 1988), especially Chapter 9, "God," Chapter 10, "Evil and Human Destiny," and Chapter 16, "What Is Religion?"

Good contemporary discussions of various arguments to prove the existence of God include Alvin Plantinga, *The Ontological Argument* (Garden City, N.Y.: Doubleday, 1965), and *God, Freedom, and Evil* (New York: Harper & Row, 1974); Donald R. Burrill (ed.), *The Cosmological Arguments* (Garden City, N.Y.: Doubleday, 1967), Wallace I. Matson, *The Existence of God* (Ithaca, New York: Cornell University Press, 1965); and Mortimer J. Adler, *How to Think about God* (New York: Bantam, 1982).

Robert Young, *Freedom, Responsibility, and God* (New York: Barnes & Noble, 1975) is a thorough study of whether the traditional western view of God as omnipotent is compatible with belief in human freedom.

Two of the best assessments of proofs for the existence of God in the Catholic tradition are John Courtney Murray, S.J., *The Problem of God* (New Haven, Conn.: Yale University Press, 1964) and Etienne Gilson, *God and Philosophy* (New Haven: Yale University Press, 1941). Another book in the Catholic tradition which only more advanced students should attempt to tackle, and which treats the subject of God within a comprehensive system of philosophy, especially in Chapter XIX, is Bernard J. F. Lonergan, S.J., *Insight: A Study of Human Understanding* (New York: Philosophical Library, 1957).

A dialogue, which all students can grasp, between two colleagues—one of whom believes in God and one of whom does not—is John Hick and Michael Goulder, *Why Believe in God?* (London: SCM, 1983).

A useful introductory source of brief readings debating whether belief in God is logically possible for a scientifically sophisticated person is David L. Bender and Bruno Leone, *Science and Religion: Opposing Viewpoints* (St. Paul, Minn.: Greenhaven: 1981).

An excellent introduction to mysticism, with selections from Hindu, Buddhist, Taoist, Jewish, Islamic, and Christian mystics, accompanied by editorial commentary, is W.T. Stace (ed.), *The Teachings of the Mystics* (New York: New American Library, 1960). William James, *The Varieties of Religious Experience* (London: Longmans, 1902) is a classic. Good recent treatments of mysticism include D. T. Suzuki, *Mysticism: Christian and Buddhist* (New York: Harper & Row, 1957) and W. T. Stace, *Mysticism and Philosophy* (London: Macmillan, 1961). For a description of the mystical and religious experiences of persons who apparently died for a short time, see Raymond A. Moody, Jr., *Life after Life* (New York: Bantam, 1975).

Important classical treatments of the problem of evil are David Hume,

Dialogues Concerning Natural Religion, Parts X and XI, many editions; and Gottfried von Leibniz, *The Theodicy in Leibniz: Selections,* edited by P. Wiener (New York: Scribner, 1951). Two good atheistic analyses of the problem of evil are E. H. Madden and P. H. Hare, *Evil and the Concept of God* (Springfield, Ill.: Charles C. Thomas, 1968) and H. J. McCloskey, *God and Evil* (The Hague: Nijhoff, 1974). Hick's defense is worked out more completely in his *Evil and the God of Love* (New York: Harper & Row, 1978). C. S. Lewis defends the Christian view in *The Problem of Pain* (New York: Macmillan, 1962).

The Nobel laureate Elie Wiesel chronicles the impact of his experience in Nazi concentration camps upon his belief in God in his powerful little volume *Night* (New York: Bantam, 1960). Rabbi Harold Kushner states his reasoned conclusions about God in the aftermath of his son's death (from progeria) in *When Bad Things Happen to Good People* (New York: Schocken, 1981). Burton Z. Cooper urges Christians to explore an alternative to the mainstream conception of God in his *Why, God?* (Atlanta, Georgia: John Knox, 1971).

Classic statements of the nontheistic, humanist position are John Dewey, *A Common Faith* (New Haven, Conn.: Yale University Press, 1934) and Bertrand Russell, *Why I Am Not A Christian* (New York: Simon & Shuster, 1957). Two comprehensive accounts of humanism by well-known American humanists are Corliss Lamont, *The Philosophy of Humanism,* 5th edition (New York: Ungar, 1965) and Paul Kurtz, *The Transcendental Temptation* (Buffalo, New York: Prometheus, 1986).

Other important humanist publications are Paul Kurtz, (ed.), *Humanist Manifestos I and II* (Buffalo, N.Y.: Prometheus, 1984); Kai Nielsen, *Philosophy and Atheism* (Buffalo, N.Y.: Prometheus Books, 1985); Peter Angeles (ed.), *Critiques of God* (Buffalo, N.Y.: Prometheus, 1976); Jim Herrick, *Against the Faith* (Buffalo, N.Y.: Prometheus, 1985), which profiles about twenty famous nonbelievers; and Delos Banning McKown, *With Faith and Fury* (Buffalo, N.Y.: Prometheus, 1985), a novel whose central figure is a young humanist professor of philosophy who takes a job at a college in the Bible belt.

A good introduction to eastern religion and the reasons for its rejection of traditional western theism is Gunapala Dharmasiri, *A Buddhist Critique of the Christian Concept of God* (Antioch, Calif.: Golden Leaves, 1988).

A response to humanism and other secular philosophies by two conservative Christian writers is John McDowell and Don Stewart, *Understanding Secular Religions* (San Bernardino, Calif.: Here's Life, 1982).

There are many articles on various aspects of the issues discussed in Part One of this text, as well as every other part of the text, in the following three important reference books: Paul Edwards (ed.), *The Encyclopedia of Philosophy* (New York: Macmillan and Free Press, 1967); Philip P. Wiener (ed.), *Dictionary of the History of Ideas* (New York: Scribner, 1974); and G. H. R. Parkinson (ed.), *The Handbook of Western Philosophy* (New York: Macmillan, 1988). The *Encyclopedia* is an eight-volume work; the index appears in volume 8. The *Dictionary* consists of four volumes plus an index. The *Handbook* is a single volume with a table of contents at the beginning and an index at the end.

PART TWO

Knowledge

THE PARADOXES OF APPEARANCE

If the scientific description of reality is closest to the truth, then we must face up to a dilemma: the world as it really is differs radically from the way it appears to us. Consider, for a moment, reality as it is portrayed by the physicist. When a thing is hot, for example, the molecules which compose it are in a state of increased vibration. The nervous system (itself a system of molecules) detects this vibration and sends signals in the form of pulses to the brain (another system of molecules). Then, and only then, do we feel heat. But the quality we experience is quite different from the motion which causes it, just as the sensation of pain is qualitatively different from the physical conditions which produce it. Other familiar qualities in the world suffer the same fate. The colors of the peacock and the blazing reds of the setting sun are but subjective qualities produced in the perceiver by a special nervous system that responds selectively to lightwaves (themselves colorless) of varying frequencies. In itself, the sun is a colorless froth of energy. The bee, the frog, and perhaps even higher life in other galaxies experience the world in ways we can only hint at. The real world, the world as described by physics, is a neutral world of colorless, soundless, odorless matter.

We have grown so accustomed to this way of thinking about the world that it no longer shocks us. But it should! Remember that this sweeping distinction between appearance and reality is usually accompanied by an emphasis on observation and experience as the building blocks of science. It has almost become an official doctrine to regard the advance of science as due to an extreme reluctance to go beyond experienced fact. Yet we certainly do not perceive the world as the scientist describes it. If we wish to assert that the world of common sense—the world of sounds, smells, colors, etc.—does not adequately represent reality, then the way we gain knowledge of reality cannot be confined to common-sense experience. We need a method which penetrates appearance—either that, or the real world must be the world of common experience and the colorless world of physics is a fiction.

There is another paradox in the scientific conception of reality. Reality, in this view, is fundamentally material. Therefore the human perceiver, like everything else, is a system of matter. Yet if this is so, it makes no sense to say that the familiar features of experience are subjective qualities in the perceiver. If color, for example, is literally "in the perceiver" and the perceiver is matter, then colors are real qualities of matter, contrary to what the theory says. To avoid this contradiction, many scientists and philosophers have argued that the perceiving self cannot be a material object. But then the world contains more than matter—it also contains *minds.*

In addition to the obvious and basic conflict *between* common sense and science, there is also conflict *within* each frame of reference. For instance, a dispute can arise among friends as to which is the best team in a particular sport. How can we determine which individual, if any, is telling the truth? None of them may be deliberately lying, but given the fact that their statements are contradictory, one would hope that there is a way to identify which statement is deserving of one's support. It would be absurd to embrace contradictory statements. Also, we have seen public demonstrations by groups, including scientists, calling for an end to nuclear power plants because they are supposedly unsafe, only to be followed within days by contradictory claims by pro-nuclear scientists. Again, there is no question of deceit; both groups are acting in good faith. Which position is sound? Which should we believe, and act upon?

The tensions between and within common sense and science raise some of the central questions of philosophy. What is the nature of the real world? How can I come to know it? What is the place of perception in knowledge? What is the nature of "mind"? How can I distinguish truth from falsity? This section presents some of the major attempts to answer these questions.

4

Skepticism and the Self

PROBLEM INTRODUCTION

In 1633, Galileo was tried by the Inquisition and found guilty of heresy. He was forced to renounce his scientific beliefs and was made to promise that he would never write or speak about them again. This dramatic event in the history of science marks a turning point of enormous proportions. Science was beginning to erode a traditional conception of the world and to erect a new one in its place.

What had Galileo said that so stirred up the forces of the Church against him? Earlier systems of thought, stemming from Aristotle, had emphasized the role of purpose and value in explaining the world. Explanations of natural phenomena were constructed in terms of "final causes." A final cause is the goal or end toward which something is moving. In Aristotelian physics, for example, an unsupported body moves downward in order to get to its natural place, which is the center of the earth. Once it reaches its natural place, it will remain at rest there until some force moves it. If this idea is consistently applied to everything, it becomes necessary to explain why the heavenly bodies continue to move? Why haven't they come to rest at their natural place? The answer is simple enough in terms of theology: God continues to keep them in motion. We also know that they move in circles, because a circle is a *perfect* geometrical form, and God would create only a perfect universe. Furthermore, since humanity is God's special creation, it is highly appropriate for the planets and the sun to move around the earth. The entire universe was a cosmic drama because the ultimate principles of explanation were formulated in terms of God's purpose. These principles seemed to be amply confirmed by observation and common sense. It was the perfect union of theology and physics.

Galileo was an advocate of the Copernican system of the world. According to this view, the earth and the rest of the planets moved around the sun. The apparent motion of the sun from horizon to horizon was caused by the rotation of the earth on its axis. Galileo's physics represented an attempt to provide the foundations for the Copernican picture. He was able to discover that the acceleration of freely falling bodies did not depend upon their weight, a thesis which ran counter to the prevailing Aristotelian view. If weight were a measure of the force with which a body was moving to its natural place, we should expect that a heavier body would get to its state of rest faster than a lighter body. But this was not so. Perhaps the most startling discovery of all was Galileo's early work on inertia. In a series of classic experiments, he discovered that a body tended to stay in its present state—whether of motion or rest. God was no longer needed as a force which keeps the universe in motion. The union of science and theology began to crumble.

The world was beginning to be seen as an elaborate mechanism. The principles of explanation which emerged in this period made no reference to God or to His purposes. The universe was matter governed by laws which could be expressed mathematically. The spirit had gone out of it, so to speak. Humans themselves were physical beings and subject to the same sort of analysis. Perhaps every action of the individual could be explained in terms of the laws of motion. Perhaps people were machines. Thomas Hobbes, the most radical materialist of the day, attempted to extend the principles of physics into psychology, ethics, and politics, in order to show that every aspect of existence could be accounted for in terms of matter and motion. For Hobbes, a desire was nothing more than a motion toward something, a thought was simply the activity of material particles in the body, and a decision, just the final resolution of warring physical forces inside the organism. To the orthodox, this was clearly a dangerous trend, for the immortal soul was hanging in the balance.

Descartes, a contemporary of Galileo and Hobbes, saw the profound changes in the state of knowledge, and recognizing the implications of these changes for the image of human nature, set himself two tasks. The first was to ascertain whether there are any beliefs immune to doubt in light of the continuous change of theories about the world. Is every belief a temporary fixture destined to be overthrown by new discoveries, or is there a sure and certain foundation of basic truths which will weather every intellectual crisis? His second task was to determine the nature of the self. Are we nothing more than our bodies, or does the human person have an aspect which is not subject to the mechanistic interpretation of ordinary matter?

What, then, can be doubted? Can I doubt the existence of the physical world? Descartes thinks that it is possible to do this. In dreams I touch, hear, smell, and see things which are nonexistent. Couldn't an evil genius of great power deceive me in my waking life by providing me with a coherent stream of perceptions similar to those I have in dreams? Indeed, couldn't such an evil genius also deceive me about my own existence? Here Descartes draws the line. I can be certain that I exist, because even my doubting requires the existence of a doubter. "I think, therefore I am": this truth is so clear and self-evident that it cannot be doubted. Truths of this sort provide the unchanging foundation for knowledge. Using such truths, Descartes attempted to prove that a good God exists who would not deceive us.* The existence of the physical world is then guaranteed.

But what about the self? What sort of thing is it? According to Descartes, the self is an immaterial thinking substance which is connected to the body in a mysterious relationship of mutual interaction. He reached this conclusion in the following way: Suppose I am a physical object. Since I can doubt the existence of all physical things, I should be able to doubt the existence of myself. But, indeed, this is the one thing it is meaningless to doubt. Therefore, the self cannot be a physical thing. In this way Descartes believed that he had shown the existence of the immortal soul. Religion need not fear the advance of science, for although the body is a machine, it is a machine activated by an immaterial mind. Once the mind sets the physical processes of the body in motion, science can explain the resultant movements. But the ultimate explanation of human behavior remains out of the reach of physical principles.

Descartes's position was a compromise between the developing scientific image of human beings and the older religious tradition. But this compromise represented an uneasy peace which was soon challenged. According to Descartes, the self is a *thing*—a nonmaterial substance—which underlies various mental states and activities. It is the thing which thinks, feels, desires, and perceives. In other words, the self is the spiritual canvas on which the mental life is painted. Some philosophers, such as David Hume, the great eighteenth-century skeptic, believed that this conception of the self would not adequately explain important facts about personal identity. If the self is a mental substance which underlies all psychological states, then it should be possible to remove all its perceptions, memories, beliefs, etc., replace them with new psychological states, and still have the same self. It would be like stripping the paint from a chair and repainting it a different color—it is still the same chair. Upon reflection, however, the self does not seem to be like this. New memories, new beliefs, new ways of thinking add up to a new self. Hume, therefore, suggests that, just as we do not think that a brick wall is something different from the many bricks which make it up, so we should not think of the self as something different from the many mental states which compose it. The wall is just a certain organization of bricks, and the self is a certain organization of memories, beliefs, and perceptions. Hume's theory is called the *bundle theory* of the self because the self is thought to be a collection rather than a single object.

The three centuries which intervene between Descartes and ourselves have produced new challenges to dualism. With the development of modern biology, physiology, and psychology, the intimate and complex relationship between the mind and the body has been increasingly uncovered. After Darwin, mental function was viewed as an evolutionary product closely tied to the

---

* Descartes uses the ontological proof to establish God's existence, since this proof does not rest on any physical assumption.

evolution of the physical body. Increasingly, biologists and psychologists explained human and animal behavior in physiological, rather than mental, terms.

Finally a bold and unorthodox position began to emerge. In an effort to make psychology "scientific," many psychologists theorized that the only appropriate *method* is one which relies exclusively on close observation and categorization of behavior. Since the realm of the mental is forever closed to public observation, these psychologists constructed a system of explanation which does not rely on mental entities. This is the doctrine of behaviorism. B. F. Skinner, the leading contemporary exponent of behaviorism, has characterized psychology as a science which searches for laws connecting environmental influences with changes in behavior.

The implications of these changes are, of course, enormous. At the time of Descartes, humans were just a little lower than the angels. We were linked to heaven by our immortal souls and tied to earth by our material bodies. But because of our dual nature we could escape the rigid physical determination of other animals. Our wills were free and capable of overcoming past determination. If behaviorists are correct in asserting that nothing mental exists, however, our link to heaven is severed and we become the natural children of the mechanistic universe.

Yet, surprisingly, not all who subscribe to the modern scientific world view see it as robbing human beings of a special or unique status within nature. This may be seen in the contemporary debate over the central question in the field of artificial intelligence, or AI: Can computers be programmed to *think?* As our final reading in this section shows, John Searle and the Dreyfus brothers, among others, argue that there is an unbridgeable gap between mind and computer, between humans and machines. However advanced, however cleverly programmed, computers can never encounter reality as a human does, they tell us. Computers are simply information processors; they have no self-consciousness, no emotions, no intuitions, no *understanding* of what they "see" or "hear." AI enthusiasts reply that such a conclusion is premature; eventually, they are confident, hardware and software will be developed that will enable a computer to exhibit every imaginable type of human experience—fear, anger, disappointment, hunger, and even confusion.

Meditations I and II
René <u>Descartes</u> (*Rationalist* + <u>Dualism</u>) *Holist*

René Descartes (1596–1650), the founder of analytical geometry, is also known as the father of modern philosophy. Born into an era of profound intellectual ferment, Descartes rejected the answers of the past. He resolved to doubt everything he had previously believed, and to accept only those truths which appeared to him to be "clear and distinct." The sense of intellectual freedom and adventure which Descartes felt is summed up in his response to a visitor who was puzzled to see so few books in his library. Descartes pointed to a corpse which he had been dissecting and replied, "This, sir, is the only book I require."

In this selection from the "Meditations," Descartes applies his systematic doubt to the very existence of the world. It is possible, he suggests, to imagine that one's entire waking life is an illusion. But even so, it is not possible to doubt one's own existence. The difficult thing, however, is to discover the nature of the self. Is the self an amalgam of perceptions and memories and feelings, or are these too, like the physical body, inessential to its real nature?

In these brief reflections, Descartes raises the central questions of modern philosophy. Is there a place in the world of matter for a spiritual being? What sort of thing could it be? Can it be known and investigated with the same methods as the physical world? Descartes's answers to these questions have intrigued thinkers for centuries because similar questions arise in each epoch that science threatens to wipe out the special place of human beings in nature.

OF THE THINGS WHICH MAY BE BROUGHT WITHIN THE SPHERE OF THE DOUBTFUL

It is now some years since I detected how many were the false beliefs that I had from my earliest youth admitted as true, and how doubtful was every-thing I had since constructed on this basis; and from that time I was convinced that I must once for all seriously undertake to rid myself of all the opinions which I had formerly accepted, and commence to build anew from the foundation, if I wanted to establish any firm and permanent structure in the sciences. But as this enterprise appeared to be a very great one, I waited until I had attained an age so mature that I could not hope that at any later date I should be better fitted to execute my design. This reason caused me to delay so long that I should feel that I was doing wrong were I to occupy in deliberation the time that yet remains to me for action. To-day, then, since very

From René Descartes, "Meditations on First Philosophy" in *The Philosophical Works of Descartes*, Elizabeth Haldane and G. R. T. Ross, trans., Cambridge University Press (1931), pp. 144–157. Reprinted by permission of the publisher.

opportunely for the plan I have in view I have delivered my mind from every care (and am happily agitated by no passions) and since I have procured for myself an assured leisure in a peaceable retirement, I shall at last seriously and freely address myself to the general upheaval of all my former opinions.

Now for this object it is not necessary that I should show that all of these are false—I shall perhaps never arrive at this end. But inasmuch as reason already persuades me that I ought no less carefully to withhold my assent from matters which are not entirely certain and indubitable than from those which appear to me manifestly to be false; if I am able to find in each one some reason to doubt, this will suffice to justify my rejecting the whole. And for that end it will not be requisite that I should examine each in particular, which would be an endless undertaking; for owing to the fact that the destruction of the foundations of necessity brings with it the downfall of the rest of the edifice, I shall only in the first place attack those principles upon which all my former opinions rested.

All that up to the present time I have accepted as most true and certain I have learned either from the senses or through the senses; but it is sometimes proved to me that these senses are deceptive, and it is wiser not to trust entirely to any thing by which we have once been deceived.

But it may be that although the senses sometimes deceive us concerning things which are hardly perceptible, or very far away, there are yet many others to be met with as to which we cannot reasonably have any doubt, although we recognise them by their means. For example, there is the fact that I am here, seated by the fire, attired in a dressing gown, having this paper in my hands and other similar matters. And how could I deny that these hands and this body are mine, were it not perhaps that I compare myself to certain persons, devoid of sense, whose cerebella are so troubled and clouded by the violent vapors of black bile, that they constantly assure us that they think they are kings when they are really quite poor, or that they are clothed in purple when they are really without covering, or who imagine that they have an earthenware head or are nothing but pumpkins or are made of glass. But they are mad, and I should not be any the less insane were I to follow examples so extravagant.

At the same time I must remember that I am a man, and that consequently I am in the habit of sleeping, and in my dreams representing to myself the same things or sometimes even less probable things, than do those who are insane in their waking moments. How often has it happened to me that in the night I dreamt that I found myself in this particular place, that I was dressed and seated near the fire, whilst in reality I was lying undressed in bed! At this moment it does indeed seem to me that it is with eyes awake that I am looking at this paper; that this head which I move is not asleep, that it is deliberately and of set purpose that I extend my hand and perceive it; what happens in sleep does not appear so clear nor so distinct as does all this. But in thinking over this I remind myself that on many occasions I have in sleep been deceived by similar illusions, and in dwelling carefully on this reflection I see so manifestly that there are no certain indications by which we may clearly distinguish wakefulness from sleep that I am lost in astonishment. And my astonishment is such that it is almost capable of persuading me that I now dream.

Now let us assume that we are asleep and that all these particulars, e.g. that we open our eyes, shake our head, extend our hands, and so on, are but false delusions; and let us reflect that possibly neither our hands nor our whole body are such as they appear to us to be. At the same time we must at least confess that the things which are represented to us in sleep are like painted representations which can only have been formed as the counterparts of something real and true, and that in this way those general things at least, i.e., eyes, a head, hands, and a whole body, are not imaginary things, but things really existent. For, as a matter of fact, painters, even when they study with the greatest skill to represent sirens and satyrs by forms the most strange and extraordinary, cannot give them natures which are entirely new, but merely make a certain medley of the members of different animals; or if their imagination is extravagant enough to invent something so novel that nothing similar has ever before been seen, and that then their work represents a thing purely fictitious and absolutely false, it is certain all the same that the colors of which this is composed are necessarily real. And for the same reason, although these general things, to wit, [a body], eyes, a head, hands, and such like, may be imaginary, we are bound at the same time to confess that there are at least some other objects yet more simple and more universal, which are real and true; and of these, things which dwell in our thoughts, whether true and real or false and fantastic, are formed.

To such a class of things pertains corporeal nature in general, and its extension, the figure of extended things, their quality or magnitude and number, as also the place in which they are, the time which measures their duration, and so on.

That is possibly why our reasoning is not unjust when we conclude from this that Physics, Astronomy, Medicine and all other sciences which have as their end the consideration of composite things, are very dubious and uncertain; but that Arithmetic, Geometry and other sciences of that kind which only treat of things that are very simple and very general, without taking great trouble to ascertain whether they are actually existent or not, contain some measure of certainty and an element of the indubitable. For whether I am awake or asleep, two and three together always form five, and the square can never have more than four sides, and it does not seem possible that truths so clear and apparent can be suspected of any falsity [or uncertainty].

Nevertheless I have long had fixed in my mind the belief that an all-powerful God existed by whom I have been created such as I am. But how do I know that He has not brought it to pass that there is no earth, no heaven, no extended body, no magnitude, no place, and that nevertheless [I possess the perceptions of all these things and that] they seem to me to exist just exactly as I now see them? And, besides, as I sometimes imagine that others deceive themselves in the things which they think they know best, how do I know that I am not deceived every time that I add two and three, or count the sides of a square, or judge of things yet simpler, if anything simpler can be imagined? But possibly God has not desired that I should be thus deceived, for He is said to be supremely good. If, however, it is contrary to His goodness to have made me such that I constantly deceive myself, it would also appear to be contrary to His goodness to permit me to be sometimes deceived, and nevertheless I cannot doubt that He does permit this.

There may indeed be those who would prefer to deny the existence of a God so powerful, rather than believe that all other things are uncertain. But let us not oppose them for the present, and grant that all that is here said of a God is a fable; nevertheless in whatever way they suppose that I have arrived at the state of being that I have reached—whether they attribute it to fate or to accident, or make out that it is by a continual succession of antecedents, or by some other method—since to err and deceive oneself is a defect, it is clear that the greater will be the probability of my being so imperfect as to deceive myself ever, as is the Author to whom they assign my origin the less powerful. To these reasons I have certainly nothing to reply, but at the end I feel constrained to confess that there is nothing in all that I formerly believed to be true, of which I cannot in some measure doubt, and that not merely through want of thought or through levity, but for reasons which are very powerful and maturely considered; so that henceforth I ought not the less carefully to refrain from giving credence to these opinions than to that which is manifestly false, if I desire to arrive at any certainty [in the sciences].

But it is not sufficient to have made these remarks. We must also be careful to keep them in mind. For these ancient and commonly held opinions still revert frequently to my mind, long and familiar custom having given them the right to occupy my mind against my inclination and rendered them almost masters of my belief; nor will I ever lose the habit of deferring to them or of placing my confidence in them, so long as I consider them as they really are, i.e. opinions in some measure doubtful, as I have just shown, and at the same time highly probable, so that there is much more reason to believe in than to deny them. That is why I consider that I shall not be acting amiss, if, taking of set purpose a contrary belief, I allow myself to be deceived, and for a certain time pretend that all these opinions are entirely false and imaginary, until at last, having thus balanced any former prejudices with my latter [so that they cannot divert my opinions more to one side than to the other], my judgment will no longer be dominated by bad usage or turned away from the right knowledge of the truth. For I am assured that there can be neither peril nor error in this course, and that I cannot at present yield too much to distrust, since I am not considering the question of action, but only of knowledge.

I shall then suppose, not that God who is supremely good and the fountain of truth, but some evil genius not less powerful than deceitful, has employed his whole energies in deceiving me; I shall consider that the heavens, the earth, colors, figures, sound, and all other external things are nought but the illusions and dreams of which this genius has availed himself in order to lay traps for my credulity; I shall consider myself as having no hands, no eyes, no flesh, no blood, nor any senses, yet falsely believing myself to possess all these things; I shall remain obstinately attached to this idea, and if by this means it is not in my power to arrive at the knowledge of any truth, I may at least do what is in my power [i.e. suspend my judgment], and with firm purpose avoid giving credence to any false thing, or being imposed upon by this arch deceiver, however powerful and deceptive he may be. But this task is a laborious one, and insensibly a certain lassitude leads me into the course of my ordinary life. And just as a captive who in sleep enjoys an imaginary liberty, when he begins to suspect that his liberty is but a dream, fears to awaken, and conspires with these agreeable illusions that the deception may be prolonged, so insensibly of my own accord I fall back into my former opinions, and I dread awakening from this slumber, lest the laborious wakefulness which would follow the tranquility of this repose should have to be spent not in daylight, but in the excessive darkness of the difficulties which have just been discussed.

OF THE NATURE OF THE HUMAN MIND

The Meditation of yesterday filled my mind with so many doubts that it is no longer in my power to forget them. And yet I do not see in what manner I can resolve them; and, just as if I had all of a sudden fallen into very deep water, I am so disconcerted that I can neither make certain of setting my feet on the bottom, nor can I swim and so support myself on the surface. I shall nevertheless make an effort and follow anew the same path as that on which I yesterday entered, i.e. I shall proceed by setting aside all that in which the least doubt could be supposed to exist, just as if I had discovered that it was absolutely false; and I shall ever follow in this road until I have met with something which is certain, or at least, if I can do nothing else, until I have learned for certain that there is nothing in the world that is certain. Archimedes, in order that he might draw the terrestrial globe out of its place, and transport it elsewhere, demanded only that one point should be fixed and immoveable; in the same way I shall have the right to conceive high hopes if I am happy enough to discover one thing only which is certain and indubitable.

I suppose, then, that all the things that I see are false; I persuade myself that nothing has ever existed of all that my fallacious memory represents to me. I consider that I possess no senses; I imagine that body, figure, extension, movement and place are but the fictions of my mind. What, then, can be esteemed as true? Perhaps nothing at all, unless that there is nothing in the world that is certain.

But how can I know there is not something different from those things that I have just considered, of which one cannot have the slightest doubt? Is there not some God, or some other being by whatever name we call it, who puts these reflections into my mind? That is not necessary, for is it not possible that I am capable of producing them myself? I myself, am I not at least something? But I have already denied that I had senses and body. Yet I hesitate, for what follows from that? Am I so dependent on body and senses that I cannot exist without these? But I was persuaded that there was nothing in all the world, that there was no heaven, no earth, that there were no minds, nor any bodies: was I not then likewise persuaded that I did not exist? Not at all; of a surety I myself did exist since I persuaded myself of something [or merely because I thought of something]. But there is some deceiver or other, very powerful and very cunning, who ever employs his ingenuity in deceiving me. Then without doubt I exist also if he deceives me, and let him deceive me as much as he will, he can never cause me to be nothing so long as I think that I am something. So that after having reflected well and carefully examined all things, we must come to the definite conclusion that this proposition: I am, I exist, is necessarily true each time that I pronounce it, or that I mentally conceive it.

But I do not yet know clearly enough what I am, I who am certain that I am; and hence I must be careful to see that I do not imprudently take some other object in place of myself, and thus that I do not go astray in respect of this knowledge that I hold to be the most certain and most evident of all that I have formerly learned. That is why I shall now consider anew what I believed myself to be before I embarked upon these last reflections; and of my former opinions I shall withdraw all that might even in a small degree be invalidated by the reasons which I have just brought forward, in order that there may be nothing at all left beyond what is absolutely certain and indubitable.

What then did I formerly believe myself to be? Undoubtedly I believed myself to be a man. But what is a man? Shall I say a reasonable animal? Certainly not; for then I should have to inquire what an animal is, and what is reasonable; and thus from a single question I should insensibly fall into an infinitude of others more difficult; and I should not wish to waste the little time and leisure remaining to me in trying to unravel subtleties like these. But I shall rather stop here to consider the thoughts which of themselves spring up in my mind, and which were not inspired by anything beyond my own nature alone when I applied myself to the consideration of my being. In the first place, then, I considered myself as having a face, hands, arms, and all that system of members composed of bones and flesh as seen in a corpse which I designated by the name of body. In addition to this I considered that I was nourished, that I walked, that I felt, and that I thought, and I referred all these actions to the soul; but I did not stop to consider what the soul was, or if I did stop, I imagined that it was something extremely rare and subtle like a wind, a flame, or an ether, which was spread throughout my grosser parts. As to body I had no manner of doubt about its nature, but I thought I had a very clear knowledge of it; and if I had desired to explain it according to the notions that I had then formed of it, I should have described it thus: By the body I understand all that which can be defined by a certain figure: something which

matter

can be confined in a certain place, and which can fill a given space in such a
way that every other body will be excluded from it; which can be perceived
either by touch, or by sight, or by hearing, or by taste, or by smell: which can
be moved in many ways not, in truth, by itself, but by something which is
foreign to it, by which it is touched [and from which it receives impressions]:
for to have the power of self-movement, as also of feeling or of thinking, I did
not consider to appertain to the nature of body: on the contrary, I was rather
astonished to find that faculties similar to them existed in some bodies.

But what am I, now that I suppose that there is a certain genius which
is extremely powerful, and, if I may say so, malicious, who employs all his
powers in deceiving me? Can I affirm that I possess the least of all those things
which I have just said pertain to the nature of body? I pause to consider, I
revolve all these things in my mind, and I find none of which I can say that
it pertains to me. It would be tedious to stop to enumerate them. Let us pass
to the attributes of soul and see if there is any one which is in me. What of
nutrition or walking [the first mentioned]? But if it is so that I have no body
it is also true that I can neither walk nor take nourishment. Another attribute
is sensation. But one cannot feel without body, and besides I have thought I
perceived many things during sleep that I recognised in my waking moments
as not having been experienced at all. What of thinking? I find here that thought
is an attribute that belongs to me: it alone cannot be separated from me. I am,
I exist, that is certain. But how often? Just when I think; for it might possibly
be the case if I ceased entirely to think, that I should likewise cease altogether
to exist. I do not now admit anything which is not necessarily true: to speak
accurately I am not more than a thing which thinks, that is to say a mind or
a soul, or an understanding, or a reason, which are terms whose significance
was formerly unknown to me. I am, however, a real thing and really exist; but
what thing? I have answered: a thing which thinks.

And what more? I shall exercise my imagination [in order to see if I am
not something more]. I am not a collection of members which we call the human body: I am not a subtle air distributed through these members, I am not
a wind, a fire, a vapor, a breath, nor anything at all which I can imagine or
conceive; because I have assumed that all these were nothing. Without changing that supposition I find that I only leave myself certain of the fact that I am
somewhat. But perhaps it is true that these same things which I supposed
were non-existent because they are unknown to me, are really not different
from the self which I know. I am not sure about this, I shall not dispute about
it now; I can only give judgment on things that are known to me. I know that
I exist, and I inquire what I am, I whom I know to exist. But it is very certain
that the knowledge of my existence taken in its precise significance does not
depend on things whose existence is not yet known to me; consequently it
does not depend on those which I can feign in imagination. And indeed the
very term *feign* in imagination proves to me my error, for I really do this if I
image myself a something, since to imagine is nothing else than to contemplate the figure or image of a corporeal thing. But I already know for certain

that I am, and that it may be that all these images, and, speaking generally, all things that relate to the nature of body are nothing but dreams [and chimeras]. For this reason I see clearly that I have as little reason to say, "I shall stimulate my imagination in order to know more distinctly what I am," than if I were to say, "I am now awake, and I perceive somewhat that is real and true: but because I do not yet perceive it distinctly enough, I shall go to sleep of express purpose, so that my dreams may represent the perception with greatest truth and evidence." And, thus, I know for certain that nothing of all that I can understand by means of my imagination belongs to this knowledge which I have of myself, and that it is necessary to recall the mind from this mode of thought with the utmost diligence in order that it may be able to know its own nature with perfect distinctness.

But what then am I? A thing which thinks. What is a thing which thinks? It is a thing which doubts, understands, [conceives], affirms, denies, wills, refuses, which also imagines and feels.

Certainly it is no small matter if all these things pertain to my nature. But why should they not so pertain? Am I not that being who now doubts nearly everything, who nevertheless understands certain things, who affirms that one only is true, who denies all the others, who desires to know more, is averse from being deceived, who imagines many things, sometimes indeed despite his will, and who perceives many likewise, as by the intervention of the bodily organs? Is there nothing in all this which is as true as it is certain that I exist, even though I should always sleep and though he who has given me being employed all his ingenuity in deceiving me? Is there likewise any one of these attributes which can be distinguished from my thought, or which might be said to be separated from myself? For it is so evident of itself that it is I who doubts, who understands, and who desires, that there is no reason here to add anything to explain it. And I have certainly the power of imagining likewise; for although it may happen (as I formerly supposed) that none of the things which I imagine are true, nevertheless this power of imagining does not cease to be really in use, and it forms part of my thought. Finally, I am the same who feels, that is to say, who perceives certain things, as by the organs of sense, since in truth I see light, I hear noise, I feel heat. But it will be said that these phenomena are false and that I am dreaming. Let it be so; still it is at least quite certain that it seems to me that I see light, that I hear noise and that I feel heat. That cannot be false; properly speaking it is what is in me called feeling, and used in this precise sense that is no other thing than thinking.

From this time I begin to know what I am with a little more clearness and distinction than before; but nevertheless it still seems to me, and I cannot prevent myself from thinking, that corporeal things, whose images are framed by thought, which are tested by the senses, are much more distinctly known than that obscure part of me which does not come under the imagination. Although really it is very strange to say that I know and understand more distinctly these things whose existence seems to me dubious, which are un-

known to me, and which do not belong to me, than others of the truth of
which I am convinced, which are known to me and which pertain to my real
nature, in a word, than myself. But I see clearly how the case stands: my mind
loves to wander, and cannot yet suffer itself to be retained within the just
limits of truth. Very good, let us once more give it the freest rein, so that, when
afterwards we seize the proper occasion for pulling up, it may the more easily
be regulated and controlled.

Let us begin by considering the commonest matters, those which we
believe to be the most distinctly comprehended, to wit, the bodies which we
touch and see; not indeed bodies in general, for these general ideas are usually
a little more confused, but let us consider one body in particular. Let us take,
for example, this piece of wax: it has been taken quite freshly from the hive,
and it has not yet lost the sweetness of the honey which it contains; it still
retains somewhat of the odour of the flowers from which it has been culled;
its color, its figure, its size are apparent; it is hard, cold, easily handled, and
if you strike it with the finger, it will emit a sound. Finally all the things which
are requisite to cause us distinctly to recognise a body, are met with in it. But
notice that while I speak and approach the fire what remained of the taste is
exhaled, the smell evaporates, the color alters, the figure is destroyed, the size
increases, it becomes liquid, it heats, scarcely can one handle it, and when one
strikes it, no sound is emitted. Does the same wax remain after this change? We
must confess that it remains; none would judge otherwise. What then did I know
so distinctly in this piece of wax? It could certainly be nothing of all that the senses
brought to my notice, since all these things which fall under taste, smell, sight,
touch, and hearing, are found to be changed, and yet the same wax remains.

Perhaps it was what I now think, viz. that this wax was not that sweet- *namely*
ness of honey, nor that agreeable scent of flowers, nor that particular white-
ness, nor that figure, nor that sound, but simply a body which a little while
before appeared to me as perceptible under these forms, and which is now
perceptible under others. But what, precisely, is it that I imagine when I form
such conceptions? Let us attentively consider this, and, abstracting from all
that does not belong to the wax, let us see what remains. Certainly nothing
remains excepting a certain extended thing which is flexible and movable. But
what is the meaning of flexible and movable? Is it not that I imagine that this
piece of wax being round is capable of becoming square and of passing from
a square to a triangular figure? No, certainly it is not that, since I imagine it
admits of an infinitude of similar changes, and I nevertheless do not know
how to compass the infinitude by my imagination, and consequently this conception which I have of the wax is not brought about by the faculty of imagination. What now is the extension? Is it not also unknown? For it becomes
greater when the wax is melted, greater when it is boiled, and greater still
when the heat increases; and I should not conceive [clearly] according to truth
what wax is, if I did not think that even this piece that we are considering is
capable of receiving more variations in extension than I have ever imagined.
We must then grant that I could not even understand through the imagination

what this piece of wax is, and that it is my mind alone which perceives it. I say
this piece of wax is particular, for as to wax in general it is yet clearer. But what
is this piece of wax which cannot be understood excepting by the [under-
standing or] mind? It is certainly the same that I see, touch, imagine, and
finally it is the same which I have always believed it to be from the beginning.
But what must particularly be observed is that its perception is neither an act
of vision, nor of touch, nor of imagination, and has never been such although
it may have appeared formerly to be so, but only an intuition of the mind,
which may be imperfect and confused as it was formerly, or clear and distinct
as it is at present, according as my attention is more or less directed to the
elements which are found in it, and of which it is composed.

Yet in the meantime I am greatly astonished when I consider [the great
feebleness of mind] and its proneness to fall [insensibly] into error; for although without giving expression to my thoughts I consider all this in my own
mind, words often impede me and I am almost deceived by the terms of ordinary language. For we say that we see the same wax, if it is present, and not
that we simply judge that it is the same from its having the same color and
figure. From this I should conclude that I knew the wax by means of vision
and not simply by the intuition of the mind; unless by chance I remember that,
when looking from a window and saying I see men who pass in the street, I
really do not see them, but infer that what I see is men, just as I say that I see
wax. And yet what do I see from the window but hats and coats which may
cover automatic machines? Yet I judge these to be men. And similarly solely
by the faculty of judgment which rests in my mind, I comprehend that which
I believed I saw with my eyes.

A man who makes it his aim to raise his knowledge above the common
should be ashamed to derive the occasion for doubting from the forms of speech
invented by the vulgar; I prefer to pass on and consider whether I had a more
evident and perfect conception of what the wax was when I first perceived it,
and when I believed I knew it by means of the external senses or at least by
the common sense as it is called, that is to say by the imaginative faculty, or
whether my present conception is clearer now that I have most carefully examined what it is, and in what way it can be known. It would certainly be
absurd to doubt as to this. For what was there in this first perception which
was distinct? What was there which might not as well have been perceived by
any of the animals? But when I distinguish the wax from its external forms,
and when, just as if I had taken from it its vestments, I consider it quite naked,
it is certain that although some error may still be found in my judgment, I can
nevertheless not perceive it thus without a human mind.

But finally what shall I say of this mind, that is, of myself, for up to this
point I do not admit in myself anything but mind? What then, I who seem to
perceive this piece of wax so distinctly, do I not know myself, not only with
much more truth and certainty, but also with much more distinctness and
clearness? For if I judge that the wax is or exists from the fact that I see it, it
certainly follows much more clearly that I am or that I exist myself from the

fact that I see it. For it may be that what I see is not really wax, it may also be that I do not possess eyes with which to see anything; but it cannot be that when I see, or (for I no longer take account of the distinction) when I think I see, that I myself who think am nought. So if I judge that the wax exists from the fact that I touch it, the same thing will follow, to wit, that I am; and if I judge that my imagination, or some other cause, whatever it is, persuades me that the wax exists, I shall still conclude the same. And what I have here marked of wax may be applied to all other things which are external to me [and which are met with outside of me]. And further, if the [notion or] perception of wax has seemed to me clearer and more distinct, not only after the sight or the touch, but also after many other causes have rendered it quite manifest to me, with how much more [evidence] and distinctness must it be said that I now know myself, since all the reasons which contribute to the knowledge of wax, or any other body whatever, are yet better proofs of the nature of my mind! And there are so many other things in the mind itself which may contribute to the elucidation of its nature, that those which depend on body such as these just mentioned, hardly merit being taken into account.

But finally here I am, having insensibly reverted to the point I desired, for, since it is now manifest to me that even bodies are not properly speaking known by the senses or by the faculty of imagination, but by the understanding only, and since they are not known from the fact that they are seen or touched, but only because they are understood, I see clearly that there is nothing which is easier for me to know than my mind. But because it is difficult to rid oneself so promptly of an opinion to which one was accustomed for so long, it will be well that I should halt a little at this point, so that by the length of my meditation I may more deeply imprint on my memory this new knowledge.

STUDY QUESTIONS

1. Why does Descartes believe that the sciences of physics, astronomy, and medicine are uncertain whereas arithmetic and geometry are not?
2. Descartes says that he will treat the existence of his body as uncertain and doubtful. Why does he do this? Do you think it is possible to doubt the existence of your own body? Would the answer to this question depend upon your historical era?
3. At one point Descartes says that he is not the same as his body. Why does he say this? Do you think the evidence is sufficient?
4. At first Descartes finds it strange that mind may be more distinctly known than matter. But then he contemplates the piece of wax. What does this case prove to him?
5. "All mere animals eat without pleasure, they cry without pain, they grow without knowing it; they desire nothing, they fear nothing, they know nothing" (Malebranche). Malebranche was a follower of Descartes. Why do you think he would say these things?

The Nature of the Self

David Hume

David Hume (1711–1776) was brought up in a rigid Calvinist home by his widowed mother. He entered the University of Edinburgh at twelve, quit school at fifteen without a degree, and decided to educate himself. His disciplined religious life combined with his growing intellectual independence to produce a mild breakdown at nineteen. But by the age of twenty-six Hume had written his masterpiece, *A Treatise of Human Nature,* from which this selection is taken. Hume was a controversial figure throughout much of his life, mostly because his brutal honesty and incisive intellect could not let any dogma pass unchallenged. His ideas on religion, psychology, history, science, and practically everything were considered "shocking." Yet in spite of his outrageous opinions, those who knew him found him to be a generous, tolerant, and friendly person.

In this selection Hume considers the doctrine that the soul is something apart from the thoughts and feelings and desires which constitute the ebb and flow of the mental life. Being a good empiricist, Hume asks whether the soul can be perceived, and finding that it cannot, argues that we cannot have an intelligible idea of it. The self, he claims, is nothing more than a series of successive perceptions. The soul is a convenient fiction.

This selection provides a fine illustration of Hume's honesty. Not satisfied with his own theory, Hume poses a problem for it, and confesses that he cannot find an answer. Perhaps you will be able to locate the source of his difficulty.

There are some philosophers who imagine we are every moment intimately conscious of what we call our *self;* that we feel its existence and its continuance in existence; and are certain, beyond the evidence of a demonstration, both of its perfect identity and simplicity. The strongest sensation, the most violent passion, say they, instead of distracting us from this view, only fix it the more intensely, and make us consider their influence on *self* either by their pain or pleasure. To attempt a further proof of this were to weaken its evidence; since no proof can be derived from any fact of which we are so intimately conscious; nor is there anything of which we can be certain if we doubt of this.

Unluckily all these positive assertions are contrary to that very experience which is pleaded for them; nor have we any idea of *self*, after the manner it is here explained. For, from what impression* could this idea be derived? This question it is impossible to answer without a manifest contradiction and absurdity; and yet it is a question which must necessarily be answered, if we would have the idea of self pass for clear and intelligible. It must be some one impression that gives rise to every real idea. But self or person is not any one impression, but that to which our several impressions and ideas are supposed

From *A Treatise of Human Nature* by David Hume, first published in 1739.
* *Editors' note:* An impression, for Hume, is a sensation presented to the mind by any of the senses.

to have a reference. If any impression gives rise to the idea of self, that impression must continue invariably the same, through the whole course of our lives; since self is supposed to exist after that manner. But there is no impression constant and invariable. Pain and pleasure, grief and joy, passions and sensations succeed each other, and never all exist at the same time. It cannot therefore be from any of these impressions, or from any other, that the idea of self is derived; and consequently there is no such idea.

But further, what must become of all our particular perceptions upon this hypothesis? All these are different, and distinguishable, and separable from each other, and may be separately considered, and may exist separately, and have no need of anything to support their existence. After what manner therefore do they belong to self, and how are they connected with it? For my part, when I enter most intimately into what I call *myself*, I always stumble on some particular perception or other, of heat or cold, light or shade, love or hatred, pain or pleasure. I never can catch *myself* at any time without a perception, and never can observe anything but the perception. When my perceptions are removed for any time, as by sound sleep, so long am I insensible of *myself*, and may truly be said not to exist. And were all my perceptions removed by death, and could I neither think, nor feel, nor see, nor love, nor hate, after the dissolution of my body, I should be entirely annihilated, nor do I conceive what is further requisite to make me a perfect nonentity. If any one, upon serious and unprejudiced reflection, thinks he has a different notion of *himself*, I must confess I can reason no longer with him. All I can allow him is, that he may be in the right as well as I, and that we are essentially different in this particular. He may, perhaps, perceive something simple and continued, which he calls *himself*; though I am certain there is no such principle in me.

But setting aside some metaphysicians of this kind, I may venture to affirm of the rest of mankind, that they are nothing but a bundle or collection of different perceptions, which succeed each other with an inconceivable rapidity, and are in a perpetual flux and movement. Our eyes cannot turn in their sockets without varying our perceptions. Our thought is still more variable than our sight; and all our other senses and faculties contribute to this change; nor is there any single power of the soul, which remains unalterably the same, perhaps for one moment. The mind is a kind of theatre, where several perceptions successively make their appearance; pass, repass, glide away, and mingle in an infinite variety of postures and situations. There is properly no *simplicity* in it at one time, nor *identity* in different, whatever natural propension we may have to imagine that simplicity and identity. The comparison of the theatre must not mislead us. They are the successive perceptions only, that constitute the mind; nor have we the most distant notion of the place where these scenes are represented, or of the materials of which it is composed.

What then gives us so great a propension to ascribe an identity to these successive perceptions, and to suppose ourselves possessed of an invariable

How can we identify these perceptions

and uninterrupted existence through the whole course of our lives? In order to answer this question we must distinguish betwixt personal identity, as it regards our thought or imagination, and as it regards our passions or the concern we take in ourselves. The first is our present subject; and to explain it perfectly we must take the matter pretty deep, and account for that identity, which we attribute to plants and animals; there being a great analogy betwixt it and the identity of a self or person.

We have a distinct idea of an object that remains invariable and uninterrupted through a supposed variation of time; and this idea we call that of *identity* or *sameness*. We have also a distinct idea of several different objects existing in succession, and connected together by a close relation; and this to an accurate view affords as perfect a notion of *diversity* as if there was no manner of relation among the objects. But though these two ideas of identity, and a succession of related objects, be in themselves perfectly distinct, and even contrary, yet it is certain that, in our common way of thinking, they are generally confounded with each other. That action of the imagination, by which we consider the uninterrupted and invariable object, and that by which we reflect on the succession of related objects, are almost the same to the feeling; nor is there much more effort of thought required in the latter case than in the former. The relation facilitates the transition of the mind from one object to another, and renders its passage as smooth as if it contemplated one continued object. This resemblance is the cause of the confusion and mistake, and makes us substitute the notion of identity, instead of that of related objects. However, at one instant we may consider the related succession as variable or interrupted, we are sure the next to ascribe to it a perfect identity, and regard it as invariable and uninterrupted. Our propensity to this mistake is so great from the resemblance above mentioned, that we fall into it before we are aware; and though we incessantly correct ourselves by reflection, and return to a more accurate method of thinking, yet we cannot long sustain our philosophy, or take off this bias from the imagination. Our last resource is to yield to it, and boldly assert that these different related objects are in effect the same, however interrupted and variable. In order to justify to ourselves this absurdity, we often feign some new and unintelligible principle, that connects the objects together, and prevents their interruption or variation. Thus we feign the continued existence of the perceptions of our senses, to remove the interruption; and run into the notion of a *soul*, and *self*, and *substance*, to disguise the variation. But, we may further observe, that where we do not give rise to such a fiction, our propension to confound identity with relation is so great, that we are apt to imagine something unknown and mysterious, connecting the parts, beside their relation; and this I take to be the case with regard to the identity we ascribe to plants and vegetables. And even when this does not take place, we still feel a propensity to confound these ideas, though we are not able fully to satisfy ourselves in that particular, nor find anything invariable and uninterrupted to justify our notion of identity.

Thus the controversy concerning identity is not merely a dispute of words.

For when we attribute identity, in an improper sense, to variable or interrupted objects, our mistake is not confined to the expression, but is commonly
attended with a fiction, either of something invariable and uninterrupted, or
of something mysterious and inexplicable, or at least with a propensity to such
fictions. What will suffice to prove this hypothesis to the satisfaction of every
fair inquirer, is to show, from daily experience and observation, that the objects which are variable or interrupted, and yet are supposed to continue the
same, are such only as consist of a succession of parts, connected together by
resemblance, contiguity, or causation. For as such a succession answers evidently to our notion of diversity, it can only be by mistake we ascribe to it an
identity; and as the relation of parts, which leads us into this mistake, is really
nothing but a quality, which produces an association of ideas, and an easy
transition of the imagination from one to another, it can only be from the
resemblance, which this act of the mind bears to that by which we contemplate one continued object, that the error arises. Our chief business, then,
must be to prove, that all objects, to which we ascribe identity, without observing their invariableness and uninterruptedness, are such as consist of a
succession of related objects.

In order to do this, suppose any mass of matter, of which the parts are
contiguous and connected, to be placed before us; it is plain we must attribute
a perfect identity to this mass, provided all the parts continue uninterruptedly
and invariably the same, whatever motion or change of place we may observe
either in the whole or in any of the parts. But supposing some very *small* or
inconsiderable part to be added to the mass, or subtracted from it; though this
absolutely destroys the identity of the whole, strictly speaking, yet as we seldom think so accurately, we scruple not to pronounce a mass of matter the
same, where we find so trivial an alteration. The passage of the thought from
the object before the change to the object after it, is so smooth and easy, that
we scarce perceive the transition, and are apt to imagine, that it is nothing but
a continued survey of the same object.

There is a very remarkable circumstance that attends this experiment;
which is, that though the change of any considerable part in a mass of matter
destroys the identity of the whole, yet we must measure the greatness of the
part, not absolutely, but by its *proportion* to the whole. The addition or dim-
inution of a mountain would not be sufficient to produce a diversity in a planet;
though the change of a very few inches would be able to destroy the identity
of some bodies. It will be impossible to account for this, but by reflecting that
objects operate upon the mind, and break or interrupt the continuity of its
actions, not according to their real greatness, but according to their proportion
to each other; and therefore, since this interruption makes an object cease to
appear the same, it must be the uninterrupted progress of the thought which
constitutes the imperfect identity.

This may be confirmed by another phenomenon. A change in any considerable part of a body destroys its identity; but it is remarkable, that where
the change is produced *gradually* and *insensibly*, we are less apt to ascribe to it

the same effect. The reason can plainly be no other, than that the mind, in following the successive changes of the body, feels an easy passage from the surveying of its condition in one moment, to the viewing of it in another, and in no particular time perceives any interruption in its actions. From which continued perception, it ascribes a continued existence and identity to the object.

But whatever precaution we may use in introducing the changes gradually, and making them proportionable to the whole, it is certain, that where the changes are at last observed to become considerable, we make a scruple of ascribing identity to such different objects. There is, however, another artifice, by which we may induce the imagination to advance a step further; and that is, by producing a reference of the parts to each other, and a combination to some *common end* or purpose. A ship, of which a considerable part has been changed by frequent reparations, is still considered as the same; nor does the difference of the materials hinder us from ascribing an identity to it. The common end, in which the parts conspire, is the same under all their variations, and affords an easy transition of the imagination from one situation of the body to another.

But this is still more remarkable, when we add a *sympathy* of parts to their *common end*, and suppose that they bear to each other the reciprocal relation of cause and effect in all their actions and operations. This is the case with all animals and vegetables; where not only the several parts have a reference to some general purpose, but also a mutual dependence on, and connection with, each other. The effect of so strong a relation is, that though every one must allow, that in a very few years both vegetables and animals endure a *total* change, yet we still attribute identity to them, while their form, size, and substance, are entirely altered. An oak that grows from a small plant to a large tree is still the same oak, though there be not one particle of matter or figure of its parts the same. An infant becomes a man, and is sometimes fat, sometimes lean, without any change in his identity.

We may also consider the two following phenomena, which are remarkable in their kind. The first is, that though we commonly be able to distinguish pretty exactly betwixt numerical and specific identity, yet it sometimes happens that we confound them, and in our thinking and reasoning employ the one for the other. Thus, a man who hears a noise that is frequently interrupted and renewed, says it is still the same noise, though it is evident the sounds have only a specific identity or resemblance, and there is nothing numerically the same but the cause which produced them. In like manner it may be said, without breach of the propriety of language, that such a church, which was formerly of brick, fell to ruin, and that the parish rebuilt the same church of freestone, and according to modern architecture. Here neither the form nor materials are the same, nor is there anything common to the two objects but their relation to the inhabitants of the parish; and yet this alone is sufficient to make us denominate them the same. But we must observe, that in these cases the first object is in a manner annihilated before the second comes into existence; by which means, we are never presented, in any one point of time, with the idea of difference and multiplicity; and for that reason are less scrupulous in calling them the same.

Secondly, we may remark, that though, in a succession of related objects, it be a manner requisite that the change of parts be not sudden nor entire, in order to preserve the identity, yet where the objects are in their nature changeable and inconstant, we admit of a more sudden transition than would otherwise be consistent with that relation. Thus, as the nature of a river consists in the motion and change of parts, though in less than four-and-twenty hours these be totally altered, this hinders not the river from continuing the same during several ages. What is natural and essential to anything is, in a manner, expected; and what is expected makes less impression, and appears of less moment than what is unusual and extraordinary. A considerable change of the former kind seems really less to the imagination than the most trivial alteration of the latter; and by breaking less the continuity of the thought, has less influence in destroying the identity.

We now proceed to explain the nature of _personal identity_, which has become so great a question in philosophy, especially of late years, in England, where all the abstruser sciences are studied with a peculiar ardor and application. And here it is evident the same method of reasoning must be continued which has so successfully explained the identity of plants, and animals, and ships, and houses, and of all compounded and changeable productions either of art or nature. The identity which we ascribe to the mind of man is only a fictitious one, and of a like kind with that which we ascribe to vegetable and animal bodies. It cannot therefore have a different origin, but must proceed from a like operation of the imagination upon like objects.

But lest this argument should not convince the reader, though in my opinion perfectly decisive, let him weigh the following reasoning, which is still closer and more immediate. It is evident that the identity which we attribute to the human mind, however perfect we may imagine it to be, is not able to run the several different perceptions into one, and make them lose their characters of distinction and difference, which are essential to them. It is still true that every distinct perception which enters into the composition of the mind, is a distinct existence, and is different, and distinguishable, and separable from every other perception, either contemporary or successive. But as, notwithstanding this distinction and separability, we suppose the whole train of perceptions to be united by identity, a question naturally arises concerning this relation of identity, whether it be something that really binds our several perceptions together, or only associates their ideas in the imagination; that is, in other words, whether, in pronouncing concerning the identity of a person, we observe some real bond among his perceptions, or only feel one among the ideas we form of them. This question we might easily decide, if we would recollect what has been already proved at large, that the understanding never observes any real connection among objects, and that even the union of cause and effect, when strictly examined, resolves itself into a customary association of ideas. For from thence it evidently follows, that identity is nothing really belonging to these different perceptions, and uniting them together, but is merely a quality which we attribute to them, because of the union of their ideas in the imagination when we reflect upon them. Now, the only qualities which can give ideas a union in the imagination, are these three relations above mentioned. These are the uniting principles in the ideal world, and without them every distinct object is separable by the mind, and may be separately considered, and appears not to have any more connection with any other object than if disjoined by the greatest difference and remoteness. It is therefore on some of these three relations of resemblance, contiguity and causation, that identity depends; and as the very essence of these relations consists in their producing an easy transition of ideas, it follows that our notions of personal identity proceed entirely from the smooth and uninterrupted progress of the thought along a train of connected ideas, according to the principles above explained.

The only question, therefore, which remains is, by what relations this uninterrupted progress of our thought is produced, when we consider the successive existence of a mind or thinking person. And here it is evident we must confine ourselves to resemblance and causation, and must drop contiguity, which has little or no influence in the present case.

To begin with *resemblance;* suppose we could see clearly into the breast of another, and observe that succession of perceptions which constitutes his mind or thinking principle, and suppose that he always preserves the memory of a considerable part of past perceptions, it is evident that nothing could more contribute to the bestowing a relation on this succession amidst all its variations. For what is the memory but a faculty, by which we raise up the images of past perceptions? And as an image necessarily resembles its object, must not the frequent placing of these resembling perceptions in the chain of thought, convey the imagination more easily from one link to another, and make the whole seem like the continuance of one object? In this particular, then, the memory not only discovers the identity, but also contributes to its production, by producing the relation of resemblance among the perceptions. The case is the same, whether we consider ourselves or others.

As to *causation;* we may observe that the true idea of the human mind, is to consider it as a system of different perceptions or different existences, which are linked together by the relation of cause and effect, and mutually produce, destroy, influence, and modify each other. Our impressions give rise to their correspondent ideas; and these ideas, in their turn, produce other impressions. One thought chases another, and draws after it a third, by which it is expelled in its turn. In this respect, I cannot compare the soul more properly to anything than to a republic or commonwealth, in which the several members are united by the reciprocal ties of government and subordination, and give rise to other persons who propagate the same republic in the incessant changes of its parts. And as the same individual republic may not only change its members, but also its laws and constitutions; in like manner the same person may vary his character and disposition, as well as his impressions and ideas, without losing his identity. Whatever changes he endures, his several parts are still connected by the relation of causation. And in this view our identity with regard to the passions serves to corroborate that with regard to the imagination, by making our distant perceptions influence each other, and by giving us a present concern for our past or future pains or pleasures.

As memory alone acquaints us with the continuance and extent of this succession of perceptions, it is to be considered, upon that account chiefly, as the source of personal identity. Had we no memory, we never should have any notion of causation, nor consequently of that chain of causes and effects, which constitute our self or person. But having once acquired this notion of causation from the memory, we can extend the same chain of causes, and consequently the identity of our persons beyond our memory, and can comprehend times, and circumstances, and actions, which we have entirely forgot, but suppose in general to have existed. For how few of our past actions are there, of which we have any memory? Who can tell me, for instance, what were his thoughts and actions on the first of January 1715, the eleventh of March 1719, and the third of August 1733? Or will he affirm, because he has entirely forgot the incidents of these days, that the present self is not the same person with the self of that time; and by that means overturn all the most established notions of personal identity? In this view, therefore, memory does not so much *produce* as *discover* personal identity, by showing us the relation of cause and effect among our different perceptions. It will be incumbent on those who affirm that memory produces entirely our personal identity, to give a reason why we can thus extend our identity beyond our memory.

The whole of this doctrine leads us to a conclusion, which is of great importance in the present affair, viz. [namely] that all the nice and subtile questions concerning personal identity can never possibly be decided, and are to be regarded rather as grammatical than as philosophical difficulties. Identity depends on the relations of ideas; and these relations produce identity, by means of that easy transition they occasion. But as the relations, and the easiness of the transition may diminish by insensible degrees, we have no just standard by which we can decide any dispute concerning the time when they acquire or lose a title to the name of identity. All the disputes concerning the identity of connected objects are merely verbal, except so far as the relation of parts gives rise to some fiction or imaginary principle of union, as we have already observed.

What I have said concerning the first origin and uncertainty of our notion of identity, as applied to the human mind, may be extended with little or no variation to that of *simplicity*. An object, whose different coexistent parts are bound together by a close relation, operates upon the imagination after much the same manner as one perfectly simple and indivisible, and requires not a much greater stretch of thought in order to its conception. From this similarity of operation we attribute a simplicity to it, and feign a principle of union as the support of this simplicity, and the centre of all the different parts and qualities of the object.

Thus we have finished our examination of the several systems of philosophy, both of the intellectual and moral world; and, in our miscellaneous way of reasoning, have been led into several topics, which will either illustrate and confirm some preceding part of this discourse, or prepare the way for our following opinions. It is now time to return to a more close examination of our subject, and to proceed in the accurate anatomy of human nature, having fully explained the nature of our judgment and understanding.

I had entertained some hopes, that however deficient our theory of the intellectual world might be, it would be free from those contradictions and absurdities which seem to attend every explication that human reason can give of the material world. But upon a more strict review of the section concerning *personal identity*, I find myself involved in such a labyrinth that, I must confess, I neither know how to correct my former opinions, nor how to render them consistent. If this be not a good *general* reason for scepticism, it is at least a sufficient one (if I were not already abundantly supplied) for me to entertain a diffidence and modesty in all my decisions. I shall propose the arguments on both sides, beginning with those that induced me to deny the strict and proper identity and simplicity of a self or thinking being.

 When we talk of _self or subsistence_, we must have an idea annexed to these terms, otherwise they are altogether unintelligible. Every idea is derived from preceding impressions; and we have no impression of self or substance, as something simple and individual. We have, therefore, no idea of them in that sense.

Whatever is distinct is distinguishable, and whatever is distinguishable is separable by the thought or imagination. All perceptions are distinct. They are, therefore, distinguishable, and separable, and may be conceived as separately existent, and may exist separately, without any contradiction or absurdity.

When I view this table and that chimney, nothing is present to me but particular perceptions, which are of a like nature with all the other perceptions. This is the doctrine of philosophers. But this table, which is present to me, and that chimney, may, and do exist separately. This is the doctrine of the vulgar, and implies no contradiction. There is no contradiction, therefore, in extending the same doctrine in all the perceptions.

In general, the following reasoning seems satisfactory. All ideas are borrowed from preceding perceptions. Our ideas of objects, therefore, are derived from that source. Consequently no proposition can be intelligible or consistent with regard to objects, which is not so with regard to perceptions. But it is intelligible and consistent to say, that objects exist distinct and independent, without any common *simple* substance or subject of inhesion. This proposition, therefore, can never be absurd with regard to perceptions.

When I turn my reflection on *myself*, I never can perceive this *self* without some one or more perceptions; nor can I ever perceive anything but the perceptions. It is the composition of these, therefore, which forms the self.

We can conceive a thinking being to have either many or few perceptions. Suppose the mind to be reduced even below the life of an oyster. Suppose it to have only one perception, as of thirst or hunger. Consider it in that situation. Do you conceive anything but merely that perception? Have you any notion of *self* or *substance*? If not, the addition of other perceptions can never give you that notion.

The annihilation which some people suppose to follow upon death, and which entirely destroys this self, is nothing but an extinction of all particular perceptions; love and hatred, pain and pleasure, thought and sensation. These, therefore, must be the same with self, since the one cannot survive the other.

Is *self* the same with *substance*? If it be, how can that question have place, concerning the substance of self, under a change of substance? If they be distinct, what is the difference betwixt them? For my part, I have a notion of neither, when conceived distinct from particular perceptions.

Philosophers begin to be reconciled to the principle, *that we have no idea of external substance, distinct from the ideas of particular qualities.* This must pave the way for a like principle with regard to the mind, *that we have no notion of it, distinct from the particular perception.*

So far I seem to be attended with sufficient evidence. But having thus loosened all our particular perceptions, when I proceed to explain the principle of connection, which binds them together, and makes us attribute to them a real simplicity and identity, I am sensible that my account is very defective, and that nothing but the seeming evidence of the precedent reasonings could have induced me to receive it. If perceptions are distinct existences, they form a whole only by being connected together. But no connections among distinct existences are ever discoverable by human understanding. We only *feel* a connection or determination of the thought to pass from one object to another. It follows, therefore, that the thought alone feels personal identity, when reflecting on the train of past perceptions that compose a mind, the ideas of them are felt to be connected together, and naturally introduce each other. However extraordinary this conclusion may seem, it need not surprise us. Most philosophers seem inclined to think, that personal identity *arises* from consciousness, and consciousness is nothing but a reflected thought or perception. The present philosophy, therefore, has so far a promising aspect. But all my hopes vanish when I come to explain the principles that unite our successive perceptions in our thought or consciousness. I cannot discover any theory which gives me satisfaction on this head.

In short, there are two principles which I cannot render consistent, nor is it in my power to renounce either of them, viz. *that all our distinct perceptions are distinct existences*, and *that the mind never perceives any real connection among distinct existences.* Did our perceptions either inhere in something simple and individual, or did the mind perceive some real connection among them, there would be no difficulty in the case. For my part, I must plead the privilege of a sceptic, and confess that this difficulty is too hard for my understanding. I pretend not, however, to pronounce it absolutely insuperable. Others, perhaps, or myself, upon more mature reflections, may discover some hypothesis that will reconcile those contradictions.

STUDY QUESTIONS

1. Hume begins by saying that we do not have an "idea" of the self. What do you think he means by the word "idea"? Could he mean "concept"?
2. At one place Hume says that the mind is like a theater which contains perceptions. Is this remark consistent with his other statements?
3. Hume says that the notion of a "soul" or "substance" is a fiction which we create. Why do we create it, according to him?
4. Toward the end of the essay, Hume is unhappy with his previous solution. What is the source of his perplexity? Can you suggest an answer?
5. "It seems to me that the greatest lesson of adult life is that one's own consciousness is not enough....What great writer would not like to share the consciousness of Shakespeare?...What I would choose would be an evolution of life whereby the essence of each of us becomes welded together into some vastly larger and more potent system" (Fred Hoyle). Would Hume say that Hoyle's dream is possible? How about Descartes?

In the Chinese Room—Do Computers Think?
George Johnson

To Descartes, what set humanity apart from the rest of nature was the immaterial soul, or mind, the seat of thinking and willing. But Hume could find no evidence of such a substance, and Darwin saw no need for one. Human behavior, Darwin proposed, emanates from physical organs which have evolved over millions of years. Thinking and willing arise from activity in the brain. If this is so, it would seem possible, in theory, to invent a machine to duplicate human behavior. In fact, the field of artificial intelligence, or AI, has been dominated since the early 1960s by researchers attempting to develop computers and programs which duplicate thinking.

    In the following article, George Johnson (1952-   ), an award-winning journalist, illuminates the debate between those who believe that computers can think (reductionists) and those who dispute such a possibility (holists). Holists, such as John Searle and the Dreyfus brothers, argue that a computer is incapable of self-consciousness, grasping the meaning of its activity, or having feelings or intuitions. To them, "mind" is more than the "hum of its parts."

As you read this selection, see if Searle's Chinese room convincingly shows that a computer cannot really think. Also, ask yourself whether the debate over the nature of mind and its relationship to body is ever likely to be settled.

In 1984 John Searle, a philosopher at the University of California's Berkeley campus, was chosen to deliver the Reith Lectures, a series of six thirty-minute talks presented each year by the British Broadcasting Company. The lectures, begun in 1948 by Bertrand Russell, are designed to introduce a general audience to some of the important intellectual and scientific issues of the day. For his presentation, Searle chose to speak about the nature of the mind and what, if anything, it has in common with a digital computer.

Searle, a short, rugged-looking man with a self-confident swagger, believes that artificial intelligence is impossible. He is not merely saying that making thinking computers is insurmountably difficult, requiring vastly better machinery, vastly smarter programmers, and a thousand or more years of progress, but that there are theoretical reasons why it can never be done. No matter how sophisticated a computer eventually becomes—even if it carries on a conversation convincing enough to pass the Turing test*—Searle would insist that it can never understand what it hears and says. Therefore it cannot be said to think.

"No one supposes that computer simulations of a five-alarm fire will burn the neighborhood down," Searle has written, in the down-home, commonsense style for which he is known, "or that a computer simulation of a rainstorm will leave us all drenched. Why on earth would anyone suppose that a computer simulation of understanding actually understood anything?" To Searle a program that passed the Turing test would be an excellent simulation of thinking, but he would insist that the map is not the territory, that the computer does not really think. Thinking is something only humans do, rooted perhaps in brain chemistry.

Searle's argument is based on the fact that a computer and its program comprise what mathematicians call a formal system. The essence of a formal system is that it consists of tokens and rules for manipulating them. Chess, checkers, tic-tac-toe, and Go all are formal systems of different levels of complexity. On a more abstract level, arithmetic is a formal system whose tokens are numbers; the rules tell how they can be manipulated using addition, subtraction, division, and multiplication. In all these systems, the nature of the

*Editors' note: Alan Turing, a British mathematician who did groundbreaking work on computing theory in the 1930s and 1940s, was convinced that, eventually, computers would be developed which could be programmed to think. To determine whether a computer could think, Turing proposed that a computer and a human being be placed in separate rooms out of sight of an interrogator. The interrogator would communicate questions to the computer and the human via teletype. If the interrogator, after receiving their responses, could not tell whether a particular response came from the computer or the human, then, according to Turing, one could reasonably conclude that computers can think.

tokens doesn't matter. Tic-tac-toe could be played on a grid of any size using pencil marks, pennies and dimes, or manhole covers and sofa cushions. Arithmetic could be carried out using colored dots in place of numerals. The details are arbitrary. It is the *form* of the games that is important, not the content. That is why they are called formal systems.

Another interesting feature of formal systems is that one can be "mapped" onto another. For example, in the game of chess, letters are often assigned to chess pieces—K for king, KB for king's bishop, Q for queen, QKt for Queen's knight, et cetera. To differentiate white pieces from black, the letters are printed in two colors, or two fonts of type. By also assigning letters and numbers to the squares of the board—QKt8 for the square eight rows in front of the one initially occupied by the Queen's knight—chess players have devised a code for describing the moves of a game.

In fact, an entire game can be translated into this system, as row after row of numbers and letters. If someone who didn't know about chess happened to encounter one of these descriptions, he would be baffled. He would have no way of knowing that it referred to the movement of little plastic statues shaped like horses, castles, and other figures on an eight-by-eight pattern of black-and-white squares. But if he examined the list carefully, he would see that there are syntactic rules for how the letters and numbers can be configured. Many combinations—KQ, QQ, or $_3$TkO$_5$, for example—are illegal and never occur. As he read through the list of plays, he might notice other, more subtle regularities: While Kkt-KR$_3$ and Kkt-KB$_3$ are legal patterns, Kkt-Kkt2 is not. These esoteric relationships reflect the fact that a knight can make L-shaped moves, but cannot advance to the square in front of it. But our naïve observer wouldn't know that. Thinking that he had found a lengthy proof written in some strange mathematics, he might set out to decipher it, devising his own set of rules—a formal system that specified how to manipulate meaningless tokens like Kkt. Then the patterns of letters and numbers all would make sense. Left in isolation, he could enjoy the intricacies of his abstract world without ever knowing that it can be mapped onto an entirely different formal system: the game of chess.

A computer can be thought of as a hierarchy of formal systems all mapped onto one another. At the highest level is the program—a word processor, for example, in which the tokens are letters of the alphabet, numerals, and punctuation marks. This system, written in some high-level language like Pascal or Lisp, is mapped onto an interpreter or compiler, which is mapped onto the computer's machine language, the system whose tokens are ιs and βs.

Artificial intelligence is based on the assumption that the mind can be described as some kind of formal system manipulating symbols that stand for things in the world. Thus it doesn't matter what the brain is made of, or what it uses for tokens in the great game of thinking. Using an equivalent set of tokens and rules, we can do thinking with a digital computer, just as we can play chess using cups, salt and pepper shakers, knives, forks, and spoons.

Using the right software, one system (the mind) can be mapped onto the other (the computer).

Searle rejects this notion. He believes that formal systems are, by their very nature, incapable of thinking.

"There is more to having a mind than having formal or syntactical processes," he said during the Reith Lectures. "Our internal mental states, by definition, have certain sorts of contents. If I am thinking about Kansas City or wishing that I had a cold beer to drink or wondering if there will be a fall in interest rates, in each case my mental state has a certain mental content in addition to whatever formal features it might have. That is, even if my thoughts occur to me in strings of symbols, there must be more to the thought than the abstract strings, because strings by themselves can't have any meaning. If my thoughts are to be *about* anything, then the strings must have a *meaning* which makes the thoughts about those things. In a word, the mind has more than a syntax, it has a semantics. The reason that no computer program can ever be a mind is simply that a computer program is only syntactical.... Minds are semantical, in the sense that they have more than a formal structure, they have a content."

Perhaps the single most important idea to artificial intelligence is that there is no fundamental difference between form and content, that meaning can be captured in a set of symbols such as a semantic net. Or, to put it another way, semantics can arise from syntax. To represent the meaning of "dog" we can, in effect, draw a box—a meaningless, empty symbol—and arbitrarily call it "dog." Then we can connect that box to other boxes. A dog is-a mammal is-a vertebrate is-a living thing is-a pet; it has-as-parts feet which have-as-parts toes...et cetera, et cetera. Then we connect those boxes to other boxes: pets are owned by humans, trained to be friendly, to be protective, to do amusing tricks. If we connect symbols to symbols in one great web, eventually we'll reach a point where the tangle of lines and boxes becomes dense enough to capture the richness and complexity the human mind associates with the word "dog," and, if the network is good enough, "pet," "human," "foot," "trick," and "living thing." The meaning of a word will not reside in any single box; the "dog" box by itself means nothing. Meaning arises from the interaction of all the boxes. It is an emergent quality, just as style arises from the interaction of Aaron's rules. While we don't yet know how to string together adequate semantic networks, most AI researchers assume that there are no theoretical barriers to doing so. If you take the mind and break it into pieces, and break the pieces into pieces, you can turn it into a medley of processes each one precise enough to be computerized.

It is this, the central dogma of artificial intelligence, that Searle refuses to accept.

"Understanding a language, or indeed, having mental states at all, involves more than just having a bunch of formal symbols," he insists. "It involves having an interpretation, or a meaning attached to those symbols." To which an AI enthusiast would reply, "Fine, so attach the meanings." Using is-a links, has-as-parts links, et cetera, you weave the symbols into a structure that is meaningful. Searle, however, would insist that no matter how good the formal system, this elusive thing called "content" will always be missing. To illustrate his point, he likes to tell a story, the parable of the Chinese Room. In this thought experiment a human (in an interesting turn of events) simulates a digital computer. In his lectures for the BBC, Searle described the situation like this:

"...[I]magine that you are locked in a room, and in this room are several baskets full of Chinese symbols. Imagine that you (like me) do not understand a word of Chinese, but that you are given a rule book in English for manipulating these Chinese symbols. The rules specify the manipulations of the symbols purely formally, in terms of their syntax, not their semantics. So the rule might say: 'Take a squiggle-squiggle sign out of basket number one and put it next to a squoggle-squoggle sign from basket number two.' Now suppose that some other Chinese symbols are passed into the room, and that you are given further rules for passing back Chinese symbols out of the room. Suppose that unknown to you the symbols passed into the room are called 'questions' by the people outside the room, and the symbols you pass back out of the room are called 'answers to the questions.' Suppose, furthermore, that the programmers are so good at designing the programs and that you are so good at manipulating the symbols, that very soon your answers are indistinguishable from those of a native Chinese speaker."

To the programmers outside, the room would appear to understand Chinese. But the human on the inside would understand nothing as he uncomprehendingly shuffled symbols. Likewise, Searle contends, a computer programmed with the very same rules would not understand Chinese, even though it would be capable of passing the Turing test. So, Searle concluded, while a computer might be programmed to simulate intelligence, that doesn't mean that it is actually thinking. Just because something acts as though it is intelligent doesn't necessarily mean that it has mental states, or that it is experiencing the subjective feeling of being aware and conscious.

Upon first hearing it, many people feel that Searle's parable is a convincing argument against artificial intelligence. Naturally, supporters of AI are ready with a number of responses. For example, suppose that we take the room, the human, the baskets of symbols, and the rules for matching squiggles and squoggles and somehow shrink them all down and implant the whole thing in someone's head. Now, when *this* person begins conversing in Chinese how can we say that he does not understand what he is doing? And if we switch the conversation to English (his native tongue) what is it about his behavior now that makes it genuine comprehension, and not just symbol shuffling in an internal Chinese room?

In order to speak English don't we have to have something in our head that is equivalent, on some level, to a Chinese room? If not, then how do we understand? If having uncomprehending symbol shufflers is not enough, then

Counter attacking Chinese room

presumably we'd need the equivalent of a homunculus inside us that is some-how capable of "real" understanding. And it, of course, could not understand Chinese unless *it* had something inside that didn't merely shuffle symbols but that *really* understood. And so we fall head first into that infinite regress that has troubled philosophers for so many years.

In his BBC lectures, Searle made it clear that he does not consider himself a mystic who holds that there is something inexplicable about the mind. "...[A]ll mental phenomena," he said, "whether conscious or unconscious, visual or auditory, pains, tickles, itches, thoughts, indeed, all of our mental life, are caused by processes going on in the brain." He implied that we should find the philosophers' old mind-body problem no more perplexing than the "digestion-stomach" problem. Both digestion and thinking are natural pro-cesses arising from the physical actions of organs. The key word here is "nat-ural." There is something special, Searle believes, about the fact that the brain is biological. Thinking, he told his audience, is produced by something a com-puter can never have: what he calls "the causal powers of the brain."

Scientists are uncomfortable with such assertions, feeling that they smack of the philosopher's old *élan vital*, the ineffable spirit that supposedly inhabits our bodies and gives us life. But Searle's argument is more subtle. He accepts wholeheartedly that the mind—consciousness, memory, intelligence, love, de-spair, and all the rest of it—arises somehow from neurons, just as the phe-nomenon we call digestion arises from the cells and chemicals that make up the stomach and the other organs of the digestive tract. There are two levels of abstraction on which brains can be described: the neurophysiological and the psychological. On the low level all we see is a medley of electrochemical reactions; on the high level we see the behavior those reactions produce. Like-wise, the stomach can be described as muscle fibers, chemicals, et cetera, or, on a higher level, as something that digests food. We know so little about the brain that we can't yet say how chemical reactions cause thinking, as we can say how they cause digestion. But it's premature, Searle believes, to presume that the brain works like a computer.

AI researchers try to circumvent our ignorance about the brain by as-suming that it doesn't matter how the "wetware" in our heads actually op-erates. In between the low level, where neurons interact with neurons, and the high level, where behavior emerges, they interpose a middle level—the information-processing level—on which the brain can be described as a com-puter running a batch of programs called the mind. If we can use hardware and software to simulate this middle level, the result will be a computer that thinks using silicon instead of brain cells. Both will be species of this thing called information processor, a formal system that thinks.

Searle says that there is no information-processing level in the brain any more than there is in the stomach. We can simulate the stomach with a com-puter but it won't digest. If we simulate the brain it won't think. The brain only seems like a computer because scientists have been seduced by a met-aphor.

"Because we do not understand the brain very well we are constantly tempted to use the latest technology as a model for trying to understand it," Searle said. "In my childhood we were always assured that the brain was a telephone switchboard.... Freud often compared the brain to hydraulic and electromagnetic systems. Leibniz compared it to a mill, and I am told that some of the ancient Greeks thought the brain functions like a catapult. At present, obviously, the metaphor is the digital computer."

But there is something misleading about Searle's comparison between simulated stomachs and simulated minds. Of course, a computer simulation of digestion won't digest anything but simulated food. A better comparison would be between a real stomach and an artificial one made with tubes and valves, a supply of digestive acids, and perhaps a microprocessor to control its cycles. If food came in one end and what emerged was indistinguishable from digested food, then is the system merely a simulation, does it lack causal powers of the stomach? One kind of food processor has been used to simulate another. AI people believe that a simulated mind would think because the machine doing the simulation is, like the brain, an information processor.

Ultimately, then, Searle is denying that the brain works by processing information. However we think, he believes, it is not by manipulating symbols. This elusive thing called content or meaning will slip through the cracks of any formal system, not because it is flawed and could, by implication, be fixed, but because there are things about the mind that cannot be described computationally. Not all the world can be formalized.

It is an old lament: by studying the science of rainbows we ruin their beauty somehow. Light diffracting through water vapor is broken into pieces: red, orange, yellow, green, blue, indigo, and violet—each describable as a frequency, a shade on the electromagnetic scale. The opponents of artificial intelligence deny that the mind can be shattered this way. They believe, as Douglas Hofstadter whimsically wrote, that the soul is greater than "the hum of its parts," that you can't explain a thought by breaking it into pieces. Some irreducible essence will always remain—the stuff that makes us human.

Hubert Dreyfus, another Berkeley philosopher, draws on a school of philosophy called existential phenomenalism to argue that thinking cannot be reduced to computation. To Dreyfus, the world of the subjective is more important than that of the objective; reality is defined from within—in terms of the individual and his power to perceive and act, to know truths that are unutterable. Using this kind of argument Dreyfus reaches a conclusion similar to that of Searle: some of the things people do are intrinsically human and cannot be mechanized. To Searle these irreducibles are meaning, content, and the "causal powers of the brain." To Dreyfus they are intuition, insight, and comprehension—the ability to immediately grasp complex situations, resolving ambiguities, weeding the relevant from the irrelevant. All these abilities, he believes, are things that we just do; they cannot be rationally analyzed.

According to Dreyfus, the conviction that we can formalize reality, explaining everything with rules, began as far back as the days of ancient Greece and has become so dominant in the twentieth century that few people question it. With the advent of the computer, we can design formal systems so complex that we stretch their possibilities to the limit. In the ultimate act of hubris we believe that, having formalized the motions of the atoms, planets, and stars, we can now formalize the mind that did the formalizing. Dreyfus is convinced that the effort must fail, overturning the assumptions of the mainstream of philosophy and vindicating those of an opposing strain, based on ideas of Wittgenstein, Heidegger, Husserl, Merleau-Ponty, and others who hold that reality cannot be completely explained by any abstract system. According to this school of thought, our powers of reasoning are derived from the fact that we are at home in the world, that we have bodies, that we are rooted in the situations around us.

"Great artists have always sensed the truth, stubbornly denied by both philosophers and technologists, that the basis of human intelligence cannot be isolated and explicitly understood," Dreyfus wrote in his book *What Computers Can't Do*. "In *Moby-Dick* Melville writes of the tattooed savage Queequeg that he had 'written out on his body a complete theory of the heavens and the earth, and a mystical treatise on the art of attaining truth; so that Queequeg in his own proper person was a riddle to unfold; a wondrous work in one volume; but whose mysteries not even himself could read.'" Then Dreyfus quoted Yeats: "Man can embody the truth, but he cannot know it."

Dreyfus is joined in his crusade against artificial intelligence by his brother, Stuart Dreyfus, a professor of industrial engineering and operations research at Berkeley. He described their position in a presentation to the annual convention of the American Association for the Advancement of Science, which was held in Los Angeles in the spring of 1985. In an abstract of the talk (which, parodying Pamela McCorduck's book *Machines Who Think*, was called "People That (sic) Think"—the "sic" being part of the title), the brothers warned of the dangers that may befall a society whose love affair with the computer causes it to value pure reason above all else.

> The mistaken view that human skill and expertise is produced by complicated inferences drawn from masses of facts and beliefs is rooted in the thought of Socrates and Plato, was nurtured by the likes of Hobbes and Descartes, and has flowered in the era of the computer and artificial intelligence. It now permeates our society. Expert legal testimony must take the form of facts and inferences rather than experience-based intuitive judgments, although the latter are superior. Environmental impacts must be modeled, not intuitively assessed based on prior observations. If school children cannot explain why they know something, they are accused of guessing or cheating. Doctors, once trusted and admired for their wisdom, now attempt to rationalize their diagnoses and recommended therapies. Politicians impress voters, not by a record of sound judgment, but with factual knowledge and debating prowess. The list is endless.

Intuitive expertise, acquired through concrete experience, is an endangered species. We must resist the temptation to exalt calculative reason as personified by the computer. Instead, we must recognize that facts, rules and logic alone can produce neither common sense, the ability to go to the heart of a problem, or intuition, our capacity to do what works without necessarily knowing why. Only if we recognize and appreciate the unique ways in which human beings transcend any reasoning device will machines *that* think become what they rightfully are, subservient aides and assistants to people *who* think.

According to the Dreyfuses, only novices use facts and rules. When we take driver-training classes, we learn to signal when we are half a block from the intersection where we want to turn. We learn to calculate the proper distance to leave between us and the car ahead of us and to shift gears at certain speeds. But as we become expert drivers, we forget the rules and act intuitively, automatically adjusting our following distance according to speed and road conditions. We shift unconsciously by reacting to the sound of the engine, the feel of the road. We become an extension of the car. Most scientists assume that these kinds of abilities are based on the unconscious and simultaneous processing of signals coming from the eyes, the ears, and the hands. But the Dreyfuses believe that intuition defies rational powers of description, that it can't be computerized. Like judgment and wisdom it is one of the irreducibles.

In their speeches and writings, Hubert and Stuart Dreyfus raise some interesting points about the possible limits of formalizing reality. For those of us who have been steeped in the scientific tradition, it is difficult to step outside our world view and imagine that everything we believe might be wrong. It is easy for us, the keepers of Western civilization's dominant paradigm, to become smug, dismissing philosophical opponents as charlatans and mystics. It is important to have a minority to force the majority to constantly reexamine its assumptions.

Unfortunately, though, the Dreyfuses, especially Hubert, have diminished their credibility in AI circles because of the rhetoric they often use in their critiques. In 1964 Stuart, who was working for the Rand Corporation, persuaded the research institute to hire Hubert as a consultant to write a report analyzing AI from a philosopher's point of view. The result was a biting paper entitled "Alchemy and Artificial Intelligence," which was expanded into the book *What Computers Can't Do*, published in 1972 and again, in a revised edition, in 1979.

In the book, Hubert Dreyfus tries to show how existential phenomenalism can be used to refute the philosophical foundation of artificial intelligence, and, for that matter, much of Western science. It's a fascinating topic, but Dreyfus seems to spend less effort clarifying his rather obscure arguments than in ridiculing AI researchers. Minsky, whose "naïveté and faith are astonishing," makes "surprising and misleading claims" about a students' programs and engages in "the usual riot of speculation" endemic to the field. While it is instructive (and occasionally amusing) to take the overly enthusiastic predictions of AI's pioneers and compare them with what the field has accomplished so far, Dreyfus overdoes it. He is as guilty of prematurely announcing AI's death as others are of heralding its triumph. He spends page after page deriding programs for their shortcomings—ones that their inventors readily admit.

But AI researchers can be equally intolerant of the opposition. When Minsky's colleague Seymour Papert, of the MIT AI laboratory, wrote a memo about *What Computers Can't Do,* he entitled it "The Artificial Intelligence of Hubert L. Dreyfus."

* * *

Ultimately, when all the details and rhetoric are stripped away, most debates on whether or not AI is possible come down to a standoff between the reductionists and the holists—those who believe that mind can be explained as the sum of its parts, and those who believe that in any such explanation something will always elude analysis. The reductionists are excited by the possibility that what seemed ineffable—life and mind—is accessible to human inquiry. By cutting through the mystical obscurantism that has surrounded thoughts of life and soul, we will be more enlightened creatures; by freeing intelligence from its roots in the brain, we will be able to amplify it, unleash its power to shape the world in a way more beneficial to humankind. In a newspaper, photographs are reproduced by breaking them into dots, each one black or white. As the grain becomes finer and finer, the reproduction approaches a point where it is indistinguishable from the original photograph. By continuing to refine their models of thinking, the reductionists of AI believe they will eventually reach a point where a system becomes so subtle and complex that its behavior will be indistinguishable from human thought.

But perhaps thinking has no grain. Perhaps it cannot be isolated by rules and definitions, skimmed off the brain and transplanted. The holists believe that intelligence and life can never be described simply as the interaction of millions of definable functions. While Searle and the Dreyfus brothers speak philosophically of formal systems, semantics, existential phenomenalism, et cetera, their arguments seem to spring from a deep-seated, gut-level revulsion at the very suggestion that something as wonderful as a human mind might someday inhabit a computer cabinet.

They are not the first people to feel this way. In his essay "Computing Machinery and Intelligence," Alan Turing bemusedly quoted a Professor Geoffrey Jefferson, who proclaimed in a speech in 1949:

"Not until a machine can write a sonnet or compose a concerto because of thoughts and emotions felt, and not by the chance fall of symbols, could we agree that machine equals brain—that is, not only write it but know that it had written it. No mechanism could feel (and not merely artificially signal, an easy contrivance) pleasure at its successes, grief when its valves fuse, be warmed by flattery, be made miserable by its mistakes, be charmed by sex, be angry or depressed when it cannot get what it wants."

Jefferson suggests that the mind's irreducibles include creativity, consciousness, and emotions. But just as the reductionists have ready answers for those who hold that meaning and intuition are beyond the ken of computation, so they argue that there are no theoretical reasons why a machine can't know what it knows or have feelings. A computer will have consciousness as soon as we can program it with a good enough model of itself, so that it can reason about its own behavior and imagine itself in various situations. The simulation would contain its own simulation—not exact in every detail, of course, since that would lead to an infinite regress, an endless hall of mirrors. In his Society of Mind theory, Marvin Minsky shows in rich detail how the collection of software routines he calls agents—stupid homunculi that are a little like Hearsay II's experts or the "beings" in Douglas Lenat's early work— might interact to produce, through emergence, human consciousness. While agents such as SEE and GRASP know how to recognize and manipulate objects in the outside world, other agents can recognize and manipulate "objects" in the mind. Thus we can think about thinking.

What then about emotions? Could a computer ever have feelings? Could it live in fear of having its plug pulled; could it find a problem interesting or dull? If these are processes, then we should be able to program them.

In the early 1960s, while the field of artificial intelligence was just beginning, psychiatrist and computer scientist Kenneth Colby was already studying artificial neurosis. One of his early programs roughly simulated the belief system of a young woman who couldn't accept the fact that she hated her father because she believed he had abandoned her. Her repertoire of canned beliefs also included the following: "Mother is helpless," "I am defective," "I descend from royalty," "I must not marry a poor man," "I must love people," "I must love father." These beliefs, and many others, were stored in the computer's memory; each was coded with a "charge," or number describing how emotionally potent and threatening it was. The woman's overall mental state was also quantified and indicated by several "monitors," numerical scales that measured such qualities as self-esteem, well-being, and anxiety.

Once the program started running it would free associate, trying to discharge its highly negative beliefs by expressing them and thus reducing the reading on its anxiety scale. But the most negative beliefs were too threatening to admit, so the program tried to alter them into milder forms, which carried lower charges. By employing various neurotic mechanisms, it created distorted beliefs. Using deflection (as well as a subroutine called FIND-ANALOG), "I hate father" became "I hate the boss." Or, using other devices, hating father could be weakened to "I see faults in father" or "I couldn't care less about father." Through the mechanism of rationalization, the belief would become "Yes, I dislike father—because he abandoned me long ago." Using reversal it would become "I love father." Or, through reflection, "I hate myself" and, through projection, "Father hates me." Which defense mechanism was chosen depended on the current readings of the program's various emotional scales. For example, "I dislike father" could be expressed only if the program was at a fairly low anxiety level. In turn, each defense mechanism varied in how it affected anxiety, well-being, and self-esteem. As the program ran, the readings on the scales would rise and fall, beliefs accumulated charges, dissipated them, spawned distortions—all in a rough simulation of a person fighting with a mind she can't control.

The artificial neurotic was a forerunner to Colby's more renowned and sophisticated program, Parry, the artificial paranoid. Both systems were attempts to use computers to study the structures of mental illness and to suggest ways that programs might someday serve as "patients" to analysts-in-training, allowing them to make their mistakes on machines, which are more easily reprogrammed than people. More important, the programs represented a new kind of psychological theory—a dynamic model that could be run, observed, and refined until it provided a closer and closer approximation to what seemed to be happening in human minds.

Another step in the modeling of emotions and beliefs was taken by Robert Abelson, a social psychologist and a colleague of Roger Schank at Yale. Abelson used AI techniques to study the mechanisms of political belief. In the late 1960s, he wrote a program called the Ideology Machine, a simulation of the belief system of a right-wing ideologue. The program, often referred to as the Goldwater machine, contained a network of concepts such as "Communist nations," "left-leaning neutrals," "Free World Nations," "liberal dupes," and "good Americans." Paraphrased, the ideology Abelson coded into the system went like this:

"The Communists want to dominate the world and are continually using Communist schemes to bring this about; these schemes when successful bring Communist victories which will eventually fulfill their ultimate purpose; if on the other hand the Free World really uses its power, then Communist schemes will surely fail, and thus their ultimate purpose will be thwarted. However, the misguided policies of liberal dupes result in inhibition of full use of Free World power; therefore it is necessary to enlighten all good Americans with the facts so that they may expose and overturn these misguided liberal policies."

When the program was asked what would happen if Communists attacked Thailand, it replied: "If Communists attack Thailand, Communists take over unprepared nations unless Thailand ask-aid-from United States and United States give-aid-to Thailand." The program clearly lacked Goldwater's oratorical skills, but it was an interesting experiment in using computers to simulate the thought processes of the True Believer and study what Abelson called "the human penchant for interposing oversimplified symbol systems between themselves and the external world."

About a decade after Abelson designed his Goldwater machine, Jaime Carbonell, a student of Roger Schank's, wrote a more advanced program called Politics, which could simulate both conservative and liberal points of view. The system was based on Schank and Abelson's work on scripts, goals, and plans as expressed in the PTRANSs, MTRANSs, et cetera, of conceptual-dependency theory. Instead of a restaurant script, Politics contained scripts with such titles as "Confrontation" and "Invade," as well as a knowledge of some of the geopolitical goals a nation might have. It also was armed with if-then rules: "If a new weapon system is built by some agency of the armed forces of country X, then the military power of X will increase"; "To stop actor X from accomplishing his goal G(X) see if there is any goal G(A) which is mutually exclusive with G(X). If so, give high priority to accomplishing G(A)."

In one experiment, the program was set to mimic a conservative and told, "Russia massed troops on the Czech border." Then it was asked to explain why. "Because Russia thought that it could take political control of Czechoslovakia by sending troops," the program replied. "What should the United States do?" it was asked. "The United States should intervene militarily." In liberal mode, the program answered the same question like this: "The United States should denounce the Russian action to the UN."

While it is difficult to decide whether a simulation of thinking really thinks, it seems fairly clear that these simulated emotions don't feel. The programs are, as Professor Jefferson would say, "artificially signaling." Nothing happened during Parry's childhood to make it paranoid; the artificial neurotic doesn't really have a father to hate. The beliefs expressed by Politics aren't rooted in a concern for survival. The programs each contain a crude approximation of a tiny corner of a human belief system. The "emotions" are preprogrammed imitations of those that people have. (And yet, how many ideologues, right and left, are responding to rigid, patterned belief systems programmed into them through books and magazines or by forceful, charismatic leaders?)

Still, these programs suggest that emotions can be thought of as mechanisms, more gears in the machinery of the mind. After all, we can always make the simulations finer, including in the programs a more densely drawn semantic network with more general knowledge of the world. Then the artificial neurotic would know the connotations attached to "father" and "mother" and what it means for a human to love, hate, or feel pain. If we are ever able to make computers sophisticated enough to work with us as companions and colleagues, this kind of knowledge probably would be essential. Still, without a body to be caressed or beaten or to feel hunger or desire, without a social structure in which to feel acceptance or rejection, all that the machine knew about human emotions would be secondhand.

Perhaps a more interesting question is whether a computer could exhibit emotions of its own. Using Schankian structures like goals, plans, scripts, et cetera, a generally intelligent program might be given rules similar to Isaac Asimov's mythical laws of robotics:

1. A robot may not injure a human being, or through inaction allow a human being to come to harm.
2. A robot must obey the orders given it by human beings except where such orders would conflict with the First Law.
3. A robot must protect its own existence as long as such protection does not conflict with the First or Second Law.

Now, what if the machine couldn't get the data it needed to carry out its master's order? Could it be said to feel frustrated? Or suppose that the system was ordered to devise an industrial policy that, according to its own calculations, would raise the nation's Gross National Product by five percentage points annually over the next decade but would indirectly cause, through increased pollution, three more lung-cancer deaths per million people per year. Thou shalt not kill, but on the other hand, improving the economy would increase employment and the general health and well-being of the people, indirectly saving lives. As it thrashed back and forth, weighing costs and benefits (drawing perhaps on preprogrammed moral precepts), could the computer be said to be "pondering" the decision, to be caught on the horns of a dilemma? A reductionist would say yes, provided the program is sophisticated enough. A holist would say no, never, impossible.

Or perhaps computer emotions wouldn't be things that were intentionally put into the machine. Instead, they would be unpredictable, complex interactions—qualities and quirks that arose through emergence, through the combination of millions of different processes. Emotions like these might seem as foreign to us as ours would to a machine. We might not even have names for them.

As one speculates, performing one thought experiment after another, it becomes clear that for any objection a holist poses—a machine can never be intelligent because it can't do X—a reductionist will always have a ready answer: Yes, but X can be simulated. And the holist will reject the answer out of hand. A computer will never have free will. But what do we mean by that? Perhaps free will is simply a term we use to explain decisions so complex or irrational that we have difficulty grasping how they came to be made. From the outside, a complex expert system might seem to exhibit free will when it made a decision based on so many logical inferences that a human couldn't untangle them all. But still, the holist would reply, it makes that decision because it must. It has no choice. Its behavior, no matter how unfathomable, is still predetermined by the architecture of the program and the machine. So, what if we add a random element so the program will occasionally act on a whim? No, the holist would say, that's not what I meant at all. Machines, by definition, cannot have free will—or emotions, consciousness, intuition, wisdom, judgment, understanding, causal powers of the brain. Even if we someday succeed in making a computer that writes symphonies as great as Beethoven's or plays as moving as Shakespeare's, a holist would always object that it is "artificially signaling."

When people argue across a chasm, there is no middle ground.

STUDY QUESTIONS

1. What is the parable of the Chinese room? What does Searle attempt to establish with it?

2. What is the Turing test? If a computer passes this test, why does Searle insist that it still does not actually think?
3. What is a homunculus? How does one figure into the discussion in this article?
4. What is "reductionism"? What is "holism"? If Descartes and Hume were alive, which position would each embrace?
5. What does it mean to say, as Searle does, that minds are "semantical" and not merely "syntactical"?
6. The Dreyfuses claim that *intuition* cannot be computerized. What is intuition? Give some examples of intuitions which you have had recently.

5

Perception and Knowledge

PROBLEM INTRODUCTION

In 1610 Galileo turned the newly invented telescope toward the heavens. This proved to be his own undoing as well as that of the traditional theory of the cosmos, in which the earth was the center of the universe. Twenty-three years later, the Church would accuse him of heresy for his scientific views, and Galileo would live out his life under house arrest. But by then the damage was done and nothing could save the old system.

Aristotle had said that the heavenly bodies were incorruptible and perfect. But Galileo saw irregularities in the surface of the moon. It looked more like a mountainous desert than a perfect sphere. He discovered the moons of Jupiter and saw that not everything revolved around the earth. But the crowning blow came when he discovered that the phases of Venus could not be explained by the old system, but fit the new Copernican theory nicely. Yet if Copernicus was right, humanity's special place in the universe seemed threatened. Thus the telescope told a revolutionary story—the heavens were not perfect, human beings were not at the center of things, and, worst of all, there might be countless worlds beyond the old familiar ones.

Galileo published his work and invited the intellectual world to confirm his observations. The reaction was hostile. A certain professor of philosophy at the University of Padua refused to look through the telescope. In mocking words he announced that logic alone could refute Galileo. Logic alone could prove that Jupiter had no moons, that the earth was the center of the universe, and therefore that Galileo had been tricked by his new "toy." As he put it:

> There are seven windows given to animals in the domicile of the head....From this and many other similarities in nature, such as the seven metals,...we gather that the number of planets is necessarily seven. Moreover these (supposed) satellites of Jupiter are invisible to the naked eye, and therefore can exercise no influence on the earth, and therefore would be useless, and therefore do not exist. Besides (from the earliest times) men have adopted the division of the week into seven days, and named them after the seven planets. Now if we

171

increase the number of planets, this whole and beautiful system falls to
the ground.

To us this argument sounds incredible, but to many of Galileo's contemporaries it made perfectly good sense. Some things are just obviously true, and
if it comes to a choice between the obvious and experience, the sober person
chooses the obvious. This attitude is, of course, the death of curiosity. The
professor's attitude was rooted in classical Greek philosophy, which, in its
own day, represented the full flowering of the ancient mind.

In the latter half of the fifth century B.C., Greek science was developing
apace. From early, vague speculations, thinkers were now beginning to construct definite physical theories to explain events which heretofore had been
treated with great religious caution. One scientist had the audacity to suggest
that the sun was a hot rock instead of a god. Democritus constructed an atomic
theory in which he claimed that all reality was composed of tiny, unobservable
atoms. The atoms possessed the qualities of size and shape, but not the familiar qualities of color, smell, hot or cold, or taste. These latter properties
were subjective products of the perceiving mind, and not reliable sources of
truth. To some thinkers this presented a dilemma. If the ordinary world of
perception is nothing more than a subjective impression, how could anyone
ever go beyond this to the hidden reality. Protagoras, a famous teacher of the
age, announced that indeed completely objective knowledge is impossible.
When he said, "Man is the measure of all things," he certainly meant this to
cover religion and ethics. This was too much for the Athenians, and in 411
Protagoras was accused of impiety and his books were ordered burned. The
Athenians were in no mood to be gracious, for they were losing their long war
with Sparta, and the times demanded the virtues of obedience and complete
commitment. To alienate the gods at this moment meant destruction.

But the seed has been sown and nothing could have remained the same.
The relativism of Protagoras struck home in an era of increasing disillusion-
ment. In the midst of this turmoil, Plato formulated a theory designed to preserve objective knowledge. In effect, Plato agreed that the shifting impressions of sense perception could not provide a foundation for knowledge. The
objective order must lie beyond the world of perception, but it must make
sense of the world we perceive. Plato's model for a system of knowledge is the
science of geometry. What impressed Plato about geometry is the fact that the
truths discovered are not about some particular physical object, but rather are
about the form which is displayed in many things. The Pythagorean theorem,
for example, says that in a right triangle the sum of the squares of the two sides
is equal to the square of the hypotenuse. This is not a truth about some particular right triangle, but a truth about the *idea* of right-triangularity. Nor is it
a truth which is discovered by measuring various physical triangles, since clearly
no physical triangle exactly fits the bill. The mind, by itself, has the power to
see the *form* or the *idea* of right-triangularity which is manifested in many different physical triangles. Plato extends this way of thinking to all knowledge.

The world of sense is a world of flux and change which the mind must penetrate to discover the forms or ideas which lie in a realm beyond space and time. Thus, for Plato knowledge does not come from the perceptual world, nor is it fundamentally concerned with the perceptual world. Knowledge comes from the intuitions of the mind as it sees forms or ideas manifested in the flux of sensation.

Plato's conception of knowledge is a paradigm of the theory known as *rationalism.* The rationalist attributes innate powers to the mind which make it capable of discovering the nature of things by directly intuiting reality itself, bypassing the world of appearance and sensation. The dangers in such a view should be manifest. In the mind of a sloppy thinker, it is extremely easy to confuse fantasy or authority with indubitable intuition. Thus we return to the professor who refused to look through Galileo's telescope. His attitude is Platonic to the extent that he believes that the nature of reality can be discovered by the logical mind alone, but it is a corrupted form of Platonism because his logic is a mere reflection of the biases of his era.

With the development of modern science, Plato's form of rationalism seemed inconsistent with the new experimental attitude. Experience, rather than innate mental powers, was considered the source of knowledge. This new attitude toward experience was called *empiricism.* The empirical attitude was no doubt exacerbated by the fact that "logic" always seemed to be on the side of tradition and authority. Galileo found it necessary to reintroduce Democritus's distinction between kinds of qualities which objects have. Being a physicist, he claimed that the real properties of objects were those which could be measured. Such properties as velocity, shape, size, and weight were called *primary qualities.* Qualities such as color, smell, hot and cold, taste, and sound were called *secondary,* indicating their subjective character. Thus science seemed to agree with Plato that the world of sense was mere appearance, but unlike Plato, science used the familiar experienced world as the primary source for discovering the real qualities of things.

While most scientists accepted Galileo's distinction between primary and secondary qualities, it was undermined by the empiricist tradition itself. Bishop Berkeley, an eighteenth-century empiricist, brought out the hidden dilemma. If all knowledge is based on experience, and if science is correct in saying that the familiar world of experience is quite different from the real world, then how is it possible to discover the so-called real world? Berkeley's conclusion was at once reasonable and paradoxical: The real world, the only world we can know about, is the world of experience. But the qualities we experience are mental, and thus the world is mental. Samuel Johnson tried to refute Berkeley by kicking a rock, but according to Berkeley all he succeeded in doing was to make his mental image of the rock and his mental image of his foot come together, probably causing a painful sensation as well.

Needless to say, Berkeley did not find many followers, but his unusual theory provoked a period of skepticism. This skepticism found its most able spokesman in David Hume, a gentle Scot with one of the most analytic minds in history. Hume believed that all ideas were but faint remainders of past sensations and that knowledge had to be confined to what was experienced. Thus the existence of God, the external world, and even the soul became suspect. These things could not be directly experienced and hence could not be known. Turning his gaze toward science, Hume declared that even the relation between cause and effect could not stand up under examination. We believe that between the cause and the effect there is some necessary connection, making the effect inevitable upon the occurrence of the cause. But close examination of experience shows that we never perceive such a necessary connection, and hence we are not entitled to assume that there is one. Since casual laws form the basis for predicting future events, Hume would say that we have no grounds for assuming that the future will be like the past, or that the laws which worked yesterday will work today. This part of science is prejudice, because it goes beyond what can be experienced.

Hume's influence has been significant. Even today many people believe that only if science keeps its conclusions directly related to what can be measured and observed will any sort of secure system of knowledge arise. Many would claim to follow Hume to the letter, but their practice puts the lie to the claim. In every area of science, the pursuit of knowledge depends upon theories which rest on precious little, if any, factual evidence. This is one of the points emphasized by Morris R. Cohen and Ernest Nagel in the final reading on perception and knowledge. These two twentieth-century philosophers describe scientific method as scientists actually practice it. They point out that the advance of knowledge often relies on imaginative hypotheses that reflect hunches more than facts. "Facts," they say, are not given immediately in experience, but are the outcome of analysis and interpretation of experience. Cohen and Nagel subscribe neither to Plato's confidence that man can achieve certainty nor to Hume's contention that we can know virtually nothing. They would claim that knowledge is fallible—liable to error—but nevertheless reliable when achieved by following scientific method.

The Role of Perception in Knowing
Plato

Plato (c. 427 B.C.–c. 347 B.C.) came from one of the most distinguished families in Athens. He was certain to become a great politician, but he gave up this ambition in disgust at the unjust trial of Socrates, his friend and teacher. After the execution of Socrates in 399, Plato traveled extensively, convinced that Athens had abandoned its ancient ideals of justice. During these travels, he wrote several dialogues on philosophy, using the character of his friend Socrates to exemplify the dialectical process of question and answer. His philosophical powers increasing, Plato returned to Athens and formed a school, the Academy, which soon became the intellectual center of Greece. Many great mathematicians and scientists studied at the Academy, including Aristotle.

The first selection is from the *Theaetetus,* a dialogue named after an important member of the Academy who discovered solid geometry. In this dialogue the theory of Protagoras, a skeptic who claimed that knowledge was subjective, is examined. Socrates and Theaetetus come to the conclusion that knowledge requires an active mind, which must go beyond passive sense perception. How is it possible then? How does one go beyond the evidence of the senses? In the second selection—from the *Republic,* Plato's great masterpiece—his answer is given. Knowledge is never concerned with physical objects but rather with forms or ideas. These abstract objects can be known by the power of the mind alone, but it requires great effort to penetrate the illusions of perception. "The Allegory of the Cave" depicts the struggle to reach the realm of ideas. This famous story exerted a major influence on early Christian thinkers such as St. Augustine, because it seemed to correspond to the believer's search for God.

KNOWLEDGE AS PERCEPTION

SOCRATES: . . . So, Theaetetus, try to explain what knowledge is. Never say it is beyond your power; it will not be so, if heaven wills [it] and you take courage.

THEAETETUS: Well, Socrates, with such encouragement from a person like you, it would be a shame not to do one's best to say what one can. It seems to me that one who knows something is perceiving the thing he knows, and, so far as I can see at present, knowledge is nothing but perception.

SOCRATES: Good. That is the right spirit in which to express one's opinion. But now suppose we examine your offspring together and see whether it is a mere wind egg or has some life in it. Perception, you say, is knowledge.

From "The Theaetetus," in *Plato's Theory of Knowledge,* translated and with commentary by F. M. Cornford. First published in 1935 by Routledge & Kegan Paul, Ltd. (London), and reprinted with their permission.

THEAETETUS: Yes.

SOCRATES: The account you give of the nature of knowledge is not, by any means, to be despised. It is the same that was given by Protagoras though he stated it in a somewhat different way. He says you will remember, that "man is the measure of all things—alike of the being of things that are and of the not-being of things that are not." No doubt you have read that.

THEAETETUS: Yes often.

SOCRATES: He puts it in this sort of way, doesn't he, that any given thing "is to me such as it appears to me, and is to you such as it appears to you," you and I being men?

THEAETETUS: Yes that is how he puts it.

SOCRATES: Well, what a wise man says is not likely to be nonsense. So let us follow up his meaning. Sometimes, when the same wind is blowing, one of us feels chilly, the other does not, or one may feel slightly chilly, the other quite cold.

THEAETETUS: Certainly.

SOCRATES: Well, in that case are we to say that the wind in itself is cold or not cold? Or shall we agree with Protagoras that it is cold to the one who feels chilly, and not to the other?

THEAETETUS: That seems reasonable.

SOCRATES: And further that it so "appears" to each of us?

THEAETETUS: Yes.

SOCRATES: And "appears" means that he "perceives" it so?

THEAETETUS: True.

SOCRATES: "Appearing," then, is the same thing as "perceiving," in the case of what is hot or anything of that kind. They *are* to each man such as he *perceives* them.

THEAETETUS: So it seems.

SOCRATES: Perception, then, is always of something that *is*, and, as being knowledge, it is infallible.

THEAETETUS: That is clear....

SOCRATES: Well then, Theaetetus, here is a point for you to consider. The answer you gave was that knowledge is perception, wasn't it?

THEAETETUS: Yes.

SOCRATES: Now suppose you were asked, When a man sees white or black things or hears high or low tones, what does he see or hear with? I suppose you would say with eyes and ears.

THEAETETUS: Yes, I should.

SOCRATES: To use words and phrases in an easygoing way without scrutinizing them too curiously is not, in general, a mark of ill breeding; on the contrary there is something lowbred in being too precise. But sometimes there is no help for it, and this is a case in which I must take exception to the form of your answer. Consider. Is it more correct to say that we see and hear *with* our eyes and ears or *through* them?

THEAETETUS: I should say we always <u>perceive through them</u>, rather than with them.

SOCRATES: Yes, it would surely be strange that there should be a number of senses ensconced inside us, like the warriors in the Trojan horse, and all these things should not converge and meet in some single nature—a mind, or whatever it is to be called—*with* which we perceive all the objects of perception *through* the senses as instruments.

THEAETETUS: Yes, I think that is a better description.

SOCRATES: My object in being so precise is to know whether there is some part of ourselves, the same in all cases, with which we apprehend black or white through the eyes, and objects of other kinds through the other senses. Can you, if the question is put to you, refer all such acts of apprehension to the body? Perhaps, however, it would be better you should speak for yourself in reply to questions, instead of my taking the words out of your mouth. Tell me, all these instruments through which you perceive what is warm or hard or light or sweet are parts of the body, aren't they, not of anything else?

THEAETETUS: Of nothing else.

SOCRATES: Now you will also agree that the objects you perceive through one faculty cannot be perceived through another—objects of hearing, for instance, through sights, or objects of sight through hearing?

THEAETETUS: Of course I will.

SOCRATES: Then, if you have some thought about both objects at once, you cannot be having a perception including both at once through either the one or the other organ.

THEAETETUS: No.

SOCRATES: Now take sound and color. Have you not, to begin with, this thought which includes both at once—that they both exist.

THEAETETUS: I have.

SOCRATES: And, further, that each of the two is *different* from the other and the *same* as itself?

THEAETETUS: Naturally.

SOCRATES: And again, that both together are *two*, and each of them is *one?*

THEAETETUS: Yes.

SOCRATES: And also you can ask yourself whether they are *unlike* each other or *alike?*

THEAETETUS: No doubt.

SOCRATES: Then through what organ do you think all this about them both? What is common to them both cannot be apprehended either through hearing or through sight. Besides, here is further evidence for my point. Suppose it were possible to inquire whether sound and color were both brackish or not; no doubt you could tell me what faculty you would use—obviously not sight or hearing, but some other.

THEAETETUS: Of course, the faculty that works through the tongue.

SOCRATES: Very good. But now, through what organ does that faculty work, which tells you what is common not only to these objects but to all things— what you mean by the words "exists" and "does not exist" and the other terms applied to them in the questions I put a moment ago? What sort of organs can you mention, corresponding to all these terms, through which the perceiving part of us perceives each one of them?

THEAETETUS: You mean existence and nonexistence, likeness and unlikeness, sameness and difference, and also unity and numbers in general as applied to them, and clearly your question covers "even" and "odd" and all that kind of notions. You are asking through what part of the body our mind perceives these?

SOCRATES: You follow me most admirably, Theaetetus; that is exactly my question.

THEAETETUS: Really, Socrates, I could not say, except that I think there is no special organ at all for these things, as there is for the others. It is clear to me that the mind in itself is its own instrument for contemplating the common terms that apply to everything.

SOCRATES: In fact, Theaetetus, you are handsome, not ugly as Theodorus said you were, for in a discussion handsome is that handsome does. And you have treated me more than handsomely in saving me the trouble of a very long argument, if it is clear to you that the mind contemplates some things through its own instrumentality, others through the bodily faculties. That was indeed what I thought myself, but I wanted you to agree.

THEAETETUS: Well, it is clear to me.

SOCRATES: Under which head, then, do you place existence? For that is, above all, a thing that belongs to everything.

THEAETETUS: I should put it among the things that the mind apprehends by itself.

SOCRATES: And also likeness and unlikeness and sameness and difference?

THEAETETUS: Yes.

SOCRATES: And how about "honorable" and "dishonorable" and "good" and "bad"?

THEAETETUS: Those again seem to me, above all, to be things whose being is considered one in comparison with another, by the mind, when it reflects within itself upon the past and the present with an eye to the future.

SOCRATES: Wait a moment. The hardness of something hard and the softness of something soft will be perceived by the mind through touch, will they not?

THEAETETUS: Yes.

SOCRATES: But their existence and the fact that they both exist and their contrariety to one another and again the existence of this contrariety are things which the mind itself undertakes to judge for us, when it reflects upon them and compares one with another.

THEAETETUS: Certainly.

SOCRATES: Is it not true, then, that whereas all the impressions which penetrate to the mind through the body are things which men and animals alike are naturally constituted to perceive from the moment of birth, reflections about them with respect to their existence and usefulness only come, if they come at all, with difficulty through a long and troublesome process of education?

THEAETETUS: Assuredly.

SOCRATES: Is it possible, then, to reach truth when one cannot reach existence?

THEAETETUS: It is impossible.

SOCRATES: But if a man cannot reach the truth of a thing, can he possibly know that thing?

THEAETETUS: No, Socrates, how could he?

SOCRATES: If that is so, knowledge does not reside in the impressions, but in our reflection upon them. It is there, seemingly, and not in the impressions, that it is possible to grasp existence and truth.

THEAETETUS: Evidently.

SOCRATES: Then are you going to give the same name to two things which differ so widely?

THEAETETUS: Surely that would not be right.

SOCRATES: Well then, what name do you give to the first one—to seeing, hearing, smelling, feeling cold and feeling warm?

THEAETETUS: Perceiving. What other name is there for it?

SOCRATES: Taking it all together, then, you call this perception?

THEAETETUS: Necessarily.

SOCRATES: A thing which, we agree, has no part in apprehending truth, since it has none in apprehending existence.

THEAETETUS: No, it has none.

SOCRATES: Nor, consequently, in knowledge either.

THEAETETUS: No.

SOCRATES: Then, Theaetetus, perception and knowledge cannot possibly be the same thing.

THEAETETUS: Evidently not, Socrates. Indeed, it is now perfectly plain that knowledge is something different from perception.

SOCRATES: But when we began our talk it was certainly not our object to find out what knowledge is not, but what it is. Still, we have advanced so far as to see that we must not look for it in sense perception at all, but in what goes on when the mind is occupied with things by itself, whatever name you give to that.

THEAETETUS: Well, Socrates, the name for that, I imagine, is "making judgments."

SOCRATES: You are right, my friend. Now begin all over again. Blot out all we have been saying, and see if you can get a clearer view from the position you have now reached. Tell us once more what knowledge is.

THEAETETUS: I cannot say it is judgment as a whole, because there is false judgment, but perhaps true judgment is knowledge. You may take that as

my answer. If, as we go further, it turns out to be less convincing than it
seems now, I will try to find another.

SOCRATES: Good, Theaetetus. This promptness is much better than hanging
back as you did at first. If we go on like this, either we shall find what we
are after or we shall be less inclined to imagine we know something of
which we know nothing whatever, and that surely is a reward not to be
despised. And now, what is this you say—that there are two sorts of judgment, one true, the other false, and you define knowledge as judgment that
is true?...

KNOWLEDGE AS TRUE BELIEF

THEAETETUS: ...True belief is knowledge. Surely there can at least be no mistake in believing what is true, and the consequences are always satisfactory.

SOCRATES: Try, and you will see, Theaetetus, as the man said when he was
asked if the river was too deep to ford. So here, if we go forward on our
search, we may stumble upon something that will reveal the thing we are
looking for. We shall make nothing out, if we stay where we are.

THEAETETUS: True. Let us go forward and see.

SOCRATES: Well, we need not go far to see this much. You will find a whole
profession to prove that true belief is not knowledge.

THEAETETUS: How so? What profession?

SOCRATES: The profession of those paragons of intellect known as orators and
lawyers. There you have men who use their skill to produce conviction, not
by instruction, but by making people believe whatever they want them to
believe. You can hardly imagine teachers so clever as to be able, in the short
time allowed by the clock, to instruct their hearers thoroughly in the true
facts of a case of robbery or other violence which those hearers had not
witnessed.

THEAETETUS: No, I cannot imagine that, but they can convince them.

SOCRATES: And by convincing you mean making them believe something.

THEAETETUS: Of course.

SOCRATES: And when a jury is rightly convinced of facts which can be known
only by an eyewitness, then, judging by hearsay and accepting a true belief,
they are judging without knowledge, although if they find the right verdict,
their conviction is correct?

THEAETETUS: Certainly.

SOCRATES: But if true belief and knowledge were the same thing, the best of
jurymen could never have a correct belief without knowledge. It now appears that they must be different things....

Socrates & Glaucon

THE OBJECTS OF KNOWLEDGE

(Socrates is conversing with Glaucon.)

...Let me remind you of the distinction we drew earlier and have often drawn on other occasions,[1] between the multiplicity of things that we call good or beautiful or whatever it may be and, on the other hand, Goodness itself or Beauty itself and so on. Corresponding to each of these sets of many things, we postulate a single Form or real essence, as we call it.

Yes, that is so.

Further, the many things, we say, can be seen, but are not objects of rational thought; whereas the <u>Forms</u> <u>are objects of thought, but invisible</u>.

Yes, certainly.

And we see things with our eyesight, just as we hear sounds with our ears and, to speak generally, perceive any sensible thing with our sense-faculties.

Of course.

Have you noticed, then, that the artificer who designed the senses has been exceptionally lavish of his materials in making the eyes able to see and their objects visible?

That never occurred to me.

Well, look at it in this way. Hearing and sound do not stand in need of any third thing, without which the ear will not hear nor sound be heard;[2] and I think the same is true of most, not to say all, of the other senses. Can you think of one that does require anything of the sort?

No, I cannot.

But there is this need in the case of sight and its objects. You may have the power of vision in your eyes and try to use it, and color may be there in the objects; but sight will see nothing and the colors will remain invisible in the absence of a third thing peculiarly constituted to serve this very purpose.

By which you mean—?

Naturally I mean what you call <u>light</u>; and if light is a thing of value, the sense of sight and the power of being visible are linked together by a very precious bond, such as unites no other sense with its object.

No one could say that light is not a precious thing.

And of all the divinities in the skies[3] is there one whose light, above all the rest, is responsible for making our eyes see perfectly and making objects perfectly visible?

From *The Republic of Plato,* translated by F. M. Cornford (1941). Reprinted by permission of Oxford University Press.

[1] Perhaps an allusion to the *Phaedo* (especially 78 E ff.), where the theory of Forms was first explicitly stated in similar terms. The earlier passage in the *Republic* is at 475 E ff., p. 179.

[2] Plato held that the hearing of sound is caused by blows inflicted by the air (*Timaeus* 67 B, 80 A); but the air is hardly analogous to light.

[3] Plato held that the heavenly bodies are immortal living creatures, i.e. gods.

There can be no two opinions; of course you mean the Sun.

And how is sight related to this deity? Neither sight nor the eye which contains it is the sun, but of all the sense-organs it is the most sun-like; and further, the power it possesses is dispensed by the Sun, like a stream flooding the eye.[4] And again, the Sun is not vision, but it is the cause of vision and also is seen by the vision it causes.

Yes.

It was the Sun, then, that I meant when I spoke of that offspring which the Good has created in the visible world, to stand there in the same relation to vision and visible things as that which the Good itself bears in the intelligible world to intelligence and to intelligible objects.

How is that? You must explain further.

You know what happens when the colors of things are no longer irradiated by the daylight, but only by the fainter luminaries of the night; when you look at them, the eyes are dim and seem almost blind, as if there were no unclouded vision in them. But when you look at things on which the Sun is shining, the same eyes see distinctly and it becomes evident that they do contain the power of vision.

Certainly.

Apply this comparison, then, to the soul. When its gaze is fixed upon an object irradiated by truth and reality, the soul gains understanding and knowledge and is manifestly in possession of intelligence. But when it looks towards that twilight world of things that come into existence and pass away, its sight is dim and it has only opinions and beliefs which shift to and fro, and it seems like a thing that has no intelligence.

That is true.

This, then, which gives to the objects of knowledge their truth and to him who knows them his power of knowing, is the Form or essential nature of Goodness. It is the cause of knowledge and truth; and so, while you may think of it as an object of knowledge, you will do well to regard it as something beyond truth and knowledge and, precious as these both are, of still higher worth. And, just as in our analogy light and vision were to be thought of as like the Sun, but not identical with it, so here both knowledge and truth are to be regarded as like the Good, but to identify either with the Good is wrong. The Good must hold a yet higher place of honor.

You are giving it a position of extraordinary splendour, if it is the source of knowledge and truth and itself surpasses them in worth. You surely cannot mean that it is pleasure.

Heaven forbid, I exclaimed. But I want to follow up our analogy still

---

[4] Plato's theory of vision involves three kinds of fire or light: (1) daylight, a body of pure fire diffused in the air by the Sun; (2) the visual current or "vision," a pure fire similar to daylight, contained in the eyeball and capable of issuing out in a stream direct toward the object seen: (3) the colour of the external object, "a flame streaming off from every body, having particles proportioned to those of the visual current, so as to yield sensation" when the two streams meet and coalesce (*Timaeus* 45 B, 67 C).

further. You will agree that the Sun not only makes the things we see visible, but also brings them into existence and gives them growth and nourishment; yet he is not the same thing as existence.[5] And so with the objects of knowledge; these derive from the Good not only their power of being known, but their very being and reality; and Goodness is not the same thing as being, but even beyond being, surpassing it is dignity and power.

Glaucon exclaimed with some amusement at my exalting Goodness in such extravagant terms.

It is your fault, I replied; you forced me to say what I think.

Yes, and you must not stop there. At any rate, complete your comparison with the Sun, if there is any more to be said.

There is a great deal more, I answered.

Let us hear it, then; don't leave anything out.

I am afraid much must be left unspoken. However, I will not, if I can help it, leave anything that can be said on this occasion.

Please do not.

FOUR STAGES OF COGNITION. THE LINE

Conceive, then, that there are these two powers I speak of, the Good reigning over the domain of all that is intelligible, the Sun over the visible world—or the heaven as I might call it; only you would think I was showing off my skill in etymology.[6] At any rate you have these two orders of things clearly before your mind: the visible and the intelligible?

I have.

Now take a line divided into two unequal parts, one to represent the visible order, the other the intelligible; and divide each part again in the same proportion, symbolizing degrees of comparative clearness or obscurity. Then (A) one of the two sections in the visible world will stand for images. By images I mean first shadows, and then reflections in water or in close-grained, polished surfaces, and everything of that kind, if you understand.

Yes, I understand.

Let the second section (B) stand for the actual things of which the first are likenesses, the living creatures about us and all the works of nature or of human hands.

So be it.

Will you also take the proportion in which the visible world has been divided as corresponding to degrees of reality and truth, so that the likeness

[5] The ambiguity of *genesis* can hardly be reproduced. The Sun "gives things their *genesis*" (generation, birth), but "is not itself *genesis*" (becoming, the existence in time of things which begin and cease to exist, as opposed to the real being of eternal things in the intelligible world).

[6] Some connected the word for heaven...with [the word meaning] "to see" (*Cratylus* 396 B). It is sometimes used for the whole of the visible universe.

shall stand to the original in the same ratio as the sphere of appearances and belief to the sphere of knowledge?

Certainly.

Now consider how we are to divide the part which stands for the intelligible world. There are two sections. In the first (C) the mind uses as images those actual things which themselves had images in the visible world; and it is compelled to pursue its inquiry by starting from assumptions and travelling, not up to a principle, but down to a conclusion. In the second (D) the mind moves in the other direction, from an assumption up towards a principle which is not hypothetical; and it makes no use of the images employed in the other section, but only of Forms, and conducts its inquiry solely by their means.

I don't quite understand what you mean.

Then we will try again; what I have just said will help you to understand. (C) You know, of course, how students of subjects like geometry and arithmetic begin by postulating odd and even numbers, or the various figures and the three kinds of angle, and other such data in each subject. These data they take as known; and, having adopted them as assumptions, they do not feel called upon to give any account of them to themselves or to anyone else, but treat them as self-evident. Then, starting from these assumptions, they go on until they arrive, by a series of consistent steps, at all the conclusions they set out to investigate.

Yes, I know that.

You also know how they make use of visible figures and discourse about them, though what they really have in mind is the originals of which these figures are images; they are not reasoning, for instance, about this particular square and diagonal which they have drawn, but about *the* Square and *the* Diagonal; and so in all cases. The diagrams they draw and the models they make are actual things, which may have their shadows or images in water; but now they serve in their turn as images, while the student is seeking to behold those realities which only thought can apprehend.[7]

True.

This, then, is the class of things that I spoke of as intelligible, but with two qualifications: first, that the mind, in studying them, is compelled to employ assumptions, and, because it cannot rise above these, does not travel upwards to a first principle; and second, that it uses as images those actual things which have images of their own in the section below them and which, in comparison with those shadows and reflections, are reputed to be more palpable and valued accordingly.

I understand; you mean the procedure of geometry and of the kindred arts.

(D) Then by the second section of the intelligible world you may under-

---

[7] Conversely, the fact that the mathematician can use visible objects as illustrations indicates that the realities and truths of mathematics are embodied, though imperfectly, in the world of visible and tangible things; whereas the counterparts of the moral Forms can only be beheld by thought.

stand me to mean all that unaided reasoning apprehends by the power of dialectic, when it treats its assumptions, not as first principles, but as *hypotheses* in the literal sense, things "laid down" like a flight of steps up which it may mount all the way to something that is not hypothetical, the first principle of all; and having grasped this, may turn back and, holding on to the consequences which depend upon it, descend at last to a conclusion, never making use of any sensible object, but only of Forms, moving through Forms from one to another and ending with Forms.

I understand, he said, though not perfectly; for the procedure you describe sounds like an enormous undertaking. But I see that you mean to distinguish the field of intelligible reality studied by dialectic as having a greater certainty and truth than the subject-matter of the "arts," as they are called, which treat their assumptions as first principles. The students of these arts are, it is true, compelled to exercise thought in contemplating objects which the senses cannot perceive; but because they start from assumptions without going back to a first principle, you do not regard them as gaining true understanding about those objects, although the objects themselves, when connected with a first principle, are intelligible. And I think you would call the state of mind of the students of geometry and other such arts, not intelligence, but thinking, as being something between intelligence and mere acceptance of appearances.

You have understood me quite well enough, I replied. And now you may take, as corresponding to the four sections, these four states of mind: *intelligence* for the highest, *thinking* for the second, *belief* for the third, and for the last *imagining*.[8] These you may arrange as the terms in a proportion, assigning to each a degree of clearness and certainty corresponding to the measure in which their objects possess truth and reality.

I understand and agree with you. I will arrange them as you say.

THE ALLEGORY OF THE CAVE

Next, said I, here is a parable to illustrate the degrees in which our nature may be enlightened or unenlightened. Imagine the condition of men living in a sort of cavernous chamber underground, with an entrance open to the light and a long passage all down the cave.[9] Here they have been from childhood, chained by the leg and also by the neck, so that they cannot move and can see only what is in front of them, because the chains will not let them turn their heads. At some distance higher up is the light of a fire burning behind them; and

---

[8] Plato never used hard and fast technical terms. The four here proposed are not defined or strictly employed in the sequel.
[9] The *length* of the "way in"...to the chamber where the prisoners sit is an essential feature, explaining why no daylight reaches them.

between the prisoners and the fire is a track[10] with a parapet built along it, like the screen at a puppet-show, which hides the performers while they show their puppets over the top.

I see, said he.

Now behind this parapet imagine persons carrying along various artificial objects, including figures of men and animals in wood or stone or other materials, which project above the parapet. Naturally, some of these persons will be talking, others silent.[11]

It is a strange picture, he said, and a strange sort of prisoners.

Like ourselves, I replied; for in the first place prisoners so confined would have seen nothing of themselves or of one another, except the shadows thrown by the fire-light on the wall of the Cave facing them, would they?

Not if all their lives they had been prevented from moving their heads.

And they would have seen as little of the objects carried past.

Of course.

Now, if they could talk to one another, would they not suppose that their words referred only to those passing shadows which they saw?[12]

Necessarily.

And suppose their prison had an echo from the wall facing them? When one of the people crossing behind them spoke, they could only suppose that the sound came from the shadow passing before their eyes.

No doubt.

In every way, then, such prisoners would recognize as reality nothing but the shadows of those artificial objects.[13]

Inevitably.

Now consider what would happen if their release from the chains and the healing of their unwisdom should come about in this way. Suppose one of them was set free and forced suddenly to stand up, turn his head, and walk with eyes lifted to the light; all these movements would be painful, and he would be too dazzled to make out the objects whose shadows he had been used to see. What do you think he would say, if someone told him that what he had formerly seen was meaningless illusion, but now, being somewhat nearer to reality and turned towards more real objects, he was getting a truer

---

[10] The track crosses the passage into the cave at right angles, and is *above* the parapet built along it.

[11] A modern Plato would compare his Cave to an underground cinema, where the audience watch the play of shadows thrown by the film passing before a light at their backs. The film itself is only an image of "real" things and events in the world outside the cinema. For the film Plato has to substitute the clumsier apparatus of a procession of artificial objects carried on their heads by persons who are merely part of the machinery, providing for the movement of the objects and the sounds whose echo the prisoners hear. The parapet prevents these persons' shadows from being cast on the wall of the Cave.

[12] Adam's text and interpretation. The prisoners, having seen nothing but shadows, cannot think their words refer to the objects carried past behind their backs. For them shadows (images) are the only realities.

[13] The state of mind called *eikasia* in the previous chapter.

view? Suppose further that he were shown the various objects being carried by and were made to say, in reply to questions, what each of them was. Would he not be perplexed and believe the objects now shown to him to be not so real as what he formerly saw?[14]

Yes, not nearly so real.

And if he were forced to look at the fire-light itself, would not his eyes ache, so that he would try to escape and turn back to the things which he could see distinctly, convinced that they really were clearer than these other objects now being shown to him?

Yes.

And suppose someone were to drag him away forcibly up the steep and rugged ascent and not let him go until he had hauled him out into the sun-light, would he not suffer pain and vexation at such treatment, and, when he had come out into the light, find his eyes so full of its radiance that he could not see a single one of the things that he was now told were real?

Certainly he would not see them all at once.

He would need, then, to grow accustomed before he could see things in that upper world.[15] At first it would be easiest to make out shadows, and then images of men and things reflected in water, and later on the things them-selves. After that, it would be easier to watch the heavenly bodies and the sky itself by night, looking at the light of the moon and stars rather than the Sun and the Sun's light in the day-time.

Yes, surely.

Last of all, he would be able to look at the Sun and contemplate its na-ture, not as it appears when reflected in water or any alien medium, but as it is in itself in its own domain.

No doubt.

And now he would begin to draw the conclusion that it is the Sun that produces the seasons and the course of the year and controls everything in the visible world, and moreover is in a way the cause of all that he and his com-panions used to see.

Clearly he would come at last to that conclusion.

Then if he called to mind his fellow prisoners and what passed for wis-dom in his former dwelling-place, he would surely think himself happy in the change and be sorry for them. They may have had a practice of honoring and commending one another, with prizes for the man who had the keenest eye for the passing shadows and the best memory for the order in which they followed or accompanied one another, so that he could make a good guess as to which was going to come next.[16] Would our released prisoner be likely to covet those prizes or to envy the men exalted to honor and power in the Cave?

---

[14] The first effect of Socratic questioning is perplexity....

[15] Here is the moral—the need of habituation by mathematical study before discussing moral ideas and ascending through them to the Form of the Good.

[16] The empirical politician, with no philosophic insight, but only a "knack of remembering what usually happens" (*Gorg.* 501 A). He has *eikasia* = conjecture as to what is likely....

Would he not feel like Homer's Achilles, that he would far sooner "be on earth as a hired servant in the house of a landless man"[17] or endure anything rather than go back to his old beliefs and live in the old way?

Yes, he would prefer any fate to such a life.

Now imagine what would happen if he went down again to take his former seat in the Cave. Coming suddenly out of the sunlight, his eyes would be filled with darkness. He might be required once more to deliver his opinion on those shadows, in competition with the prisoners who had never been released, while his eyesight was still dim and unsteady; and it might take some time to become used to the darkness. They would laugh at him and say that he had gone up only to come back with his sight ruined; it was worth no one's while even to attempt the ascent. If they could lay hands on the man who was trying to set them free and lead them up, they would kill him.[18]

Yes, they would.

Every feature in this parable, my dear Glaucon, is meant to fit our earlier analysis. The prison dwelling corresponds to the region revealed to us through the sense of sight, and the fire-light within it to the power of the Sun. The ascent to see the things in the upper world you may take as standing for the upward journey of the soul into the region of the intelligible; then you will be in possession of what I surmise, since that is what you wish to be told. Heaven knows whether it is true; but this, at any rate, is how it appears to me. In the world of knowledge, the last thing to be perceived and only with great difficulty is the essential Form of Goodness. Once it is perceived, the conclusion must follow that, for all things, this is the cause of whatever is right and good; in the visible world it gives birth to light and to the lord of light, while it is itself sovereign in the intelligible world and the parent of intelligence and truth. Without having had a vision of this Form no one can act with wisdom, either in his own life or in matters of state.

So far as I can understand, I share your belief.

Then you may also agree that it is no wonder if those who have reached this height are reluctant to manage the affairs of men. Their souls long to spend all their time in the upper world—naturally enough, if here once more our parable holds true. Nor, again, is it at all strange that one who comes from the contemplation of divine things to the miseries of human life should appear awkward and ridiculous when, with eyes still dazed and not yet accustomed to the darkness, he is compelled, in a law-court or elsewhere, to dispute about the shadows of justice or the images that cast those shadows, and to wrangle over the notions of what is right in the minds of men who have never beheld Justice itself.[19]

It is not at all strange.

---

[17] This verse . . . being spoken by the ghost of Achilles, suggests that the Cave is comparable with Hades.

[18] An allusion to the fate of Socrates.

[19] In the *Gorgias* 486 A, Callicles, forecasting the trial of Socrates, taunts him with the philosopher's inability to defend himself in a court.

No; a sensible man will remember that the eyes may be confused in two ways—by a change from light to darkness or from darkness to light; and he will recognize that the same thing happens to the soul. When he sees it troubled and unable to discern anything clearly, instead of laughing thoughtlessly, he will ask whether, coming from a brighter existence, its unaccustomed vision is obscured by the darkness, in which case he will think its condition enviable and its life a happy one; or whether, emerging from the depths of ignorance, it is dazzled by excess of light. If so, he will rather feel sorry for it; or, if he were inclined to laugh, that would be less ridiculous than to laugh at the soul which has come down from the light.

That is a fair statement.

If this is true, then, we must conclude that education is not what it is said to be by some, who profess to put knowledge into a soul which does not possess it, as if they could put sight into blind eyes. On the contrary, our own account signifies that the soul of every man does possess the power of learning the truth and the organ to see it with; and that, just as one might have to turn the whole body round in order that the eye should see light instead of darkness, so the entire soul must be turned away from this changing world, until its eye can bear to contemplate reality and that supreme splendor which we have called the Good. Hence there may well be an art whose aim would be to effect this very thing, the conversion of the soul, in the readiest way; not to put the power of sight into the soul's eye, which already has it, but to ensure that, instead of looking in the wrong direction, it is turned the way it ought to be.

Yes it may well be so.

It looks, then, as though wisdom were different from those ordinary virtues, as they are called, which are not far removed from bodily qualities, in that they can be produced by habituation and exercise in a soul which has not possessed them from the first. Wisdom, it seems, is certainly the virtue of some diviner faculty, which never loses its power, though its use for good or harm depends on the direction towards which it is turned. You must have noticed in dishonest men with a reputation for sagacity the shrewd glance of a narrow intelligence piercing the objects to which it is directed. There is nothing wrong with their power of vision, but it has been forced into the service of evil, so that the keener its sight, the more harm it works.

STUDY QUESTIONS

1. Socrates distinguishes between seeing "with" the eyes and "through" the eyes. What is he trying to explain? What do you think perception would be like if this distinction were not made?
2. Through what organ does Theaetetus say we perceive "sameness," "difference," "existence," etc.? Why can these things not be sensed in the usual way? Do you think Descartes would agree with Plato on this point?

3. Plato's doctrine is often called a *theory of innate ideas*. Briefly, such a theory would hold that we are born with certain concepts, such as "sameness," and we do not acquire them from experience. To what extent do you agree with this? Can you think of experiments which would test this theory?
4. In the selection from the *Republic*, Plato says that the many things which are sensed are not the objects of rational thought. What are the objects of thought, then? Can anything in the *Theaetetus* help explain this?
5. In the section on the stages of cognition, Plato divides the intelligible world into two parts. He uses geometry to explain the kind of thinking that occurs in the first division (C). Can you explain the difference between this sort of thinking and that which occurs in the second division (D)? Can you think of any analogies which might bring out the difference?

Perception and Matter

George Berkeley

George Berkeley (1685–1753) was the first great philosopher to visit America. He and his wife lived in Rhode Island for three years, hoping to establish a college in Bermuda. But the money for this project never arrived from England, and, after the death of their baby daughter, the Berkeleys returned to Ireland. Because of a poem he wrote, however, Berkeley was honored by the New World—a small California town was named after him.

Berkeley was an Anglican bishop, who believed that materialism was the foundation of atheism. His new philosophy of "immaterialism" was designed to show that matter does not exist and that reality is fundamentally spiritual. Following John Locke, he claimed that we never perceive anything but our own ideas. Matter cannot be the cause of our ideas because the concept of "material substance" is meaningless. Here Berkeley uses the fundamental tenet of empiricism—that all our ideas come from perception—to demonstrate that the only things which can exist are mental. He summed it up in the phrase *Esse est percipi*: To be is to be perceived.

One day after church, Samuel Johnson, the great literary critic of the age, was asked his opinion of this new doctrine of immaterialism. He is reported to have kicked a large rock, saying, "I refute it thus." After reading the following selection, you may decide for yourself whether Johnson's common sense prevails.

HYLAS: You were represented in last night's conversation, as one who maintained the most extravagant opinion that ever entered into the mind of man, to wit, that there is no such thing as *material substance* in the world.

From *Three Dialogues between Hylas and Philonous*, 1713, by George Berkeley. First Dialogue.

Berkeley

PHILONOUS: That there is no such thing as what Philosophers call *material substance*, I am seriously persuaded; but, if I were made to see anything absurd or sceptical in this, I should then have the same reason to renounce this that I imagine I have now to reject the contrary opinion.

HYLAS: What! can anything be more fantastical, more repugnant to common sense, or a more manifest piece of Scepticism, than to believe there is no such thing as *matter?*

PHILONOUS: Softly, good Hylas. What if it should prove, that you, who hold there is, are, by virtue of that opinion, a greater sceptic, and maintain more paradoxes and repugnances to common sense, than I who believe no such thing?

HYLAS: You may as soon persuade me, the part is greater than the whole, as that, in order to avoid absurdity and Scepticism, I should ever be obliged to give up my opinion in this point.

PHILONOUS: Well then, are you content to admit that opinion for true, which, upon examination, shall appear most agreeable to common sense, and remote from Scepticism?

HYLAS: With all my heart. Since you are for raising disputes about the plainest things in nature, I am content for once to hear what you have to say.

PHILONOUS: Pray, *Hylas*, what do you mean by a *sceptic?*

HYLAS: I mean what all men mean, one that doubts of everything.

PHILONOUS: He then who entertains no doubt concerning some particular point, with regard to that point cannot be thought a sceptic.

HYLAS: I agree with you.

PHILONOUS: Whether doth doubting consist in embracing the affirmative or negative side of a question?

HYLAS: In neither; for whoever understands English cannot but know that *doubting* signifies a suspense between both.

PHILONOUS: He then that denieth any point, can no more be said to doubt of it, than he who affirmeth it with the same degree or assurance.

HYLAS: True.

PHILONOUS: And, consequently, for such his denial is no more to be esteemed a sceptic than the other.

HYLAS: I acknowledge it.

PHILONOUS: How cometh it to pass then, *Hylas*, that you pronounce me a *sceptic*, because I deny what you affirm, to wit, the existence of Matter? Since, for aught you can tell, I am as peremptory in my denial, as you in your affirmation.

HYLAS: Hold, *Philonous*, I have been a little out in my definition; but every false step a man makes in discourse is not to be insisted on. I said indeed that a *sceptic* was one who doubted of everything; but I should have added, or who denies the reality and truth of things.

PHILONOUS: What things? Do you mean the principles and theorems of sciences? But these you know are universal intellectual notions, and consequently independent of Matter; the denial therefore of this doth not imply the denying them.

HYLAS: I grant it. But are there no other things? What think you of distrusting
the senses, of denying the real existence of sensible things, or pretending
to know nothing of them. Is not this sufficient to denominate a man a *sceptic?*

PHILONOUS: Shall we therefore examine which of us it is that denies the reality
of sensible things, or professes the greatest ignorance of them; since, if I
take you rightly, he is to be esteemed the greatest *sceptic?*

HYLAS: That is what I desire.

PHILONOUS: What mean you by Sensible Things?

HYLAS: Those things which are perceived by the senses. Can you imagine that
I mean anything else?

PHILONOUS: Pardon me, *Hylas,* if I am desirous clearly to apprehend your notions, since this may much shorten our inquiry. Suffer me then to ask you
this farther question. Are those things only perceived by the senses which
are perceived immediately? Or, may those things properly be said to be
sensible which are perceived mediately, or not without the intervention of
others?

HYLAS: I do not sufficiently understand you.

PHILONOUS: In reading a book, what I immediately perceive are the letters,
but mediately, or by means of these, are suggested to my mind the notions
of God, virtue, truth, &c. Now, that the letters are truly sensible things, or
perceived by sense, there is no doubt: but I would know whether you take
the things suggested by them to be so too.

HYLAS: No certainly; it were absurd to think God or *virtue* sensible things,
though they may be signified and suggested to the mind by sensible marks,
with which they have an arbitrary connexion.

PHILONOUS: It seems then, that by *sensible things* you mean those only which
can be perceived *immediately* by sense?

HYLAS: Right.

PHILONOUS: Doth it not follow from this, that though I see one part of the sky
red, and another blue, and that my reason doth thence evidently conclude
there must be some cause of that diversity of colours, yet that cause cannot
be said to be a sensible thing, or perceived by the sense of seeing?

HYLAS: It doth.

PHILONOUS: In like manner, though I hear variety of sounds, yet I cannot be
said to hear the causes of those sounds?

HYLAS: You cannot.

PHILONOUS: And when by my touch I perceive a thing to be hot and heavy,
I cannot say, with any truth or propriety, that I feel the cause of its heat or
weight?

HYLAS: To prevent any more questions of this kind, I tell you once for all, that
by *sensible things* I mean those only which are perceived by sense, and that
in truth the senses perceive nothing which they do not perceive immediately, for they make no inferences. The deducing therefore of causes or

occasions from effects and appearances, which alone are perceived by sense, entirely relates to reason.

PHILONOUS: This point then is agreed between us—that *sensible things are those only which are immediately perceived by sense.* You will farther inform me, whether we immediately perceive by sight anything beside light, and colours, and figures; or by hearing, anything but sounds; by the palate, anything besides tastes; by the smell, beside odours; or by the touch, more than tangible qualities.

HYLAS: We do not.

PHILONOUS: It seems, therefore, that if you take away all sensible qualities, there remains nothing sensible?

HYLAS: I grant it.

PHILONOUS: Sensible things therefore are nothing else but so many sensible qualities, or combinations of sensible qualities?

HYLAS: Nothing else.

PHILONOUS: *Heat* is then a sensible thing?

HYLAS: Certainly.

PHILONOUS: Doth the reality of sensible things consist in being perceived? or, is it something distinct from their being perceived, and that bears no relation to the mind?

HYLAS: To *exist* is one thing, and to be *perceived* is another.

PHILONOUS: I speak with regard to sensible things only; and of these I ask, whether by their real existence you mean a subsistence exterior to the mind, and distinct from their being perceived?

HYLAS: I mean a real absolute being, distinct from, and without any relation to their being perceived.

PHILONOUS: Heat therefore, if it be allowed a real being, must exist without the mind?

HYLAS: It must.

PHILONOUS: Tell me, *Hylas,* is real existence equally compatible to all degrees of heat, which we perceive; or is there any reason why we should attribute it to some, and deny it to others? and if there be, pray let me know that reason.

HYLAS: Whatever degree of heat we perceive by sense, we may be sure the same exists in the object that occasions it.

PHILONOUS: What! the greatest as well as the least?

HYLAS: I tell you, the reason is plainly the same in respect of both: they are both perceived by sense; nay, the greater degree of heat is more sensibly perceived; and consequently, if there is any difference, we are more certain of its real existence than we can be of the reality of a lesser degree.

PHILONOUS: But is not the most vehement and intense degree of heat a very great pain?

HYLAS: No one can deny it.

PHILONOUS: And is any unperceiving thing capable of pain or pleasure?

HYLAS: No certainly.

PHILONOUS: Is your material substance a senseless being, or a being endowed with sense and perception?

HYLAS: It is senseless without doubt.

PHILONOUS: It cannot therefore be the subject of pain?

HYLAS: By no means.

PHILONOUS: Nor consequently of the greatest heat perceived by sense, since you acknowledge this to be no small pain?

HYLAS: I grant it.

PHILONOUS: What shall we say then of your external object; is it a material substance, or no?

HYLAS: It is a material substance with the sensible qualities inhering in it.

PHILONOUS: How then can a great heat exist in it, since you own it cannot in a material substance? I desire you would clear this point.

HYLAS: Hold, *Philonous*, I fear I was out in yielding intense heat to be a pain. It should seem rather, that pain is something distinct from heat, and the consequences or effect of it.

PHILONOUS: Upon putting your hand near the fire, do you perceive one simple uniform sensation, or two distinct sensations?

HYLAS: But one simple sensation.

PHILONOUS: Is not the heat immediately perceived?

HYLAS: It is.

PHILONOUS: And the pain?

HYLAS: True.

PHILONOUS: Seeing therefore they are both immediately perceived at the same time, and the fire affects you only with one simple, or uncompounded idea, it follows that this same simple idea is both the intense heat immediately perceived, and the pain; and, consequently, that the intense heat immediately perceived, is nothing distinct from a particular sort of pain.

HYLAS: It seems so.

PHILONOUS: Again, try in your thought, *Hylas,* if you can conceive a vehement sensation to be without pain or pleasure.

HYLAS: I cannot.

PHILONOUS: Or can you frame to yourself an idea of sensible pain or pleasure, in general, abstracted from every particular idea of heat, cold, tastes, smells? &c.

HYLAS: I do not find that I can.

PHILONOUS: Doth it not therefore follow, that sensible pain is nothing distinct from those sensations or ideas—in an intense degree?

HYLAS: It is undeniable; and, to speak the truth, I begin to suspect a very great heat cannot exist but in a mind perceiving it.

PHILONOUS: What! are you then in that *sceptical* state of suspense, between affirming and denying?...

HYLAS: But, after all, can anything be more absurd than to say, *there is no heat in the fire?*

PHILONOUS: To make the point still clearer, tell me whether, in two cases exactly alike, we ought not to make the same judgment?

HYLAS: We ought.

PHILONOUS: When a pin pricks your finger, doth it not rend and divide the fibres of your flesh?

HYLAS: It doth.

PHILONOUS: And when a coal burns your finger, doth it any more?

HYLAS: It doth not.

PHILONOUS: Since, therefore, you neither judge the sensation itself occasioned by the pin, nor anything like it to be in the pin, you should not, conformably to what you have now granted, judge the sensation occasioned by the fire, or anything like it, to be in the fire.

HYLAS: Well, since it must be so, I am content to yield this point, and acknowledge that heat and cold are only sensations existing in our minds, But there still remain qualities enough to secure the reality of external things....

PHILONOUS: The objects you speak of are, I suppose, corporeal substances existing without the mind.

HYLAS: They are.

PHILONOUS: And have true and real colours inhering in them?

HYLAS: Each visible object hath that colour which we see in it.

PHILONOUS: How! Is there anything visible but what we perceive by sight?

HYLAS: There is not.

PHILONOUS: And do we perceive anything by sense, which we do not perceive immediately?

HYLAS: How often must I be obliged to repeat the same thing? I tell you, we do not.

PHILONOUS: Have patience, good *Hylas;* and tell me once more, whether there is any thing immediately perceived by the senses, except sensible qualities. I know you asserted there was not, but I would now be informed, whether you still persist in the same opinion.

HYLAS: I do.

PHILONOUS: Pray, is your corporeal substance either a sensible quality, or made up of sensible qualities?

HYLAS: What a question that is! who ever thought it was?

PHILONOUS: My reason for asking was, because in saying, *each visible object hath colour which we see in it*, you make visible objects to be corporeal substances; which implies either that corporeal substances are sensible qualities, or else that there is something beside sensible qualities perceived by sight; but as this point was formerly agreed between us, and is still maintained by you, it is a clear consequence, that your corporeal substance is nothing distinct from sensible qualities.

HYLAS: You may draw as many absurd consequences as you please, and endeavour to perplex the plainest things, but you shall never persuade me out of my senses. I clearly understand my own meaning.

PHILONOUS: I wish you would make me understand it too. But since you are unwilling to have your notion of corporeal substance examined, I shall urge that point no farther. Only be pleased to let me know, whether the same colours which we see exist in external bodies, or some other.

HYLAS: The very same.

PHILONOUS: What! are then the beautiful red and purple we see on yonder clouds, really in them? Or do you imagine they have in themselves any other form, than that of a dark mist or vapour?

HYLAS: I must own, *Philonous,* those colours are not really in the clouds as they seem to be at this distance. They are only apparent colours.

PHILONOUS: *Apparent* call you them? how shall we distinguish these apparent colours from real?

HYLAS: Very easily. Those are to be thought apparent, which appearing only at a distance, vanish upon a nearer approach.

PHILONOUS: And those I suppose are to be thought real, which are discovered by the most near and exact survey.

HYLAS: Right.

PHILONOUS: Is the nearest and exactest survey made by the help of a microscope, or by the naked eye?

HYLAS: By a microscope, doubtless.

PHILONOUS: But a microscope often discovers colours in an object different from those perceived by the unassisted sight. And in case we had microscopes magnifying to any assigned degree, it is certain, that no object whatsoever viewed through them, would appear in the same colour which it exhibits to the naked eye.

HYLAS: And what will you conclude from all this? You cannot argue that there are really and naturally no colours on objects, because by artificial managements they may be altered, or made to vanish.

PHILONOUS: I think it may evidently be concluded from your own concessions, that all the colours we see with our naked eyes, are only apparent as those on the clouds, since they vanish upon a more close and accurate inspection, which is afforded us by a microscope. Then as to what you say by way of prevention, I ask you, whether the real and natural state of an object is better discovered by a very sharp and piercing sight, or by one which is less sharp?

HYLAS: By the former without doubt.

PHILONOUS: Is it not plain from *dioptrics*, that microscopes make the sight more penetrating, and represent objects as they would appear to the eye, in case it were naturally endowed with a most exquisite sharpness?

HYLAS: It is.

PHILONOUS: Consequently the microscopical representation is to be thought that which best sets forth the real nature of the thing, or what it is in itself. The colours therefore by it perceived, are more genuine and real, than those perceived otherwise.

HYLAS: I confess there is something in what you say.

PHILONOUS: Besides, it is not only possible but manifest, that there actually are animals, whose eyes are by Nature framed to perceive those things, which by reason of their minuteness escape our sight. What think you of those inconceivably small animals perceived by glasses? Must we suppose they are all stark blind? Or, in case they see, can it be imagined their sight hath not the same use in preserving their bodies from injuries, which appears in that of all other animals? And if it hath, is it not evident, they must see particles less than their own bodies, which will present them with a far different view in each object, from that which strikes our senses? Even our own eyes do not always represent objects to us after the same manner. In the *jaundice*, every one knows that all things seem yellow. Is it not therefore highly probable, those animals in whose eyes we discern a very different texture from that of ours, and whose bodies abound with different humours, do not see the same colours in every object that we do? From all which, should it not seem to follow, that all colours are equally apparent, and that none of those which we perceive are really inherent in any outward object?

HYLAS: It should.

PHILONOUS: The point will be past all doubt, if you consider, that in case colours were real properties or affections inherent in external bodies, they could admit of no alteration, without some change wrought in the very bodies themselves; but is it not evident from what hath been said, that upon the use of microscopes, upon a change happening in the humours of the eye, or a variation of distance, without any manner of real alteration in the thing itself, the colours of any object are either changed, or totally disappear? Nay all other circumstances remaining the same, change but the situation of some objects, and they shall present different colours to the eye. The same thing happens upon viewing an object in various degrees of light. And what is more known, than that the same bodies appear differently coloured by candle-light, from what they do in the open day? Add to these the experiment of a prism, which separating the heterogeneous rays of light, alters the colour of any object; and will cause the whitest to appear of a deep blue or red to the naked eye. And now tell me, whether you are still of [the] opinion, that every body hath its true real colour inhering in it; and if you think it hath, I would fain know farther from you, what certain distance and position of the object, what peculiar texture and formation of the eye, what degree or kind of light is necessary for ascertaining that true colour, and distinguishing it from apparent ones.

HYLAS: I own myself entirely satisfied, that they are all equally apparent; and that there is no such thing as colour really inhering in external bodies, but that it is altogether in the light. And what confirms me in this opinion is, that in proportion to the light, colours are still more or less vivid; and if there be no light, then are there no colours perceived. Besides, allowing there are colours on external objects, yet how is it possible for us to perceive them? For no external body affects the mind, unless it act first on our organs of sense. But the only action of bodies is motion; and motion cannot be communicated otherwise than by impulse. A distant object therefore cannot act on the eye, nor consequently make itself or its properties perceivable to the soul. Whence it plainly follows, that it is immediately some contiguous substance, which operating on the eye occasions a perception of colours; and such is light.

PHILONOUS: How! is light then a substance?

HYLAS: I tell you, *Philonous,* external light is nothing but a thin fluid substance, whose minute particles being agitated with a brisk motion, and in various manners reflected from the different surfaces of outward objects to the eyes, communicate different motions to the optic nerves; which being propagated to the brain, cause therein various impressions; and these are attended with the sensations of red, blue, yellow, &c.

PHILONOUS: It seems then, the light doth no more than shake the optic nerves.

HYLAS: Nothing else.

PHILONOUS: And consequent to each particular motion of the nerves the mind is affected with a sensation, which is some particular colour.

HYLAS: Right.

PHILONOUS: And these sensations have no existence without the mind.

HYLAS: They have not.

PHILONOUS: How then do you affirm that colours are in the light, since by *light* you understand a corporeal substance external to the mind?

HYLAS: Light and colours, as immediately perceived by us, I grant cannot exist without the mind. But in themselves they are only the motions and configurations of certain insensible particles of matter.

PHILONOUS: Colours then in the vulgar sense, or taken for the immediate objects of sight, cannot agree to any but a perceiving substance.

HYLAS: That is what I say.

PHILONOUS: Well then, since you give up the point as to those sensible qualities, which are alone thought colours by all mankind beside, you may hold what you please with regard to those invisible ones of the philosophers. It is not my business to dispute about them; only I would advise you to bethink your self, whether considering the inquiry we are upon, it be prudent for you to affirm, *the red and blue which we see are not real colours, but certain unknown motions and figures which no man ever did or can see, are truly so.* Are not these shocking notions, and are not they subject to as many ridiculous inferences, as those you were obliged to renounce before in the case of sounds?

HYLAS: I frankly own, *Philonous,* that it is in vain to stand out any longer. Colours, sounds, tastes, in a word, all those termed *secondary qualities,* have certainly no existence without the mind. But by this acknowledgment I must not be supposed to derogate any thing from the reality of matter or external objects, seeing it is no more than several philosophers maintain, who nevertheless are the farthest imaginable from denying matter. For the clearer understanding of this, you must know sensible qualities are by philosophers divided into *primary* and *secondary.* The former are extension, figure,

solidi̲t̲y, gra̲v̲ity, m̲o̲t̲ion, and r̲est. And these they hold exist really in bodies. The latter are those above enumerated; or briefly, all sensible qualities
beside the primary, which they assert are only so many sensations or ideas
existing no where but in the mind. But all this, I doubt not, you are already
apprised of. For my part, I have been a long time sensible there was such
an opinion current among philosophers, but was never thoroughly convinced of its truth till now.

PHILONOUS: You are still then of [the] opinion, that extension and figure are
inherent in external unthinking substances.

HYLAS: I am.

PHILONOUS: But what if the same arguments which are brought against secondary qualities, will hold good against these also?

HYLAS: Why then I shall be obliged to think, they too exist only in the mind.

PHILONOUS: Is it your opinion, the very figure and extension which you perceive by sense, exist in the outward object or material substance?

HYLAS: It is.

PHILONOUS: Have all other animals as good grounds to think the same of the
figure and extension which they see and feel?

HYLAS: Without doubt, if they have any thought at all.

PHILONOUS: Answer me, *Hylas*. Think you the senses were bestowed upon all
animals for their preservation and well-being in life? or were they given to
men alone for this end?

HYLAS: I make no question but they have the same use in all other animals.

PHILONOUS: If so, is it not necessary they should be enabled by them to perceive their own limbs, and those bodies which are capable of harming them?

HYLAS: Certainly.

PHILONOUS: A mite therefore must be supposed to see his own foot, and things
equal or even less than it, as bodies of some considerable dimension; though
at the same time they appear to you scarce discernible, or at best as so many
visible points.

HYLAS: I cannot deny it.

PHILONOUS: And to creatures less than the mite they will seem yet larger.

HYLAS: They will.

PHILONOUS: Insomuch that what you can hardly discern, will to another extremely minute animal appear as some huge mountain.

HYLAS: All this I grant.

PHILONOUS: Can one and the same thing be at the same time in itself of different dimensions?

HYLAS: That were absurd to imagine.

PHILONOUS: But from what you have laid down it follows, that both the extension by you perceived, and that perceived by the mite itself, as likewise
all those perceived by lesser animals, are each of them the true extension
of the mite's foot, that is to say, by your own principles you are led into an
absurdity.

HYLAS: There seems to be some difficulty in the point.

PHILONOUS: Again, have you not acknowledged that no real inherent property of any object can be changed, without some change in the thing itself?

HYLAS: I have.

PHILONOUS: But as we approach to or recede from an object, the visible extension varies, being at one distance ten or an hundred times greater than at another. Doth it not therefore follow from hence likewise, that it is not really inherent in the object?

HYLAS: I own I am at a loss what to think.

PHILONOUS: Your judgment will soon be determined, if you will venture to think as freely concerning this quality, as you have done concerning the rest. Was it not admitted as a good argument, that neither heat nor cold was in the water, because it seemed warm to one hand, and cold to the other?

HYLAS: It was.

PHILONOUS: Is it not the very same reasoning to conclude, there is no extension or figure in an object, because to one eye it shall seem little, smooth, and round, when at the same time it appears to the other, great, uneven, and angular?

HYLAS: The very same. But doth this latter fact ever happen?

PHILONOUS: You may at any time make the experiment, by looking with one eye bare, and with the other through a microscope.

HYLAS: I know not how to maintain it, and yet I am loth to give up *extension,* I see so many odd consequences following upon such a concession.

PHILONOUS: Odd, say you? After the concessions already made, I hope you will stick at nothing for its oddness. But on the other hand should it not seem very odd, if the general reasoning which includes all other sensible qualities did not also include extension? If it be allowed that no idea nor any thing like an idea can exist in an unperceiving substance, then surely it follows, that no figure or mode of extension, which we can either perceive or imagine, or have any idea of, can be really inherent in matter; not to mention the peculiar difficulty there must be, in conceiving a material substance, prior to and distinct from extension, to be the *substratum* of extension. Be the sensible quality what it will, figure, or sound, or colour; it seems alike impossible it should subsist in that which doth not perceive it. . . .

HYLAS: I acknowledge, *Philonous,* that, upon a fair observation of what passes in my mind, I can discover nothing else but that I am a thinking being, affected with variety of sensations; neither is it possible to conceive how a sensation should exist in an unperceiving substance. But then, on the other hand, when I look on sensible things in a different view, considering them as so many modes and qualities, I find it necessary to suppose a material substratum, without which they cannot be conceived to exist.

PHILONOUS: *Material substratum* call you it? Pray, by which of your senses came you acquainted with that being?

HYLAS: It is not itself sensible; its modes and qualities only being perceived by the senses.

PHILONOUS: I presume then it was by reflection and reason you obtained the idea of it?

HYLAS: I do not pretend to any proper positive idea of it. However, I conclude it exists, because qualities cannot be conceived to exist without a support.

PHILONOUS: It seems then you have only a relative notion of it, or that you conceive it not otherwise than by conceiving the relation it bears to sensible qualities?

HYLAS: Right.

PHILONOUS: Be pleased therefore to let me know wherein that relation consists.

HYLAS: Is it not sufficiently expressed in the term *substratum* or *substance?*

PHILONOUS: If so, the word *substratum* should import that it is spread under the sensible qualities or accidents?

HYLAS: True.

PHILONOUS: And consequently under extension?

HYLAS: I own it.

PHILONOUS: It is therefore somewhat in its own nature entirely distinct from extension?

HYLAS: I tell you, extension is only a mode, and Matter is something that supports modes. And is it not evident the thing supported is different from the thing supporting?

PHILONOUS: So that something distinct from, and exclusive of, extension is supposed to be the *substratum* of extension?

HYLAS: Just so.

PHILONOUS: Answer me, *Hylas.* Can a thing be spread without extension? or is not the idea of extension necessarily included in *spreading?*

HYLAS: It is.

PHILONOUS: Whatsoever therefore you suppose spread under anything must have in itself an extension distinct from the extension of that thing under which it is spread?

HYLAS: It must.

PHILONOUS: Consequently, every corporeal substance being the substratum of extension must have in itself another extension, by which it is qualified to be a *substratum,* and so on to infinity? And I ask whether this be not absurd in itself, and repugnant to what you granted just now, to wit, that the *substratum was something distinct from and exclusive of extension?*

HYLAS: Aye, but *Philonous,* you take me wrong. I do not mean that Matter is *spread* in a gross literal sense under extension. The world *substratum* is used only to express in general the same thing with *substance.*

PHILONOUS: Well then, let us examine the relation implied in the term *substance.* Is it not that it stands under accidents?

HYLAS: The very same.

PHILONOUS: But, that one thing may stand under or support another, must it not be extended?

HYLAS: It must.

PHILONOUS: Is not therefore this supposition liable to the same absurdity with the former?

HYLAS: You still take things in a strict literal sense; that is not fair, *Philonous.*

PHILONOUS: I am not for imposing any sense on your words; you are at liberty to explain them as you please. Only, I beseech you, make me understand something by them. You tell me Matter supports or stands under accidents. How? Is it as your legs support your body?

HYLAS: No; that is the literal sense.

PHILONOUS: Pray let me know any sense, literal or not literal, that you understand it in.... How long must I wait for an answer, *Hylas?*

HYLAS: I declare I know not what to say. I once thought I understood well enough what was meant by Matter's supporting accidents. But now, the more I think on it the less can I comprehend it; in short I find that I know nothing of it.

STUDY QUESTIONS

1. Samuel Johnson claimed to have refuted Berkeley by kicking a large rock. What do you think of his "refutation"?
2. Some religious groups who accepted Berkeley's doctrine refused medical help for their illnesses. Since the body is mental, they argued, all that is required to cure disease is the right mental attitude. Do you think this follows from Berkeley's doctrine?
3. "To be is to be perceived" seems to mean that things disappear when I am no longer looking at them. Berkeley's response is summed up in this limerick:

> There was a young man who said, "God
> Must think it exceedingly odd
> > If he finds that this tree
> > Continues to be
> When there's no one about in the Quad"

> *Reply*
> *Dear Sir:*
> > Your astonishment's odd.
> I am always about in the Quad
> > And that's why the tree
> > Will continue to be
> Since observed by
> > Yours faithfully,
> > God.
> > (Ronald Knox)

Do you think God's reply is sufficient to account for an objective world?
4. Can you think how Berkeley might analyze the sense of touch? Is this sense ever subject to illusion?

5. Berkeley is not content to deny the existence of matter, for he also wants to say that the concept of matter is "nonsensical." What makes a concept meaningful according to Berkeley? Do you think that the concept of "God" is meaningful?
6. Do you think one could be a scientist and accept Berkeley's theory? What would you say to Bertrand Russell's claim that "physical objects are those series of appearances whose matter obeys the laws of physics"?

Our Knowledge of Cause and Effect
David Hume

In this selection, David Hume (see biography on pp. 36 and 146) brings his skepticism to its ultimate conclusion. He insists that knowledge cannot go beyond *experience,* and he limits experience to passive sense perception. God, the self, the external world, are rendered beyond human comprehension by this strict form of empiricism. In this selection, Hume's target is the assumption which seems to underlie all experience—the assumption that there is a real connection between the events we experience. We believe, for example, that cause and effect are necessarily connected. That is, if the cause occurs, the effect must follow. The bread we ate yesterday should produce the same nourishing effects today. The water which satisfied thirst a few seconds ago should do so again. But with infuriating logic Hume argues that this assumption is a blind prejudice.

Many contemporary scientists have accepted part of what Hume wants us to believe, namely, that the only evidence we have for the cause-effect relation is our perception of a constant correlation between two observable events. In fact, many scientists claim that this is all we can ever know about nature. While most do not accept the consequences of this for prediction, still it is probably accurate to say that this essay has had a great influence on the contemporary picture of science.

I

All the objects of human reason or inquiry may naturally be divided into two kinds, to wit, *Relations of Ideas,* and *Matters of Fact.* Of the first kind are the sciences of Geometry, Algebra, and Arithmetic; and in short, every affirmation which is either intuitively or demonstratively certain. *That the square of the hypotenuse is equal to the square of the two sides,* is a proposition which expresses a relation between these figures. *That three times five is equal to the half of thirty,*

From *An Enquiry concerning Human Understanding,* by David Hume, first published in 1748.

expresses a relation between these numbers. Propositions of this kind are discoverable by the mere operation of thought, without dependence on what is anywhere existent in the universe. Though there never were a circle or triangle in nature, the truths demonstrated by Euclid would forever retain their certainty and evidence.

Matters of fact, which are the second objects of human reason, are not ascertained in the same manner; nor is our evidence of their truth, however great, of a like nature with the foregoing. The contrary of every matter of fact is still possible; because it can never imply a contradiction, and is conceived by the mind with the same facility and distinctness, as if ever so conformable to reality. *That the sun will not rise tomorrow* is no less intelligible a proposition, and implies no more contradiction than the affirmation, *that it will rise.* Were it demonstratively false, it would imply a contradiction, and could never be distinctly conceived by the mind.

It may, therefore, be a subject worthy of curiosity, to inquire what is the nature of that evidence which assures us of any real existence and matter of fact, beyond the present testimony of our senses, or the records of our memory. This part of philosophy, it is observable, has been little cultivated, either by the ancients or moderns; and therefore our doubts and errors, in the prosecution of so important an inquiry, may be the most excusable; while we march through such difficult paths without any guide or direction. They may even prove useful, by exciting curiosity, and destroying that implicit faith and security, which is the bane of all reasoning and free inquiry. The discovery of defects in the common philosophy, if any such there be, will not, I presume, be a discouragement, but rather an incitement, as is usual, to attempt something more full and satisfactory than has yet been proposed to the public.

All reasonings concerning matter of fact seem to be founded on the relation of *Cause and Effect.* By means of that relation alone we can go beyond the evidence of our memory and senses. If you were to ask a man, why he believes any matter of fact, which is absent; for instance, that his friend is in the country, or in France; he would give you a reason; and this reason would be some other fact; as a letter received from him, or the knowledge of his former resolutions and promises. A man finding a watch or any other machine in a desert island, would conclude that there had once been men in that island. All our reasonings concerning fact are of the same nature. And here it is constantly supposed that there is a connection between the present fact and that which is inferred from it. Were there nothing to bind them together, the inference would be entirely precarious. The hearing of an articulate voice and rational discourse in the dark assures us of the presence of some person. Why? Because these are the effects of the human make and fabric, and closely connected with it. If we anatomize all the other reasonings of this nature, we shall find that they are founded on the relation of cause and effect, and that this relation is either near or remote, direct or collateral. Heat and light are collateral effects of fire, and the one effect may justly be inferred from the other.

If we would satisfy ourselves, therefore, concerning the nature of that evidence, which assures us of matters of fact, we must inquire how we arrive at the knowledge of cause and effect.

I shall venture to affirm, as a general proposition, which admits of no exception, that the knowledge of this relation is not, in any instance, attained by reasonings *a priori*; but arises entirely from experience, when we find that any particular objects are constantly conjoined with each other. Let an object be presented to a man of ever so strong natural reason and abilities; if that object be entirely new to him, he will not be able, by the most accurate examination of its sensible qualities, to discover any of its causes or effects. Adam, though his rational faculties be supposed, at the very first, entirely perfect, could not have inferred from the fluidity and transparency of water that it would suffocate him, or from the light and warmth of fire that it would consume him. No object ever discovers, by the qualities which appear to the senses, either the causes which produced it, or the effects which will arise from it; nor can our reason, unassisted by experience, ever draw any inference concerning real existence and matter of fact.

This proposition, *that causes and effects are discoverable, not by reason but by experience,* will readily be admitted with regard to such objects, as we remember to have once been altogether unknown to us; since we must be conscious of the utter inability, which we then lay under, of foretelling what would arise from them. Present two smooth pieces of marble to a man who has no tincture of natural philosophy; he will never discover that they will adhere together in such a manner as to require great force to separate them in a direct line, while they make so small a resistance to a lateral pressure. Such events, as bear little analogy to the common course of nature, are also readily confessed to be known only by experience; nor does any man imagine that the explosion of gunpowder, or the attraction of a loadstone, could ever be discovered by arguments *a priori*. In like manner, when an effect is supposed to depend upon an intricate machinery or secret structure of parts, we make no difficulty in attributing all our knowledge of it to experience. Who will assert that he can give the ultimate reason, why milk or bread is proper nourishment for a man, not for a lion or a tiger?

But the same truth may not appear, at first sight, to have the same evidence with regard to events, which have become familiar to us from our first appearance in the world, which bear a close analogy to the whole course of nature, and which are supposed to depend on the simple qualities of objects, without any secret structure of parts. We are apt to imagine that we could discover these effects by the mere operation of our reason, without experience. We fancy, that were we brought on a sudden into this world, we could at first have inferred that one Billiard-ball would communicate motion to another upon impulse; and that we needed not to have waited for the event, in order to pronounce with certainty concerning it. Such is the influence of custom, that, where it is strongest, it not only covers our natural ignorance, but even conceals itself, and seems not to take place, merely because it is found in the highest degree.

But to convince us that all the laws of nature, and all the operations of bodies without exception, are known only by experience, the following reflections may, perhaps, suffice. Were any object presented to us, and were we required to pronounce concerning the effect, which will result from it, without consulting past observation; after what manner, I beseech you, must the mind proceed in this operation? It must invent or imagine some event, which it ascribes to the object as its effect; and it is plain that this invention must be entirely arbitrary. The mind can never possibly find the effect in the supposed cause, by the most accurate scrutiny and examination. For the effect is totally different from the cause, and consequently can never be discovered in it. Motion in the second Billiard-ball is a quite distinct event from motion in the first; nor is there anything in the one to suggest the smallest hint of the other. A stone or piece of metal raised into the air, and left without any support, immediately falls; but to consider the matter *a priori*, is there anything we discover in this situation which can beget the idea of a downward, rather than an upward, or any other motion, in the stone or metal?

And as the first imagination or invention of a particular effect, in all natural operations, is arbitrary, where we consult not experience; so must we also esteem the supposed tie or connection between the cause and effect, which binds them together, and renders it impossible that any other effect could result from the operation of that cause. When I see, for instance, a Billiard-ball moving in a straight line towards another; even suppose motion in the second ball should by accident be suggested to me, as the result of their contact or impulse; may I not conceive, that a hundred different events might as well follow from that cause? May not both these balls remain at absolute rest? May not the first ball return in a straight line, or leap off from the second in any line or direction? All these suppositions are consistent and conceivable. Why then should we give the preference to one, which is no more consistent or conceivable than the rest? All our reasonings *a priori* will never be able to show us any foundation for this preference.

In a word, then, every effect is a distinct event from its cause. It could not, therefore, be discovered in the cause, and the first invention or conception of it, *a priori*, must be entirely arbitrary. And even after it is suggested, the conjunction of it with the cause must appear equally arbitrary; since there are always many other effects, which, to reason, must seem fully as consistent and natural. In vain, therefore, should we pretend to determine any single event, or infer any cause or effect, without the assistance of observation and experience.

Hence we may discover the reason why no philosopher, who is rational and modest, has ever pretended to assign the ultimate cause of any natural operation, or to show distinctly the action of that power, which produces any single effect in the universe. It is confessed, that the utmost effort of human reason is to reduce the principles, productive of natural phenomena, to a greater simplicity, and to resolve the many particular effects into a few general causes, by means of reasonings from analogy, experience, and observation. But as to the causes of these general causes, we should in vain attempt their discovery; nor shall we ever be able to satisfy ourselves, by any particular explication of them. These ultimate springs and principles are totally shut up from human curiosity and inquiry. Elasticity, gravity, cohesion of parts, communication of motion by impulse; these are probably the ultimate causes and principles which we shall ever discover in nature; and we may esteem ourselves sufficiently happy, if, by accurate inquiry and reasoning, we can trace up the particular phenomena to, or near to, these general principles. The most perfect philosophy of the natural kind only staves off our ignorance a little longer, as perhaps the most perfect philosophy of the moral or metaphysical kind serves only to discover large portions of it. Thus the observation of human blindness and weakness is the result of all philosophy, and meets us at every turn, in spite of our endeavors to elude or avoid it.

II

But we have not yet attained any tolerable satisfaction with regard to the question first proposed. Each solution still gives rise to a new question as difficult as the foregoing, and leads us on to farther inquiries. When it is asked, *What is the nature of all our reasonings concerning matter of fact?* the proper answer seems to be, that they are founded on the relation of cause and effect. When again it is asked, *What is the foundation of all our reasonings and conclusions concerning that relation?* it may be replied in one word, Experience. But if we still carry on our sifting humor, and ask *What is the foundation of all conclusions from experience?* this implies a new question, which may be of more difficult solution and explication. Philosophers, that give themselves airs of superior wisdom and sufficiency, have a hard task when they encounter persons of inquisitive dispositions, who push them from every corner to which they retreat, and who are sure at last to bring them to some dangerous dilemma. The best expedient to prevent this confusion, is to be modest in our pretensions; and even to discover the difficulty ourselves before it is objected to us. By this means, we may make a kind of merit of our very ignorance.

I shall content myself, in this section, with an easy task, and shall pretend only to give a negative answer to the question here proposed. I say then, that, even after we have experience of the operations of cause and effect, our conclusions from that experience are not founded on reasoning, or any process of the understanding. This answer we must endeavor both to explain and to defend.

It must certainly be allowed, that nature has kept us at a great distance from all her secrets, and has afforded us only the knowledge of a few superficial qualities of objects; while she conceals from us those powers and principles on which the influence of those objects entirely depends. Our senses inform us of the color, weight, and consistence of bread; but neither sense nor reason can ever inform us of those qualities which fit it for the nourishment and support of a human body. Sight or feeling conveys an idea of the actual motion of bodies; but as to that wonderful force or power, which would carry on a moving body forever in a continued change of place, and which bodies never lose but by communicating it to others; of this we cannot form the most distant conception. But notwithstanding this ignorance of natural powers[1] and principles, we always presume, when we see like sensible qualities, that they have like secret powers, and expect that effects, similar to those which we have experienced, will follow from them. If a body of like color and consistence with that bread, which we have formerly eaten, be presented to us, we make no scruple of repeating the experiment, and foresee, with certainty, like nourishment and support. Now this is a process of the mind or thought, of which I would willingly know the foundation. It is allowed on all hands that there is no known connection between the sensible qualities and the secret powers; and consequently, that the mind is not led to form such a conclusion concerning their constant and regular conjunction, by anything which it knows of their nature. As to past *Experience,* it can be allowed to give *direct* and *certain* information of those precise objects only, and that precise period of time, which fell under its cognizance; but why this experience should be extended to future times, and to other objects, which for aught we know, may be only in appearance similar; this is the main question on which I would insist. The bread, which I formerly eat, nourished me; that is, a body of such sensible qualities was, at that time, endued with such secret powers; but does it follow, that other bread must also nourish me at another time, and that like sensible qualities must always be attended with like secret powers? The consequence seems nowise necessary. At least, it must be acknowledged that there is here a consequence drawn by the mind; that there is a certain step taken; a process of thought, and an inference, which wants to be explained. These two propositions are far from being the same, *I have found that such an object has always been attended with such an effect,* and *I forsee, that other objects, which are, in appearance, similar, will be attended with similar effects.* I shall allow, if you please, that the one proposition may justly be inferred from the other. I know, in fact, that it always is inferred. But if you insist that the inference is made by a chain of reasoning, I desire you to produce that reasoning. The connection between these propositions is not intuitive. There is required a medium, which may enable the mind to draw such an inference, if indeed it be drawn by reasoning and argument. What that medium is, I must confess, passes my comprehension; and it is incumbent on those to produce it, who assert that it really exists, and is the origin of all our conclusions concerning matter of fact.

This negative argument must certainly, in process of time, become altogether convincing, if many penetrating and able philosophers shall turn their inquiries this way and no one be ever able to discover any connecting proposition or intermediate step, which supports the understanding in this con-

---

[1] The word, Power, is here used in a loose and popular sense. The more accurate explication of it would give additional evidence to this argument.

clusion. But as the question is yet new, every reader may not trust so far to his own penetration, as to conclude, because an argument escapes his inquiry, that therefore it does not really exist. For this reason it may be requisite to venture upon a more difficult task; and enumerating all the branches of human knowledge, endeavor to show that none of them can afford such an argument.

All reasonings may be divided into two kinds, namely, demonstrative reasoning, or that concerning relations of ideas, and moral reasoning, or that concerning matter of fact and existence. That there are no demonstrative arguments in the case seems evident; since it implies no contradiction that the course of nature may change, and that an object, seemingly like those which we have experienced, may be attended with different or contrary effects. May I not clearly and distinctly conceive that a body, falling from the clouds, and which, in all other respects, resembles snow, has yet the taste of salt or feeling of fire? Is there any more intelligible proposition than to affirm, that all the trees will flourish in December and January, and decay in May and June? Now whatever is intelligible, and can be distinctly conceived, implies no contradiction, and can never be proved false by any demonstrative argument or abstract reasoning *a priori*.

If we be, therefore, engaged by arguments to put trust in past experience, and make it the standard of our future judgment, these arguments must be probable only, or such as regard matter of fact and real existence, according to the division above mentioned. But that there is no argument of this kind, must appear, if our explication of that species of reasoning be admitted as solid and satisfactory. We have said that all arguments concerning existence are founded on the relation of cause and effect; that our knowledge of that relation is derived entirely from experience; and that all our experimental conclusions proceed upon the supposition that the future will be conformable to the past. To endeavor, therefore, the proof of this last supposition by probable arguments, or arguments regarding existence, must be evidently going in a circle, and taking that for granted, which is the very point in question.

In reality, all arguments from experience are founded on the similarity which we discover among natural objects, and by which we are induced to expect effects similar to those which we have found to follow from such objects. And though none but a fool or madman will ever pretend to dispute the authority of experience, or to reject that great guide of human life, it may surely be allowed a philosopher to have so much curiosity at least as to examine the principle of human nature, which gives this mighty authority to experience, and makes us draw advantage from that similarity which nature has placed among different objects. From causes which appear *similar* we expect similar effects. This is the sum of all our experimental conclusions. Now it seems evident that, if this conclusion were formed by reason, it would be as perfect at first, and upon one instance, as after ever so long a course of experience. But the case is far otherwise. Nothing so like as eggs; yet no one, on account of this appearing similarity, expects the same taste and relish in all of them. It is only after a long course of uniform experiments in any kind, that we attain a firm reliance and security with regard to a particular event. Now where is that process of reasoning which, from one instance draws a conclusion so different from that which it infers from a hundred instances that are nowise different from that single one? This question I propose as much for the sake of information, as with an intention of raising difficulties. I cannot find, I cannot imagine any such reasoning. But I keep my mind still open to instruction, if any one will vouchsafe to bestow it on me.

Should it be said that, from a number of uniform experiments, we *infer* a connection between the sensible qualities and the secret powers; this, I must confess, seems the same difficulty, couched in different terms. The question still recurs, on what process of argument this *inference* is founded? Where is the medium, the interposing ideas, which join propositions so very wide of each other? Is it confessed that the color, consistence, and other sensible qualities of bread appear not, of themselves, to have any connection with the secret powers of nourishment and support? For otherwise we could infer these secret powers from the first appearance of these sensible qualities, without the aid of experience; contrary to the sentiment of all philosophers, and contrary to plain matter of fact. Here, then, is our natural state of ignorance with regard to the powers and influence of all objects. How is this remedied by experience? It only shows us a number of uniform effects, resulting from certain objects, and teaches us that those particular objects, at that particular time, were endowed with such powers and forces. When a new object, endowed with similar sensible qualities, is produced, we expect similar powers and forces, and look for a like effect. From a body of like color and consistence with bread we expect like nourishment and support. But this surely is a step or progress of the mind, which wants to be explained. When a man says, *I have found, in all past instances, such sensible qualities conjoined with such secret powers;* And when he says, *Similar sensible qualities will always be conjoined with similar secret powers,* he is not guilty of a tautology, nor are these propositions in any respect the same. You say that the one proposition is an inference from the other. But you must confess that the inference is not intuitive; neither is it demonstrative. Of what nature is it, then? To say it is experimental, is begging the question. For all inferences from experiences suppose, as their foundation, that the future will resemble the past, and that similar powers will be conjoined with similar sensible qualities. If there be any suspicion that the course of nature may change, and that the past may be no rule for the future, all experience becomes useless, and can give rise to no inference or conclusion. It is impossible, therefore, that any arguments from experience can prove this resemblance of the past to the future; since all these arguments are founded on the supposition of that resemblance. Let the course of things be allowed hitherto ever so regular; that alone, without some new argument or inference, proves not that, for the future, it will continue so. In vain do you pretend to have learned the nature of bodies from your past experience. Their secret nature, and consequently all their effects and influence, may change, without any change in their sensible qualities. This happens sometimes, and with regard to some objects. Why may it not happen always, and with regard to all objects? What logic, what process of argument secures you against this supposition? My practice, you say, refutes my doubts. But you mistake the purport of my question. As an agent, I am quite satisfied in the point; but as a philosopher, who has some share of curiosity, I will not say skepticism, I want to learn the foundation of this inference. No reading, no inquiry has yet been able to remove my difficulty, or give me satisfaction in a matter of such importance. Can I do better than propose the difficulty to the public, even though, perhaps, I have small hopes of obtaining a solution? We shall at least, by this means, be sensible of our ignorance, if we do not augment our knowledge.

I must confess that a man is guilty of unpardonable arrogance who concludes, because an argument has escaped his own investigation, that therefore it does not really exist. I must also confess that, though all the learned, for several ages, should have employed themselves in fruitless search upon any subject, it may still, perhaps, be rash to conclude positively that the subject must, therefore, pass all human comprehension. Even though we examine all the sources of our knowledge, and conclude them unfit for such a subject, there may still remain a suspicion, that the enumeration is not complete, or the examination not accurate. But with regard to the present subject, there are some considerations which seem to remove all this accusation of arrogance or suspicion of mistake.

It is certain that the most ignorant and stupid peasants—nay infants, nay even brute beasts—improve by experience, and learn the qualities of natural objects, by observing the effects which result from them. When a child has felt the sensation of pain from touching the flame of a candle, he will be careful not to put his hand near any candle; but will expect a similar effect from a cause which is similar in its sensible qualities and appearance. If you assert, therefore, that the understanding of the child is led into this conclusion by any process of argument or ratiocination, I may just require you to produce that argument; nor have you any pretence to refuse so equitable a demand. You cannot say that the argument is abstruse, and may possibly escape your inquiry; since you confess that it is obvious to the capacity of a mere infant. If you hesitate, therefore, a moment, or if, after reflection, you produce any intricate or profound argument, you, in a manner, give up the question, and confess that it is not reasoning which engages us to suppose the past resembling the future, and to expect similar effects from causes which are, to appearance, similar. This is the proposition which I intended to enforce in the present section. If I be right, I pretend not to have made any mighty discovery. And if I be wrong, I must acknowledge myself to be indeed a very backward scholar; since I cannot now discover an argument which, it seems, was perfectly familiar to me long before I was out of my cradle.

STUDY QUESTIONS

1. Hume says that causes and effects are discovered not by reason, but by experience. What does he mean by the words "reason" and "experience"?
2. Hume suggests that it is possible to imagine stuff falling from the sky which resembles snow in every respect, except that it is hot instead of cold. What is his point? Do you agree that such an event is possible?
3. "Since bread has nourished me in the past, it will continue to do so in the future." Would Hume say that this is a valid inference? Why? Do you think that the future resembles the past?
4. "The terms 'cause' and 'effect' are no longer widely used in science.... The terms which replace them, however, refer to the same factual core.... The new terms do not suggest *how* a cause causes its effect: they merely assert that different events tend to occur together in a certain order" (B. F. Skinner). Would Hume think that Skinner's conception of cause and effect is correct? How do you think Skinner would locate the "causes" of human behavior?
5. What do you think Hume would say to someone who thought that the moon stays in orbit because the earth *attracts* it through the force of gravity?

Scientific Method
Morris R. Cohen and Ernest Nagel

Morris R. Cohen (1880–1947) was born in Russia, emigrated to America at age twelve; lived in New York, where he attended college; took a philosophy degree from Harvard; and eventually became one of America's most respected twentieth-century philosophers. Cohen taught at several universities, including the City College of New York, the University of Chicago, and the New School for Social Research. He contributed important ideas to several branches of philosophy, especially logic, the philosophy of science, and legal philosophy. His major works include *Reason and Nature: An Essay on the Meaning of Scientific Method* (1931), *Law and the Social Order: Essays in Legal Philosophy* (1933), *A Preface to Logic* (1945), and *An Introduction to Logic and Scientific Method* (1934), with his former student, Ernest Nagel.

In this excerpt from the last book, Cohen and Nagel (see the biographical information on p. 48) outline the method of science, the most effective way to acquire reliable knowledge, in their view. While they write in the empirical tradition which includes Hume, they reject his narrow brand of empiricism. Science does not proceed merely by collecting facts based on observations. Indeed, a "fact" is not ascertained without analysis and interpretation. Scientific method, they argue, relies heavily on hypotheses— tentative assertions, often flowing from a hunch or guess—which rest on very little factual evidence. Science involves an interplay of theories and facts, with each necessarily open to reassessment as time passes. Often scientific theories are speculative explanations meant to inform us as to how unobserved forces and events cause observed forces and events; they acquire authority from their predictive power.

FACTS AND SCIENTIFIC METHOD

The method of science does not seek to impose the desires and hopes of men upon the flux of things in a capricious manner. It may indeed be employed to satisfy the desires of men. But its successful use depends upon seeking, in a deliberate manner, and irrespective of what men's desires are, to recognize, as well as to take advantage of, the structure which the flux possesses.

Consequently, scientific method aims to discover what the facts truly are, and the use of the method must be guided by the discovered facts. But, as we have repeatedly pointed out, what the facts are cannot be discovered without reflection. Knowledge of the facts cannot be equated to the brute immediacy of our sensations. When our skin comes into contact with objects having high temperatures or with liquid air, the immediate experiences may be similar. We cannot, however, conclude without error that the temperatures of the substances touched are the same. Sensory experience sets the *problem* for knowledge, and just because such experience is immediate and final it must become informed by reflective analysis before knowledge can be said to take place.

Every inquiry arises from some felt problem, so that no inquiry can even get under way unless some selection or sifting of the subject matter has taken place. Such selection requires, we have been urging all along, some hypothesis, preconception, prejudice, which guides the research as well as delimits the subject matter of inquiry. Every inquiry is specific in the sense that it has a definite problem to solve, and such solution terminates the inquiry. It is idle to collect "facts" unless there is a problem upon which they are supposed to bear.

The ability to formulate problems whose solution may also help solve other problems is a rare gift, requiring extraordinary genius. The problems which meet us in daily life can be solved, if they can be solved at all, by the application of scientific method. But such problems do not, as a rule, raise far-reaching issues. The most striking applications of scientific method are to be found in the various natural and social sciences.

The "facts" for which every inquiry reaches out are propositions for whose truth there is considerable evidence. Consequently what the "facts" are must be determined by inquiry, and cannot be determined antecedently to inquiry.

Moreover, what we believe to be the facts clearly depends upon the stage of our inquiry. There is therefore no sharp line dividing facts from guesses or hypotheses. During any inquiry the status of a proposition may change from that of hypothesis to that of fact, or from that of fact to that of hypothesis. Every so-called fact, therefore, *may* be challenged for the evidence upon which it is asserted to be a fact, even though no such challenge is actually made.

HYPOTHESES AND SCIENTIFIC METHOD

The method of science would be impossible if the hypotheses which are suggested as solutions could not be elaborated to reveal what they imply. The full meaning of a hypothesis is to be discovered in its implications.

Hypotheses are suggested to an inquirer by something in the subject matter under investigation, and by his previous knowledge of other subject matters. No rules can be offered for obtaining fruitful hypotheses, any more than rules can be given for discovering significant problems.

Hypotheses are required at every stage of an inquiry. It must not be forgotten that what are called general principles of laws (which may have been confirmed in a previous inquiry) can be applied to a present, still unterminated inquiry only with some risk. For they may not in fact be applicable. The general laws of any science function as hypotheses, which guide the inquiry in all its phases.

Hypotheses can be regarded as suggestions of possible connections between actual facts or imagined ones. The question of the truth of hypotheses need not, therefore, always be raised. The necessary feature of a hypothesis, from this point of view, is that it should be statable in a determinate form, so that its implications can be discovered by logical means.

The number of hypotheses which may occur to an inquirer is without limit, and is a function of the character of his imagination. There is a need, therefore, for a technique to choose between the alternative suggestions, and to make sure that the alternatives are in fact, and not only in appearance, *different* theories. Perhaps the most important and best explored part of such a technique is the technique of formal inference. For this reason, the structure of formal logic has been examined at some length. The object of that examination has been to give the reader an adequate sense of what formal validity means, as well as to provide him with a synoptic view of the power and range of formal logic.

It is convenient to have on hand—in storage, so to speak—different hypotheses whose consequences have been carefully explored. It is the task of mathematics to provide and explore alternative hypotheses. Mathematics receives hints concerning what hypotheses to study from the natural sciences; and the natural sciences are indebted to mathematics for suggestions concerning the type of order which their subject matter embodies.

The deductive elaboration of hypotheses is not the sole task of scientific method. Since there is a plurality of possible hypotheses, it is the risk of inquiry to determine which of the possible explanations or solutions of the problem is in best agreement with the facts. Formal considerations are therefore never sufficient to establish the material truth of any theory.

No hypothesis which states a general proposition can be demonstrated as absolutely true. We have seen that all inquiry which deals with matters of fact employs probable inference. The task of such investigations is to select that hypothesis which is the most probable on the factual evidence; and it is the task of further inquiry to find other factual evidence which will increase or decrease the probability of such a theory.

EVIDENCE AND SCIENTIFIC METHOD

Scientific method pursues the road of systematic doubt. It does not doubt *all* things, for this is clearly impossible. But it does question whatever lacks adequate evidence in its support.

Science is not satisfied with psychological certitude, for the mere intensity with which a belief is held is no guarantee of its truth. Science demands and looks for logically adequate grounds for the propositions it advances.

No single proposition dealing with matters of fact is beyond every significant doubt. No proposition is so well supported by evidence that other evidence may not increase or decrease its probability. However, while no single proposition is indubitable, the body of knowledge which supports it, and of which it is itself a part, is better grounded than any alternative body of knowledge.

Science is thus always ready to abandon a theory when the facts so demand. But the facts must really demand it. It is not unusual for a theory to be modified so that it may be retained in substance even though "facts" contradicted an earlier formulation of it. Scientific procedure is therefore a mixture of a willingness to change, and an obstinacy in holding on to, theories apparently incompatible with facts.

The verification of theories is only approximate. Verification simply shows that, within the margin of experimental error, the experiment is *compatible* with the verified hypothesis.

SYSTEM IN THE IDEAL OF SCIENCE

The ideal of science is to achieve a systematic interconnection of facts. Isolated propositions do not constitute a science. Such propositions serve merely as an opportunity to find the logical connection between them and other propositions.

"Common sense" is content with a miscellaneous collection of information. As a consequence, the propositions it asserts are frequently vague, the range of their application is unknown, and their mutual compatibility is generally very questionable. The advantages of discovering a system among facts is therefore obvious. A condition for achieving a system is the introduction of accuracy in the assertions made. The limit within which propositions are true is then clearly defined. Moreover, inconsistencies between propositions asserted become eliminated gradually because propositions which are part of a system must support and correct one another. The extent and accuracy of our information is thus increased. In fact, scientific method differs from other methods in the accuracy and number of facts it studies.

When, as frequently happens, a science abandons one theory for another, it is a mistake to suppose that science has become "bankrupt" and that it is incapable of discovering the structure of the subject matter it studies. Such changes indicate rather that the science is progressively realizing its ideal. For such changes arise from correcting previous observations or reasoning, and such correction means that we are in possession of more reliable facts.

The ideal of system requires that the propositions asserted to be true should be connected without the introduction of further propositions for which the evidence is small or nonexistent. In a system the number of unconnected propositions and the number of propositions for which there is no evidence are at a minimum. Consequently, in a system the requirements of simplicity, as expressed in the principle of Occam's razor, are satisfied in a high degree. For that principle declares that entities should not be multiplied beyond necessity. This may be interpreted as a demand that whatever is capable of proof should be proved. But the idea of system requires just that.

The evidence for propositions which are elements in a system accumulates more rapidly than that for isolated propositions. The evidence for a proposition may come from its own verifying instances, or from the verifying instances of *other* propositions which are connected with the first in a system. It is this systematic character of scientific theories which gives such high probabilities to the various individual propositions of a science.

THE SELF-CORRECTIVE NATURE
OF SCIENTIFIC METHOD

Science does not desire to obtain conviction for its propositions in *any* manner and at *any* price. Propositions must be supported by logically acceptable evidence, which must be weighed carefully and tested by the well-known canons of necessary and probable inference. It follows that the *method* of science is more stable, and more important to men of science, than any particular result achieved by its means.

In virtue of its method, the enterprise of science is a self-corrective process. It appeals to no special revelation or authority whose deliverances are indubitable and final. It claims no infallibility, but relies upon the methods of developing and testing hypotheses for assured conclusions. The canons of inquiry are themselves discovered in the process of reflection, and may themselves become modified in the course of study. The method makes possible the noting and correction of errors by continued application of itself.

General propositions can be established only by the method of repeated sampling. Consequently, the propositions which a science puts forward for study are either confirmed in all possible experiments or modified in accordance with the evidence. It is this self-corrective nature of the method which allows us to challenge any proposition, but which also assures us that the theories which science accepts are more probable than any alternative theories. By not claiming more certainty than the evidence warrants, scientific method succeeds in obtaining more logical certainty than any other method yet devised.

In the process of gathering and weighing evidence, there is a continuous appeal from facts to theories or principles, and from principles to facts. For there is nothing intrinsically indubitable, there are no absolutely first principles, in the sense of principles which are self-evident or which must be known prior to everything else.

The method of science is thus essentially circular. We obtain evidence for principles by appealing to empirical material, to what is alleged to be "fact"; and we select, analyze, and interpret empirical material on the basis of principles. In virtue of such give and take between facts and principles, everything that is dubitable falls under careful scrutiny at one time or another.

THE ABSTRACT NATURE OF SCIENTIFIC THEORIES

No theory asserts *everything* that can possibly be asserted about a subject matter. Every theory selects certain aspects of it and excludes others. Unless it were possible to do this—either because such other aspects are irrelevant or because their influence on those selected is very minute—science as we know it would be impossible.

All theories involve abstraction from concrete subject matter. No rule can be given as to which aspects of a subject matter should be abstracted and so studied independently of other aspects. But in virtue of the goal of science— the achievement of a systematic interconnection of phenomena—in general those aspects will be abstracted which make a realization of this goal possible. Certain common elements in the phenomenon studied must be found, so that the endless variety of phenomena may be viewed as a system in which their structure is exhibited.

Because of the abstractness of theories, science often seems in patent contradiction with "common sense." In "common sense" the unique character and the pervasive character of things are not distinguished, so that the attempt by science to disclose the invariant features often gives the appearance of artificiality. Theories are then frequently regarded as "convenient fictions" or as "unreal." However, such criticisms overlook the fact that it is just certain *selected invariant relations* of things in which science is interested, so that many familiar properties of things are necessarily neglected by the sciences. Moreover, they forget that "common sense" itself operates in terms of abstractions, which are familiar and often confused, and which are inadequate to express the complex structure of the flux of things.

TYPES OF SCIENTIFIC THEORIES

Scientific explanation consists in subsuming under some rule or law which expresses an invariant character of a group of events, the particular events it is said to explain. Laws themselves may be explained, and in the same manner, by showing that they are consequences of more comprehensive theories. The effect of such progressive explanation of events by laws, laws by wider laws or theories, is to reveal the interconnection of many apparently isolated propositions.

It is clear, however, that the process of explanation must come to a halt at some point. Theories which cannot be shown to be special consequences from a wider connection of facts must be left unexplained, and accepted as a part of the brute fact of existence. Material considerations, in the form of contingent matters of fact, must be recognized in at least two places. There is contingency at the level of sense: just *this* and not *that* is given in sense experience. And there is contingency at the level of explanation: a definite system, although not the only possible one from the point of view of formal logic, is found to be exemplified in the flux of things.

In a previous chapter we have enumerated several kinds of "laws" which frequently serve as explanations of phenomena. There is, however, another interesting distinction between theories. Some theories appeal to an easily imagined *hidden mechanism* which will explain the observable phenomena; other theories eschew all reference to such hidden mechanisms, and make use of *relations* abstracted from the phenomena actually observable. The former are called *physical* theories; the latter are called *mathematical* or *abstractive* theories.

It is important to be aware of the difference between these two kinds of theories, and to understand that some minds are especially attracted to one kind, while others are comfortable only with the other kind. But it is also essential not to suppose that either kind of theory is more fundamental or more valid than the other. In the history of science there is a constant oscillation between theories of these two types; sometimes both types of theories are used successfully on the same subject matter. Let us, however, make clear the difference between them.

The English physicist Rankine explained the distinction as follows: There are two methods of framing a theory. In a mathematical or abstractive theory, "a class of objects or phenomena is defined...by describing...that assemblage of properties which is common to all the objects or phenomena composing the class, as perceived by the senses, without introducing anything hypothetical." In a physical theory "a class of objects is defined...as being constituted, in a manner not apparent to the senses, by a modification of some other class of objects or phenomena whose laws are already known."[1]

In the second kind of theory, some visualizable model is made the pattern for a mechanism hidden from the senses. Some physicists, like Kelvin, cannot be satisfied with anything less than a mechanical explanation of observable phenomena, no matter how complex such a mechanism may be. Examples of this kind of theory are the atomic theory of chemistry, the kinetic theory of matter as developed in thermodynamics and the behavior of gases, the theory of the gene in studies on heredity, the theory of lines of force in electrostatics, and the recent Bohr model of the atom in spectroscopy.

In the mathematical type of theory, the appeal to hidden mechanisms is eliminated, or at any rate is at a minimum. How this may be done is graphically described by Henri Poincaré: "Suppose we have before us any machine; the initial wheel work and the final wheel work alone are visible, but the transmission, the intermediary machinery by which the movement is communicated from one to the other, is hidden in the interior and escapes our view; we do not know whether the communication is made by gearing or by belts, by connecting-rods or by other contrivances. Do we say that it is impossible for us to understand anything about this machine so long as we are not permitted to take it to pieces? You know well we do not, and that the principle of the conservation of energy suffices to determine for us the most interesting point. We easily ascertain that the final wheel turns ten times less quickly than the initial wheel, since these two wheels are visible; we are able thence to conclude that a couple applied to the one will be balanced by a couple ten times greater applied to the other. For that there is no need to penetrate the mechanism of this equilibrium and to know how the forces compensate each other in the interior of the machine."[2] Examples of such theories are the theory of gravitation, Galileo's laws of falling bodies, the theory of the flow of heat, the theory of organic evolution, and the theory of relativity.

As we suggested, it is useless to quarrel as to which type of theory is the more fundamental and which type should be universally adopted. Both kinds of theories have been successful in coordinating vast domains of phenomena, and fertile in making discoveries of the most important kind. At some periods in the history of a science, there is a tendency to mechanical models and atomicity; at others, to general principles connecting characteristics abstracted from directly observable phenomena; at still others, to a fusion or synthesis of these two points of view. Some scientists, like Kelvin, Faraday, Lodge, Maxwell, show an exclusive preference for "model" theories; other scientists, like Rankine, Ostwald, Duhem, can work best with the abstractive theories; and still others, like Einstein, have the unusual gift of being equally at home with both kinds.

[1] W. J. M. Rankine, *Miscellaneous Scientific Paper,* 1881, p. 210.
[2] Op. cit., pp. 290–291.

THE LIMITS AND THE VALUE OF SCIENTIFIC METHOD

The desire for knowledge for its own sake is more widespread than is generally recognized by anti-intellectualists. It has its roots in the animal curiosity which shows itself in the cosmological questions of children and in the gossip of adults. No ulterior utilitarian motive makes people want to know about the private lives of their neighbors, the great, or the notorious. There is also a certain zest which makes people engage in various intellectual games or exercises in which one is required to find out something. But while the desire to know is wide, it is seldom strong enough to overcome the more powerful organic desires, and few indeed have both the inclination and the ability to face the arduous difficulties of scientific method in more than one special field. The desire to know is not often strong enough to sustain critical inquiry. Men generally are interested in the results, in the story or romance of science, not in the technical methods whereby these results are obtained and their truth continually is tested and qualified. Our first impulse is to accept the plausible as true and to reject the uncongenial as false. We have not the time, inclination, or energy to investigate everything. Indeed, the call to do so is often felt as irksome and joy-killing. And when we are asked to treat our cherished beliefs as mere hypotheses, we rebel as violently as when those dear to us are insulted. This provides the ground for various movements that are hostile to rational scientific procedure (though their promoters do not often admit that it is science to which they are hostile).

Mystics, intuitionists, authoritarians, voluntarists, and fictionalists are all trying to undermine respect for the rational methods of science. These attacks have always met with wide acclaim and are bound to continue to do so, for they strike a responsive note in human nature. Unfortunately they do not offer any reliable alternative method for obtaining verifiable knowledge. The great French writer Pascal opposed to logic the spirit of subtlety or finesse (*esprit géometrique* and *esprit de finesse*) and urged that the heart has its reasons as well as the mind, reasons that cannot be accurately formulated but which subtle spirits apprehend none the less. Men as diverse as James Russell Lowell and George Santayana are agreed that:

> "The soul is oracular still,"
>   and
> "It is wisdom to trust the heart...
> To trust the soul's invincible surmise."

Now it is true that in the absence of omniscience we must trust our soul's surmise; and great men are those whose surmises or intuitions are deep or penetrating. It is only by acting on our surmise that we can procure the evidence in its favor. But only havoc can result from confusing a surmise with a proposition for which there is already evidence. Are all the reasons of the heart sound? Do all oracles tell the truth? The sad history of human experience is distinctly discouraging to any such claim. Mystic intuition may give men absolute subjective certainty, but can give no proof that contrary intuitions are erroneous. It is obvious that when authorities conflict we must weigh the evidence in their favor logically if we are to make a rational choice. Certainly, when a truth is questioned it is no answer to say, "I am convinced," or, "I prefer to rely on this rather than on another authority." The view that physical science is no guide to proof, but is a mere fiction, fails to explain why it has enabled us to anticipate phenomena of nature and to control them. These attacks on scientific method receive a certain color of plausibility because of some indefensible claims made by uncritical enthusiasts. But it is of the essence of scientific method to limit its own pretension. Recognizing that we do not know everything, it does not claim the ability to solve all of our practical problems. It is an error to suppose, as is often done, that science denies the truth of all unverified propositions. For that which is unverified today may be verified tomorrow. We may get at truth by guessing or in other ways. Scientific method, however, is concerned with verification. Admittedly the wisdom of those engaged in this process has not been popularly ranked as high as that of the sage, the prophet, or the poet. Admittedly, also, we know of no way of supplying creative intelligence to those who lack it. Scientists, like all other human beings, may get into ruts and apply their techniques regardless of varying circumstances. There will always be formal procedures which are fruitless. Definitions and formal distinctions may be a sharpening of tools without the wit to use them properly, and statistical information may conform to the highest technical standards and yet be irrelevant and inconclusive. Nevertheless, scientific method is the only way to increase the general body of tested and verified truth and to eliminate arbitrary opinion. It is well to clarify our ideas by asking for the precise meaning of our words, and to try to check our favorite ideas by applying them to accurately formulated propositions.

In raising the question as to the social need for scientific method, it is well to recognize that the suspension of judgment which is essential to that method is difficult or impossible when we are pressed by the demands of immediate action. When my house is on fire, I must act quickly and promptly—I cannot stop to consider the possible causes, nor even to estimate the exact probabilities involved in the various alternative ways of reacting. For this reason, those who are bent upon some specific course of action often despise those devoted to reflection; and certain ultramodernists seem to argue as if the need for action guaranteed the truth of our decision. But the fact that I must either vote for candidate X or refrain from doing so does not of itself give me adequate knowledge. The frequency of our regrets makes this obvious. Wisely ordered society is therefore provided with means for deliberation and reflection *before* the pressure of action becomes irresistible. In order to assure the most thorough investigation, all possible views must be canvassed, and this means toleration of views that are *prima facie* most repugnant to us.

In general the chief social condition of scientific method is a widespread desire for truth that is strong enough to withstand the powerful forces which make us cling tenaciously to old views or else embrace every novelty because it is a change. Those who are engaged in scientific work need not only leisure for reflection and material for their experiment, but also a community that respects the pursuit of truth and allows freedom for the expression of intellectual doubt as to its most sacred or established institutions. Fear of offending established dogmas has been an obstacle to the growth of astronomy and geology and other physical sciences; and the fear of offending patriotic or respected sentiment is perhaps one of the strongest hindrances to scholarly history and social science. On the other hand, when a community indiscriminately acclaims every new doctrine the love of truth becomes subordinated to the desire for novel formulations.

On the whole it may be said that the safety of science depends on there being men who care more for the justice of their methods than for any results obtained by their use. For this reason it is unfortunate when scientific research in the social field is largely in the hands of those not in a favorable position to oppose established or popular opinion.

We may put it the other way by saying that the physical sciences can be more liberal because we are sure that foolish opinions will be readily eliminated by the shock of facts. In the social field, however, no one can tell what harm may come of foolish ideas before the foolishness is finally, if ever, demonstrated. None of the precautions of scientific method can prevent human life from being an adventure, and no scientific investigator knows whether he will reach his goal. But scientific method does enable large numbers to walk with surer steps. By analyzing the possibilities of any step or plan, it becomes possible to anticipate the future and adjust ourselves to it in advance. Scientific method thus minimizes the shock of novelty and the uncertainty of life. It enables us to frame policies of actions and of moral judgment fit for a wider outlook than those of immediate physical stimulus or organic response.

Scientific method is the only effective way of strengthening the love of truth. It develops the intellectual courage to face difficulties and to overcome illusions that are pleasant temporarily but destructive ultimately. It settles differences without any external force by appealing to our common rational nature. The way of science, even if it is up a steep mountain, is open to all. Hence, while sectarian and partisan faiths are based on personal choice or temperament and divide men, scientific procedure unites men in something nobly devoid of all pettiness. Because it requires detachment, disinterestedness, it is the finest flower and test of a liberal civilization.

STUDY QUESTIONS

1. What do Cohen and Nagel mean by a hypothesis? When do they suggest we may rationally believe one?
2. The article makes a brief reference to Occam's razor. This sounds like a shaving product. Why is it mentioned in an essay on scientific method?

3. Cohen and Nagel refer to physical theories and mathematical or abstractive theories. What is the difference, and what are examples of each?
4. The article says that science appeals to "no special revelation or authority whose deliverances are indubitable and final." Does this mean that scientists, and others who use the method of science, cannot possibly be religious?
5. What exactly is a "fact"? Does the article ever give a definition of one, implicitly or explicitly?

6

Truth

PROBLEM INTRODUCTION

"Don't believe everything you read!" People who chose to ignore this old but wise maxim would turn into mindless, irresponsible fools. They would have no basis on which to justify or defend their acceptance of particular statements, and before long they would affirm contradictory statements. In addition, if people were to believe whatever they read or heard, they would be pathetic puppets. In the political arena, for instance, cover-ups, fabrications, and exaggerations are routine, and so politicians could manipulate them. Also, in the commercial world, the advertising industry, a multi-billion-dollar annual enterprise, inundates us with slick appeals whose purpose is to condition our behavior, not illuminate the truth. Incredibly the average American has seen 350,000 television commercials before graduating from high school.* In such circumstances, a good dose of skepticism is welcome and necessary. Yet, "Don't believe *everything* you read," is not the same as "Don't believe *anything* you read." While most people would endorse a mild form of skepticism as healthy, few would endorse a radical form, thereby surrendering altogether the hope of acquiring accurate and reliable knowledge. This is certainly the case in the philosophical community. In the main philosophers over the centuries have tried to identify the characteristics of true statements and to determine the meaning or definition of truth, and in this section of the book you will find three authors—William James, Bertrand Russell, and Brand Blanshard—who represent the three main lines of thinking on the problem of truth.

A word, first, however, about the philosophical minority: the radical skeptics. Since the very beginning of philosophical reflection, even before Socrates, there have been thinkers who denied the possibility of acquiring genuine knowledge, of distinguishing true statements from false ones. Legend has it that one of these early radical skeptics, Cratylus, was so adamant that our quest for

---

* Robert N. Bellah, *The Broken Covenant: American Civil Religion in Time of Trial* (New York: Seabury, 1975), p. 133.

knowledge is doomed, that he actually refused to speak, believing that his statements could not possibly be truthful. People who share this position face logical difficulties if they choose to defend it. If they say, in effect, "We can know nothing for sure," we might ask whether they are sure of that statement. If they answer "yes," they have contradicted their claim by asserting at least a single truth; if they answer "no," they are retracting the claim and thus opening the door to an opposite claim—namely that one can know *something* for sure. Furthermore, if they offer arguments in support of their claim, they are presuming that both the premises and the conclusion are sound—truthful, if you will—and again they are trapped. Furthermore, radical skeptics' living usually puts the lie to their talking. If you examine their behavior, you will find that they act on statements or beliefs which they accept implicitly as truthful. They wear clothes to protect themselves from the elements, pay their bills on time, and eat regularly—all of which actions show that they implicitly affirm some truths about themselves and their surroundings.

Another simplistic response to the problem of truth deserves a mention. This is the appeal to authority. If you wish to know the truth, consult an authority, a person thoroughly trained and educated in a particular field. Historically, this view has its roots in the philosophy of Plato. Plato argued that a select few in society possess a superior intellectual endowment, which, when cultivated, enables them to grasp unchanging truths. Based on insight into the "forms" or "essences" of things, the wisdom of the intelligentsia is beyond the reach of ordinary people who lack the native intellectual powers and the extraordinary self-discipline required to be truly wise. In Plato's *Republic,* his sketch of an ideal society, those possessing wisdom—absolute knowledge—are entitled to absolute political power.

While we would be foolish to ignore the advice of authorities, it would be even more foolish to follow them slavishly, accepting their judgment as final, uncritically. Again, Galileo's case is instructive. His theories flew in the face of encrusted views; both scientific and ecclesiastical authorities condemned him and subjected him to a cruel and terrifying ordeal. Generally speaking, the authorities of the day shared a consensus, which, however, proved to be flawed. Further, in our complex, changing, technological world of the late twentieth century, unanimity among authorities is the exception more than the rule. For instance, it is quite common for congressional hearings to turn up contradictory claims from authorities, on questions ranging from military weapons to health insurance, to drug abuse, to the economy, to energy. Imagine the frustration of a well-intentioned legislator who wants to make an intelligent, responsible decision on a critical public issue. Finally, even authorities, when they form judgments, apply standards and procedures to ensure that particular claims, statements, or hypotheses are sound. Either implicitly or explicitly they too recognize that sound, or truthful, statements have identifiable characteristics. Even the most dogmatic of them would be unlikely to say "X is true because I say so." They would give reasons which they expected others to understand and accept. They accept a particular assertion because it meets those criteria which they associate with truth. Thus, for all the reasons cited, the appeal to authority is no substitute for the hard philosophical work of discovering the basic distinguishing characteristics of truth.

One theory of truth is the *pragmatic* theory. Pragmatism, a native American philosophical school which began with the work of Charles Sanders Peirce in the nineteenth century, emphasizes the close relationship between thinking and acting. Indeed, thinking is viewed by pragmatists as problem-solving activity; ideas are plans of action; the meaning of ideas or terms is reducible to their concrete, practical implications. On the subject of truth, pragmatists tell us that a statement is true if, when we act upon it, we actually encounter the consequences which the statement implies, anticipates, or predicts. Every meaningful statement, they argue, can be translated into a set of consequences which is supposed to follow if specific operations are performed. So perform the operations, and observe whether the consequences ensue; if so, the statement is true; if not, it is false. For instance, let us suppose that your doctor diagnoses an ailment of yours as an allergy to chlorine, which you encounter frequently since swimming is one of your hobbies. Is his or her diagnosis, formulated in the statement, "You are allergic to chlorine," true or false? This statement implies that should you stop swimming and exposing yourself to chlorine for a time, then the ailment will disappear. If you do the former, and the latter ensues, a pragmatist would say that the doctor's statement is true; if the ailment continues, however, the diagnosis would be false.

Peirce, William James, and John Dewey, the three most important pragmatists, did not state the pragmatic theory identically. James's version is reprinted here, and you should know that both Peirce and Dewey found fault with it; in fact, both would share at least some of the criticisms recited in the article by Bertrand Russell which follows the one by James. One of the reasons that James invited criticism is his use of ordinary language in discussing complicated philosophical problems. For instance, he defines truth variously as "that which works" or "that which pays." To his critics this "loose" talk meant sloppy thinking and imprecision. Also, James always emphasized, no doubt reflecting his early career as a psychologist, that man is both a *rational* and a *passional* animal. For James our beliefs have to fulfill both parts of our nature. As a result James endorsed affirming beliefs, such as belief in God, in the absence of verification, on the basis that holding such beliefs is satisfying, and that holding them may result, eventually, in the evidence which substantiates them. To the critic such as Russell, who insists that our beliefs correspond to confirming *facts* before we embrace them, James is sacrificing objectivity at the altar of self-satisfaction. The rational in man bows to the passional.

Perhaps on the subject of God, and other metaphysical issues, James was mistaken. Yet he seems to have hit on a genuine insight about the indispensable role of human endeavor in "making" the truth. By accepting a belief, and acting upon it, we can at times bring about the consequences which confirm the belief. For instance, an athlete who hopes to set a new record in an event must first believe that he or she can do so; without this vital assumption the

athlete would not proceed to sharpen his or her skills through intensive training and top-flight competition; and without the training and competition he
or she could not break the record. Most philosophers today have come to see
this side of James. Yet they would insist that the athlete's belief is not arbitrary
or reckless; surely past performances and the coach's advice would serve as
the basis for such self-confidence. Further, most would say, holding the belief,
in this case, is a *necessary* but not a *sufficient* condition for its truthfulness. This
means that the belief must be held as a condition of its being proven true, but
that the mere holding of it is not enough to guarantee its truth; there has to
be an eventual record-breaking performance—a fact—to establish truth. Russell,
both criticizing James and arguing on behalf of the correspondence theory of
truth, would no doubt be among those who reason along these lines.

The pragmatic and correspondence tests are not the only ones. The third
major test is called the "coherence" test because it argues that a statement is
true if it coheres—is consistent—with the scheme or system of beliefs which
we have come to accept. This view, supported in the readings by Brand
Blanshard, an influential American philosopher, presumes that the *object* of
knowledge—humans and Nature—is ordered and systematic, and that knowledge itself is therefore ordered and systematic. Each advance in knowledge
uncovers intrinsic features in objects which tie them together increasingly into
one comprehensive system of reality. Likewise, statements about reality are
increasingly systematic; more and more they entail one another, like the pieces
of a giant puzzle. So, from the perspective of the coherence test, if a statement
is consistent with the body of knowledge which has been formed over time,
and which is taken to be sound, then it is true; if not, it is false.

Critics of the coherence test allege that it militates against the discovery
of new knowledge. The advance of knowledge, they say, means, at least occasionally, accepting beliefs which are at odds with those held now and in the
past. Sometimes there is a need for a wholesale change in the "system." To
the extent that the coherence test favors the *status quo,* to the extent it resists
the new in principle, it detracts from the discovery of truth. Blanshard and
others have tried to defend the coherence test against such criticisms; you
should decide whether the defense is successful after you have read and analyzed all three articles.

Thus, to determine truth and falsity, the pragmatic theory focuses on a
statement's relation to *predicted experiences;* the correspondence theory focuses
on a statement's relation to *facts;* and the coherence theory focuses on a statement's relation to *other statements.* Perhaps, in the end, there is no single relation of a statement which qualifies it as true. Perhaps the more of these three
possible relations a statement has, the more confident we can be of its truthfulness, and the fewer it has, the less confident we can be. As you read the
following selections, see if you can endorse one of the three classical positions,
or perhaps formulate your own more adequate theory of truth.

The Pragmatic Test
William James

William James (1842–1910) was one of the boldest thinkers America has produced. His early aspirations were to become an artist, but he chose medicine instead, obtaining a medical degree from Harvard in 1869. Branching out from medicine, he turned first to physiology and then to psychology. His book *The Principles of Psychology* was published in 1890, and for decades was the definitive text. From psychology James moved next into the study of religious experience and philosophy. During this period he produced such masterpieces as *The Varieties of Religious Experience* (1902) and *Pragmatism* (1907). Throughout his career his work was characterized by a vitality and intensity which bring theory into close connection with life.

In the following classic essay, James describes the pragmatic theory of truth. Although he defines truth in several different ways, the most popular one is truth is "that which works." James suggests that statements, or beliefs, bear implicit or explicit predictions about what will follow if one acts upon them. When, if one acts upon a statement, the predicted consequences actually follow, the statement is true; if they do not, it is false.

James's critics claimed that his endorsing beliefs that were doubtfully, if at all, subject to factual confirmation in the usual way, such as belief in God, meant that "works" is reducible to whatever produces personal satisfaction. James protested, but with little apparent impact. As you read James, try to determine what he means by truth as "that which works." Does he endorse holding a belief which makes one feel good in the absence of confirming evidence, or in the presence of disconfirming evidence? Also, pay attention to his references to the "copy" theory of truth, and his explanation as to why the pragmatic theory is supposedly superior.

Truth, as any dictionary will tell you, is a property of certain of our ideas. It means their "agreement," as falsity means their disagreement, with "reality." Pragmatists and intellectualists both accept this definition as a matter of course. They begin to quarrel only after the question is raised as to what may precisely be meant by the term "reality," when reality is taken as something for our ideas to agree with.

In answering these questions the pragmatists are more analytic and painstaking, the intellectualists more offhand and irreflective. The popular notion is that a true idea must copy its reality. Like other popular views, this one follows the analogy of the most usual experience. Our true ideas of sensible things do indeed copy them. Shut your eyes and think of yonder clock on the wall, and you get just such a true picture or copy of its dial. But your idea of its "works" (unless you are a clock-maker) is much less of a copy, yet it passes muster, for it in no way clashes with the reality. Even though it should shrink

Taken from William James, *Pragmatism: A New Name for Some Old Ways of Thinking*, originally published in New York in 1907.

to the mere word "works," that word still serves you truly; and when you speak of the "time-keeping function" of the clock, or of its spring's "elasticity," it is hard to see exactly what your ideas can copy.

You perceive that there is a problem here. Where our ideas cannot copy definitely their object, what does agreement with that object mean? Some idealists seem to say that they are true whenever they are what God means that we ought to think about that object. Others hold the copy-view all through, and speak as if our ideas possessed truth just in proportion as they approach to being copies of the Absolute's eternal way of thinking.

These views, you see, invite pragmatistic discussion. But the great assumption of the intellectualists is that truth means essentially an inert static relation. When you've got your true idea of anything, there's an end of the matter. You're in possession; you *know;* you have fulfilled your thinking destiny. You are where you ought to be mentally; you have obeyed your categorical imperative; and nothing more need follow on that climax of your rational destiny. Epistemologically you are in stable equilibrium.

Pragmatism, on the other hand, asks its usual question. "Grant an idea or belief to be true," it says, "what concrete difference will its being true make in any one's actual life? How will the truth be realized? What experiences will be different from those which would obtain if the belief were false? What, in short, is the truth's cash-value in experiential terms?"

The moment pragmatism asks this question, it sees the answer: *True ideas are those that we can assimilate, validate, corroborate and verify. False ideas are those that we can not.* That is the practical difference it makes to us to have true ideas; that, therefore, is the meaning of truth, for it is all that truth is known as.

This thesis is what I have to defend. The truth of an idea is not a stagnant property inherent in it. Truth *happens* to an idea. It *becomes* true, is *made* true by events. Its verity *is* in fact an event, a process: the process namely of its verifying itself, its veri-*fication.* Its validity is the process of its valid-*ation.*

But what do the words verification and validation themselves pragmatically mean? They again signify certain practical consequences of the verified and validated idea. It is hard to find any one phrase that characterizes these consequences better than the ordinary agreement formula—just such consequences being what we have in mind whenever we say that our ideas "agree" with reality. They lead us, namely, through the acts and other ideas which they instigate, into or up to, or towards, other parts of experience with which we feel all the while—such feeling being among our potentialities—that the original ideas remain in agreement. The connexions and transitions come to us from point to point as being progressive, harmonious, satisfactory. This function of agreeable leading is what we mean by an idea's verification. Such an account is vague and it sounds at first quite trivial, but it has results which it will take the rest of my hour to explain.

Let me begin by reminding you of the fact that the possession of true thoughts means everywhere the possession of invaluable instruments of action; and that our duty to gain truth, so far from being a blank command from out of the blue, or a "stunt" self-imposed by our intellect, can account for itself by excellent practical reasons.

The importance to human life of having true beliefs about matters of fact is a thing too notorious. We live in a world of realities that can be infinitely useful or infinitely harmful. Ideas that tell us which of them to expect count as the true ideas in all this primary sphere of verification, and the pursuit of such ideas is a primary human duty. The possession of truth, so far from being here an end in itself, is only a preliminary means towards other vital satisfactions. If I am lost in the woods and starved, and find what looks like a cow-path, it is of the utmost importance that I should think of a human habitation at the end of it, for if I do so and follow it, I save myself. The true thought is useful here because the house which is its object is useful. The practical value of true ideas is thus primarily derived from the practical importance of their objects to us. Their objects are, indeed, not important at all times. I may on another occasion have no use for the house; and then my idea of it, however verifiable, will be practically irrelevant, and had better remain latent. Yet since almost any object may some day become temporarily important, the advantage of having a general stock of *extra* truths, of ideas that shall be true of merely possible situations, is obvious. We store such extra truths away in our memories, and with the overflow we fill our books of reference. Whenever such an extra truth becomes practically relevant to one of our emergencies, it passes from cold-storage to do work in the world and our belief in it grows active. You can say of it then either that "it is useful because it is true" or that "it is true because it is useful." Both these phrases mean exactly the same thing, namely that here is an idea that gets fulfilled and can be verified. True is the name for whatever idea starts the verification-process, useful is the name for its completed function in experience. True ideas would never have been singled out as such, would never have acquired a class-name, least of all a name suggesting value, unless they had been useful from the outset in this way.

From this simple cue pragmatism gets her general notion of truth as something essentially bound up with the way in which one moment in our experience may lead us towards other moments which it will be worth while to have been led to. Primarily, and on the common-sense level, the truth of a state of mind means this function of *a leading that is worth while*. When a moment in our experience, of any kind whatever, inspires us with a thought that is true, that means that sooner or later we dip by that thought's guidance into the particulars of experience again and make advantageous connexion with them. This is a vague enough statement, but I beg you to retain it, for it is essential.

Our experience meanwhile is all shot through with regularities. One bit of it can warn us to get ready for another bit, can "intend" or be "significant of" that remoter object. The object's advent is the significance's verification. Truth, in these cases, meaning nothing but eventual verification, is manifestly incompatible with waywardness on our part. Woe to him whose beliefs play fast and loose with the order which realities follow in his experience; they will lead him nowhere or else make false connexions.

By "realities" or "objects" here, we mean either things of common sense, sensibly present, or else common-sense relations, such as dates, places, distances, kinds, activities. Following our mental image of a house along the cowpath, we actually come to see the house; we get the image's full verification. *Such simple and fully verified leadings are certainly the originals and prototypes of the truth-process.* Experience offers indeed other forms of truth-process, but they are all conceivable as being primary verifications arrested, multiplied or substituted one for another.

Take, for instance, yonder object on the wall. You and I consider it to be a "clock," altho no one of us has seen the hidden works that make it one. We let our notion pass for true without attempting to verify. If truths mean verification-process essentially, ought we then to call such unverified truths as this abortive? No, for they form the overwhelmingly large number of the truths we live by. Indirect as well as direct verifications pass muster. Where circumstantial evidence is sufficient, we can go without eye-witnessing. Just as we here assume Japan to exist without ever having been there, because it *works* to do so, everything we know conspiring with the belief, and nothing interfering, so we assume that thing to be a clock. We *use* it as a clock, regulating the length of our lecture by it. The verification of the assumption here means its leading to no frustration or contradiction. Verifi*ability* of wheels and weights and pendulum is as good as verification. For one truth-process completed there are a million in our lives that function in this state of nascency. They turn us *towards* direct verification; lead us into the *surroundings* of the objects they envisage; and then, if everything runs on harmoniously, we are so sure that verification is possible that we omit it, and are usually justified by all that happens.

Truth lives, in fact, for the most part on a credit system. Our thoughts and beliefs "pass," so long as nothing challenges them, just as bank-notes pass so long as nobody refuses them. But this all points to direct face-to-face verifications somewhere, without which the fabric of truth collapses like a financial system with no cash-basis whatever. You accept my verification of one thing, I yours of another. We trade on each other's truth. But beliefs verified concretely by *somebody* are the posts of the whole superstructure.

Another great reason—beside economy of time—for waiving complete verification in the usual business of life is that all things exist in kinds and not singly. Our world is found once for all to have that peculiarity. So that when we have once directly verified our ideas about one specimen of a kind, we consider ourselves free to apply them to other specimens without verification. A mind that habitually discerns the kind of thing before it, and acts by the law of the kind immediately, without pausing to verify, will be a "true" mind in ninety-nine out of a hundred emergencies, proved so by its conduct fitting everything it meets, and getting no refutation.

Indirectly or only potentially verifying processes may thus be true as well as full verification-processes. They work as true processes would work, give us the same advantages, and claim our recognition for the same reasons. All this on the common-sense level of matters of fact, which we are alone considering.

But matters of fact are not our only stock in trade. *Relations among purely mental ideas* form another sphere where true and false beliefs obtain, and here the beliefs are absolute, or unconditional. When they are true they bear the name either of definitions or of principles. It is either a principle or a definition that 1 and 1 make 2, that 2 and 1 make 3, and so on; that white differs less from gray than it does from black; that when the cause begins to act the effect also commences. Such propositions hold of all possible "ones," of all conceivable "whites" and "grays" and "causes." The objects here are mental objects. Their relations are perceptually obvious at a glance, and no sense-verification is necessary. Moreover, once true, always true, of those same mental objects. Truth here has an "eternal" character. If you can find a concrete thing anywhere that is "one" or "white" or "gray" or an "effect," then your principles will everlastingly apply to it. It is but a case of ascertaining the kind, and then applying the law of its kind to the particular object. You are sure to get truth if you can but name the kind rightly, for your mental relations hold good of everything of that kind without exception. If you then, nevertheless, failed to get truth concretely, you would say that you had classed your real objects wrongly.

In this realm of mental relations, truth again is an affair of leading. We relate one abstract idea with another, framing in the end great systems of logical and mathematical truth, under the respective terms of which the sensible facts of experience eventually arrange themselves, so that our eternal truths hold good of realities also. This marriage of fact and theory is endlessly fertile. What we say is here already true in advance of special verification, *if we have subsumed our objects rightly.* Our ready-made ideal framework for all sorts of possible objects follows from the very structure of our thinking. We can no more play fast and loose with these abstract relations than we can do so with our sense-experiences. They coerce us; we must treat them consistently, whether or not we like the results. The rules of addition apply to our debts as rigorously as to our assets. The hundredth decimal of ξ, the ratio of the circumference to its diameter, is predetermined ideally now, tho no one may have computed it. If we should ever need the figure in our dealings with an actual circle we should need to have it given rightly, calculated by the usual rules; for it is the same kind of truth that those rules elsewhere calculate.

Between the coercions of the sensible order and those of the ideal order, our mind is thus wedged tightly. Our ideas must agree with realities, be such realities concrete or abstract, be they facts or be they principles, under penalty of endless inconsistency and frustration.

So far, intellectualists can raise no protest. They can only say that we have barely touched the skin of the matter.

Realities mean, then, either concrete facts, or abstract kinds of things and relations perceived intuitively between them. They furthermore and thirdly mean, as things that new ideas of ours must no less take account of, the whole body of other truths already in our possession. But what now does "agreement" with such threefold realities mean?—to use again the definition that is current.

Here it is that pragmatism and intellectualism begin to part company. Primarily, no doubt, to agree means to copy, but we saw that the mere word "clock" would do instead of a mental picture of its works, and that of many realities our ideas can only be symbols and not copies. "Past time," "power," "spontaneity,"—how can our mind copy such realities?

To "agree" in the widest sense with a reality *can only mean to be guided either straight up to it or into its surroundings, or to be put into such working touch with it as to handle either it or something connected with it better than if we disagreed.* Better either intellectually or practically! And often agreement will only mean the negative fact that nothing contradictory from the quarter of that reality comes to interfere with the way in which our ideas guide us elsewhere. To copy a reality is, indeed, one very important way of agreeing with it, but it is far from being essential. The essential thing is the process of being guided. Any idea that helps us to *deal,* whether practically or intellectually, with either the reality or its belongings, that doesn't entangle our progress in frustrations, that *fits,* in fact, and adapts our life to the reality's whole setting, will agree sufficiently to meet the requirement. It will hold true of that reality.

Thus, *names* are just as "true" or "false" as definite mental pictures are. They set up similar verification-processes, and lead to fully equivalent practical results.

All human thinking gets discursified; we exchange ideas; we lend and borrow verifications, get them from one another by means of social intercourse. All truth thus gets verbally built out, stored up, and made available for every one. Hence, we must *talk* consistently just as we must *think* consistently: for both in talk and thought we deal with kinds. Names are arbitrary, but once understood they must be kept to. We mustn't now call Abel "Cain" or Cain "Abel." If we do, we ungear ourselves from the whole book of Genesis, and from all its connexions with the universe of speech and fact down to the present time. We throw ourselves out of whatever truth that entire system of speech and fact may embody.

The overwhelming majority of our true ideas admit of no direct or face-to-face verification—those of past history, for example, as of Cain and Abel. The stream of time can be remounted only verbally, or verified indirectly by the present prolongations or effects of what the past harbored. Yet if they agree with these verbalities and effects, we can know that our ideas of the past are true. *As true as past time itself was,* so true was Julius Caesar, so true were antediluvian monsters, all in their proper dates and settings. That past time itself was, is guaranteed by its coherence with everything that's present. True as the present *is,* the past *was* also.

Agreement thus turns out to be essentially an affair of leading—leading that is useful because it is into quarters that contain objects that are important. True ideas lead us into useful verbal and conceptual quarters as well as directly up to useful sensible termini. They lead to consistency, stability and flowing human intercourse. They lead away from eccentricity and isolation, from foiled and barren thinking. The untrammelled flowing of the leading-process, its general freedom from clash and contradiction, passes for its indirect verification; but all roads lead to Rome, and in the end and eventually, all true processes must lead to the face of directly verifying sensible experiences *somewhere*, which somebody's ideas have copied.

Such is the large loose way in which the pragmatist interprets the word agreement. He treats it altogether practically. He lets it cover any process of conduction from a present idea to a future terminus, provided only it run prosperously. It is only thus that "scientific" ideas, flying as they do beyond common sense, can be said to agree with their realities. It is, as I have already said, *as if* reality were made of ether, atoms or electrons, but we mustn't think so literally. The term "energy" doesn't even pretend to stand for anything "objective." It is only a way of measuring the surface of phenomena so as to string their changes on a simple formula.

Yet in the choice of these man-made formulas we can not be capricious with impunity any more than we can be capricious on the common-sense practical level. We must find a theory that will *work*; and that means something extremely difficult; for our theory must mediate between all previous truths and certain new experiences. It must derange common sense and previous belief as little as possible, and it must lead to some sensible terminus or other that can be verified exactly. To "work" means both these things; and the squeeze is so tight that there is little loose play for any hypothesis. Our theories are wedged and controlled as nothing else is. Yet sometimes alternative theoretic formulas are equally compatible with all the truths we know, and then we choose between them for subjective reasons. We choose the kind of theory to which we are already partial; we follow "elegance" or "economy." Clerk-Maxwell somewhere says it would be "poor scientific taste" to choose the more complicated of two equally well-evidenced conceptions; and you will all agree with him. Truth in science is what gives us the maximum possible sum of satisfactions, taste included, but consistency both with previous truth and with novel fact is always the most imperious claimant.

"The true," to put it very briefly, is only the expedient in the way of our thinking, just as "the right" is only the expedient in the way of our behaving. Expedient in almost any fashion; and expedient in the long run and on the whole of course; for what meets expediently all the experience in sight won't necessarily meet all farther experiences equally satisfactorily. Experience, as we know, has ways of *boiling over*, and making us correct our present formulas.

The "absolutely" true, meaning what no farther experience will ever alter, is that ideal vanishing-point towards which we imagine that all our temporary truths will some day converge. It runs on all fours with the perfectly wise man, and with the absolutely complete experience; and, if these ideals are ever realized, they will all be realized together. Meanwhile we have to live to-day by what truth we can get to-day, and be ready to-morrow to call it falsehood. Ptolemaic astronomy, euclidean space, aristotelian logic, scholastic metaphysics, were expedient for centuries, but human experience has boiled over those limits, and we now call these things only relatively true, or true within those borders of experience. "Absolutely" they are false; for we know that those limits were casual, and might have been transcended by past theorists just as they are by present thinkers.

When new experiences lead to retrospective judgments, using the past tense, what these judgments utter *was* true, even tho no past thinker had been led there. We live forwards, a Danish thinker has said, but we understand backwards. The present sheds a backward light on the world's previous processes. They may have been truth-processes for the actors in them. They are not so for one who knows the later revelations of the story.

This regulative notion of a potential better truth to be established later, possibly to be established some day absolutely, and having powers of retroactive legislation, turns its face, like all pragmatist notions, towards concreteness of fact, and towards the future. Like the half-truths, the absolute truth will have to be *made*, made as a relation incidental to the growth of a mass of verification-experience, to which the half-true ideas are all along contributing their quota.

I have already insisted on the fact that truth is made largely out of previous truths. Men's beliefs at any time are so much experience *funded*. But the beliefs are themselves parts of the sum total of the world's experience, and become matter, therefore, for the next day's funding operations. So far as reality means experienceable reality, both it and the truths men gain about it are everlastingly in process of mutation—mutation towards a definite goal, it may be—but still mutation.

Mathematicians can solve problems with two variables. On the Newtonian theory, for instance, acceleration varies with distance, but distance also varies with acceleration. In the realm of truth-processes facts come independently and determine our beliefs provisionally. But these beliefs make us act, and as fast as they do so, they bring into sight or into existence new facts which re-determine the beliefs accordingly. So the whole coil and ball of truth, as it rolls up, is the product of a double influence. Truths emerge from facts; but they dip forward into facts again and add to them; which facts again create or reveal new truth (the word is indifferent) and so on indefinitely. The "facts" themselves meanwhile are not *true*. They simply *are*. Truth is the function of the beliefs that start and terminate among them.

STUDY QUESTIONS

1. What does James mean when he speaks about truth as an "expedient" and Ptolemaic astronomy and Euclidean space as expedients?
2. James believed in God. Applying his own pragmatic test of truth, is the statement "God exists" or "There is a God" true?
3. Is a statement true only once it is actually verified, or was it true all along?

4. Can you think of beliefs which are true, but which are also dissatisfying?
5. James speaks about verification. What does that mean for him? Does it mean factual confirmation?
6. Does James sanction affirming a belief personally prior to verification? Must verification be public, or only private?
7. List the several specific phrases in which James defines or describes his theory of truth. Do they have the same meaning?

Truth as Correspondence: A Reply to James
Bertrand Russell

Bertrand Russell (1872–1970) was an internationally famous British philosopher with both a professional and a public audience. He made important contributions to the foundations of mathematics, logic, theory of knowledge, social philosophy, educational philosophy, and other areas of investigation. During World War I he was imprisoned for his pacifist activities, and when he was eighty-seven he was arrested for demonstrating against nuclear weapons. In 1940 he was invited to lecture at the City College of New York, but was prevented from teaching there through the vigorous opposition of a group of religious and political leaders who maintained that he was morally unfit. The court invalidated Russell's contract on the basis that his appointment would adversely affect "the public health, safety, and morals of the community." In 1950 he was awarded the Nobel Prize for Literature, in spite of the fact that he was not a poet or a 'novelist.

In the selection which follows, Russell takes issue with the pragmatic theory of truth as interpreted by William James, and discusses the "correspondence" theory, which he finds to be more adequate. Probably the most important element in the article is the emphasis on "facts." According to Russell a statement is true only if it corresponds with actual observable conditions. One should not affirm statements in the absence of such confirming evidence, according to Russell, no matter how much comfort or personal satisfaction a belief may produce. He claims that what James does is to permit embracing a belief which produces "general agreeableness" but which may not conform "with observed phenomena." Satisfaction is fine, he says, providing it flows from the fact, not the belief.

The pragmatic theory of truth is the central doctrine of pragmatism, and we must consider it at some length. William James states it in various ways, some of which I shall now quote. He says: "Ideas (which themselves are but parts

From Bertrand Russell, *Philosophical Essays* (New York: Simon and Schuster, 1966), pp. 116–126.

of our experience) become true just in so far as they help us to get into satisfactory relation with other parts of our experience." Again: "Truth is *one species of good,* and not, as is usually supposed, a category distinct from good, and co-ordinate with it. *The true is the name of whatever proves itself to be good in any way of belief, and good, too, for definite, assignable reasons.*" That truth means "agreement with reality" may be said by a pragmatist as well as by any one else, but the pragmatist differs from others as to what is meant by *agreement,* and also (it would seem) as to what is meant by *reality.* William James gives the following definition of agreement: "To 'agree' in the widest sense with a reality *can only mean to be guided either straight up to it or into its surroundings, or to be put into such working touch with it as to handle either it or something connected with it better than if we disagreed.*" This language is rather metaphorical, and a little puzzling; it is plain, however, that "agreement" is regarded as practical, not as merely intellectual. This emphasis on practice is, of course, one of the leading features of pragmatism.

In order to understand the pragmatic notion of truth, we have to be clear as to the basis of *fact* upon which truths are supposed to rest. Immediate sensible experience, for example, does not come under the alternative of *true* and *false.* "Day follows day," says James, "and its contents are simply added. The new contents themselves are not true, they simply *come* and *are.* Truth is *what we say about* them." Thus when we are merely aware of sensible objects, we are not to be regarded as knowing any truth, although we have a certain kind of contact with reality. It is important to realise that the *facts* which thus lie outside the scope of truth and falsehood supply the material which is presupposed by the pragmatic theory. Our beliefs have to agree with matters of fact: it is an essential part of their "satisfactoriness" that they should do so. James also mentions what he calls "relations among purely mental ideas" as part of our stock-in-trade with which pragmatism starts. He mentions as instances "1 and 1 make 2," "white differs less from grey than it does from black," and so on. All such propositions as these, then, we are supposed to know for certain before we can get under way. As James puts it: "Between the coercions of the sensible order and those of the ideal order, our mind is thus wedged tightly. Our ideas must agree with realities, be such realities concrete or abstract, be they facts or be they principles, under penalty of endless inconsistency and frustration." Thus it is only when we pass beyond plain matters of fact and *a priori* truisms that the pragmatic notion of truth comes in. It is, in short, the notion to be applied to doubtful cases, but it is not the notion to be applied to cases about which there can be no doubt. And that there are cases about which there can be no doubt is presupposed in the very statement of the pragmatist position. "Our account of truth," James tells us, "is an account...of processes of leading, realised *in rebus* [in things—*Editors*], and having only this quality in common, that they *pay.*" We may thus sum up the philosophy in the following definition: "A truth is anything which it pays to believe." Now, if this definition is to be useful, as pragmatism intends it to be, it must be possible to know that it pays to believe something without knowing anything that pragmatism would call a truth. Hence the knowledge that a certain belief pays must be classed as knowledge of a sensible fact or of a "relation among purely mental ideas," or as some compound of the two, and must be so easy to discover as not to be worthy of having the pragmatic test applied to it. There is, however, some difficulty in this view. Let us consider for a moment what it means to say that a belief "pays." We must suppose that this means that the consequences of entertaining the belief are better than those of rejecting it. In order to know this, we must know what are the consequences of entertaining it, and what are the consequences of rejecting it; we must know also what consequences are good, what bad, what consequences are better, and what worse. Take, say, belief in the Roman Catholic Faith. This, we may agree, causes a certain amount of happiness at the expense of a certain amount of stupidity and priestly domination. Such a view is disputable and disputed, but we will let that pass. But then comes the question whether, admitting the effects to be such, they are to be classed as on the whole good or on the whole bad; and this question is one which is so difficult that our test of truth becomes practically useless. It is far easier, it seems to me, to settle the plain question of fact: "Have Popes been always infallible?" than to settle the question whether the effects of thinking them infallible are on the whole good. Yet this question, of the truth of Roman Catholicism, is just the sort of question that pragmatists consider specially suitable to their method.

The notion that it is quite easy to know when the consequences of a belief are good, so easy, in fact, that a theory of knowledge need take no account of anything so simple—this notion, I must say, seems to be one of the strangest assumptions for a theory of knowledge to make. Let us take another illustration. Many of the men of the French Revolution were disciples of Rousseau, and their belief in his doctrines had far-reaching effects, which make Europe at this day a different place from what it would have been without that belief. If, on the whole, the effects of their belief have been good, we shall have to say that their belief was true; if bad, that it was false. But how are we to strike the balance? It is almost impossible to disentangle what the effects have been; and even if we could ascertain them, our judgment as to whether they have been good or bad would depend upon our political opinions. It is surely far easier to discover by direct investigation that the *Contrat Social* is a myth than to decide whether belief in it has done harm or good on the whole.

Another difficulty which I feel in regard to the pragmatic meaning of "truth" may be stated as follows: Suppose I accept the pragmatic criterion, and suppose you persuade me that a certain belief is useful. Suppose I thereupon conclude that the belief is true. Is it not obvious that there is a transition in my mind from seeing that the belief is useful to actually holding that the belief is true? Yet this could not be so if the pragmatic account of truth were valid. Take, say, the belief that other people exist. According to the pragmatists, to say "it is true that other people exist" *means* "it is useful to believe that other people exist." But if so, then these two phrases are merely different words for the same proposition; therefore when I believe the one I believe the other. If this were so, there could be no transition from the one to the other, as plainly there is. This shows that the word "true" represents for us a different idea from that represented by the phrase "useful to believe," and that, therefore, the pragmatic definition of truth ignores, without destroying, the meaning commonly given to the word "true," which meaning, in my opinion, is of fundamental importance, and can only be ignored at the cost of hopeless inadequacy.

This brings me to the difference between *criterion* and *meaning*—a point on which neither James nor Dr. Schiller* is very clear. I may best explain the difference, to begin with, by an instance. If you wish to know whether a certain book is in a library, you consult the catalogue: books mentioned in the catalogue are presumably in the library, books not mentioned in it are presumably not in the library. Thus the catalogue affords a *criterion* of whether a book is in the library or not. But even supposing the catalogue perfect, it is obvious that when you say the book is in the library you do not *mean* that it is mentioned in the catalogue. You mean that the actual book is to be found somewhere in the shelves. It therefore remains an intelligible hypothesis that there are books in the library which are not yet catalogued, or that there are books catalogued which have been lost and are no longer in the library. And it remains an inference from the discovery that a book is mentioned in the catalogue to the conclusion that the book is in the library. Speaking abstractly, we may say that a property A is a *criterion* of a property B when the same objects possess both; and A is a *useful* criterion of B if it is easier to discover whether an object possesses the property A than whether it possesses the property B. Thus being mentioned in the catalogue is a *useful* criterion of being in the library, because it is easier to consult the catalogue than to hunt through the shelves.

Now if pragmatists only affirmed that utility is a *criterion* of truth, there would be much less to be said against their view. For there certainly seem to be few cases, if any, in which it is clearly useful to believe what is false. The chief criticism one would then have to make on pragmatism would be to deny that utility is a *useful* criterion, because it is so often harder to determine whether a belief is useful than whether it is true. The arguments of pragmatists are almost wholly directed to proving that utility is a *criterion*; that utility is the *meaning* of truth is then supposed to follow. But, to return to our illustration of the library, suppose we had conceded that there are no mistakes in the British Museum catalogue: would it follow that the catalogue would do without the books? We can imagine some person long engaged in a comparative study of libraries, and having, in the process, naturally lost all taste for reading, declaring that the catalogue is the only important thing—as for the books, they are useless lumber; no one ever wants them, and the principle of economy should lead us to be content with the catalogue. Indeed, if you consider the matter with an open mind, you will see that the catalogue *is* the library, for it tells you everything you can possibly wish to know about the library. Let

* *Editors' note:* F. C. S. Schiller (1864–1937) was a British Pragmatist, influenced heavily by James, who helped to popularize Pragmatism in Europe.

us, then, save the taxpayers' money by destroying the books: allow free access
to the catalogue, but condemn the desire to read as involving an exploded
dogmatic realism.

This analogy of the library is not, to my mind, fantastic or unjust, but as
close and exact an analogy as I have been able to think of. The point I am trying
to make clear is concealed from pragmatists, I think, by the fact that their
theories start very often from such things as the general hypotheses of science—
ether, atoms, and the like. In such cases, we take little interest in the hypotheses themselves, which, as we well know, are liable to rapid change. What we
care about are the inferences as to sensible phenomena which the hypotheses
enable us to make. All we ask of the hypotheses is that they should "work"—
though it should be observed that what constitutes "working" is not the general agreeableness of their results, but the conformity of these results with
observed phenomena. But in the case of these general scientific hypotheses,
no sensible man believes that they are true as they stand. They are believed
to be true in part, and to work because of the part that is true; but it is expected
that in time some element of falsehood will be discovered, and some truer
theory will be substituted. Thus pragmatism would seem to derive its notion
of what constitutes belief from cases in which, properly speaking, belief is
absent, and in which—what is pragmatically important—there is but a slender
interest in truth or falsehood as compared to the interest in what "works."

But when this method is extended to cases in which the proposition in
question has an emotional interest on its own account, apart from its working,
the pragmatic account becomes less satisfactory. This point has been well
brought out by Prof. Stout in *Mind*,[1] and what I have to say is mostly contained in his remarks. Take the question whether other people exist. It seems
perfectly possible to suppose that the hypothesis that they exist will always
work, even if they do not in fact exist. It is plain, also, that it makes for happiness to believe that they exist—for even the greatest misanthropist would
not wish to be deprived of the objects of his hate. Hence the belief that other
people exist is, pragmatically, a true belief. But if I am troubled by solipsism,
the discovery that a belief in the existence of others is "true" in the pragmatist's sense is not enough to allay my sense of loneliness: the perception that
I should profit by rejecting solipsism is not alone sufficient to make me reject
it. For what I desire is not that the belief in solipsism should be false in the
pragmatic sense, but that other people should in fact exist. And with the pragmatist's meaning of truth, these two do not necessarily go together. The belief
in solipsism might be false even if I were the only person or thing in the universe.

This paradoxical consequence would, I presume, not be admitted by pragmatists. Yet it is an inevitable outcome of the divorce which they make between *fact* and *truth*. Returning to our illustration, we may say that "facts" are
represented by the books, and "truths" by the entries in the catalogue. So long

---

[1] October, 1907, pp. 586–588. This criticism occurs in the course of a very sympathetic review of
Dr. Schiller's *Studies in Humanism*.

as you do not wish to read the books, the "truths" will do in place of the "facts," and the imperfections of your library can be remedied by simply making new entries in the catalogue. But as soon as you actually wish to read a book, the "truths" become inadequate, and the "facts" become all-important. The pragmatic account of truth assumes, so it seems to me, that no one takes any interest in facts, and that the truth of the proposition that your friend exists is an adequate substitute for the fact of his existence. "Facts," they tell us, are neither true nor false, therefore truth cannot be concerned with them. But the truth "A exists," if it is a truth, is concerned with A, who in that case is a fact; and to say that "A exists" may be true even if A does not exist is to give a meaning to "truth" which robs it of all interest. Dr. Schiller is fond of attacking the view that truth must correspond with reality; we may conciliate him by agreeing that *his* truth, at any rate, need not correspond with reality. But we shall have to add that reality is to us more interesting than such truth.

I am, of course, aware that pragmatists minimise the basis of "fact," and speak of the "making of reality" as proceeding *pari passu* with the "making of truth." It is easy to criticise the claim to "make reality" except within obvious limits. But when such criticisms are met by pointing to the pragmatist's admission that, after all, there must be a basis of "fact" for our creative activity to work upon, then the opposite line of criticism comes into play. Dr. Schiller, in his essay on "the making of reality," minimises the importance of the basis of "fact," on the ground (it would seem) that "facts" will not submit to pragmatic treatment, and that, if pragmatism is true, they are unknowable.[2] Hence, on pragmatistic principles, it is useless to think about facts. We therefore return to fictions with a sigh of relief, and soothe our scruples by calling them "realities." But it seems something of a *petitio principii* [begging the question— *Editors*] to condemn "facts" because pragmatism, though it finds them necessary, is unable to deal with them. And William James, it should be said, makes less attempt than Dr. Schiller does to minimise facts. In this essay, therefore, I have considered the difficulties which pragmatism has to face if it admits "facts" rather than those (no less serious) which it has to face if it denies them.

It is chiefly in regard to religion that the pragmatist use of "truth" seems to me misleading. Pragmatists boast much of their ability to reconcile religion and science, and William James, as we saw, professes to have discovered a position combining the merits of tender-mindedness and tough-mindedness. The combination is really effected, if I am not mistaken, in a way of which pragmatists are not themselves thoroughly aware. For their position, if they fully realised it, would, I think, be this: "We cannot know whether, in fact, there is a God or a future life, but we can know that the belief in God and a future life is true." This position, it is to be feared, would not afford much comfort to the religious if it were understood, and I cannot but feel some sympathy with the Pope in his condemnation of it.

"On pragmatic principles," James says, "we cannot reject any hypothesis if consequences useful to life flow from it." He proceeds to point out that

---

[2] Cf. *Studies in Humanism*, pp. 434–436.

consequences useful to life flow from the hypothesis of the Absolute, which is therefore so far a true hypothesis. But it should be observed that these useful consequences flow from the hypothesis that the Absolute is a fact, not from the hypothesis that useful consequences flow from belief in the Absolute. But we cannot believe the hypothesis that the Absolute is a fact merely because we perceive that useful consequences flow from this hypothesis. What we can believe on such grounds is that this hypothesis is what pragmatists call "true," i.e. that it is useful; but it is not from this belief that the useful consequences flow, and the grounds alleged do not make us believe that the Absolute is a fact, which is the useful belief. In other words, the useful belief is that the Absolute is a fact, and pragmatism shows that this belief is what it calls "true." Thus pragmatism persuades us that belief in the Absolute is "true," but does not persuade us that the Absolute is a fact. The belief which it persuades us to adopt is therefore not the one which is useful. In ordinary logic, if the belief in the Absolute is true, it follows that the Absolute is a fact. But with the pragmatist's meaning of "true" this does not follow; hence the proposition which he proves is not, as he thinks, the one from which comforting consequences flow.

In another place James says: "On pragmatistic principles, if the hypothesis of God works satisfactorily in the widest sense of the word, it is true." This proposition is, in reality, a mere tautology. For we have laid down the definition: "The word 'true' means 'working satisfactorily in the widest sense of the word.'" Hence the proposition stated by James is merely a verbal variant on the following: "On pragmatistic principles, if the hypothesis of God works satisfactorily in the widest sense of the word, then it works satisfactorily in the widest sense of the word." This would hold even on other than pragmatistic principles; presumably what is peculiar to pragmatism is the belief that this is an important contribution to the philosophy of religion. The advantage of the pragmatic method is that it decides the question of the truth of the existence of God by purely mundane arguments, namely, by the effects of belief in His existence upon our life in this world. But unfortunately this gives a merely mundane conclusion, namely, that belief in God is true, i.e. useful, whereas what religion desires is the conclusion that God exists, which pragmatism never even approaches. I infer, therefore, that the pragmatic philosophy of religion, like most philosophies whose conclusions are interesting, turns on an unconscious play upon words. A common word—in this case, the word "true"—is taken at the outset in an uncommon sense, but as the argument proceeds the usual sense of the word gradually slips back, and the conclusions arrived at seem, therefore, quite different from what they would be seen to be if the initial definition had been remembered.

The point is, of course, that, so soon as it is admitted that there are things that exist, it is impossible to avoid recognising a distinction, to which we may give what name we please, between believing in the existence of something that exists and believing in the existence of something that does not exist. It is common to call the one belief true, the other false. But if, with the pragmatists, we prefer to give a different meaning to the words "true" and "false," that does not prevent the distinction commonly called the distinction of "true" and "false" from persisting. The pragmatist attempt to ignore this distinction fails, as it seems to me, because a basis of fact cannot be avoided by pragmatism, and this basis of fact demands the *usual* antithesis of "true" and "false." It is hardly to be supposed that pragmatists will admit this conclusion. But it may be hoped that they will tell us in more detail how they propose to avoid it.

STUDY QUESTIONS

1. Are there any points in the article where Russell may have misinterpreted James?
2. What important points does Russell attempt to make by using the example of a card catalogue in a library?
3. How would Russell decide the truth or falsity of this statement: "Susan loves Michael"?
4. Must one suspend judgment, and remain uncommitted, when the facts required to verify a statement are in dispute? For instance, if someone says, "Nuclear power plants are safe," is the statement true or false? Presuming the matter is arguable, must one be silent and disinterested?
5. "George, unless you stop your drinking, you'll be dead by the time you're forty!" How would Russell deal with the truthfulness of such a statement in contrast to James? Would they differ at all?
6. In the previous reading, James spoke about the "copy" theory of truth. Is that the same as Russell's "correspondence" theory?
7. What does Russell mean by a "fact"?

Truth as Coherence
Brand Blanshard

Brand Blanshard (1892–1988) taught at Michigan, Swarthmore, and Yale.
Before his retirement in 1961, he was chairman of the philosophy department
and Sterling Professor of Philosophy at Yale. He was one of America's most
distinguished philosophers, and a leading exponent of rationalism and
idealism. His major works include *The Nature of Thought* (1939), *Reason*

From Brand Blanshard, *The Nature of Thought*, Volume II (New York: The Macmillan Company; and London: Allen and Unwin, 1939), pp. 260–269. Reprinted with the permission of Unwin Hyman, Ltd.

and Goodness (1961), *Reason and Analysis* (1962), and *Reason and Belief* (1975).

In the following selection from *The Nature of Thought*, Blanshard argues that the advance of knowledge over the centuries shows that reality is "completely ordered and fully intelligible"; in other words reality is systematic. The more we know, the more we find interconnections in Nature. Since thought aims to uncover reality, and since reality is systematic, thought itself must be systematic. "Hence," he says, "at any given time the degree of truth of a particular proposition is the degree of system it has achieved." In other words, a proposition is true if it *coheres* with other propositions in the system. If it entails the others, or is entailed by them, it is true; if not, it is false. Ideally, Blanshard observes, "if any proposition were lacking (in a system), it could be supplied by the rest."

Notice that Blanshard speaks about coherence as both the "test" of truth *and* the "meaning" of truth. Make sure that you understand the distinction, and then ask yourself whether you agree with Blanshard on this point. Also, consider this. Could you have two systems of statements which are internally coherent but mutually incompatible?

It has been contended in the last chapter that coherence is in the end our sole criterion of truth. We have now to face the question whether it also gives us the nature of truth. We should be clear at the beginning that these are different questions, and that one may reject coherence as the definition of truth while accepting it as the test. It is conceivable that one thing should be an accurate index of another and still be extremely different from it. There have been philosophers who held that pleasure was an accurate gauge of the amount of good in experience, but that to confuse good with pleasure was a gross blunder. There have been a great many philosophers who held that for every change in consciousness there was a change in the nervous system and that the two corresponded so closely that if we knew the laws connecting them we could infallibly predict one from the other; yet it takes all the hardihood of a behaviourist to say that the two are the same. Similarly it has been held that though coherence supplies an infallible measure of truth, it would be a very grave mistake to identify it with truth.

The view that truth *is* coherence rests on a theory of the relation of thought to reality, and since this is the central problem of the theory of knowledge, to begin one's discussion by assuming the answer to it or by trying to make one out of whole cloth would be somewhat ridiculous. But as this was our main problem in the long discussions of Book II, we may be pardoned here for brevity. First we shall state in *résumé* the relation of thought to reality that we were there driven to accept, and sketch the theory of truth implicit in it. We shall then take up one by one the objections to this theory and ask if they can pass muster.

To think is to seek understanding. And to seek understanding is an activity of mind that is marked off from all other activities by a highly distinctive aim. This aim, as we saw in our chapter on the general nature of understanding, is to achieve systematic vision, so to apprehend what is now unknown to us as to relate it, and relate it necessarily, to what we know already. We think to solve problems; and our method of solving problems is to build a bridge of intelligible relation from the continent of our knowledge to the island we wish to include in it. Sometimes this bridge is causal, as when we try to explain a disease; sometimes teleological, as when we try to fathom the move of an opponent over the chess board; sometimes geometrical, as in Euclid. But it is always systematic; thought in its very nature is the attempt to bring something unknown or imperfectly known into a sub-system of knowledge, and thus also into that larger system that forms the world of accepted beliefs. That is what explanation is. *Why* is it that thought desires this ordered vision? Why should such a vision give satisfaction when it comes? To these questions there is no answer, and if there were, it would be an answer only because it had succeeded in supplying the characteristic satisfaction to this unique desire.

But may it not be that what satisfies thought fails to conform to the real world? Where is the guarantee that when I have brought my ideas into the form my ideal requires, they should be *true?* Here we come round again to the tortured problem of Book II. In our long struggle with the relation of thought to reality we saw that if thought and things are conceived as related only externally, then knowledge is luck; there is no necessity whatever that what satisfies intelligence should coincide with what really is. It may do so, or it may not; on the principle that there are many misses to one bull's-eye, it more probably does not. But if we get rid of the misleading analogies through which this relation has been conceived, of copy and original, stimulus and organism, lantern and screen, and go to thought itself with the question what reference to an object means, we get a different and more hopeful answer. To think of a thing is to get that thing itself in some degree within the mind. To think of a colour or an emotion is to have that within us which if it *were developed and completed*, would identify itself with the object. In short, if we accept its own report, thought is related to reality as the partial to the perfect fulfillment of a purpose. The more adequate its grasp the more nearly does it approximate, the more fully does it realize in itself, the nature and relations of its objects.

Thought thus appears to have two ends, one immanent, one transcendent. On the one hand it seeks fulfillment in a special kind of satisfaction, the satisfaction of systematic vision. On the other hand it seeks fulfillment in its object. Now it was the chief contention of our second book that these ends are one. Indeed unless they are accepted as one, we could see no alternative to scepticism. If the pursuit of thought's own ideal were merely an elaborate self-indulgence that brought us no nearer to reality, or if the apprehension of reality did not lie in the line of thought's interest, or still more if both of these held at once, the hope of knowledge would be vain. Of course it may really be vain. If any one cares to doubt whether the framework of human logic has any bearing on the nature of things, he may be silenced perhaps, but he cannot be conclusively answered. One may point out to him that the doubt itself is framed in accordance with that logic, but he can reply that thus we are taking advantage of his logico-centric predicament; further, that any argument we can offer accords equally well with his hypothesis and with ours, with the view that we are merely flies caught in a logical net and the view that knowledge reveals reality. And what accords equally well with both hypotheses does not support either to the exclusion of the other. But while such doubt is beyond reach by argument, neither is there anything in its favour. It is a mere suspicion which is, and by its nature must remain without any positive ground; and as such it can hardly be discussed. Such suspicions aside, we can throw into the scale for our theory the impressive fact of the advance of knowledge. It has been the steadfast assumption of science whenever it came to an unsolved problem that there was a key to it to be found, that if things happened thus rather than otherwise they did so for a cause or reason, and that if this were not forthcoming it was never because it was lacking, but always because of a passing blindness in ourselves. Reflection has assumed that pursuit of its own immanent end is not only satisfying but revealing, that so far as the immanent end is achieved we are making progress toward the transcendent end as well. Indeed, that these ends coincide is the assumption of every act of thinking whatever. To think is to raise a question; to raise a question is to seek an explanation; to seek an explanation is to assume that one may be had; so to assume is to take for granted that nature in that region is intelligible. Certainly the story of advancing knowledge unwinds as if self-realization in thought meant also a coming nearer to reality.

That these processes are really one is the metaphysical base on which our belief in coherence is founded. If one admits that the pursuit of a coherent system has actually carried us to what everyone would agree to call knowledge, why not take this ideal as a guide that will conduct us farther? What better key can one ask to the structure of the real? Our own conviction is that we should take this immanent end of thought in all seriousness as the clue to the nature of things. We admit that it may prove deceptive, that somewhere thought may end its pilgrimage in frustration and futility before some blank wall of the unintelligible. There are even those who evince their superior insight by taking this as a foregone conclusion and regarding the faith that the real is rational as the wishful thinking of the "tender-minded." Their attitude appears to us a compound made up of one part timidity, in the form of a refusal to hope lest they be disillusioned; one part muddled persuasion that to be sceptical is to be sophisticated; one part honest dullness in failing to estimate rightly the weight of the combined postulate and success of knowledge; one part genuine insight into the possibility of surds in nature. But whatever its motives, it is a view that goes less well with the evidence than the opposite and brighter view. That view is that reality is a system, completely ordered and fully intelligible, with which thought in its advance is more and more identifying itself. We may look at the growth of knowledge, individual or social, either as an attempt by our own minds to return to union with things as they are in their ordered wholeness, or the affirmation through our minds of the ordered whole itself. And if we take this view, our notion of truth is marked out for us. Truth is the approximation of thought to reality. It is thought on its way home. Its measure is the distance thought has travelled, under guidance of its inner compass, toward that intelligible system which unites its ultimate object with its ultimate end. Hence at any given time the degree of truth in our experience as a whole is the degree of system it has achieved. The degree of truth of a particular proposition is to be judged in the first instance by its coherence with experience as a whole, ultimately by its coherence with that further whole, all-comprehensive and fully articulated, in which thought can come to rest.

But it is time we defined more explicitly what coherence means. To be sure, no fully satisfactory definition can be given; and as Dr. Ewing says, "it is wrong to tie down the advocates of the coherence theory to a precise definition. What they are doing is to describe an ideal that has never yet been completely clarified but is none the less immanent in all our thinking."[1] Certainly this ideal goes far beyond mere consistency. Fully coherent knowledge would be knowledge in which every judgment entailed, and was entailed by, the rest of the system. Probably we never find in fact a system where there is so much of interdependence. What it means may be clearer if we take a number of familiar systems and arrange them in a series tending to such coherence as a limit. At the bottom would be a junk-heap, where we could know every item but one and still be without any clue as to what that remaining item was. Above this would come a stone-pile, for here you could at least infer that what you could find next would be a stone. A machine would be higher again, since from the remaining parts one could deduce not only the general character of a missing part, but also its special form and function. This is a high degree of coherence, but it is very far short of the highest. You could remove the engine from a motorcar while leaving the other parts intact, and replace it with any one of thousands of other engines, but the thought of such an interchange among human heads or hearts shows at once that the interdependence in a machine is far below that of the body. Do we find then in organic bodies the highest conceivable coherence? Clearly not. Though a human hand, as Aristotle said, would hardly be a hand when detached from the body, still it would be something definite enough; and we can conceive systems in which even this something would be gone. Abstract a number from the number series and it would be a mere unrecognizable x; similarly, the very thought of a straight line involves the thought of the Euclidean space in which it falls. It is perhaps in such systems as Euclidean geometry that we get the most perfect examples of coherence that have been constructed. If any proposition were lacking, it could be supplied from the rest; if any were altered, the repercussions would be felt through the length and breadth of the system. Yet even such a system as this falls short of ideal system. Its postulates are unproved; they are independent of each other, in the sense that none of them could be derived from any other or even from all the others together; its clear necessity is bought by an abstractness so extreme as to have left out nearly everything that belongs to the character of actual things. A completely satisfactory system would have none

[1] *Idealism*, p. 231.

of these defects. No proposition would be arbitrary, every proposition would be entailed by the others jointly and even singly,[2] no proposition would stand outside the system. The integration would be so complete that no part could be seen for what it was without seeing its relation to the whole, and the whole itself could be understood only through the contribution of every part.

It may be granted at once that in common life we are satisfied with far less than this. We accept the demonstrations of the geometer as complete, and do not think of reproaching him because he begins with postulates and leaves us at the end with a system that is a skeleton at the best. In physics, in biology, above all in the social sciences, we are satisfied with less still. We test judgments by the amount of coherence which in that particular subject-matter it seems reasonable to expect. We apply, perhaps unconsciously, the advice of Aristotle, and refrain from asking demonstration in the physical sciences, while in mathematics we refuse to accept less. And such facts may be thought to show that we make no actual use of the ideal standard just described. But however much this standard may be relaxed within the limits of a particular science, its influence is evident in the grading of the sciences generally. It is precisely in those sciences that approach most nearly to system as here defined that we achieve the greatest certainty, and precisely in those that are most remote from such system that our doubt is greatest whether we have achieved scientific truth at all. Our immediate exactions shift with the subject-matter; our ultimate standard is unvarying.

Now if we accept coherence as the test of truth, does that commit us to any conclusions about the *nature* of truth or reality? I think it does, though more clearly about reality than about truth. It is past belief that the fidelity of our thought to reality should be rightly measured by coherence if reality itself were not coherent. To say that the nature of things may be *in*coherent, but we shall approach the truth about it precisely so far as our thoughts become coherent, sounds very much like nonsense. And providing we retained coherence as the test, it would still be nonsense even if truth were conceived as correspondence. On this supposition we should have truth when, our thought having achieved coherence, the correspondence was complete between that thought and its object. But complete correspondence between a coherent thought and an incoherent object seems meaningless. It is hard to see, then, how anyone could consistently take coherence as the test of truth unless he took it also as a character of reality.

Does acceptance of coherence as a test commit us not only to a view about the structure of reality but also to a view about the nature of truth? This is a more difficult question. As we saw at the beginning of the chapter, there

---

[2] Coherence can be defined without this point, which, as Dr. Ewing remarks (*Idealism*, p. 231), makes the case harder to establish. In no mathematical system, for example, would anyone dream of trying to deduce all the other propositions from any proposition taken singly. But when we are describing an ideal, such a fact is not decisive, and I follow Joachim in holding that in a perfectly coherent system every proposition would entail all others, if only for the reason that its meaning could never be fully understood without apprehension of the system in its entirety.

have been some highly reputable philosophers who have held that the answer to "What is the test of truth?" is "Coherence," while the answer to "What is the nature or meaning of truth?" is "Correspondence." These questions are plainly distinct. Nor does there seem to be any direct path from the acceptance of coherence as the test of truth to its acceptance as the nature of truth. Nevertheless there is an indirect path. If we accept coherence as our test, we must use it everywhere. We must therefore use it to test the suggestion that truth *is* other than coherence. But if we do, we shall find that we must reject the suggestion as leading to *in*coherence. Coherence is a pertinacious concept and, like the well-known camel, if one lets it get its nose under the edge of the tent, it will shortly walk off with the whole.

Suppose that, accepting coherence as the test, one rejects it as the nature of truth in favor of some alternative; and let us assume, for example, that this alternative is correspondence. This, we have said, is incoherent; why? Because if one holds that truth is correspondence, one cannot intelligibly hold either that it is tested by coherence or that there is any dependable test at all. Consider the first point. Suppose that we construe experience into the most coherent picture possible, remembering that among the elements included will be such secondary qualities as colours, odours, and sounds. Would the mere fact that such elements as these are coherently arranged prove that anything precisely corresponding to them exists "out there"? I cannot see that it would, even if we knew that the two arrangements had closely corresponding patterns. If on one side you have a series of elements a, b, c..., and on the other a series of elements α, β, γ..., arranged in patterns that correspond, you have no proof as yet that the *natures* of these elements correspond. It is therefore impossible to argue from a high degree of coherence within experience to its correspondence in the same degree with anything outside. And this difficulty is typical. If you place the nature of truth in one sort of character and its test in something quite different, you are pretty certain, sooner or later, to find the two falling apart. In the end, the only test of truth that is not misleading is the special nature or character that is itself constitutive of truth.

Feeling that this is so, the adherents of correspondence sometimes insist that correspondence shall be its own test. But then the second difficulty arises. If truth does consist in correspondence, no test can be sufficient. For in order to know that experience corresponds to fact, we must be able to get at that fact, unadulterated with idea, and compare the two sides with each other. And we have seen in the last chapter that such fact is not accessible. When we try to lay hold of it, what we find in our hands is a judgment which is obviously not itself the indubitable fact we are seeking, and which must be checked by some fact beyond it. To this process there is no end. And even if we did get at the fact directly, rather than through the veil of our ideas, that would be no less fatal to correspondence. This direct seizure of fact presumably gives us truth, but since that truth no longer consists in correspondence of idea with fact, the main theory has been abandoned. In short, if we can know fact only through the medium of our own ideas, the original forever eludes us; if we can get at the facts directly, we have knowledge whose truth is not correspondence. The theory is forced to choose between scepticism and self-contradiction.

Thus the attempt to combine coherence as the test of truth with correspondence as the nature of truth will not pass muster by its own test. The result is incoherence. We believe that an application of the test to other theories of truth would lead to a like result. The argument is: assume coherence as the test, and you will be driven by the incoherence of your alternatives to the conclusion that it is also the nature of truth.

STUDY QUESTIONS

1. What makes up the "system" which is the basis for deciding whether a particular statement is true or false in the coherence theory?
2. According to Blanshard, the correspondence theory of truth is doomed either to skepticism or to self-contradiction. Why? Do you agree?
3. If the coherence theory had been applied to Copernicus's heliocentric theory when he first published it, would it have been judged true or false?
4. Blanshard says that we cannot fully appreciate the meaning of a statement without relating it to the "system" in its entirety. Since we are unlikely ever to grasp the "system" in its entirety, can we ever hope to have legitimate confidence in our beliefs? If so, what would be the basis for such confidence?
5. "The coherence test has a conservative bias. It judges statements true or false in line with their coherence with accepted common-sense and scientific beliefs. Yet new knowledge is born on the grave of old knowledge; an advance in knowledge usually requires that we reject some of what we have customarily accepted. The coherence doctrine militates against this." Do you agree?
6. "A strange thing happened this morning; the sun rose in the west." Which theory of truth would you most likely apply in judging the truth of this statement?

SELECTED READINGS FOR PART TWO

One of the most famous contemporary arguments against Descartes's radical skepticism is G. E. Moore, "Proof of an External World," reprinted in his *Philosophical Papers* (London: G. Allen, 1959; New York: Collier Books, 1962). A. Kenny, *Descartes: A Study of His Philosophy* (New York: Random House, 1968), and H. G. Frankfurt, *Demons, Dreamers, and Madmen* (Indianapolis: Bobbs-Merrill, 1970) are good, recent critical studies of Cartesian skepticism. Some of the best writing on the mind-body problem is collected in A. Flew (ed.), *Body, Mind, and Death* (New York: Macmillan, 1964), G. N. A. Vesey (ed.), *Body and Mind* (London: G. Allen, 1964), and Sidney Hook (ed.), *Dimensions of Mind* (New York: Collier Books, 1961). A readable explanation of six classical theories of the mind-body relationship is F. F. Centore, *Persons: A Comparative Account of the Six Possible Theories* (Westport, Conn., and London, England: Greenwood Press, 1979). A fine source of criticisms of Cartesian dualism by modern philosophers is Stuart F. Spicker (ed.), *The Philosophy of the Body* (Chicago: Quadrangle, 1970). Probably the best-known contemporary critic of Descartes's view of the mind-body relationship is Gilbert Ryle. See especially his *The Concept of Mind* (New York: Harper & Row, 1949), pp. 11–18 and 167–172. Ryle's views are critically evaluated in O. P. Wood and G. Pitcher (eds.), *Ryle: A Collection of Critical Essays* (Garden City, N.Y.: Doubleday, 1970). One of the earliest and most provocative statements of the behaviorist position was made by the psychologist John B. Watson in *Behaviorism* (New York: Norton, 1924). By far the most famous contemporary spokesman is Nobel laureate B. F. Skinner. For a general statement of his views, see his *Science and Human Behavior* (New York: Macmillan, 1953). Skinner's political thought can be seen in his utopian novel, *Walden Two* (New York: Macmillan, 1948), and *Beyond Freedom and Dignity* (New York: Knopf, 1971). He both restates the essentials of behaviorism and defends it against its critics in his *About Behaviorism* (New York: Knopf, 1974). Interesting critiques of behaviorism by a psychologist and a philosopher respectively are contained in W. Köhler, *Gestalt Psychology* (New York: Liveright, 1929), and Bertrand Russell, *Outline of Philosophy* (London: G. Allen; New York: Norton, 1927).

For a look at very recent debate on the mind-body problem, see Jerry A. Fodor, "The Mind-Body Problem," in *Scientific American,* January, 1981, pp. 114–123. In this overview, Fodor shows how a theory called *functionalism* aims to overcome deficiencies in traditional dualist and materialist accounts of the nature of mind. Also, important sources of information on current research into the workings of the mind include George Johnson, *Machinery of the Mind* (New York: Times Books, 1986), and Colin Blakemore and Susan Greenfield (eds.), *Mindwaves* (New York: Basil Blackwell, 1987). Johnson's book, from which one of our readings is taken, has an extensive bibliography on pp. 321–323. An important and controversial contribution to epistemology is Richard Rorty, *Philosophy and the Mirror of Nature* (Princeton, N.J.: Princeton University Press, 1979). Rorty reviews classical and contemporary theories of knowledge, particularly in relation to the mind-body problem.

The first four chapters in Bertrand Russell, *The Problems of Philosophy* (London: Oxford, 1912) raise the problem of perception and knowledge in a clear and thought-provoking way. A more technical account can be found in Russell, *Our Knowledge of the External World,* 2d ed. (London: G. Allen, 1926). F. M. Cornford's *Plato's Theory of Knowledge* (London: Routledge, 1935), from which our Plato selection was taken, is a very good book. Cornford adds rich commentary to the text, so that the beginning student can read Plato as well as have important philosophical points explained and set into a historical context. For the more advanced student, Brand Blanshard, *The Nature of Thought,* vol. II (London: G. Allen, 1939) gives a good defense of rationalism and compares it with other theories. G. J. Warnock, *Berkeley* (Harmondsworth: Penguin, 1953) is a good general account of Berkeley's philosophy. For more extensive reading on idealism, see A. C. Ewing (ed.), *The Idealist Tradition from Berkeley to Blanshard* (New York: Free Press, 1957). For advanced students, an excellent source of articles which describe and criticize Hume's philosophy is a special commemorative issue on Hume in the *Review of Metaphysics*, vol. XXX, no. 1, September 1976. For advanced work in the philosophy of science, see C. G. Hempel, *Philosophy of Natural Science* (Englewood Cliffs, N.J.: Prentice-Hall, 1966), N. R. Hanson, *Patterns of Discovery* (Cambridge, Mass.: Harvard, 1958), Karl Popper, *The Logic of Scientific Discovery* (New York: Basic Books, 1959), and Thomas S. Kuhn, *The Structure of Scientific Revolutions* (Chicago: University of Chicago Press, 1962). A good introduction to the subject is George Gale, *Theory of Science* (New York: McGraw-Hill, 1979). Probably the most thorough and exhaustive collection of essays on the philosophy of science is Frederick Suppe (ed.), *The Structure of Scientific Theories*, 2d ed. (Urbana: University of Illinois Press, 1977).

For excellent historical and descriptive accounts of the three classical theories of truth, see various articles in Paul Edwards (ed.), *The Encyclopedia of Philosophy* (New York: Macmillan and Free Press, 1967); on the pragmatic theory see Gertrude Ezorsky, "Pragmatic Theory of Truth," vol. 6, pp. 427–430; on the correspondence theory, see A. N. Prior, "Correspondence Theory of Truth," vol. 2, pp. 223–232; and for the coherence theory, see Alan R. White, "Coherence Theory of Truth," vol. 2, pp. 130–133. This encyclopedia is available in most college libraries. For C. S. Peirce's early formulation of the pragmatic test of meaning, see Charles Hartshorne and Paul Weiss (eds.), vol. 5, *Collected Papers of Charles Sanders Peirce* (Cambridge, Mass.: Harvard, 1931–58); the specific relevant article in this volume is "How to Make Our Ideas Clear," pp. 248–271; this article is usually available in anthologies of American philosophy as well. A fine edition of James's writings is Horace M. Kallen (ed.), *The Philosophy of William James* (New York: Modern Library, n.d.). John Dewey gives a critical discussion of James's version of the pragmatic test of truth, and also clarifies his own stance, in his *Essays in Experimental Logic*, chap. 12 (New York: Dover, n.d.), pp. 303–329. For a useful collection of readings on the problem of truth, see George Pitcher (ed.), *Truth* (Englewood Cliffs, N.J.: Prentice-Hall, 1964). A helpful essay on the meaning of "true" and "false" and "truth" and "falsity," as well as an analysis of three classical and three contemporary theories of truth, is Alan R. While, *Truth* (New York: Macmillan, 1970). In his *The Correspondence Theory of Truth* (London: Hutchinson, 1975), D. J. O'Connor examines contemporary versions of the correspondence theory, including those of Tarski and J. L. Austin. Impressive attempts to revive the coherence theory and defend it against major criticisms are Nicholas Rescher, *The Coherence Theory of Truth* (London: Oxford University Press, 1973), and Keith Lehrer, *Knowledge* (London: Oxford University Press, 1974).

PART THREE

Free Will
and Determinism

THE PARADOX OF FREEDOM

I have quit smoking. The cigarettes lie on the desk before me. I remember the delightful sensation of smoke filling my lungs. My fingers begin to twitch. I force myself to think of the consequences of resuming the habit— the health dangers, the responsibilities I have to others. But I am especially nervous today and smoking would calm me down. Besides, just one couldn't hurt....I pick up the pack. But then I hesitate, gather myself together, and throw them away. I have won against powerful forces within myself. I am not a passive victim, for I have exerted my will.

This sort of struggle is a familiar story to everyone. As we experience it, we feel that we can go one way or another. The future is open, and the outcome is under our control. But there are facts which cloud this assumption. If every event has a cause, as science seems to say, how can we be in control of things? In a burst of scientific enthusiasm, the nineteenth-century mathematician La Place remarked that if a person of great intelligence knew the exact configuration of atoms at any specific time, as well as the laws which govern the movement of matter, that person could predict every future state of the universe with absolute certainty. Every event is conditioned to be just as it is by what immediately precedes it, and those events by what precedes them, and so on. A million years ago God could have predicted that I would throw the cigarettes away. Whatever happens *must* happen—there is no alternative.

The dominant image of life which emerges from this dilemma seems clearly pessimistic. The individual is a passive object, manipulated by hidden forces that are impossible to resist. Try as we might, we cannot alter the future which is laid down at the beginning of time. In our own time, new developments in psychology have added detail to this picture.

Many psychologists emphasize the extent to which our choices are governed by unconscious forces created by early childhood experiences. Our lives are depicted as the working out of blind mechanical processes over which we have no control.

Yet the feeling of freedom persists. At least some of the time, we believe that we are in control of our future. Above all, we see ourselves as morally responsible agents, ready to stand accountable for what we do, because we could have done otherwise. Is this feeling of freedom an unscientific illusion, or is the realm of choice somehow exempt from the laws of causality?

7

Choice: From Chance to Compulsion

PROBLEM INTRODUCTION

Determinism is the view that every event has a cause. At first glance, this seems to be a reasonable assumption, but it is one which has confounded every thinker who has pondered its implications. Modern science assumes that the universe is a deterministic system. To explain, predict, and establish lawful relations between things requires that the past and the future be connected, and this, in turn, seems to mean that the future flows necessarily from the past. If things and events are caused, then it is possible to specify a set of conditions which, when present, produce the effect *without exception.* On the other hand, an indeterministic universe would be one where sometimes events would lead up to what appeared to be an inevitable consequence, and yet something new might occur—something which could not be predicted from the past, not even by God.

How does the issue of determinism affect our belief that we are free agents? The most natural position to adopt is that a deterministic universe rules out free will. If this assumption is correct, then one is forced to choose between free will and determinism. The position known as *hard-determinism* rejects free will, whereas its opposite counterpart, *libertarianism,* or *indeterminism,* asserts that determinism is false.

The hard-determinist claims that the human personality is within the normal course of nature, and so free will cannot exist. If it did exist, it would be possible for a person to choose a course of action against all the forces of heredity and training which have been building in the opposite direction. But the hard-determinist believes that every choice can be completely explained by previous causes, and so the subjective feeling of freedom to choose between alternatives is an illusion. Naturally, this affects the normal view of moral responsibility. Character—that is, habits, beliefs, values, dispositions, and capacities—is a unique product of heredity and environment. Our decisions flow from our character with the same necessity as an unfolding chem-

255

ical reaction. But we are not responsible for our character, and so we cannot be held responsible for the actions produced by it.

It is very easy to confuse hard-determinism with fatalism. The central idea of fatalism is that *specific* events are unavoidable. It leads to the resignation expressed by many soldiers in the slogan "There's a bullet out there with my name on it," indicating that a specific mode of dying at a specific time and place is inevitable. Strictly speaking, however, fatalism is not a form of determinism. To say that something is inevitable is to assert that it will occur *no matter what* precedes it. No determinist can accept this. If the world is deterministic, then the future is conditioned to be what it is by the past. If conditions in the past were altered, the future would be altered also. Since human activity is part and parcel of nature, there is no reason to suppose that it cannot serve as a cause for future events. A hard-determinist, therefore, believes that human effort is not futile. But hard-determinists would also say that whether we put forth that effort or not is determined, and we are not free to control *that*.

It is not easy, however, to reject the nagging feeling of freedom that most people experience in their daily lives. Libertarianism, like hard-determinism, is based on the assumption that free will cannot exist in a deterministic universe. Because of the experienced quality of freedom the libertarian denies that the universe is completely deterministic. William James, for example, believed that chance is an ultimate factor in nature. Most libertarians do not go so far as James for fear of denying the obvious successes of science. Rather than regarding the uniformities of nature as a series of happy coincidences, they grant that most events are under the rule of causal necessity. There is, however, a range of events where alternative possibilities are available— namely, the events of human choice. Therefore, libertarians all agree that some decisions cannot be completely explained by prior causes.

Libertarianism is a doctrine which seeks to preserve the sense of self-control which is required for moral responsibility. People do not merely passively respond to the world. The person is a well-spring of creative activity which stands over against the flow of events and controls them. Determinism, consequently, is a view that runs counter to the predominant trend of experience. William James argues that our feelings of regret do not make sense in a determined world. We regret the occurrence of things that are bad. But according to the determinist, they *must* occur. How can we regret something that must be? We might as well regret the falling of a stone when we drop it. As a result, James held that determinism leads to moral complacency, for, without regrets, we must be satisfied with the world as it is.

We seem to be on the horns of a dilemma: give up free will or give up determinism. Either alternative is intellectually discomforting. But there is a middle position. This is the theory called *soft-determinism*. Soft-determinists claim that free will and determinism are compatible. Indeed, soft-determinists believe that determinism is a necessary condition for moral responsibility. William James called this view a "quagmire of evasion."

The soft-determinist maintains that our actual moral practices cannot be squared with indeterminism, and that they make sense only if we suppose that a person's behavior is caused by certain ingredients of the personality. If someone commits a murder while under the influence of a hypnotist, for example, it is absurd to hold that person responsible. The chief cause of the action lay outside the person's character—in this case, in the character of the hypnotist. Similarly, if someone behaves irrationally because of a brain tumor, or as a result of excruciating pain, responsibility is diminished. Once again, these are causes which lie outside the wants and desires that make up the personality. The reason that we do not punish individuals under these conditions is that the punishment would not affect such behavior under similar circumstances. Punishment, like rewards, makes sense only under the assumption that *it will serve as a cause for future behavior.* Libertarianism, therefore, cannot provide an adequate account of moral responsibility because it is a theory in which decisions are not caused by the central mechanisms of the personality. If a person's decisions do not spring from the personality—if they simply "pop" into existence—then they are capricious. In such a world, the person is a victim of chance, not a free agent. Moral freedom is not freedom from all causes, but rather it is freedom from certain *kinds* of causes. When we are prevented by an external constraint from acting as we want to act, or when our actions result from causes foreign to our personality, we are not free. We are free when our actions result from the uncompelled choices of the personality.

According to soft-determinism, both libertarianism and hard-determinism are founded on a shared misconception. Both positions have correctly noted that freedom requires that more than one alternative be available to the agent. They have interpreted this to mean that a free agent must be able to act independently of prior causes. But this is an error. When we say that a person has alternatives available, we simply mean that no matter which course of action is chosen, there are no external constraints which would prevent the person from acting on that choice. A free agent could have done otherwise, in the sense that nothing stood in the way of doing otherwise, *if another choice had been made.*

What are the practical consequences of these theories? Does accepting one of them make a difference? The answer to this is an unqualified "yes." To see the practical effect of a belief in hard-determinism, read Clarence Darrow's moving defense of Leopold and Loeb, two admitted murderers. Darrow argues that the death penalty is cruel and senseless because the defendants were not responsible for what they did. Indeed, Darrow would argue that punishment of any kind is unjustified. If people are to be locked up, it is only to protect society—not because they deserve it. A libertarian, on the other hand, believes that wrongdoing merits retribution. That is, punishment is justified because the agent *could have done otherwise.* Also, the libertarian position supposes that the human person cannot be fully analyzed by the methods of science, and therefore transcends the normal order of nature. Soft-determinism accepts something from both positions. It counsels mercy, because the sole function of punishment is to reform. Like Darrow, the soft-determinist cannot regard the infliction of punishment as retribution for past wrongs. Therefore, the doctrine of eternal punishment, which is a feature of many religions, is senseless. But like the libertarian, the soft-determinist believes that people can be held responsible for their actions under certain conditions, because holding them responsible serves to cause socially desired behavior.

Leopold and Loeb:
The Crime of Compulsion
Clarence Darrow

In 1924, America was shocked at the brutal kidnapping and murder of fourteen-year-old Bobby Franks. The confessed killers were two brilliant students: Nathan Leopold, Jr., eighteen, and Richard Loeb, seventeen. Both came from wealthy Chicago families. Leopold was the youngest graduate of the University of Chicago, and Loeb was the youngest graduate of the University of Michigan. In order to demonstrate their contempt for conventional morality, the two made a pact to commit the "perfect" crime. The state demanded the death penalty.

They were defended by Clarence Darrow (1867–1938), America's best-known criminal attorney. At this time Darrow was already famous for his many defenses of unpopular causes. He was, for example, an early supporter of organized labor when it was considered an anarchist movement. Early in his career, when he was the general counsel for the Chicago and North Western Railroad Company, he quit his position to defend union strikers against his former company.

Darrow believed that the case of Leopold and Loeb would allow him to present his views against capital punishment. He attempted to show that the two boys were helpless victims of heredity and environment. Killing them, he argued, would be a pointless brutality.

For over twelve hours, Darrow pleaded for mercy for the two boys. At the end of his summation, the courtroom was quiet and the judge was weeping openly. The defendants were sentenced to life in prison.

I have tried to study the lives of these two most unfortunate boys. Three months ago, if their friends and the friends of the family had been asked to pick out the most promising lads of their acquaintance, they probably would have picked these two boys. With every opportunity, with plenty of wealth, they would have said that those two would succeed.

In a day, by an act of madness, all this is destroyed, until the best they can hope for now is a life of silence and pain, continuing to the end of their years.

How did it happen?

Let us take Dickie Loeb first.

I do not claim to know how it happened; I have sought to find out. I know that something, or some combination of things, is responsible for this mad act. I know that there are no accidents in nature. I know that effect follows cause. I know that, if I were wise enough, and knew enough about this case, I could lay my finger on the cause. I will do the best I can, but it is largely speculation.

The child, of course, is born without knowledge.

Impressions are made upon its mind as it goes along. Dickie Loeb was a child of wealth and opportunity. Over and over in this court Your Honor has been asked, and other courts have been asked, to consider boys who have no chance; they have been asked to consider the poor, whose home had been the street, with no education and no opportunity in life, and they have done it, and done it rightfully.

But, Your Honor, it is just as often a great misfortune to be the child of the rich as it is to be the child of the poor. Wealth has its misfortunes. Too much, too great opportunity and advantage, given to a child has its misfortunes, and I am asking Your Honor to consider the rich as well as the poor (and nothing else). Can I find what was wrong? I think I can. Here was a boy at a tender age, placed in the hands of a governess, intellectual, vigorous, devoted, with a strong ambition for the welfare of this boy. He was pushed in his studies, as plants are forced in hothouses. He had no pleasures, such as a boy should have, except as they were gained by lying and cheating.

Now, I am not criticizing the nurse. I suggest that some day Your Honor look at her picture. It explains her fully. Forceful, brooking no interference, she loved the boy, and her ambition was that he should reach the highest perfection. No time to pause, no time to stop from one book to another, no time to have those pleasures which a boy ought to have to create a normal life. And what happened? Your Honor, what would happen? Nothing strange or unusual. This nurse was with him all the time, except when he stole out at night, from two to fourteen years of age. He, scheming and planning as healthy boys would do, to get out from under her restraint; she, putting before him the best books, which children generally do not want; and he, when she was not looking, reading detective stories, which he devoured, story after story, in his young life. Of all this there can be no question.

What is the result? Every story he read was a story of crime. We have a statute in this state, passed only last year, if I recall it, which forbids minors reading stories of crime. Why? There is only one reason. Because the legislature in its wisdom felt that it would produce criminal tendencies in the boys who read them. The legislature of this state has given its opinion, and forbidden boys to read these books. He read them day after day. He never stopped. While he was passing through college at Ann Arbor he was still reading them. When he was a senior he read them, and almost nothing else.

Now, these facts are beyond dispute. He early developed the tendency to mix with crime, to be a detective; as a little boy shadowing people on the street; as a little child going out with his fantasy of being the head of a band of criminals and directing them on the street. How did this grow and develop in him? Let us see. It seems to be as natural as the day following the night. Every detective story is a story of a sleuth getting the best of it: trailing some unfortunate individual through devious ways until his victim is finally landed in jail or stands on the gallows. They all show how smart the detective is, and where the criminal himself falls down.

This boy early in his life conceived the idea that there could be a perfect crime, one that nobody could ever detect; that there could be one where the detective did not land his game—a perfect crime. He had been interested in the story of Charley Ross, who was kidnaped. He was interested in these things all his life. He believed in his childish way that a crime could be so carefully planned that there would be no detection, and his idea was to plan and accomplish a perfect crime. It would involve kidnaping and involve murder.

There had been growing in Dickie's brain, dwarfed and twisted—as every act in this case shows it to have been dwarfed and twisted—there had been growing this scheme, not due to any wickedness of Dickie Loeb, for he is a child. It grew as he grew; it grew from those around him; it grew from the lack of the proper training until it possessed him. He believed he could beat the police. He believed he could plan the perfect crime. He had thought of it and talked of it for years—had talked of it as a child, had worked at it as a child—this sorry act of his, utterly irrational and motiveless, a plan to commit a perfect crime which must contain kidnaping, and there must be ransom, or else it could not be perfect, and they must get the money....

The law knows and has recognized childhood for many and many a long year. What do we know about childhood? The brain of the child is the home of dreams, of castles, of visions, of illusions and of delusions. In fact, there could be no childhood without delusions, for delusions are always more alluring than facts. Delusions, dreams and hallucinations are a part of the warp and woof of childhood. You know it and I know it. I remember, when I was a child, the men seemed as tall as the trees, the trees as tall as the mountains. I can remember very well when, as a little boy, I swam the deepest spot in the river for the first time. I swam breathlessly and landed with as much sense of glory and triumph as Julius Caesar felt when he led his army across the Rubicon. I have been back since, and I can almost step across the same place, but it seemed an ocean then. And those men whom I thought so wonderful were dead and left nothing behind. I had lived in a dream. I had never known the real world which I met, to my discomfort and despair, and that dispelled the illusions of my youth.

The whole life of childhood is a dream and an illusion, and whether they take one shape or another shape depends not upon the dreamy boy but on what surrounds him. As well might I have dreamed of burglars and wished to be one as to dream of policemen and wished to be one. Perhaps I was lucky, too, that I had no money. We have grown to think that the misfortune is in not having it. The great misfortune in this terrible case is the money. That has destroyed their lives. That has fostered these illusions. That has promoted this mad act. And, if Your Honor shall doom them to die, it will be because they are the sons of the rich....

I know where my life has been molded by books, amongst other things.

We all know where our lives have been influenced by books. The nurse, strict and jealous and watchful, gave him one kind of book; by night he would steal off and read the other.

Which, think you, shaped the life of Dickie Loeb? Is there any kind of question about it? A child. Was it pure maliciousness? Was a boy of five or six or seven to blame for it? Where did he get it? He got it where we all get our ideas, and these books became a part of his dreams and a part of his life, and as he grew up his visions grew to hallucinations.

He went out on the street and fantastically directed his companions, who were not there, in their various moves to complete the perfect crime. Can there be any sort of question about it?

Suppose, Your Honor, that instead of this boy being here in this court, under the plea of the State that Your Honor shall pronounce a sentence to hang him by the neck until dead, he had been taken to a pathological hospital to be analyzed, and the physicians had inquired into his case. What would they have said? There is only one thing that they could possibly have said. They would have traced everything back to the gradual growth of the child.

That is not all there is about it. Youth is hard enough. The only good thing about youth is that it has no thought and no care; and how blindly we can do things when we are young!

Where is the man who has not been guilty of delinquencies in youth? Let us be honest with ourselves. Let us look into our own hearts. How many men are there today—lawyers and congressmen and judges, and even state's attorneys—who have not been guilty of some mad act in youth? And if they did not get caught, or the consequences were trivial, it was their good fortune.

We might as well be honest with ourselves, Your Honor. Before I would tie a noose around the neck of a boy I would try to call back into my mind the emotions of youth. I would try to remember what the world looked like to me when I was a child. I would try to remember how strong were these instinctive, persistent emotions that moved my life. I would try to remember how weak and inefficient was youth in the presence of the surging, controlling feelings of the child. One that honestly remembers and asks himself the question and tries to unlock the door that he thinks is closed, and calls back the boy, can understand the boy.

But, Your Honor, that is not all there is to boyhood. <u>Nature is strong and she is pitiless. She works in her own mysterious way, and we are her victims</u>. We have not much to do with it ourselves. Nature takes this job in hand, and we play our parts. In the words of old Omar Khayyam, we are only:

> But helpless pieces in the game He plays
> Upon this checkerboard of nights and days;
> Hither and thither moves, and checks, and slays,
> And one by one back in the closet lays.

What had this boy to do with it? He was not his own father; he was not his own mother; he was not his own grandparents. All of this was handed to him. He did not surround himself with governesses and wealth. He did not make himself. And yet he is to be compelled to pay.

There was a time in England, running down as late as the beginning of the last century, when judges used to convene court and call juries to try a horse, a dog, a pig, for crime. I have in my library a story of a judge and jury and lawyers trying and convicting an old sow for lying down on her ten pigs and killing them.

What does it mean? Animals were tried. Do you mean to tell me that Dickie Loeb had any more to do with this making than any other product of heredity that is born upon the earth?...

For God's sake, are we crazy? In the face of history, of every line of philosophy, against the teaching of every religionist and seer and prophet the world has ever given us, we are still doing what our barbaric ancestors did when they came out of the caves and the woods.

From the age of fifteen to the age of twenty or twenty-one, the child has the burden of adolescence, of puberty and sex thrust upon him. Girls are kept at home and carefully watched. Boys without instruction are left to work the period out for themselves. It may lead to excess. It may lead to disgrace. It may lead to perversion. Who is to blame? Who did it? Did Dickie Loeb do it?

Your Honor, I am almost ashamed to talk about it. I can hardly imagine that we are in the twentieth century. And yet there are men who seriously say that for what nature has done, for what life has done, for what training has done, you should hang these boys.

Now, there is no mystery about this case, Your Honor. I seem to be criticizing their parents. They had parents who were kind and good and wise in their way. But I say to you seriously that the <u>parents are more responsible than these boys</u>. And yet few boys had better parents.

Your Honor, it is the easiest thing in the world to be a parent. We talk of motherhood, and yet every woman can be a mother. We talk of fatherhood, and yet every man can be a father. Nature takes care of that. It is easy to be a parent. But to be wise and farseeing enough to understand the boy is another thing; only a very few are so wise and so farseeing as that. When I think of the light way nature has of picking our parents and populating the earth, having them born and die, I cannot hold human beings to the same degree of responsibility that young lawyers hold them when they are enthusiastic in a prosecution. I know what it means.

I know there are not better citizens in Chicago than the fathers of these poor boys. I know there were no better women than their mothers. But I am going to be honest with this court, if it is at the expense of both. I know that one of two things happened to Richard Loeb: <u>that this terrible crime was inherent in his organism, and came from some ancestor;</u> or that it came through <u>his education</u> and his training after he was born. Do I need to prove it? Judge Crowe said at one point in this case, when some witness spoke about their wealth, that "probably that was responsible."

To believe that any boy is responsible for himself or his early training is an absurdity that no lawyer or judge should be guilty of today. Somewhere this came to the boy. If his failing came from his heredity, I do not know where or how. None of us are bred perfect and pure; and the color of our hair, the color of our eyes, our stature, the weight and fineness of our brain, and everything about us could, with full knowledge, be traced with absolute certainty to somewhere. If we had the pedigree it could be traced just the same in a boy as it could in a dog, a horse or a cow.

I do not know what remote ancestors may have sent down the seed that corrupted him, and I do not know through how many ancestors it may have passed until it reached Dickie Loeb.

All I know is that it is true, and there is not a biologist in the world who will not say that I am right.

If it did not come that way, then I know that if he was normal, if he had been understood, if he had been trained as he should have been it would not have happened. Not that anybody may not slip, but I know it and Your Honor knows it, and every schoolhouse and every church in the land is an evidence of it. Else why build them?

Every effort to protect society is an effort toward training the youth to keep the path. Every bit of training in the world proves it, and it likewise proves that it sometimes fails. I know that if this boy had been understood and properly trained—properly for him—and the training that he got might have been the very best for someone; but if it had been the proper training for him he would not be in this courtroom today with the noose above his head. If there is responsibility anywhere, it is back of him; somewhere in the infinite number of his ancestors, or in his surroundings, or in both. And I submit, Your Honor, that under every principle of natural justice, under every principle of conscience, of right, and of law, he should not be made responsible for the acts of someone else....

It is when these dreams of boyhood, these fantasies of youth still linger, and the growing boy is still a child—a child in emotion, a child in feeling, a child in hallucinations—that you can say that it is the dreams and the hallucinations of childhood that are responsible for his conduct. There is not an act in all this horrible tragedy that was not the act of a child, the act of a child wandering around in the morning of life, moved by the new feelings of a boy, moved by the uncontrolled impulses which his teaching was not strong enough to take care of, moved by the dreams and the hallucinations which haunt the brain of a child. I say, Your Honor, that it would be the height of cruelty, of injustice, of wrong and barbarism to visit the penalty upon this poor boy.

STUDY QUESTIONS

1. Darrow begins by tracing the causes of Loeb's mental framework. Why does he do this? Is there anything special about Loeb's background which exempts him from responsibility?

2. At one point Darrow quotes Omar Khayyam, and says that nature is piti-less. Why is nature pitiless? Do you agree?

3. Where does Darrow wish to place the responsibility for the crime? Can he consistently place responsibility anywhere?

4. What do you think it means to say that people are responsible for what they do? Is it possible to be responsible and to have causes for what we choose?

5. "What's it to me that nobody's guilty and I know it—I need revenge or I'd kill myself. And revenge not in some far off eternity, somewhere, some-time, but here and now, on earth, so that I can see it" (Dostoyevsky, *The Brothers Karamazov*). What would Darrow say about the sentiment expressed in this quotation? What do you say? Do you think that the desire for re-venge is rational?

6. "In conformity, therefore, to the clear doctrine of Scripture we assert, that by an eternal and immutable counsel, God has once for all determined, both whom he would admit to salvation, and whom he would condemn to destruction" (John Calvin, *The Institutes of the Christian Religion*). If Calvin's God were the judge in the Leopold-Loeb case, what would the verdict be?

The Dilemma of Determinism

LIBERTARIAN

William James

William James (see biographical sketches on p. 109 and p. 228) called himself a "possibility man." This means that he regarded the universe as an unfolding system which cannot be completely predicted from past events. When we think of the future, we can imagine many different possibilities, and none of them is logically inconsistent with what went before. Therefore, he says, possibility or chance is a real factor in things. This must be so, James believes, to make sense of our moral experience.

James's critics have claimed that if human choice involves "chance," then anything should be possible—at any time; saints may suddenly "choose" to become fiends, or as you read this, you may "choose" to start eating the carpet. Keep this in mind as you read one of the most provocative essays ever written on the nature of freedom.

A common opinion prevails that the juice has ages ago been pressed out of the free-will controversy, and that no new champion can do more than warm up stale arguments which every one has heard. This is a radical mistake. I know of no subject less worn out, or in which inventive genius has a better chance of breaking open new ground—not, perhaps, of forcing a conclusion or of coercing assent, but of deepening our sense of what the issue between the two

An Address to the Harvard Divinity Students, published in the *Unitarian Review*, September 1884.

parties really is, of what the ideas of fate and of free-will imply.... The arguments I am about to urge all proceed on two suppositions: first, when we make theories about the world and discuss them with one another, we do so in order to attain a conception of things which shall give us subjective satisfaction; and, second, if there be two conceptions, and the one seems to us, on the whole, more rational than the other, we are entitled to suppose that the more rational one is the truer of the two. I hope that you are all willing to make these suppositions with me; for I am afraid that if there be any of you here who are not, they will find little edification in the rest of what I have to say. I cannot stop to argue the point; but I myself believe that all the magnificent achievements of mathematical and physical science—our doctrines of evolution, of uniformity of law, and the rest—proceed from our indomitable desire to cast the world into a more rational shape in our minds than the shape into which it is thrown there by the crude order of our experience. The world has shown itself, to a great extent, plastic to this demand of ours for rationality. How much farther it will show itself plastic no one can say. Our only means of finding out is to try; and, I, for one, feel as free to try conceptions of moral as of mechanical or of logical rationality. If a certain formula for expressing the nature of the world violates my moral demand, I shall feel as free to throw it overboard, or at least to doubt it, as if it disappointed my demand for uniformity of sequence, for example; the one demand being, so far as I can see, quite as subjective and emotional as the other is. The principle of causality, for example,—what is it but a postulate, an empty name covering simply a demand that the sequence of events shall some day manifest a deeper kind of belonging of one thing with another than the mere arbitrary juxtaposition which now phenomenally appears? It is as much an altar to an unknown god as the one that Saint Paul found at Athens. All our scientific and philosophic ideals are altars to unknown gods. Uniformity is as much so as is free-will. If this be admitted, we can debate on even terms. But if any one pretends that while freedom and variety are, in the first instance, subjective demands, necessity and uniformity are something altogether different, I do not see how we can debate at all.

To begin, then, I must suppose you acquainted with all the usual arguments on the subject. I cannot stop to take up the old proofs from causation, from statistics, from the certainty with which we can fortell one another's conduct, from the fixity of character, and all the rest. But there are two *words* which usually encumber these classical arguments, and which we must immediately dispose of if we are to make any progress. One is the eulogistic word *freedom*, and the other is the opprobrious word *chance*. The word "chance" I wish to keep, but I wish to get rid of the word "freedom." Its eulogistic associations have so far overshadowed all the rest of its meaning that both parties claim the sole right to use it, and determinists to-day insist that they alone are freedom's champions. Old-fashioned determinism was what we may call *hard* determinism. It did not shrink from such words as fatality, bondage of the will, necessitation, and the like. Nowadays, we have a *soft* determinism

which abhors harsh words, and, repudiating fatality, necessity, and even pre-
determination, says that its real name is freedom; for freedom is only necessity
understood, and bondage to the highest is identical with true freedom.

Now, all this is a quagmire of evasion under which the real issue of fact
has been entirely smothered.... But there *is* a problem, an issue of fact and not
of words, an issue of the most momentous importance, which is often decided
without discussion in one sentence,—nay, in one clause of a sentence,—by
those very writers who spin out whole chapters in their efforts to show what
"true" freedom is; and that is the question of determinism, about which we
are to talk to-night.

Fortunately, no ambiguities hang about this word or about its opposite,
indeterminism. Both designate an outward way in which things may happen,
and their cold and mathematical sound has no sentimental associations that
can bribe our partiality either way in advance. Now, evidence of an external
kind to decide between determinism and indeterminism is, as I intimated a
while back, strictly impossible to find. Let us look at the difference between
them and see for ourselves. What does determinism profess?

It professes that those parts of the universe already laid down absolutely
appoint and decree what the other parts shall be. The future has no ambiguous possibilities hidden in its womb: the part we call the present is compatible with only one totality. Any other future complement than the one fixed
from eternity is impossible. The whole is in each and every part, and welds
it with the rest into an absolute unity, an iron block, in which there can be no
equivocation or shadow of turning.

> With earth's first clay they did the last man knead,
> And there of the last harvest sowed the seed.
> And the first morning of creation wrote
> What the last dawn of reckoning shall read.

Indeterminism, on the contrary, says that the parts have a certain amount
of loose play on one another, so that the laying down of one of them does not
necessarily determine what the others shall be. It admits that possibilities may
be in excess of actualities, and that things not yet revealed to our knowledge
may really in themselves be ambiguous. Of two alternative futures which we
conceive, both may now be really possible; and the one become impossible
only at the very moment when the other excludes it by becoming real itself.
Indeterminism thus denies the world to be one unbending unit of fact. It says
there is a certain ultimate pluralism in it; and, so saying, it corroborates our
ordinary unsophisticated view of things. To that view, actualities seem to float
in a wider sea of possibilities from out of which they are chosen; and *somewhere*, indeterminism says, such possibilities exist, and form a path of truth.

Determinism, on the contrary, says they exist *nowhere*, and that necessity
on the one hand and impossibility on the other are the sole categories of the
real. Possibilities that fail to get realized are, for determinism, pure illusions:
they never were possibilities at all. There is nothing inchoate, it says, about

this universe of ours, all that was or is or shall be actual in it having been from eternity virtually there. The cloud of alternatives our minds escort this mass of actuality withal is a cloud of sheer deceptions, to which "impossibilities" is the only name that rightfully belongs.

The issue, it will be seen, is a perfectly sharp one, which no eulogistic terminology can smear over or wipe out. The truth *must* lie with one side or the other, and its lying with one side makes the other false.

The question relates solely to the existence of possibilities, in the strict sense of the term, as things that may, but need not, be. Both sides admit that a volition, for instance, has occurred. The indeterminists say another volition might have occurred in its place: the determinists swear that nothing could possibly have occurred in its place. Now, can science be called in to tell us which of these two point-blank contradicters of each other is right? Science professes to draw no conclusions but such as are based on matters of fact, things that have actually happened; but how can any amount of assurance that something actually happened give us the least grain of information as to whether another thing might or might not have happened in its place? Only facts can be proved by other facts. With things that are possibilities and not facts, facts have no concern. If we have no other evidence than the evidence of existing facts, the possibility-question must remain a mystery never to be cleared up....

The sting of the word "chance" seems to lie in the assumption that it means something positive, and that if anything happens by chance, it must needs be something of an intrinsically irrational and preposterous sort. Now, chance means nothing of the kind. It is a purely negative and relative term, giving us no information about that of which it is predicated, except that it happens to be disconnected with something else,—not controlled, secured, or necessitated by other things in advance of its own actual presence. As this point is the most subtile one of the whole lecture, and at the same time the point on which all the rest hinges, I beg you to pay particular attention to it. What I say is that it tells us nothing about what a thing may be in itself to call it "chance." It may be a bad thing, it may be a good thing. It may be lucidity, transparency, fitness incarnate, matching the whole system of other things, when it has once befallen, in an unimaginably perfect way. All you mean by calling it "chance" is that this is not guaranteed, that it may also fall out otherwise.

Nevertheless, many persons talk as if the minutest dose of disconnectedness of one part with another, the smallest modicum of independence, the faintest tremor of ambiguity about the future, for example, would ruin everything, and turn this goodly universe into a sort of insane sand-heap or nulliverse, no universe at all. Since future human volitions are as a matter of fact the only ambiguous things we are tempted to believe in, let us stop for a moment to make ourselves sure whether their independent and accidental character need be fraught with such direful consequences to the universe as these.

What is meant by saying that my choice of which way to walk home after the lecture is ambiguous and matter of chance as far as the present moment is concerned? It means that both Divinity Avenue and Oxford Street are called; but that only one, and that *either* one, shall be chosen. Now, I ask you seriously to suppose that this ambiguity of my choice is real; and then to make the impossible hypothesis that the choice is made twice over, and each time falls on a different street. In other words, imagine that I first walk through Divinity Avenue, and then imagine that the powers governing the universe annihilate ten minutes of time with all that it contained, and set me back at the door of this hall just as I was before the choice was made. Imagine then that, everything else being the same, I now make a different choice and traverse Oxford Street. You, as passive spectators, look on and see the two alternative universes,—one of them with me walking through Divinity Avenue in it, the other with the same me walking through Oxford Street. Now, if you are determinists you believe one of these universes to have been from eternity impossible: you believe it to have been impossible because of the intrinsic irrationality or accidentality somewhere involved in it. But looking outwardly at these universes, can you say which is the impossible and accidental one, and which the rational and necessary one? I doubt if the most ironclad determinist among you could have the slightest glimmer of light on this point. In other words, either universe *after the fact* and once there would, to our means of observation and understanding, appear just as rational as the other. There would be absolutely no criterion by which we might judge one necessary and the other matter of chance. Suppose now we relieve the gods of their hypothetical task and assume my choice, once made, to be made forever. I go through Divinity Avenue for good and all. If, as good determinists, you now begin to affirm, what all good determinists punctually do affirm, that in the nature of things I *couldn't* have gone through Oxford Street,—had I done so it would have been chance, irrationality, insanity, a horrid gap in nature,—I simply call your attention to this, that your affirmation is what the Germans call a *Machtspruch*, a mere conception fulminated as a dogma and based on no insight into details. Before my choice, either street seemed as natural to you as to me. Had I happened to take Oxford Street, Divinity Avenue would have figured in your philosophy as the gap in nature; and you would have so proclaimed it with the best deterministic conscience in the world. . . .

And this at last brings us within sight of our subject. We have seen what determinism means: we have seen that indeterminism is rightly described as meaning chance; and we have seen that chance, the very name of which we are urged to shrink from as from a metaphysical pestilence, means only negative fact that no part of the world, however big, can claim to control absolutely the destinies of the whole. But although, in discussing the word "chance," I may at moments have seemed to be arguing for its real existence, I have not meant to do so yet. We have not yet ascertained whether this be a world of chance or no; at most, we have agreed that it seems so. And I now repeat what I said at the outset, that, from any strict theoretical point of view, the question is insoluble. To deepen our theoretic sense of the *difference* between a world with chances in it and a deterministic world is the most I can hope to do; and this I may now at last begin upon, after all our tedious clearing of the way.

I wish first of all to show you just what the notion that this is a deterministic world implies. The implications I call your attention to are all bound up with the fact that it is a world in which we constantly have to make what I shall, with your permission, call judgments of regret. Hardly an hour passes in which we do not wish that something might be otherwise; and happy indeed are those of us whose hearts have never echoed the wish of Omar Khayam—

> That we might clasp, ere closed, the book of fate,
> And make the writer on a fairer leaf
> Inscribe our names, or quite obliterate.
>
> Ah! Love, could you and I with fate conspire
> To mend this sorry scheme of things entire,
> Would we not shatter it to bits, and then
> Remould it nearer to the heart's desire?

Now, it is undeniable that most of these regrets are foolish, and quite on a par in point of philosophic value with the criticisms on the universe of that friend of our infancy, the hero of the fable The Atheist and the Acorn,—

> Fool! had that bough a pumpkin bore,
> Thy whimsies would have worked no more, etc.

Even from the point of view of our own ends, we should probably make a botch of remodelling the universe. How much more then from the point of view of ends we cannot see! Wise men therefore regret as little as they can. But still some regrets are pretty obstinate and hard to stifle,—regrets for acts of wanton cruelty or treachery, for example, whether performed by others or by ourselves. Hardly any one can remain *entirely* optimistic after reading the confession of the murderer at Brockton the other day: how, to get rid of the wife whose continued existence bored him, he inveigled her into a desert spot, shot her four times, and then, as she lay on the ground and said to him, "You didn't do it on purpose, did you dear?" replied, "No, I didn't do it on purpose," as he raised a rock and smashed her skull. Such an occurrence, with the mild sentence and self-satisfaction of the prisoner, is a field for a crop of regrets, which one need not take up in detail. We feel that, although a perfect mechanical fit to the rest of the universe, it is a bad moral fit, and that something else would really have been better in its place.

But for the deterministic philosophy the murder, the sentence, and the prisoner's optimism were all necessary from eternity; and nothing else for a moment had a ghost of a chance of being put into their place. To admit such a chance, the determinists tell us, would be to make a suicide of reason; so we must steel our hearts against the thought. And here our plot thickens, for we see the first of those difficult implications of determinism and monism which

it is my purpose to make you feel. If this Brockton murder was called for by
the rest of the universe, if it had to come at its preappointed hour, and if
nothing else would have been consistent with the sense of the whole, what are
we to think of the universe? Are we stubbornly to stick to our judgment of
regret, and say, though it *couldn't* be, yet, it *would* have been a better universe
with something different from this Brockton murder in it? That, of course,
seems the natural and spontaneous thing for us to do; and yet it is nothing
short of deliberately espousing a kind of pessimism. The judgment of regret
calls the murder bad. Calling a thing bad means, if it mean anything at all, that
the thing ought not to be, that something else ought to be in its stead. Determinism, in denying that anything else can be in its stead, virtually defines
the universe as a place in which what ought to be is impossible,—in other
words, as an organism whose constitution is afflicted with an incurable taint,
an irremediable flaw. The pessimism of a Schopenhauer says no more than
this,—that the murder is a symptom; and that it is a vicious symptom because
it belongs to a vicious whole, which can express its nature no otherwise than
by bringing forth just such a symptom as that at this particular spot. Regret
for the murder must transform itself, if we are determinists and wise, into a
larger regret. It is absurd to regret the murder alone. Other things being what
they are, *it* could not be different. What we should regret is that whole frame
of things of which the murder is one member. I see no escape whatever from
this pessimistic conclusion, if, being determinists, our judgment of regret is to
be allowed to stand at all.

The only deterministic escape from pessimism is everywhere to abandon
the judgment of regret. That this can be done, history shows to be not impossible. The devil, *quoad existentiam,* may be good. That is, although he be a
principle of evil, yet the universe, with such a principle in it, may practically
be a better universe than it could have been without. On every hand, in a
small way, we find that a certain amount of evil is a condition by which a
higher form of good is bought. There is nothing to prevent anybody from
generalizing this view, and trusting that if we could but see things in the largest of all ways, even such matters as this Brockton murder would appear to
be paid for by the uses that follow in their train. An optimism *quand même,* a
systematic and infatuate optimism like that ridiculed by Voltaire in his *Candide,*
is one of the possible ideal ways in which a man may train himself to look on
life. Bereft of dogmatic hardness and lit up with the expression of a tender and
pathetic hope, such an optimism has been the grace of some of the most religious characters that ever lived.

> Throb thine with Nature's throbbing breast,
> And all is clear from east to west.

Even cruelty and treachery may be among the absolutely blessed fruits
of time, and to quarrel with any of their details may be blasphemy. The only
real blasphemy, in short, may be that pessimistic temper of the soul which lets
it give way to such things as regrets, remorse, and grief.

Thus, our deterministic pessimism may become a deterministic optimism at the price of extinguishing our judgments of regret.

But does not this immediately bring us into a curious logical predicament? Our determinism leads us to call our judgments of regret wrong, because they are pessimistic in implying that what is impossible yet ought to be. But how then about the judgments of regret themselves? If they are wrong, other judgments, judgments of approval presumably, ought to be in their place. But as they are necessitated, nothing else *can* be in their place; and the universe is just what it was before,—namely, a place in which what ought to be appears impossible. We have got one foot out of the pessimistic bog, but the other one sinks all the deeper. We have rescued our actions from the bonds of evil, but our judgments are now held fast. When murders and treacheries cease to be sins, regrets are theoretic absurdities and errors. The theoretic and the active life thus play a kind of seesaw with each other on the ground of evil. The rise of either sends the other down. Murder and treachery cannot be good without regret being bad: regret cannot be good without treachery and murder being bad. Both, however, are supposed to have been foredoomed; so something must be fatally unreasonable, absurd, and wrong in the world. It must be a place of which either sin or error forms a necessary part. From this dilemma there seems at first sight no escape. Are we then so soon to fall back into the pessimism from which we thought we had emerged?...

Let me, then, without circumlocution say just this. The world is enigmatical enough in all conscience, whatever theory we may take up toward it. The indeterminism I defend, the free-will theory of popular sense based on the judgment of regret, represents that world as vulnerable, and liable to be injured by certain of its parts if they act wrong. And it represents their acting wrong as a matter of possibility or accident, neither inevitable nor yet to be infallibly warded off. In all this, it is a theory devoid either of transparency or of stability. It gives us a pluralistic, restless universe, in which no single point of view can ever take in the whole scene; and to a mind possessed of the love of unity at any cost, it will, no doubt, remain forever inacceptable. A friend with such a mind once told me that the thought of my universe made him sick, like the sight of the horrible motion of a mass of maggots in their carrion bed.

But while I freely admit that the pluralism and the restlessness are repugnant and irrational in a certain way, I find that every alternative to them is irrational in a deeper way. The indeterminism with its maggots, if you please to speak so about it, offends only the native absolutism of my intellect,—an absolutism which, after all, perhaps, deserves to be snubbed and kept in check. But the determinism with its necessary carrion, to continue the figure of speech, and with no possible maggots to eat the latter up, violates my sense of moral reality through and through. When, for example, I imagine such carrion as the Brockton murder, I cannot conceive it as an act by which the universe, as a whole, logically and necessarily expresses its nature without shrinking from complicity with such a whole. And I deliberately refuse to keep on terms of loyalty with the universe by saying blankly that the murder, since it does flow from the nature of the whole, is not carrion. There are *some* instinctive reactions which I, for one, will not tamper with. The only remaining alternative, the attitude of gnostical romanticism, wrenches my personal instincts in quite as violent a way. It falsifies the simple objectivity of their deliverance. It makes the goose-flesh the murder excites in me a sufficient reason for the perpetration of the crime.

No! better a thousand times, than such systematic corruption of our moral sanity, the plainest pessimism, so that it be straightforward; but better far than that the world of chance. Make as great an uproar about chance as you please, I know that chance means pluralism and nothing more. If some of the members of the pluralism are bad, the philosophy of pluralism, whatever broad views it may deny me, permits me, at least, to turn to the other members with a clean breast, of affection and an unsophisticated moral sense. And if I still wish to think of the world as a totality, it lets me feel that a world with a *chance* in it of being altogether good, even if the chance never come to pass, is better than a world with no such chance at all. That "chance" whose very notion I am exhorted and conjured to banish from my view of the future as the suicide of reason concerning it, that "chance" is—what? Just this,—the chance that in moral respects the future may be other and better than the past has been. This is the only chance we have any motive for supposing to exist. Shame, rather, on its repudiation and its denial! For its presence is the vital air which lets the world live, the salt which keeps it sweet.

STUDY QUESTIONS

1. What is the difference between determinism and indeterminism? How would a deterministic world affect our choices?
2. What does James mean by "chance"? Can you think of other meanings? Do you think that James would regard the throw of dice as a matter of chance?
3. The example about Oxford Street and Divinity Avenue is supposed to show that choice is "ambiguous." What does this mean? Does the example show this, do you think?
4. James argues that in a deterministic universe the feeling of regret makes no sense. Why is this? Why does determinism lead to pessimism?
5. James suggests that the determinist gets into a logical predicament. What is this predicament?
6. "There are some instinctive reactions which I, for one, will not tamper with." What reactions does James have in mind here? Do you think he is irrational on this issue?
7. "If some great power would agree to always make me think what is true and do what is right, on condition of being turned into a sort of clock and wound up every morning before I got out of bed, I should instantly close with the offer" (T.H. Huxley). Do you agree with Huxley? Which universe do you think would be best—Huxley's or James's?

will power - ability to carry out choices (restricted by heredity + environ.

will-agency) - innate ability to consider alternatives + to try

to make 1 of 2 possibilities into reality.

Free Will and Self-Creation *Libertarian!*
Peter Bertocci

Peter Anthony Bertocci (1910–   ) is emeritus professor of philosophy at Boston University. He is well known for his defense of the teleological argument in proving the existence of God. In this selection he considers a familiar slogan which determinists often use to excuse someone from responsibility: "We don't create ourselves." Bertocci, on the contrary, believes that to some extent we can create our own character.

Bertocci's argument softens James's position somewhat. Possibility is still a real element in the universe, but, as far as the personality is concerned, there are restrictions. We must distinguish between "will-agency" and "will-power." We may will to do something but be unable to carry it out—this is a failure of will-power. The ability to carry out choices depends upon many factors, including heredity and environment. However, these restrictions on will-power do not affect the reality of will-agency, which is an innate ability to consider alternatives and to try to make one of two possibilities into a reality. The final behavior of the person is the result of will-agency working within a restricted framework of will-power. Our habits, developed traits, learned capacities, are tools with which we confront our own natures as well as the world. We cannot do more than our tools allow. Therefore, much of our behavior may be predictable because these ingredients of our will-power and their limitations are known. Within these limitations, however, we are free to build our own characters.

A human being's *personality*, we may say, *is his unique and dynamic mode of adjustment to his own nature and the world*. In the process of living, a person's nature is affected by the influences coming to bear upon him; the home, school, playground, church, social organizations, work-environment challenge his capacities and leave their marks on his particular structure. However, he is far from neutral to these influences. He is more responsive and plastic in some ways than others, and he ploughs the course his own basic developing nature makes possible.

Thus, children brought up in the same home and community develop different personalities because their natures differ in responsiveness to their world as they each seek an adequate *modus vivendi*. As they grow older they find themselves having to deal not only with other persons and the world but also with the habits and dispositions which make up their own developing personalities. Once certain habits and attitudes are formed, they stand as obstacles to new adjustments the children should make; the personality pattern, itself a product of learning, is beginning to restrict ease of choice and further development. This is a very interesting and important fact. Even language

From Peter Anthony Bertocci, *Introduction to the Philosophy of Religion,* Chapter IX, Prentice-Hall, Inc., 1951. Reprinted by permission of the author.

habits illustrate it. Do we not learn to express our thoughts through a specific language and then find that it becomes almost impossible for us to think except in terms of that language? Similarly, we find that the personalities we develop restrict the channels for the expression of native wants and abilities.

Other persons see us in our personalities. However, although what other people think of us may be important, our personality is our own more or less unified pattern of adjustment, much of which is hidden from observers, and some of which we ourselves are not aware of. The patterning of our responses is more intricate than we understand, but we cannot deny the fact that as our personality-formation "sets," our adaptability is reduced. How difficult it is for us now to act like persons who worked out their life-adjustment in China! Yet had we been born in other homes, we could (with the same innate constitutions) have developed different emphases in our personalities.

It should now be clear that we as *persons* (as unified activities of wanting, knowing, feeling, willing, and oughting) are not coextensive with our *personalities*. If these unified activities (*persons*) had been brought up in China, they would have developed different modes of adjustment (*personalities*). These same wants and abilities might have found different expressions—other personalities could have been built from the same raw materials, as it were.

Now let us assume that a given person comes to the point where he does not approve his personality (or parts of it). Can he change it? Indeed, given the inheritance he had and the environmental forces which surrounded him from the moment of conception, could he really have developed any other personality than the one he has? This brings us face to face with the problem of free will. Is it true that a person's personality is *wholly* the product of the forces, hereditary and environmental, which meet in him?

We are here confronting one of the most important problems of philosophy and life. . . . So many other issues come to lodge at the entrance and at the exits of this problem that one hardly knows where to begin, especially if the discussion must be brief. It seems best here to define what we find in our conscious experience before moving to other considerations. It may help if the description is expressed in personal terms so that the reader may check the account by his own introspection.

From the time that I began to be conscious of myself as an active agent, I have had many experiences of confronting at least two alternative courses of action and then of *choosing to enact one*. A book falls. I consider: Shall I pick it up now or not? At the moment I have no doubt that I can, if I decide to, but I actually decide not to pick it up now. Again: the telephone rings. Shall I start at once to answer it, or shall I let it ring while I finish a sentence? I can go immediately, I feel, but I decide to finish the sentence. There are many examples of such simple choices. And they are not to be confused with those run-of-the-mill routine actions in which the strongest impulse is obeyed before any question comes up.

In most instances where alternatives come before my thought *as* problems of choice, I find myself leaning toward or wanting one alternative more than the other; to stay in bed rather than shiver temporarily in the cold, and to work in the garden rather than study, for example. If I did not stop to think about the situation, the ensuing action would surely be the one toward which I had the stronger leaning, and too often, even though I do stop to think about it, the wanted action still ensues!

Two things are clear so far. When I am conscious of alternatives, I am free at least to think about them. Since I do not have to go on thinking about them, and since I frequently do not want to continue thinking about them, the first act of will is the *willing to think or not to think* about any alternatives.

I use the word *will* to designate not the fact that I want to think but that I shall try to think even though it would be easier not to think. My *will* seems to be an activity of my person and an activity whereby I concentrate on an alternative which would have died had I not exerted effort on its behalf and withheld consent from the other wanted activity. My self (person) is a complex activity-unit whose life *in the main* consists of moving along in the wake of the dominant concourse of feeling, wanting, and thinking. But as conflicting courses present themselves in it, I must try (or try not) to "make up my mind" as to which course I, as a whole, *will* pursue.

In the last chapter we emphasized the importance of considering personal activities as different modes of one complex unity. It is equally important for us to remember that fact here. For the *will* must not be thought of as some separate faculty of the self, engaged in a struggle with other faculties or "components" of the self. It refers to that one of my self-activities in which I hold possible courses of action before myself, and, at least, think about them before I allow any one simply to dominate the path of action. While we shall, for brevity, go on speaking about the will as if it were one of the players on the team composing the person, it is untrue to fact to consider it in this way. A person is nothing apart from his varied distinguishable activities.

The next point to note is that I may not only will to think and, to that extent, delay the course of possible action, but having thought that one alternative is the better one for me to pursue, I may then *will* that one. William James properly, I think, called this effortful fact, *fiat*.[1] Since I cannot define it further, I can only appeal to my reader to identify in his own experience the state of consciousness in which one throws the total energy at his disposal on the side of one of his alternatives and "pushes" that.

This *fiat*—this setting oneself in support of one course of action in opposition to another—is the most vivid and the clearest expression of the will. The self may not succeed in the course it thus sets itself to realize, but that it can think about the alternative and that it can assign itself to the task of supporting the approved goal seems clear. So far as I know, nothing can keep me from exerting whatever energy I have toward the realization of an approved objective.

But note: I have not asserted that I know or can guarantee the amount

---

[1] See William James, *Psychology*. New York: Henry Holt & Co., 1896, II, 559 ff.

of control I have. Furthermore, I do know there are some things I cannot do. Free will does not mean that I can add an inch to the stature of any given endowment beyond the limits set by nature. Free will does not mean that I can create some new ability. I can operate only within the limits and possibilities of my given wants and abilities *and* of my environment. All free will, then, is freedom within limits of a person's inborn capabilities and of the world in which he lives.

However, whereas I cannot add to the ultimate potentialities of my wants and abilities—to my I.Q., for example—is it, then, the environment which comes in to determine what form my adjustment, given my capacities, will take? Not completely, for the environment cannot force me to do my best. Between the "floor" and the "ceiling" of my nature I can choose. Thus it is up to me, whatever environment I am in, to decide whether I will think my hardest and go on thinking even though fatigue is setting in. It is up to me whether I will persevere in certain activities beyond the point at which they would normally "carry themselves," especially when difficulty or pain are involved.

If, however, I develop habits of work and other attitudes which do not take full advantage of what is really available to me, if my personality is more limited than my endowment allows, I may not be able to realize my full endowment later when I might wish to. In other words, the choices I made along the way have determined my present mode of adjustment, and this in turn may restrict the range of freedom I *now* have.

Here we are brought to a point at which a distinction must be carefully drawn between *free will* (or *will-agency* as we shall now call it) and *will-power*. Our conception of human freedom will be clearer if this distinction—it is a distinction and not a separation—is kept in mind.

To what in experience does *will-power* refer? It is one thing to will to think, to do one's best to realize one alternative. But it is another thing to succeed in the face of the obstacles, internal and external, one confronts. The power of will (*will-power*) refers to the actual efficacy, as opposed to the effort being expended by the person, of the willing to realize a chosen objective. *How much power* willing has is frequently a matter of great uncertainty, for we never can be sure what obstacles willing may confront. *Free will is not acquired.* The power of that will to realize the approved goal depends not completely on the activity of willing but on factors within the personality and the environment impinging upon the person at the time of choice.

Thus, *power* or *strength of will* refers not to the possibility of free will (will-agency) to begin with, but to the ability of will-agency to overcome opposition or actually to bring the approved to fruition. To repeat, the basic capacities of the individual, the strength of the opposition, be it conscious or unconscious personality-segments already formed, or those external conditions surrounding a given choice—all of these may be more influential than the agent realizes. It should, therefore, be clear that the question of whether there is free will (will-agency) is a different one from the question of how much power (in terms of effect) the will actually has in given situations. Only one with complete knowledge of all the ingredients in a situation of choice could predict with high *probability* whether the person, *if* he chose to will one alternative, would be victorious (that is, would have enough will-power).

It is at this point that psychological analyses could contribute to our understanding, since the light thrown on the formation of personality is light thrown on the nature of the organization which will-agency has to face as the person chooses to effect changes in his life. A person with an ingrained trait of honesty, gradually built into his personality through the years, may try (will) to be dishonest, but he may actually fail (have no will-power in this respect). When the author urged a graduate student to borrow available funds in order that he could complete his graduate work, the student replied that much as his mind approved of finishing his work, he simply could not bring himself to get into debt; the training his mother had given him was telling more than he or she had ever realized that it would. *Will-power, then, is one of the by-products of the organization of the personality; but will-agency itself is a property of the person who builds and changes his personality within the ultimate limits of his given nature and the opportunities or obstacles afforded by his acquired habits, attitudes, and traits.*

To press the point of our distinction: if a psychologist knew the ultimate potentialities of a given person, and if he knew the present structure of habits, sentiments, traits (and other ingredients) of his personality, he might be able to predict failure or success in objective terms because he knows the relative hold of these upon the person. He might well have predicted, for example, that this graduate student would not borrow the money. But from such facts would the conclusion be warranted that the student has no will-agency? No. All we can say is that the student has inadequate will-power at present to alter the course of events in a certain area of his life. The fact that a person does not seem to alter his *behavior* is far from proof that he has no free will. The psychologist did not witness the battle going on in the individual as he fought his strong sentiment about indebtedness. The student was willing to break his sentiment, and his willing delayed the failure.

There has been some fear that a recognition of free will would actually demoralize human beings. For, it has been argued, if one can alter his behavior at will, then what point is there in struggling to form good habits. The child who has been brought up to be honest or to hate indebtedness can at any time change that habit. Thus neither he nor his parents can expect stability in his character.

This objection would be serious against any view which asserted freedom of will without limits, but it certainly does not hold against views, such as the one here presented, which hold that the effect of habit and of personality structure will constantly influence the amount of will-power one actually can exert.

When a person wills, he wills as a person with definite capacities, innate and acquired. He wills to think this, to continue wanting that—he wills, in other words, to realize what another part of his total nature makes possible.

(margin annotation: grad. student)

What his willing accomplishes is not the simple result of "an act of will" but of the total situation he confronts at the moment of willing. Thus the honest person will not find it easy to do something dishonest, and the habitually dishonest person will hardly become honest overnight because he has free will. Stability of character is not undermined by the existence of a will which operates within the total possibilities his nature and development allow.

But deny free will altogether and take the denial seriously. Then the very possibility of moral or immoral life vanishes; moral development becomes a meaningless process. To a person intent on realizing ideals, the fact that the effort can be made, the fact that the evil action is at least delayed, the fact that a person goes down in defeat against his best willing—all these are considerations which determine whether he can have any self-respect. If a person were convinced that he simply could not alter his behavior, what *good reason* would there be for trying or for urging *trying*? Indeed, if his trying is simply the outcome of circumstances, if it is "in the cards" to try, he will; if not, he will not, and that's the end of it. For any action will be the by-product of what was going on in him at a given moment in the light of the past and of the environmental forces venting themselves through him.

Are not those who say that "one can still praise or blame a man for what he really *had* to do" using words without meaning? Praise and blame are meaningless unless there is both will-agency and obstacle to will-agency in human life. We do not praise a man for being a male, but we do praise him for being one kind of man when he could have been another. We do not praise him simply so that he will be influenced to be better. We praise him because we think that he has already chosen a path which was not forced upon him, and because we believe that he will be able to make our praise help him in the future. We as part of his environment influence him, but we do so because he is willing to let praise help him.

Similarly, to consider actions morally right or wrong is meaningless, unless the possibility of choice is real.... When we say: "John did right to tell the truth," we presuppose that he meant to tell the truth when falsehood was open to him. Otherwise we might as well say that John did right to breathe, to digest, to blink his eyes—all actions appropriate for survival but not right in the sense intended when we say he did right to tell the truth. Right and wrong as moral terms are nonsense syllables if we apply them to actions which involve no choice. For if any action is the only action really possible to the person, the problem of right *or* wrong does not apply. If we do not say it is right for the match to burn the paper (since we know that given the proper conditions no other effect is ever produced), why say that a given act is right (or wrong) if we know no other could have resulted?

But an even more far-reaching consequence issues from the denial of free will. If there is no free will, then "true" and "false" become meaningless. If this is so, it makes no sense to say that determinism is true and free will is false. Let us see why this is so.

What do I mean when I say: "John's conclusion is truer than Mary's?"

[margin notes, handwritten:]
"no free will = no moral life"

H.Def.

no praise or blame w/out will-agency + obstacle to will agency

I mean that given the problem and the data, John had developed a better evaluation of the data than had Mary.

But the process of discovering truth is not a simple one. In solving the problem there were likes and dislikes, sympathies and antipathies in both Mary and John which might tempt them to favor solutions not adequately grounded in the data. This of course would hold all the more if their interests were vitally affected by the solution. Accordingly, in saying that John's solution is truer than Mary's, I am asserting that John was able, whatever the difficulties in the problem and whatever the prejudices affecting him, to develop a solution which was fair to the evidence. Assuming that Mary and John had the same ability and opportunities, I am asserting that Mary was not able to control her desires or to use her ability in such a way as to arrive at an unbiased interpretation of the problem.

But if I believe in determinism, I must say that given John's nature and given Mary's nature there could be no other account of the data than the one each actually gave. If Mary denied John's conclusion (or if John denied Mary's), both condemnations would be the result of past and present determination. All we could say is: This is what John concluded, and this is what Mary concluded. They could do nothing else!

If then someone should ask me: "Why do you think your observation about John and Mary is any truer than Mary's conclusion?" the situation becomes quite serious. For if all my actions are determined, then my judgment too is as determined as Mary's and John's; it is the product of all the subjective forces and the data making their impact on my mind. I was compelled to come to my conclusion just as much as Mary and John were. There are three conclusions now, John's and Mary's, and mine about theirs. Is there any reason for supposing that one is truer than the other? If each of us could come to no other conclusion, if no one of us was free to control his own subjective attitudes toward the data and the possible solutions, why trust any statement.

The only one who can know what judgment is true is a person who can analyze and think freely about the data, a person who is able to resist any conclusion which is not based on the evidence before him. The person who cannot will to think and keep thinking about the evidence and different interpretations of it will *have* conclusions; but his conclusions are not necessarily *from* the evidence.

If what we have said is true, the person who holds that scientific investigation presupposes that all events are determined is in an embarrassing position. For if there is no freedom of will, there is no meaning to scientific truth. Hold that the mind, in its reasoning about events, is just as determined as the events are, and there is no basis for holding that the scientist's conclusion is truer than that of the layman. Indeed, no one is left to know which conclusion is less partial than the other, for everyone's conclusion proceeds not from relatively free or detached observation of the facts but from the nexus of events in his brain. But why is one flurry of electrical events truer than another, unless we can have some basis for believing that subjective desires and prejudices, for example, can be *will*-fully resisted in accordance with an ideal of proper investigation?

To summarize our conception of free will: man is free to will within uncertain limits. His will-agency is not arbitrary in the sense that it can operate without regard for his own nature, his past development, and his present opportunities. Will-agency represents the capacity of man to build his own world within the possible worlds provided by his environment and his capacities. But in willing man wills what is possible to his own nature, and in doing so he finds himself effective to different extents. Thus man is more than a responsive creature; he is a responsible creature. His plastic needs and abilities provide the raw materials from which he must build his own character and personality. He cannot be blamed for the raw materials, but he can be blamed for the kind of structure he wills to create out of them.

STUDY QUESTIONS

1. What does Bertocci mean by "free will"? What exactly do his examples from experience show? Do they show, for example, that both alternatives are really possible for the agent?
2. What does Bertocci mean by a "fiat" of the will? Is such a thing compatible with determinism?
3. Can you give some everyday examples which would illustrate the difference between will-agency and will-power? Are there some features of the personality which restrict will-power and which will-agency could choose to eliminate? If so, provide an example.
4. Some people have argued that the claim that God is the first cause of things does not provide an adequate explanation for the universe because God would need an explanation for God's choices. What do you think Bertocci would say?
5. "No one says: It is useless to offer wages for work that you wish done, because people may prefer starvation. If free-will were common, all social organization would be impossible, since there would be no way of influencing their actions" (Bertrand Russell, *Human Society in Ethics and Politics*). How do you think Bertocci would reply to Russell?
6. "It is my contention that all beliefs are caused by the application of rewards and punishment. We find believing that the earth is round rewarding—teachers pat us on the head when we believe it—and so it becomes part of our intellectual system. Years of study and experiment by psychologists have proved this beyond a doubt." What would Bertocci say about this claim? Can it be "true"?

Can a Robot Have Free Will?

J. J. C. Smart   SOFT DET.

J. J. C. Smart (1920-   ) is one of the most famous contemporary defenders
of the view that mental processes are nothing more than physical events in
the brain. Consequently, the human decision-making process is a sequence of
physical events which is as determined as any other material process. In this
essay, Smart argues that determinism is not inconsistent with the common
notion of free will.

Smart argues that while there may be some degree of indeterminacy in the
behavior of atomic particles, this does not affect the free-will issue. A
machine can act "rationally" even though its choices are caused. Sometimes
there is equal evidence on either side of an issue, and in such cases, a
"random" or "uncaused" selection procedure can be rational. But most of the
time, a condition of rationality is that the choice is caused by the weight of
evidence.

Those who insist that free will is uncaused seem to believe that if this were
not so, then many common practices, such as punishment, would no longer
make sense. But Smart denies this implication of determinism. To hold
someone responsible, for example, is justified on the ground that punishment
and blame will serve as *causes* for altering future behavior. The question is not
whether we are all "programmed," but whether our programs can be altered
by our being held responsible.

Does pure chance imply free will, and does the absence of pure chance imply
the absence of free will? That is, are free will and determinism incompatible?
I wish to argue that the question of pure chance or determinism is irrelevant
to the question of free will, though, so far from free will and determinism
being incompatible with one another, a close approximation to determinism
on the macro-level is required for free will.

Consider two decision-making computers A and B. Suppose that they
are designed to select candidates for a staff training course for some organization. (I do not wish to argue here that selection of candidates should at
present be automated in this way: my illustration is here meant purely to illustrate a metaphysical point.) Into the inputs of the computers all available
information is fed by means of punched cards. The information consists of
detailed records of examination results, gradings of mental character (e.g.,
"honest," "moderately honest," etc., "bad tempered," "easy tempered," etc.)
and in short all possible information which might be of interest to a human
selector. The machines have been programmed in such a way that we would
be happy with the candidates selected (e.g., none of them are too stupid, too
dishonest, too bad tempered).

Suppose that there are 20 vacancies and that the computer selects 19 candidates first. For the 20th (and last) place there are two equally good candidates. This last candidate is then selected from the two possibilities by means of a <u>randomizing device</u>. Suppose that Smith and Jones are the two candidates between which, on the available criteria, the machine so far cannot choose. The randomizing device is such that it gives a probability of ½ of choosing each candidate. In the case of machine A the randomizer consists of a roulette wheel on which there is an electrical contact. If the wheel stops with "red" opposite a fixed contact it causes the machine to choose Smith, whereas if "black" is opposite the fixed contact Jones is chosen. In the case of machine B the randomizer consists of a <u>Geiger counter</u> near a small quantity of a radioactive substance such that there is a probability of ½ of the Geiger counter being actuated in the nth second after the start of operation of the machine, where n is an odd number, and there is a probability of ½ of it being actuated in the mth second where m is an even number. If the Geiger counter is actuated in an even numbered second the machine chooses Jones. Let us suppose that in fact, in the case of each machine, Smith happens to be the candidate chosen.

The machine A as described above can be regarded as a deterministic machine, since its behavior can be described with a close enough approximation by means of classical physics. We may say that the choice by machine A of Smith as against Jones was a deterministic one, since with sufficient knowledge of the inputs to the machine and of the initial state and working of the machine the choice of Smith as against Jones could have been predicted. On the other hand the machine B is an indeterministic machine, since the choice of Smith depended on an <u>indeterministic quantum mechanical effect</u>.

Was the choice of Smith as made by machine A any more or less "rational" than the same choice as made by machine B? Surely not. Was the choice of Smith by B "more rational" than the choice of the first nineteen candidates, whose qualifications were such that no use of the randomizer was necessary in their case? <u>We may say that the indeterministic machine B is neither more nor less "free" than is the deterministic machine A. For this reason I hold that the principle of quantum mechanical indeterminacy has nothing whatever to do with the problem of free will.</u> Whether our brains are (near enough) deterministic machines or whether they contain "pure chance" randomizers, they are neither more nor less possessed of free will.

Some philosophers would object to my implicit assumption above that choice is a matter of a largely causal computation process. They ~~would say that~~ →indet. in free choice we act from reasons, not from causes, and they <u>would say that</u> <u>acting from reasons is neither caused nor a matter of pure chance</u>. I find this unintelligible. The machine which chose the twentieth man by a quantum mechanical randomizer did not do so on account of a cause, but did so by pure chance. It had no reason to choose the one candidate rather than another. On the other hand the machine in choosing the first nineteen candidates did behave in a deterministic way and could be said to have been caused to make the choices it did. It was programmed in such a way that its causes corresponded to reasons; for example it was programmed in such a way that it chose the most intelligent, sensible, etc., candidates, and so it was programmed to act in accordance with what we would call "good reasons." It acted from reasons precisely because it was caused.

It may be objected, however, that here is the trouble. It was *programmed* to do so, whereas we act freely. In reply to this we may make two rejoinders. In the first place are we not ourselves "programmed"? That is, on account of our genetic endowment, together with certain environmental influences both when we were embryos and ever since, our brains have been caused to have a certain structure. They therefore compute in certain ways. People with certain brain structures will make certain choices, and people with other brain structures will make other choices. The second rejoinder is as follows. If the view that we are largely deterministic machines is taken to imply that we do not have free will, we may concede indeed that we also do not have free will in the sense which the objector has in mind. It is not clear, however, what this sense is: the free choice is supposed to be not deterministic and not a matter of pure chance in the way in which a quantum jump is supposed to be pure chance. It is supposed to be pure chance in the sense of "not being determined" but the suggestion is that it is also not merely random and is "acting from reason." The previous paragraph suggests, however, that acting from reasons is not merely random precisely because it is also acting from causes.

It is possible that the plain man's concept of free will has inconsistent elements in it. He may demand of free will that it be both random and yet not random. If so, we should feel no compunction about denying the existence of free will in the plain man's sense. This does not mean, however, that we do not have at our disposal the means to make most of the contrasts which the plain man makes by asserting or denying free will. A determinist can still make the distinction between the condition of a man who goes for a walk because he wants to do so (being determined by his desire, which we may take to be a state of neural interconnections in his brain) and a man in a prison cell who does not go for a walk, even though he dearly desires to do so. (The latter man would be caused by the state of his brain to go for a walk but he is prevented from doing so by the bolts and bars of his cell.) Being caused by your internal state of desire in the former way is, *ceteris paribus*, pleasant, and being prevented by external constraints is, *ceteris paribus*, unpleasant. Similarly we do not deny that there is an important difference between doing a thing X, because we want to do it and have no conflicting desires, and the case where we do X because of some threat. A man who gives money to charity because he wishes to help that good cause acts in a way which is relatively pleasant. A man who hands over money in a police court because he has to pay a fine also in a sense does what he wants to do, but he wants to hand over the money only in the sense that he dislikes the alternative of going to prison even more.

Once more the determinist can make the relevant distinction, and whether or not he does so by means of the words "free" and "unfree" is not very important.

What about the contrast between a psychopathic offender (say a kleptomaniac) and an ordinary criminal (say a burglar)? In both cases their desires cause the behavior. The plain man and the criminal law both tend to contrast the case of the kleptomaniac and the ordinary burglar by denying that the kleptomaniac was fully free. We can make the required contrast (which is all that the criminal law should need) by saying that the kleptomaniac is not easily caused by threats of punishment to act otherwise, whereas the ordinary burglar is amenable to threats. On account of this we can give a rational justification for treating kleptomaniacs differently from burglars, and we can do so without involving the questionable concept of free will. Once more we conclude that if the plain man's concept of free will is a denial both of determinism and of randomness, then its apparent inconsistency does not matter all that much, since we can nevertheless make most of the distinctions which the plain man wishes to make without its aid.

Now let us consider a piece of science fiction. Instead of having our brains "programmed" by our genes and environment let us suppose that they could be programmed (or reprogrammed) by means of a machine. Suppose that it were possible to change a person's whole character by applying a number of electrodes to his head, so that in some (at present technologically inconceivable) way the interconnections between his neurons (and possibly also whatever constitutes his memory store) are radically altered. Perhaps we could apply such a machine to a humanitarian poet and turn him into a diabolical technologist who is an able inventor of lethal weapons. It might be said that such a "reprogrammed" man, however little he was thwarting contrary desires, would not be free, and would merit neither praise nor blame for his activities. In reply to this we could contend that he would merit praise or blame exactly as much or as little as would an ordinary person (i.e., a person who had not had his brain changed in this way). If it were useful (for deterrent reasons) to punish the ordinary person, so would it be useful (for deterrent reasons) to punish the reprogrammed person. (I neglect here the possibility that in the fictional case better results might be achieved by punishing not the programmed but the programmer.) The only good reasons for punishment or reward, praise or blame, seem to me to be their social effects. A philosopher who thinks that it is not right to blame or punish an ordinary person, is surely forgetting that the ordinary person is also programmed by his heredity and environment. Such a philosopher may have the extraordinary idea, when thinking of a vicious murderer, that if *he* had had the murderer's bad brain and bad environment he would nevertheless have acted differently. I think that such a view is unintelligible.

My conclusion therefore is that even though the brain should be a deterministic mechanism, we are still able to make the important contrasts which we normally signalize by calling behavior either "free" or "unfree." It is a matter of somewhat arbitrary choice whether or not we say that the ordinary man's concept of free will is contrary to determinism, and that the view of the mind as a deterministic (or largely deterministic) machine implies that we have not got free will. A lot depends on what plain man we catch, and on whether or not we catch him in a metaphysical frame of mind. If we do say that the plain man's concept of free will is incompatible with determinism, then even so we can also say that our denial of free will does not have the startling consequences which it would have had if it had implied also the denial of the important contrasts which have been discussed above. Alternatively we can use "free" and "unfree" in order to make the above mentioned contrasts, in which case determinism is perfectly compatible with free will.

What has science to say about the question whether the brain is a deterministic machine? A good many philosophers have held that the indeterministic nature of quantum mechanics leaves a loophole for free will. Our discussion of free will should have shown what is wrong with this. It is abstractly possible that the brain might contain indeterministic trigger mechanisms, like the Geiger counter of machine B above. Nevertheless this would mean only that the brain contained an indeterministic randomizer: if it contained instead a deterministic randomizer like that of machine A how would this affect the question of its freedom? We must not entirely discount the possibility of very small events, possibly below the level of quantum mechanical uncertainty, which occur in the synaptic knobs of single neurons, being amplified by neuronal mechanisms so as to produce behavioral effects. No less a neurophysiologist than Sir John Eccles has indeed proposed such a mechanism. Eccles thinks that in this way events in an immaterial mind can have effects on the brain. Many scientists would perhaps think that the idea of an immaterial mind produces more difficulties than it solves. For one thing the postulation of an immaterial mind seems to raise difficulties for the genetical theory of evolution by natural selection. It is not difficult to see in a general way how mutations in genes lead, *via* the biochemistry of embryology, to slightly differently convoluted brains, and hence ultimately to the sort of potentialities for behavior which leads us to say that an organism has a mind. But it is hard to see how the production of an immaterial mind could come to be reconciled with the chemical approach to genetics. Eccles regards the existence of the immaterial mind as vouched for by introspection, but we shall here avoid discussing this issue, which raises large and controversial questions in the philosophy of mind. Let us remark, however, that the postulation of an immaterial mind does not help to illuminate the problem of free will. For once more we can ask whether events in the immaterial mind are caused, or whether they are random, or supposing that they are neither caused nor random, we can ask what this third possibility consists in.

STUDY QUESTIONS

1. Smart compares two decision-making computers. Some of the time, both computers use a randomizing device to make their selections. Why does it not make any difference whether such a device is deterministic or indeterministic? If the indeterministic device made *all* choices of the candidates, would such a procedure be rational?

2. Smart claims that the computers acted from "good reasons" precisely because they were caused. What would Bertocci say about that? Would Bertocci agree that indeterminism means random choice?

3. Smart maintains that even if the ordinary notion of free will is inconsistent, determinism is compatible with the sorts of contrasts which the ordinary notion is used to make. What are these contrasts? How do you think Smart would finish the following:
   a. Smith freely gave his money to charity because...
   b. Smith did not freely hand over his money to the man in the mask because...
   c. Smith remained in jail of his own free will because... What does Smart mean by "free" and "unfree"?

4. "Praise and blame, rewards and punishments, and the whole apparatus of the criminal law, are rational on the deterministic hypothesis, but not on the hypothesis of free will, for they are all mechanisms designed to cause volitions that are in harmony with the interests of the community..." (Bertrand Russell, *Human Society in Ethics and Politics*). Would Smart agree with this? Do you?

5. Does Smart believe that if someone could prove the existence of the "soul," the problem of free will would be solved? Do you?

8

Moral Responsibility
in a Determined World

PROBLEM INTRODUCTION

Consider the behavior of the solitary wasp *Sphex*. When the time for egg-laying approaches, this little wasp carefully digs a burrow to serve as the hatchery for her young. Then she searches for a cricket. She stings the cricket in just the right place so as to paralyze it, and carries it to her burrow. Leaving the cricket just outside her carefully prepared nest, she goes inside for a last-minute check to clear out any unwanted debris which may have gotten in. Then she drags the cricket inside the hatchery and lays her eggs beside it. When the eggs hatch, the young wasps will feed on the living host that their mother has so graciously placed in suspended animation. Her task complete, the wasp leaves the burrow, covers it up, and flies away—the future of her children secured.

Complex behavior of this sort in insects, fish, and lower mammals has intrigued scientists for centuries. On the surface, it bears all the marks of intelligent, purposeful, and free action. Yet, in spite of appearances, the elaborate behavior pattern of the wasp is simply a sequence of automatic stages. If, for example, the cricket host is removed a few inches from the edge of the burrow while the wasp is inside making her last-minute check, she will drag it to the edge of the burrow again and go through the same routine. Again and again, this poor harried mother can be made to repeat her housecleaning chores by moving the cricket a few inches from the lip of the nest. This shows that the wasp has no executive control over the entire operation. Each stage of this complex sequence of behavior is "triggered" by an earlier stage in the chain. If part of the chain is interfered with, the insect reacts in response to the last completed part of the chain, even if this means doing the same thing over and over again indefinitely. The wasp is a helpless victim of her own internal wiring.

In one of the readings that follow, John Hospers argues that people cannot alter their drives, wants, and emotions, and therefore cannot be held responsible for actions which such features of the personality produce. No doubt if wasps were conscious, they would have the feeling of freedom. Each time the mother wasp dragged the cricket back to the entrance of the burrow, she would say to herself, "Should I check the burrow again?" and each time, with the inevitability of clockwork, she would answer, "Yes." Given the circumstances, and the programming of the wasp, it cannot *choose* otherwise. The appearance of alternatives, the possibility of an option, is an illusion. Hospers believes that, like the wasp, we too must think and choose as our "wiring" programs us to think and choose, and this means that freedom disappears.

The case of the wasp raises some interesting questions about the major positions on free will. In the previous section, we identified three main theories about free will. Hard-determinism assumes that free will and moral responsibility are incompatible with a universe in which all events are caused. Since the hard-determinist believes that the world is deterministic, free will is held to be impossible. The libertarian, on the other hand, believes that experience reveals the reality of free will, and so denies that determinism is true. Between these two opposing views there is a compromise position called *soft-determinism*, which is an attempt to make freedom compatible with determinism. Surely this would be the ideal theory, if it could be justified, for then the ethical and the scientific pictures of humanity would not be in conflict.

The soft-determinist tries to reconcile freedom and determinism by claiming that moral responsibility does not depend upon being free from all causes but merely upon being free from certain *kinds* of causes. Any action of ours which is principally caused by factors outside our own personalities is one for which we cannot be held responsible. The soft-determinist says that if an action issues from our own wants and desires, it is free. A free agent can do otherwise, is free to do otherwise, if there is nothing which would prevent the exercise of an alternative choice. This is called the *hypothetical interpretation of freedom*, since it says that a free agent can do otherwise *if* some other choice is made.

Both hard-determinists and libertarians believe that this analysis is superficial. The real issue, they argue, is not whether someone can act differently if a different choice is made. The real issue is whether someone can *choose* differently. Freedom of action must be distinguished from freedom of the will. The wasp which repeats the cleaning operation over and over enjoys freedom of action. There is nothing preventing her from dragging the cricket into the burrow *if she chooses to do so*. But of course she cannot choose to do so! It is this fact which prompts us to declare that the wasp is not free.

C. A. Campbell is a libertarian who believes that since the hypothetical freedom of soft-determinism still leaves choices under the reign of necessity, the central problem of free will remains. A person could have *chosen* differently, according to the soft-determinist, only if some aspect of his or her personality were altered. But Campbell insists that what we want to know is whether the same person, with the same desires and beliefs, could have chosen differently in the same circumstances. This is impossible in a deterministic universe. Campbell recognizes that soft-determinism has rightly rejected the indeterminism of William James. If choice is ruled by chance, if anything is possible, then choice does not reflect the self and so the self cannot be held responsible. Although he admits that choices are caused by the self, he insists that the self is something distinct from the formed character. The self has the ability to stand against the flow of environmental pressures, even to stand against its own habits and desires, and to choose in a new direction—a direction which cannot be explained or predicted by the forces which have molded character. It is possible, therefore, for the autonomous self to creatively choose duty over its own strongest desire. This form of libertarianism is not strictly indeterminism, since choices are caused by the self; but the self is something which stands outside of the usual flow of events, and its action cannot be causally explained.

The soft-determinist cannot ignore these criticisms. Moral freedom must be more than freedom from external forces. We can be victimized by our own natures, as well as by the external environment, and any theory which ignores this—any theory that says that the wasp is free—is surely false. Soft-determinism, therefore, must be able to distinguish between causes which deprive us of free will and those which create free will, whether those causes be internal or external. To the libertarian and the hard-determinist, such a distinction is unintelligible. All forms of necessity destroy human freedom, they argue, because necessity means that one cannot make another choice. How can the soft-determinist meet this objection? Can the choices of a free agent come about by necessity?

The answer to this paradox, according to the soft-determinist, depends on how the word "necessity" is understood. In a deterministic universe, to say that a choice is necessitated is simply to say that given the prior conditions, that choice, and no other, must occur. The word "necessitated," however, suggests that choices are fated and uncontrollable. It suggests that certain decisions will be made no matter what we try to do to alter them, and our most fervent efforts to change ourselves are useless. Now surely this is true some of the time. There are some features of our personality which no one can change, just as there are physical events which cannot be altered by human design. But many features of the personality are caused by human effort—if not by one's own effort, then by the effort of others. Our parents, for example, cause us to react and behave in certain ways through the training they provide. If someone else's effort can shape my personality, then surely mine can too.

"Aha!" says the hard-determinist, "certainly you can change your own personality to some extent *if you desire to do so*. But your desire to change is itself caused by factors which you cannot control." This is surely correct. Does this mean, however, that self-control is lost? The soft-determinist says, "No." In fact, determinism is required for self-control.

Remember that free will is something valuable. Even the hard-determinist regrets that it doesn't exist, much like the atheist regards the prospect of heaven. Free will is valuable because it is required for self-control, and this, in turn, is valuable because it allows us to alter ourselves and our reactions so as to avoid frustrations, pain, and unhappiness. The absence of self-control means that there is no flexibility, no possibility of alternative responses, in a world of change. It is to be locked into a system of mechanical habits which remain rigid and unyielding in the face of a shifting environment. What does it take to be the master of myself? When I have an appreciation of my most fundamental needs, those which are essential to my self-identity and happiness, I will try to satisfy them in the most efficient way. Of course, whether I am successful depends upon how accurately I can predict the consequences of my actions. This, in turn, depends upon my knowledge of the world in which I shall act. To know the conditions for happiness, to know the world enough to see the avenues for achieving it, and to have the motivation to set oneself on those avenues—*this is self-control.* In other words, self-control is having our choices caused by the most rational appraisal of ourselves and our environment.

There is a temptation to suppose that this is not enough. The libertarian, for example, would insist that even if the system of causes produces the best choices, it is still true that no other choices are possible. Unless a person could have chosen otherwise, he or she is not free.

In order to formulate the soft-determinist response to this, let us return to the case of the harassed wasp. The wasp does not exhibit self-control because it cannot alter its behavior to achieve its goal. When we say that the wasp "cannot do otherwise" we mean that it is incapable of responding flexibly, in light of its own needs, to changing situations. Someone who is in control is open to new information and new circumstances in a way that allows for alternative choices *if the information warrants it.* An intelligent and rational agent will alter certain habits and dispositions, *if these are no longer effective in achieving basic goals.* The capacity to do otherwise is valuable only when doing otherwise is the rational thing to do. Therefore, someone who is caused to behave by a system of rationality possesses the ability to choose otherwise in the only meaningful sense of that expression. This is a hypothetical sense, it is true, because it makes choice depend on the introduction of new causal factors (new information), but any other sense would deprive the person of self-control. The wasp is a victim, not because its behavior is necessitated, but because the necessitating causes are automatic and inflexible.

Man neither Free nor Responsible

John Hospers   HARD DET.

At one time, insanity was treated as a crime, and the mentally deranged were punished in particularly vicious ways. The very fact that we now talk about mental "illness" and classify some psychological disorders as "diseases" indicates that many forms of behavior which were once thought to deserve punishment have been shown to be the result of factors beyond the agent's control. With the development of modern psychiatry and psychology, more and more is being discovered about the causes of fairly typical behavior patterns. John Hospers (1918–   ), professor of philosophy at the University of Southern California, believes that as this trend continues we shall find that ultimately no one is responsible.

Hospers is particularly interested in the consequences of psychotherapy on the doctrine of free will. The psychoanalyst does not blame someone for being unable to cope with the world and does not praise someone for possessing the capacity to handle life's problems. Everyone's reaction to the world is the result of forces which shaped their psychological dispositions for better or for worse. In order to be held morally responsible, a person should have been able to do otherwise. But Hospers claims that the ability to do otherwise hinges on the ability to have different desires than those which caused the action. This is impossible, he claims, and so the usual conception of responsibility is wrong.

I*

... There are many actions—not those of an insane person (however the term "insane" be defined), nor of a person ignorant of the effects of his action, nor ignorant of some relevant fact about the situation, nor in any obvious way mentally deranged—for which human beings in general and the courts in particular are inclined to hold the doer responsible, and for which, I would say, he should not be held responsible. The deed may be planned, it may be carried out in cold calculation, it may spring from the agent's character and be continuous with the rest of his behavior, and it may be perfectly true that he could have done differently *if* he had wanted to; nonetheless his behavior was brought about by unconscious conflicts developed in infancy, over which he had no control and of which (without training in psychiatry) he does not even have knowledge. He may even *think* he knows why he acted as he did, he may *think* he has conscious control over his actions, he may even *think* he is fully responsible for them; but he is not. Psychiatric casebooks provide hundreds of examples. The law and common sense, though puzzled sometimes by such cases, are gradually becoming aware that they exist; but at this early stage

From *Determinism and Freedom in the Age of Modern Science,* by Sidney Hook (ed.), © 1958 by New York University. Reprinted by permission of Sidney Hook.
Editors' note: The division of this reading is the editors'.

countless tragic blunders still occur because neither the law nor the public in general is aware of the genesis of criminal actions. The mother blames her daughter for choosing the wrong men as candidates for husbands; but though the daughter thinks she is choosing freely and spends a considerable amount of time "deciding" among them, the identification with her sick father, resulting from Oedipal fantasies in early childhood, prevents her from caring for any but sick men, twenty or thirty years older than herself. Blaming her is beside the point; she cannot help it, and she cannot change it. Countless criminal acts are thought out in great detail; yet the participants are (without their own knowledge) acting out fantasies, fears, and defenses from early childhood, over whose coming and going they have no conscious control.

Let us suppose it were established that a man commits murder only if, sometime during the previous week, he has eaten a certain combination of foods—say, tuna fish salad at a meal also including peas, mushroom soup, and blueberry pie. What if we were to track down the factors common to all murders committed in this country during the last twenty years and found this factor present in all of them, and only in them? The example is of course empirically absurd; but may it not be that there is *some* combination of factors that regularly leads to homicide. . . . When such specific factors are discovered, won't they make it clear that it is foolish and pointless, as well as immoral, to hold human beings responsible for crimes? Or, if one prefers biological to psychological factors, suppose a neurologist is called in to testify at a murder trial and produces X-ray pictures of the brain of the criminal; anyone can see, he argues, that the *cella turcica* was already calcified at the age of nineteen; it should be a flexible bone, growing, enabling the gland to grow.[1] All the defendant's disorders might have resulted from this early calcification. Now, this particular explanation may be empirically false; but who can say that no such factors, far more complex, to be sure, exist?

When we know such things as these, we no longer feel so much tempted to say that the criminal is responsible for his crime; and we tend also (do we not?) to excuse him—not legally (we still confine him to prison) but morally; we no longer call him a monster or hold him personally responsible for what he did. Moreover, we do this in general, not merely in the case of crime: "You must excuse Grandmother for being irritable, she's really quite ill and is suffering some pain all the time." Or: "The dog always bites children after she's had a litter of pups; you can't blame her for it; she's not feeling well, and besides she naturally wants to defend them." Or: "She's nervous and jumpy, but do excuse her; she has a severe glandular disturbance."

Let us note that the more *thoroughly* and *in detail* we know the causal factors leading a person to behave as he does, the more we tend to exempt him from responsibility. When we know nothing of the man except what we see him do, we say he is an ungrateful cad who expects much of other people and does nothing in return, and we are usually indignant. When we learn that his parents were the same way and, having no guilt feelings about this mode of

[1] Meyer Levin, *Compulsion* (New York: Simon and Schuster, 1956), p. 403.

behavior themselves, brought him up to be greedy and avaricious, we see that we could hardly expect him to have developed moral feelings in this direction. When we learn, in addition, that he is not aware of being ungrateful or selfish, but unconsciously represses the memory of events unfavorable to himself, we feel that the situation is unfortunate but "not really his fault." When we know that this behavior of his, which makes others angry, occurs more constantly when he feels tense or insecure, and that he now feels tense and insecure, and that relief from pressure will diminish it, then we tend to "feel sorry for the poor guy" and say he's more to be pitied than censured. We no longer want to say that he is personally responsible; we might rather blame nature or his parents for having given him an unfortunate constitution or temperament.

> In recent years a new form of punishment has been imposed on middle aged and elderly parents. Their children, now in their twenties, thirties or even forties, present them with a modern grievance. "My analysis proves that *you* are responsible for my neurosis." Overawed by these authoritative statements, the poor tired parents fall easy victims to the newest variations on the scapegoat theory.
>
> In my opinion, this senseless cruelty—which disinters educational sins which had been buried for decades, and uses them as the basis for accusations which the victims cannot answer—is unjustified. Yes, "the truth loves to be centrally located" (Melville), and few parents—since they are human—have been perfect. But granting their mistakes, they acted as *their* neurotic difficulties forced them to act. To turn the tables and declare the children not guilty because of the *impersonal* nature of their own neuroses, while at the same time the parents are *personally* blamed, is worse than illogical; it is profoundly unjust.[2]

And so, it would now appear, neither of the parties is responsible: "they acted as their neurotic difficulties forced them to act." The patients are not responsible for their neurotic manifestations, but then neither are the parents responsible for theirs; and so, of course, for their parents in turn, and theirs before them. It is the twentieth-century version of the family curse, the curse on the House of Atreus.

"But," a critic complains, "it's immoral to exonerate people indiscriminately in this way. I might have thought it fit to excuse somebody because he was born on the other side of the tracks, if I didn't know so many bank presidents who were also born on the other side of the tracks." Now, I submit that the most immoral thing in this situation is the critic's caricature of the conditions of the excuse. Nobody is excused merely because he was born on the other side of the tracks. But if he was born on the other side of the tracks *and* was a highly narcissistic infant to begin with *and* was repudiated or neglected by his parents *and*...(here we list a finite number of conditions), and if this complex of factors is *regularly* followed by certain behavior traits in adulthood, and moreover *unavoidably* so—that is, they occur no matter what he or anyone

---

[2] Edmund Bergler, *The Superego* (New York: Grune and Stratton, 1952), p. 320.

else tries to do—then we excuse him morally and say he is not responsible for his deed. If he is not responsible for A, a series of events occurring in his babyhood, then neither is he responsible for B, a series of things he does in adulthood, provided that B inevitably—that is, unavoidably—follows upon the occurrence of A. And according to psychiatrists and psychoanalysts, this often happens.

But one may still object that so far we have talked only about neurotic behavior. Isn't nonneurotic or normal or not unconsciously motivated (or whatever you want to call it) behavior still within the area of responsibility? There are reasons for answering "No" even here; for the normal person no more than the neurotic one has caused his own character, which makes him what he is. Granted that neurotics are not responsible for their behavior (that part of it which we call neurotic) because it stems from undigested infantile conflicts that they had no part in bringing about, and that are external to them just as surely as if their behavior had been forced on them by a malevolent deity (which is indeed one theory on the subject); but the so-called normal person is equally the product of causes in which his volition took no part. And if, unlike the neurotic's, his behavior is changeable by rational consideration, and if he has the willpower to overcome the effects of an unfortunate early environment, this again is no credit to him; he is just lucky. If energy is available to him in a form in which it can be mobilized for constructive purposes, this is no credit to him, for this too is part of his psychic legacy. Those of us who can discipline ourselves and develop habits of concentration of purpose tend to blame those who cannot, and call them lazy and weak-willed; but what we fail to see is that they literally *cannot* do what we expect; if their psyches were structured like ours, they could, but as they are burdened with a tyrannical superego (to use psychoanalytic jargon for the moment), and a weak defenseless ego whose energies are constantly consumed in fighting endless charges of the superego, they simply cannot do it, and it is irrational to expect it of them. We cannot with justification blame them for their inability, any more than we can congratulate ourselves for our ability. This lesson is hard to learn, for we constantly and naïvely assume that other people are constructed as we ourselves are.

But, one persists, it isn't a matter simply of luck; it is a matter of effort. Very well then, it's a matter of effort; without exerting the effort you may not overcome the deficiency. But whether or not you are the kind of person who has it in him to exert the effort is a matter of luck.

All this is well known to psychoanalysts. They can predict, from minimal cues that most of us don't notice, whether a person is going to turn out to be lucky or not. "The analyst," they say, "must be able to use the residue of the patient's unconscious guilt so as to remove the symptom or character trait that creates the guilt. The guilt must not only be present, but *available* for use, *mobilizable*. If it is used up (absorbed) in criminal activity, or in an excessive amount of self-damaging tendencies, then it cannot be used for therapeutic purposes, and the prognosis is negative." Not all philosophers will relish the analyst's way of putting the matter, but at least as a physician he can soon detect whether the patient is lucky or unlucky—and he knows that whichever it is, it *isn't the patient's fault*. The patient's conscious volition cannot remedy the deficiency. Even whether he will cooperate with the analyst is really out of the patient's hands: if he continually projects the denying-mother fantasy on the analyst and unconsciously identifies him always with the cruel, harsh forbidder of the nursery, thus frustrating any attempt at impersonal observation, the sessions are useless; yet if it happens that way, he can't help that either. That fatal projection is not under his control; whether it occurs or not depends on how his unconscious identifications have developed since his infancy. He can try, yes—but the ability to try enough for the therapy to have effect is also beyond his control; the capacity to try more than just so much is either there or it isn't—and either way "it's in the lap of the gods."

The position, then, is this: if we *can* overcome the effects of early environment, the ability to do so is itself a product of the early environment. We did not give ourselves this ability; and if we lack it we cannot be blamed for not having it. Sometimes, to be sure, moral exhortation brings out an ability that is there but not being used, and in this lies its *occasional* utility; but very often its use is pointless, because the ability is not there. The only thing that can overcome a desire, as Spinoza said, is a stronger contrary desire; and many times there simply is no wherewithal for producing a stronger contrary desire. Those of us who do have the wherewithal are lucky.

There is one possible practical advantage in remembering this. It may prevent us (unless we are compulsive blamers) from indulging in righteous indignation and committing the sin of spiritual pride, thanking God that we are not as this publican here. And it will protect from our useless moralizings those who are least equipped by nature for enduring them.

As with responsibility, so with deserts. Someone commits a crime and is punished by the state; "he deserved it," we say self-righteously—as if we were moral and he immoral, when in fact we are lucky and he is unlucky—forgetting that there, but for the grace of God and a fortunate early environment, go we. Or, as Clarence Darrow said in his speech for the defense in the Loeb-Leopold case:

> I do not believe that people are in jail because they deserve to be. . . . I know what causes the emotional life. . . . I know it is practically left out of some. Without it they cannot act with the rest. They cannot feel the moral shocks which safeguard others. Is [this man] to blame that his machine is imperfect? Who is to blame? I do not know. I have never in my life been interested so much in fixing blame as I have in relieving people from blame. I am not wise enough to fix it.[3]

II

I want to make it quite clear that I have not been arguing for determinism. Though I find it difficult to give any sense to the term "indeterminism," be-

---

[3] Levin, op. cit., pp. 439–469.

cause I do not know what it would be like to come across an uncaused event, let us grant indeterminists everything they want, at least in words—influences that suggest but do not constrain, a measure of acausality in an otherwise rigidly causal order, and so on—whatever these phrases may mean. With all this granted, exactly the same situation faces the indeterminist and the determinist; all we have been saying would still hold true. "Are our powers innate or acquired?"

> Suppose the powers are declared innate; then the villain may sensibly ask whether he is responsible for what he was born with. A negative reply is inevitable. Are they then acquired? Then the ability to acquire them—was *that* innate? or acquired? it is innate? Very well then.... [4]

The same fact remains—that we did not cause our characters, that the influences that made us what we are are influences over which we had no control and of whose very existence we had no knowledge at the time. This fact remains for "determinism" and "indeterminism" alike. And it is this fact to which I would appeal, not the specific tenets of traditional forms of "determinism," which seem to me, when analyzed, empirically empty.

"But," it may be asked, "isn't it your view that nothing ultimately *could* be other than it is? And isn't this deterministic? And isn't it deterministic if you say that human beings could never act otherwise than they do, and that their desires and temperaments could not, when you consider their antecedent conditions, be other than they are?"

I reply that all these charges rest on confusions.

1 To say that nothing *could* be other than it is, is, taken literally, nonsense; and if taken as a way of saying something else, misleading and confusing. If you say, "I can't do it," this invites the question, "No? Not even if you want to?" "Can" and "could" are power words, used in the context of human action; when applied to nature they are merely anthropomorphic. "Could" has no application to nature—unless, of course, it is uttered in a theological context; one might say that God *could* have made things different. But with regard to inanimate nature "could" has no meaning. Or perhaps it is intended to mean that the order of nature is in some sense *necessary*. But in that case the sense of "necessary" must be specified. I know what "necessary" means when we are talking about propositions, but not when we are talking about the sequence of events in nature.

2 What of the charge that we could never have acted otherwise than we did? This, I submit, is simply not true. Here the exponents of Hume-Mill-Schlick-Ayer "soft determinism" are quite right. I could have gone to the opera today instead of coming here; that is, if certain conditions had been different, I should have gone. I could have done many other things instead of what I did, if some condition or other had been different, specifically if my desire had been dif-

[4] W. I. Matson, "The Irrelevance of Free Will to Moral Responsibility," *Mind*, LXV (October 1956), p. 495.

ferent. I repeat that "could" is a power word, and "I could have done this" means approximately "I *should* have done this *if* I had wanted to." In this sense, all of us could often have done otherwise than we did. I would not want to say that I should have done differently even if *all* the conditions leading up to my action had been the same (this is generally not what we mean by "could" anyway); but to assert that I could have is empty, for if I *did* act differently from the time before, we would automatically say that one or more of the conditions were different, whether we had independent evidence for this or not, thus rendering the assertion immune to empirical refutation. (Once again, the vacuousness of "determinism.")

3 Well, then, <u>could we ever have</u>, not acted, <u>but desired otherwise than we did desire</u>? This gets us once again to the heart of the matter we were discussing in the previous section. Russell said, "We can do as we please but we can't please as we please." But I am persuaded that even this statement conceals a fatal mistake. Let us follow the same analysis through. "I could have done X" means "<u>I should have done X if I had wanted to</u>." "I could have wanted X" by the same analysis would mean "I should have wanted X if I had wanted to"—which seems to make no sense at all. (What does Russell want? To please as he doesn't please?)

What does this show? It shows, I think, that the only meaningful context of "can" and "could have" is that of *action*. "Could have acted differently" makes sense; "could have desired <u>differently</u>," as we have just seen, does not. Because a word or phrase makes good sense in one context, let us not assume that it does so in another.

I conclude, then, with the following suggestion: <u>that we operate on two levels of moral discourse</u>, which we shouldn't confuse; one (let's call it the upper level) is that of <u>actions;</u> the other (the lower, or deeper, level) is that of the <u>springs of action.</u> Most moral talk occurs on the upper level. It is on this level that the Hume-Mill-Schlick-Ayer analysis of freedom fully applies. As we have just seen, "can" and "could" acquire their meaning on this level; so, I suspect, does "freedom." So does the distinction between compulsive and noncompulsive behavior, and among the senses of "responsibility," discussed in the first section of this paper, according to which we are responsible for some things and not for others. All these distinctions are perfectly valid on this level (or in this dimension) of moral discourse; and it is, after all, the usual one—we are practical beings interested in changing the course of human behavior, so it is natural enough that 99 per cent of our moral talk occurs here.

But when we descend to what I have called the lower level of moral discourse, as we occasionally do in thoughtful moments when there is no immediate need for action, <u>then we must admit</u> that we are ultimately the kind of persons we are because of conditions occurring outside us, over which we had no control. But while this is true, we should beware of extending the moral terminology we used on the other level to this one also. "Could" and "can," as we have seen, no longer have meaning here. "Right" and "wrong," which apply only to actions, have no meaning here either. I suspect that the same is true of "responsibility," for now that we have recalled often forgotten facts about our being the product of outside forces, we must ask in all seriousness what would be added by saying that we are not *responsible* for our own characters and temperaments. What would it mean even? Has it a significant opposite? What would it be like to be responsible for one's own character? What possible situation is describable by this phrase? Instead of saying that it is *false* that we are responsible for our own characters, I should prefer to say that the utterance is meaningless—meaningless in the sense that it describes no possible situation, though it *seems* to because the word "responsible" is the same one we used on the upper level, where it marks a real distinction. If this is so, the result is that *moral* terms—at least the terms "could have" and "responsible"—simply drop out on the lower level. What remains, shorn now of moral terminology, is the point we tried to bring out in Part [I]: whether or not we have personality disturbances, whether or not we have the ability to overcome deficiencies of early environment, is like the answer to the question whether or not we shall be struck down by a dread disease: "it's all a matter of luck." It is important to keep this in mind, for people almost always forget it, with consequences in human intolerance and unnecessary suffering that are incalculable.

STUDY QUESTIONS

1. Hospers says that the more thoroughly we know the causes of someone's behavior, the more we tend to exempt that person from responsibility. Why is this? Do you think this is true for all kinds of causes—neurotic and nonneurotic?
2. "Darrow argued that Leopold and Loeb should be excused because they had been conditioned to do whatever they did by their background of wealth and luxury. But there are plenty of wealthy children who do not grow up to be criminals." How would Hospers respond to this criticism?
3. "Perhaps what Hospers says is true about neurotic people, but it is certainly not true about normal people. Most people are rational; they can alter their behavior in the face of discomforting situations. So it makes sense to hold most people responsible for what they do." What would Hospers say to this? Do you agree with him?
4. Does Hospers believe that a person "could have done something other than what he or she did"?
5. What would Hospers reply to someone who claimed that one could have desired differently? Do you agree with him on this point?
6. Hospers says that there are two levels of moral discourse. What are these two levels? Do you think he would maintain that it is possible to be responsible for what you do, even though you are not responsible for what you are?

The Self and Free Will

C. A. Campbell

C. A. Campbell (1897–1974) was an outstanding exponent of libertarianism. At the core of his theory is the belief that the "self" is more than the elaborate system of habits and dispositions which we call a person's "character." The self is something which "has" a character, but is not identical with it. The self has the power to resist the inclinations of its character, to rise above all caused dispositions, and to act "creatively."

Campbell does not believe that the usual varieties of soft-determinism provide any genuine answer to the problem of free will. A condition for moral responsibility is that the agent "could have done otherwise." Soft-determinists interpret this to mean that the agent "could have done otherwise, *if* he or she had chosen otherwise." But Campbell insists that this is not enough. The real question, he believes, is whether the agent could have "chosen otherwise," in spite of the urgings of character. This ability to choose "creatively" is known to exist by everyone's experience of it.

Campbell denies that free will is inconsistent with prediction or that it leads to capricious choice. On rare occasions, the individual is required to choose between moral duty and the impulses of character. Only then is the situation indeterminate.

I

...It is something of a truism that in philosophic enquiry the exact formulation of a problem often takes one a long way on the road to its solution. In the case of the Free Will problem I think there is a rather special need of careful formulation. For there are many sorts of human freedom; and it can easily happen that one wastes a great deal of labour in proving or disproving a freedom which has almost nothing to do with the freedom which is at issue in the traditional problem of Free Will. The abortiveness of so much of the argument for and against Free Will in contemporary philosophical literature seems to me due in the main to insufficient pains being taken over the preliminary definition of the problem....

Fortunately we can at least make a beginning with a certain amount of confidence. It is not seriously disputable that the kind of freedom in question is the freedom which is commonly recognized to be in some sense a precondition of moral responsibility. Clearly, it is on account of this integral connection with moral responsibility that such exceptional importance has always been felt to attach to the Free Will problem. But in what precise sense is free will a precondition of moral responsibility, and thus a postulate of the moral life in general? This is an exceedingly troublesome question; but until we have

From C. A. Campbell, *On Selfhood and Godhood,* George Allen & Unwin Ltd., 1957. Reprinted by permission of Unwin Hyman, Ltd.

satisfied ourselves about the answer to it, we are not in a position to state, let alone decide, the question whether ''Free Will'' in its traditional, ethical, significance is a reality....

The first point to note is that the freedom at issue (as indeed the very name ''Free *Will* Problem'' indicates) pertains primarily not to overt acts but to inner acts. The nature of things has decreed that, save in the case of one's self it is only overt acts which one can directly observe. But a very little reflection serves to show that in our moral judgments upon others their overt acts are regarded as significant only in so far as they are the expression of inner acts. We do not consider the acts of a robot to be morally responsible acts; nor do we consider the acts of a man to be so save in so far as they are distinguishable from those of a robot by reflecting an inner life of choice. Similarly, from the other side, if we are satisfied (as we may on occasion be, at least in the case of ourselves) that a person has definitely elected to follow a course which he believes to be wrong, but has been prevented by external circumstances from translating his inner choice into an overt act, we still regard him as morally blameworthy. Moral freedom, then, pertains to *inner* acts.

The next point seems at first sight equally obvious and uncontroversial; but, as we shall see, it has awkward implications if we are in real earnest with it (as almost nobody is). It is the simple point that the act must be one of which the person judged can be regarded as the *sole* author. It seems plain enough that if there are any *other* determinants of the act, external to the self, to that extent the act is not an act which the *self* determines, and to that extent not an act for which the self can be held morally responsible. The self is only part-author of the act, and his moral responsibility can logically extend only to those elements within the act (assuming for the moment that these can be isolated) of which he is the *sole* author....

Thirdly, we come to a point over which much recent controversy has raged. We may approach it by raising the following question. Granted an act of which the agent is sole author, does this ''sole authorship'' suffice to make the act a morally free act? We may be inclined to think that it does, until we contemplate the possibility that an act of which the agent is sole author might conceivably occur as a necessary expression of the agent's nature; the way in which, e.g. some philosophers have supposed the Divine act of creation to occur. This consideration excites a legitimate doubt; for it is far from easy to see how a person can be regarded as a proper subject for moral praise or blame in respect of an act which he *cannot help* performing—even if it be his own ''nature'' which necessitates it. Must we not recognize it as a condition of the morally free act that the agent ''could have acted otherwise'' than he in fact did? It is true, indeed, that we sometimes praise or blame a man for an act about which we are prepared to say, in the light of our knowledge of his established character, that he ''could no other.'' But I think that a little reflection shows that in such cases we are not praising or blaming the man strictly for what he does *now* (or at any rate we ought not to be), but rather for those past acts of his which have generated the firm habit of mind from which his *present* act follows "necessarily." In other words, our praise and blame, so far as justified, are really retrospective, being directed not to the agent *qua* performing *this* act, but to the agent *qua* performing those past acts which have built up his present character, and in respect to which we presume that he *could* have acted otherwise, that there really *were* open possibilities before him. These cases, therefore, seem to me to constitute no valid exception to what I must take to be the rule, viz. that a man can be morally praised or blamed for an act only if he could have acted otherwise.

Now philosophers today are fairly well agreed that it is a postulate of the morally responsible act that the agent "could have acted otherwise" in *some* sense of that phrase. But sharp differences of opinion have arisen over the way in which the phrase ought to be interpreted. There is a strong disposition to water down its apparent meaning by insisting that it is not (as a postulate of moral responsibility) to be understood as a straightforward categorical proposition, but rather as a disguised hypothetical proposition. All that we really require to be assured of, in order to justify our holding X morally responsible for an act, is, we are told, that X could have acted otherwise *if* he had *chosen* otherwise or perhaps that X could have acted otherwise *if* he had had a different character, or *if* he had been placed in different circumstances.

I think it is easy to understand, and even, in a measure, to sympathise with, the motives which induce philosophers to offer these counter-interpretations. It is not just the fact that "X could have acted otherwise," as a bald categorical statement, is incompatible with the universal sway of causal law—though this is, to some philosophers, a serious stone of stumbling. The more wide-spread objection is that at least it looks as though it were incompatible with that causal continuity of an agent's character with his conduct which is implied when we believe (surely with justice) that we can often tell the sort of thing a man will do from our knowledge of the sort of man he is.

We shall have to make our accounts with that particular difficulty later. At this stage I wish merely to show that neither of the hypothetical propositions suggested—and I think the same could be shown for *any* hypothetical alternative—is an acceptable substitute for the categorical proposition "X could have acted otherwise" as the presupposition of moral responsibility.

Let us look first at the earlier suggestion—"X could have acted otherwise *if* he had chosen otherwise." Now clearly there are a great many acts with regard to which we are entirely satisfied that the agent is thus situated. We are often perfectly sure that—for this is all it amounts to—if X had chosen otherwise, the circumstances presented no external obstacle to the translation of that choice into action. For example, we often have no doubt at all that X, who in point of fact told a lie, could have told the truth *if* he had so chosen. But does our confidence on this score allay all legitimate doubts about whether X is really blameworthy? Does it entail that X is free in the sense required for moral responsibility? Surely not. The obvious question immediately arises: "But *could* X have *chosen* otherwise than he did?" It is doubt about the true answer to *that* question which leads most people to doubt the reality of moral responsibility.

Yet on this crucial question the hypothetical proposition which is offered as a sufficient statement of the condition justifying the ascription of moral responsibility gives us no information whatsoever.

Indeed this hypothetical substitute for the categorical "X could have acted otherwise" seems to me to lack all plausibility unless one contrives to forget why it is, after all, that we ever come to feel fundamental doubts about man's moral responsibility. Such doubts are born, surely, when one becomes aware of certain reputable world-views in religion or philosophy, or of certain reputable scientific beliefs, which in their several ways imply that man's actions are necessitated, and thus could not be otherwise than they in fact are. But clearly a doubt so based is not even touched by the recognition that a man could very often act otherwise *if* he so chose. That proposition is entirely compatible with the necessitarian theories which generate our doubt: indeed it is this very compatibility that has recommended it to some philosophers, who are reluctant to give up either moral responsibility or Determinism. The proposition which we *must* be able to affirm if moral praise or blame of X is to be justified is the categorical proposition that X could have acted otherwise because—not if—he could have chosen otherwise; or, since it is essentially the inner side of the act that matters, the proposition simply that X could have chosen otherwise.

For the second of the alternative formulae suggested we cannot spare more than a few moments. But its inability to meet the demands it is required to meet is almost transparent. "X could have acted otherwise," as a statement of a precondition of X's moral responsibility, really means (we are told) "X could have acted otherwise *if* he were differently constituted, or *if* he had been placed in different circumstances." It seems a sufficient reply to this to point out that the person whose moral responsibility is at issue is X; a specific individual, in a specific set of circumstances. It is totally irrelevant to X's moral responsibility that we should be able to say that some person differently constituted from X, or X in a different set of circumstances, could have done something different from what X did. . . .

II

That brings me to the second, and more constructive, part of this lecture. From now on I shall be considering whether it is reasonable to believe that man does in fact possess a free will of the kind specified in the first part of the lecture. If so, just how and where within the complex fabric of the volitional life are we to locate it?—for although free will must presumably belong (if anywhere) to the volitional side of human experience, it is pretty clear from the way in which we have been forced to define it that it does not pertain simply to volition as such; not even to all volitions that are commonly dignified with the name of "choices." It has been, I think, one of the more serious impediments to profitable discussion of the Free Will problem that Libertarians and Determinists alike have so often failed to appreciate the comparatively narrow area within which the free will that is necessary to "save" morality is required to operate. It goes without saying that this failure has been gravely prejudicial to the case for Libertarianism. I attach a good deal of importance, therefore, to the problem of locating free will correctly within the volitional orbit. Its solution forestalls and annuls, I believe, some of the more tiresome clichés of Determinist criticism.

We saw earlier that Common Sense's practice of "making allowances" in its moral judgments for the influence of heredity and environment indicates Common Sense's conviction, both that a just moral judgment must discount determinants of choice over which the agent has no control, and also (since it still accepts moral judgments as legitimate) that *something* of moral relevance survives which can be regarded as genuinely self-originated. We are now to try to discover what this "something" is. And I think we may still usefully take Common Sense as our guide. Suppose one asks the ordinary intelligent citizen *why* he deems it proper to make allowances for X, whose heredity and/or environment are unfortunate. He will tend to reply, I think, in some such terms as these: that X has more and stronger temptations to deviate from what is right than Y or Z, who are normally circumstanced, so that he must put forth a *stronger moral effort* if he is to achieve the same level of external conduct. The intended implication seems to be that X is just as morally praiseworthy as Y or Z *if* he exerts an equivalent moral effort, even though he may not thereby achieve an equal success in conforming his will to the "concrete" demands of duty. And this implies, again, Common Sense's belief that *in moral effort* we have something for which a man is responsible *without qualification,* something that is *not* affected by heredity and environment but depends *solely* upon the self itself.

Now in my opinion Common Sense has here, in principle, hit upon the one and only defensible answer. Here, and here alone, so far as I can see, in the act of deciding whether to put forth or withhold the moral effort required to resist temptation and rise to duty, is to be found an act which is free in the sense required for moral responsibility; an act of which the self is sole author, and of which it is true to say that "it could be" (or, after the event, "could have been") "otherwise." Such is the thesis which we shall now try to establish.

The species of argument appropriate to the establishment of a thesis of this sort should fall, I think, into two phases. First, there should be a consideration of the evidence of the moral agent's own inner experience. What *is* the act of moral decision, and what does it imply, from the standpoint of the actual participant? Since there is no way of knowing the act of moral decision— or for that matter any other form of activity—except by actual participation in it, the evidence of the subject, or agent, is on an issue of this kind of palmary importance. It can hardly, however, be taken as in itself conclusive. For even if that evidence should be overwhelmingly to the effect that moral decision does have the characteristics required by moral freedom, the question is bound to be raised—and in view of considerations from other quarters pointing in a contrary direction is *rightly* raised—Can we *trust* the evidence of inner experience? That brings us to what will be the second phase of the argument. We shall have to go on to show, if we are to make good our case, that the extraneous considerations so often supposed to be fatal to the belief in moral freedom are in fact innocuous to it. . . .

These arguments can, I think, be reduced in principle to no more than two: first, the argument from "predictability"; second, the argument from the alleged meaninglessness of an act supposed to be the self's act and yet not an expression of the self's character. Contemporary criticism of free will seems to me to consist almost exclusively of variations on these two themes. I shall deal with each in turn.

Let us remind ourselves briefly of the setting within which, on our view, free will functions. There is X, the course which we believe we ought to follow, and Y, the course towards which we feel our desire is strongest. The freedom which we ascribe to the agent is the freedom to put forth or refrain from putting forth the moral effort required to resist the pressure of desire and do what he thinks he ought to do.

But then there is surely an immense range of practical situations—covering by far the greater part of life—in which there is no question of a conflict within the self between what he most desires to do and what he thinks he ought to do. Indeed such conflict is a comparatively rare phenomenon for the majority of men. Yet over that whole vast range there is nothing whatever in our version of Libertarianism to prevent our agreeing that character determines conduct. In the absence, real or supposed, of any "moral" issue, what a man chooses will be simply that course which, after such reflection as seems called for, he deems most likely to bring him what he most strongly desires; and that is the same as to say the course to which his present character inclines him.

Over by far the greater area of human choices, then, our theory offers no more barrier to successful prediction on the basis of character than any other theory. For where there is no clash of strongest desire with duty, the free will we are defending has no business. There is just nothing for it to do.

But what about the situations—rare enough though they may be—in which there *is* this clash and in which free will does therefore operate? Does our theory entail that there at any rate, as the critic seems to suppose, "anything may happen"?

Not by any manner of means. In the first place, and by the very nature of the case, the range of the agent's possible choices is bounded by what he thinks he ought to do on the one hand, and what he most strongly desires on the other. The freedom claimed for him is a freedom of decision to make or withhold the effort required to do what he thinks he ought to do. There is no question of a freedom to act in some "wild" fashion, out of all relation to his characteristic beliefs and desires. This so-called "freedom of caprice," so often charged against the Libertarian, is, to put it bluntly, a sheer figment of the critic's imagination, with no *habitat* in serious Libertarian theory. Even in situations where free will does come into play it is perfectly possible, on a view like ours, given the appropriate knowledge of a man's character, to predict within certain limits how he will respond.

I claim, therefore, that the view of free will I have been putting forward is consistent with predictability of conduct on the basis of character over a very wide field indeed. And I make the further claim that that field will cover all the situations in life concerning which there is any empirical evidence that successful prediction is possible.

Let us pass on to consider the second main line of criticism. This is, I think, much the more illuminating of the two, if only because it compels the Libertarian to make explicit certain concepts which are indispensable to him, but which, being desperately hard to state clearly, are apt not to be stated at all. The critic's fundamental point might be stated somewhat as follows:

"Free will as you describe it is completely unintelligible. On your own showing no *reason* can be given, because there just *is* no reason, why a man decides to exert rather than to withhold moral effort, or *vice versa*. But such an act—or more properly, such an 'occurrence'—it is nonsense to speak of as an act of a *self*. If there is nothing in the self's character to which it is, even in principle, in any way traceable, the self has nothing to do with it. Your so-called 'freedom,' therefore, so far from supporting the self's moral responsibility, destroys it as surely as the crudest Determinism could do."

If we are to discuss this criticism usefully, it is important, I think, to begin by getting clear about two different senses of the word "intelligible."

If, in the first place, we mean by an "intelligible" act one whose occurrence is in principle capable of being inferred, since it follows necessarily from something (though we may not know in fact from what), then it is certainly true that the Libertarian's free will is unintelligible. But that is only saying, is it not, that the Libertarian's "free" act is not an act which follows necessarily from something! This can hardly rank as a *criticism* of Libertarianism. It is just a description of it. That there can be nothing unintelligible in *this* sense is precisely what the Determinist has got to *prove*.

Yet it is surprising how often the critic of Libertarianism involves himself in this circular mode of argument. Repeatedly it is urged against the Libertarian, with a great air of triumph, that on this view he can't say *why* I now decide to rise to duty or now decide to follow my strongest desire in defiance of duty. Of course he can't. If he could he wouldn't *be* a Libertarian. To "account for" a "free" act is a contradiction in terms. A free will is *ex hypothesi* the sort of thing of which the request for an *explanation* is absurd. The assumption that an explanation must be in principle possible for the act of moral decision deserves to rank as a classic example of the ancient fallacy of "begging the question."

But the critic usually has in mind another sense of the word "unintelligible." He is apt to take it for granted that an act which is unintelligible in the *above* sense (as the morally free act of the Libertarian undoubtedly is) is unintelligible in the *further* sense that we can attach no meaning to it. And this is an altogether more serious matter. If it could really be shown that the Libertarian's "free will" were unintelligible in this sense of being meaningless, that, for myself at any rate, would be the end of the affair. Libertarianism would have been conclusively refuted.

But it seems to me manifest that this can *not* be shown. The critic has allowed himself, I submit, to become the victim of a widely accepted but fundamentally vicious assumption. He has assumed that whatever is meaningful must exhibit its meaningfulness to those who view it from the standpoint of external observation. Now if one chooses thus to limit one's self to the rôle of external observer, it is, I think, perfectly true that one can attach no meaning to an act which is the act of something we call a "self" and yet follows from nothing in that self's character. But then *why should we* so limit ourselves, when what is under consideration is a subjective activity? For the apprehension of subjective acts there is *another* standpoint available, that of *inner experience,* of the practical consciousness in its actual functioning. If our free will should turn out to be something to which we can attach a meaning from *this* standpoint, no more is required. And no more ought to be expected. For I must repeat that only from the inner standpoint of living experience *could* anything of the nature of "activity" be directly grasped. Observation from without is in the nature of the case impotent to apprehend the active *qua* active. We can from without observe sequences of states. If into these we read activity (as we sometimes do), this can only be on the basis of what we discern in ourselves from the inner standpoint. It follows that if anyone insists upon taking his criterion of the meaningful simply from the standpoint of external observation, he is really deciding in advance of the evidence that the notion of activity, and *a fortiori* the notion of a free will, is "meaningless." He looks for the free act through a medium which is in the nature of the case incapable of revealing it, and then, because inevitably he doesn't find it, he declares that it doesn't exist!

But if, as we surely ought in this context, we adopt the inner standpoint, then (I am suggesting) things appear in a totally different light. From the inner standpoint, it seems to me plain, there is no difficulty whatever in attaching meaning to an act which is the self's act and which nevertheless does not follow from the self's character. So much I claim has been established by the phenomenological analysis, in this and the previous lecture, of the act of moral decision in face of moral temptation. It is thrown into particularly clear relief where the moral decision is to make the moral effort required to rise to duty. For the very function of moral effort, as it appears to the agent engaged in the act, is to enable the self to act against the line of least resistance, against the line to which his character as so far formed most strongly inclines him. But if the self is thus conscious here of *combating* his formed character, he surely cannot possibly suppose that the act, although his own act, *issues from* his formed character? I submit, therefore, that the self knows very well indeed—from the inner standpoint—what is meant by an act which is the *self's* act and which nevertheless does not follow from the self's *character.*

What this implies—and it seems to me to be an implication of cardinal importance for any theory of the self that aims at being more than superficial—is that the nature of the self is for itself something more than just its character as so far formed. The "nature" of the self and what we commonly call the "character" of the self are by no means the same thing, and it is utterly vital that they should not be confused. The "nature" of the self comprehends, but is not without remainder reducible to, its "character"; it must, if we are to be true to the testimony of our experience of it, be taken as including *also* the authentic creative power of fashioning and re-fashioning "character."

STUDY QUESTIONS

1. Campbell says that a condition of moral responsibility is that the agent be the sole author of the act in question. There is, however, a further condition for moral responsibility. What is it?
2. What is the hypothetical interpretation of the expression, "X could have done otherwise"? Why does Campbell believe that the various hypothetical interpretations are inadequate for moral responsibility?
3. Campbell admits that it is proper to make allowances for those individuals whose environment has been unfortunate. But he says this does not mean that such persons do not have a free will. Why is this? Do you agree?
4. In B. F. Skinner's novel *Walden II*, individuals are conditioned by behavioral engineering to become "perfect" citizens in a utopian community. At one point, the mastermind of the project, a psychologist by the name of Frazier, makes the following observation about free will: "I deny that freedom exists at all. I must deny it—or my program would be absurd. You cannot have a science about a subject matter which hops capriciously about." How would Campbell respond to this comment? Do you think his answer is sufficient?
5. Why does Campbell believe that the "inner standpoint" is the preferred standpoint in the matter of free will? What can be seen in inner experience which cannot be appreciated from an external position? Do you agree with this view?

Moral Freedom in a Determined World

Sidney Hook   SOFT DET.

Sidney Hook (1902–1989) was one of America's most outstanding political philosophers. At the time of his death he was professor emeritus at New York University and senior research fellow at the Hoover Institution on War, Revolution and Peace. He was the author of many books on social and political philosophy, including *Reason, Social Myths, and Democracy* (1940) and *The Paradoxes of Freedom* (1967). In the following essay, Hook does a masterful job of rallying the best criticisms of both indeterminism and hard-determinism.

Indeterminism, he argues, is unintelligible. To the extent that indeterminists wish to locate human freedom in the ability to reflect and reason, such ability is consistent with determinism. Hard-determinism, on the other hand, is an inconsistent doctrine that has morally undesirable consequences. It is a doctrine which leads to personal inertia and prevents the full exercise of human powers. Indeed, the belief that we are responsible, and that others will hold us responsible, serves as a cause for new effort and new direction in our actions. The justification for blame in a determined world is the fact that it is a cause for behavior which would not have occurred without it.

In the last year of the Weimar Republic, when ordinary criminals were some-times more philosophical than the judges of Hitler's Third Reich subsequently proved to be, a strange case was tried before the tribunal of Hanover. The evidence showed that one Waldemar Debbler had been guilty of burglary, and the prosecutor proposed two years of penal servitude. Whereupon the prisoner rose and said:

"Gentlemen, you see in me the victim of an unwavering destiny. So-called freedom of decision does not exist. Every human action in this world is determined. The causes are given by the circumstances and the results inevitable. By my inclinations of character, for which I am not responsible, since they were born in me, by my upbringing, my experiences, I was predetermined to become what I am. If you, gentlemen, had a heredity similar to mine and had been subjected to the same influence as I, you would also have committed the burglary in this particular situation. With this theory I am in good company. I refer you to Spinoza and Leibnitz. Even St. Augustine and, later, Calvin attributed all human actions to the immutable decree of destiny. As I have only done what I had to do, you have no moral right to punish me, and I therefore plead for my acquittal."

To which peroration the court answered:

"We have followed the prisoner's reasoning with attention. Whatever happens is the necessary and immutable sequel of preceding causes which, once given, could not be other than it is. Consequently the prisoner, by reason of his character and experience, was destined to commit the burglary. On the other hand, destiny also decrees that the court, as a result of the submitted testimony, must judge the prisoner guilty of burglary. The causes—the deed, the law, the nature of the judge—being given, the sentence of guilty and punishment follows as a natural consequence."

When asked whether he accepted the sentence, the prisoner declared: "Destiny demands that I appeal." To which the judge replied: "That may be. However, destiny will see to it that your appeal is rejected."

This story, for whose authenticity with respect to exact detail I will not vouch, confuses the concept of <u>determinism</u> with that of <u>fatalism</u>. It confuses an event whose occurrence depends upon, or is caused by, what the individual in this particular situation desires and does, with an event whose occurrence does not depend upon any event antecedent to it, and which would occur no matter what the antecedent event was. It confuses conditional necessity with unconditional necessity, what is *predetermined* with what is predictable with reference to certain laws and initial data. It further fails to distinguish clearly between the concept of punishment and the concept of moral responsibility. Nonetheless, in its appeal to a double standard of judgment it illustrates a defect which appears in the writings of more sophisticated philosophers who have returned to the theme of determinism and moral responsibility in recent years.

Those philosophers who have thought that progress in philosophy consists in part in showing that the traditional problems of philosophy are either pseudo-problems, or a confusing mixture of psychology, logic, and sociology, have been rudely awakened from their complacency by a revival of interest in the question of free will, determinism, and responsibility. It had been widely assumed that the whole problem of whether the *will* is free had been replaced, in consequence of the writings of Hobbes, Locke, Hume, Mill, and the modern naturalists and positivists, by the problem of the *conditions* under which men's actions are free. The general solution had been that *men* are free when their actions are determined by their own will, and not by the will of others, or by factors which lead us to say that their actions were involuntary. To the extent that conditions exist which prevent a man from acting as he wishes (*e.g.,* ignorance, physical incapacity, constraint used upon his body and mind) he is unfree. This view accepts the postulate of determinism as valid, regardless of whether a man's action is free or coerced—in one case his action is determined by his own volition, in the other not. The fact that my volition, say, to undergo an operation, is caused by a complex of factors, among which the existence of sickness or disease, is normally a necessary condition, does not make my action less free. <u>After all, it would be absurd to suggest that my action in undergoing an operation would be free only if there were no cause or reason to undergo it</u>. If one insisted on undergoing an operation when one knew there was no cause for the operation, one would normally be regarded as insane. That there would be a cause for the decision, for the insistence on the unnecessary operation, would not affect our judgment of it. On this view, the distinction between free and unfree acts, sane or insane acts, lies in the specific character of the causes at work, not in the presence or absence of causes.

What has been until recently considered a commonplace is now in several quarters described and repudiated as a wild paradox. That an action can be characterized as both "determined" and "free," or "determined" and "responsible," is denied from two different points of view. The first view accepts determinism, indeed insists on it, because of the findings of modern medicine and psychotherapy, and then argues the invalidity of judgments of responsibility in any and every case. The second accepts the validity of the principle of responsibility, but denies the validity of the postulate of determinism or of its universal applicability.

Those who believe that one cannot legitimately square the doctrine of determinism with the acceptance of responsibility argue generally as follows: an individual is neither responsible nor blamable for his actions unless he could have acted differently from the way he did. Given the sum total of conditions which preceded his action, the latter is in principle always predictable or determined, and therefore unavoidable. But if an action is unavoidable, then no one can be held morally responsible for it.

The usual retort to this is to point out that an act is determined, among other things, by a wish or desire or volition for which we shall use the generic term "choice." Consequently it is sometimes true to say that if an individual had chosen differently, he would have acted differently. To which the rejoinder comes that this is merely an evasion. If every event is in principle predictable and therefore determined, then the choice itself, given all the antecedent conditions, is unavoidable. An individual cannot be held morally responsible for his choice if it could not have been other than it was. And even if it were true that his choice now was a consequence of an earlier choice, which *if* it had been different *would* have led to [a] different present choice and action, that earlier choice *could not* have been different, given its antecedent conditions, and so on for any other choice in the series. And since the choice could not have been different, we cannot blame the person choosing since he is not morally responsible. He is "a victim of circumstances."

There is a certain ambiguity in the writings of those who, accepting the principle of determinism, criticize the attribution of moral responsibility to individuals or the judgment of blameworthiness on their actions. Sometimes their criticism has an air of high moral concern. They imply that under certain circumstances, which they often spell out in advance, individuals are being improperly considered responsible. They inveigh against the injustice of improperly blaming those who, because their desires and choices are determined, are the victims, not the agents of misfortune. This plea is sometimes forensically very effective, as the legal career of Clarence Darrow shows. Defending the accused in the Leopold-Loeb murder case, which is now enjoying a revival in popular concern, he said in his closing address to the jury, after quoting Housman's poem, the soliloquy of a boy about to be hanged, "I do not know what it was that made these boys do this mad act, but I know there is a reason for it. I know they did not beget themselves. I know that any one of an infinite number of causes reaching back to the beginning might be working out in these boys' minds, whom you are asked to hang in malice and in hatred and injustice, because someone in the past has sinned against them."

One does not, of course, look for precision in an *ex parte* plea. To a determinist, what difference does it make whether human beings are begotten by others, whether they reproduce by fission or by spontaneous generation in test tubes? In any case the process is determined. Of course we did not choose to be born. But suppose we did choose to be born: would that make us more responsible? The choice to be born would not be any less determined. And if the argument is that in a determined world, where our choices are bound to be what they are, it is unfair to blame anybody for any action to which that choice leads, how would we be better off, *i.e.*, more responsible, if we chose to be born? And if it is unjust to tax anyone with sinning who is not responsible for his being born, is it any more legitimate to speak of his being sinned against? If children cannot sin against parents, neither can parents sin against children.

Darrow's inconsistencies are less surprising than the fact that some sophisticated philosophers have adopted pretty much the same position. They fortify it with complex and subtle elaborations of the findings of psychoanalysis as these bear upon the motives and compulsive behavior of men. Yet the logic of their argument makes all the evidence of psychoanalysis irrelevant to the question of blame and responsibility. For if every psychoanalytical theory were discarded as false, the life of mind would still be determined if one accepts the postulate of universal determinism. The piling up of the data which exhibit the specific mechanism of determination adds only a rhetorical force to the position. Further, it is one thing to imply that the concept of moral responsibility is empty, that although in fact no individuals are morally responsible, there are conditions or circumstances under which they could be legitimately held responsible; it is quite another thing to hold that the concept of moral responsibility is completely *vacuous*, that no matter what the specific conditions are under which men choose to act, it would still be inappropriate to hold them morally responsible or blame them. And it is this view, *i.e.*, that moral responsibility is a vacuous or unintelligible expression, which seems to me to be entailed by those who urge Darrow's position, for they never seem able to indicate the rule or condition for its proper use. If one cannot indicate any possible situation on a deterministic view under which actions can be blamed, the term "blame" is cognitively meaningless.

Nonetheless, the paradox of the position is that those who hold it, blame us for blaming others. Just as the burglar in our story makes an appeal whose sense depends upon there being alternatives, that is upon the possibility of making or not making that specific appeal, so some philosophers find us blameworthy for not acting on the recognition that in a determined world in which no one chooses to be born, no one can be held at fault. . . .

The great difficulty with the indeterminist view in most forms is the suggestion it carries that choices and actions, if not determined, are capricious. Caprice and responsibility are more difficult to reconcile than determinism and responsibility, for it seems easier to repudiate a choice or action which does not follow from one's character, or history, or nature, or self, than an act which does follow. Consequently, the more thoughtful indeterminists are those who do not deny the operation of determining forces or tendencies altogether, but insist upon a certain kind of determination which manifests itself in addition to, or over and above, the factors extrinsic to the particular situation in which the choosing individual finds himself. For example, they believe that the free action is not the habitual action, not the coerced action, not the instinctive or impulsive action, but the action which is determined by reflection. And as we shall see, there is a sense in which ordinarily we do characterize an action as responsible, depending upon whether it was intended, and if intended, upon the character and extent of the reflection which preceded it. But so long as "reasons" are not disembodied entities but express reflective choices of men in nature, there is nothing here at which a determinist need boggle. On the contrary, he may define the locus of moral freedom and responsibility in the capacity of the human creature, using his insight and foresight to modify his preferences and control his inclinations whenever they conflict or lead to "actions involving others."

Not only indeterminists who recognize moral responsibility, but some determinists who regard it as an empty concept, write as if a person would be responsible if he could "ultimately and completely shape or choose his own character." Surely the notion of ultimately and completely shaping or choosing one's own character is more difficult to grasp than any it would illumine. Since every decision to shape or choose one's character, to be responsibly attributed to oneself, must be one's own, and therefore is already an indication of the kind of person one is, the notion that one can ultimately and completely shape or choose one's character seems to be unintelligible. C. A. Campbell distinguishes between a choice which is the expression of a formed character, and therefore determined, and a choice of a self. But aside from the difficulty of separating self from character, it is hard to understand why we should be more willing to accept responsibility or blame for the decision of a raw or pure self that has no history, than to accept responsibility or blame for the choices of our formed characters.

We return now to consider some of the difficulties which the determinist faces who attributes blame or responsibility to himself or others. If all actions are in principle predictable or unavoidable, how can he blame the actor? If every judgment of "ought" or "should" implies a "can" or "could," and if of every act we can say (once given its antecedent conditions) that it cannot or could not have been avoided, why blame, why praise, why, indeed, in a determined universe, pass any moral judgment whatsoever, whether it be on a petty sneak-thief or on a Hitler or Stalin?

I shall try to show that the difficulty lies uniquely in the use of the concept of blame, not of praise, and not of moral judgment *per se*. The difficulty in the concept of blame is that ordinary usage is itself confusing, that the confusion requires a reconstruction of our use in such a way as to bring out more consistently and systematically the pragmatic character of judgments of blame. I do not believe that if we guide ourselves by ordinary usage we can make ends meet, because in this instance ordinary usage is vague and inconsistent.

First of all, although it may be difficult to square the belief that all choices are determined with judgments of blame and responsibility, I do not see that there is any difficulty in squaring the belief that all choices are determined with the moral judgment that these choices, and the actions to which they lead, are good or bad. Pain is evil, and an intentional action which imposes unnecessary pain, or a desire to impose unnecessary pain, is wicked. After all, we blame persons only for those acts of omission or commission which we condemn. If such actions were not initially or antecedently judged good or bad, we could not blame anybody for failing to do the one, or failing to prevent the other. No matter whether an action is determined or undetermined, accidental or intentional, I can still pronounce it good or bad. We may not blame the child whose actions cause the house to burn, or the maniac who kills those who minister to his wants; but we can and do deplore and condemn these actions as bad. And I believe that this is legitimate from the standpoint of any analysis of the meaning of "good" or "bad" which philosophers have offered, except the Kantian analysis. So, too, although there are difficulties about feelings of "remorse" similar to those about judgments of blame, I can only feel remorse about something I regret, and the qualities of the action I regret are what they are, independently of whether the action is determined or not.

It is sometimes said that if it is unwarranted to pass judgments of blame on actions that are predictable or unavoidable, it is also unwarranted to pass judgments of praise. I am not so sure of this, because of the broader semantic range of judgments of praise. When we praise a person for his or her beauty, talent, intelligence, charm, personality, warmth, etc., etc., we do not have in mind at all whether or not the person could help being or doing that which evokes our praise. Formally, we can always praise a person for not committing an act that we would blame, and in this sense the logic of the judgments is symmetrical. But aside from such cases, and some others in which praise seems to be justified because an individual might have acted differently, e.g., in which he fights against odds instead of running away, there is an indefinitely large number of situations in which we unembarrassedly praise, regardless of whether the person can help being as he is or acting as he does. And when judgments of praise do not have this character, they may plausibly be regarded as having the social function of inducing individuals to do what we regard as desirable and to forego doing the undesirable. But if it is possible to carry out such an analysis without difficulty for judgments of praise, is it possible to do so for judgments of blame and attributions of moral responsibility?

The facts of responsibility must be distinguished from their justification. By facts of responsibility I mean that in every society there are social relations

or institutional arrangements which are regarded as binding on human behavior, for violations of which human beings are called to account. When individuals are called to account, this involves the possibility that sanctions may
be applied. These facts of responsibility are an anthropological datum—varied
and multiform. In some cultures children are held responsible for their parents; in others, parents for children. Leaving aside questions of legal responsibility, or rather legal liability, which are often only matters of social convenience and rules of the road, the justification of responsibility is a moral
question. Should a child be held personally responsible for the sins of its father, not only for the Biblical three generations, but even for one? Should a
parent ever be held responsible for the misdeeds of his children? Now those
who hold that determinism is incompatible with reasoned judgments of blame
presumably do not mean to deny the existence of the facts of responsibility.
They simply contest the justification of the facts—not the justification of any
specific fact of responsibility, but the possibility of any justification whatsoever in the determinist view. If this were true, then, since social life is impossible without recognition of some kind of responsibility in behavior, the
whole basis of social life would appear utterly unintelligible, or if justified,
only by some extrinsic consideration that had no moral relevance. But, as our
illustration shows, there are obviously good reasons why in general we regard
it as more justifiable to blame parents up to a point for the misdeeds of their
children than to blame children for the misdeeds of their parents. First, we
know there is some causal connection between the training or absence of training which parents give their children and the children's behavior outside the
home, a causal connection which is not reversible; second, and more important, we blame parents for their children rather than children for their parents,
primarily because in this way we can get more desirable conduct on the part
of both parents and children. We influence the future by our judgments of
blame and, to the extent that they are not merely judgments of spontaneous
admiration or excellence, by our judgments of praise as well.

There are some obvious difficulties with this interpretation of judgments
of blame. For example, as C. A. Campbell observes, we can influence the future behavior of infants and animals by punishment, but we certainly do not
blame them when we are reflective. On the other hand, we do not seem to be
able to influence the future behavior of the hardened criminal, but we certainly do blame him. Further, how explain remorse, as distinct from regret, for
actions committed long ago?

Because the behavior of children and animals is modifiable by appropriate reward and deprivation, we punish them, even though we may hesitate
to use the term to identify what we do. We do not "blame" them, however,
even when we find it necessary to punish, because blame is directed to volitions, or, if we do not believe in volitions, to intentions. If children's actions
reveal intentions or if we suspect, as we sometimes do, that animals have
intentions, we count upon the sting of our blame to prod them to different
behavior. Otherwise there is no point in blaming. But, it is objected, this only

tells us whether our blame is effective rather than deserved. The blame is "deserved" if the action we wish to correct is bad, and the worse the action the more deserved—provided the blame has point in the first place. When we distribute blame—as when we say "I blame you more than I do him"—it is because we believe that the intentions (or volitions) of the one had a greater role in the commission of the act, or could have a greater role in preventing similar actions in the future, than the intention of the other. We must be able to answer the question: what is the use of blaming any individual? before we can properly distribute blame among individuals. I can see no earthly use of blaming an individual save directly or indirectly to prevent the undesirable act from being repeated in the future. This is the justification for blame in a determined world.

Another element enters into the picture. The more rational an individual is, the more susceptible he is to understanding and giving reasons, the more blameworthy we hold him—not because the intelligent man's choice is less determined than that of the stupid man's but because the choice, which is determined among other things by insight into reasons, is generally more informed, more persistent, and more decisive in redetermining the stream of events. We blame children more as they approach the age of rationality, not because they come into possession of a soul, not because they become more subject to causal laws, but because the growth of intelligence enhances the subtlety, range, and effectiveness of their choice. And if animals could think or respond to reasons, we would blame them, too, because we could build up within them a sense of blame, shame, and responsibility. A sense of blame, shame, and responsibility has a sound therapeutic use in the moral education of men.

Why, then, do we blame the hardened criminal for his actions, when the continued life of crime makes blame and punishment almost as inefficacious in his case—so it is said—as in the case of an alcoholic, a dope addict, or a kleptomaniac? I believe here that most people in blaming a hardened offender are blaming him for the entire series of his actions and not only for his latest action; what revolts them is the cumulative series of evil things done; and they make the mistake of running these evils together, as if it were one great evil which one great blame or punishment might effectively forestall in the future, if not for the offender in question then for others. If, however, one were to isolate the latest dereliction of the hardened offender, and show that no blame or punishment one can devise is more likely to modify his conduct than blame or punishment can prevent an alcoholic addict from drinking or a kleptomaniac from stealing or a pyromaniac from arson, then I believe blame of the hardened criminal would be pointless. We would tend to regard him as criminally insane, confine him without blaming him.

It is sometimes said that we can legitimately blame only when the person blamed has failed to do his duty or live up to an obligation, and that wherever a person has a duty, wherever we say he "ought" to do something, then he in fact "could have" done so. As I have already indicated, I am not at all sure

they are capable of doing better, is it so absurd to hold them at least partly responsible for not doing better? Do we not know from our own experience that our belief that we are responsible, or that we will be held responsible, enables us to do things which had previously seemed beyond our power?

What often passes as irremediable evil in the world, or the inevitable ills and suffering to which the flesh is heir, is a consequence of our failure to act in time. We are responsible, whether we admit it or not, for what it is in our power to do; and most of the time we can't be sure what is in our power to do until we attempt it. If only we are free to try, we don't have to claim also to be free to try to try, or look for an ultimate footing in some prime metaphysical indeterminate to commit ourselves responsibly. Proximate freedom is enough. And although what we are now is determined by what we were, what we will be is still determined also by what we do now. Human effort can within limits redetermine the direction of events even though it cannot determine the conditions which make human effort possible. It is time enough to reconcile oneself to what is unalterable, or to disaster, after we have done our best to overcome them.

STUDY QUESTIONS

1. "You can't blame me for what I've done. I didn't choose to be born. I didn't choose my parents. I didn't choose my environment." Why does Hook think that such an argument is inconsistent?
2. What does Hook identify as the greatest difficulty in the indeterminist position? What does he mean by a "thoughtful indeterminist"? Would Campbell qualify?
3. What is the justification for blame in a determined world, according to Hook? Why do we treat some people as more blameworthy than others?
4. Suppose it were possible to correct the behavior of criminals by giving them a certain sort of pill, depending upon the crime. Murderers, for example, would be given antimurder pills, rapists would be given antirape pills, etc. Imagine, then, that every convicted criminal is made to take the appropriate pill. Would you want to punish them also? Would they still "deserve" to be punished? What would Hook say?
5. Hospers argues that the more that is known about the causes of someone's behavior, the more we tend to excuse that person from responsibility. To what extent would Hook agree?
6. Hook says that Darrow's kind of hard-determinism is mischievous. Why does he think so? Do you?

SELECTED READINGS FOR PART THREE

There are several good anthologies which give the student an appreciation of the problem of free will: Willard Enteman, *The Problem of Free Will* (New York:

Scribner, 1967); Sidney Morgenbesser and James Walsh, *Free Will* (Englewood Cliffs, N.J.: Prentice-Hall, 1962); D. F. Pears, *Freedom and the Will* (London: Macmillan, 1963); and Robert E. Dewey and James A. Gould, *Freedom: Its History, Nature, and Varieties* (New York: Macmillan, 1970), especially Part 3. Sidney Hook (ed.), *Determinism and Freedom in the Age of Modern Science* (New York: New York University Press, 1958), from which our selection by Hospers comes, provides good coverage of many modern philosophers.

Fatalism and predestination especially bothered Christian theologians, since responsibility for evil seemed to rest with God. St. Augustine's views can be found in his *City of God,* Book IX, chap. 21, and in Morgenbesser and Walsh cited above. Defenses of predestination by John Calvin and Jonathan Edwards have been reprinted in Enteman, cited above. St. Thomas's opinions can be found in *Summa Theologica,* Part I, question 14, article 3. An interesting contemporary defense of fatalism is given by Richard Taylor, *Metaphysics* (Englewood Cliffs, N.J.: Prentice-Hall, 1963), chap. 5.

Brand Blanshard gives a clear and forceful statement of hard-determinism in "The Case for Determinism" in the Hook anthology cited above. One of the classical presentations of hard-determinism is Baron D'Holbach in his *System of Nature,* originally published in 1770. Arthur Eddington, *New Pathways in Science* (New York: Cambridge, 1935), presents arguments against hard-determinism from the viewpoint of twentieth-century physics; in chapter XIII Eddington tries to rebut criticisms of his views.

The first complete statement of soft-determinism was given by the seventeenth-century materialist Thomas Hobbes. His position is reprinted in R. S. Peters (ed.), *Body, Mind, and Citizen* (New York: Collier Books, 1962). This theory became the accepted view for most of the British empiricists down to the present time. David Hume states the position forcefully in Section 8 of his *Enquiry Concerning Human Understanding.* The classic nineteenth-century presentation was John Stuart Mill, *An Examination of Sir William Hamilton's Philosophy* (London: Longmans, 1872), chap. 26. Bertrand Russell, *Philosophical Essays,* rev. ed. (London: G. Allen, 1966), and C. J. Ducasse, *Nature, Mind, and Death* (La Salle, Ill.: Open Court, 1951) have good, clear discussions of the position. In his *Religion and the Modern Mind* (Philadelphia: Lippincott, 1952), W. T. Stace gives a clear and provocative account of soft-determinism in a manner reminiscent of Hume. For a soft-determinist stance which stresses responsibility, see Moritz Schlick, *Problems of Ethics* (New York: Dover, 1939). In "A Plea for Excuses," *Proceedings of the Aristotelian Society,* 1956–57, John Austin, a soft-determinist, gives a perceptive, often humorous examination of the notion of responsibility from the "ordinary language" viewpoint that teases out aspects of philosophical problems not usually noticed in the classic literature.

There are many kinds of libertarianism. C. A. Campbell, who appears in our readings, criticizes Schlick's soft-determinism (see above) and clarifies his version of libertarianism in "Is 'Free Will' a Pseudo-Problem?" in *Mind,* vol. 60, 1951. Campbell's sort of theory has its historical counterpart in Thomas

Reid (1710–1796), *Essays on the Active Powers of Man*, in many editions. A similar position is advocated in H. D. Lewis, *Morals and Revelation* (London: G. Allen, 1951). A Jamesian position of objective chance is defended in Corliss Lamont, *Freedom of Choice Affirmed* (New York: Horizon Press, 1957), and an extreme theory of self-creation is urged by the popular existentialist Jean-Paul Sartre in *Being and Nothingness*, trans. H. E. Barnes (New York: Philosophical Library, 1956). Sartre moderates this view in his later social and political writings, especially *Search for a Method* (New York: Knopf, 1967) and *Critique of Dialectical Reason* (London: NLB, 1976).

Additional information on the issues discussed in Part Three can be found in the following important reference books: Paul Edwards (ed.), *The Encyclopedia of Philosophy* (New York: Macmillan and Free Press, 1967); Philip P. Wiener (ed.), *Dictionary of the History of Ideas* (New York: Scribner, 1974); and G. H. R. Parkinson (ed.), *The Handbook of Western Philosophy* (New York: Macmillan, 1988). The *Encyclopedia* is an eight-volume work; the index appears in volume 8. The *Dictionary* consists of four volumes plus an index. The *Handbook* is a single volume with a table of contents in the beginning and an index at the end.

PART FOUR

Morality

THE PARADOX OF MORAL EXPERIENCE

In Dostoyevsky's famous novel *The Brothers Karamazov,* one of the characters describes the following scene:

> One day a serf boy, a little child of eight, threw a stone in play and hurt the paw of the general's favorite hound. "Why is my favorite dog lame?" He is told that the boy threw a stone that hurt the dog's paw. "So you did it." The general looked the child up and down. "Take him." He was taken—taken from his mother and kept shut up all night. Early the next morning the general comes out on horseback, with the hounds, his dependents, dog-boys, and huntsmen, all mounted around him in full hunting parade. The servants are summoned for their edification, and in front of them all stands the mother of the child. The child is brought forward. It's a gloomy, cold, foggy autumn day, a perfect day for hunting....*"Make him run,"* commands the general. *"Run, run,"* shout the dog-boys. The boy runs....*"At him!"* yells the general, and he sets the whole pack of hounds after the child. The hounds catch him and tear him to pieces before the mother's eyes....

As this moral horror unfolds, powerful feelings and judgments intrude upon the reader. Rage, pity, and indignation emerge, along with the immediate and convincingly clear judgment that the suffering of the child is bad, that the punishment is unfair, and that the general is evil.

These are the facts of moral experience. The question for philosophy is how to understand them. Why do we feel these powerful urgings and sentiments? There are thousands of common events which do not call forth these feelings, so what is special about the death of the child? When we judge that the boy's suffering is bad, what exactly do we mean and what justifies our mental attitude? Is there something in the nature of things which demands a specific moral response, much as the nature of a triangle demands a certain intellectual judgment about it, or do we instead project our subjective feelings onto an objectively neutral circumstance?

323

Historically, theories have been developed on both sides. Moral subjectivism interprets our reactions as nonrational emotional responses which have been conditioned by training and which can be altered by training. On this view, there is no objective moral quality to the situation described by Dostoyevsky and there is nothing in human nature which *must* find it abhorrent. Perhaps in the future, in some new culture, audiences will watch such things for entertainment, and scholars will find our reactions somewhat curious and primitive. Thus for the moral subjectivist, our moral judgments are but expressions of taste, and taste is capricious and arbitrary. On the other hand, objectivists view our moral judgments in the same way as other judgments. Moral judgments are true or false, depending upon the objective nature of things. Although disagreeing in detail, objectivists all agree that moral evaluation can be a rational affair.

Both positions, of course, can be supported with reasons. As you begin the readings, you will be confronted with the paradoxes of our moral experience. The rest is discovery.

9

Sources of Morality: God, Society, and the Individual

PROBLEM INTRODUCTION

In 399 B.C. Socrates was executed by the Athenian court on trumped-up charges of atheism and corrupting youth. He probably could have escaped the death sentence if he had been willing to leave Athens or cease his philosophical activity, but, convinced that the unexamined life is not worth living, Socrates chose death over silence. In his speech to the court, he announced that his consuming passion was to examine the nature of virtue—what it is and how it is acquired. Socrates devoted his life to interrogating the citizens of Athens about morality, attempting to show them that, in spite of their firm convictions, they did not really know what virtue was. Since some of the things he was saying appeared to be an affront to religion, and were finding acceptance among the young, he was considered a threat to the established order.

Two moral theories found acceptance in the Athens of Socrates's day. The traditionalists maintained that the gods set forth a system of rules which all people were required to obey. For this group, moral and religious behavior were inseparable. This view was opposed by a new and unorthodox theory which took morality to be a set of rules used to further the interests of the strong. According to this theory, right and wrong, good and evil are not real qualities in the world but merely conventions designed to protect the prevailing mode of life. To the traditionalist, this new conception of morality threatened to undermine the foundations of civilized society. How could people be motivated to follow the dictates of duty, often against their own self-interest, if morality is considered a human convention, destined to be replaced with new social conditions? On the other hand, the proponents of the new morality saw themselves as a progressive force in society, liberated from the dogmas of religion and custom.

Plato found himself in the middle of this controversy. Like Socrates, his teacher, he disagreed with both sides. The simple picture of moral obligation presented by the traditionalists is complicated by two persistent facts: one,

325

human opinion about the will of the gods is extremely varied, and two, there is no certain method for choosing among conflicting opinion. In addition, the fact that the gods call some things good and other things evil tells us nothing about the nature of good and evil. The following important questions remain: Why do the gods command us to do certain things and not others? Is it mere caprice, or is there some reason behind the choice? Why should the gods be viewed as moral authorities? Does might make right? Unless satisfactory answers to these questions can be given, adherence to the will of the gods is blind obedience to dogmatic authority. Unlike the proponents of the new morality, Plato believed that some things are good by their very nature. That is, goodness is an objective quality in the world which does not alter with each new regime; nor does it depend on the changing character of human opinion. Plato first raised these questions and asserted the independence of morality from religion in his famous dialogue, the *Euthyphro*. In our readings Plato's point of view is expressed by a contemporary philosopher, Kai Nielsen, in an article which is sure to make many believers uneasy.

The conception of morality as a system of objective, universally binding rules has come under attack in our own era from the social sciences. Advocating a theory which is reminiscent of the "new morality" of Plato's time, many social scientists are convinced that moral values are nothing more than conventions which have evolved within the special environment of each distinct culture. Ruth Benedict, a noted cultural anthropologist who is representative of this group of scientists, observed that forms of behavior vary so extensively from culture to culture that no universally approved practices can be found. Because of this, she adopted the position called *ethical relativism*. Ethical relativists tend to view ethical systems as arbitrary conventions which have no logical basis in human nature or any other objective fact. Therefore, morality varies from culture to culture, and each culture's morality is correct for it, for there are no criteria for determining which, if any, is the superior system of rules. In some ways this sort of relativism strikes a progressive and reasonable note. Social scientists have long been aware of the disastrous effects of one culture rigidly imposing its system of morality on another. We recognize that, in many instances, to suppress different customs in the name of morality is an expression of an outworn puritanism or a presumptuous egotism. But ethical relativism, if pushed to its logical limits, penetrates deep into the moral values of all cultures and declares that they stand on the same nonrational level. Many serious thinkers reject relativism because of this implication. If whatever a culture approves of is right for that culture, then there is no point in trying to change any dominant practice. In fact, in a culture where slavery, for example, is the dominant social practice, it would be wrong to try to change things. When cultural approval becomes the sole criterion for right, moral progress does not seem possible. Indeed, the progressive and tolerant appearance of relativism begins to recede into moral complacency.

A second critique of relativism challenges one of its basic assumptions—that the values of various cultures are fundamentally different. It is true, for example, that some societies approve of infanticide while others do not. But this sort of difference concerning a specific practice may not indicate a difference in fundamental attitude. The same act may not have the same meaning in different cultural contexts because of divergent beliefs about the world. Thus, a culture which practices infanticide may view the infant in exactly the same way as we view the newly formed fetus, or perhaps even as we view a plant. Consequently, the act has a different psychological significance to people in that culture. James Rachels maintains that because ethical relativists do not consider the full context in which people moralize, they are inclined to interpret opposing practices as signs of opposing values. Rachels suggests that if we probe deeply enough into the beliefs which give meaning to various cultural practices, we may find a common network of values.

Whatever the overall merit of ethical relativism, one component is no longer a matter of serious dispute. There is a strong consensus in support of the claim of relativists that every member of a society is continually exposed to powerful conditioning forces which shape his or her values. In modern society, we are barraged with messages on television and radio, and in films, newspapers, magazines, and other media, aimed not merely to inform, or misinform, but to instill or preserve certain values, and to evoke certain responses. Among the students of social conditioning in modern society are feminist writers who are convinced that all the major forms of communication and entertainment today denigrate women and promote the domination of women by men. Jane Caputi marshalls evidence from a variety of sources to substantiate this thesis. Anyone serious about gender equality, she cautions, can no longer ignore the devastating impact of modern mass communication on our values. And anyone serious about determining whether values are subjective or objective, one might add, needs to understand the subtle and complex ways in which values are imbued and perpetuated in today's high-tech world.

It is not an exaggeration to call ours the *era of subjectivism*. Never before in the history of thought have so many intelligent and educated people rejected belief in a universal, objective system of values. Indeed, much of the recent resurgence of religious sentiment is grounded in the belief that moral chaos is the inevitable consequence of a godless universe. Many eminent thinkers simply believe that the logical problems confronting an objective ethics are insurmountable. However, before you form an opinion, you should study the next series of readings, in which several philosophers discuss the most notable formulations of an objective ethics.

The Connection between Morality and Religion

Kai Nielsen

Kai Nielsen (1926–   ) is a widely respected philosopher of religion who has published extensively, producing six books and more than 200 articles. He has taught at Hamilton College, Amherst College, Harpur College, New York University, Brooklyn College, the University of Ottawa, and the University of Calgary. Due to his deep opposition to American prosecution of the Vietnam war, he renounced his American citizenship, moved to Canada, and became a Canadian citizen.

The subject under discussion here is the relation of morality to religion. Many people not only believe in God, but believe that "x" is right or wrong because God says so. For instance, a Christian might say that stealing is wrong because it violates one of God's commandments. Nielsen takes issue with this point of view. It presumes, he says, that God is good, and therefore a being worthy of worship and an authoritative moral voice. To say that God is good, however, implies that one already knows what goodness is, for without this prior understanding one could not even grasp the meaning of the sentence, "God is good." Thus, "goodness" is independent of "Godness" and morality is independent of religion. To put it another way, stealing is wrong not because the Bible says so, according to Nielsen, but the Bible says so because stealing is wrong.

Nielsen does not merely play the role of critic. In his book *Ethics without God*, from which the following selection is taken, he attempts to outline an alternative to a religiously-grounded ethic. His secular alternative is based on "happiness," "self-consciousness," and a sense of "self-identity," all of which he claims are intrinsically good. Although Nielsen's positive proposals are not reprinted here, you should ask yourself whether a secular ethic will work. Can we expect most human beings to behave morally unless they believe that there is a God, that God wants them to do some things and avoid others, and that God will appropriately reward or punish them in the afterlife? In other words, does religion furnish the only effective incentive for people to be moral? If you answer this in the affirmative, your next challenge is to respond to the claim that the usefulness of a belief (God, afterlife, etc.) does not necessarily mean that it is true. For this, see Bertrand Russell's reply to James in Part Two. Perhaps by now you are beginning to appreciate how complex and interconnected philosophical problems are.

It is the claim of many influential Jewish and Christian theologians (Brunner, Buber, Barth, Niebuhr and Bultmann—to take outstanding examples) that the only genuine basis for morality is in religion. And any old religion is not good enough. The only truly adequate foundation for moral belief is a religion that

From Kai Nielsen, *Ethics without God* (Buffalo, N.Y.: Prometheus Books, 1973). Reprinted by permission of the publisher.

acknowledges the absolute sovereignty of the Lord found in the prophetic religions....

Is this frequently repeated claim justified? Are our moral beliefs and conceptions based on or grounded in a belief in the God of Judaism, Christianity and Islam?...

I shall argue that the fact that God wills something—if indeed that is a fact—cannot be a fundamental criterion for its being morally good or obligatory and thus it cannot be the only criterion or the only adequate criterion for moral goodness or obligation....

In asking about the basis or authority for our moral beliefs we are not asking about how we came to have them. If you ask someone where he got his moral beliefs, he, to be realistic, should answer that he got them from his parents, parent surrogates, teachers.[1] They are beliefs which he has been conditioned to accept. But the validity or soundness of a belief is independent of its origin. When one person naively asks another where he got his moral beliefs, most likely he is not asking how he came by them, but rather, (a) on what authority he holds these beliefs, or (b) what good reasons or justification he has for these moral beliefs. He should answer that he does not and cannot hold these beliefs on any authority. It is indeed true that many of us turn to people for moral advice and guidance in moral matters, but if we do what we do simply because it has been authorized, we cannot be reasoning and acting as moral agents; for to respond as a moral agent, one's moral principle must be something which is subscribed to by one's own deliberate commitment, and it must be something for which one is prepared to give reasons....

Suppose we say that we ought to do what God wills because God will punish us if we do not obey him. This may indeed be a cogent self-interested or prudential reason for doing what God commands, but it is hardly a morally good reason for doing what he commands since such considerations of self-interest cannot be an adequate basis for morality. A powerful being—an omnipotent and omniscient being—speaking out of the whirlwind cannot by his mere commands create an obligation. Ewing...assert[s]: "Without a prior conception of God as good or his commands as right, God would have no more claim on our obedience than Hitler or Stalin except that he would have more power than even they had to make things uncomfortable for those who disobey him."[2] Unless we assume that God is morally perfect, unless we assume the perfect goodness of God, there can be no necessary "relation between being commanded or willed by God and being obligatory or good."[3]

...Good is a concept which can be understood quite independently of any reference to the deity;...morality without religion, without theism, is quite possible. In fact, just the reverse is the case. Christianity, Judaism and theistic

---

[1] Nowell-Smith, P. H. (1966), "Morality: Religious and Secular" in Ramsey, Ian (ed.), *Christian Ethics and Contemporary Philosophy*, London: SCM Press.
[2] Ewing, A. C. (1961), "The Autonomy of Ethics" in Ramsey, Ian (ed.), *Prospect for Metaphysics*, London: Allen and Unwin, p. 40.
[3] Ibid., p. 41.

religions of that sort could not exist if people did not have a moral understanding that was, logically speaking, quite independent of such religions. We
could have no understanding of the truth of "God is good" or of the concept
God unless we had an independent understanding of goodness.

That this is so can be seen from the following considerations. If we had
no understanding of the word young, and if we did not know the criteria for
deciding whether a dog was young, we could not know how correctly to apply
the word puppy. Without such a prior understanding of what it is to be young,
we could not understand the sentence "puppies are young." Similarly, if we
had no understanding of the use of the word good, and if we did not know
the criteria for deciding whether a being (or if you will, a power or a force) was
good, we could not know how correctly to apply the word God. Without such
a prior understanding of goodness, we could not understand the sentence
"God is good." This clearly shows that our understanding of morality and
knowledge of goodness are independent of any knowledge that we may or
may not have of the divine. Indeed, without a prior and logically independent
understanding of good and without some non-religious criterion for judging
something to be good, the religious person could have no knowledge of God,
for he could not know whether that powerful being who spoke out of the
whirlwind and laid the foundations of the earth was in fact worthy of worship
and perfectly good.

From my argument we should conclude that we cannot decide whether
something is good or whether it ought to be done simply from finding out
(assuming that we can find out) that God commanded it, willed it, enjoined
it. Furthermore, whether "God is good" is synthetic (substantive) or analytic
(a truth of language), the concept of good must be understood as something
distinct from the concept of God; that is to say, a man could know how to use
"good" properly and still not know how to use "God." Conversely, a man
could not know how to use "God" correctly unless he already understood
how to use "good." An understanding of goodness is logically prior to, and
is independent of, any understanding or acknowledgment of God.

In attempting to counter my argument for the necessary independence
of morality—including a central facet of religious morality—from any beliefs
about the existence or powers of the deity, the religious moralist might begin
by conceding that (a) there are secular moralities that are logically independent of religion, and (b) that we must understand the meanings of moral terms
independently of understanding what it means to speak of God. He might
even go so far as to grant that only a man who understood what good and bad
were could come to believe in God. "Good," he might grant, does not mean
"willed by God" or anything like that; and "there is no God, but human happiness is nonetheless good" is indeed perfectly intelligible as a moral utterance. But granting that, it is still the case that Jew and Christian do and must—
on pain of ceasing to be Jew or Christian—take God's will as their final court
of appeal in the making of moral appraisals or judgments. Any rule, act or
attitude that conflicts with what the believer sincerely believes to be the will

of God must be rejected by him. It is indeed true that in making moral judgments the Jew or Christian does not always use God's will as a criterion for what is good or what ought to be done. When he says "fluoridation is a good thing" or "the resumption of nuclear testing is a crime," he need not be using God's will as a criterion for his moral judgment. But where any moral judgment or any other moral criterion conflicts with God's ordinances, or with what the person making the judgment honestly takes to be God's ordinances, he must accept those ordinances, or he is no longer a Jew or a Christian. This acceptance is a crucial test of his faith. In this way, God's will is his fundamental moral criterion.

That the orthodox Jew or Christian would reason in this way is perfectly true, but though he says that God's will is his fundamental criterion, it is still plain that he has a yet more fundamental criterion which he must use in order to employ God's will as a moral criterion. Such a religious moralist must believe and thus be prepared to make the moral claim that there exists a being whom he deems to be perfectly good or worthy of worship and whose will should always be obeyed. But to do this he must have a moral criterion (a standard for what is morally good) that is independent of God's will or what people believe to be God's will. In fact, the believer's moral criterion—"because it is willed by God"—is in logical dependence on some distinct criterion in virtue of which the believer judges that something is perfectly good, is worthy of worship. And in making this very crucial judgment he cannot appeal to God's will as a criterion, for, that there is a being worthy of the appellation "God," depends in part on the above prior moral claim. Only if it is correct, can we justifiably say that there is a God.

It is crucial to keep in mind that "a wholly good being exists who is worthy of worship" is not analytic, is not a truth of language, though "God is wholly good" is. The former is rather a substantive moral statement (expressing a moral judgment) and a very fundamental one indeed, for the believer's whole faith rests on it. Drop this and everything goes.

It is tempting to reply to my above argument in this vein: "but it is blasphemy to judge God; no account of the logical structure of the believer's argument can be correct if it says that the believer must judge that God is good." Here we must beware of verbal magic and attend very carefully to precisely what it is we are saying. I did not—and could not on pain of contradiction—say that God must be judged worthy of worship, perfectly good; for God by definition is worthy of worship, perfectly good. I said something quite different, namely that the believer and non-believer alike must decide whether there exists or could conceivably exist a force, a being ("ground of being") that is worthy of worship or perfectly good; and I further said that in deciding this, one makes a moral judgment that can in no way be logically dependent on God's will. Rather, the moral standard, "because it is willed by God," is dependent for its validity on the acceptance of the claim that there is a being worthy of worship. And as our little word "worthy" indicates, this is unequivocally a moral judgment for believer and non-believer alike....

The dialectic of our general argument about morality and divine commands should not end here. There are some further considerations which need to be brought to the forefront. Consider the theological claim that there is an infinite self-existent being, upon whom all finite realities depend for their existence, but who in turn depends on nothing. Assuming the intelligibility of the key concepts in this claim and assuming also that we know this claim to be true, it still needs to be asked how we can know, except by the use of our own moral understanding, that this infinite, self-existent being is good or is a being whose commands we ought to obey. Since he—to talk about this being anthropomorphically by the use of personal pronouns—is powerful enough, we might decide that it would be "the better part of valour" to obey him, but this decision would not at all entail that we ought to obey him. How do we know that this being is good, except by our own moral discernment? We could not discover that this being is good or just by discovering that he "laid the foundation of the world" or "created man in his image and likeness." No information about the behavior patterns of this being would of itself tell us that he was good, righteous or just. We ourselves would have to decide that, or, to use the misleading idiom of the ethical intuitionist, we would have to intuit or somehow come to perceive or understand that the unique ethical properties of goodness, righteousness and justness apply to this strange being or "ground of all being" that we somehow discover to exist. Only if we independently knew what we would count as good, righteous, just, would we be in a position to know whether this being is good or whether his commands ought to be obeyed. That most Christians most of the time unquestionably assume that he is good only proves that this judgment is for them a fundamental moral judgment. But this should hardly be news....

By simply considering the reality allegedly denoted by the word "God," we cannot discover whether this "reality" is good. If we simply let Z stand for this reality, we can always ask, "Is it good?" This is never a self-answering question in the way it is if we ask, "Is murder evil?" Take away the evaluative force of the word God and you have no ground for claiming that it must be the case that God is good; to make this claim, with our admittedly fallible moral understanding, we must decide if this Z is good.

"But"—it will be countered—"you have missed the significance of the very point you have just made. As you say yourself, 'God' is not just a descriptive word and God-sentences are not by any means used with a purely descriptive aim. 'God' normally has an evaluative use and God-sentences have a directive force. You cannot begin to understand them if you do not take this into consideration. You cannot just consider what Z designates or purports to designate."

My reply to this is that we can and must if we are going to attain clarity in these matters. Certain crucial and basic sentences like "God created the Heavens and the earth" and "God is in Christ," are by no means just moral or practical utterances and they would not have the evaluative force they do if it were not thought that in some strange way they described a mysterious objective power. The religious quest is a quest to find a Z such that Z is worthy of worship. This being the case, the evaluative force of the words and of the utterance is dependent on the descriptive force. How else but by our own moral judgment that Z is a being worthy to be worshipped are we enabled to call this Z "my Lord and my God"? Christians say there is a Z such that Z should be worshipped. Non-believers deny this or remain sceptical. Findlay,[4] for example, points out that his atheism is in part moral because he does not believe that there can possibly be a Z such that Z is a worthy object of worship. Father Copleston,[5] on the other hand, says there is a Z such that Z ought to be worshipped. This Z, Father Copleston claims, is a "necessary being" whose non-existence is in some important sense inconceivable. But both Findlay and Copleston are using their own moral understanding in making their respective moral judgments. Neither is deriving or deducing his moral judgment from the statement "there is a Z" or from noticing or adverting to the fact—if it is a fact—that Z is "being-itself," "a reality whose non-existence is unthinkable," "the ground of being" or the like.

Morality cannot be based on religion. If anything, the opposite is partly true, for nothing can be God unless he or it is an object worthy of worship and it is our own moral insight that must tell us if anything at all could possibly be worthy of worship....

We have already seen that if so-and-so is called a divine command or an ordinance of God, then it is obviously something that the person who believes it to be a divine command or ordinance of God will believe he ought to obey, for he would not call anything a *divine* command or an ordinance of *God* unless he thought he ought to obey it. But we ourselves, by our own moral insight, must judge that such commands or promulgations are worthy of such an appellation. Yet no moral conceptions follow from a command or law as such. And this would be true at any time whatsoever. It is a logical and not a historical consideration.

Now it is true that if you believe in God in such a way as to accept God as your Lord and Master, and if you believe that something is an ordinance of God, then you ought to try to follow this ordinance. But if you behave like this it is not because you base morals on religion or on a law concept of morality, but because he who can bring himself to say "my God" uses "God" and cognate words evaluatively. To use such an expression is already to make a moral evaluation; the man expresses a decision that he is morally bound to do whatever God commands. "I ought to do whatever this Z commands" is an expression of moral obligation. To believe in God, as we have already seen, involves the making of a certain value judgment; that is to say, the believer

[4] Findlay, J. N. (1955), "Can God's Existence Be Disproved?" in Antony Flew and Alasdair MacIntyre (eds.), *New Essays in Philosophical Theology*, New York: Macmillan Company, pp. 47–56.
[5] Russell, Bertrand, and Copleston, F. C. (1957), "The Existence of God: A Debate" in Bertrand Russell, *Why I Am Not a Christian*, London: Allen and Unwin, pp. 145–147.

believes that there is a Z such that Z is worthy of worship. But his value judgment cannot be derived from just examining Z, or from hearing Z's commands or laws. Without a pro-attitude on the part of the believer toward Z, without a decision by the individual concerned that Z is worthy of worship, nothing of moral kind follows. But no decision of this sort is entailed by discoveries about Z or by finding out what Z commands or wishes. It is finally up to the individual to decide that this Z is worthy of worship, that this Z ought to be worshipped, that this Z ought to be called his Lord and Master. We have here a moral use of "ought" that is logically prior to any law conception of ethics. The command gains obligatory force because it is judged worthy of obedience. If someone says, "I do not pretend to appraise God's laws, I just simply accept them because God tells me to," similar considerations obtain. This person judges that there is a Z that is a proper object of obedience. This expresses his own moral judgment, his own sense of what he is obliged to do.

A religious belief depends for its viability on our sense of good and bad—our own sense of worth—and not vice versa. It is crucial to an understanding of morality that this truth about the uses of our language be understood. Morality cannot be based on religion and I (like Findlay) would even go so far as to deny in the name of morality that any Z whatsoever could be an object or being worthy of worship. But whether or not I am correct in this last judgment, it remains the case that each person with his own finite and fallible moral awareness must make decisions of this sort for himself. This would be so whether he was in a Hebrew-Christian tradition or in a "corrupt" and "shallow" consequentialist tradition or in any tradition whatsoever. A moral understanding must be logically prior to any religious assent.

STUDY QUESTIONS

1. Does Nielsen ever define "goodness" or tell us how we come to distinguish between "good" and "evil"?
2. In Plato's famous dialogue *Euthyphro* Socrates asks: "Is the pious or holy beloved by the gods because it is holy, or holy because it is beloved of the gods?" How would Nielsen answer the question?
3. "There is no morality; there are only moralities, and one is as valid as the next." How would Nielsen respond to this statement? How would you respond to it?
4. What does Nielsen mean when he says that it is more accurate to say that religion is based on morality than morality on religion?
5. If it is the case that God's commands and the good are logically separable, is it perhaps possible, nevertheless, that they always coincide?

Culture and Morality
Ruth Benedict

Ruth Benedict (1887–1948) was one of America's leading cultural anthropologists. Her *Patterns of Culture* (1934) is a classic study in comparative anthropology. Benedict viewed a culture as a coherent system of ideas and practices which evolve around a central preference or mode of behavior. Once these core values have been selected, habits and ideas are chosen which are congenial with them. Practices which conflict with the core preferences are discarded, and over long periods of time a systematic pattern of behavior is built up.

Benedict believed that human beings are, for the most part, fairly adaptive. Widely divergent preferences may be expressed by different cultures, even to the point of whole cultures behaving in ways we would characterize as "crazy." But she surveys this diversity with moral neutrality. In this essay she claims that morality is nothing more than habit. What is moral for a culture is what is normal for that culture; and there is no fixed human nature which determines that only one behavior pattern can be normal.

Benedict's theory is a form of subjectivism. There is no hint given that some attitudes are more reasonable than others. In fact, some of the things she says suggest that "rationality," like morality, may be a culturally defined trait. This theory gives new life to the saying of the ancient Greek philosopher Protagoras: "Man is the measure of all things."

Modern social anthropology has become more and more a study of the varieties and common elements of cultural environment and the consequences of these in human behavior. For such a study of diverse social orders primitive peoples fortunately provide a laboratory not yet entirely vitiated by the spread of a standardized worldwide civilization. Dyaks and Hopis, Fijians and Yakuts are significant for psychological and sociological study because only among these simpler peoples has there been sufficient isolation to give opportunity for the development of localized social forms. In the higher cultures the standardization of custom and belief over a couple of continents has given a false sense of the inevitability of the particular forms that have gained currency, and we need to turn to a wider survey in order to check the conclusions we hastily base upon this near-universality of familiar customs. Most of the simpler cultures did not gain the wide currency of the one which, out of our experience, we identify with human nature, but this was for various historical reasons, and certainly not for any that gives us as its carriers a monopoly of social good or of social sanity. Modern civilization, from this point of view, becomes not a necessary pinnacle of human achievement but one entry in a long series of possible adjustments.

From "Anthropology and the Abnormal," by Ruth Benedict, *The Journal of General Psychology*, 1934, 10, 59–82. Reprinted with permission of the Helen Dwight Reid Educational Foundation. Published by Heldref Publications, 4000 Albemarle St., N.W., Washington, D.C. 20016. Copyright © 1934.

These adjustments, whether they are in mannerisms like the ways of showing anger, or joy, or grief in any society, or in major human drives like those of sex, prove to be far more variable than experience in any one culture would suggest. In certain fields, such as that of religion or of formal marriage arrangements, these wide limits of variability are well known and can be fairly described. In others it is not yet possible to give a generalized account, but that does not absolve us of the task of indicating the significance of the work that has been done and of the problems that have arisen.

One of these problems relates to the customary modern normal-abnormal categories and our conclusions regarding them. In how far are such categories culturally determined, or in how far can we with assurance regard them as absolute? In how far can we regard inability to function socially as diagnostic of abnormality, or in how far is it necessary to regard this as a function of the culture?

As a matter of fact, one of the most striking facts that emerge from a study of widely varying cultures is the ease with which our abnormals function in other cultures. It does not matter what kind of "abnormality" we choose for illustration, those which indicate extreme instability, or those which are more in the nature of character traits like sadism or delusions of grandeur or of persecution, there are well-described cultures in which these abnormals function at ease and with honor, and apparently without danger or difficulty to the society.

The most notorious of these is trance and catalepsy. Even a very mild mystic is aberrant in our culture. But most peoples have regarded even extreme psychic manifestations not only as normal and desirable, but even as characteristic of highly valued and gifted individuals. This was true even in our own cultural background in that period when Catholicism made the ecstatic experience the mark of sainthood. It is hard for us, born and brought up in a culture that makes no use of the experience, to realize how important a role it may play and how many individuals are capable of it, once it has been given an honorable place in any society.

Cataleptic and trance phenomena are, of course, only one illustration of the fact that those whom we regard as abnormals may function adequately in other cultures. Many of our culturally discarded traits are selected for elaboration in different societies. Homosexuality is an excellent example, for in this case our attention is not constantly diverted, as in the consideration of trance, to the interruption of routine activity which it implies. Homosexuality poses the problem very simply. A tendency toward this trait in our culture exposes an individual to all the conflicts to which all aberrants are always exposed, and we tend to identify the consequences of this conflict with homosexuality. But these consequences are obviously local and cultural. Homosexuals in many societies are not incompetent, but they may be such if the culture asks adjustments of them that would strain any man's vitality. Wherever homosexuality has been given an honorable place in any society, those to whom it is congenial have filled adequately the honorable roles society assigns to them. Plato's *Republic* is, of course, the most convincing statement of such a reading of homosexuality. It is presented as one of the major means to the good life, and it was generally so regarded in Greece at that time.

The cultural attitude toward homosexuals has not always been on such a high ethical plane, but it has been very varied. Among many American Indian tribes there exists the institution of the berdache, as the French called them. These men-women were men who at puberty or thereafter took the dress and the occupations of women. Sometimes they married other men and lived with them. Sometimes they were men with no inversion, persons of weak sexual endowment who chose this rôle to avoid the jeers of the women. The berdaches were never regarded as of first-rate supernatural power, as similar men-women were in Siberia, but rather as leaders in women's occupations, good healers in certain diseases, or, among certain tribes, as the genial organizers of social affairs. In any case, they were socially placed. They were not left exposed to the conflicts that visit the deviant who is excluded from participation in the recognized patterns of his society.

The most spectacular illustrations of the extent to which normality may be culturally defined are those cultures where an abnormality of our culture is the cornerstone of their social structure. It is not possible to do justice to these possibilities in a short discussion. A recent study of an island of northwest Melanesia by Fortune describes a society built upon traits which we regard as beyond the border of paranoia. In this tribe the exogamic groups look upon each other as prime manipulators of black magic, so that one marries always into an enemy group which remains for life one's deadly and unappeasable foes. They look upon a good garden crop as a confession of theft, for everyone is engaged in making magic to induce into his garden the productiveness of his neighbors'; therefore no secrecy in the island is so rigidly insisted upon as the secrecy of a man's harvesting of his yams. Their polite phrase at the acceptance of a gift is, "And if you now poison me, how shall I repay you this present?" Their preoccupation with poisoning is constant; no woman ever leaves her cooking pot for a moment untended. Even the great affinal economic exchanges that are characteristic of this Melanesian culture area are quite altered in Dobu since they are incompatible with this fear and distrust that pervades the culture. They go farther and people the whole world outside their own quarters with such malignant spirits that all-night feasts and ceremonials simply do not occur here.* They have even rigorous religiously enforced customs that forbid the sharing of seed even in one family group. Anyone else's food is deadly poison to you, so that communality of stores is out of the question. For some months before harvest the whole society is on the verge of starvation, but if one falls to the temptation and eats up one's seed yams, one is an outcast and a beachcomber for life. There is no coming back. It involves, as a matter of course, divorce and the breaking of all social ties.

Now in this society where no one may work with another and no one may share with another, Fortune describes the individual who was regarded

---

*Editors' note: This sentence is reprinted exactly as in the original journal article.

by all his fellows as crazy. He was not one of those who periodically ran amok and, beside himself and frothing at the mouth, fell with a knife upon anyone he could reach. Such behavior they did not regard as putting anyone outside the pale. They did not even put the individuals who were known to be liable to these attacks under any kind of control. They merely fled when they saw the attack coming on and kept out of the way. "He would be all right tomorrow." But there was one man of sunny, kindly disposition who liked work and liked to be helpful. The compulsion was too strong for him to repress it in favor of the opposite tendencies of his culture. Men and women never spoke of him without laughing; he was silly and simple and definitely crazy. Nevertheless, to the ethnologist used to a culture that has, in Christianity, made his type the model of all virtue, he seemed a pleasant fellow.

An even more extreme example, because it is of a culture that has built itself upon a more complex abnormality, is that of the North Pacific Coast of North America. The civilization of the Kwakiutl, at the time when it was first recorded in the last decades of the nineteenth century, was one of the most vigorous in North America. It was built up on an ample economic supply of goods, the fish which furnished their food staple being practically inexhaustible and obtainable with comparatively small labor, and the wood which furnished the material for their houses, their furnishings, and their arts being, with however much labor, always procurable. They lived in coastal villages that compared favorably in size with those of any other American Indians and they kept up constant communication by means of sea-going dug-out canoes.

It was one of the most vigorous and zestful of the aboriginal cultures of North America, with complex crafts and ceremonials, and elaborate and striking arts. It certainly had none of the earmarks of a sick civilization. The tribes of the Northwest Coast had wealth, and exactly in our terms. That is, they had not only a surplus of economic goods, but they made a game of the manipulation of wealth. It was by no means a mere direct transcription of economic needs and the filling of those needs. It involved the idea of capital, of interest, and of conspicuous waste. It was a game with all the binding rules of a game, and a person entered it as a child. His father distributed wealth for him, according to his ability, at a small feast or potlatch, and each gift the receiver was obliged to accept and to return after a short interval with interest that ran to about 100 per cent a year. By the time the child was grown, therefore, he was well launched, a larger potlatch had been given for him on various occasions of exploit or initiation, and he had wealth either out at usury or in his own possession. Nothing in the civilization could be enjoyed without validating it by the distribution of this wealth. Everything that was valued, names and songs as well as material objects, were passed down in family lines, but they were always publicly assumed with accompanying sufficient distributions of property. It was the game of validating and exercising all the privileges one could accumulate from one's various forbears, or by gift, or by marriage, that made the chief interest of the culture. Everyone in his degree took part in it, but many, of course, mainly as spectators. In its highest form it was played out between rival chiefs representing not only themselves and their family lines but their communities, and the object of the contest was to glorify oneself and to humiliate one's opponent. On this level of greatness the property involved was no longer represented by blankets, so many thousand of them to a potlatch, but by higher units of value. These higher units were like our bank notes. They were incised copper tablets, each of them named, and having a value that depended upon their illustrious history. This was as high as ten thousand blankets, and to possess one of them, still more to enhance its value at a great potlatch, was one of the greatest glories within the compass of the chiefs of the Northwest Coast.

The details of this manipulation of wealth are in many ways a parody on our own economic arrangements, but it is with the motivations that were recognized in this contest that we are concerned in this discussion. The drives were those which in our own culture we should call megalomaniac. There was an uncensored self-glorification and ridicule of the opponent that it is hard to equal in other cultures outside of the monologues of the abnormal....

All of existence was seen in terms of insult. Not only derogatory acts performed by a neighbor or an enemy, but all untoward events, like a cut when one's axe slipped, or a ducking when one's canoe overturned, were insults. All alike threatened first and foremost one's ego security, and the first thought one was allowed was how to get even, how to wipe out the insult.

In their behavior at great bereavements this set of the culture comes out most strongly. Among the Kwakiutl it did not matter whether a relative had died in bed of disease, or by the hand of an enemy, in either case death was an affront to be wiped out by the death of another person. The fact that one had been caused to mourn was proof that one had been put upon. A chief's sister and her daughter had gone up to Victoria, and either because they drank bad whiskey or because their boat capsized they never came back. The chief called together his warriors. "Now I ask you, tribes, who shall wail? Shall I do it or shall another?" The spokesman answered, of course, "Not you, Chief. Let some other of the tribes." Immediately they set up the war pole to announce their intention of wiping out the injury, and gathered a war party. They set out, and found seven men and two children asleep and killed them. "Then they felt good when they arrived at Sebaa in the evening."

The point which is of interest to us is that in our society those who on that occasion would feel good when they arrived at Sebaa that evening would be the definitely abnormal. There would be some, even in our society, but it is not a recognized and approved mood under the circumstances. On the Northwest Coast those are favored and fortunate to whom that mood under those circumstances is congenial, and those to whom it is repugnant are unlucky. This latter minority can register in their own culture only by doing violence to their congenial responses and acquiring others that are difficult for them. The person, for instance, who, like a Plains Indian whose wife has been taken from him, is too proud to fight, can deal with the Northwest Coast civilization only by ignoring its strongest bents. If he cannot achieve it, he is the deviant in that culture, their instance of abnormality.

This head-hunting that takes place on the Northwest Coast after a death is no matter of blood revenge or of organized vengeance. There is no effort to tie up the subsequent killing with any responsibility on the part of the victim for the death of the person who is being mourned. A chief whose son has died goes visiting wherever his fancy dictates, and he says to his host, "My prince has died today, and you go with him." Then he kills him. In this, according to their interpretation, he acts nobly because he has not been downed. He has thrust back in return. The whole procedure is meaningless without the fundamental paranoid reading of bereavement. Death, like all the other untoward accidents of existence, confounds man's pride and can only be handled in the category of insults.

Behavior honored upon the Northwest Coast is one which is recognized as abnormal in our civilization, and yet it is sufficiently close to the attitudes of our own culture to be intelligible to us and to have a definite vocabulary with which we may discuss it. The megalomaniac paranoid trend is a definite danger in our society. It is encouraged by some of our major preoccupations, and it confronts us with a choice of two possible attitudes. One is to brand it as abnormal and reprehensible, and is the attitude we have chosen in our civilization. The other is to make it an essential attribute of ideal man, and this is the solution in the culture of the Northwest Coast.

These illustrations, which it has been possible to indicate only in the briefest manner, force upon us the fact that normality is culturally defined. An adult shaped to the drives and standards of either of these cultures, if he were transported into our civilization, would fall into our categories of abnormality. He would be faced with the psychic dilemmas of the socially unavailable. In his own culture, however, he is the pillar of society, the end result of socially inculcated mores, and the problem of personal instability in his case simply does not arise.

No one civilization can possibly utilize in its mores the whole potential range of human behavior. Just as there are great numbers of possible phonetic articulations, and the possibility of language depends on a selection and standardization of a few of these in order that speech communication may be possible at all, so the possibility of organized behavior of every sort, from the fashions of local dress and houses to the dicta of a people's ethics and religion, depends upon a similar selection among the possible behavior traits. In the field of recognized economic obligations or sex tabus this selection is as nonrational and subconscious a process as it is in the field of phonetics. It is a process which goes on in the group for long periods of time and is historically conditioned by innumerable accidents of isolation or of contact of peoples. In any comprehensive study of psychology, the selection that different cultures have made in the course of history within the great circumference of potential behavior is of great significance.

Every society, beginning with some slight inclination in one direction or another, carries its preference farther and farther, integrating itself more and more completely upon its chosen basis, and discarding those types of behavior that are uncongenial. Most of those organizations of personality that seem to us most uncontrovertibly abnormal have been used by different civilizations in the very foundations of their institutional life. Conversely the most valued traits of our normal individuals have been looked on in differently organized cultures as aberrant. Normality, in short, within a very wide range, is culturally defined. It is primarily a term for the socially elaborated segment of human behavior in any culture; and abnormality, a term for the segment that that particular civilization does not use. The very eyes with which we see the problem are conditioned by the long traditional habits of our own society.

It is a point that has been made more often in relation to ethics than in relation to psychiatry. We do not any longer make the mistake of deriving the morality of our locality and decade directly from the inevitable constitution of human nature. We do not elevate it to the dignity of a first principle. We recognize that morality differs in every society, and is a convenient term for socially approved habits. Mankind has always preferred to say, "It is morally good," rather than "It is habitual," and the fact of this preference is matter enough for a critical science of ethics. But historically the two phrases are synonymous.

The concept of the normal is properly a variant of the concept of the good. It is that which society has approved. A normal action is one which falls well within the limits of expected behavior for a particular society. Its variability among different peoples is essentially a function of the variability of the behavior patterns that different societies have created for themselves, and can never be wholly divorced from a consideration of culturally institutionalized types of behavior.

Each culture is a more or less elaborate working-out of the potentialities of the segment it has chosen. In so far as a civilization is well integrated and consistent within itself, it will tend to carry farther and farther, according to its nature, its initial impulse toward a particular type of action, and from the point of view of any other culture those elaborations will include more and more extreme and aberrant traits.

Each of these traits, in proportion as it reinforces the chosen behavior patterns of that culture, is for that culture normal. Those individuals to whom it is congenial either congenitally, or as the result of childhood sets, are accorded prestige in that culture, and are not visited with the social contempt or disapproval which their traits would call down upon them in a society that was differently organized. On the other hand, those individuals whose characteristics are not congenial to the selected type of human behavior in that community are the deviants, no matter how valued their personality traits may be in a contrasted civilization.

The Dobuan who is not easily susceptible to fear of treachery, who enjoys work and likes to be helpful, is their neurotic and regarded as silly. On the Northwest Coast the person who finds it difficult to read life in terms of an insult contest will be the person upon whom fall all the difficulties of the culturally unprovided for. The person who does not find it easy to humiliate a neighbor, nor to see humiliation in his own experience, who is genial and loving, may, of course, find some unstandardized way of achieving satisfactions in his society, but not in the major patterned responses that his culture requires of him. If he is born to play an important rôle in a family with many hereditary privileges, he can succeed only by doing violence to his whole personality. If he does not succeed, he has betrayed his culture; that is, he is abnormal.

I have spoken of individuals as having sets toward certain types of behavior, and of these sets as running sometimes counter to the types of behavior which are institutionalized in the culture to which they belong. From all that we know of contrasting cultures it seems clear that differences of temperament occur in every society. The matter has never been made the subject of investigation, but from the available material it would appear that these temperament types are very likely of universal recurrence. That is, there is an ascertainable range of human behavior that is found wherever a sufficiently large series of individuals is observed. But the proportion in which behavior types stand to one another in different societies is not universal. The vast majority of the individuals in any group are shaped to the fashion of that culture. In other words, most individuals are plastic to the moulding force of the society into which they are born. In a society that values trance, as in India, they will have supernormal experience. In a society that institutionalizes homosexuality, they will be homosexual. In a society that sets the gathering of possessions as the chief human objective, they will amass property. The deviants, whatever the type of behavior the culture has institutionalized, will remain few in number, and there seems no more difficulty in moulding the vast malleable majority to the "normality" of what we consider an aberrant trait, such as delusions of reference, than to the normality of such accepted behavior patterns as acquisitiveness. The small proportion of the number of the deviants in any culture is not a function of the sure instinct with which that society has built itself upon the fundamental sanities, but of the universal fact that, happily, the majority of mankind quite readily take any shape that is presented to them....

STUDY QUESTIONS

1. What examples are used by Benedict to demonstrate that normalcy is culturally defined? What is her discussion of normalcy supposed to show about morality?
2. What does Benedict say happens to an individual who is transported to a culture which has a different conception of normalcy? What is the importance of this claim?

3. How does the recognition of the cultural relativity of normalcy affect our conception of morality, according to Benedict?
4. Why is it said that the concept of normalcy is a variant of the concept of the good? Do you think that this is true? Why or why not?
5. "National Socialists [that is, Nazis] say: Legality is that which does the German people good; illegality is that which harms the German people" (William Frick—Nazi minister of the Interior). Would Benedict say that Frick is on solid logical ground? How would Benedict respond to the Nuremberg trials?

The Challenge of Cultural Relativism
James Rachels

In one society, we find sexual promiscuity; in another, a stern, ascetic, puritanical attitude toward sexual indulgence. In one society the aged are abandoned and left to die; in another, they are protected and cared for. Obviously, different societies have different routine practices. Cultural relativists say that calling an action "right" means that it coincides with what is customarily done in a given society, and that there is no measure of right and wrong other than the practices of one's own society. Is this the case? Does it follow from the fact that customary behavior differs from society to society that there are no objective standards of behavior? No, argues James Rachels (1940–   ), professor of philosophy and dean of the School of Humanities at the University of Alabama. After clarifying the meaning of cultural relativism and tracing its harmful consequences, Rachels focuses on what he views as the main defect in relativism. Relativists are mistaken when they interpret differences in behavior as differences in moral values. For instance, people in society A may eat the meat of cows while people in society B refuse to do so. This refusal may follow upon the religious belief in society B that the souls of deceased humans inhabit the bodies of cows, a belief foreign to society A. Yet both societies may embrace the moral principle that human beings should not be eaten.

Rachels also argues that some rules are needed in all societies as a condition of social life. If a society did not encourage truth-telling, there could be no communication; and if it did not discourage murder, the very survival of its members would be at risk.

Despite his reservations about relativism, Rachels believes that relativists can help us to see that some of the practices and attitudes which we think are "natural" are really only cultural products.

From James Rachels, *The Elements of Moral Philosophy* (New York: Random House, Inc., 1986). Reprinted by permission of Random House, Inc.

Morality differs in every society, and is a convenient term for socially approved habits.
                                            Ruth Benedict, *Patterns of Culture* (1934)

HOW DIFFERENT CULTURES
HAVE DIFFERENT MORAL CODES

Darius, a king of ancient Persia, was intrigued by the variety of cultures he
encountered in his travels. He had found, for example, that the Callatians (a
tribe of Indians) customarily ate the bodies of their dead fathers. The Greeks,
of course, did not do that—the Greeks practiced cremation and regarded the
funeral pyre as the natural and fitting way to dispose of the dead. Darius
thought that a sophisticated understanding of the world must include an appreciation of such differences between cultures. One day, to teach this lesson,
he summoned some Greeks who happened to be present at his court and
asked them what they would take to eat the bodies of their dead fathers. They
were shocked, as Darius knew they would be, and replied that no amount of
money could persuade them to do such a thing. Then Darius called in some
Callatians, and while the Greeks listened asked them what they would take
to burn their dead fathers' bodies. The Callatians were horrified and told Darius
not even to mention such a dreadful thing.

This story, recounted by Herodotus in his *History*, illustrates a recurring
theme in the literature of social science: different cultures have different moral
codes. What is thought right within one group may be utterly abhorrent to the
members of another group, and vice versa. Should we eat the bodies of the
dead or burn them? If you were a Greek, one answer would seem obviously
correct; but if you were a Callatian, the opposite would seem equally certain.

It is easy to give additional examples of the same kind. Consider the
Eskimos. They are a remote and inaccessible people. Numbering only about
25,000, they live in small, isolated settlements scattered mostly along the north-
ern fringes of North America and Greenland. Until the beginning of this century, the outside world knew little about them. Then explorers began to bring
back strange tales.

Eskimo customs turned out to be very different from our own. The men
often had more than one wife, and they would share their wives with guests,
lending them for the night as a sign of hospitality. Moreover, within a community, a dominant male might demand—and get—regular sexual access to
other men's wives. The women, however, were free to break these arrangements simply by leaving their husbands and taking up with new partners—
free, that is, so long as their former husbands chose not to make trouble. All
in all, the Eskimo practice was a volatile scheme that bore little resemblance
to what we call marriage.

But it was not only their marriage and sexual practices that were different. The Eskimos also seemed to have less regard for human life. Infanticide,
for example, was common. Knud Rasmussen, one of the most famous early
explorers, reported that he met one woman who had borne twenty children
but had killed ten of them at birth. Female babies, he found, were especially

liable to be destroyed, and this was permitted simply at the parents' discretion, with no social stigma attached to it. Old people also, when they became too feeble to contribute to the family, were left out in the snow to die. So there seemed to be, in this society, remarkably little respect for life.

To the general public, these were disturbing revelations. Our own way of living seems so natural and right that for many of us it is hard to conceive of others living so differently. And when we do hear of such things, we tend immediately to categorize those other peoples as "backward" or "primitive." But to anthropologists and sociologists, there was nothing particularly surprising about the Eskimos. Since the time of Herodotus, enlightened observers have been accustomed to the idea that conceptions of right and wrong differ from culture to culture. If we assume that *our* ideas of right and wrong will be shared by all peoples at all times, we are merely naive.

CULTURAL RELATIVISM

To many thinkers, this observation—"Different cultures have different moral codes"—has seemed to be the key to understanding morality. The idea of universal truth in ethics, they say, is a myth. The customs of different societies are all that exist. These customs cannot be said to be "correct" or "incorrect," for that implies we have an independent standard of right and wrong by which they may be judged. But there is no such independent standard; every standard is culture-bound. The great pioneering sociologist William Graham Sumner, writing in 1906, put the point like this:

> The "right" way is the way which the ancestors used and which has been
> handed down. The tradition is its own warrant. It is not held subject
> to verification by experience. The notion of right is in the folkways.
> It is not outside of them, of independent origin, and brought to test them.
> In the folkways, whatever is, is right. This is because they are traditional,
> and therefore contain in themselves the authority of the ancestral ghosts.
> When we come to the folkways we are at the end of our analysis.

This line of thought has probably persuaded more people to be skeptical about ethics than any other single thing. *Cultural Relativism*, as it has been called, challenges our ordinary belief in the objectivity and universality of moral truth. It says, in effect, that there is no such thing as universal truth in ethics; there are only the various cultural codes, and nothing more. Moreover, our own code has no special status; it is merely one among many.

As we shall see, this basic idea is really a compound of several different thoughts. It is important to separate the various elements of the theory because, on analysis, some parts of the theory turn out to be correct, whereas others seem to be mistaken. As a beginning, we may distinguish the following claims, all of which have been made by cultural relativists:

1. Different societies have different moral codes.
2. There is no objective standard that can be used to judge one societal code better than another.

3. The moral code of our own society has no special status; it is merely one among many.
4. There is no "universal truth" in ethics—that is, there are no moral truths that hold for all peoples at all times.
5. The moral code of a society determines what is right within that society; that is, if the moral code of a society says that a certain action is right, then that action *is* right, at least within that society.
6. It is mere arrogance for us to try to judge the conduct of other peoples. We should adopt an attitude of tolerance toward the practices of other cultures.

Although it may seem that these six propositions go naturally together, they are independent of one another, in the sense that some of them might be true even if others are false. In what follows, we will try to identify what is correct in Cultural Relativism, but we will also be concerned to expose what is mistaken about it.

THE CULTURAL DIFFERENCES ARGUMENT

Cultural Relativism is a theory about the nature of morality. At first blush it seems quite plausible. However, like all such theories, it may be evaluated by subjecting it to rational analysis; and when we analyze Cultural Relativism we find that it is not so plausible as it first appears to be.

The first thing we need to notice is that at the heart of Cultural Relativism there is a certain *form of argument*. The strategy used by cultural relativists is to argue from facts about the differences between cultural outlooks to a conclusion about the status of morality. Thus we are invited to accept this reasoning:

1. The Greeks believed it was wrong to eat the dead, whereas the Callatians believed it was right to eat the dead.
2. Therefore, eating the dead is neither objectively right nor objectively wrong. It is merely a matter of opinion, which varies from culture to culture.

Or, alternatively:

1. The Eskimos see nothing wrong with infanticide, whereas Americans believe infanticide is immoral.
2. Therefore, infanticide is neither objectively right nor objectively wrong. It is merely a matter of opinion, which varies from culture to culture.

Clearly, these arguments are variations of one fundamental idea. They are both special cases of a more general argument, which says:

1. Different cultures have different moral codes.
2. Therefore, there is no objective "truth" in morality. Right and wrong are only matters of opinion, and opinions vary from culture to culture.

We may call this the *Cultural Differences Argument*. To many people, it is very persuasive. But from a logical point of view, is it a *sound* argument?

It is not sound. The trouble is that the conclusion does not really follow from the premise—that is, even if the premise is true, the conclusion still might be false. The premise concerns what people *believe:* in some societies, people believe one thing; in other societies, people believe differently. The conclusion, however, concerns *what really is the case.* The trouble is that this sort of conclusion does not follow logically from this sort of premise.

Consider again the example of the Greeks and Callatians. The Greeks believed it was wrong to eat the dead; the Callatians believed it was right. Does it follow, *from the mere fact that they disagreed,* that there is no objective truth in the matter? No, it does not follow; for it *could* be that the practice was objectively right (or wrong) and that one or the other of them was simply mistaken.

To make the point clearer, consider a very different matter. In some societies, people believe the earth is flat. In other societies, such as our own, people believe the earth is (roughly) spherical. Does it follow, *from the mere fact that they disagree,* that there is no "objective truth" in geography? Of course not; we would never draw such a conclusion because we realize that, in their beliefs about the world, the members of some societies might simply be wrong. There is no reason to think that if the world is round everyone must know it. Similarly, there is no reason to think that if there is moral truth everyone must know it. The fundamental mistake in the Cultural Differences Argument is that it attempts to derive a substantive conclusion about a subject (morality) from the mere fact that people disagree about it.

It is important to understand the nature of the point that is being made here. We are *not* saying (not yet, anyway) that the conclusion of the argument is false. Insofar as anything being said here is concerned, it is still an open question whether the conclusion is true. We *are* making a purely logical point and saying that the conclusion does not *follow from* the premise. This is important, because in order to determine whether the conclusion is true, we need arguments in its support. Cultural Relativism proposes this argument, but unfortunately the argument turns out to be fallacious. So it proves nothing.

THE CONSEQUENCES OF TAKING CULTURAL RELATIVISM SERIOUSLY

Even if the Cultural Differences Argument is invalid, Cultural Relativism might still be true. What would it be like if it were true?

In the passage quoted above, William Graham Sumner summarizes the essence of Cultural Relativism. He says that there is no measure of right and wrong other than the standards of one's society: "The notion of right is in the folkways. It is not outside of them, of independent origin, and brought to test them. In the folkways, whatever is, is right."

Suppose we took this seriously. What would be some of the consequences?

1. *We could no longer say that the customs of other societies are morally inferior to our own.* This, of course, is one of the main points stressed by Cultural Relativism. We would have to stop condemning other societies merely because they are "different." So long as we concentrate on certain examples, such as the funerary practices of the Greeks and Callatians, this may seem to be a sophisticated, enlightened attitude.

    However, we would also be stopped from criticizing other, less benign practices. Suppose a society waged war on its neighbors for the purpose of taking slaves. Or suppose a society was violently anti-Semitic and its leaders set out to destroy the Jews. Cultural Relativism would preclude us from saying that either of these practices was wrong. We would not even be able to say that a society tolerant of Jews is *better* than the anti-Semitic society, for that would imply some sort of transcultural standard of comparison. The failure to condemn *these* practices does not seem "enlightened"; on the contrary, slavery and anti-Semitism seem wrong *wherever* they occur. Nevertheless, if we took Cultural Relativism seriously, we would have to admit that these social practices also are immune from criticism.

2. *We could decide whether actions are right or wrong just by consulting the standards of our society.* Cultural Relativism suggests a simple test for determining what is right and what is wrong: all one has to do is ask whether the action is in accordance with the code of one's society. Suppose a resident of South Africa is wondering whether his country's policy of *apartheid*—rigid racial segregation—is morally correct. All he has to do is ask whether this policy conforms to his society's moral code. If it does, there is nothing to worry about, at least from a moral point of view.

    This implication of Cultural Relativism is disturbing because few of us think that our society's code is perfect—we can think of ways it might be improved. Yet Cultural Relativism would not only forbid us from criticizing the codes of *other* societies; it would stop us from criticizing our *own*. After all, if right and wrong are relative to culture, this must be true for our own culture just as much as for others.

3. *The idea of moral progress is called into doubt.* Usually, we think that at least some changes in our society have been for the better. (Some, of course, may have been changes for the worse.) Consider this example: Throughout most of Western history the place of women in society was very narrowly circumscribed. They could not own property; they could not vote or hold political office; with a few exceptions, they were not permitted to have paying jobs; and generally they were under the almost absolute control of their husbands. Recently much of this has changed, and most people think of it as progress.

If Cultural Relativism is correct, can we legitimately think of this as progress? Progress means replacing a way of doing things with a *better* way. But by what standard do we judge the new ways as better? If the old ways were in accordance with the social standards of their time, then Cultural Relativism would say it is a mistake to judge them by the standards of a different time. Eighteenth-century society was, in effect, a different society from the one we have now. To say that we have made progress implies a judgment that present-day society is better, and that is just the sort of transcultural judgment that, according to Cultural Relativism, is impermissible.

Our idea of social *reform* will also have to be reconsidered. A reformer such as Martin Luther King, Jr., seeks to change his society for the better. Within the constraints imposed by Cultural Relativism, there is one way this might be done. If a society is not living up to its own ideals, the reformer may be regarded as acting for the best: the ideals of the society are the standard by which we judge his or her proposals as worthwhile. But the "reformer" may not challenge the ideals themselves, for those ideals are by definition correct. According to Cultural Relativism, then, the idea of social reform makes sense only in this very limited way.

These three consequences of Cultural Relativism have led many thinkers to reject it as implausible on its face. It does make sense, they say, to condemn some practices, such as slavery and anti-Semitism, wherever they occur. It makes sense to think that our own society has made some moral progress, while admitting that it is still imperfect and in need of reform. Because Cultural Relativism says that these judgments make no sense, the argument goes, it cannot be right.

WHY THERE IS LESS DISAGREEMENT THAN IT SEEMS

The original impetus for Cultural Relativism comes from the observation that cultures differ dramatically in their views of right and wrong. But just how much do they differ? It is true that there are differences. However, it is easy to overestimate the extent of those differences. Often, when we examine what *seems* to be a dramatic difference, we find that the cultures do not differ nearly as much as it appears.

Consider a culture in which people believe it is wrong to eat cows. This may even be a poor culture, in which there is not enough food; still, the cows are not to be touched. Such a society would *appear* to have values very different from our own. But does it? We have not yet asked why these people will not eat cows. Suppose it is because they believe that after death the souls of humans inhabit the bodies of animals, especially cows, so that a cow may be someone's grandmother. Now do we want to say that their values are different from ours? No; the difference lies elsewhere. The difference is in our belief systems, not in our values. We agree that we shouldn't eat Grandma; we simply disagree about whether the cow *is* (or could be) Grandma.

The general point is this. Many factors work together to produce the customs of a society. The society's values are only one of them. Other matters, such as the religious and factual beliefs held by its members and the physical circumstances in which they must live, are also important. We cannot conclude, then, merely because customs differ, that there is a disagreement about *values*. The difference in customs may be attributable to some other aspect of social life. Thus there may be less disagreement about values than there appears to be.

Consider the Eskimos again. They often kill perfectly normal infants, especially girls. We do not approve of this at all; a parent who did this in our society would be locked up. Thus there appears to be a great difference in the values of our two cultures. But suppose we ask *why* the Eskimos do this. The explanation is not that they have less affection for their children or less respect for human life. An Eskimo family will always protect its babies if conditions permit. But they live in a harsh environment, where food is often in short supply. A fundamental postulate of Eskimo thought is: "Life is hard, and the margin of safety small." A family may want to nourish its babies but be unable to do so.

As in many "primitive" societies, Eskimo mothers will nurse their infants over a much longer period of time than mothers in our culture. The child will take nourishment from its mother's breast for four years, perhaps even longer. So even in the best of times there are limits to the number of infants that one mother can sustain. Moreover, the Eskimos are a nomadic people—unable to farm, they must move about in search of food. Infants must be carried, and a mother can carry only one baby in her parka as she travels and goes about her outdoor work. Other family members can help, but this is not always possible.

Infant girls are more readily disposed of because, first, in this society the males are the primary food providers—they are the hunters, according to the traditional division of labor—and it is obviously important to maintain a sufficient number of food gatherers. But there is an important second reason as well. Because the hunters suffer a high casualty rate, the adult men who die prematurely far outnumber the women who die early. Thus if male and female infants survived in equal numbers, the female adult population would greatly outnumber the male adult population. Examining the available statistics, one writer concluded that "were it not for female infanticide...there would be approximately one-and-a-half times as many females in the average Eskimo local group as there are food-producing males."

So among the Eskimos, infanticide does not signal a fundamentally different attitude toward children. Instead, it is a recognition that drastic measures are sometimes needed to ensure the family's survival. Even then, however, killing the baby is not the first option considered. Adoption is common; childless couples are especially happy to take a more fertile couple's "surplus."

Killing is only the last resort. I emphasize this in order to show that the raw data of the anthropologists can be misleading; it can make the differences in values between cultures appear greater than they are. The Eskimos' values are not all that different from our values. It is only that life forces upon them choices that we do not have to make.

HOW ALL CULTURES HAVE
SOME VALUES IN COMMON

It should not be surprising that, despite appearances, the Eskimos are protective of their children. How could it be otherwise? How could a group survive that did *not* value its young? This suggests a certain argument, one which shows that all cultural groups must be protective of their infants:

1. Human infants are helpless and cannot survive if they are not given extensive care for a period of years.
2. Therefore, if a group did not care for its young, the young would not survive, and the older members of the group would not be replaced. After a while the group would die out.
3. Therefore, any cultural group that continues to exist must care for its young. Infants that are *not* cared for must be the exception rather than the rule.

Similar reasoning shows that other values must be more or less universal. Imagine what it would be like for a society to place no value at all on truth telling. When one person spoke to another, there would be no presumption at all that he was telling the truth—for he could just as easily be speaking falsely. Within that society, there would be no reason to pay attention to what anyone says. (I ask you what time it is, and you say "Four o'clock." But there is no presumption that you are speaking truly; you could just as easily have said the first thing that came into your head. So I have no reason to pay attention to your answer—in fact, there was no point in my asking you in the first place!) Communication would then be extremely difficult, if not impossible. And because complex societies cannot exist without regular communication among their members, society would become impossible. It follows that in any complex society there *must* be a presumption in favor of truthfulness. There may of course be exceptions to this rule: there may be situations in which it is thought to be permissible to lie. Nevertheless, these will be exceptions to a rule that *is* in force in the society.

Let me give one further example of the same type. Could a society exist in which there was no prohibition on murder? What would this be like? Suppose people were free to kill other people at will, and no one thought there was anything wrong with it. In such a "society," no one could feel secure. Everyone would have to be constantly on guard. People who wanted to survive would have to avoid other people as much as possible. This would inevitably result in individuals trying to become as self-sufficient as possible—

after all, associating with others would be dangerous. Society on any large scale would collapse. Of course, people might band together in smaller groups with others that they *could* trust not to harm them. But notice what this means: they would be forming smaller societies that *did* acknowledge a rule against murder. The prohibition of murder, then, is a necessary feature of all societies.

There is a general theoretical point here, namely, that *there are some moral rules that all societies will have in common, because those rules are necessary for society to exist.* The rules against lying and murder are two examples. And in fact, we do find these rules in force in all viable cultures. Cultures may differ in what they regard as legitimate exceptions to the rules, but this disagreement exists against a background of agreement on the larger issues. Therefore, it is a mistake to overestimate the amount of difference between cultures. Not *every* moral rule can vary from society to society.

WHAT CAN BE LEARNED FROM CULTURAL RELATIVISM

At the outset, I said that we were going to identify both what is right and what is wrong in Cultural Relativism. Thus far I have mentioned only its mistakes: I have said that it rests on an invalid argument, that it has consequences that make it implausible on its face, and that the extent of cultural disagreement is far less than it implies. This all adds up to a pretty thorough repudiation of the theory. Nevertheless, it is still a very appealing idea, and the reader may have the feeling that all this is a little unfair. The theory *must* have something going for it, or else why has it been so influential? In fact, I think there *is* something right about Cultural Relativism, and now I want to say what that is. There are two lessons we should learn from the theory, even if we ultimately reject it.

1 Cultural Relativism warns us, quite rightly, about the danger of assuming that all our preferences are based on some absolute rational standard. They are not. Many (but not all) of our practices are merely peculiar to our society, and it is easy to lose sight of that fact. In reminding us of it, the theory does a service.

Funerary practices are one example. The Callatians, according to Herodotus, were "men who eat their fathers"—a shocking idea, to us at least. But eating the flesh of the dead could be understood as a sign of respect. It could be taken as a symbolic act that says: We wish this person's spirit to dwell within us. Perhaps this was the understanding of the Callatians. On such a way of thinking, burying the dead could be seen as an act of rejection, and burning the corpse as positively scornful. If this is hard to imagine, then we may need to have our imaginations stretched. Of course we may feel a visceral repugnance at the idea of eating human flesh in any circumstances. But what of it? This repugnance may be, as the relativists say, only a matter of what is customary in our particular society.

There are many other matters that we tend to think of in terms of objective right and wrong, but that are really nothing more than social conventions. Should women cover their breasts? A publicly exposed breast is scandalous in our society, whereas in other cultures it is unremarkable. Objectively speaking, it is neither right nor wrong—there is no objective reason why either custom is better. Cultural Relativism begins with the valuable insight that many of our practices are like this—they are only cultural products. Then it goes wrong by concluding that, because *some* practices are like this, *all* must be.

2 The second lesson has to do with keeping an open mind. In the course of growing up, each of us has acquired some strong feelings: we have learned to think of some types of conduct as acceptable, and others we have learned to regard as simply unacceptable. Occasionally, we may find those feelings challenged. We may encounter someone who claims that our feelings are mistaken. For example, we may have been taught that homosexuality is immoral, and we may feel quite uncomfortable around gay people and see them as alien and "different." Now someone suggests that this may be a mere prejudice; that there is nothing evil about homosexuality; that gay people are just people, like anyone else, who happen, through no choice of their own, to be attracted to others of the same sex. But because we feel so strongly about the matter, we may find it hard to take this seriously. Even after we listen to the arguments, we may still have the unshakable feeling that homosexuals *must*, somehow, be an unsavory lot.

Cultural Relativism, by stressing that our moral views can reflect the prejudices of our society, provides an antidote for this kind of dogmatism. When he tells the story of the Greeks and Callatians, Herodotus adds:

> For if anyone, no matter who, were given the opportunity of choosing from amongst all the nations of the world the set of beliefs which he thought best, he would inevitably, after careful consideration of their relative merits, choose that of his own country. Everyone without exception believes his own native customs, and the religion he was brought up in, to be the best.

Realizing this can result in our having more open minds. We can come to understand that our feelings are not necessarily perceptions of the truth—they may be nothing more than the result of cultural conditioning. Thus when we hear it suggested that some element of our social code is *not* really the best and we find ourselves instinctively resisting the suggestion, we might stop and remember this. Then we may be more open to discovering the truth, whatever that might be.

We can understand the appeal of Cultural Relativism, then, even though the theory has serious shortcomings. It is an attractive theory because it is based on a genuine insight—that many of the practices and attitudes we think so natural are really only cultural products. Moreover, keeping this insight firmly in view is important if we want to avoid arrogance and have open minds.

These are important points, not to be taken lightly. But we can accept these points without going on to accept the whole theory.

STUDY QUESTIONS

1. Rachels says that infanticide among Eskimos does not necessarily signal a different attitude toward children from that which exists elsewhere. Why? Do you agree with him on this point?
2. Rachels says that the consequences of cultural relativism are so harmful that many thinkers have rejected it as a plausible theory. What are these consequences, according to Rachels?
3. Why, according to Rachels, do differences in customary behavior not always imply differences in moral beliefs?
4. What values do all societies have in common, according to Rachels? Do you agree with him?
5. What lessons do cultural relativists teach us, according to Rachels?

Seeing Elephants: The Myths of Phallotechnology

Jane Caputi

Ruth Benedict (author of a previous selection) and other cultural anthropologists have helped us appreciate the fact that there are powerful influences which condition us as we grow up to adopt the dominant beliefs, practices, and values in our society, and to view these, ethnocentrically, as "God-given," or "good," or "normal."

In the provocative article below, Jane Caputi, (1953–   ), who took her Ph.D. in American Culture from Bowling Green State University, whose *Age of Sex* won the Emily Toth Award in 1988, and who teaches in the Department of American Studies at the University of New Mexico, directs our attention to how we are conditioned to adopt and maintain values in a modern technological society. With the aid of slick techniques of mass communication, Caputi argues, government and business, including the film industry, conspire to ensure the preservation of patriarchy (male dominance), to glorify technology as a panacea, and to bifurcate human beings from nature (the "Elemental").

According to Caputi, too often mass communication means mass indoctrination or manipulation. This is sometimes accomplished

This article is reprinted from *Feminist Studies*, Volume 14, Number 3 (Fall 1988): 487-524, by permission of the publisher, *Feminist Studies*, Inc., 40 Women's Studies Program, University of Maryland, College Park, MD 20742.

"subliminally," so that we are not even aware of the "hidden messages" which we receive.

The principal, but not the exclusive victims of the high-tech propaganda machine, Caputi insists, are women. Although the law and popular moral codes may proclaim the coequality of men and women, they are reduced to empty, insignificant slogans in the wake of the constant visual and auditory reinforcement of images of women as inferior to men, as decorations or satisfiers of men's needs and desires.

As you read this extraordinary analysis by Professor Caputi, try to determine what she means by "really seeing the elephants." By entreating us to see the elephants, is she implicitly affirming that we can neutralize attempts to program our values?

On January 24, Apple computer will introduce Macintosh and you'll see why 1984 won't be like "1984."

TV ad for Apple Computer

1984: Orwell Was Wrong

Ad for the Olivetti M20 personal computer, *Newsweek*, 12 Dec. 1983.

[Winston's] mind slid away into the labyrinthine world of double-think. To know and not to know . . . to forget, whatever it was necessary to forget, then to draw it back into memory again at the moment when it was needed, and then promptly to forget it again, and above all, to apply the same process to the process itself—that was the ultimate subtlety. . . .

George Orwell, *1984*

During election week of 1984, a particularly memorable commercial was shown on a nightly network news broadcast.[1*] It wasn't an overtly political commercial. It wasn't, for example, the Reagan campaign's red-baiting "Bear in the Woods" spot.[2] Rather, this one was about elephants. Elephants in the city. Elephants on Wall Street, to be exact.

The ad opens with an establishing shot of Wall Street. Centered directly in our view is Federal Hall with its statue of George Washington standing midway up the entrance stairs. The scene is utterly deserted, desolate. There is a quick cut to an empty subway entrance; the wind is blowing and steam billows up from the underground system. An ominous drum resounds, soon accompanied by the ubiquitous male voice-over: "To help American business remember better/What American business *has* to remember/Help is on the way." During this exhortation, trumpeting animal cries merge with the drum, and the camera turns to introduce a herd of elephants now charging up Wall Street: "Introducing Elephant Premium Floppy Discs for business. They're designed to protect your data when other discs won't. Elephant Premium Floppy Discs. Because Elephant Never Forgets." The last shot places us back at Federal Hall. There, a heavily tusked beast gives one last triumphant cry in front of the statue of Washington and the ad is over.

If elephants don't forget, neither did I as images from the ad continued to replay in my mind. Indeed, the ad is all about *memory*. Fundamentally, it

* *Editors' note*: See pages 377–381 for footnotes.

is about organic/animal memory being captive to, contained, and perhaps even replaced by artificial/computer "memory"—a process ineffably expressed by the image of elephants in a city. Moreover, the ad is explicitly about *having* to remember; still, it wasn't until a few days after the first viewing that I realized how deeply this ad is also about *having* to forget.

On the morning after the elections, a friend told me a funny dream she'd had the night before, a dream in which little baby elephants were running all through her house, an image she immediately connected to the Republican presidential victory.[3] Only as I laughed did I connect her dream to my commercial, only then did I remember what I had been forgetting all along—that elephants are the well-known symbol of the Republican party—and only then did I realize that the ad I had seen had been an unannounced political message wrapped in the guise of the consumer product commercial. Recall the key words: *American, business, elephant, protect.* Link those to the presidential statue, Federal Hall, and the setting of Wall Street, and the message is not only blatant but, arguably, deliberately contrived.

Recalling the second image of the commercial—the stairway down to the subway system—we might also bear in mind this ad's entrance into our own underground or subliminal system. For the communication method here clearly involves what Wilson Bryan Key has termed "subliminal seduction,"[4] the implanting of hidden messages into ads, billboards, newspaper and magazine copy and images, movies, and so on. Such messages are engineered so that they will be perceptible only to the subconscious mind. Thus, they bypass the critical faculty of the conscious, and the viewer is left unaware of even having received a message or suggestion.

Although Key is expressly critical of such methods, others endorse them, although usually not naming them as subliminal manipulations. Adman Tony Schwartz, for example (the one who designed the daisy countdown to nuclear explosion for the 1964 Johnson presidential campaign), explains what he terms the "resonance principle."

> The critical task is to design our package of stimuli so that it resonates with information already stored within an individual and thereby induces the desired learning or behavioral effect. Resonance takes place when the stimuli put into our communication evoke *meaning* in a listener or viewer. That which we put into the communication has no meaning in itself. The meaning of our communication is what a listener or viewer *gets out* of his experience with the communicator's stimuli. The listener's or viewer's brain is an indispensable component of the total communication system. His life experiences, as well as his expectations of the stimuli he is receiving, interact with the communicator's output in determining the meaning of the communication. . . . In communicating at electronic speed, we no longer direct information into an audience, but try to evoke stored information out of them, in a patterned way.[5]

The elephant commercial works by subconsciously evoking the viewer's stored memories linking elephants, Republicans, and big business. It probably was somewhat effective in inducing the "desired learning or behavioral effect," that is, voting Republican, or, if you were already convinced, grafting your partisan enthusiasms to the product itself and causing you to favor Elephant Premium Floppy Discs.

Beyond these particulars, however, it is essential to realize that the ubiquity of subliminal messages creates an environment that in effect cracks the mind. In all subliminal ads there are deliberately constructed split-level meanings; as such, the viewer's mind must divide in order to receive them. Thus, even if one disagrees with the hidden message, disregards it, and remains behaviorally resolute, such methods continually condition us to fragment our perception, to remember and forget at the same time, to keep a secret, effectively, by hiding it from ourselves. Again, in the elephant "package," viewers are called upon to remember that elephant equals Republican but simultaneously to forget/repress/hide that fact for, as our expectations of the stimuli set us up to believe, this is *only* a commercial. George Orwell might recognize this structural mode of keeping secrets from oneself, of remembering and forgetting at the same time, as a form of doublethink. And, computer company pronouncements notwithstanding, George Orwell might be right.

Moreover, Schwartz's description of the viewer's brain and the communication process itself, with his key words of *design, stimuli, information, component, system, output, stored,* and *patterned,* is reminiscent of that other even deeper meaning of the elephant commercial—the replacement of organic memory by an artificial substitute. For Schwartz models the mind *after* the computer, not the other way around as we might reasonably expect. However absurd such technological metaphors for the organic might seem, metaphors such as these—along with the more common *breaking down, turning on, screwing,* and even *accessing* or *interfacing*—are actively altering modern consciousness. For metaphor not only extends meaning through a sometimes ridiculous, if evocative, comparison, but, as Philip Wheelright argues, can actually lead to "the creation of new meaning by juxtaposition and synthesis."[6] Thus, metaphor can work to *create* a similarity, adjusting consciousness to perceive and feel a previously unknown and unfelt connection. David Edge comments, "To use a metaphor is to overlap two images...our sense of both is subtly altered, by a sort of elision."[7] Under the influence of such metaphors, humans and machines slur/blur ever into one another, the humans becoming more cold, the machines acquiring soul.

Rather than merging with this vision, we can instead develop our own and even begin to "see elephants." Really *seeing* the elephants means seeing the ghosts that haunt mass communications, recognizing the apparitions beneath the bland and smiling surfaces. Seeing elephants means seeing through the doublethink and hearing beyond the doubletalk of mass communications. And finally, seeing elephants means, as in the old story of the blind men and the elephants, to no longer be blind through fragmentation to the total picture. It means, taking a concept from Mary Daly, to *re-member,*[8] to no longer accept the part as the whole, to perceive and act upon essential connections.

Of course, once you start to look around you find there are elephants everywhere. Here I will consider several of these, chosen particularly for the ways they involve remembering and forgetting, making connections, and the replacement of the organic with the artificial. These are, respectively, (1) the use of Charlie Chaplin's Little Tramp character to sell the IBM personal computer, (2) the irresistible application of the nickname "Star Wars" to the Reagan administration's Strategic Defense Initiative, (3) various instances of what Marshall McLuhan designated as "mechanical bride" imagery, and (4) the use of the bitten, artificial apple as the trademark for Apple Computer.

REMEMBERING AND FORGETTING

> Chiefly, we wanted something that people would remember. Using the Chaplin character was one way to create ads with stopping power. (P. David McGovern, ad director at IBM)

> The Tramp campaign has been so successful that it has created a new image for IBM. The firm has always been seen as efficient and reliable, but it has also been regarded as somewhat cold and aloof. The Tramp, with his ever present red rose, has given IBM a human face. (*Time,* 11 July 1983)

> Soldiers! Don't give yourselves to these brutes. . . . Don't give yourselves to these unnatural men—machine men with machine minds and machine hearts. (Charlie Chaplin, *The Great Dictator,* 1939)

Stuck with a multinational, cold, colossus, remote, and even a totalitarian "Big Brother" public image, IBM took the plunge and set out to manufacture some warmer and more sympathetic associations for itself and its "personal" computer. Investing a quick 36 million, it mounted one of the largest ad campaigns ever for a computer, producing ads calling the PC "a tool for modern times" and using Charlie Chaplin's internationally recognized and beloved character, the Little Tramp. These ads proved to be both extraordinarily memorable and successful, winning not only business gains but also acclaim and awards from the advertising world.[9]

The method of these spots, as with so many others, was to set up a metaphor—to link a particular product with some positive symbol or association already held by the viewers, to induce "resonance." Once again, literal absurdity is by no means a disqualifier for such metaphors. Consider cigarette advertising whereby cigarettes are said to be "only natural," to taste "like Springtime," or are consistently linked with fresh, outdoor, and highly physical activities. Such ads use nature the way the military uses camouflage. And although they may seem merely ridiculous, metaphors such as these further the pollution and destruction of both environments—the body and the ecosystem—by bridging our feelings about each with, of all things, a cigarette.

The absurdity of the smoking ads, however, is more than matched by the contradictions inherent in the IBM campaign. In these, the Little Tramp, "perhaps the most famous creation in any art medium of the 20th century,"[10] provides the positive associations, for Charlie the Tramp was a clown whose "appeal was virtually universal."[11] His very image came to immediately signify humanity, survival, innocence, the beauty of the commonplace, and, above all, the soul or spirit. James Agee has written that "the Tramp is as centrally representative of humanity, as many-sided and as mysterious as Hamlet, and it seems unlikely that any dancer or actor can ever have excelled him in eloquence, variety, or poignancy of motion."[12] Thus does IBM acquire a human face and graft a soul onto its new machine. The method is virtually indistinguishable from the way that Salem bonds itself to Springtime or Marlboro to the western landscape. All are highly *memorable* ads, ones with "stopping power."

But of course the IBM ads, like the elephant ad, are as much about forgetting as remembering for, although they evoke those positive memories of Charlie, they simultaneously arrest and reverse the recollection that Chaplin himself was expressly opposed to big business, mechanization, and those technological goals and/or gods of timekeeping, speed, and efficiency. Those views, evident throughout much of his work, are nowhere more clearly expressed than in the 1936 *Modern Times,* Chaplin's last film to feature the Tramp, a character he had then played for over twenty years. It was in *Modern Times,* as Parker Tyler has observed, that, "the Machine was the thoroughly identified enemy, the robber of art and poetry."[13] Now, however, in perfect accord with doublethink, the home computer is plugged as "a tool for modern times," and the image of the Tramp is made to perform as the thoroughly identified advocate, indeed *tool,* of the Machine—International Business Machines to be precise.

In *Modern Times,* Chaplin as the Tramp is a worker in some colossal factory, his job to tighten the nuts on some unidentifiable product as it comes down an assembly line. The line becomes a synchronized mechanical dance, and each time Charlie takes a break his shoulders and arms twitch in helpless repetition of the nut-tightening gesture. In one of the most celebrated scenes from the film, the Big Brother-like boss of the factory orders a speedup on the line and Charlie snaps. Jumping onto the assembly line, he plunges headfirst into the machine and is swallowed though finally disgorged by the gigantic gears. Emerging from the machine, he frolics and spins out his own outrageous ballet in response to the monotone of the line, spreading sheer chaos throughout the factory. The sequence closes with him being taken off to a mental hospital.

Thus, in Chaplin's own account, the Machine might swallow him, temporarily, but it could not digest him and had to spit him out. Now, however, IBM figuratively swallows him whole, thoroughly assimilates and converts him, effectively erasing his original message by producing a doppelgänger who now befriends and promotes the Machine and its order—and all accompanied by studied references to *Modern Times.*

For example, one of the print ads in this series features the Chaplin figure dashing madly by on a bicycle; his hat flies off and tie swings back to register the velocity. A computer is strapped to the back of his bike. The copy reads: "How to move with modern times and take your PC with you." A television spot portrays the Tramp straddling the intersection of two assembly lines in a bakery. He is placing decorated cakes from one line into boxes from the other. But the cakes don't match the boxes, the machinery starts going haywire, and chaos results. The scene then changes by means of a wipe taking the form of a hand sweeping round a clock's face, and next we see the Tramp seated in front of a personal computer. His problems, we know, will soon be techno-magically solved. And indeed, next he is back at the factory, but this time a baker has taken his place on the line. The Tramp is there only to put the decoration on a cake and present it to a purely decorative female. The moral of this thirty-second parable is clear. The Tramp, backed by the Machine, has *restored* Order; he is now the Owner, the Boss; he gets kissed by the Girl; the End.

These very specific and specifically reversed references to *Modern Times* indicate something of a willful effort to undercut the integrity of that film and indeed of Chaplin himself. Although the question was raised early in the campaign as to whether the Tramp and this film actually represented an "antitechnology sentiment," both IBM and the ad agency concluded, in the words of an IBM director, that the character actually "stands fear of technology on its head."[14] Of course, it is really the Chaplin character who is being stood on his head and shaken until the original content and message have been expunged, leaving only an empty if still appealing image to be infused with new meaning by IBM. Or, as O'Brien said to Winston in *1984*, "You will be hollow. We shall squeeze you empty, and then we shall fill you with ourselves."[15] The final punch or stopping power of these ads thus lies in their subtle suggestion that the dissident has been assimilated and converted. Just as Winston finally loves Big Brother, "Charlie" now loves the Machine.

Although the link between *Modern Times* and the IBM personal computer is a deceptive one, deliberately forged to induce a particular response, another metaphorical connection between a popular movie and a technology rings alarmingly true. I refer of course to *Star Wars* which, obviously, isn't *only* a movie anymore.

SEEING STARS

"What are the stars?" said O'Brien indifferently. "They are bits of fire a few kilometers away. We could reach them if we wanted to. Or we could blot them out." (George Orwell, *1984*)

Star Wars, directed by George Lucas and released in 1977, is one of the most phenomenally successful films in motion picture history. It has become a landmark of popular culture and has entered deeply into collective memory. When it was first released, most reviewers hailed the sheer entertainment value of the movie and stressed that it was utterly pure escapism, a science fiction

movie *without* a message, a fun, heroic, traditionally moral and optimistic fable
in the best U.S. tradition. Vincent Canby spoke for many when he not only
joined in the general applause but also further declared that the film "made
absolutely no meaningful comment on contemporary concerns such as nuclear war, overpopulation, depersonalization and sex."[16] Reversals abound
here, however, for *Star Wars* is deeply about all of these and more.

One of the film's initially striking aspects is that it is science fiction (conventionally the "future") set in the past; the action, we are told, takes place
"a long time ago in a galaxy far, far away." Thus evoking mythic time, *Star
Wars* serves as the perfect vehicle for implanting traditional patriarchal values
into the present and future. The movie gives us powerful old men, both good
and evil, and two young, blonde, male heroes. All the human beings in the
movie are white (although the embodiment of evil, Darth Vader, is encased in
all-black garb and his voice is that of a Black actor). There are machines as
slaves, robots with, as many critics delightedly pointed out, far more personality than their human counterparts. There are inferior and servile living species as well. Chewbacca the Wookie, one of the main characters, is an ani-
malistic "primitive" who lives apart from any of his people and wordlessly
plays the role of Tonto to Han Solo's space cowboy—a stereotyping as com-
municative of racism as that former formulaic duo. For female relief, we have
virtually *one* woman in the entire movie, a Princess in distress, the predictably
spunky token in a movie whose sexual composition resembles that of a gang
rape, a common media structure for subliminally communicating and con-
structing male dominance.[17] The idealized future/past of *Star Wars* is an all-
white, all-male world and, like the Westerns and war movies it is modeled on,
reserves its principal commitments for violence, male bonding, and war. Indeed, *Star Wars* takes war figuratively and literally to the heavens and gives
us not only a space combat but also a holy war, a just war, a war in which God
or "the Force" is ultimately on "our" side.

As Dan Rubey has noted, "If *Star Wars* is 'about' anything, it is about
power—and the source of ultimate power in the film is the Force."[18] He continues by accurately naming that power as inextricable from the *patriarchal*
power of fathers and sons. Moreover, the Force is identified throughout the
movie as an explicitly religious or sacred power and, as in other patriarchal
religious visions, is given dualistic form, having both a good and a bad (or
"dark") side. Nevertheless, both the "good" and the "bad" sides are really the
same, for they are bound together by their identical use for combat, death, and
destruction. Thus, despite the warrior-priest Obi Wan Kenobe's sanctimonious
drivel on the Force as an "energy field created by all living things that surrounds and penetrates us; it binds the galaxy together," this "life" force is, at
base, a death dealer.

Star Wars is indeed about *power,* and of principal concern is the possession of that power by the "good" group and their ability to channel that Force
into an energy which aids them in their righteous destruction of "evil." Translating from film symbol to social reality, the precise contemporary analog of

the Force is nuclear power, and *Star Wars*—Vincent Canby's pronouncements notwithstanding—is manifestly a film about *nuclear war*. Nowhere is this hidden message more evident than in the infectious nicknaming of the Strategic Defense Initiative (the proposed space-based missile defense system) as "Star Wars." That nickname was given to the SDI by its critics and then enthusiastically and irrevocably adopted by the mass media. Now nearly all but those professionally connected to the Reagan administration regularly use it. Obviously there are now *two* Star Wars and although one is a movie, a commercial fantasy, and the other a "historic" technological, political, and military event, the two phenomena, as the naming reveals, are generically linked, culturally twinned. To illustrate this, we might begin by hearing some sample testimony from each side, for the rhetoric surrounding each Star Wars phenomenon displays an astonishing similarity.

Episode 4: A New Hope (Subtitle of *Star Wars*[19]).

> I have reached a decision which offers a new hope for our children in the twenty-first century. (Ronald Reagan, "Star Wars" speech, 23 March 1983)

It is a period of civil war. Rebel spaceships, striking from a hidden base, have won their first victory against the Evil Galactic Empire (Introductory title from *Star Wars*).

> So in your discussions of the nuclear freeze proposals, I urge you to beware the temptation of pride—the temptation blithely to declare yourself above it all and label both sides equally at fault, to ignore the facts of history and the aggressive impulses of an evil empire, to simply call the arms race a giant misunderstanding and thereby remove yourself from the struggle between right and wrong, good and evil. (Ronald Reagan, 8 March 1983)

The message of *Star Wars* is religious: God isn't dead, He's there if you want him to be (Dale Pollock, *Skywalking: The Life and Films of George Lucas*, New York: Harmony Books, 1983, 139).

> Regrettably, our national debate over President Reagan's suggestion that the country develop a strategic defense against a Soviet nuclear attack is taking on a theological dimension. (Zbigniew Brzesinski, Robert Jastrow, and Max M. Kampelman, *New York Times Magazine*, 27 January 1985)

I thought: we all know what a terrible mess we have made of the world, we all know how wrong we were in Vietnam. We also know, as every movie in the last ten years points out, how terrible we are, how we have ruined the world and what schmucks we are and how rotten everything is. And I said, what we really need is something more positive (George Lucas, *Rolling Stone*, 15 August 1977).

> Although President Reagan's proposal was dubbed Star Wars so its opponents could ridicule it, remarkably enough, a considerable

proportion of the population took that designation in a most positive manner. (Edward Teller, *Popular Mechanics*, July 1984)

It [*Star Wars*] was a subtle suggestion that opening the door and going out there, no matter what the risk, is sometimes worth the effort (George Lucas, in *Skywalking*).

> My fellow Americans, tonight we are launching an effort which holds the promise of changing the course of human history. There will be risks, and results take time. But I believe we can do it. As we cross this threshold, I ask for your prayers and your support. Thank you, good night, and God bless you. (Ronald Reagan, "Star Wars" speech)

On 23 March 1983, Ronald Reagan, relying heavily on a rhetoric of *hope, defense, vision, peace, morality, promise, risk,* and the *future,* delivered what has subsequently registered in collective memory as his "Star Wars" speech. In it he called upon "the scientific community in our country... to give us the means of rendering... nuclear weapons impotent and obsolete."[20] This presidential speech "on a new defense" succeeded in launching the most massive weapons research project ever, known officially as the "Strategic Defense Initiative." That project involves the development of a hypothetical "third generation"[21] of nuclear weapons (in perfect harmony with the reigning doublethink, one scientist working on these arms passionately declares them to be "weapons of life"), as well as the construction of an equally hypothetical antimissile system in space, what Caspar Weinberger dispassionately promotes as an "impenetrable shield" (what we could think of as a diaphragm in space).[22]

Within a few days of the presidential exhortation, Democratic opposition charged that Reagan was concocting a "Star Wars' scenario" in order to incite fear of the Soviets. Considering not only the sci-fi aspects of the proposal itself, but also Reagan's characterization of the Soviet Union as an "evil empire," indeed the very "focus of evil in the modern world," that movie metaphor seemed completely appropriate. Still, the Democrats knew not what they had wrought. The "Star Wars" nickname proved both irresistible and irrevocable. And although Reagan and crew have intermittently expressed pique with the name-calling (after all, it does get *war* into the title instead of *defense*), on the whole they have nothing to worry about. Even Edward Teller (a principal instigator of the SDI) has affirmed that the linking of that project to one of the most mythic, popular, and all-American movies ever, one invariably described in terms of *vision, hope, optimism, positive messages, fun, morality,* and *universal themes,* a film that has become deeply embedded in our "shared media environment," can only serve to familiarize, popularize, and ultimately embed the project itself.[23]

Still, if the Democratic opposition to the SDI unwittingly stepped into the role of publicists for it, they were only giving utterance to an undeniable if largely subliminal connection; for there is far more than a superficial or fortuitous bond between *Star Wars* the symbolic fantasy and cinematic blockbuster and "Star Wars" the strategic vision and technomilitary extravaganza.

Indeed, just as the movie *Star Wars* is fundamentally about nuclear war, its counterpart, "Star Wars," is fundamentally a fantasy, a political symbol produced for the purpose of manipulating emotions, perceptions, and behaviors. As one analyst observed, "The MX missile, whatever its military usefulness may be, is often seen as a weapon whose importance is largely symbolic, more a tool for manipulating perceptions, than for fulfilling a real military need."[24] Manifestly, the SDI, like the MX, performs primarily as a symbol, a motivating myth, for it is not the actual deployment or even the (much disputed) feasibility of the projected space shield which is the true significance of the "Star Wars" project. Rather, its actual meaning is to set new economic, military, and technological priorities, to legitimate the channeling of vast sums of money into weapons research, to step up the arms race, to cut off any movement toward disarmament, and to revision the Soviet Union as a diabolical enemy and global evil, with the United States as the true champion of morality and the good.

The joint Star Wars phenomenon reveals not only the use of myth in politics but, equally, the mythic function of popular fictions and films. For gazing more deeply into *Star Wars,* we can see that film as itself a precursor of the SDI, the cultural herald of this giant step into both the space and nuclear ages, supremely entertaining propaganda and preparation for both war itself and its new theater—space.

THE JOY OF WAR

I loved the war. It was a big deal when I was growing up.
(George Lucas)

Star Wars is the first war movie of a new age of electronic combat, a
prediction of what war will feel like for combatants completely encased
in technology. (Dan Rubey)

As many critics have noted, popular culture has rallied mightily to the cause of restoring/reshaping collective memory of the U.S. war on Vietnam, forgetting it as a hateful U.S. aggression and remembering it as a "call to glory." And, although long before the 1985 movie *Rambo,* and not specifically about Vietnam, *Star Wars* should be reckoned as one of the first and most powerful media forces in the restoration of that glorious image of war: war as a testing ground and initiation rite for young men; an arena of heroism; a just struggle for the good; and war as just plain fun. Erasing the horror of Vietnam, Lucas painted us into a past which, as one critic noted, was actually "not so far away."[25] Rather, his principal imagery was taken from the popular storehouse of collective memories and images associated with a war Americans still felt good about—World War II—hence, the profusion of references to Nazi helmets and stormtroopers, dogfights and a romanticized air war, a nuclear explosion to end the action, and, astonishingly, a visual quote from Leni Riefenstahl's 1935 *Triumph of the Will* (Der Triumph des Willens), the key Nazi propaganda film and a precursor of both total Nazi domination of Germany and World War II. Curiously enough, in the last scene, Lucas has his heroes parading in the footsteps of Adolf Hitler, Heinrich Himmler, and Viktor Lutze in a visual reenactment of their movement to the Nüremberg memorial monument. Those few critics who actually noted some of the many fascist themes in the film itself—its "Nazi mixture of heroism, self-sacrifice and mysticism," its sanctification of violence, its paeons to individual and triumphant will, its sexism and racism—nevertheless tended to dismiss this reference as merely attributable to the former film student's good humor and boyish highjinks.[26] However, from the perspective of post-1983 and the now-proposed SDI, we might open our eyes and see this filmic quotation not only as a structural acknowledgment of the film's underlying fascism but also as an internal prediction of the key propaganda role that *Star Wars* would soon come to play in the projected militarization of space.

Although visually reminiscent of much of World War II, *Star Wars* is really about much more modern warfares—both the contemporary and the futuristic. Writing in *Jump Cut,* Dan Rubey argues that the electronic warfare of the film is the cinematic equivalent of the electronic battlefield that characterized the air war in Vietnam. Drawing upon the writings of Robert Jay Lifton, he points to the state of mind induced by such technologies, particularly the "numbing" of sensibilities induced by the technological reduction of the enemy to mere blips on a radar screen as well as a concomitant sensorial merging between pilot and machine: "The sensory equipment of the machines becomes an extension of the pilot's sensory equipment—a substitute for it—and along with it the pilots seem to take on the machine's lack of moral sensibility as well." He quotes one flyer who participated in the bombings on Laos: "You become part of the machine as you really do it.... The key is to be able to bomb without really thinking about it, automatically...instinctively." As Rubey notes, this statement is an apt description of Luke Skywalker's mystical consciousness during his final hazardous military mission—the attack on the Death Star space station. In this scene, he is part of a team of individual flyers who must travel up a long, narrow tunnel and try to shoot their missiles into a tiny hole, the "vulnerable spot," which will cause the gigantic, round Death Star to explode (this movie could also have been called "Sperm Wars"). After most of the flyers have died trying, Obi Wan Kenobe appears to Luke and exhorts him to turn off his computer and instead to rely upon the Force to guide his aim. Luke complies and in Rubey's words, "releases the missile instinctively, in a fantasy of bionic fusion with his ship made possible by the Force."[27]

Leaving this admittedly fantastic film for a moment, we might also start to consider what actual forces in contemporary myth and metaphor work to cement this identification of man with machine or, more accurately, man with weapon. Susan Sontag has spoken of the "predilection of the fascist leaders...for sexual metaphor,"[28] and such metaphors abound in the imageries of both *Star Wars* and "Star Wars." Recalling Reagan's oft-quoted vow to render nuclear weapons "impotent," we might wonder about this common conjunction of male sexuality and weaponry, as evident in slang, jokes, popular imagery, and erudite theory as it is in political persuasions. Thinking about that fusion is particularly critical in this era when manifestations of both the weaponry and male sexuality have paralleled each other in a continually accelerating lethality.

SPERM WARS: IN THE IMAGE AND LIKENESS OF MAN

> Sex is the weapon of life, the shooting sperm sent like an army of guerrillas to penetrate the egg's defenses—the only victory that really matters. (William Broyles, Jr., "Why Men Love War," *Esquire*, November 1984)

> As you drove into town when it was lit up, you could see that missile standing straight up in the air, and it just gave you—I don't know—a warm, strong feeling about how strong a man he was. ("Shorty" Kiefer, cited in David Chamberlain, "Missile Center—USA," *Harper's*, March 1985)

> It makes me mad—it's a masculine thing—competing with each other to see who's got the biggest bomb. (Girl interviewed by the American Psychiatric Association surveying children's nuclear awareness, quoted in Robert J. Lifton and Richard Falk's *Indefensible Weapons: The Political and Psychological Case against Nuclearism*)

A political cartoon by Lou Myers shows two military men dueling with extended penises, actually missiles, one marked "U.S.," the other "U.S.S.R."[29] *Public Illumination* magazine, a small artists' publication, serves up their version of nuclear safety: a drawing of an exploding mushroom cloud with a diaphragm attempting to contain it. "Better Safe than Sorry," they advise.[30] What these mock, however, is the subject of a 1984 ad for a Northrop Tigershark fighter plane's genuflection. This ad (appearing in the January 1984 *Atlantic*) features a black and white picture, not of the plane but of its "control stick." That stick, in huge close-up, dominates the page. The copy reads:

> Pilot and aircraft are one. He thinks; the plane responds. . . . Systems and human engineering . . . have coupled the pilot with the world's most advanced avionics through an anatomically designed control stick. All vital controls are strategically positioned on the stick and throttle. . . . The competitive edge is his.

What Chaplin was recoiling from in horror—the structural fusion between the mechanical and organic—Northrop is promoting as a source of joy, epitomized in its flaunted "joystick." Moreover, this picture exposes the mythic force which is being used to facilitate that fusion, for this is manifestly a sexual fantasy. The key image is that "anatomically designed" stick, lovingly fashioned in the image and likeness of man and thereby eliciting, or at least intending to elicit, a biological identification, a species bonding, loyalty and support.

Reagan made supreme use of this mythic force in his postgame remarks at Superbowl 1984. Speaking on split-screen television to Coach Flores of the Los Angeles Raiders, the president said, "I've already gotten a call from Moscow. They think Marcus Allen is a new secret weapon. They insist we dismantle it." Warming to his metaphors, the Great Communicator continued, stating that the game "had given me an idea about that team of yours. If you would turn them over to us, we'd put them in silos and we wouldn't have to build the MX missile."[31] Idealized virility is thus gleefully fused to weaponry and to an unprecedented and earth-destroying lethality.

In her exquisitely titled *Missile Envy: The Arms Race and Nuclear War*, Helen Caldicott writes:

> I recently watched a filmed launching of an MX missile. It rose slowly
> out of the ground, surrounded by smoke and flames and elongated into
> the air—it was indeed a very sexual sight, and when armed with the
> ten warheads it will explode with the most almighty orgasm. The
> names that the military uses are laden with psycho-sexual overtones:
> missile erector, thrust-to-weight ratio, soft lay down, deep penetration,
> hard line and soft line.[32]

And "Star Wars," although confounded by the doublethink of *defense*, proudly carries on this tradition of missile envy. No longer content to merely measure, the explicit vow is now to *unman* the enemy—a fate, however, which is intended only for the non-U.S. missiles. For however much "Star Wars" proponents want to emasculate their rivals, they desire only to bone up the home team. About 10 percent of the SDI's budget is explicitly for nuclear weapons, what the *New York Times* coyly refers to as the "dark side."[33] Such research includes items such as advanced "penetration aids" to help the obviously still potent U.S. missiles reach their targets, as well as high-speed projectiles and the futuristic laser and particle beams. As laser expert John D.G. Rather, also a strong advocate of "Star Wars," wrote in a 1982 article, any country that was the sole possessor of space lasers would thus possess "the longest 'big stick' in history."[34] This obsession with lengths, measurements, and comparisons of "sticks" points to one further supreme reversal: it is not *women* who have penis envy.[35]

There is one further connection I would like to make here. For this common bond between male sexuality, force, and destruction (as obvious in the words *fuck* and *screw* and the institution of rape as in the MX missile) clearly provides a touchstone for the identification of patriarchal ideologies, paradigms, and practices.[36] Hence, the patriarchal state's nuclear age began with a "fathered" bomb nicknamed "Little Boy" and dropped on a city chosen because it provided a "virgin" target. It has subsequently been marked by the development of ever more mature and destructive phallic devices. But at the same time, another form of that bond between sex and violence structures a parallel patriarchal age, an age I have elsewhere called "The Age of Sex Crime."[37] By this I mean the modern phenomenon of the random, serial sexual murder (men killing predominantly women) which has been on the rise throughout this century, now reaching "epidemic" proportions.[38]

Just as the nuclear age had a profoundly mythic initiating event—the Trinity explosion in the New Mexico desert in July 1945—the Age of Sex Crime was first blasted into being in London 1888, with the essentially unprecedented crimes of Jack the Ripper.[39] That still-anonymous killer actually invented modern sex crime; we might think of him as its "father." These murders provided a mythic paradigm for subsequent killers such as the "Boston Strangler," "Jack the Stripper," the "Hillside Strangler," the "Son of Sam," the "Yorkshire Ripper," and the "Green River Killer," to name only a few of the most sensationalized.

Jack the Ripper did not rape his victims; he first slit their throats and then mutilated their sex organs. Like their original model, the modern sex killers frequently do not actually rape their victims. Instead of using their penis as a weapon, they use a fetishized weapon as their penis: knives, guns, machine tools, clubs, and so forth. This breed of sex killer, so known today, was in 1888 an unprecedented anomaly, at first incomprehensible to his culture. Sex, weaponry, and mutilation were not yet interchangeable in the public consciousness. However, by 1891, Richard von Krafft-Ebing was able to articulate the soon-to-be common consciousness: "He does not seem to have had sexual intercourse with his victims but very likely the murderous act and subsequent mutilation of the corpse were equivalents for the sexual act."[40] Within a few years, Sigmund Freud would lay down his theory of sexual symbolism, explicitly equating the penis with deadly force. He wrote that the male organ first finds symbolic equivalents in things which "resemble it in shape" and, second, in things which resemble it in function, "in objects which share with the thing they represent the characteristic of penetrating into the body and injuring—thus sharp *weapons* of every kind, *knives, daggers, spears, sabres*, but also fire-arms, *rifles, pistols,* and *revolvers.*"[41] Consider the consequences to female life now that that list has expanded to include nuclear weaponry. Consider as well the parallel consequences to *planetary* life now that cultural perceptions of male sexuality and weaponry have been metaphorically bridged by the likes of the MX missile. Listening carefully, we might realize that whenever Reagan or anyone else sexualizes/fetishizes his weaponry, he is actually pronouncing himself the political equivalent of Jack the Ripper.

Thus far, I have concentrated largely on the implicit aggression and destructiveness of "Star Wars." Yet what of this much vaunted *defense*, this "impenetrable shield," this diaphragm in space which will purportedly cover and protect us from the enemy emissions? Like Princess Leia in the otherwise all-male world of *Star Wars*, like Athena sprung from the head of Zeus, or like the Virgin Mary beside the men's association of the Christian trinity, the space shield seems to provide some traditional feminine symbolism—covering, protection, impregnability—to what is otherwise a flagrantly all-male venture. Yet, although those other females—the Space Princess, Warrior Goddess, or Queen of Heaven—are indubitably token women, they also still manage to evoke some memories of archaic female power.[42] The feminized space shield, however, moves beyond this level and into a more total realm of control, for it speaks without any memory and only to a future annihilation and replacement of female power and presence. The symbolic meaning of the feminized space shield resides precisely in what McLuhan was moving toward understanding when he identified the contemporary symbol cluster of the "mechanical bride."

MECHANICAL BRIDES...OR, WHY A SPACE SHIELD IS LIKE A BEAUTIFUL WOMAN

WHY IS A BEAUTIFUL WOMAN LIKE A NUCLEAR POWER PLANT? In order to remain beautiful she must take good care of herself....She schedules her rest regularly....When she is not feeling well she sees her doctor...she never lets herself get out of shape....She is as trim now as she was ten years ago....In other words, *she is a perfect example of preventative maintenance.* (Ad for the Crouse group of companies, *Nuclear News Buyer's Guide,* mid-February 1976)

It was McLuhan, in his 1951 book, *The Mechanical Bride: Folklore of Industrial Man,* who first pointed to what he found to be "one of the most peculiar features of our world—the interfusion of sex and technology...a widely occurring cluster image of sex, technology, and death which constitutes the mystery of the mechanical bride."[43] At the heart of this mystery, according to McLuhan, rests the pervasive sexualization (that is, feminization) of technology—engines, cars, "bodies by Fisher," even an atomic bomb nicknamed "Gilda" after Rita Hayworth—and the corresponding mechanization of the female body into a set of fragmented, fetishized, and replaceable parts—the legs, breasts, buttocks forming what is basically a plastic mechanism, a hot number, sex object, sex bomb, living doll, love machine.

Since 1951, the patterns that McLuhan pinpointed have only grown and prospered. In ads, fashion and pornography, on television, in popular novels, films, and songs, the mechanical bride is everywhere. To cite only a few of the more telling examples for his first category—the technological container of feminine symbolism—I would begin by pointing to those most explicit of mechanical come-ons, the car ads. One ad for a 1964 Pontiac told its viewers that "any car that is this responsive, obedient, and satisfying to drive simply has no right to be this good looking." More recently, an ad for Volvo urges: "Fall in love in 6.8 seconds flat," and one for Nissan informs us: "The headlights wink; the engine growls; the styling flirts." Recall as well National Airlines sensational 1971 "Fly Me" campaign in which a woman and an airplane are posited as equals. A 1980s' ad for Technics portable stereo shows its product surrounded by curling smoke and attended by a black cat; the copy reads: "Technology Made Seductive."

The second of McLuhan's categories—the fragmentation/mechanization

of the images of women—continues full force. One of McLuhan's original illustrations is an ad for nylon stockings depicting the frankly disembodied "legs
on a pedestal." Of course, this symbolic dismemberment has always been
normative in pornography. Still, it is illuminating to realize how common the
pornographic composition is in mainstream imagery. For example, a 1979 ad
for "Tame" hair conditioner routinely chops up a female body in order to ask:
"Is there a part of you that's overconditioned?" A 1981 ad for Almay eye shadow
simply presents a V-shaped design of disembodied, although colorful, female
eyes. Another, a 1980 ad for Yves Saint Laurent stockings, shows a pair of
high-heeled legs, cut off at the waist and waving in the air.

Moreover, the woman need not be thus dismembered but can simply be
presented as a mechanical doll, a perfect plastic copy (a mode superbly par-
odied by Ira Levin in his novel, *The Stepford Wives*).[44] Consider, for example,
a 1982 ad for Fuji audiocassettes. Against a grid of lines superimposed upon
black space, a shiny, faceless mechanical woman is curled up in the fetal position. The copy reads: "Imagination has just become reality." And, indeed,
it is partially through such contemporary creation myths, through the perva-
sion of such symbols and visualizations, that a new technological reality is
being summoned into being.

Another line from that same ad offers further testimony on the meaning
of the mechanical bride: "Audiocassettes of such remarkable accuracy and clarity that differences between original and recording virtually vanish." Similarly, Memorex audio and video tapes swear that their products will leave us
forever wondering: "Is it live, or is it Memorex?" while an ad for Gould Elec-
tronics, a company which proclaims that it is "leading the way in nuclear power
plant simulations," avers in a 1983 ad: "AT GOULD SIMULATION IS REALITY." Yet
when life becomes so indistinguishable from its imitations, it is due not so
much to the accuracy of the copy as to a willingness to forsake the original, as
well as a fundamental alteration and atrophy of sense perceptions themselves.[45]

An identical message, and an identical use of mechanical bride symbolism, is eerily echoed in fashion photography. A late 1970s' ad for Christian
Dior sunglasses displays six "female" heads grouped in a clocklike circle. One,
at the very bottom, seems conclusively real; four of the others are mannequins, clear fakes. Yet another at mid-left is questionable. Consider as well the
fashion/pornography of such celebrated photographers as Helmut Newton and
Guy Bourdin. Newton, for one, has made a specialty of using nudity, pros-
thetic props, and scenes of sexual slavery and ritual murder in his renowned
fashion photography. Moreover, he regularly mixes wax mannequins in with
his female models and shoots them as if they too were actual women. An
introduction to one of his books meticulously explains that approach:

> But above all, here is a man who loves women so passionately, so
> completely, that he has to carry this love to its ultimate conclusion.
> Look, he says, in a brace, a plaster cast, even in an artificial limb, she
> remains beautiful and desirable. And since models and mannequins are
> objects, to be manipulated at will, why not attempt the final

> manipulation, the mingling of real life and wax models? Do we really
> know the difference—not only here, but also in real life?[46]

Such abject objectification is but the extreme version of the normative objectification of women which structures phallic image production, most mark-
edly in pornography and fashion. Moreover, as this passage indicates, the
mechanical bride is as much an icon for the Age of Sex Crime as it is for the
Age of Mechanical Reproduction. Indeed, such a final manipulator as serial
sex killer Ted Bundy (who referred to his victims as *dolls, puppets, symbols,* and
images) also refused to distinguish between life and its imitations. After his
capture, Bundy frankly pointed to the mass objectification of women as both
inducement to and clear justification for mass murder.[47]

And the nuclear age itself gives just as ardent an embrace to the mechanical bride. In early 1984, the *New York Times* reported on a group of dedicated young scientists hard at work on "Star Wars" research at the Lawrence
Livermore Laboratory, young men striving to invent that "third generation"
of nuclear weapons.

> Behind fences topped with barbed wire and doors equipped with
> combination locks, dozens of young physicists and engineers at the
> Lawrence Livermore National Laboratory work late into the night, six
> and seven days a week, on classified projects aimed at creating the next
> generation of nuclear weapons.
>
> Their dream, they say, is to end the nuclear arms race.

That perfected doublethink is more than matched by many other such reversals throughout the article. For example, meet Mr. West, a physicist who is
questioned about the morality involved in working on "weapons of death."
He replies: "I don't think I fall into this category of working on weapons of
death.... We're working on weapons of life, ones that will save people from
weapons of death." That feat of inversion accomplished, we move on to learn
that "here the average scientist is in his 20s and few, if any, wear wedding
rings. No women are present except for secretaries. The kitchen has a microwave oven, a hot plate, a refrigerator, and a mountain of empty Coke bottles."[48]

Here, surrounded by culinary evocations of the mechanical bride (but no
actual women to disturb their security), these young priests swallow Coke,
dream of their weapons, and tinker with world destruction. Their desires are
for potency; they want to father that third generation of nuclear weapons.
They happily follow the fathers before them: J. Robert Oppenheimer (named
"Father of the Year" in 1945 by the American Baby Association for his "Little
Boy"), the five fathers of plutonium,[49] Edward Teller ("Father of the Hydrogen Bomb"), and, of course, Dr. Victor Frankenstein. It can still give one pause
to realize how prophetic, how hauntingly accurate Mary Shelley was when
she conceived the exemplary monster of technological myth to be a purely
fathered (from dead flesh) and utterly unmothered creation.

Here we can also receive intense intuitions on McLuhan's "mystery" of
the mechanical bride. For this symbol is also a metaphor, one that links tech-

nology to creation via an artificial woman/wife/mother. As such, it cannot help but expose the enmity that technological man declares not only for living flesh and blood creation—nature, motherhood, the womb[50]—but also for female *reality*. It further signals the longed-for replacement of the elemental world by an indistinguishable artificial substitute, brought forth from that faked female, the controlled womb/tomb of the mechanical bride. And assuredly this is "stale male mating,"[51] for the mechanical bride is absolutely empty of any genuine femaleness, as false a female as "Mother Church" or "Ma Bell." Rather, it is a technological Tootsie, veritably a transsexed image of themselves and their technology for whom these young priests lust. It is "she" to whom they are truly wed, "she" with whom they couple to produce their inventions/sons/ monsters. And, increasingly, the consummation of that union presages the destruction of the elemental earth and the final ensconcement in a totally artificial and dead environment—again, something like the parable of the Stepford husbands who preferred to murder their wives and bury themselves into beautiful, acquiescent, man-made, and lifeless mechanical brides and, concomitantly, something like the ritual action of the sex killer who attacks and destroys the womb, the place of original generation.[52] Finally, an inescapable meaning of the mechanical bride is that—like the Lawrence Livermore Lab, like the idealized world of *Star Wars*, like the world of Sex Crime, and like the Stepford world the phallotechnic fathers are wishing us into—in the deepest meaning of the word, no women are *present*.

The "Star Wars" fantasy of Reagan is a variant on the mechanical bride motif in that it too is "technology made seductive"—not only by its implicit vision of potent, charging missiles but also by its subtle evocation of a companion feminine stereotype. The rhetoric surrounding the hypothetical space shield is strangely suggestive of a sort of Princess Leia-like space virgin, one who is untouchable, immaculate, impenetrable, impregnable, and, above all, moral.[53] "Star Wars" further evokes the mechanical bride in that it envisions a final technological container or envelope for the earth. This is the ultimate extension of the mall or bubble mentality—the consummate controlled environment, the planet as Astrodome, the world in a plastic bag, the earth itself contained by the artificial womb of the mechanical bride, the "Future Eve"[54] finally ensconced in an artificial paradise.

EATING APPLES

At Apple we only have one rule. Rules are made to be broken....When you set out to change the rules, you wind up changing the world. (Ad for Apple Computer, *Newsweek*, November/December 1984)

She's *changed*, Walter! She doesn't talk the same, doesn't *think* the same—and I'm not going to wait around for it to happen to me. (Joanna, in *The Stepford Wives*)

> We do not merely destroy our enemies; we change them. (O'Brien, in *1984*)

> To her who asks the nature of her crime they answer that it was identical with that of the woman of whom it was written that she saw that the tree of the garden was good to eat, tempting to see, and that it was the tree requisite for gaining understanding.... The women say with an oath, it was by a trick that he expelled you from the earthly paradise. (Monique Wittig, *Les Guérillères*)

Let's go back once more to the time of the 1984 elections. To commemorate what it termed an "avalanche," *Newsweek* put out a special edition (November/December 1984) with only one sponsor—Apple Computer. Moreover, all the ads formed a continuum, telling the story of the new Macintosh personal computer. It is here that Apple announces that it intends to change the world. Of course, what we might immediately realize is that one of the ways it plans to accomplish this is through technological myth-making, essentially (as evidenced by their logo—the artificial apple with the bite taken out) by altering the central creation myth of Judeo-Christian culture.

Clearly, that myth in its biblical version has functioned to make the world exactly what it is today. Thinkers such as Elizabeth Cady Stanton, Karen Horney, Kate Millett, Mary Daly, and many others[55] have long pointed to the absurdities and misogyny of the Adam and Eve story: its negation and scapegoating of Eve; the ludicrous reversal of Eve's birth from Adam; the further reversal of blame and/or shame affixed to Eve's daring move toward knowledge, despite the deceptive injunctions of the gardener; and the myth's carte blanche legitimation of man's total domination over nature.

Yet within this myth still linger stray memories of the earthly paradise, the Wilderness/Eden,[56] the living food, the snake and the tree, and the daring originality of the woman. And that original apple signified not only knowledge, but also a knowledge rooted in the earth. It signified a vital wisdom quite literally from the trees, something Mary Daly writes of in *Pure Lust* as an "Elemental" knowing or philosophy, "a form of philosophical being/thinking that emerges together with metapatriarchal consciousness—consciousness that is in harmony with the Wild in nature and in the Self.... It is the force of reason rooted in instinct, intuition and passion... rooted in love for the earth and for things that are naturally on earth.[57] The original apple signifies as well the Elemental world *as* Paradise—the earthly paradise.

Apple Computer, however, neatly erases and reverses all of this. The symbol of knowledge disappears and is replaced by a plastic dummy—something like a Stepford wife. Now, the apple represents artificial intelligence, and perhaps we will become what we eat as surely as we become what we behold. Moreover, what the Apple logo promotes and promises is an artificial paradise, indeed the artificial *as* paradise.

Laurie Anderson sings, "It's a sky blue sky; the satellites are out tonight."[58] We now not only have satellite stars, mechanical brides, and plastic apples, but also nuclear power *plants* and *breeders, generations* of weapons, *smart* and *baby* bombs, electronic *bugs,* computer *memory,* mushroom *clouds,* space *pods,* missile *skin,* radar *eyes,* Ford *Mustangs,* black and acid *rains,* nuclear *winter*—all sorts of dummy replacements for the Elemental world. Moreover, all such "changes" are contingent upon the destruction, in memory and in fact, of the original sources, as well as our final inability to distinguish life from its replacements/imitations/limitations.

This destructive opposition to a nature metaphorically bonded to women is marked throughout much of the patriarchal tradition.[59] Daly specifically traces this theme throughout Western Christianity. She demonstrates a distinctive Christian warfare against the "elemental spirits of the universe," citing Paul's demands that we not only "die to" such spirits but that we set our "mind on things that are above, not on things that are on the earth." Consider as well this Peter passage: "But the day of the Lord will come like a thief, and then the heavens will pass away with a loud noise, and the elements will be dissolved with fire, and the earth and the works that are upon it will be burned up." Daly quotes this biblical Ripper and then comments that "as self-fulfilling prophecy and manifesto of necrophilic faith, this 'inspired' text is one among many that have paved the way for modern technological war against the elements, which takes such forms as nuclearism and chemical contamination."[60] Clearly the Apple update, that technological version of Genesis, is not so much a fundamental alteration of the original myth, as a logical progression of the Christian credo, for it too implies and encourages the destruction of the "Elemental."

And indeed, that message is found everywhere today. In film, song, story, advertising, politics, language, and technique, from science fiction to fundamentalist religion,[61] a complex of patriarchal symbolisms and practices propagate the diminishment, replacement, and destruction of the earth. In the summer of 1984, for example, two very telling ads appeared in the business section of the *New York Times.* The first (25 June) was for Saudia Airlines. A split-screen composition was used. On the left hung an image of the earth, the globe as if seen from space; it was captioned: "The Problem." On the right are pictured four long jet planes, made to seem as if they are larger than the planet itself and aiming directly at the earth. This was captioned: "And how we got round it." On the very next day, *Science* magazine took out an ad to promote its upcoming fifth anniversary issue, one to be devoted to "20 DISCOVERIES THAT SHAPED THE 20TH CENTURY." To impress that upon their viewers, they visualized two gigantic male hands grasping, shaping, crushing, and dwarfing a puny, malleable, pathetic, and vulnerable earth. Other recent ads resound the message. To cite only a few, one 1984 ad for Perrier water shows a giant bottle triumphantly bursting out of the top of a now-dwarfed and violated planet. Another 1984 ad for Cobra phone answering machines depicts that machine floating over the surface of a planet which is no longer even composed of land and water but, instead, of Cobra phone answering machines. A 1984 ad for a *Newsweek* publication chops the globe in half, announcing that it is "ON TOP DOWN UNDER." Finally, a 1984 ad for Rockwell International (a major contractor for both the MX missile and the B-1 bomber) headlines itself with the deformed word "man•ij" in boldface, assuring viewers that Rockwell is "not out to change the world. Just to supply the technology to make it better." To illustrate this "man•ijed" planet, the earth is depicted as if it were a projection on a computer screen. The top half of the sphere is sectioned into four pieces; the bottom disappears into the omnipresent abstract grid. Bolts penetrate the planet at both axes as well as through the middle.

Such visualizations of the earth closely parallel many of the depictions of women as artificial and/or fragmented "mechanical brides," indicating here the presence of McLuhan's mysterious modern cluster of "sex, technology, and death." Further clues to that mystery can be found in two other nonadvertising images. The first illustrates an article in the *Nation* (25 February 1984). It shows a grinning Henry Kissinger raping a woman whose head is the planet earth. The second image is once again from that crucial election month of November 1984. It is the cover of the *Atlantic* and refers to an inside article on nuclear winter. The illustration depicts a man (we see only his military arms labeled "U.S.") holding a glowing, irradiated earth in his hands. Moreover, the shrunken planet is now serving as the dot underneath a hovering question mark of black smoke; once again *he* has the whole world in his hands, once again the planet is diminutive to the man. And just as a woman on her back with legs spread-eagled is the characteristic icon of female defeat in the Age of Sex Crime,[62] these images of the raped—the shrunken, violated, manipulated, and replicated earth—are the characteristic icons in a pornography of the nuclear age. And like that other age, the nuclear age presages the escalation of the paradigmatic rape of the "Mother" into a final act of sexual murder; for such images are meant not only to sell a particular product or illustrate a particular concept, but also to reflect, sell, and embed a world view in which these products and conceptions attain a reality. Both Annette Kolodny and Carolyn Merchant have demonstrated the historical role of female metaphors for the earth and nature in influencing, constraining, legitimating, and even mandating certain behaviors.[63] Such visualizations of a planet traditionally understood as "Mother Earth" not only legitimates male domination and violation of women but also enacts and anticipates the domination/destruction of the earth and symbolically urges the actualization of that "ultimate" reality.

With this pattern in mind, let's return briefly to the movie *Star Wars*. Throughout most of that movie, the only colors we see are black and white, gold and silver; this is a mechanical world. Moreover, we are usually out in space somewhere. Our longest time on a planet is the bleak, desert world from which Luke happily escapes. But for one significant moment we do glimpse a resonant shimmer of blue and green. It is when Darth Vader and his crew are trying to wrest information from Princess Leia. They show us her home planet of Alderaan on their space screen. "Tell us what you know, or we'll blow it up," they threaten. She pretends to comply, hoping to save her planet, but they blow it up anyway just so that they can demonstrate the destructive power of their "Death Star." Viewers of this most viewed of films then see a very graphic depiction of what a planet like the earth would look like being annihilated by a beam weapon. I suggest that, on some level, most viewers get the message that Alderaan equals earth. It looks just like the earth and frankly it is the only thing in the movie that does; moreover, it is linked with the only woman in the movie. Here we arrive precisely at the deep conjunction between *Star Wars,* the movie, and "Star Wars," the technomilitary extravaganza. The shared naming is completely logical for each visualizes/portends the complete destruction of the earth.

And the ramifications of that "fantasy" go far beyond the movies. Consider the front page of the *Boston Globe* for Christmas Eve of 1984. Two stories at the top of the page command our attention. The first, on the left, is about the Ethiopian famine. There is a photograph of a mother and her infant son grotesquely posed to look like the Christian Madonna and child. The headline reads: "Amid famine and war, hope and faith survive." If those key words sound familiar, our expectations are soon met for when we turn to the immediate right there is a story about "Star Wars." Its headline reads: "Weinberger: No Give on 'Star Wars'" and beneath that a quote from the man himself: "It's the one thing that offers any real hope to the world and we will not give that up."

Both stories are part of *one* continuing story.[64] One part is about the earth, the Mother, real food, Africa—the cradle of human life, the "primitive," the "past," the expendable. The other is about space, the Father, the Final Frontier, technology, the "future." No matter how many public tears are shed or publicity trips are taken by politicians, Africa and its people are in the phallotechnic scheme of things completely, perhaps even necessarily, expendable. Not only do the white heavenly fathers pour 3 billion dollars per year into death star research while those people starve, but that genocide in Africa is spurred not only by racism and neocolonialism, but also by the time-honored patriarchal war against the Elemental. For Caspar Weinberger, like Paul his brother before him, has set his mind "on things that are above, not on things that are on the earth."

Weinberger possesses hope; Reagan has a vision; computers are full of memory. But what of our own? If we see the world only through news, films, commercials, and the rhetorical reversals of bad actors and politicians, we see ourselves and the world objectified, mechanized, destroyed, and replaced. Must we then believe what we see? Do we become what we behold? Do we accept being mirrored in and by elephants caged in the city, clowns replaced by puppets, shooting death stars, mechanical brides, artificial apples, and raped and shrunken earths? Siegfried Kracauer has written that "the deep feelings of uneasiness *Triumph of the Will* arouses in unbiased minds originates in the fact that before our eyes palpable life becomes an apparition."[65] That very same intent and strategy inform every piece of propaganda discussed here. Moreover, under the influence of such systematic lying, we are expected to forget and forego originality and/or reality, finally accepting the apparitions as the inevitable or preferred replacements for the palpable life.

In 1952, Rachel Carson drew a connection between the increasing artificialization of the environment and what she perceived to be an increasing destructiveness in "mankind."

> I myself am convinced that there has never been a greater need than there is today for the reporter and interpreter of the natural world. Mankind has...sought to insulate himself, in his cities of steel and concrete, from the realities of earth and water and the growing seed. Intoxicated with a sense of his own power, he seems to be going farther and farther into more experiments for the destruction of himself and his world.

> There is certainly no single remedy for this condition and I am offering no panacea. But it seems reasonable to believe—and I do believe—that the more clearly we can focus our attention on the wonders and reality of the universe about us the less taste we shall have for the destruction of our race.[66]

By "seeing elephants," then, I suggest that we are really doing two things. First, we can see through the unrealities, the deceptions. For example, we can realize that the rose-colored vision of "Star Wars" which Ronald Reagan so sincerely asks us to share with him is actually a lethal hallucination, that the apple in the computer is a man-made dummy, promoting knowledge that, if not wholly artificial, remains ontologically incomplete. Second, we can move on to focus our attention, to remember and see the elephants as well as the stars, apples, and the earth itself, not as possessed symbolic projections, but in their wonder, in their Elemental and continuing originality, in their *reality*.

NOTES

1 "ABC World News Tonight," with Peter Jennings, ABC, 5 Nov. 1984.
2 This political spot was fairly obvious in its play upon anti-Soviet sentiments. An Indian (!) was shown in the woods. The voice-over spoke of the danger of the "bear" (i.e., Russia) in the woods and that although some scoffed, saying that "the bear" didn't even exist, it was best to be prepared.
3 Conversation with Trisha Franzen, 6 Nov. 1984.
4 Wilson Bryan Key, *Subliminal Seduction* (Englewood Cliffs, N.J.: Prentice-Hall, 1973). See also Wilson Bryan Key, *The Clam-Plate Orgy* (Englewood Cliffs, N.J.: Prentice-Hall, 1980).
5 Tony Schwartz, *The Responsive Chord* (New York: Anchor Books, 1973), 24–25.
6 Philip Wheelwright, *Metaphor and Reality* (Bloomington: Indiana University Press, 1962), 72.
7 D.O. Edge, "Technological Metaphor," in *Meaning and Control*, ed. D.O. Edge and J.N. Wolfe (London: Tavistock, 1973), 31–59.
8 Mary Daly, *Gyn/Ecology: The Metaethics of Radical Feminism* (Boston: Beacon Press, 1978), 23.

9 Kathy Root, "Kudos for a Tramp and a Motor Mouth," *Nation's Business,* April 1984, 44–45; "Softening a Starchy Image," *Time,* 11 July 1983, 54.

10 R.A.E. Pickard, *Dictionary of 1,000 Best Films* (New York: Association Press, 1971), 296.

11 Louis Giannetti, *Masters of the American Cinema* (Englewood Cliffs, N.J.: Prentice-Hall, 1981), 83.

12 James Agee, "Comedy's Greatest Era," in *Film Theory and Criticism,* 2d ed., edited by Gerald Mast and Marshall Cohen (New York: Oxford University Press, 1979), 535–58.

13 Parker Tyler, *Chaplin: Last of the Clowns* (New York: Horizon Press, 1972), 158.

14 "Softening a Starchy Image," 54.

15 George Orwell, *1984* (New York: New American Library, Signet Classic, 1961), 211. Originally published in 1949.

16 Vincent Canby, "Not since 'Flash Gordon Conquers the Universe' . . . ," *New York Times,* 5 June 1977, sec. 2, p. 15, col. 1.

17 George Gerbner and Gaye Tuchman term this technique "symbolic annihilation" and mean it to include the tactics of both derogatory stereotyping and deliberate absences. See George Gerbner, "Violence in Television Drama: Trends and Symbolic Functions," in *Media Content and Control,* ed. G.A. Comstock and E.A. Rubinstein (Washington, D.C.: GPO, 1972), 28–187; and Gaye Tuchman, "The Symbolic Annihilation of Women by the Mass Media," in *Hearth and Home: Images of Women in the Mass Media,* ed. Gaye Tuchman, A.K. Daniels, and James Benet (New York: Oxford University Press, 1978), 3–38.

18 Dan Rubey, "*Star Wars:* Not So Far Away," *Jump Cut* 18 (August 1978): 9–14.

19 Although it was the first in the series, *Star Wars* is actually episode four of a projected nine-part series, three of which have already been completed.

20 This speech is transcribed in the *New York Times,* 24 Mar. 1983, sec. 1, p. 20, col. 1.

21 "Third-generation" nuclear technology is different from "first generation" (the atom bomb) and "second generation" (the hydrogen bomb) in that it posits devices such as X-ray lasers, directed microwave weapons, and others still undisclosed. These weapons will have a small nuclear bomb at their core; the explosive energy, it is posited, can be channeled into tight beams of radiation that can then be directed at targets. See William J. Broad, "The Young Physicists: Atoms and Patriotism amid the Coke Bottles," *New York Times,* 31 Jan. 1984, p. 17, col. 2.

22 An ad for Planned Parenthood (full page, *New York Times,* 23 Oct. 1984), shows a diaphragm flying through space; the copy reads: "When it comes to birth control, our technology isn't exactly space age." Did the national debate over the "impenetrable shield" in space, however subtly, influence the format of this ad?

23 Somewhat later, President Reagan himself came around to acknowledging the positive propaganda value of the "Star Wars" nickname. Doublespeaking to the National Space Club, he reminded his listeners: "The Strategic Defense Initiative has been labeled 'Star Wars,' but it isn't about war, it's about peace. It isn't about retaliation, it's about prevention. It isn't about fear, it's about hope . . . and in that struggle, if you will pardon my stealing a film line, the force is with us." See *Albuquerque Tribune,* 30 Mar. 1985, p. 1, col. 4.

24 Daniel Goleman, "Political Forces Come under New Scrutiny of Psychology" *New York Times,* 2 Apr. 1985, p. 17, col. 1.

25 Rubey, 9.

26 See Arthur Lubow, "A Space 'Illiad': The STAR WARS War: I," *Film Comment*, 13 (July-August 1977), 20–21. Lubow is most explicit in observing some of the fascist themes but then largely dismisses them.

27 Rubey, 10.

28 Susan Sontag, "Fascinating Fascism," in *Under the Sign of Saturn* (New York: Vintage Books, 1980), 73–105.

29 Steven Heller, *War Heads: Cartoonists Draw the Line* (New York: Penguin Books, 1983), 66.

30 *Public Illumination*, 21 June 1982, 14. The artist is Mimi Smith.

31 Quoted in Bob Bach, Letter, *New York Times*, 2 Feb. 1984, sec. A, p. 18, col. 5.

32 Helen Caldicott, *Missile Envy: The Arms Race and Nuclear War* (New York: Morrow, 1984), 297.

33 Philip M. Boffey, "Dark Side of 'Star Wars': System Could Also Attack," *New York Times*, 7 Mar. 1985, 1.

34 John D. Rather, quoted in Boffey.

35 For a new definition of penis envy see Mary Daly in Cahoots with Jane Caputi, *Websters' First New Intergalactic Wickedary of the English Language* (Boston: Beacon Press, 1987), 215–16.

36 A number of feminist theorists have made this point. These include Kate Millett, *Sexual Politics* (Garden City, N.Y.: Doubleday, 1970), 44; Andrea Dworkin, esp. *Pornography: Men Possessing Women* (New York: Perigee, 1981), 129–98; Catharine A. MacKinnon, "Feminist, Marxism, Method, and the State: Toward Feminist Jurisprudence," *Signs* 8 (Summer 1983): 635–58.

37 See Jane Caputi, *The Age of Sex Crime* (Bowling Green, Ohio: Bowling Green University Popular Press, 1987).

38 See Robert Lindsey, "Officials Cite Rise in Killers Who Roam U.S. for Victims," *New York Times*, 21 Jan. 1984, sec. A, p. 1, col. 5. See also "The Random Killers," *Newsweek*, 26 Nov. 1984, 100-6D.

39 This point is made by Colin Wilson in his introduction to *The Complete Jack the Ripper*, by Donald Rumbelow (Boston: New York Graphic Society, 1975), vii. The assertion that the Ripper's crimes were unprecedented and at first incomprehensible can be substantiated by a review of newspaper reporting at that time. See Caputi 4–6, 10-2. Although assuredly there were prior isolated instances in which men murdered and mutilated women, the crimes of the Ripper—the single, territorial serial killer who victimized a socially stigmatized class of women in a ritual manner—transformed cultural consciousness, entered into cultural mythology, and provided an initiating myth for future emulation. For additional commentary on the mythic role of Jack the Ripper, see Judith R. Walkowitz, "Jack the Ripper and the Myth of Male Violence," *Feminist Studies* 8 (Fall 1982): 543–74.

40 Richard von Kraft-Ebing, *Psychopathia Sexualis*, trans. from the twelfth German edition and with an introduction by Franklin S. Klaf (New York: Stein and Day, 1965), 58–59.

41 Sigmund Freud, "Dreams," *The Standard Edition of the Complete Psychological Works of Sigmund Freud*, vol. 15 (London: Hogarth, 1953), 154.

42 See Mary Daly's analysis of patriarchal archetypes as well as her discussion of the "Arch-Image" (the controlled, Christian Madonna symbol) as contrasted with the "Arch-image" (the "Original Witch within") in *Pure Lust: Elemental Feminist Philosophy* (Boston: Beacon Press, 1984), 78–121.

43 Marshall McLuhan, *The Mechanical Bride: Folklore of Industrial Man* (Boston: Beacon Press, 1951, 98, 101.

44 Ira Levin, *The Stepford Wives* (New York: Random, 1972); see also the 1974 film directed by Bryan Forbes. This is a parable of an upper-middle-class suburban "Men's Association" whose members, with the help of high technology and skills learned at Disneyland, bond to kill their wives and replace them with beautiful, eminently screwable, and very clean robot wives.

45 For analysis of this, see Walter Benjamin, "The Work of Art in the Age of Mechanical Reproduction," in *Illuminations*, ed. Hannah Arendt, trans. Harry Zohn (New York: Schocken, 1969), 217–51.

46 Edward Behr, introduction to *Sleepless Nights* by Helmut Newton (New York: Congreve, 1978), n. p.

47 See Stephen G. Michaud and Hugh Aynesworth, *The Only Living Witness* (New York: Simon & Schuster, 1983), 130.

48 Broad, 17.

49 The most prominent of these is Glenn Seaborg.

50 For an analysis of technological attempts to both control and replace biological motherhood, see Gena Corea, *The Mother Machine: Reproductive Technologies from Artificial Insemination to Artificial Wombs* (New York: Harper & Row, 1985).

51 See Daly, *Gyn/Ecology*, 63.

52 Jack the Ripper not only mutilated female genitals and wombs, but he also took the womb from the body of one of his victims, Annie Chapman.

53 For example, Paul C. Warnke stated, "It's ["Star Wars"] all things to all people. . . . To Defense Secretary Weinberger, it is a technological stepping-stone from missile defense to the President's larger conception of *immaculate* defense. . . . To . . . the President, it is *untouchable*" (quoted in Leslie H. Gelb, "Vision of Space Defense Posing New Challenges," *New York Times*, 3 Mar. 1985, sec. 1, p. 1, col. 1).

54 *The Future Eve* is an 1887 French novel by Villiers de l'Isle Adam in which a rejected lover asks the inventor Thomas Edison to construct a perfect mechanical replica of his lost love. Edison complies. This novel is discussed in Edmund Bergler, *Fashion and the Unconscious* (New York: Robert Brunner, 1953), 271–72.

55 Elizabeth Cady Stanton, Letter to the Editor, *The Critic* (1896), cited in *Up from the Pedestal: Selected Writings in the History of American Feminism*, ed. Aileen S. Kraditor (Chicago:Quadrangle Books, 1968), 119; Karen Horney, "The Distrust between the Sexes," in *Feminine Psychology*, ed. Harold Kelman (New York: Norton, 1967), 107–18; Millett, *Sexual Politics*, 52–54; Mary Daly, *Beyond God the Father: Toward a Philosophy of Women's Liberation* (Boston: Beacon Press, 1973), 44–68.

56 See Alice Walker's poem, "Without Commercials," in *Horses Make a Landscape Look More Beautiful* (New York: Harcourt Brace Jovanovich, 1984), 55–58.

57 Daly, *Pure Lust*, 7–8.

58 Laurie Anderson, "Let X Λ X," *Big Science*, Warner Brothers, BSK 3674, 1981.

59 See Susan Griffin, *Woman and Nature: The Roaring inside Her* (New York: Harper & Row, 1978); Annette Kolodny, *The Lay of the Land: Metaphor As Experience and History in American Letters* (Chapel Hill: University of North Carolina Press, 1975); Carolyn Merchant, *The Death of Nature: Women, Ecology, and the Scientific Revolution* (San Francisco: Harper & Row, 1980).

60 Daly, *Pure Lust*, 10.

61 See Arthur Clarke's classic science fiction novel, *Childhood's End* (New York:

Ballantine, 1953); and Hal Lindsey with C.C. Carlson, *The Late Great Planet Earth* (Toronto:Bantam, 1970). Lindsey was named by the *New York Times* as the best-selling author of the 1970s.

62 The original "spread eagle"—the figure of an eagle with wings and legs spread—is the emblem on the Great Seal of the United States. *Webster's Unabridged Dictionary* (1986) reports that as a verb, *spread eagle* means "defeat completely."

63 Kolodny; Merchant.

64 A basic principle of media analysis is that media content is organized according to *flow*, that is, the arrangement of stories and commercials on television and in other media for comprehensive comment and counterpoint—meant to achieve a unified experience. For a discussion of flow in television content see Raymond Williams, *Television: Technology and Cultural Form* (Glasgow: Fontana/Collins, 1974), 78–118.

65 Siegfried Kracauer, *From Caligari to Hitler: A Psychological History of the German Film* (Princeton: Princeton University Press, 1947), 303.

66 Carol B. Gartner, *Rachel Carson* (New York: Frederick Ungar, 1983), 124–25.

STUDY QUESTIONS

1. How, according to Caputi, did the Reagan administration seek to capitalize on the movie *Star Wars?* Is this movie, as Caputi claims, one which implants "traditional patriarchal values"?

2. Who was Charlie Chaplin? Why does Caputi take issue with IBM's use of the Little Tramp, a character created by Chaplin?

3. Caputi indicts modern technology for divorcing human beings from nature. What does she mean by this? What evidence does she cite to support this claim?

4. Caputi alleges that images used in advertising legitimate domination of women by men. Do you agree with her? Why?

5. Traditional interpretations of the Bible story of Adam and Eve contribute to misogyny, according to Caputi. What does this mean? Do you agree with her on this point? Why?

6. Caputi says that modern advertising seeks to manipulate us by winning our loyalty to a product by associating that product with a person or animal or thing which we love or value. Is she correct on this point? Can you cite instances from your own experience where this has been attempted?

10

The Search for Objectivity: Classical Ethical Theories

PROBLEM INTRODUCTION

Most of us, in our everyday lives, believe that there is something called *moral truth*. That is, we act as though there is a genuine difference between good and evil, right and wrong. We attempt to assess the direction of our lives and to guide ourselves by ideals which appear to us to be much more than sentiment, social convention, or mere whim. We do not regard morality as something we just come up with on the spur of the moment, but instead we actively strive to overcome our passions, prejudices, and narrow social or economic contexts in order to see the world as it really is. In other words, we regard morality as rooted in the nature of things, part and parcel of the world, as discoverable as the other facts of nature. Can we find a standpoint from which to justify this attitude?

The first giant step in the search for objectivity was taken by the Greek philosophers Plato and Aristotle. Plato saw clearly that morality must be severed from religion and made into an independent intellectual enterprise. This means that God is not enough to justify objectivity. Even if the moral law is a divine commandment, God must be able to provide good reasons for God's law. Without this, the divine will is simply irrational whim. But if morality is rooted in the nature of things, then it should be accessible to the inquiring mind, whether that mind be divine or human. The importance of this step cannot be stressed enough, for it eliminates forever the comfortable stupor of intellectual and moral dependency. Fact, rather than power, has become the source of moral authority.

But what facts are important? To Aristotle, the answer to this question was clear: an objective morality must be founded on the facts of human nature. A simple example can demonstrate what led Aristotle to this conclusion. In general, we have no difficulty evaluating many common objects and events. We can tell a good shoe from a bad shoe, a good chess player from a bad one, or a good mathematician from a bad one. How do we make such value judgments? First, we ask for the definition of the thing in question. This tells us what it is, what features of the object set it apart from other things. The definition of a shoe, for example, specifies that it is an object having a certain function. This gives us a criterion of excellence. A good shoe is one which functions as it is the nature of shoes to function. In general, a thing is good when it functions as its definition specifies. So it is for baseballs, mathematicians, houses, hands, legs, eyes, and other objects. Indeed, so it is for human beings. People, like other objects, have a definite nature which sets them off from the rest of creation. The good life for human beings, then, is one in which this essential nature is most completely manifested. Aristotle's ethics is the ethics of self-realization. The Greek poet Pindar expressed it in the credo: "Become what you are."

What are we then? What is our essential nature? Aristotle was struck by the fact that human beings are equipped by nature to pursue intellectual activities. We are rational animals. Therefore, the good life, the life of happiness, must consist in rational activity. If we were gods, without physical needs, we would be happy in pure contemplation. But since we are animals, other needs must be satisfied as well. These needs can be met in rational or irrational ways. Moral virtue, then, is the state of character which leads to intelligent and rational choices in our pursuit of happiness. In our practical affairs the rational path usually lies between two irrational extremes. Bravery, for example, is a virtue which lies between the extremes of cowardice and rashness. Aristotle is careful to point out that the rational choice is always relative to the person and the circumstances. A skilled warrior may exhibit bravery in a certain course of action, whereas an untried soldier would be foolish to do the same thing. Therefore, moral virtue cannot be set down in a rigidly defined code of behavior.

This point is extremely important. The search for objectivity cannot result in a list of moral recipes for every situation. An example from geometry can show why. Proving a theorem in geometry is a rational affair if anything is. It involves seeing connections between definitions, axioms, and other theorems. Yet even in this formal, logical activity, there is no set of rules which will tell the student how to construct proofs for any problem. Basic principles must be mastered, and after some practice, it is assumed that intelligence will show the way to a solution. Similarly, in scientific activity there are no rules which one can study and then use to construct good, fruitful experiments for every problem. Yet experimental design, like proving a theorem, is a highly rational procedure. Intelligent people, through experience and practice, learn to prove theorems, design experiments, and choose wisely. This is what Aristotle calls "practical wisdom."

Aristotle's theory represents a revolution in thought. It brings morality down from the heavens and places it squarely in the lap of humanity. It emphasizes that the source of value is within our own nature. Human nature is not intrinsically corrupt—it is intrinsically good. Furthermore, we possess the power to become happy and virtuous. Virtue is not a gift, a sign of the gods' favor. It is the result of training, of the application of intelligence to living. The total effect of Aristotle's thought is to ennoble humanity and to increase personal responsibility.

Within the basic framework set down by Aristotle, there is a great deal of room for alternative theories. The eighteenth-century philosopher Immanuel Kant believed, as did Aristotle, that the key to moral objectivity lay in the rationality of humans. But unlike Aristotle, Kant rejected the idea that happiness was intrinsically good. There are some persons who do not *deserve* to be happy. A world of happy Hitlers is not the best of all possible worlds. Kant argues that the only thing that is intrinsically good is a *good will*. In other words, the virtuous person is one who has certain *motives*, regardless of whether those motives lead to his or her own happiness. What, then, is a good reason for moral action? According to Kant, the only reason which makes an act praiseworthy is that it was done out of a regard for duty. The truly moral agent acts out of the recognition that the moral law demands it—and for no other reason. The moral law must be universal and apply to everyone alike. Given this condition, it must have a certain form. It must command us to behave in ways which we recognize to be legitimate for everyone. Such a law, Kant maintains, rules out selfishness and sometimes our own happiness.

Kant's moral theory is called a *rationalistic theory of value* because he believes that reason alone, through the investigation of our moral concepts, can discover what we ought to do. But empirically minded philosophers of the nineteenth century wished to bring ethics into the realm of science, and so returned to the Aristotelian assumption that morality must be founded on an empirical study of human nature. The nineteenth century was a period of great social reform. In England, France, and the United States, the pursuit of happiness became the rallying cry of change. John Stuart Mill, an English philosopher and social reformer, the most famous exponent of the doctrine of utilitarianism, stated that all policies of the individual and government must be aimed at increasing the general happiness of humanity. The most important undertaking in Mill's theory is his proof of utilitarianism. In a manner similar to Aristotle, Mill argues that the only proof of something's value is whether people value it. Happiness is good, he says, because people desire it. Most philosophers have strongly disagreed with this sort of "proof." In addition, Mill's theory requires that individuals sometimes sacrifice their own happiness for the general happiness. But how can this be justified? After all, it is not obvious that everyone does, in fact, desire the general happiness.

The emphasis on human nature can lead in many directions, depending upon one's theory of human nature. Aristotle, Kant, and Mill, for example, take a rather charitable view of humanity. In general, they depict people as basically rational, other-regarding, sincere, and capable of overcoming impulses which are contrary to these traits. Yet one of the most popular moral theories does not accept this picture of human psychology. Ethical egoism is the view that people ought to be concerned with their own interests first and always, even if this means neglecting the interests of others. This ethical doctrine is based on a harsh conception of humanity. People are basically selfish and egoistic. They are moved by desires such as self-preservation, self-esteem, or love of power; and these desires are so elemental that they cannot be eliminated. Self-realization, according to this scheme of things, demands that each person satisfy himself or herself to the greatest extent possible. If we must treat others with kindness and charity, it can only be because there is some payoff in it for us. Any other reason requires us to go against our nature. In our readings Jesse Kalin defends this conception of morality against common criticisms.

In the end, the objective standpoint may be incapable of proof, in the usual sense of that word. After all, how do you prove to people that something is red? If they look at it, they see it. If they do not see it, either they have misunderstood the instructions or they are color-blind. Morality may be the same way. Many philosophers have been intuitionists, believing that the ultimate test for the morality of an action is moral vision—an immediate intuition of the rightness or wrongness of the act. However, it should be pointed out that this does not eliminate the role of reason. We must still know what the facts are, because our moral insights are based on what we believe to be the real representation of the moral situation. Once reason has reported all the facts, however, we just "see" whether the act is right or wrong, or whether the consequences of it are good or evil. The final selection by William Gass represents a kind of intuitionist position.

The world has always been brutalized by people who claim to be bearers of the "true" morality. But dogmatism is not more likely under the objective standpoint than under any other. In fact, to the extent that the objective standpoint depends upon the use of reason to discover moral truth, it should discourage dogmatism. If we take science as our model, then we can regard our moral theories as hypotheses. They are capable of revision, of expansion and change as new experience reveals unforeseen circumstances. This does not mean that we cannot be guided by our beliefs with fervor and intensity. It does mean, however, that we should strive to keep open the means by which our own ideals can be disproved in case we are wrong.

Virtue and Rationality
Aristotle

Aristotle (384 B.C.–322 B.C.) studied at Plato's Academy. He is surely one of
the greatest philosophers of all time. His work in biology and physics stood
as the principal theories until the scientific revolution in the seventeenth
century. Even Darwin admitted that Aristotle was the greatest biologist to
have ever lived. This empirical temper stands in marked contrast to the
rationalistic emphasis of his teacher, Plato. After Plato's death, Aristotle
traveled and was largely engaged in marine biology. In 342 B.C., he became
the tutor of Alexander the Great, and in 336, he returned to Athens, where
he established his own school, the Lyceum. With the death of Alexander in
323, Aristotle became involved in the political upheaval which followed. The
Athenians trumped up charges of impiety against him, and recalling the fate
of Socrates, he fled Athens so that the city would not "offend twice against
philosophy."

Aristotle believed that the good was happiness. But happiness can be
defined only after the fundamental facts of human nature have been
uncovered. The entire structure of human psychology reveals that humans
are animals who are directed in their activities by rational principles. Rational
activity, therefore, is the highest good according to Aristotle. But living
requires action, and virtue is a state of character which produces rational
action. Aristotle does not attempt to lay down rules for everyone to obey,
since what is rational will depend to some extent upon the context. Still, this
is not subjectivism since happiness is an objective and universal goal.

1

Every art and every inquiry, and similarly every action and pursuit, is thought
to aim at some good; and for this reason the good has rightly been declared
to be that at which all things aim. But a certain difference is found among
ends; some are activities, others are products apart from the activities that
produce them. Where there are ends apart from the actions, it is the nature of
the products to be better than the activities. Now, as there are many actions,
arts, and sciences, their ends also are many; the end of the medical art is health,
that of shipbuilding a vessel, that of strategy victory, that of economics wealth.
But where such arts fall under a single capacity—as bridle-making and the
other arts concerned with the equipment of horses fall under the art of riding,
and this and every military action under strategy, in the same way other arts
fall under yet others—in all of these the ends of the master arts are to be preferred to all the subordinate ends; for it is for the sake of the former that the
latter are pursued. It makes no difference whether the activities themselves

From *Nichomachean Ethics,* translated by W. D. Ross, in *The Oxford Translation of Aristotle,* edited
by W.D. Ross, Volume 9, 1925. Reprinted by permission of Oxford University Press.

life, but its discussions start from these and are about these; and, further, since he tends to follow his passions, his study will be vain and unprofitable, because the end aimed at is not knowledge but action. And it makes no difference whether he is young in years or youthful in character; the defect does not depend on time, but on his living, and pursuing each successive object, as passion directs. For to such persons, as to the incontinent, knowledge brings no profit; but to those who desire and act in accordance with a rational principle knowledge about such matters will be of great benefit.

Let us resume our inquiry and state, in view of the fact that all knowledge and every pursuit aims at some good, what it is that we say political science aims at and what is the highest of all goods achievable by action. Verbally there is very general agreement; for both the general run of men and people of superior refinement say that it is happiness, and identify living well and doing well with being happy; but with regard to what happiness is they differ, and the many do not give the same account as the wise. For the former think it is some plain and obvious thing, like pleasure, wealth, or honor; they differ, however, from one another—and often even the same man identifies it with different things, with health when he is ill, with wealth when he is poor; but, conscious of their ignorance, they admire those who proclaim some great ideal that is above their comprehension. Now some[1] thought that apart from these many goods there is another which is self-subsistent and causes the goodness of all these as well. To examine all the opinions that have been held were perhaps somewhat fruitless; enough to examine those that are most prevalent or that seem to be arguable. . . .

To judge from the lives that men lead, most men, and men of the most vulgar type, seem (not without some ground) to identify the good, or happiness, with pleasure; which is the reason why they love the life of enjoyment. For there are, we may say, three prominent types of life—that just mentioned, the political, and thirdly the contemplative life. Now the mass of mankind are evidently quite slavish in their tastes, preferring a life suitable to beasts, but they get some ground for their view from the fact that many of those in high places share the tastes of Sardanapalus. A consideration of the prominent types of life shows that people of superior refinement and of active disposition identify happiness with honor; for this is, roughly speaking, the end of the political life. But it seems too superficial to be what we are looking for, since it is thought to depend on those who bestow honor rather than on him who receives it, but the good we divine to be something proper to a man and not easily taken from him. Further, men seem to pursue honor in order that they may be assured of their goodness; at least it is by men of practical wisdom that they seek to be honored, and among those who know them, and on the ground of their virtue; clearly, then, according to them, at any rate, virtue is better. And perhaps one might even suppose this to be, rather than honor, the end of the political life. But even this appears somewhat incomplete; for possession of

---

[1] The Platonic School.

are the ends of the actions, or something else apart from the activities, a the case of the sciences just mentioned.

If, then, there is some end of the things we do, which we desire for own sake (everything else being desired for the sake of this), and if we do n choose everything for the sake of something else (for at that rate the proces would go on to infinity, so that our desire would be empty and vain), clearly this must be the good and the chief good. Will not the knowledge of it, then, have a great influence on life? Shall we not, like archers who have a mark to aim at, be more likely to hit upon what is right? If so, we must try, in outline at least to determine what it is, and of which of the sciences or capacities it is the object. It would seem to belong to the most authoritative art and that which is most truly the master art. And politics appears to be of this nature; for it is this that ordains which of the sciences should be studied in a state, and which each class of citizens should learn and up to what point they should learn them; and we see even the most highly esteemed of capacities to fall under this, e.g., strategy, economics, rhetoric; now, since politics uses the rest of the sciences, and since, again, it legislates as to what we are to do and what we are to abstain from, the end of this science must include those of the others, so that this end must be the good for man. For even if the end is the same for a single man and for a state, that of the state seems at all events something greater and more complete whether to attain or to preserve; though it is worthwhile to attain the end merely for one man, it is finer and more godlike to attain it for a nation or for city-states. These, then, are the ends at which our inquiry aims, since it is political science, in one sense of that term.

Our discussion will be adequate if it has as much clearness as the subject matter admits of, for precision is not to be sought for alike in all discussions, any more than in all the products of the crafts. Now fine and just actions, which political science investigates, admit of much variety and fluctuation of opinion, so that they may be thought to exist only by convention, and not by nature. And goods also give rise to a similar fluctuation because they bring harm to many people; for before now men have been undone by reason of their wealth, and others by reason of their courage. We must be content, then, in speaking of such subjects and with such premises to indicate the truth roughly and in outline, and in speaking about things which are only for the most part true and with premises of the same kind to reach conclusions that are no better. In the same spirit, therefore, should each type of statement be *received*; for it is the mark of an educated man to look for precision in each class of things just so far as the nature of the subject admits; it is evidently equally foolish to accept probable reasoning from a mathematician and to demand from a rhetorician scientific proofs.

Now each man judges well the things he knows, and of these he is a good judge. And so the man who has been educated in a subject is a good judge of that subject, and the man who has received an all-round education is a good judge in general. Hence a young man is not a proper hearer of lectures on political science; for he is inexperienced in the actions that occur in

virtue seems actually compatible with being asleep, or with lifelong inactivity, and further, with the greatest sufferings and misfortunes; but a man who was living so no one would call happy, unless he were maintaining a thesis at all costs. But enough of this; for the subject has been sufficiently treated even in the current discussions. Third comes the contemplative life, which we shall consider later.

The life of moneymaking is one undertaken under compulsion, and wealth is evidently not the good we are seeking; for it is merely useful and for the sake of something else. And so one might rather take the aforenamed objects to be ends; for they are loved for themselves. But it is evident that not even these are ends; yet many arguments have been thrown away in support of them. Let us leave this subject, then. . . .

Let us again return to the good we are seeking, and ask what it can be. It seems different in different actions and arts; it is different in medicine, in strategy, and in the other arts likewise. What then is the good of each? Surely that for whose sake everything else is done. In medicine this is health, in strategy victory, in architecture a house, in any other sphere something else, and in every action and pursuit the end; for it is for the sake of this that all men do whatever else they do. Therefore, if there is an end for all that we do, this will be the good achievable by action, and if there are more than one, these will be the goods achievable by action.

So the argument has by a different course reached the same point; but we must try to state this even more clearly. Since there are evidently more than one end, and we choose some of these (e.g., wealth, flutes, and, in general, instruments) for the sake of something else, clearly not all ends are final ends; but the chief good is evidently something final. Therefore, if there is only one final end, this will be what we are seeking, and if there are more than one, the most final of these will be what we are seeking. Now we call that which is in itself worthy of pursuit more final than that which is worthy of pursuit for the sake of something else, and that which is never desirable for the sake of something else more final than the things that are desirable both in themselves and for the sake of that other thing, and therefore we call final without qualification that which is always desirable in itself and never for the sake of something else.

Now such a thing as happiness, above all else, is held to be; for this we choose always for itself and never for the sake of something else, but honor, pleasure, reason, and every virtue we choose indeed for themselves (for if nothing resulted from them we should still choose each of them), but we choose them also for the sake of happiness, judging that by means of them we shall be happy. Happiness, in the other hand, no one chooses for the sake of these, nor, in general, for anything other than itself.

From the point of view of self-sufficiency the same result seems to follow; for the final good is thought to be self-sufficient. Now by self-sufficient we do not mean that which is sufficient for a man by himself, for one who lives a solitary life, but also for parents, children, wife, and in general for his friends and fellow citizens, since man is born for citizenship. But some limit must be set to this; for if we extend our requirement to ancestors and descendants and friends' friends we are in for an infinite series. Let us examine this question, however, on another occasion; the self-sufficient we now define as that which when isolated makes life desirable and lacking in nothing; and such we think happiness to be; and further we think it most desirable of all things, without being counted as one good thing among others—if it were so counted it would clearly be made more desirable by the addition of even the least of goods; for that which is added becomes an excess of goods, and of goods the greater is always more desirable. Happiness, then, is something final and self-sufficient, and is the end of action.

Presumably, however, to say that happiness is the chief good seems a platitude, and a clearer account of what it is is still desired. This might perhaps be given, if we could first ascertain the function of man. For just as for a flute-player, a sculptor, or any artist, and, in general, for all things that have a function or activity, the good and the "well" is thought to reside in the function, so would it seem to be for man, if he has a function. Have the carpenter, then, and the tanner certain functions or activities, and has man none? Is he born without a function? Or as eye, hand, foot, and in general each of the parts evidently has a function, may one lay it down that man similarly has a function apart from all these? What then can this be? Life seems to be common even to plants, but we are seeking what is peculiar to man. Let us exclude, therefore, the life of nutrition and growth. Next there would be a life of perception, but it also seems to be common even to the horse, the ox, and every animal. There remains, then, an active life of the element that has a rational principle; of this, one part has such a principle in the sense of being obedient to one, the other in the sense of possessing one and exercising thought. And, as "life of the rational element" also has two meanings, we must state that life in the sense of activity is what we mean; for this seems to be the more proper sense of the term. Now if the function of man is an activity of soul which follows or implies a rational principle, and if we say "a so-and-so" and "a good so-and-so" have a function which is the same in kind, e.g., a lyre player and a good lyre player, and so without qualification in all cases, eminence in respect of goodness being added to the name of the function (for the function of a lyre player is to play the lyre, and that of a good lyre player is to do so well): if this is the case, [and we state the function of man to be a certain kind of life, and this to be an activity or actions of the soul implying a rational principle, and the function of a good man to be the good and noble performance of these, and if any action is well performed when it is performed in accordance with the appropriate excellence: if this is the case,] human good turns out to be activity of soul in accordance with virtue, and if there are more than one virtue, in accordance with the best and most complete.

But we must add "in a complete life." For one swallow does not make a summer, nor does one day; and so too one day, or a short time, does not make a man blessed and happy....

Yet evidently, as we said, it [happiness] needs the external goods as well; for it is impossible, or not easy, to do noble acts without the proper equipment. In many actions we use friends and riches and political power as instruments; and there are some things the lack of which takes the luster from happiness, as good birth, goodly children, beauty; for the man who is very ugly in appearance or ill-born or solitary and childless is not very likely to be happy, and perhaps a man would be still less likely if he had thoroughly bad children or friends or had lost good children or friends by death. As we said then, happiness seems to need this sort of prosperity in addition; for which reason some identify happiness with good fortune, though others identify it with virtue. . . .

2

Virtue, then, being of two kinds, intellectual and moral, intellectual virtue in the main owes both its birth and its growth to teaching (for which reason it requires experience and time), while moral virtue comes about as a result of habit, whence also its name *ethike* is one that is formed by a slight variation from the word *ethos* (habit). From this it is also plain that none of the moral virtues arises in us by nature; for nothing that exists by nature can form a habit contrary to its nature. For instance the stone which by nature moves downwards cannot be habituated to move upwards, not even if one tries to train it by throwing it up ten thousand times; nor can fire be habituated to move downwards, nor can anything else that by nature behaves in one way be trained to behave in another. Neither by nature, then, nor contrary to nature do the virtues arise in us; rather we are adapted by nature to receive them, and are made perfect by habit.

Again, of all the things that come to us by nature we first acquire the potentiality and later exhibit the activity (this is plain in the case of the senses; for it was not by often seeing or often hearing that we got these senses, but on the contrary we had them before we used them, and did not come to have them by using them); but the virtues we get by first exercising them, as also happens in the case of the arts as well. For the things we have to learn before we can do them, we learn by doing them, e.g., men become builders by building and lyre players by playing the lyre, so too we become just by doing just acts, temperate by doing temperate acts, brave by doing brave acts.

This is confirmed by what happens in states; for legislators make the citizens good by forming habits in them, and this is the wish of every legislator, and those who do not effect it miss their mark, and it is in this that a good constitution differs from a bad one.

Again, it is from the same causes and by the same means that every virtue is both produced and destroyed, and similarly every art; for it is from playing the lyre that both good and bad lyre players are produced. And the corresponding statement is true of builders and of all the rest; men will be good or bad builders as a result of building well or badly. For if this were not so, there would have been no need of a teacher, but all men would have been born good or bad at their craft. This, then, is the case with the virtues also; by doing the acts that we do in our transactions with other men we become just or unjust, and by doing the acts that we do in the presence of danger, and being habituated to feel fear or confidence, we become brave or cowardly. The same is true of appetites and feelings of anger; some men become temperate and good-tempered, others self-indulgent and irascible, by behaving in one way or the other in the appropriate circumstances. Thus, in one word, states of character arise out of like activities. This is why the activities we exhibit must be of a certain kind; it is because the states of character correspond to the differences between these. It makes no small difference, then, whether we form habits of one kind or of another from our very youth; it makes a very great difference, or rather *all* the difference.

Since, then, the present inquiry does not aim at theoretical knowledge like the others (for we are inquiring not in order to know what virtue is, but in order to become good, since otherwise our inquiry would have been of no use), we must examine the nature of actions, namely how we ought to do them; for these determine also the nature of the states of character that are produced, as we have said. Now, that we must act according to the right rule is a common principle and must be assumed—it will be discussed later, i.e., both what the right rule is, and how it is related to the other virtues. But this must be agreed upon beforehand, that the whole account of matters of conduct must be given in outline and not precisely, as we said at the very beginning that the accounts we demand must be in accordance with the subject matter; matters concerned with conduct and questions of what is good for us have no fixity, any more than matters of health. The general account being of this nature, the account of particular cases is yet more lacking in exactness; for they do not fall under any art of precept but the agents themselves must in each case consider what is appropriate to the occasion, as happens also in the art of medicine or of navigation.

But though our present account is of this nature we must give what help we can. First, then, let us consider this, that it is the nature of such things to be destroyed by defect and excess, as we see in the case of strength and of health (for to gain light on things imperceptible we must use the evidence of sensible things); both excessive and defective exercise destroys the strength, and similarly drink or food which is above or below a certain amount destroys the health, while that which is proportionate both produces and increases and preserves it. So too is it, then, in the case of temperance and courage and the other virtues. For the man who flies from and fears everything and does not stand his ground against anything becomes a coward, and the man who fears nothing at all but goes to meet every danger becomes rash; and similarly the man who indulges in every pleasure and abstains from none becomes self-indulgent, while the man who shuns every pleasure, as boors do, becomes in a way insensible; temperance and courage, then, are destroyed by excess and defect, and preserved by the mean.

But not only are the sources and causes of their origination and growth the same as those of their destruction but also the sphere of their actualization will be the same; for this is also true of the things which are more evident to sense, e.g., of strength; it is produced by taking much food and undergoing much exertion, and it is the strong man that will be most able to do these things. So too is it with the virtues; by abstaining from pleasures we become temperate, and it is when we have become so that we are most able to abstain from them; and similarly too in the case of courage; for by being habituated to despise things that are terrible and to stand our ground against them we become brave, and it is when we have become so that we shall be most able to stand our ground against them.

We must take as a sign of states of character the pleasure or pain that ensues on acts; for the man who abstains from bodily pleasures and delights in this very fact is temperate, while the man who is annoyed at it is self-indulgent, and he who stands his ground against things that are terrible and delights in this or at least is not pained is brave, while the man who is pained is a coward. For moral excellence is concerned with pleasures and pains; it is on account of the pleasure that we do bad things, and on account of the pain that we abstain from noble ones. Hence we ought to have been brought up in a particular way from our very youth, as Plato says, so as both to delight in and to be pained by the things that we ought; for this is the right education. . . .

Next we must consider what virtue is. Since things that are found in the soul are of three kinds—passions, faculties, states of character—virtue must be one of these. By passions I mean appetite, anger, fear, confidence, envy, joy, friendly feeling, hatred, longing, emulation, pity, and in general the feelings that are accompanied by pleasure or pain; by faculties the things in virtue of which we are said to be capable of feeling these, e.g., of becoming angry or being pained or feeling pity; by states of character the things in virtue of which we stand well or badly with reference to the passions, e.g., with reference to anger we stand badly if we feel it violently or too weakly, and well if we feel it moderately; and similarly with reference to the other passions.

Now neither the virtues nor the vices are *passions,* because we are not called good or bad on the ground of our passions, but are so called on the ground of our virtues and our vices, and because we are neither praised nor blamed for our passions (for the man who feels fear or anger is not praised, nor is the man who simply feels anger blamed, but the man who feels it in a certain way), but for our virtues and our vices we *are* praised or blamed.

Again, we feel anger and fear without choice, but the virtues are modes of choice or involve choice. Further, in respect of the passions we are said to be moved, but in respect of the virtues and the vices we are said not to be moved but to be disposed in a particular way.

For these reasons also they are not *faculties;* for we are neither called good nor bad, nor praised nor blamed, for the simple capacity of feeling the passions; again, we have the faculties by nature, but we are not made good or bad by nature; we have spoken of this before.

If, then, the virtues are neither passions nor faculties, all that remains is that they should be *states of character*.

Thus we have stated what virtue is in respect of its genus.

We must, however, not only describe virtue as a state of character, but also say what sort of state it is. We may remark, then, that every virtue or excellence both brings into good condition the thing of which it is the excellence and makes the work of that thing be done well; e.g., the excellence of the eye makes both the eye and its work good; for it is by the excellence of the eye that we see well. Similarly the excellence of the horse makes a horse both good in itself and good at running and at carrying its rider and at awaiting the attack of the enemy. Therefore, if this is true in every case, the virtue of man also will be the state of character which makes a man good and which makes him do his own work well.

How this is to happen we have stated already, but it will be made plain also by the following consideration of the specific nature of virtue. In everything that is continuous and divisible it is possible to take more, less, or an equal amount, and that either in terms of the thing itself or relatively to us; and the equal is an intermediate excess and defect. By the intermediate in the object I mean that which is equidistant from each of the extremes, which is one and the same for all men; by the intermediate relatively to us that which is neither too much nor too little—and this is not one, nor the same for all. For instance, if ten is many and two is few, six is the intermediate, taken in terms of the object; for it exceeds and is exceeded by an equal amount; this is intermediate according to arithmetical proportion. But the intermediate relatively to us is not to be taken so; if ten pounds are too much for a particular person to eat and two too little, it does not follow that the trainer will order six pounds; for this also is perhaps too much for the person who is to take it, or too little— too little for Milo, too much for the beginner in athletic exercises. The same is true of running and wrestling. Thus a master of any art avoids excess and defect, but seeks the intermediate and chooses this—the intermediate not in the object but relatively to us.

It is thus, then, that every art does its work well—by looking to the intermediate and judging its works by this standard (so that we often say of good works of art that it is not possible either to take away or to add anything, implying that excess and defect destroy the goodness of works of art, while the mean preserves it; and good artists, as we say, look to this in their work), and if, further, virtue is more exact and better than any art, as nature also is, then virtue must have the quality of aiming at the intermediate. I mean moral virtue; for it is this that is concerned with passions and actions, and in these there is excess, defect, and the intermediate. For instance, both fear and confidence and appetite and anger and pity and in general pleasure and pain may be felt both too much and too little, and in both cases not well; but to feel them at the right times, with reference to the right objects, towards the right people, with the right motive, and in the right way, is what is both intermediate and best, and this is characteristic of virtue. Similarly with regard to actions also there is excess, defect, and the intermediate. Now virtue is concerned with passions and actions, in which excess is a form of failure, and so is defect, while the intermediate is praised and is a form of success; and being praised and being successful are both characteristics of virtue. Therefore virtue is a kind of mean, since, we have seen, it aims at what is intermediate.

Again, it is possible to fail in many ways (for evil belongs to the class of the unlimited, as the Pythagoreans conjectured, and good to that of the limited), while to succeed is possible only in one way (for which reason also one is easy and the other difficult—to miss the mark easy, to hit it difficult); for these reasons also, then, excess and defect are characteristic of vice, and the mean of virtue;

For men are good in but one way, but bad in many.

Virtue, then, is a state of character concerned with choice, lying in a mean, i.e., the mean relative to us, this being determined by a rational principle, and by that principle by which the man of practical wisdom would determine it. Now it is a mean between two vices, that which depends on excess and that which depends on defect; and again it is a mean because the vices respectively fall short of or exceed what is right in both passions and actions, while virtue both finds and chooses that which is intermediate. Hence in respect of its substance and the definition which states its essence virtue is a mean, with regard to what is best and right an extreme.

But not every action nor every passion admits of a mean; for some have names that already imply badness, e.g., spite, shamelessness, envy, and in the case of actions adultery, theft, murder; for all of these and suchlike things imply by their names that they are themselves bad, and not the excesses or deficiencies of them. It is not possible, then, ever to be right with regard to them; one must always be wrong. Nor does goodness or badness with regard to such things depend on commiting adultery with the right woman, at the right time, and in the right way, but simply to do any of them is to go wrong. It would be equally absurd, then, to expect that in unjust, cowardly, and voluptuous action there should be a mean, an excess, and a deficiency; for at that rate there would be a mean of excess and of deficiency, and excess of excess, and a deficiency of deficiency. But as there is no excess and deficiency of temperance and courage because what is intermediate is in a sense an extreme, so too of the actions we have mentioned there is no mean nor any excess and deficiency, but however they are done they are wrong; for in general there is neither a mean of excess and deficiency, nor excess and deficiency of a mean.

STUDY QUESTIONS

1. How does Aristotle define "the chief good"? Why are honor and virtue not chief goods? Do you agree with Aristotle's argument on this point?
2. When we talk about a good knife, a good tennis ball, a good carpenter, and a good hand, what common quality makes all of these things good? How does Aristotle apply this quality to "man"? In what sense does Aristotle try to make goodness a function of *human nature?*
3. Rationality is, for Aristotle, a central part of human nature. Is this enough, do you think, to adequately define humanity?
4. What is Aristotle's definition of happiness? Has he left anything out? Do you think that happiness can be defined alike for everyone?
5. How does one become virtuous, according to Aristotle? What do you think the role of intellect is in such a process?
6. Suppose you do not know what to do in a puzzling moral situation. Does Aristotle's theory contain any practical advice?
7. The first line of Tolstoy's *Anna Karenina* reads: "Happy families are all alike; every unhappy family is unhappy in its own way." What do you think Tolstoy is trying to say about happiness? Would Aristotle agree?

The Categorical Imperative

Immanuel Kant

Immanuel Kant (1724–1804) was an immensely innovative and influential philosopher. His *Critique of Pure Reason* (1781) introduced a revolution in thinking which set the tone for all nineteenth-century philosophy, and which is still felt today. Kant lived most of his life in obscurity in Konigsberg, East Prussia, teaching at the University of Konigsberg. He was a man of great discipline and regular habits, and it is said that the people of Konigsberg set their clocks by his daily walks to the university.

There are two related questions raised in Kant's selection: What makes an act right, and what makes a person morally praiseworthy? The latter question has a fairly direct answer. A person is morally praiseworthy only when that person acts from a love for duty. Self-regard, pity, sympathy, or social inclinations of whatever sort are not morally respectable motives. Duty is a perfectly rational consideration which is determined by the *categorical imperative*. In order to determine whether an action is right, according to Kant, the moral agent must be able to imagine the action as something which he or she would want everyone to do in similar circumstances. Whatever can be so universalized into a law for everyone is right. Of course, this is Kant's version of the Golden Rule. Kant gave a variety of formulations of the categorical imperative, two of which are included here.

As you look at the examples Kant gives as illustrations of his ethics, ask yourself whether they embody the principles he says they do. His critics have suggested that the examples actually employ self-interest as a fundamental moral tenet.

Nothing in the world—indeed nothing even beyond the world—can possibly be conceived which could be called good without qualification except a *good will*. Intelligence, wit, judgment, and the other talents of the mind, however they may be named, or courage, resoluteness, and perseverance as qualities of temperament, are doubtless in many respects good and desirable. But they can become extremely bad and harmful if the will, which is to make use of these gifts of nature and which in its special constitution is called character, is not good. It is the same with the gifts of fortune. Power, riches, honor, even health, general well-being, and the contentment with one's condition which is called happiness, make for pride and even arrogance if there is not a good will to correct their influence on the mind and on its principles of action so as to make it universally comfortable to its end. It need hardly be mentioned that the sight of being adorned with no feature of a pure and good will, yet enjoying uninterrupted prosperity, can never give pleasure to a rational impartial observer. Thus the good will seems to constitute the indispensable condition even of worthiness to be happy.

Some qualities seem to be conducive to this good will and can facilitate its action, but, in spite of that, they have no intrinsic unconditional worth. They rather presuppose a good will, which limits the high esteem which one otherwise rightly has for them and prevents their being held to be absolutely good. Moderation in emotions and passions, self-control, and calm deliberation not only are good in many respects but even seem to constitute a part of the inner worth of the person. But however unconditionally they were esteemed by the ancients, they are far from being good without qualification. For without the principle of good will they can become extremely bad, and the coolness of a villain makes him not only far more dangerous but also more directly abominable in our eyes than he would have seemed without it.

The good will is not good because of what it effects or accomplishes or because of its adequacy to achieve some proposed end; it is good only because of its willing, i.e., it is good of itself. And, regarded for itself, it is to be esteemed incomparably higher than anything which could be brought about by it in favor of any inclination or even of the sum total of all inclinations. Even if it should happen that, by a particularly unfortunate fate or by the niggardly provision of a stepmotherly nature, this will should be wholly lacking in power to accomplish its purpose, and if even the greatest effort should not avail it to achieve anything of its end, and if there remained only the good will (not as a mere wish but as the summoning of all the means in our power), it would sparkle like a jewel in its own right, as something that had its full worth in itself. Usefulness or fruitlessness can neither diminish nor augment this worth. Its usefulness would be only its setting, as it were, so as to enable us to handle it more conveniently in commerce or to attract the attention of those who are not yet connoisseurs, but not to recommend it to those who are experts or to determine its worth.

But there is something so strange in this idea of the absolute worth of the will alone, in which no account is taken of any use, that, not withstanding the agreement even of common sense, the suspicion must arise that perhaps only high-flown fancy is its hidden basis, and that we may have misunderstood the purpose of nature in its appointment of reason as the ruler of our will. We shall therefore examine this idea from this point of view.

In the natural constitution of an organized being, i.e., one suitably adapted to life, we assume as an axiom that no organ will be found for any purpose which is not the fittest and best adapted to that purpose. Now if its preservation, its welfare—in a word, its happiness—were the real end of nature in a being having reason and will, then nature would have hit upon a very poor arrangement in appointing the reason of the creature to be the executor of this purpose. For all the actions which the creature has to perform with this intention, and the entire rule of its conduct, would be dictated much more exactly by instinct, and that end would be far more certainly attained by instinct than it ever could be by reason. And if, over and above this, reason should have been granted to the favored creature, it would have served only to let it contemplate the happy constitution of its nature, to admire it, to rejoice in it, and to be grateful for it to its beneficent cause. But reason would not have been given in order that the being should subject its faculty of desire to that weak and delusive guidance and to meddle with the purpose of nature. In a word, nature would have taken care that reason did not break forth into practical use nor have the presumption, with its weak insight, to think out for itself the plan of happiness and the means of attaining it. Nature would have taken over not only the choice of ends but also that of the means, and with wise foresight she would have entrusted both to instinct alone.

And, in fact, we find that the more a cultivated reason deliberately devotes itself to the enjoyment of life and happiness, the more the man falls short of true contentment. From this fact there arises in many persons, if only they are candid enough to admit it, a certain degree of misology, hatred of reason. This is particularly the case with those who are most experienced in its use. After counting all the advantages which they draw—I will not say from the invention of the arts of common luxury—from the sciences (which in the end seem to be also a luxury of the understanding), they nevertheless find that they have actually brought more trouble on their shoulders instead of gaining in happiness; they finally envy, rather than despise, the common run of men who are better guided by mere natural instinct and who do not permit their reason much influence on their conduct. And we must at least admit that a morose attitude or ingratitude to the goodness with which the world is governed is by no means found always among those who temper or refute the boasting eulogies which are given of the advantages of happiness and contentment with which reason is supposed to supply us. Rather their judgment is based on the idea of another and far more worthy purpose of their existence for which, instead of happiness, their reason is properly intended, this purpose, therefore, being the supreme condition to which the private purposes of men must for the most part defer.

Reason is not, however, competent to guide the will safely with regard to its objects and the satisfaction of all our needs (which it in part multiplies), and to this end an innate instinct would have led with far more certainty. But reason is given to us as a practical faculty, i.e., one which is meant to have an influence on the will. As nature has elsewhere distributed capacities suitable to the functions they are to perform, reason's proper function must be to produce a will good in itself and not one good merely as a means, for to the former reason is absolutely essential. This will must indeed not be the sole and complete good but the highest good and the condition of all others, even of the desire for happiness. In this case it is entirely compatible with the wisdom of nature that the cultivation of reason, which is required for the former unconditional purpose, at least in this life restricts in many ways—indeed can reduce to less than nothing—the achievement of the latter conditional purpose, happiness. For one perceives that nature here does not proceed unsuitably to its purpose, because reason, which recognizes its highest practical vocation in the establishment of a good will, is capable of a contentment of its own kind, i.e., one that springs from the attainment of a purpose which is determined by reason, even though this injures the ends of inclination.

We have, then, to develop the concept of a will which is to be esteemed as good of itself without regard to anything else. It dwells already in the natural sound understanding and does not need so much to be taught as only to be brought to light. In the estimation of the total worth of our actions it always takes first place and is the condition of everything else. In order to show this, we shall take the concept of duty. It contains that of a good will, though with certain subjective restrictions and hindrances; but these are far from concealing it and making it unrecognizable, for they rather bring it out by contrast and make it shine forth all the brighter.

I here omit all actions which are recognized as opposed to duty, even though they may be useful in one respect or another, for with these the question does not arise at all as to whether they may be carried out *from* duty, since they conflict with it. I also pass over the actions which are really in accordance with duty and to which one has not direct inclination, rather executing them because impelled to do so by another inclination. For it is easily decided whether an action in accord with duty is performed from duty or for some selfish purpose. It is far more difficult to note this difference when the action is in accordance with duty and, in addition, the subject has a direct inclination to do it. For example, it is in fact in accordance with duty that a dealer should not overcharge an inexperienced customer, and wherever there is much business the prudent merchant does not do so, having a fixed price for everyone, so that a child may buy of him as cheaply as any other. Thus the customer is honestly served. But this is far from sufficient to justify the belief that the merchant has behaved in this way from duty and principles of honesty. His own advantage required this behavior; but it cannot be assumed that over and above that he had a direct inclination to the purchaser and that, out of love, as it were, he gave none an advantage in price over another. Therefore the action was done neither from duty nor from direct inclination but only for a selfish purpose.

On the other hand, it is a duty to preserve one's life, and moreover everyone has a direct inclination to do so. But for that reason the often anxious care which most men take of it has no intrinsic worth, and the maxim of doing so has no moral import. They preserve their lives according to duty, but not from duty. But if adversities and hopeless sorrow completely take away the relish for life, if an unfortunate man, strong in soul, is indignant rather than despondent or dejected over his fate and wishes for death, and yet preserves his life without loving it and from neither inclination nor fear but from duty— then his maxim has a moral import.

To be kind where one can is duty, and there are, moreover, many persons so sympathetically constituted that without any motive of vanity or selfishness they find an inner satisfaction in spreading joy, and rejoice in the contentment of others which they have made possible. But I say that, however dutiful and amiable it may be, that kind of action has no true moral worth. It is on a level with [actions arising from] other inclinations, such as the inclination to honor, which, if fortunately directed to what in fact accords with duty and is generally useful and thus honorable, deserve praise and encouragement but no esteem. For the maxim lacks the moral import of an action done not from inclination but from duty. But assume that the mind of that friend to mankind was clouded by a sorrow of his own which extinguished all sympathy with the lot of others and that he still had the power to benefit others in distress, but that their need left him untouched because he was preoccupied with his own need. And now suppose him to tear himself, unsolicited by inclination, out of this dead insensibility and to perform this action only from duty and without any inclination—then for the first time his action has genuine moral worth. Furthermore, if nature has put little sympathy in the heart of man, and if he, though an honest man, is by temperament cold and indifferent to the sufferings of others, perhaps because he is provided with special gifts of patience and fortitude and expects or even requires that others should have the same—and such a man would certainly not be the meanest product of nature—would not he find himself a source from which to give himself a far higher worth than he could have got by having a good-natured temperament? This is unquestionably true even though nature did not make him philanthropic, for it is just here that the worth of the character is brought out, which is morally and incomparably the highest of all: he is beneficent not from inclination but from duty.

To secure one's own happiness is at least indirectly a duty, for discontent with one's condition under pressure from many cares and amid unsatisfied wants could easily become a great temptation to transgress duties. But without any view to duty all men have the strongest and deepest inclination to happiness, because in this idea all inclinations are summed up. But the precept of happiness is often so formulated that it definitely thwarts some inclinations, and men can make no definite and certain concept of the sum of satisfaction of all inclinations which goes under the name of happiness. It is not to be wondered at, therefore, that a single inclination, definite as to what it promises and as to the time at which it can be satisfied, can outweigh a fluctuating idea, and that, for example, a man with the gout can choose to enjoy what he likes and to suffer what he may, because according to his calculations at least on this occasion he has not sacrificed the enjoyment of the present moment to a perhaps groundless expectation of a happiness supposed to lie in health. But even in this case, if the universal inclination to happiness did not determine his will, and if health were not at least for him a necessary factor in these calculations, there yet would remain, as in all other cases, a law that he ought to promote his happiness, not from inclination but from duty. Only from this law would his conduct have true moral worth.

It is in this way, undoubtedly, that we should understand those passages of Scripture which command us to love our neighbor and even our enemy, for love as an inclination cannot be commanded. But beneficence from duty, when no inclination impels it and even when it is opposed by a natural and unconquerable aversion, is practical love, not pathological love; it resides in the will and not in the propensities of feeling, in principles of action and not in tender sympathy; and it alone can be commanded.

[Thus the first proposition of morality is that to have moral worth an action must be done from duty.] The second proposition is: An action performed from duty does not have its moral worth in the purpose which is to be achieved through it but in the maxim by which it is determined. Its moral value, therefore, does not depend on the realization of the object of the action but merely on the principle of volition by which the action is done, without any regard to the objects of the faculty of desire. From the preceding discussion it is clear that the purposes we may have for our actions and their effects as ends and incentives of the will cannot give the actions any unconditional and moral worth. Wherein, then, can this worth lie, if it is not in the will in relation to its hoped-for effect? It can lie nowhere else than in the principle of the will, irrespective of the ends which can be realized by such action. For the will stands, as it were, at the crossroads halfway between its *a priori* principle which is formal and its *a posteriori* incentive which is material. Since it must be determined by something, if it is done from duty it must be determined by the formal principle of volition as such since every material principle has been withdrawn from it.

The third principle, as a consequence of the two preceding, I would express as follows: Duty is the necessity of an action executed from respect for law. I can certainly have an inclination to the object as an effect of the proposed action, but I can never have respect for it precisely because it is a mere effect and not an activity of a will. Similarly, I can have no respect for any inclination whatsoever, whether my own or that of another; in the former case I can at most approve of it and in the latter I can even love it, i.e., see it as favorable to my own advantage. But that which is connected with my will merely as ground and not as consequence, that which does not serve my inclination but overpowers it or at least excludes it from being considered in making a choice—in a word, law itself—can be an object of respect and thus a command. Now as an act from duty wholly excludes the influence of inclination and therewith every object of the will, nothing remains which can determine the will objectively except the law, and nothing subjectively except pure respect for this practical law. This subjective element is the maxim[1] that I ought to follow such a law even if it thwarts all my inclinations.

Thus the moral worth of an action does not lie in the effect which is expected from it or in any principle of action which has to borrow its motive from this expected effect. For all these effects (agreeableness of my own condition, indeed even the promotion of the happiness of others) could be brought about through other causes and would not require the will of a rational being, while the highest and unconditional good can be found only in such a will. Therefore, the preeminent good can consist only in the conception of the law in itself (which can be present only in a rational being) so far as this conception and not the hoped-for effect is the determining ground of the will. This preeminent good, which we call moral, is already present in the person who acts according to this conception, and we do not have to look for it first in the result.[2]

But what kind of a law can that be, the conception of which must de-

---

[1] A maxim is the subjective principle of volition. The objective principle (i.e., that which would serve all rational beings also subjectively as a practical principle if reason had full power over the faculty of desire) is the practical law.

[2] It might be objected that I seek to take refuge in an obscure feeling behind the word "respect," instead of clearly resolving the question with a concept of reason. But though respect is a feeling, it is not one received through any [outer] influence but is self-wrought by a rational concept: thus it differs specifically from all feelings of the former kind which may be referred to inclination or fear. What I recognize directly as a law for myself I recognize with respect, which means merely the consciousness of the submission of my will to a law without the intervention of other influences on my mind. The direct determination of the will by the law and the consciousness of this determination is respect; thus respect can be regarded as the effect of the law on the subject and not as the cause of the law. Respect is properly the conception of a worth which thwarts my self-love. Thus it is regarded as an object neither of inclination nor of fear, though it has something analogous to both. The only object of respect is the law, and indeed only the law which we impose on ourselves and yet recognize as necessary in itself. As a law, we are subject to it without consulting self-love; as imposed on us by ourselves, it is a consequence of our will. In the former respect it is analogous to fear and in the latter to inclination. All respect for a person is only respect for the law (of righteousness, etc.) of which the person provides an example. Because we see the improvement of our talents as a duty, we think of a person of talents as the example of a law, as it were (the law that we should by practice become like him in his talents), and that constitutes our respect. And so-called moral interest consists solely in respect for the law.

termine the will without reference to the expected result? Under this condition alone the will can be called absolutely good without qualification. Since I have robbed the will of all impulses which could come to it from obedience to any law, nothing remains to serve as a principle of the will except universal conformity of its action to law as such. That is, I should never act in such a way that I could not also will that my maxim should be a universal law. Mere conformity to law as such (without assuming any particular law applicable to certain actions) serves as the principle of the will, and it must serve as such a principle if duty is not to be a vain delusion and chimerical concept. The common reason of mankind in its practical judgments is in perfect agreement with this and has this principle constantly in view.

Let the question, for example, be: May I, when in distress, make a promise with the intention not to keep it? I easily distinguish the two meanings which the question can have, viz., whether it is prudent to make a false promise, or whether it conforms to my duty. Undoubtedly the former can often be the case, though I do see clearly that it is not sufficient merely to escape from the present difficulty by this expedient, but that I must consider whether inconveniences much greater than the present one may not later spring from this lie. Even with all my supposed cunning, the consequences cannot be so easily foreseen. Loss of credit might be far more disadvantageous than the misfortune I now seek to avoid, and it is hard to tell whether it might not be more prudent to act according to a universal maxim and to make it a habit not to promise anything without intending to fulfill it. But it is soon clear to me that such a maxim is based only on an apprehensive concern with consequences.

To be truthful from duty, however, is an entirely different thing from being truthful out of fear of disadvantageous consequences, for in the former case the concept of the action itself contains a law for me, while in the latter I must first look about to see what results for me may be connected with it. For to deviate from the principle of duty is certainly bad, but to be unfaithful to my maxim of prudence can sometimes be very advantageous to me, though it is certainly safer to abide by it. The shortest but most infallible way to find the answer to the question as to whether a deceitful promise is consistent with duty is to ask myself: Would I be content that my maxim (of extricating myself from difficulty by a false promise) should hold as a universal law for myself as well as for others? And could I say to myself that everyone may make a false promise when he is in a difficulty from which he otherwise cannot escape? I immediately see that I could will the lie but not a universal law to lie. For with such a law there would be no promises at all, inasmuch as it would be futile to make a pretense of my intention in regard to future actions to those who would not believe in this pretense or—if they overhastily did so—who would pay me back in my own coin. Thus my maxim would necessarily destroy itself as soon as it was made a universal law.

I do not, therefore, need any penetrating acuteness in order to discern what I have to do in order that my volition may be morally good. Inexperienced in the course of the world, incapable of being prepared for all its contingencies, I ask myself only: Can I will that my maxim become a universal law? If not, it must be rejected, not because of any disadvantage accruing to myself or even to others, but because it cannot enter as a principle into a possible universal legislation, and reason extorts from me an immediate respect for such legislation. I do not as yet discern on what it is grounded (a question the philosopher may investigate), but I at least understand that it is an estimation of the worth which far outweighs all the worth of whatever is recommended by the inclinations, and that the necessity of my actions from pure respect for the practical law constitutes duty. To duty every other motive must give place, because duty is the condition of a will good in itself, whose worth transcends everything. . . .

There is, therefore, only one categorical imperative. It is: Act only according to that maxim by which you can at the same time will that it should become a universal law.

Now if all imperatives of duty can be derived from this one imperative as a principle, we can at least show what we understand by the concept of duty and what it means, even though it remain undecided whether that which is called duty is an empty concept or not.

The universality of law according to which effects are produced constitutes what is properly called nature in the most general sense (as to form), i.e., the existence of things so far as it is determined by universal laws. [By analogy], then, the universal imperative of duty can be expressed as follows: Act as though the maxim of your action were by your will to become a universal law of nature.

We shall now enumerate some duties, adopting the usual division of them into duties to ourselves and to others and into perfect and imperfect duties.[3]

1. A man who is reduced to despair by a series of evils feels a weariness with life but is still in possession of his reason sufficiently to ask whether it would not be contrary to his duty to himself to take his own life. Now he asks whether the maxim of his action could become a universal law of nature. His maxim, however, is: For love of myself, I make it my principle to shorten my life when by a longer duration it threatens more evil than satisfaction. But it is questionable whether this principle of self-love could become a universal law of nature. One immediately sees a contradiction in a system of nature whose law would be to destroy life by the feeling whose special office is to impel the improvement of life. In this case it would not exist as

---

[3] It must be noted here that I reserve the division of duties for a future *Metaphysics of Morals* and that the division here stands as only an arbitrary one (chosen in order to arrange my examples). For the rest, by a perfect duty I here understand a duty which permits no exception in the interest of inclination; thus I have not merely outer but also inner perfect duties. This runs contrary to the usage adopted in the schools, but I am not disposed to defend it here because it is all one to my purpose whether this is conceded or not.

nature; hence that maxim cannot obtain as a law of nature, and thus it wholly contradicts the supreme principle of all duty.

2. Another man finds himself forced by need to borrow money. He well knows that he will not be able to repay it, but he also sees that nothing will be loaned him if he does not firmly promise to repay it at a certain time. He desires to make such a promise, but he has enough conscience to ask himself whether it is not improper and opposed to duty to relieve his distress in such a way. Now, assuming he does decide to do so, the maxim of his action would be as follows: When I believe myself to be in need of money, I will borrow money and promise to repay it, although I know I shall never do so. Now this principle of self-love or of his own benefit may very well be compatible with his whole future welfare, but the question is whether it is right. He changes the pretension of self-love into a universal law and then puts the question: How would it be if my maxim became a universal law? He immediately sees that it could never hold as a universal law of nature and be consistent with itself; rather it must necessarily contradict itself. For the universality of a law which says that anyone who believes himself to be in need could promise what he pleased with the intention of not fulfilling it would make the promise itself and the end to be accomplished by it impossible; no one would believe what was promised to him but would only laugh at any such assertion as vain pretense.

3. A third finds in himself a talent which could, by means of some cultivation, make him in many respects a useful man. But he finds himself in comfortable circumstances and prefers indulgence in pleasure to troubling himself with broadening and improving his fortunate natural gifts. Now, however, let him ask whether his maxim of neglecting his gifts, besides agreeing with his propensity to idle amusement, agrees also with what is called duty. He sees that a system of nature could indeed exist in accordance with such a law, even though man (like the inhabitants of the South Sea Islands) should let his talents rust and resolve to devote his life merely to idleness, indulgence, and propagation—in a word, to pleasure. But he cannot possibly will that this should become a universal law of nature or that it should be implanted in us by a natural instinct. For, as a rational being, he necessarily wills that all his faculties should be developed, inasmuch as they are given to him for all sorts of possible purposes.

4. A fourth man, for whom things are going well, sees that others (whom he could help) have to struggle with great hardships, and he asks, "What concern of mine is it? Let each one be as happy as heaven wills, or as he can make himself; I will not take anything from him or even envy him; but to his welfare or to his assistance in time of need I have no desire to contribute." If such a way of thinking were a universal law of nature, certainly the human race could exist, and without doubt even better than in a state where everyone talks of sympathy and good will, or even exerts himself occasionally to practice them while, on the other hand, he cheats when he can and betrays or otherwise violates the rights of man. Now although it is

possible that a universal law of nature according to that maxim could exist, it is nevertheless impossible to will that such a principle should hold everywhere as a law of nature. For a will which resolved this would conflict with itself, since instances can often arise in which he would need the love and sympathy of others, and in which he would have robbed himself, by such a law of nature springing from his own will, of all hope of the aid he desires.

The foregoing are a few of the many actual duties, or at least of duties we hold to be actual, whose derivation from the one stated principle is clear. We must be able to will that a maxim of our action become a universal law; this is the canon of the moral estimation of our action generally. Some actions are of such a nature that their maxim cannot even be *thought* as a universal law of nature without contradiction, far from it being possible that one could will that it should be such. In others this internal impossibility is not found, though it is still impossible to *will* that their maxim should be raised to the universality of a law of nature, because such a will would contradict itself. We easily see that the former maxim conflicts with the stricter or narrower (imprescriptible) duty, the latter with broader (meritorious) duty. Thus all duties, so far as the kind of obligation (not the object of their action) is concerned, have been completely exhibited by these examples in their dependence on the one principle.

When we observe ourselves in any transgression of a duty, we find that we do not actually will that our maxim should become a universal law. That is impossible for us; rather, the contrary of this maxim should remain as a law generally, and we only take the liberty of making an exception to it for ourselves or for the sake of our inclination, and for this one occasion. Consequently, if we weighed everything from one and the same standpoint, namely, reason, we would come upon a contradiction in our own will, viz., that a certain principle is objectively necessary as a universal law and yet subjectively does not hold universally but rather admits exceptions. However, since we regard our action at one time from the point of view of a will wholly conformable to reason and then from that of a will affected by inclinations, there is actually no contradiction, but rather an opposition of inclination to the precept of reason (*antagonismus*). In this the universality of the principle (*universalitas*) is changed into mere generality (*generalitas*), whereby the practical principle of reason meets the maxim halfway. Although this cannot be justified in our own impartial judgment, it does show that we actually acknowledge the validity of the categorical imperative and allow ourselves (with all respect to it) only a few exceptions which seem to us to be unimportant and forced upon us....*

The will is thought of as a faculty of determining itself to action in accordance with the conception of certain laws. Such a faculty can be found only

Editors' note: This concludes Kant's first formulation of the categorical imperative. Now he proceeds to a second formulation.

in rational beings. That which serves the will as the objective ground of its self-determination is an end, and, if it is given by reason alone, it must hold alike for all rational beings. On the other hand, that which contains the ground of the possibility of the action, whose result is an end, is called the means. The subjective ground of desire is the incentive, while the objective ground of volition is the motive. Thus arises the distinction between subjective ends, which rest on incentives, and objective ends, which depend on motives valid for every rational being. Practical principles are formal when they disregard all subjective ends; they are material when they have subjective ends, and thus certain incentives, as their basis. The ends which a rational being arbitrarily proposes to himself as consequences of his action are material ends and are without exception only relative, for only their relation to a particularly constituted faculty of desire in the subject gives them their worth. And this worth cannot, therefore, afford any universal principles for all rational beings or valid and necessary principles for every volition. That is, they cannot give rise to any practical laws. All these relative ends, therefore, are grounds for hypothetical imperatives only.

But suppose that there were something the existence of which in itself had absolute worth, something which, as an end in itself, could be a ground of definite laws. In it and only in it could lie the ground of a possible categorical imperative, i.e., of a practical law.

Now, I say, man and, in general, every rational being exists as an end in himself and not merely as a means to be arbitrarily used by this or that will. In all his actions, whether they are directed to himself or to other rational beings, he must always be regarded at the same time as an end. All objects of inclination have only a conditional worth, for if the inclinations and the needs founded on them did not exist, their object would be without worth. The inclinations themselves as the sources of needs, however, are so lacking in absolute worth that the universal wish of every rational being must be indeed to free himself completely from them. Therefore, the worth of any objects to be obtained by our actions is at all times conditional. Beings whose existence does not depend on our will but on nature, if they are not rational beings, have only a relative worth as means and are therefore called "things"; on the other hand, rational beings are designated "persons" because their nature indicates that they are ends in themselves, i.e., things which may not be used merely as means. Such a being is thus an object of respect and, so far, restricts all (arbitrary) choice. Such beings are not merely subjective ends whose existence as a result of our action has a worth for us, but are objective ends, i.e., beings whose existence in itself is an end. Such an end is one for which no other end can be substituted, to which these beings should serve merely as means. For, without them, nothing of absolute worth could be found, and if all worth is conditional and thus contingent, no supreme practical principle for reason could be found anywhere.

Thus if there is to be a supreme practical principle and a categorical imperative for the human will, it must be one that forms an objective principle of the will from the conception of that which is necessarily an end for everyone because it is an end in itself. Hence this objective principle can serve as a universal practical law. The ground of this principle is: rational nature exists as an end in itself. Man necessarily thinks of his own existence in this way; thus far it is a subjective principle of human actions. Also every other rational being thinks of his existence by means of the same rational ground which holds also for myself; thus it is at the same time an objective principle from which, as a supreme practical ground, it must be possible to derive all laws of the will. The practical imperative, therefore, is the following: Act so that you treat humanity, whether in your own person or in that of another, always as an end and never as a means only.

STUDY QUESTIONS

1. What does Kant mean by a "good will"? What does he mean by claiming that it is good "without qualification"?
2. What argument does Kant give to show that happiness is not good in itself? What do you think of the argument?
3. The following are statements of motives. How would Kant analyze them?
   a. I helped him because I could not stand to see him suffering.
   b. I helped her because the Bible says it is my duty to help others.
   c. I helped him because I want to promote social behavior that may prove beneficial to myself.
4. Kant distinguishes between an action done from duty and one done from inclination. In fact he says that it is possible to disregard all inclinations and follow duty. Do you think this is possible? Do you think Kant should count the love for duty as an inclination?
5. How do you think Kant would define freedom of the will? Why would a free will be a condition for moral responsibility?
6. Do you see any difference between Kant's categorical imperative and the Golden Rule?
7. How do you think Kant would analyze the morality of abortion? What maxim is involved? Do his other examples provide hints about how he would treat such a maxim?
8. Kant distinguishes between treating human beings as means and as ends. What is the meaning of this distinction? What bearing does it have on our behavior? Possibly the most important word in the second formulation is the adverb "only." Why?

The Greatest Happiness Principle
John Stuart Mill

John Stuart Mill (1806–1873) was one of the outstanding thinkers of the
nineteenth century. His father, James Mill, himself a famous economist and
social philosopher, and Jeremy Bentham, the founder of utilitarianism, raised
Mill according to a strict plan. They set out to make young Mill into a
democratic, intellectual, social reformer who would carry on their own liberal
projects. Denied the usual pastimes of youth, he quickly adapted to a
rigorous schedule of study, and by the age of twelve he had mastered Latin
and Greek, read the classics, and worked his way beyond the differential
calculus. The plan worked, and in his maturity, Mill was an explosion of
talents devoted to a progressive and democratic society.

   Mill's utilitarianism was the logical backbone of his attempts at social
reform. Human happiness is the only thing which is intrinsically valuable,
and right conduct is that which tends to maximize happiness. It is important
to point out that utilitarianism is not egoistic, for to maximize happiness may
require personal sacrifice. In the first part of our selection, he attempts to
clarify the utilitarian standard. In the latter part, he discusses how it may be
proved. Mill's conception of how ethical principles are proved is one of the
most debated issues in moral philosophy. As you read this section, keep in
mind that he has to prove *two* things: that happiness is intrinsically valuable,
and that each person ought to be concerned with the happiness of others.

WHAT UTILITARIANISM IS

A passing remark is all that needs be given to the ignorant blunder of supposing that those who stand up for utility as the test of right and wrong use
the term in that restricted and merely colloquial sense in which utility is opposed to pleasure. An apology is due to the philosophical opponents of utilitarianism for even the momentary appearance of confounding them with anyone capable of so absurd a misconception; which is the more extraordinary,
inasmuch as the contrary accusation, of referring everything to pleasure, and
that, too, in its grossest form, is another of the common charges against utilitarianism: and, as has been pointedly remarked by an able writer, the same
sort of persons, and often the very same persons, denounce the theory "as
impracticably dry when the word 'utility' precedes the word 'pleasure,' and
as too practically voluptuous when the word 'pleasure' precedes the word
'utility.'" Those who know anything about the matter are aware that every
writer, from Epicurus to Bentham, who maintained the theory of utility meant
by it, not something to be contradistinguished from pleasure, but pleasure
itself, together with exemption from pain; and instead of opposing the useful
to the agreeable or the ornamental, have always declared that the useful means

From *Utilitarianism* by John Stuart Mill, published in 1863. Many editions, chaps. 2 and 4.

these, among other things. Yet the common herd, including the herd of writers, not only in newspapers and periodicals, but in books of weight and pretension, are perpetually falling into this shallow mistake. Having caught up the word "utilitarian," while knowing nothing whatever about it but its sound, they habitually express by it the rejection or the neglect of pleasure in some of its forms: of beauty, of ornament, or of amusement. Nor is the term thus ignorantly misapplied solely in disparagement, but occasionally in compliment, as though it implied superiority to frivolity and the mere pleasures of the moment. And this perverted use is the only one in which the word is popularly known, and the one from which the new generation are acquiring their sole notion of its meaning. Those who introduced the word, but who had for many years discontinued it as a distinctive appellation, may well feel themselves called upon to resume it if by doing so they can hope to contribute anything toward rescuing it from this utter degradation.

The creed which accepts as the foundation of morals "utility" or the "greatest happiness principle" holds that actions are right in proportion as they tend to promote happiness; wrong as they tend to produce the reverse of happiness. By happiness is intended pleasure and the absence of pain; by unhappiness, pain and the privation of pleasure. To give a clear view of the moral standard set up by the theory, much more requires to be said; in particular, what things it includes in the ideas of pain and pleasure, and to what extent this is left an open question. But these supplementary explanations do not affect the theory of life on which this theory of morality is grounded— namely, that pleasure and freedom from pain are the only things desirable as ends; and that all desirable things (which are as numerous in the utilitarian as in any other scheme) are desirable either for pleasure inherent in themselves or as means to the promotion of pleasure and the prevention of pain.

Now such a theory of life excites in many minds, and among them in some of the most estimable in feeling and purpose, inveterate dislike. To suppose that life has (as they express it) no higher end than pleasure—no better and nobler object of desire and pursuit—they designate as utterly mean and groveling, as a doctrine worthy only of swine, to whom the followers of Epicurus were, at a very early period, contemptuously likened; and modern holders of the doctrine are occasionally made the subject of equally polite comparisons by its German, French, and English assailants.

When thus attacked, the Epicureans have always answered that it is not they, but their accusers, who represent human nature in a degrading light, since the accusation supposes human beings to be capable of no pleasures except those of which swine are capable. If this supposition were true, the charge could not be gainsaid, but would then be no longer an imputation; for if the sources of pleasure were precisely the same to human beings and to swine, the rule of life which is good enough for the one would be good enough for the other. The comparison of the Epicurean life to that of beasts is felt as degrading, precisely because a beast's pleasures do not satisfy a human being's conceptions of happiness. Human beings have faculties more elevated than the animal appetites and, when once made conscious of them, do not regard anything as happiness which does not include their gratification. I do not, indeed, consider the Epicureans to have been by any means faultless in drawing out their scheme of consequences from the utilitarian principle. To do this in any sufficient manner, many Stoic, as well as Christian, elements require to be included. But there is no known Epicurean theory of life which does not assign to the pleasures of the intellect, of the feelings and imagination, and of the moral sentiments a much higher value as pleasures than to those of mere sensation. It must be admitted, however, that utilitarian writers in general have placed the superiority of mental over bodily pleasures chiefly in the greater permanency, safety, uncostliness, etc., of the former—that is, in their circumstantial advantages rather than in their intrinsic nature. And on all these points utilitarians have fully proved their case; but they might have taken the other and, as it may be called, higher ground with entire consistency. It is quite compatible with the principle of utility to recognize the fact that some kinds of pleasure are more desirable and more valuable than others. It would be absurd that, while in estimating all other things quality is considered as well as quantity, the estimation of pleasure should be supposed to depend on quantity alone.

If I am asked what I mean by difference of quality in pleasures, or what makes one pleasure more valuable than another, merely as a pleasure, except its being greater in amount, there is but one possible answer. Of two pleasures, if there be one to which all or almost all who have experience of both give a decided preference, irrespective of any feeling of moral obligation to prefer it, that is the more desirable pleasure. If one of the two is, by those who are competently acquainted with both, placed so far above the other that they prefer it, even though knowing it to be attended with a greater amount of discontent, and would not resign it for any quantity of the other pleasure which their nature is capable of, we are justified in ascribing to the preferred enjoyment a superiority in quality so far outweighing quantity as to render it, in comparison, of small account.

Now it is an unquestionable fact that those who are equally acquainted with and equally capable of appreciating and enjoying both do give a most marked preference to the manner of existence which employs their higher faculties. Few human creatures would consent to be changed into any of the lower animals for a promise of the fullest allowance of a beast's pleasures; no intelligent human being would consent to be a fool, no instructed person would be an ignoramus, no person of feeling and conscience would be selfish and base, even though they should be persuaded that the fool, the dunce, or the rascal is better satisfied with his lot than they are with theirs. They would not resign what they possess more than he for the most complete satisfaction of all the desires which they have in common with him. If they ever fancy they would, it is only in cases of unhappiness so extreme that to escape from it they would exchange their lot for almost any other, however undesirable in their own eyes. A being of higher faculties requires more to make him happy, is capable probably of more acute suffering, and certainly accessible to it at more points, than one of an inferior type; but in spite of these liabilities, he can never really wish to sink into what he feels to be a lower grade of existence. We may give what explanation we please of this unwillingness; we may attribute it to pride, a name which is given indiscriminately to some of the most and to some of the least estimable feelings of which mankind are capable; we may refer it to the love of liberty and personal independence, an appeal to which was with the Stoics one of the most effective means for the inculcation of it; to the love of power or to the love of excitement, both of which do really enter into and contribute to it; but its most appropriate appellation is a sense of dignity, which all human beings possess in one form or other, and in some, though by no means in exact, proportion to their higher faculties, and which is so essential a part of the happiness of those in whom it is strong that nothing which conflicts with it could be otherwise than momentarily an object of desire to them. Whoever supposes that this preference takes place at a sacrifice of happiness—that the superior being, in anything like equal circumstances, is not happier than the inferior—confounds the two very different ideas of happiness and content. It is indisputable that the being whose capacities of enjoyment are low has the greatest chance of having them fully satisfied; and a highly endowed being will always feel that any happiness which he can look for, as the world is constituted, is imperfect. But he can learn to bear its imperfections, if they are at all bearable; and they will not make him envy the being who is indeed unconscious of the imperfections, but only because he feels not at all the good which those imperfections qualify. It is better to be a human being dissatisfied than a pig satisfied; better to be Socrates dissatisfied than a fool satisfied. And if the fool, or the pig, are of a different opinion, it is because they only know their own side of the question. The other party to the comparison knows both sides....

I have dwelt on this point as being a necessary part of a perfectly just conception of utility or happiness considered as the directive rule of human conduct. But it is by no means an indispensable condition to the acceptance of the utilitarian standard; for that standard is not the agent's own greatest happiness, but the greatest amount of happiness altogether; and if it may possibly be doubted whether a noble character is always the happier for its nobleness, there can be no doubt that it makes other people happier, and that the world in general is immensely a gainer by it. Utilitarianism, therefore, could only attain its end by the general cultivation of nobleness of character, even if each individual were only benefited by the nobleness of others, and his own, so far as happiness is concerned, were a sheer deduction from the benefit. But the bare enunciation of such an absurdity as this last renders refutation superfluous.

According to the greatest happiness principle, as above explained, the ultimate end, with reference to and for the sake of which all other things are desirable—whether we are considering our own good or that of other people—is an existence exempt as far as possible from pain, and as rich as possible in enjoyments, both in point of quantity and quality; the test of quality and the rule for measuring it against quantity being the preference felt by those who, in their opportunities of experience, to which must be added their habits of self-consciousness and self-observation, are best furnished with the means of comparison. This, being according to the utilitarian opinion the end of human action, is necessarily also the standard of morality, which may accordingly be defined "the rules and precepts for human conduct," by the observance of which an existence such as has been described might be, to the greatest extent possible, secured to all mankind; and not to them only, but, so far as the nature of things admits, to the whole sentient creation. . . .

OF WHAT SORT OF PROOF
THE PRINCIPLE OF UTILITY IS SUSCEPTIBLE

. . . Questions of ultimate ends do not admit of proof, in the ordinary acceptation of the term. To be incapable of proof by reasoning is common to all first principles, to the first premises of our knowledge, as well as to those of our conduct. But the former, being matters of fact, may be the subject of a direct appeal to the faculties which judge of fact—namely, our senses and our internal consciousness. Can an appeal be made to the same faculties on questions of practical ends? Or by what other faculty is cognizance taken of them?

Questions about ends are, in other words, questions what things are desirable. The utilitarian doctrine is that happiness is desirable, and the only thing desirable, as an end; all other things being only desirable as means to that end. What ought to be required of this doctrine, what conditions is it requisite that the doctrine should fulfill—to make good its claim to be believed?

The only proof capable of being given that an object is visible is that people actually see it. The only proof that a sound is audible is that people hear it; and so of the other sources of our experience. In like manner, I apprehend, the sole evidence it is possible to produce that anything is desirable is that people do actually desire it. If the end which the utilitarian doctrine proposes to itself were not, in theory and in practice, acknowledged to be an end, nothing could ever convince any person that it was so. No reason can be given why the general happiness is desirable, except that each person, so far as he believes it to be attainable, desires his own happiness. This, however, being a fact, we have not only all the proof which the case admits of, but all which it is possible to require, that happiness is a good, that each person's happiness is a good to that person, and the general happiness, therefore, a good to the aggregate of all persons. Happiness has made out its title as *one* of the ends of conduct and, consequently, one of the criteria of morality.

But it has not, by this alone, proved itself to be the sole criterion. To do that, it would seem, by the same rule, necessary to show, not only that people desire happiness, but that they never desire anything else. Now it is palpable that they do desire things which, in common language, are decidedly distinguished from happiness. They desire, for example, virtue and the absence of vice no less really than pleasure and the absence of pain. The desire of virtue is not as universal, but it is as authentic a fact as the desire of happiness. And hence the opponents of the utilitarian standard deem that they have a right to infer that there are other ends of human action besides happiness, and that happiness is not the standard of approbation and disapprobation.

But does the utilitarian doctrine deny that people desire virtue, or maintain that virtue is not a thing to be desired? The very reverse. It maintains not only that virtue is to be desired, but that it is to be desired disinterestedly, for itself. Whatever may be the opinion of utilitarian moralists as to the original conditions by which virtue is made virtue, however they may believe (as they do) that actions and dispositions are only virtuous because they promote another end than virtue, yet this being granted, and it having been decided, from considerations of this description, what *is* virtuous, they not only place virtue at the very head of the things which are good as means to the ultimate end, but they also recognize as a psychological fact the possibility of its being, to the individual, a good in itself, without looking to any end beyond it; and hold that the mind is not in a right state, not in a state conformable to utility, not in the state most conducive to the general happiness, unless it does love virtue in this manner—as a thing desirable in itself, even although, in the individual instance, it should not produce those other desirable consequences which it tends to produce, and on account of which it is held to be virtue. This opinion is not, in the smallest degree, a departure from the happiness principle. The ingredients of happiness are very various, and each of them is desirable in itself, and not merely when considered as swelling an aggregate. The principle of utility does not mean that any given pleasure, as music, for instance, or any given exemption from pain, as for example health, is to be looked upon as means to a collective something termed happiness, and to be desired, on that account. They are desired and desirable in and for themselves; besides being means, they are a part of the end. Virtue, according to the utilitarian doctrine, is not naturally and originally part of the end, but it is capable of becoming so; and in those who live it disinterestedly it has become so, and is desired and cherished, not as a means to happiness, but as a part of their happiness.

To illustrate this further, we may remember that virtue is not the only thing originally a means, and which if it were not a means to anything else would be and remain indifferent, but which by association with what it is a means to comes to be desired for itself, and that too with the utmost intensity. What, for example, shall we say of the love of money? There is nothing originally more desirable about money than about any heap of glittering pebbles. Its worth is solely that of the things which it will buy; the desires for other things than itself, which it is a means of gratifying. Yet the love of money is not only one of the strongest moving forces of human life, but money is, in many cases, desired in and for itself; the desire to possess it is often stronger than the desire to use it, and goes on increasing when all the desires which point to ends beyond it, to be compassed by it, are falling off. It may, then, be said truly that money is desired not for the sake of an end, but as part of the end. From being a means to happiness, it has come to be itself a principal ingredient of the individual's conception of happiness. The same may be said of the majority of the great objects of human life: power, for example, or fame, except that to each of these there is a certain amount of immediate pleasure annexed, which has at least the semblance of being naturally inherent in them— a thing which cannot be said of money. Still, however, the strongest natural attraction, both of power and of fame, is the immense aid they give to the attainment of our other wishes; and it is the strong association thus generated between them and all our objects of desire which gives to the direct desire of them the intensity it often assumes, so as in some characters to surpass in strength all other desires. In these cases the means have become a part of the end, and a more important part of it than any of the things which they are means to. What was once desired as an instrument for the attainment of happiness has come to be desired for its own sake. In being desired for its own sake it is, however, desired as *part* of happiness. The person is made, or thinks he would be made, happy by its mere possession; and is made unhappy by failure to obtain it. The desire of it is not a different thing from the desire of happiness any more than the love of music or the desire of health. They are included in happiness. They are some of the elements of which the desire of happiness is made up. Happiness is not an abstract idea but a concrete whole; and these are some of its parts. And the utilitarian standard sanctions and approves their being so. Life would be a poor thing, very ill provided with sources of happiness, if there were not this provision of nature by which things originally indifferent, but conducive to, or otherwise associated with, the satisfaction of our primitive desires, become in themselves sources of pleasure more valuable than the primitive pleasures, both in permanency, in the space of human existence that they are capable of covering, and even in intensity.

Virtue, according to the utilitarian conception, is a good of this description. There was no original desire of it, or motive to it, save its conduciveness to pleasure, and especially to protection from pain. But through the association thus formed it may be felt a good in itself, and desired as such with as great intensity as any other good; and with this difference between it and the love of money, of power, or of fame—that all of these may, and often do, render the individual noxious to the other members of the society to which he belongs, whereas there is nothing which makes him so much a blessing to them as the cultivation of the disinterested love of virtue. And consequently, the utilitarian standard, while it tolerates and approves those other acquired desires, up to the point beyond which they would be more injurious to the general happiness than promotive of it, enjoins and requires the cultivation of the love of virtue up to the greatest strength possible, as being above all things important to the general happiness.

It results from the preceding considerations that there is in reality nothing desired except happiness. Whatever is desired otherwise than as a means to some end beyond itself, and ultimately to happiness, is desired as itself a part of happiness, and is not desired for itself until it has become so. Those who desire virtue for its own sake desire it either because the consciousness of it is a pleasure, or because the consciousness of being without it is a pain, or for both reasons united; as in truth the pleasure and pain seldom exist separately, but almost always together—the same person feeling pleasure in the degree of virtue attained, and pain in not having attained more. If one of these gave him no pleasure, and the other no pain, he would not love or desire virtue, or would desire it only for the other benefits which it might produce to himself or to persons whom he cared for.

We have now, then, an answer to the question, of what sort of proof the principle of utility is susceptible. If the opinion which I have now stated is psychologically true—if human nature is so constituted as to desire nothing which is not either a part of happiness or a means of happiness—we can have no other proof, and we require no other, that these are the only things desirable. If so, happiness is the sole end of human action, and the promotion of it the test by which to judge of all human conduct; from whence it necessarily follows that it must be the criterion of morality, since a part is included in the whole.

And now to decide whether this is really so, whether mankind do desire nothing for itself but that which is a pleasure to them, or of which the absence is a pain, we have evidently arrived at a question of fact and experience, dependent, like all similar questions, upon evidence. It can only be determined by practiced self-consciousness and self-observation, assisted by observation of others. I believe that these sources of evidence, impartially consulted, will declare that desiring a thing and finding it pleasant, aversion to it and thinking of it as painful, are phenomena entirely inseparable or, rather, two parts of the same phenomenon—in strictness of language, two different modes of naming the same psychological fact; that to think of an object as desirable (unless for the sake of its consequences) and to think of it as pleasant are one and the same thing; and that to desire anything except in proportion as the idea of it is pleasant is a physical and metaphysical impossibility.

So obvious does this appear to me that I expect it will hardly be disputed; and the objection made will be, not that desire can possibly be directed to anything ultimately except pleasure and exemption from pain, but that the will is a different thing from desire; that a person of confirmed virtue or any other person whose purposes are fixed carries out his purposes without any thought of the pleasure he has in contemplating them or expects to derive from their fulfillment, and persists in acting on them, even though these pleasures are much diminished by changes in his character or decay of his passive sensibilities, or are outweighed by the pains which the pursuit of the purposes may bring upon him. All this I fully admit and have stated it elsewhere as positively and emphatically as anyone. Will, the active phenomenon, is a different thing from desire, the state of passive sensibility, and, though originally an offshoot from it, may in time take root and detach itself from the parent stock, so much so that in the case of a habitual purpose, instead of willing the thing because we desire it, we often desire it only because we will it. This, however, is but an instance of that familiar fact, the power of habit, and is nowise confined to the case of virtuous actions. Many indifferent things which men originally did from a motive of some sort they continue to do from habit. Sometimes this is done unconsciously, the consciousness coming only after the action; at other times with conscious volition, but volition which has become habitual and is put in operation by the force of habit, in opposition perhaps to the deliberate preference, as often happens with those who have contracted habits of vicious or hurtful indulgence. Third and last comes the case in which the habitual act of will in the individual instance is not in contradiction to the general intention prevailing at other times, but in fulfillment of it, as in the case of the person of confirmed virtue and of all who pursue deliberately and consistently any determinate end. The distinction between will and desire thus understood is an authentic and highly important psychological fact; but the fact consists solely in this—that will, like all other parts of our constitution, is amenable to habit, and that we may will from habit what we no longer desire for itself, or desire only because we will it. It is not the less true that will, in the beginning, is entirely produced by desire, including in that term the repelling influence of pain as well as the attractive one of pleasure. Let us take into consideration no longer the person who has a confirmed will to do right, but him in whom that virtuous will is still feeble, conquerable by temptation, and not to be fully relied on; by what means can it be strengthened? How can the will to be virtuous, where it does not exist in sufficient force, be implanted or awakened? Only by making the person *desire* virtue— by making him think of it in a pleasurable light, or of its absence in a painful one. It is by associating the doing right with pleasure, or the wrong with pain, or by eliciting and impressing and bringing home to the person's experience the pleasure naturally involved in the one or the pain in the other, that it is possible to call forth that will to be virtuous which, when confirmed, acts without any thought of either pleasure or pain. Will is the child of desire, and passes out of the dominion of its parent only to come under that of habit. That which is the result of habit affords no presumption of being intrinsically good; and there would be no reason for wishing that the purpose of virtue should become independent of pleasure and pain were it not that the influence of the pleasurable and painful associations which prompt to virtue is not sufficiently to be depended on for unerring constancy of action until it has acquired the support of habit. Both in feeling and in conduct, habit is the only thing which imparts certainty; and it is because of the importance to others of being able to rely absolutely on one's feelings and conduct, and to oneself of being able to rely on one's own, that the will to do right ought to be cultivated into this habitual independence. In other words, this state of the will is a means to good, not intrinsically a good; and does not contradict the doctrine that nothing is a good to human beings but in so far as it is either itself pleasurable or a means of attaining pleasure or averting pain.

But if this doctrine be true, the principle of utility is proved. Whether it is so or not must now be left to the consideration of the thoughtful reader.

STUDY QUESTIONS

1. Happiness, according to Mill, is a life of pleasure. How does Mill distinguish between kinds of pleasures? To what sort of pleasure does the principle of utility refer?
2. What is the test for determining the quality of pleasure? Suppose someone were to say that the highest pleasures were to be found in eating, drinking, sex, and sleep. Would Mill agree? Why not? What would Aristotle say?
3. What is the distinction between happiness and contentment? How can Mill say that it is *better* to be Socrates dissatisfied than a fool satisfied?
4. Mill argues that the only proof that something is desirable is that people actually do desire it. Many philosophers have argued that this "proof" is completely fallacious. What do you think? Does Mill supplement this proof of utility?
5. How does Mill prove that the general happiness is a good? Does he prove that *each* individual ought to desire the general happiness?
6. Kant insists that the love of duty is the only morally respectable motive for action. Does Mill's defense of the "disinterested love of virtue" allow him to agree with Kant?
7. Do you think that Kant and Mill would disagree on the relation between *desire* and *will?* Does Mill think it is possible for the will to operate independently of desire? If free will is required for moral responsibility, do you think that Mill would say a free will is one that is not "caused"?

A Defense of Ethical Egoism

Jesse Kalin

Jesse Kalin (1940–   ) teaches philosophy at Vassar College. In several important articles Kalin has defended ethical egoism against widely accepted criticisms. One such criticism is that egoism is self-contradictory. Egoism is the doctrine that every person ought to act in his or her self-interest. The contradiction lies in the fact, says the critic, that the theory urges all of us to pursue our self-interest, when in fact, the success of some necessitates the failure of others, due to the fact that interests are in conflict. Kalin argues that

From "In Defense of Egoism" by Jesse Kalin, in *Morality and Rational Self-Interest*, edited by David P. Gauthier (Englewood Cliffs, New Jersey: Prentice-Hall, Inc., 1970). Reprinted by permission of Professor Gauthier and Professor Kalin.

egoism survives the conflict of interests intact. A key distinction in his defense is that between "approving" and "wanting." For instance, two teams can *approve* of the principle that their opponent ought to try to win, while not *wanting* the opponent to win. Professor Kalin also tells us that pursuing self-interest intelligently means seeking long-term and not merely short-term satisfaction, and that helping others is perfectly appropriate *if* it produces benefits for oneself.

Egoism poses a dilemma for many people. Many of us want to help others even when there is no identifiable benefit to be had; indeed, many help others even when personal losses are entailed. Likewise, some people would prefer to avoid harming others, despite the benefits that could follow. These considerations prompt some questions. What is to become of quite common sentiments of fellow-feeling and compassion? To the extent that egoism requires that we act against strong social impulses, is it a contrived and artificial ethic? The egoist reply to this is that traditional morality has encouraged an altruistic frame of mind, one which places the interests of others ahead of our own, and that the so-called social impulses need to be curbed so that people begin living for themselves and not for others.

As you read Kalin, study his distinction between "approving" and "wanting," and reflect on the implications of the term "enlightened" in his definition of ethical egoism. If you were to seriously seek your enlightened self-interest, would your lifestyle have to change?

I

Ethical egoism is the view that it is morally right—that is, morally permissible, indeed, morally obligatory—for a person to act in his own self-interest even when his self-interest conflicts or is irreconcilable with the self-interest of another. The point people normally have in mind in accepting and advocating this ethical principle is that of justifying or excusing their own self-interested actions by giving them a moral sanction.

This position is sometimes construed as saying that selfishness is moral, but such an interpretation is not quite correct. "Self-interest" is a general term usually used as a synonym for "personal happiness" and "personal welfare," and what would pass as selfish behavior frequently would not pass as self-interested behavior in this sense. Indeed, we have the suspicion that selfish people are characteristically, if not always, unhappy. Thus, in cases where selfishness tends to a person's unhappiness it is not in his self-interest, and as an egoist he ought not to be selfish. As a consequence, ethical egoism does not preclude other-interested, non-selfish, or altruistic behavior, as long as [the] behavior also leads to the individual's own welfare.

That the egoist may reasonably find himself taking an interest in others and promoting their welfare perhaps sounds nonegoistic, but it is not. Ethical egoism's justification of such behavior differs from other accounts in the following way: The ethical egoist acknowledges no general obligation to help people in need. Benevolence is never justified unconditionally or "categorically." The egoist has an obligation to promote the welfare only of those whom he likes, loves, needs, or can use. The source of this obligation is his interest in them. No interest, no obligation. And when his interest conflicts or is irreconcilable with theirs, he will reasonably pursue his own well-being at their expense, even when this other person is his wife, child, mother, or friend, as well as when it is a stranger or enemy.

Such a pursuit of one's own self-interest is considered *enlightened*. The name Butler provides for ethical egoism so interpreted is "cool self-love."[1] On this view, a person is to harmonize his natural interests, perhaps cultivate some new interests, and optimize their satisfaction. Usually among these interests will be such things as friendships and families (or perhaps one gets his greatest kicks from working for UNICEF). And, of course, it is a part of such enlightenment to consider the "long run" rather than just the present and immediate future.

Given this account of ethical egoism plus the proper circumstances, a person could be morally justified in cheating on tests, padding expense accounts, swindling a business partner, being a slum landlord, draft-dodging, lying, and breaking promises, as well as in contributing to charity, helping friends, being generous or civic minded, and even undergoing hardship to put his children through college. Judged from inside "standard morality," the first actions would clearly be immoral, while the preceding paragraphs suggest the latter actions would be immoral as well, being done from a vicious or improper motive.

With this informal account as background, I shall now introduce a formal definition of ethical egoism, whose coherence will be the topic of the subsequent discussion:

(i) (x) (y) (x ought to do y if and only if y is in x's overall self-interest)

In this formalization, "x" ranges over persons and "y" over particular actions, or kinds of action; "ought" has the sense "ought, all things considered." (i) may be translated as: "A person ought to do a specific action, all things considered, if and only if that action is in that person's overall (enlightened) self-interest."

(i) represents what Medlin calls "universal egoism."[2] The majority of philosophers have considered universalization to be necessary for a sound moral theory, though few have considered it sufficient. This requirement may

---

[1] Butler, Joseph, *Fifteen Sermons Preached at the Rolls Chapel*, 1726. Standard anthologies of moral philosophy include the most important of these sermons; or see the Library of Liberal Arts Selection, *Five Sermons* (New York: The Bobbs-Merrill Company, Inc., 1950). See particularly Sermons I and XI. In XI, Butler says of rational self-love that "the object the former pursues is something internal—our own happiness, enjoyment, satisfaction. . . . The principle we call 'self-love' never seeks anything external for the sake of the thing, but only as a means of happiness or good." Butler is not, however, an egoist for there is also in man conscience and "a natural principle of benevolence" (see Sermon I).

[2] Medlin, Brian, "Ultimate Principles and Ethical Egoism," *Australasian Journal of Philosophy*, XXXV (1957), pp. 111–118.

be expressed as follows: If it is reasonable for A to do s in C, it is also reasonable for any similar person to do similar things in similar circumstances. Since everyone has a self-interest and since the egoist is arguing that his actions are right simply because they are self-interested, it is intuitively plausible to hold that he is committed to regarding everyone as morally similar and as morally entitled (or even morally obligated) to be egoists. His claim that his own self-interested actions are right thus entails the claim that all self-interested actions are right. If the egoist is to reject this universalization, he must show that there are considerations in addition to self-interest justifying his action, considerations making him relevantly different from all others such that his self-interested behavior is justified while theirs is not. I can't imagine what such considerations would be. In any case, egoism has usually been advanced and defended in its universalized form, and it is in this form that it will most repay careful examination. Thus, for the purposes of this paper, I shall assume without further defense the correctness of the universalization requirement.

It has also been the case that the major objections to ethical egoism have been derived from this requirement. Opponents have argued that once egoism is universalized, it can readily be seen to be incoherent. Frankena[3] and Medlin each advance an argument of this sort. In discussing their positions, I shall argue that the universalization of egoism given by (i) is coherent.... The result will be that egoism can with some plausibility be defended as an ultimate practical principle. At the least, if egoism is incorrect, this is not due to any incoherence arising from the universalization requirement.

II

One purpose of a moral theory is to provide criteria for first person moral judgments (such as "I ought to do s in C"); another purpose is to provide criteria for second and third person moral judgments (such as "Jones ought to do s in C"). Any theory which cannot coherently provide such criteria must be rejected as a moral theory. Can ethical egoism do this? Frankena argues that it cannot.

Frankena formulates egoism as consisting of two principles:

a If A is judging about himself, then A is to use this criterion: A ought to do y if and only if y is in A's overall self-interest.

b If A is a spectator judging about anyone else, B, then A is to use this criterion: B ought to do y if and only if y is in A's overall self-interest.

Frankena thinks that [(a) & (b)] is the only interpretation of (i) "consistent with the spirit of ethical egoism."

But isn't it the case that (a) and (b) taken together produce contradictory

---

[3] Frankena, William, *Ethics* (Englewood Cliffs, New Jersey: Prentice-Hall, Inc., 1963), pp. 16–18. References to Frankena in Part II are from this book.

moral judgments about an important subset of cases, namely those where people's self-interests conflict or are irreconcilable? If this is so, egoism as formulated by Frankena is incoherent and must be rejected.

To illustrate, let us suppose that B does s, and that s is in B's overall self-interest, but not in A's. Is s right or wrong? Ought, or ought not B do s? The answer depends on who is making the judgment. If A is making the judgment, then "B ought not to do s" is correct. If B is making the judgment, then "B ought to do s" is correct. And, of course, when both make judgments, both "B ought to do s" and "B ought not to do s" are correct. Surely any principle which has this result as a possibility is incoherent.

This objection may be put another way. The ethical egoist claims that there is one ultimate moral principle applicable to everyone. This is to claim that (i) is adequate for all moral issues, and that all applications of it can fit into a logically coherent system. Given the above illustration, "B ought to do s" does follow from (a), and "B ought not to do s" does follow from (b), but the fact that they cannot coherently be included in a set of judgments shows that (a) and (b) are not parts of the same ultimate moral principle. Indeed, these respective judgments can be said to follow from a moral principle at all only if they follow from *different* moral principles. Apparently, the ethical egoist must choose between (i)'s parts if he is to have a coherent ethical system, but he can make no satisfactory choice. If (a) is chosen, second and third person judgments become impossible. His moral theory, however, must provide for both kinds of judgment. Ethical egoism needs what it logically cannot have. Therefore, it can only be rejected.

The incompatibility between (a) and (b) and the consequent incoherence of (i) manifests itself in still a third way. Interpreted as a system of judgments, [(a) & (b)] is equivalent to: Everyone ought to pursue A's self-interest, and everyone ought to pursue B's self-interest, and everyone ought to pursue C's self-interest, and...[4] When the interests of A and B are incompatible, one

---

[4] This can be shown as follows:
    i. Suppose A is the evaluator, then
        What ought A to do? A ought to do what's in A's interest.
            (by (a))
        What ought B to do? B ought to do what's in A's interest.
            (by (b))
        What ought C to do? C ought to do what's in A's interest.
            (by (b))
        etc.
        Therefore, everyone ought to do what's in A's interest.
            (by (a) & (b))
    ii. Suppose B is the evaluator, then
        What ought A to do? A ought to do what's in B's interest.
            (by (b))
        What ought B to do? B ought to do what's in B's interest.
            (by (a))
        What ought C to do? C ought to do what's in B's interest.
            (by (b))
        etc.

must pursue both of these incompatible goals, which, of course, is impossible. On this interpretation, ethical egoism must fail in its function of guiding conduct (one of the most important uses of moral judgments). In particular, it must fail with respect to just those cases for which the guidance is most wanted—conflicts of interests. In such situations, the theory implies that one must both do and not do a certain thing. Therefore, since ethical egoism cannot guide conduct in these crucial cases, it is inadequate as a moral theory and must be rejected.

Ethical egoism suffers from three serious defects if it is interpreted as [(a) & (b)]. These defects are closely related. The first is that the theory implies a contradiction, namely, that some actions are both right *and* wrong. The second defect is that the theory, if altered and made coherent by rejecting one of its parts, cannot fulfill one of its essential tasks: Altered, it can provide for first person moral judgments *or* for second and third person moral judgments, but not for both. The third defect is that the theory cannot guide conduct and must fail in its advice-giving function because it advises (remember: advises, all things considered) a person to do what it advises him not to do.

Any one of these defects would be sufficient to refute the theory, and indeed they do refute ethical egoism when it is defined as [(a) & (b)]. The only plausible way to escape these arguments is to abandon Frankena's definition and reformulate egoism so that they are no longer applicable. Clearly, (a) must remain, for it seems central to any egoistic position. However, we can replace (b) with the following:

> c If A is a spectator judging about anyone else, B, then A is to use this criterion: B ought to do y if and only if y is in B's overall self-interest.

The objections to [(a) & (b)] given above do not apply to [(a) & (c)]. [(a) & (c)] yields no contradictions, even in cases where self-interests conflict or are irreconcilable. When we suppose that B is the agent, that s is in B's overall self-interest, and that s is against A's overall self-interest, both B and A will agree in their moral judgments about this case, that is, both will agree that B ought to do s. And, of course, the theory provides for all moral judgments, whether first, second, or third person; since it yields no contradictions, there

---

Therefore, everyone ought to do what's in B's interest.
    (by (a) & (b))
iii. Suppose C is the evaluator, then

   .

   .

   .

  etc.

Conclusion:
Everyone ought to do what's in A's interest, and
everyone ought to do what's in B's interest, and...etc.

is no need to make it coherent by choosing between its parts and thereby making it inadequate.

Finally, this interpretation avoids the charge that ethical egoism cannot adequately fulfill its conduct guiding function. Given [(a) & (c)], it will never truly be the case that an agent ought to pursue anyone's self-interest except his own. Any judgment of the form "A ought to pursue B's self-interest" will be false, unless it is understood to mean that pursuit of B's self-interest is a part of the pursuit of A's self-interest (and this, of course, would not contribute to any incoherence in the theory). Thus, the theory will have no difficulty in being an effective practical theory; it will not give contradictory advice, even in situations where interests conflict. True, it will not remove such conflicts—indeed, in practice it might well encourage them; but a conflict is not a contradiction. The theory tells A to pursue a certain goal, and it tells B to pursue another goal, and does this unequivocally. That both cannot succeed in their pursuits is irrelevant to the coherence of the theory and its capacity to guide conduct, since both *can* do what they are advised to do, all things considered—pursue their own self-interests....

There remains the question whether [(a) & (c)] is a plausible interpretation of (i), that is, whether it is "consistent with the spirit of ethical egoism." It is certainly consistent with the "spirit" behind the "ethical" part of egoism in its willingness to universalize the doctrine. It is also consistent with the "egoistic" part of the theory in that if a person does faithfully follow (a) he will behave as an egoist. Adding the fact that [(a) & (c)] is a coherent theory adequate to the special ethical chores so far discussed, do we have any reason for rejecting it as an interpretation of (i) and ethical egoism? So far, I think not. Therefore, I conclude that Frankena has failed to refute egoism. It has thus far survived the test of universalization and still remains as a candidate for "the one true moral theory."

III

In his article, "Ultimate Principles and Ethical Egoism," Brian Medlin maintains that ethical egoism cannot be an ultimate principle because it fails to guide our actions, tell us what to do, or determine our choice between alternatives. He bases this charge on his view that because ethical egoism is the expression of inconsistent desires, it will always tell people to do incompatible things. Thus:

> I have said from time to time that the egoistic principle is inconsistent. I have not said it is contradictory. This for the reason that we can, without contradiction, express inconsistent desires and purposes. To do so is not to say anything like "Goliath was ten feet tall and not ten feet tall." Don't we all want to have our cake and eat it too? And when we say we do we aren't asserting a contradiction whether we be making an avowal of our attitudes or stating a fact about them. We all have

conflicting motives. None of this, however, can do the egoist any good.
For we assert our ultimate principles not only to express our own
attitudes but also to induce similar attitudes in others, to dispose them
to conduct themselves as we wish. In so far as their desires conflict,
people don't know what to do. And, therefore, no expression of
incompatible desires can ever serve for an ultimate principle of human
conduct.

That egoism could not successfully guide one's conduct was a criticism
discussed and rebutted in section II. There, it rested upon Frankena's formulation of egoism as equal to [(a) & (b)] and was easily circumvented by replacing principle (b) with principle (c). Medlin's charge is significant, however, because it appears to be applicable to [(a) & (c)] as well[5] and therefore
must be directly refuted if egoism is to be maintained.

The heart of Medlin's argument is his position that to affirm a moral
principle is to express approval of any and all actions following from that principle. This means for Medlin not only that the egoist is committed to approving all egoistic actions but also that such approval will involve wanting those
actions to occur and trying to bring them about, even when they would be to
one's own detriment.

> But is not to believe that someone should act in a certain way to try to
> persuade him to do so? Of course, we don't always try to persuade
> people to act as we think they should act. We may be lazy, for instance.
> But insofar as we believe that Tom should do so and so, we have a
> tendency to induce him to do so and so. Does it make sense to say: "Of
> course you should do this, but for goodness' sake don't"? Only where
> we mean: "You should do this for certain reasons, but here are even

---

[5] Medlin himself does not distinguish between (b) and (c). Some of his remarks suggest (c). Thus,
at one point he says:

> When he [the egoist] tries to convince me that he should look after himself, he is attempting
> so to dispose me that I shall approve when he drinks my beer and steals Tom's wife. I cannot
> approve of his looking after himself alone without so far approving of his achieving his hap-
> piness, regardless of the happiness of myself and others.

This passage implies that as a spectator assessing another's conduct, I should employ principle
(c) and approve of A's doing y whenever y promotes A's interest, even if this is at the expense
of my welfare.
But other of his remarks suggest (b). Thus, the above passage continues:

> So that when he sets out to persuade me that he should look after himself regardless of others,
> he must also set out to persuade me that I should look after him regardless of myself and
> others. Very small chance he has!

Here, the implication is that the egoist as spectator and judge of another should assess the
other's behavior according to his own interests, not the other's which would be in accordance
with (b).
Perhaps Medlin is arguing that the egoist is committed to accepting both (b) and (c), as well
as (a). This interpretation is consistent with his analysis of "approval."

more persuasive reasons for not doing it." If the egoist believes ultimately that others should mind themselves alone, then, he must persuade them accordingly. If he doesn't persuade them, he is no universal egoist.

According to Medlin, if I adopt ethical egoism and am thereby led to approve of A's egoistic actions [as would follow from (c)], I must also *want* A to behave in that way and must want him to be happy, to come out on top, and so forth where wanting is interpreted as setting an end for my own actions and where it tends (according to the intensity of the want, presumably) to issue in my "looking after him."

Of course, I will also approve of my pursuing my own welfare [as would follow from (a)] and will want myself to be happy, to come out on top, and so forth. Since I want my own success, I will want A's noninterference. Indeed, what I will want A to do, and will therefore approve of A's doing, is to pursue my welfare, rather than his own.

It is thus the case that whenever my interest conflicts with A's interest, I will approve of inconsistent ends and will want incompatible things ("I want myself to come out on top and I want Tom to come out on top"). Since I approve of incompatible ends, I will be motivated in contrary directions—both away from and toward my own welfare, for instance. However, this incompatibility of desires is not sufficient to produce inaction and does not itself prove Medlin's point, for one desire may be stronger than the other. If the egoist's approval of his own well-being were always greater than his approval of anyone else's well-being, the inconsistent desires constituting egoism would not prevent (i) from decisively guiding conduct. Unfortunately for the egoist, his principle will in fact lead him to inaction, for in being universal (i) expresses equal approval of each person's pursuing his own self-interest, and therefore, insofar as his desires follow from this principle, none will be stronger than another.

We can now explain Medlin's conclusion that "the proper objection to the man who says 'Everyone should look after his own interests regardless of the interests of others' is not that he isn't speaking the truth, but simply that he isn't speaking." Upon analysis, it is clear that the egoist is "saying" that others should act so that he himself comes out on top and should not care about Tom, Dick, *et al.*, but they should also act so that Tom comes out on top and should not care about himself, Dick, the others, and so forth. This person *appears* to be saying how people should act, and that they should act in a definite way. But his "directions" can guide no one. They give one nothing to do. Therefore, such a man has in fact said nothing.

I think Medlin's argument can be shown to be unsuccessful without a discussion of the emotivism in which it is framed. The egoist can grant that there is a correct sense in which affirmation of a moral principle is the expression of approval. The crux of the issue is Medlin's particular analysis of approbation, and this can be shown to be incorrect.

We may grant that the egoist is committed to approving of anyone's egoistic behavior at least to the extent of believing that the person ought so to behave. Such approval will hold of all egoistic actions, even those that endanger his own welfare. But does believing that A ought to do y commit one to wanting A to do y? Surely not. This is made clear by the analogy with competitive games. Team A has no difficulty in believing that team B ought to make or try to make a field goal while not wanting team B to succeed, while hoping that team B fails, and, indeed, while trying to prevent team B's success. Or consider this example: I may see how my chess opponent can put my king in check. That is how he ought to move. But believing that he ought to move his bishop and check my king does not commit me to wanting him to do that, nor to persuading him to do so. What I ought to do is sit there quietly, hoping he does not move as he ought.

Medlin's mistake is to think that believing that A ought to do y commits one to *wanting* A to do y and hence to encouraging or otherwise helping A to do y. The examples from competitive games show that this needn't be so. The egoist's reply to Medlin is that just as team A's belief that team B ought to do so and so is compatible with their not wanting team B to do so and so, so the egoist's belief that A ought to do y is compatible with the egoist's not wanting A to do y. Once this is understood, egoism has no difficulty in decisively guiding conduct, for insofar as (i) commits the egoist to wanting anything, it only commits him to wanting his own welfare. Since he does not want incompatible goals, he has no trouble in deciding what to do according to (a) and in judging what others ought to do according to (c).

IV

There is in Medlin's paper confusion concerning what the egoist wants or values and why he believes in ethical egoism. The egoist does not believe that everyone ought to pursue their own self-interest merely because *he* wants to get *his* goodies out of life. If this were all there were to his position, the egoist would not bother with (i) or with moral concepts at all. He would simply go about doing what he wants. What reason, then, does he have to go beyond wanting his own welfare to ethical egoism? On Medlin's emotivist account, his reason must be that he also wants B to have B's goodies, and wants D to have his, and so forth, even when it is impossible that everybody be satisfied. But I argued in the preceding section that the egoist is not committed to wanting such states, and that it is not nonsense for him to affirm (i) and desire his own welfare yet not desire the welfare of others. Therefore, the question remains—why affirm egoism at all?

The egoist's affirmation of (i) rests upon both teleological and deontological elements. What he finds to be of ultimate value is his own welfare. He needn't be selfish or egocentric in the ordinary sense (as Medlin sometimes suggests by such paraphrases as "Let each man do what he wants regardless of what anyone else wants"), but he will value his own interest above that of others. Such an egoist would share Sidgwick's view that when "the painful necessity comes for another man to choose between his own happiness and the general happiness, he must as a reasonable being prefer his own."[6] When this occasion does arise, the egoist will want the other's welfare less than he wants his own, and this will have the practical effect of not wanting the other's welfare at all. It is in terms of this personal value that he guides his actions, judging that he ought to do y if and only if y is in his overall self-interest. This is the teleological element in his position.

However, there is no reason that others should find his well-being to be of value to them and it is much more likely that each will find his own welfare to be his own ultimate value. But if it is reasonable for the egoist to justify his behavior in terms of what he finds to be of ultimate value, than it is also reasonable for others to justify their behavior in terms of what they find to be of ultimate value. This follows from the requirement of universalization and provides the deontological element. Interpreted as "Similar things are right for similar people in similar circumstances," the universalization principle seems undeniable. Failing to find any relevant difference between himself and others, the egoist must admit that it can be morally permissible for him to pursue his self-interest only if it is morally permissible for each person to pursue his self-interest. He therefore finds himself committed to (i), even though he does not *want* others to compete with him for life's goods.

STUDY QUESTIONS

1. In his formulation of egoism, Kalin uses the phrase "all things considered." What does this mean? Can a person ever consider "all things" in making a decision?
2. What does Kalin mean by selfishness and self-interest?
3. Would an ethical egoist do the following if he or she intended to be faithful to the principle of enlightened self-interest: use hallucinogenic drugs, smoke cigarettes, drink alcoholic beverages to excess, become overweight, or avoid regular exercise?
4. According to Kalin I should help another person only when helping him or her produces benefits for me. Suppose that I want to help a person, but that doing so would produce no benefits, except perhaps for a sense of self-satisfaction. Would Kalin consider the self-satisfaction a benefit sufficient to justify helping another?
5. Does ethical egoism say that I should harm others if harming them produces benefits for me in the long run?

---

[6] Henry Sidgwick, *The Methods of Ethics*, 7th ed. (London: Macmillan and Co., 1907), preface to the 6th edition, p. xvii.

The Case of the Obliging Stranger
William Gass

William Gass (1924–   ) is David May Distinguished University Professor in Humanities at Washington University in St. Louis. In addition to his philosophical writing, he has published several short stories and a novel, *Omensetter's Luck* (1966). In this selection, Gass challenges the usual account of moral reasoning. He argues that moral problems are not solved in real life by appealing to "principles." Instead, the elaborate theories of moralists, along with the abstract principles of right and good they are designed to justify, are themselves justified by ordinary moral experience.

 Gass claims that there are "clear" cases of immoral (and moral) conduct. Only a lunatic—or a philosopher—could look at such cases and seriously ask, "But is it really wrong?" These clear cases are unmistakable data, and no moral theory which conflicts with these data can be correct. Moral principles, he maintains, are actually convenient summaries of some of the outstanding features of the clear cases. A tendency to lead to the greatest happiness, for example, is a feature of some clear cases of moral action. But it is not this tendency which makes it moral, any more than the tendency of a rooster to crow at sunrise makes it into a rooster. Other principles provide different distinguishing marks of clear cases. But when principles conflict, we must throw them aside and return to moral experience, which Gass says requires no explanation.

I

Imagine I approach a stranger on the street and say to him, "If you please, sir, I desire to perform an experiment with your aid." The stranger is obliging, and I lead him away. In a dark place conveniently by, I strike his head with the broad of an axe and cart him home. I place him, buttered and trussed, in an ample electric oven. The thermostat reads 450°F. Thereupon I go off to play poker with friends and forget all about the obliging stranger in the stove. When I return, I realize I have overbaked my specimen, and the experiment, alas, is ruined.

 Something has been done wrong. Or something wrong has been done.

 Any ethic that does not roundly condemn my action is vicious. It is interesting that none is vicious for this reason. It is also interesting that no more convincing refutation of any ethic could be given than by showing that it approved of my baking the obliging stranger.

 This is really all I have to say, but I shall not stop on that account. Indeed, I shall begin again.

From "The Case of the Obliging Stranger" by William Gass. *Philosophical Review*, LXVI (1957), 193–204. Reprinted by permission of the editor and the author.

II

The geometer cannot demonstrate that a line is beautiful. The beauty of lines is not his concern. We do not chide him when he fails to observe uprightness in his verticals, when he discovers no passions between sinuosities. We could not judge it otherwise than foolish to berate him for neglecting to employ the methods successful in biology or botany merely because those methods dealt fairly with lichens and fishes. Nor do we despair of him because he cannot give us reasons for doing geometry which will equally well justify our drilling holes in teeth. There is a limit, as Aristotle said, to the questions which we may sensibly put to each man of science; and however much we may desire to find unity in the purposes, methods, and results of every fruitful sort of inquiry, we must not allow that desire to make mush of their necessary differences.

Historically, with respect to the fundamental problems of ethics, this limit has not been observed. Moreover, the analogy between mathematics and morals, or between the methods of empirical science and the good life, has always been unfairly one-sided. Geometers never counsel their lines to be moral, but moralists advise men to be like lines and go straight. There are triangles of lovers, but no triangles in love. And who says the organism is a state?

For it is true that the customary methods for solving moral problems are the methods which have won honors by leaping mathematical hurdles on the one hand or scientific and physical ones on the other: the intuitive and deductive method and the empirical and inductive one. Nobody seems to have minded very much that the moral hurdle has dunked them both in the pool beyond the wall, for they can privately laugh at each other for fools, and together they can exclaim how frightfully hard is the course.

The difficulty for the mathematical method is the discovery of indubitable moral first premises which do not themselves rest on any inductive foundation and which are still applicable to the complicated tissue of factors that make up moral behavior. The result is that the premises are usually drawn from metaphysical speculations having no intimate relation to moral issues or from rational or mystical revelations which only the intuiter and his followers are willing to credit. For the purposes of deduction, the premises have to be so broad and, to satisfy intuition, so categorically certain, that they become too thin for touch and too heavy for bearing. All negative instances are pruned as unreal or parasitic. Consequently, the truth of the ultimate premises is constantly called into question by those who have intuited differently or have men and actions in mind that they want to call good and right but cannot.

Empirical solutions, so runs the common complaint, lop off the normative branch altogether and make ethics a matter of expediency, taste, or conformity to the moral etiquette of the time. One is told what people do, not what they ought to do; and those philosophers who still wish to know what people ought to do are told, by some of the more uncompromising, that they can have no help from empiricism and are asking a silly question. Philosophers, otherwise empiricists, who admit that moral ends lie beyond the reach of factual debate turn to moral sentiment or some other *bonum ex machina*, thus generously embracing the perplexities of both methods.

III

Questions to which investigators return again and again without success are very likely improperly framed. It is important to observe that the ethical question put so directly as "What is good?" or "What is right?"[1] aims in its answer not, as one might immediately suppose, at a catalogue of the world's good, right things. The moralist is not asking for a list of sheep and goats. The case of the obliging stranger is a case of immoral action, but this admission is not an answer, even partially, to the question, "What is wrong?"

Furthermore, the ethical question is distressingly short. "Big" questions, it would seem, ought to be themselves big, but they almost never are; and they tend to grow big simply by becoming short—too short, in fact, ever to receive an answer. I might address, to any ear that should hear me, the rather less profound-sounding, but none the less similar question, "Who won?" or perhaps the snappier, "What's a winner?" I should have to ask this question often because, if I were critical, I should never find an answer that would suit me; while at the same time there would be a remarkable lot of answers that suited a remarkable lot of people. The more answers I had—the more occasions on which I asked the question—the more difficult, the more important, the more "big" the question would become.

If the moralist does not want to hear such words as "Samson," "money," or "brains" when he asks his question, "What is good?" what does he want to hear? He wants to hear a word like "power." He wants to know what is good in the things that are good that makes them good. It should be perfectly clear it is not the things themselves that he thinks good or bad but the qualities they possess, the relations they enter into, or the consequences they produce. Even an intuitionist, who claims to perceive goodness directly, perceives a property of things when he perceives goodness, and not any *thing*, except incidentally. The wrong done the obliging stranger was not the act of cooking him but was something belonging to the act in some one of many possible ways. It is not I who am evil (if I am not mad) but something which I *have* that is; and while, of course, I may be adjudged wicked for having whatever it is I have that is bad, it is only because I have it that I am wicked—as if I owned a vicious and unruly dog.

I think that so long as I look on my act in this way, I wrong the obliging stranger a second time.

The moralist, then, is looking for the ingredient that perfects or spoils the

---

[1] The order in which these questions are asked depends on one's view of the logical primacy of moral predicate. I shall not discriminate among them since I intend my remarks to be indiscriminate.

He wants to hear the word "power." He wants to know what is good what is good that makes it good; and the whole wretched difficulty is that one is forced to reply either that what is good in what is good makes the good in what is good good, or that it is, in fact, made good by things which are not in the least good at all. So the next question, which is always, "And why is power good?" is answered by saying that it is good because it is power and power is good; or it is put off by the promise that power leads to things worth much; or it is shrugged aside with the exclamation, "Well, that's life!" This last is usually accompanied by an exhortation not to oppose the inevitable course of nature.

You cannot ask questions forever. Sooner or later the questioning process is brought up short by statements of an apparently dogmatic sort. Pleasure is sought for pleasure's sake. The principle of utility is susceptible of no demonstration. Every act and every inquiry aims at well-being. The nonnatural property of goodness fastens itself to its object and will remain there whatever world the present world may madly become. Frustrated desires give rise to problems, and problems are bad. We confer the title of The Good upon our natural necessities.

I fail to see why, if one is going to call a halt in this way, the halt cannot be called early, and the evident, the obvious, the axiomatic, the indemonstrable, the intrinsic, or whatever one wants to name it, be deemed those clear cases of moral goodness, badness, obligation, or wrong which no theory can cloud, and for which men are prepared to fight to the last ditch. For if someone asks me, now I am repentant, why I regard my act of baking the obliging stranger as wrong, what can I do but point again to the circumstances comprising the act? "Well, I put this fellow in an oven, you see. The oven was on, don't you know." And if my questioner persists, saying: "Of course, I know all about *that*; but what I want to know is, why is *that* wrong?", I should recognize there is no use in replying that it is wrong because the kind of act it is, a wrong one, for my questioner is clearly suffering from a sort of *folie de doute morale* which forbids him to accept any final answer this early in the game, although he will have to accept precisely the same kind of answer at some time or other.

Presumably there is some advantage in postponing the stop, and this advantage lies in the explanatory power of the higher-level answer. It cannot be that my baking the stranger is wrong for no reason at all. It would then be inexplicable. I do not think this is so, however. It is not inexplicable; it is transparent. Furthermore, the feeling of elucidation, of greater insight or knowledge, is a feeling only. It results, I suspect, from the satisfaction one takes in having an open mind. The explanatory factor is always more inscrutable than the event it explains. The same questions can be asked of it as were asked of the original occasion. It is either found in the situation and brought forward to account for all, as one might advance pain, in this case, out of the roaster; or it resides there mysteriously, like an essence, the witch in the oven; or it hovers, like a coil of smoke, as hovers the greatest unhappiness of the greatest number.

But how ludicrous are the moralist's "reasons" for condemning my baking the obliging stranger. They sound queerly unfamiliar and out of place. This is partly because they intrude where one expects to find denunciation only and because it is true they are seldom if ever *used*. But their strangeness is largely due to the humor in them.

Consider:

My act produced more pain than pleasure.
Baking this fellow did not serve the greatest good to the greatest
    number.
I acted wrongly because I could not consistently will that the maxim of
    my action become a universal law.
God forbade me, but I paid no heed.
Anyone can apprehend the property of wrongness sticking plainly to
    the whole affair.
Decent men remark it and are moved to tears.

But I should say that my act was wrong even if my stranger were tickled into laughter while he cooked; or even if his baking did the utmost good it could; or if, in spite of all, I could consistently will that whatever maxim I might have had might become a universal law; or even if God had spoken from a bush to me, "Thou shalt!" How redundant the property of wrongness, as if one needed *that*, in such a case! And would the act be right if the whole world howled its glee? Moralists can say, with conviction, that the act is wrong; but none can *show* it.

Such cases, like that of the obliging stranger, are cases I call clear. They have the characteristic of moral transparency, and they comprise the core of our moral experience. When we try to explain why they are instances of good or bad, of right or wrong, we sound comic, as anyone does who gives elaborate reasons for the obvious, especially when these reasons are so shame-faced before reality, so miserably beside the point. What we must explain is not why these cases have the moral nature they have, for that needs no explaining, but *why they are so clear*. It is an interesting situation: any moralist will throw over his theory if it reverses the decision on cases like the obliging stranger's. The most persuasive criticism of any ethical system has always been the demonstration, on the critic's part, that the system countenances moral absurdities, despite the fact that, in the light of the whole theoretical enterprise, such criticisms beg the question. Although the philosopher who is caught by a criticism of this sort may protest its circularity or even manfully swallow the dreadful conclusion, his system has been scotched, if it has not been killed.

Not all cases are clear. But the moralist will furrow his brow before even this one. He will pursue principles which do not apply. He does not believe in clear cases. He refuses to believe in clear cases. Why?

.ıs disbelief is an absolute presupposition with him. It is a part of his methodological commitments and a part of his notion of profundity and of the nature
of philosophy. It is a part of his reverence for intellectual humility. It is a part of
his fear of being arbitrary. So he will put the question bravely to the clear cases,
even though no state of fact but only his state of mind brings the question up,
and even though putting the question, revealing the doubt, destroys immediately the validity of any answer he has posed the question to announce.

Three children are killed by a drunken driver. A family perishes in a sudden fire. Crowded bleachers collapse. Who is puzzled, asking why these things
are terrible, why these things are wrong? When is such a question asked? It is
asked when the case is not clear, when one is in doubt about it. "Those impious
creatures!... At the movies... today,... which is the Lord's!" Is that so bad? Is
being impious, even, so bad? I do not know. It is unclear, so I ask why. Or I
disagree to pick a quarrel. Or I am a philosopher whose business it is to be puzzled. But do I imagine there is nothing the matter when three children are run
over by drunkenness, or when a family goes up in smoke, or when there is a
crush of people under timbers under people? There is no lack of clarity here,
there is only the philosopher: patient, persistent as the dung beetle, pushing
his "whys" up his hillocks with his nose. His doubts are never of the present case.
They are always general. They are doubts in legion, regiment, and principle.

The obliging stranger is overbaked. I wonder whether this is bad or not.
I ask about it. Presumably there is a reason for my wonderment. What is it?
Well, of course there is not any reason that is a reason about the obliging
stranger. There is only a reason because I am a fallibilist, or because one must
not be arbitrary, or because all certainties in particular cases are certain only
when deduced from greater, grander certainties. The reason I advance may be
advanced upon itself. The entire moral structure tumbles at once. It is a test
of the clarity of cases that objections to them are objections in principle; that
the principle applies as well to all cases as to any one; and that these reasons
for doubt devour themselves with equal right and the same appetite. That is
why the moralist is really prepared to fight for the clear cases to the last ditch;
why, when he questions them, he does so to display his philosophical breeding, because it is good form: he knows that if these cases are not clear, none
are, and if none are, the game is up.

If there are clear cases, and if every moralist, at bottom, behaves as if
there were, why does he still, at the top, behave as if there were none?

V

He may do so because he is an empiricist practicing induction. He believes,
with Peirce, that "the inductive method springs directly out of dissatisfaction
with existing knowledge." To get more knowledge he must become dissat-

isfied with what he has, all of it, by and large, often for no reason whatever. Our knowledge is limited, and what we do know, we know inexactly. In the sphere of morals the moralist has discovered how difficult it is to proceed from facts to values, and although he has not given up, his difficulties persuade him not that no one knows but that no one can be sure.

Above all, the empiricist has a hatred of certainty. His reasons are not entirely methodological. Most are political: certainty is evil; it is dictatorial; it is undemocratic; all cases should be scrutinized equally; there should be no favoritism; the philosopher is fearless. "Thought looks into the pit of hell and is not afraid."

The moralist may behave as if there were no clear cases because he is a rationalist practicing deduction. He knows all about the infinite regress. He is familiar with the unquestioned status of first principles. He is beguiled by the precision, rigor, and unarguable moves of logical demonstration. Moreover, he is such an accomplished doubter of the significance of sensation that he has persuaded the empiricist also to doubt that significance. He regards the empiricist as a crass, anti-intellecutal booby, a smuggler where he is not an honest skeptic, since no fact, or set of facts, will account for the value we place on the obliging stranger unless we are satisfied to recount again the precise nature of the case.

Suppose our case concerned toads. And suppose we were asking of the toads, "Why? Why are you toads?" They would be unable to reply, being toads. How far should we get in answering our own question if we were never sure of any particular toad that he was? How far should we get with our deductions if we were going to deduce one from self-evident toadyisms? What is self-evident about toads except that some are toads? And if we had a toad before us, and we were about to investigate him, and someone doubted that we had a toad before us, we could only say our creature was tailless and clumsy and yellow-green and made warts. So if someone still wanted to doubt our toad, he would have to change the definition of "toad," and someone might want to do that; but who wants to change our understanding of the word "immoral" so that the baking of the obliging stranger is not to be called immoral?

The empiricist is right: the deductive ethic rests upon arbitrary postulation. The rationalist is right: the inductive ethic does not exist; or worse, it consists of arbitrary values disguised as facts. Both are guilty of the most elaborate and flagrant rationalizations. Both know precisely what it is they wish to save. Neither is going to be surprised in the least by what turns out to be good or bad. They are asking of their methods answers that their methods cannot give.

VI

It is confusion which gives rise to doubt. What about the unclear cases? I shall be satisfied to show that there are clear ones, but the unclear ones are more interesting, and there are more of them. How do we decide about blue laws, supposing that there is nothing to decide about the obliging stranger except how to prevent the occurrence from happening again? How do we arbitrate conflicts of duty where each duty, even, may be clear? What of principles, after all? Are there none? Are they not used by people? Well, they talk about them more than they use them, but they use them a little.

I should like to try to answer these questions another time. I can only indicate, quite briefly, the form these answers will take.

I think we decide cases where there is some doubt by stating what it is about them that puzzles us. We hunt for more facts, hoping that the case will clear:

"She left her husband with a broken hand and took the children."

"She did!"

"He broke his hand on her head."

"Dear me; but even so!"

"He beat her every Thursday after tea and she finally couldn't stand it any longer."

"Ah, of course, but the poor children?"

"He beat them, too."

"My, my, and was there no other way?"

"The court would grant her no injunction."

"Why not?"

"Judge Bridlegoose is a fool."

"Ah, of course, she did right, no doubt about it."

If more facts do not clear the case, we redescribe it, emphasizing first this fact and then that until it is clear, or until we have several clear versions of the original muddle. Many ethical disputes are due to the possession, by the contending parties, of different accounts of the same occasion, all satisfactorily clear, and this circumstance gives the disputants a deep feeling for the undoubted rightness of each of their versions. Such disputes are particularly acrimonious, and they cannot be settled until an agreement is reached about the true description of the case.

There are, of course, conflicts of duty which are perfectly clear. I have promised to meet you at four to bowl, but when four arrives I am busy rescuing a baby from the jaws of a Bengal tiger and cannot come. Unclear conflicts we try to clarify. And it sometimes happens that the tug of obligations is so equal as to provide no reasonable solution. If some cases are clear, others are undecidable.

It is perfectly true that principles are employed in moral decisions—popular principles, I mean, like the golden rule and the laws of God. Principles really obscure matters as often as they clear them. They are generally flags and slogans to which the individual is greatly attached. Attack the principle and you attack the owner: his good name, his reputation, his sense of righteousness. Love me, love my maxims. People have been wrongly persuaded that principles decide cases and that a principle which fails in one case fails in all.

So principles are usually vehicles for especially powerful feelings and frequently get in the way of good sense. We have all observed the angry arguer who grasps the nettle of absurdity to justify his bragging about the toughness of his skin.

I should regard useful principles as summaries of what may be present generally in clear cases, as for instance: cases where pain is present are more often adjudged bad than not. We might, if the reverse were true for pleasure, express our principle briefly in hedonistic terms: pleasure is the good. But there may be lots of principles of this sort, as there may be lots of rather common factors in clear cases. Principles state more or less prevalent identifying marks, as cardinals usually nest in low trees, although there is nothing to prevent them from nesting elsewhere, and the location of the nest is not the essence of the bird. When I appeal to a principle, then, the meaning of my appeal consists of the fact that before me is a case about which I can reach no direct decision; of the fact that the principle I invoke is relevant, since not every principle is (the laws of God do not cover everything, for instance). In this way I affirm my loyalty to those clear cases the principle so roughly summarizes and express my desire to remain consistent with them.

VII

Insofar as present moral theories have any relevance to our experience, they are elaborate systems designed to protect the certainty of the moralist's last-ditch data. Although he may imagine he is gathering his principles from the purest vapors of the mind, the moralist will in fact be prepared to announce as such serenities only those which support his most cherished goods. And if he is not careful to do just this, he will risk being charged with irrelevancy by those who will employ the emptiness and generality of his principles to demonstrate the value of trivialities: as for example, the criticism of the categorical imperative that claims one can universally will all teeth be brushed with powder in the morning, and so on in like manner.

Ethics, I wish to say, is about something, and in the rush to establish principles, to elicit distinctions from a recalcitrant language, and to discover "laws," those lovely things and honored people, those vile seducers and ruddy villains our principles and laws are supposed to be based upon and our ethical theories to be about are overlooked and forgotten.

STUDY QUESTIONS

1. According to Gass, moralists are looking for some property that makes all good things good. Does he think this search will lead to an answer?
2. Gass thinks that the moralist's reasons for not baking the stranger sound ludicrous. He argues that none of the familiar principles could justify such an act. Do you agree? If not, which principle could justify it?

3. Suppose you simply observed the case of the obliging stranger. That is, you watched someone struck, killed, and baked until overdone. Do you think that this is enough to know that the action is immoral? If not, what else do you have to know? Does your answer affect Gass's analysis of moral reasoning?

4. What is Gass's account of moral argument? What is the role of rationality in this account?

5. Some early Portuguese explorers reported that there was a tribe in the jungles of Brazil which practiced cannibalism. The children of captured tribes were raised to adolescence and then cooked and eaten by the adoptive tribe. Would this sort of case undermine what Gass has to say about "clear" cases: What facts would someone like Rachels claim are relevant here? Would Rachels agree with Gass's analysis of moral reasoning?

SELECTED READINGS FOR PART FOUR

Plato's view that morality is independent of religion may be found in his *Euthyphro*, which is available in many editions. Kai Nielsen's similar view is spelled out in his *Ethics Without God* (London: Pemberton Books: Buffalo, N.Y.: Prometheus Books, 1973). The claim that an objective morality depends upon the existence of God is defended in A. E. Taylor, *The Faith of a Moralist* (London: Macmillan, 1930), and given a thorough airing in H. J. Paton, *The Modern Predicament* (New York: Collier Books, 1962), chap. 21. Some of the most important works in the literature on ethical relativity are R. Benedict, *Patterns of Culture* (Boston: Houghton Mifflin, 1934), M. Herskovits, *Man and His Works* (New York: Knopf, 1948), and E. Westermarck, *Ethical Relativity* (New York: Harcourt, Brace, 1932). W. T. Stace, *The Concept of Morals* (New York: Macmillan, 1937) is one of the most comprehensive and clear criticisms of relativism.

A popular form of relativism in the twentieth century is emotivism, the view that moral statements are simply an expression of the feelings or emotions of the speaker. Bertrand Russell embraced this theory in his *Religion and Science* (London: T. Butterworth-Nelson; and New York: Holt, 1935). The doctrine was refined and given its most popular expression in A. J. Ayer, *Language, Truth, and Logic* (New York: Dover, 1946). C. L. Stevenson further refined the position and gave a complex defense of it in *Ethics and Language* (New Haven, Conn.: Yale, 1943). S. Hook and J. Buchler criticize Russell's theory in P. A. Schilpp (ed.), *The Philosophy of Bertrand Russell* (Evanston, Ill.: Northwestern University Press, 1944). Russell responds to his critics in this volume, but indicates that he is unsatisfied with his position. For a careful and comprehensive evaluation of emotivism, see J. O. Urmson, *The Emotive Theory of Ethics* (Berkeley: University of California Press, 1954).

Two good books which clearly and interestingly compare the major traditions in ethics are J. Hospers, *Human Conduct* (New York: Harcourt, Brace &

World, 1961), and W. K. Frankena, *Ethics* (Englewood Cliffs, N.J.: Prentice-Hall, 1963). Aristotle's moral theory is set in the context of the rest of his philosophy in J. H. Randall, *Aristotle* (New York: Columbia, 1960), and W. D. Ross, *Aristotle* (New York: Barnes & Noble, 1955). Jeremy Bentham, who had a close hand in Mill's education, was an early defender of utility. His *Principles of Morals and Legislation* laid the groundwork for Mill's theory. Bentham's book is especially interesting because, unlike Mill, he made pleasurable sensations intrinsically good. He even provided a "calculus" for measuring pleasures. Mill's *Autobiography* (New York: Columbia, 1924) provides many insights into the travails of his intense childhood. A readable, interesting defense of utilitarianism is Rolf E. Sartorius, *Individual Conduct and Social Norms* (Encino and Belmont, Calif.: Dickenson, 1975). An excellent debate on utilitarianism is J. J. C. Smart and Bernard Williams, *Utilitarianism: For and Against* (London: Cambridge, 1973). For an explanation and debate of contemporary humanist interpretations of utilitarianism, see Morris B. Storer (ed.), *Humanist Ethics* (Buffalo, N.Y.: Prometheus, 1980). The classical attack on egoism is Bishop Joseph Butler's *Fifteen Sermons upon Human Nature*, first printed in 1726. The relevant sections of this work can be found in R. Brandt (ed.), *Value and Obligation* (New York: Harcourt, Brace & World, 1961). An interesting contemporary treatment of egoism is K. Baier, *The Moral Point of View* (Ithaca, N.Y.: Cornell, 1958). Ayn Rand, who has done much to popularize ethical egoism, presents her highly controversial version in her *The Virtue of Selfishness* (New York: New American Library, 1961). Robert G. Olson argues that self-interest cannot be divorced logically or practically from the interests of others in his *The Morality of Self-Interest* (New York: Harcourt, Brace, 1965). In this century, G. E. Moore's criticism of ethical naturalism is most responsible for the decline of utilitarianism and the rise of nonnaturalist theories. Moore's critique of naturalism and his own intuitionism are presented in *Principia Ethica* (New York: Cambridge, 1959). Two other forms of intuitionism are defended in W. D. Ross, *Foundations of Ethics* (Oxford: Clarendon Press, 1939), and D. D. Raphael, *The Moral Sense* (London: Oxford, 1957).

For discussion and debate on the morality of various stances on a variety of current issues, see the following: James Rachels (ed.), *Moral Problems* (New York: Harper & Row, 1971); Robert Baum (ed.), *Ethical Arguments for Analysis*, 2d ed. (New York: Holt, 1976); Thomas A. Mappes and Jane S. Zembaty (eds.), *Social Ethics* (New York: McGraw-Hill, 1977); D. P. Verene (ed.), *Sexual Love and Western Morality* (New York: Harper & Row, 1972); Robert Baker and Frederick Elliston (eds.), *Philosophy and Sex* (Buffalo, N.Y.: Prometheus Books, 1975); and Marvin Kohl (ed.), *Benificent Euthanasia* (Buffalo, N.Y.: Prometheus Books, 1975). For a useful introduction to the enormously complex issues in medical ethics, see Joseph Fletcher, *Humanhood: Essays in Biomedical Ethics* (Buffalo, N.Y.: Prometheus Books, 1979). Ronald Munson, *Intervention and Reflection: Basic Issues in Medical Ethics* (Belmont, Calif.: Wadsworth, 1979) is a very helpful medical ethics primer for students, featuring clear and incisive exposition, case studies, and readings.

Possibly the best nontechnical introduction to moral theory is James Rachels, *The Elements of Moral Philosophy* (Philadelphia: Temple University Press, 1986), from which the critique of cultural relativism which appears in the readings has been taken. Two other recent, but difficult and challenging works in ethics which more advanced students should consult are Alasdair Macintyre, *After Virtue*, 2d ed. (Notre Dame, Ind.: University of Notre Dame Press, 1984), and David Gauthier, *Morals By Agreement* (New York: Oxford University Press, 1986). Macintyre argues that the theory and practice of morality in the contemporary world are in a state of "grave disorder," and Gauthier attempts to build a basis for moral rules on cooperation agreed to by the members of society, and not considerations of personal utility.

To see the points of convergence and divergence between classical western ethical theories and those embraced in the far east, consult Gunapala Dharmasiri, *Fundamental of Buddhist Ethics* (Antioch, Calif.: Golden Leaves, 1988).

Informative reference sources on virtually all aspects of ethics are Paul Edwards (ed.), *The Encyclopedia of Philosophy* (New York: Macmillan and Free Press, 1967); Philip P. Wiener (ed.), *Dictionary of the History of Ideas* (New York: Scribner, 1974); and G. H. R. Parkinson (ed.), *The Handbook of Western Philosophy* (New York: Macmillan, 1988). The *Encyclopedia* is an eight-volume work; the index appears in volume 8. The *Dictionary* consists of four volumes plus an index. The *Handbook* is a single volume with a table of contents in the beginning and an index at the end.

PART FIVE

Political Philosophy

THE PARADOXES OF AUTHORITY

"It is not desirable to cultivate a respect for the law so much as for the right. The only obligation I have a right to assume is to do at any time what I think right" (Henry David Thoreau in *Civil Disobedience*).

"A man must do what his city and his country order him; or he must change their view of what is just.... He who disobeys [the laws] is thrice wrong; first because in disobeying [them] he is disobeying his parents; secondly because [they] are the authors of his education; thirdly because he has made an agreement with [them] that he will duly obey [their] commands" (Socrates in the *Crito,* on the occasion of an opportunity to escape prison and execution). *tacit consent*

"The sole end for which mankind are warranted, individually or collectively, in interfering in the liberty of action of any of their number, is self-protection.... The only purpose for which power can be rightfully exercised on any member of a civilized community, against his will, is to prevent harm to others..." (John Stuart Mill, *On Liberty*).

"There are also many positive acts for the benefit of others, which he may rightfully be compelled to perform; such as to give evidence in a court of justice, to bear his fair share in the common defense, or in any other joint work necessary to the interest of the society of which he enjoys the protection" (John Stuart Mill, *On Liberty*).

"I think we all have moral obligations to obey just laws. On the other hand, I think that we have moral obligations to disobey unjust laws because non-cooperation with evil is just as much a moral obligation as cooperation with good" (Rev. Martin Luther King, Jr.).

"Submit yourselves to every ordinance of men for the Lord's sake; whether it be to the king, as supreme; or unto the governors, as unto them that are sent by him for the punishment of evil-doers and for the praise of them that do well" (1 Peter 2:13–14).

441

"The working class, in the course of its development, will substitute for the old civil society an association which will exclude classes and their antagonism, and there will be no more political power properly so-called, since political power is precisely the official expression of antagonism in civil society" (Karl Marx, *Poverty of Philosophy*).

"The task of the leaders is not to put into effect the wishes and will of the masses....In the recent past we have encountered the phenomenon of certain categories of workers acting *against* their interests. What is the task of a leader in such a situation? Is it mechanically to implement incorrect ideas? No, it is not....If the will of the masses does not coincide with progress, then one must lead the masses in another direction..." (Jan Kadar, Address to the Hungarian National Assembly on May 11, 1957, explaining the need to suppress workers after the 1956 Budapest uprising).

11

The State and the Individual

PROBLEM INTRODUCTION

In ancient Greece Socrates was charged with <u>blasphemy</u> and the <u>corruption of youth</u> by misguided Athenians who had questionable political motives and who feared the consequences of his encouraging young people to question traditional beliefs. Although we do not have all the facts, apparently his trial left much to be desired, the outcome foreordained even before the evidence was presented. Socrates was found guilty as charged and was sentenced to death. The irony of it all! Athens had turned against its most brilliant and virtuous citizen. To his friends this was a scandal, an outrage that had to be met with resistance. Therefore, a group of them conspired to free Socrates while he was awaiting his execution, and to spirit him out of Athens to a distant place where he would be safe. They sent <u>Crito</u> to visit Socrates and to secure his cooperation in the escape plan. <u>Plato</u> reports their discussion in a dialogue entitled *Crito,* in which Crito and Socrates raise some of the most basic questions about a citizen's obligations to the State. <u>Indeed, the position taken by Socrates has become part of the foundation of Western political life</u>.

obey all laws

     Socrates listened intently to Crito's plea, but in the end he rejected the idea of escape and chose instead to accept his sentence, not because he wished to be a martyr, <u>but because he genuinely believed that it was his obligation to do so</u>. His justification is simple but profound. As young people grow up, Socrates tells us, they have ample opportunity to become acquainted with the way of life in the community by observing customs, traditions, institutional life, the workings of government, and citizens exercising rights and duties. A <u>young person who finds this offensive may go elsewhere</u>, to a place where the surroundings are more suitable and satisfactory. Should the young person stay, however, he or she must accept the duties of a citizen as the price of the rights of a citizen. Implicitly, Socrates says, an adult enters into a *contract* with the State which involves these terms: The State promises to promote the individual's well-being, and, in turn, the individual promises to respect the State and to obey its laws. Should a citizen object to a particular law, the contract requires him or her to obey it until the individual succeeds in securing a

tacit consent by staying

change through procedures for that purpose provided in the law. On this basis, Socrates points out that if he were to agree to escape, he would violate his promise to obey the law. He was not prepared to repudiate his obligation merely because the law had worked to his detriment in the case at hand. It would *seem*, then, for Socrates, that a citizen should obey all of the laws all of the time, being neither selective nor inconsistent.

On the other hand, Socrates himself may have opened the door to resistance to the State. As Socrates tells it, in the contract entered into by the citizens and the State, the State obligates itself to promote the welfare of the citizens, and to provide a mechanism for changing the law when its "commands are unjust." Now suppose that the State defaults on its part of the bargain. Suppose it becomes self-serving and tyrannical at the expense of the people at large, or deprives one group of the rights and privileges which it accords to others, or blocks any initiatives to change a law which many believe to be unwise or immoral. Perhaps in such circumstances a citizen would no longer have a duty to obey the government.

Not long ago, civil rights leaders in the United States faced these agonizing questions. Years of struggle within the law to end segregation had failed, especially but not exclusively in the south. Blacks were denied many rights, including the right to vote. Blacks were humiliated because many restaurants, lodgings, amusement parks, schools and colleges, stores, and restrooms were reserved for whites and closed to them. Blacks were the last hired and the first fired. Appeal to the courts was usually ineffective. Black extremists appeared on the scene, condemning whites as devils and calling on blacks to employ any means, including violence, to redress their long-standing grievances. The future of relations between the races looked bleak indeed.

As if on cue, an eloquent voice of moderation in the person of Dr. Martin Luther King, Jr., appeared on the scene. Eschewing violence because, like Gandhi before him, he viewed it as an immoral and counterproductive strategy which could only escalate violence and hatred between oppressor and oppressed, Dr. King, a Baptist minister, called for active but nonviolent resistance to discriminatory laws. His justification of this course, following a tradition with roots in Cicero, Augustine, and Aquinas, was that no citizen has a duty to obey an unjust law, and clearly laws that "degrade human personality," such as the "Jim Crow" laws, did just that. He said that segregation relegates blacks to the status of things, and deprives them of the opportunity to participate in their government through voting. Yet, he cautioned, to show that their cause is moral, blacks and their supporters must break the unjust laws "openly, lovingly, and with a willingness to accept the penalty."

Despite the fact that many condemned Dr. King as disruptive of law and order, he never once questioned the authority of the American government, or any government in principle, to make and enforce laws—in other words, to wield political authority. His aim was to improve government, not destroy it. His critique of government was much less radical than that of *philosophical anarchists*, such as Robert Paul Wolff, who deny that the State has any authority to command obedience from the citizens. Wolff affirms this on the basis of his view of what it means to be a moral agent. A moral agent, Wolff says, must be autonomous, or self-legislating, thinking and judging for himself or herself, and accepting responsibility for his or her actions. The individual citizen can never relinquish autonomy, thereby permitting others to dictate how he or she should act, and yet remain a moral agent. The obvious implication of this is that the State cannot issue binding commands to individuals. A citizen, therefore, has no *duty* to obey a law simply because his or her government has enacted it, even though he or she may do so *for other reasons.*

The crux of the issue, then, seems to be whether the autonomy of the individual and the authority of the State are compatible. Can the individual remain autonomous, or self-legislating, while at the same time recognizing a government as legitimate, as possessing the authority to make and enforce laws which he or she has a duty to obey? Carl Cohen answers in the affirmative. According to Cohen, there is one form of government—democracy— in which a person makes his or her own laws. This is done by participation in the process of lawmaking through one's own vote or through the votes and decisions of those representatives whom one elected. When individuals participate in the process of lawmaking, they pledge to respect the laws resulting from the process, even if some are disagreeable to them.

Yet even Cohen draws back from any suggestion that a citizen has a duty to obey each and every law. Although I make a promise to obey the laws which are the outcome of the lawmaking process in which I participate, and although I have a serious obligation to obey such laws, this obligation is *conditional* or *qualified,* not absolute. Exceptional circumstances could arise where a more important moral obligation would require me to break my promise. For instance, if I promise to help you paint a room on Saturday, but I come across a serious accident along the way, then it is my moral duty to attend to the injured and break my promise. The duty to save lives is more important than the duty to keep a promise to help a friend paint a room.

From these considerations it is obvious that the problem of *law or conscience* is very complicated. Try to formulate your own position as you read these landmark statements on the problem. As you do, you will probably find, in your frustration, as so many have, that "the speculative line of demarcation where obedience ought to end and resistance must begin, is faint, obscure, and not easily definable."*

---

*Edmund Burke, *Reflections on the Revolution in France* (Indianapolis: Library of Liberal Arts, 1955), p. 34.

Our Duty to the Law
Plato

In 404 B.C. the Peloponnesian War ended with the defeat of Athens. The victorious Spartans set up a puppet regime of thirty men who proceeded to terrorize the citizens with mass arrests and executions of dissenters. When the supporters of democracy came back into power and made peace with the Spartans, they, in turn, took reprisals against those who had sided with what became known as the "Tyranny of the Thirty." Socrates, the friend and teacher of Plato (see biographical information, p. 175), was suspected of complicity in some of the brutalities of the Thirty. But this was untrue, and since nothing could be proved against him, his enemies accused him of corrupting the youth and of being impious. Although he denied the charges, he was found guilty, and was executed in 399.

Plato knew that Socrates was innocent and that the legal process had been corrupted by prejudice. Nevertheless, in the following selection, Plato has Socrates defending the right of the State to take his life and arguing that he is obliged to allow it. Plato had seen what life was like when the rule of law disappeared—more Athenians were killed during the year-long reign of the Thirty than in the previous twenty-seven years of the war. The rule of law is our only protection against anarchy.

But the law can be unfair or immoral, or the legal process can be perverted, and when this occurs, why should we surrender our own conscience and our own sense of justice—indeed our very lives—to some remote ideal of social order? Plato's answers to these questions may not satisfy you, but you can be sure that they were agonizingly reached by a man who saw his best friend unjustly executed by the Athenian court.

CRITO: ...But, oh! my beloved Socrates, let me entreat you once more to take my advice and escape. For if you die I shall not only lose a friend who can never be replaced, but there is another evil: people who do not know you and me will believe that I might have saved you if I had been willing to give money, but that I did not care. Now, can there be a worse disgrace than this—that I should be thought to value money more than the life of a friend? For the many will not be persuaded that I wanted you to escape, and that you refused.

SOCRATES: But why, my dear Crito, should we care about the opinion of the many? Good men, and they are the only persons who are worth considering, will think of these things truly as they occurred.

CRITO: But you see, Socrates, that the opinion of the many must be regarded, for what is happening shows that they can do the greatest evil to any one who has lost their good opinion.

SOCRATES: I only wish it were so, Crito; and that the many could do the greatest evil; for then they would also be able to do the greatest good—and what

From *The Crito*, in *The Dialogues of Plato*, Benjamin Jowett, trans. (The Macmillan Company, Ltd., 1892).

a fine thing this would be! But in reality they can do neither; for they cannot make a man either wise or foolish; and whatever they do is the result of chance.

CRITO: Well, I will not dispute with you; but please tell me, Socrates, whether you are not acting out of regard to me and your other friends: are you not afraid that if you escape from prison we may get into trouble with the informers for having stolen you away, and lose either the whole or a great part of our property; or that even a worse evil may happen to us? Now, if you fear on our account, be at ease; for in order to save you, we ought surely to run this, or even a greater risk; be persuaded, then, and do as I say.

SOCRATES: Yes, Crito, that is one fear which you mention, but by no means the only one.

CRITO: Fear not—there are persons who are willing to get you out of prison at no great cost; and as for the informers, they are far from being exorbitant in their demands—a little money will satisfy them. My means, which are certainly ample, are at your service, and if you have a scruple about spending all mine, here are strangers who will give you the use of theirs; and one of them, Simias the Theban, has brought a large sum of money for this very purpose; and Cebes and many others are prepared to spend their money in helping you to escape. I say, therefore, do not hesitate on our account, and do not say, as you did in court, that you will have a difficulty in knowing what to do with yourself anywhere else. For men will love you in other places to which you may go, and not in Athens only; there are friends of mine in Thessaly, if you like to go to them, who will value and protect you, and no Thessalian will give you any trouble. Nor can I think that you are at all justified, Socrates, in betraying your own life when you might be saved; in acting thus you are playing into the hands of your enemies, who are hurrying on your destruction. And further I should say that you are deserting your own children; for you might bring them up and educate them; instead of which you go away and leave them, and they will have to take their chance; and if they do not meet with the usual fate of orphans, there will be small thanks to you. No man should bring children into the world who is unwilling to persevere to the end in their nurture and education. But you appear to be choosing the easier part, not the better and manlier, which would have been more becoming in one who professes to care for virtue in all his actions, like yourself. And indeed, I am ashamed not only of you, but of us who are your friends, when I reflect that the whole business will be attributed entirely to our want of courage. The trial need never have come on, or might have been managed differently; and this last act, or crowning folly, will seem to have occurred through our negligence and cowardice, who might have saved you, if you had been good for anything; and you might have saved yourself, for there was no difficulty at all. See now, Socrates, how sad and discreditable are the consequences, both to us and you. Make up your mind then, or rather have your mind already made up, for the time of deliberation is over, and there is only one thing to be done, which must be done this very night, and if we delay at all will be no longer practicable or possible; I beseech you therefore, Socrates, be persuaded by me, and do as I say.

SOCRATES: Dear Crito, your zeal is invaluable, if a right one; but if wrong, the greater the zeal the greater the danger; and therefore we ought to consider whether I shall or shall not do as you say. For I am and always have been one of those natures who must be guided by reason, whatever the reason may be which upon reflection appears to me to be the best; and now that this chance has befallen me, I cannot repudiate my own words: the principles which I have hitherto honoured and revered I still honour, and unless we can at once find other and better principles, I am certain not to agree with you; no, not even if the power of the multitude could inflict many more imprisonments, confiscations, deaths, frightening us like children with hobgoblin terrors. What will be the fairest way of considering the question? Shall I return to your old argument about the opinions of men?—we are saying that some of them are to be regarded, and others not. Now were we right in maintaining this before I was condemned? And has the argument which was once good now proved to be talk for the sake of talking—mere childish nonsense? That is what I want to consider with your help, Crito: whether, under my present circumstances, the argument appears to be in any way different or not; and is to be allowed by me or disallowed. That argument, which, as I believe, is maintained by many persons of authority, was to the effect, as I was saying, that the opinions of some men are to be regarded, and of other men not to be regarded. Now you, Crito, are not going to die tomorrow—at least, there is no human probability of this—and therefore you are disinterested and not liable to be deceived by the circumstances in which you are placed. Tell me then, whether I am right in saying that some opinions, and the opinions of some men only, are to be valued, and that other opinions, and the opinions of other men, are not to be valuable. I ask you whether I was right in maintaining this?

CRITO: Certainly.

SOCRATES: The good are to be regarded, and not the bad?

CRITO: Yes.

SOCRATES: And the opinions of the wise are good, and the opinions of the unwise are evil?

CRITO: Certainly.

SOCRATES: And what was said about another matter? Is the pupil who devotes himself to the practice of gymnastics supposed to attend to the praise and blame and opinion of every man, or of one man only—his physician or trainer, whoever he may be?

CRITO: Of one man only.

SOCRATES: And he ought to fear the censure and welcome the praise of that one only, and not of the many?

CRITO: Clearly so.

SOCRATES: And he ought to act and train, and eat and drink in the way which seems good to his single master who has understanding, rather than according to the opinion of all other men put together?

CRITO: True.

SOCRATES: And if he disobeys and disregards the opinion and approval of the one, and regards the opinion of the many who have no understanding, will he not suffer evil?

CRITO: Certainly he will.

SOCRATES: And what will the evil be, whither tending and what affecting, in the disobedient person?

CRITO: Clearly, affecting the body; that is what is destroyed by the evil.

SOCRATES: Very good; and is not this true, Crito, of other things which we need not separately enumerate? In questions of just and unjust, fair and foul, good and evil, which are the subjects of our present consultation, ought we to follow the opinion of the many and to fear them; or the opinion of the one man who has understanding? ought we not to fear and reverence him more than all the rest of the world: and if we desert him shall we not destroy and injure that principle in us which may be assumed to be improved by justice and deteriorated by injustice;—there is such a principle?

CRITO: Certainly there is, Socrates.

SOCRATES: Take a parallel instance:—if, acting under the advice of those who have no understanding, we destroy that which is improved by health and is deteriorated by disease, would life be worth having? And that which has been destroyed is—the body?

CRITO: Yes.

SOCRATES: Could we live, having an evil and corrupted body?

CRITO: Certainly not.

SOCRATES: And will life be worth having, if that higher part of man be destroyed, which is improved by justice and depraved by injustice? Do we suppose that principle, whatever it may be in man, which has to do with justice and injustice, to be inferior to the body?

CRITO: Certainly not.

SOCRATES: More honourable than the body?

CRITO: Far more.

SOCRATES: Then, my friend, we must not regard what the many say of us: but what he, the one man who has understanding of just and unjust, will say, and what the truth will say. And therefore you begin in error when you advise that we should regard the opinion of the many about just and unjust, good and evil, honourable and dishonourable,—"Well," some one will say, "but the many can kill us."

CRITO: Yes, Socrates: that will clearly be the answer.

SOCRATES: And it is true: but still I find with surprise that the old argument is unshaken as ever. And I should like to know whether I may say the same of another proposition—that not life, but a good life, is to be chiefly valued?

CRITO: Yes, that also remains unshaken.

SOCRATES: And a good life is equivalent to a just and honourable one—that holds also?

CRITO: Yes, it does.

SOCRATES: From these premisses I proceed to argue the question whether I ought or ought not to try and escape without the consent of the Athenians: and if I am clearly right in escaping, then I will make the attempt; but if not, I will abstain. The other considerations which you mention, of money and loss of character and the duty of educating one's children are, I fear, only the doctrines of the multitude, who would be as ready to restore people to life, if they were able, as they are to put them to death—and with as little reason. But now, since the argument has thus far prevailed, the only question which remains to be considered is, whether we shall do rightly either in escaping or in suffering others to aid in our escape and paying them in money and thanks, or whether in reality we shall not do rightly; and if the latter, then death or any other calamity which may ensue on my remaining here must not be allowed to enter into the calculation.

CRITO: I think that you are right, Socrates; how then shall we proceed?

SOCRATES: Let us consider the matter together, and do you either refute me if you can, and I will be convinced; or else cease, my dear friend, from repeating to me that I ought to escape against the wishes of the Athenians: for I highly value your attempts to persuade me to do so, but I may not be persuaded against my own better judgment. And now please to consider my first position, and try how you can best answer me.

CRITO: I will.

SOCRATES: Are we to say that we are never intentionally to do wrong, or that in one way we ought and in another we ought not to do wrong, or is doing wrong always evil and dishonourable, as I was just now saying, and as has been already acknowledged by us? Are all our former admissions which were made within a few days to be thrown away? And have we, at our age, been earnestly discoursing with one another all our life long only to discover that we are no better than children? Or, in spite of the opinion of the many, and in spite of consequences whether better or worse, shall we insist on the truth of what was then said, that injustice is always an evil and dishonour to him who acts unjustly? Shall we say so or not?

CRITO: Yes.

SOCRATES: Then we must do no wrong?

CRITO: Certainly not.

SOCRATES: Nor when injured injure in return, as the many imagine; for we must injure no one at all?

CRITO: Clearly not.

SOCRATES: Again, Crito, may we do evil?

CRITO: Surely not, Socrates.

SOCRATES: And what of doing evil in return for evil, which is the morality of the many—is that just or not?

CRITO: Not just.

SOCRATES: For doing evil to another is the same as injuring him?

CRITO: Very true.

SOCRATES: Then we ought not to retaliate or render evil for evil to any one, whatever evil we may have suffered from him. But I would have you consider, Crito, whether you really mean what you are saying. For this opinion has never been held, and never will be held, by any considerable number of persons; and those who are agreed and those who are not agreed upon this point have no common ground, and can only despise one another when they see how widely they differ. Tell me, then, whether you agree with and assent to my first principle, that neither injury nor retaliation nor warding off evil by evil is ever right. And shall that be the premise of our argument? Or do you decline and dissent from this? For so I have ever thought, and continue to think; but, if you are of another opinion, let me hear what you have to say. If, however, you remain of the same mind as formerly, I will proceed to the next step.

CRITO: You may proceed, for I have not changed my mind.

SOCRATES: Then I will go on to the next point, which may be put in the form of a question:—Ought a man to do what he admits to be right, or ought he to betray the right?

CRITO: He ought to do what he thinks right.

SOCRATES: But if this is true, what is the application? In leaving the prison against the will of the Athenians, do I wrong any? or rather do I not wrong those whom I ought least to wrong? Do I not desert the principles which were acknowledged by us to be just—what do you say?

CRITO: I cannot tell, Socrates; for I do not know.

SOCRATES: Then consider the matter in this way: Imagine that I am about to play truant (you may call the proceeding by any name which you like), and the laws and the government come and interrogate me: "Tell us, Socrates," they say, "what are you about? are you not going by an act of yours to overturn us—the laws, and the whole state, as far as in you lies? Do you imagine that a state can subsist and not be overthrown, in which the decisions of law have no power, but are set aside and trampled upon by individuals?" What will be our answer, Crito, to these and the like words? Any one, and especially a rhetorician, will have a good deal to say on behalf of the law which requires a sentence to be carried out. He will argue that this law should not be set aside; and shall we reply, "Yes, but the state has injured us and given an unjust sentence." Suppose I say that?

CRITO: Very good, Socrates.

SOCRATES: "And was that our agreement with you?" the law would answer, "or were you to abide by the sentence of the state?" And if I were to express my astonishment at their words, the law would probably add: "Answer, Socrates, instead of opening your eyes—you are in the habit of asking and answering questions. Tell us,—What complaint have you to make against us which justifies you in attempting to destroy us and the state? In the first place did we not bring you into existence? Your father married your mother by our aid and begat you. Say whether you have any objection to urge against those of us who regulate marriage?" None, I should reply. "Or against those of us who after birth regulate the nurture and education of children, in which you also were trained? Were not the laws, which have the charge of education, right in commanding your father to train you in music and gymnastic?" Right, I should reply. "Well then, since you were brought into the world and nurtured and educated by us, can you deny in the first place that you are our child and slave, as your fathers were before you? And if this is true you are not on equal terms with us; nor can you think that you have a right to do to us what we are doing to you. Would you have any right to strike or revile or do any other evil to your father or your master, if you had one, because you have been struck or reviled by him, or received some other evil at his hands?—you would not say this? And because we think right to destroy you, do you think that you have any right to destroy us in return, and your country as far as in you lies? Will you, O professor of true virtue, pretend that you are justified in this? Has a philosopher like you failed to discover that our country is more to be valued and higher and holier far than mother or father or any ancestor, and more to be regarded in the eyes of the gods and of men of understanding? Also to be soothed, and gently and reverently entreated when angry, even more than a father, and either to be persuaded, or if not persuaded, to be obeyed? And when we are punished by her, whether with imprisonment or stripes, the punishment is to be endured in silence; and if she leads us to wounds or death in battle, thither we follow as is right; neither may any one yield or retreat or leave his rank, but whether in battle or in a court of law, or in any other place, he must do what his city and his country order him; or he must change their view of what is just: and if he may do no violence to his father or mother, much less may he do violence to his country." What answer shall we make to this, Crito? Do the laws speak truly, or do they not?

CRITO: I think that they do.

SOCRATES: Then the laws will say, "Consider, Socrates, if we are speaking truly that in your present attempt you are going to do us an injury. For, having brought you into the world, and nurtured and educated you, and given you and every other citizen a share in every good which we had to give, we further proclaim to any Athenian by the liberty which we allow him, that if he does not like us when he has become of age and has seen the ways of the city, and made our acquaintance, he may go where he pleases and take his goods with him. None of us laws will forbid him or interfere with him. Any one who does not like us and the city, and who wants to emigrate to a colony or to any other city, may go where he likes, retaining his property. But he who has experience of the manner in which we order justice and administer the state, and still remains, has entered into an implied contract that he will do as we command him. And he who disobeys us is, as we maintain, thrice wrong; first, because in disobeying us he is

tacit consent

tacit consent

disobeying his parents; secondly, because we are the authors of his education; thirdly, because he has made an agreement with us that he will duly obey our commands; and he neither obeys them nor convinces us that our commands are unjust; and we do not rudely impose them, but give him the alternative of obeying or convincing us;—that is what we offer, and he does neither.

"These are the sort of accusations to which, as we were saying, you, Socrates, will be exposed if you accomplish your intentions; you, above all other Athenians." Suppose now I ask, why I rather than anybody else? they will justly retort upon me that I above all other men have acknowledged the agreement. "There is clear proof," they will say, "Socrates, that we and the city were not displeasing to you. Of all Athenians you have been the most constant resident in the city, which, as you never leave, you may be supposed to love. For you never went out of the city either to see the games, except once when you went to the Isthmus, or to any other place unless when you were on military service; nor did you travel as other men do. Nor had you any curiosity to know other states or their laws; your affections did not go beyond us and our state; we were your special favourites, and you acquiesced in our government of you; and here in this city you begat your children, which is a proof of your satisfaction. Moreover, you might in the course of the trial, if you had liked, have fixed the penalty at banishment; the state which refuses to let you go now would have let you go then. But you pretended that you preferred death to exile, and that you were not unwilling to die. And now you have forgotten these fine sentiments, and pay no respect to us the laws, of whom you are the destroyer; and are doing what only a miserable slave would do, running away and turning your back upon the compacts and agreements which you made as a citizen. And first of all answer this very question: Are we right in saying that you agreed to be governed according to us in deed, and not in word only? Is that true or not?" How shall we answer, Crito? Must we not assent?

CRITO: We cannot help it, Socrates.

SOCRATES: Then will they not say: "You, Socrates, are breaking the covenants and agreements which you made with us at your leisure, not in any haste or under any compulsion or deception, but after you have had seventy years to think of them, during which time you were at liberty to leave the city, if we were not to your mind, or if our covenants appeared to you to be unfair. You had your choice, and might have gone either to Lacedaemon or Crete, both which states are often praised by you for their good government, or to some other Hellenic or foreign state. Whereas you, above all other Athenians, seemed to be so fond of the state, or, in other words, of us her laws (and who would care about a state which has no laws?), that you never stirred out of her; the halt, the blind, the maimed were not more stationary in her than you were. And now you run away and forsake your agreements. Not so, Socrates, if you will take our advice; do not make yourself ridiculous by escaping out of the city.

"For just consider, if you transgress and err in this sort of way, what good will you do either to yourself or to your friends? That your friends will be driven into exile and deprived of citizenship, or will lose their property, is tolerably certain; and you yourself, if you fly to one of the neighboring cities, as, for example, Thebes or Megara, both of which are well governed, will come to them as an enemy, Socrates, and their government will be against you, and all patriotic citizens will cast an evil eye upon you as a subverter of the laws, and you will confirm in the minds of the judges the justice of their own condemnation of you. For he who is a corrupter of the laws is more than likely to be a corrupter of the young and foolish portion of mankind. Will you then flee from well-ordered cities and virtuous men? and is existence worth having on these terms? Or will you go to them without shame, and talk to them, Socrates? And what will you say to them? What you say here about virtue and justice and institutions and laws being the best things among well-governed states to Crito's friends in Thessaly, where there is great disorder and licence, they will be charmed to hear the tale of your escape from prison, set off with ludicrous particulars of the manner in which you were wrapped in a goatskin or some other disguise, and metamorphosed as the manner is of runaways; but will there be no one to remind you that in your old age you were not ashamed to violate the most sacred laws from a miserable desire of a little more life? Perhaps not, if you keep them in a good temper; but if they are out of temper you will hear many degrading things; you will live, but how?—as the flatterer of all men, and the servant of all men; and doing what?—eating and drinking in Thessaly, having gone abroad in order that you may get a dinner. And where will be your fine sentiments about justice and virtue? Say that you wish to live for the sake of your children—you want to bring them up and educate them—will you take them into Thessaly and deprive them of Athenian citizenship? Is this the benefit which you will confer upon them? Or are you under the impression that they will be better cared for and educated here if you are still alive, although absent from them; for your friends will take care of them? Do you fancy that if you are an inhabitant of Thessaly they will take care of them, and if you are an inhabitant of the other world that they will not take care of them? Nay; but if they who call themselves friends are good for anything, they will—to be sure they will.

"Listen, then, Socrates, to us who have brought you up. Think not of life and children first, and of justice afterwards, but of justice first, that you may be justified before the princes of the world below. For neither will you nor any that belong to you be happier or holier or juster in this life, or happier in another, if you do as Crito bids. Now you depart in innocence, a sufferer and not a doer of evil; a victim, not of the laws but of men. But if you go forth, returning evil for evil, and injury for injury, breaking the covenants and agreements which you have made with us, and wronging those whom you ought least of all to wrong, that is to say, yourself, your friends, your country, and us, we shall be angry with you while you live, and our brethren, the laws of the world below, will receive you as an enemy; for they will know that you have done your best to destroy us. Listen, then, to us and not to Crito."

This, dear Crito, is the voice which I seem to hear murmuring in my ears, like the sound of the flute in the ears of the mystic; that voice, I say, is humming in my ears and prevents me from hearing any other. And I know that anything more which you may say will be in vain. Yet speak, if you have anything to say.

CRITO: I have nothing to say, Socrates.

SOCRATES: Leave me then, Crito, to fulfil the will of God, and to follow whither he leads.

STUDY QUESTIONS

1. Socrates characterizes his relationship to the State as that of a child to its parent. What facts support this analogy? Do you agree with the comparison?

2. What are the limits of authority of parents over their children? When may a child rightfully reject the demands of parents? Do these considerations apply in Socrates's case?

3. Socrates argues that he is obliged to obey the law because he has contractually promised to do so. What facts are adduced to support the claim that he is under an implied contract to obey the law? Do you think the evidence is sufficient to demonstrate that a contract exists?

4. Surely contracts are not binding under any and all circumstances. What sorts of considerations would justify the breaking of a contract? Do you think that any of them obtain in this case?

5. Would Socrates grant amnesty to those who resisted the draft during the war in Viet Nam? Would you?

6. "An ordered society cannot exist if every man may determine which laws he will obey...that only 'just' laws need be obeyed and that every man is free to determine for himself the question of 'justness'" (Lewis F. Powell, Jr.). To what extent would Socrates agree with this? Would he accept it unqualifiedly?

Letter From Birmingham Jail
Martin Luther King, Jr.

In 1968 an assassin's bullet stilled the eloquent voice of a towering figure in
the twentieth century. How ironic that an act of violence cut down this
champion of nonviolence and recipient of the Nobel Peace Prize! As though
he had a premonition of his impending fate, Martin Luther King, Jr. (1929–
1968), told a group of followers only days before his death that he had seen
the promised land of equal opportunity for blacks in America, but that he
would not be there with his brothers and sisters to enjoy it.

   Dr. King was the heart and soul of the civil rights movement in America in
the 1950s and 1960s. In countless speeches, sermons, writings, and public
demonstrations, he worked to rid America of the vestiges of slavery. Those
who were resistant to change, and with it a new status for blacks, not only
spoke disparagingly of him, but subjected him to electronic surveillance,
physical assaults, and threats. A lesser person would not have exhibited the
self-restraint which marked his service to his race and his nation.

   Dr. King's activism was founded upon a framework of beliefs which is set
out in the following excerpt from a letter which he wrote in a jail cell in
Birmingham, Alabama, in response to criticisms of local clergy who described
the civil rights demonstration which he led there in 1963 as "unwise and
untimely." In the letter Dr. King argues within the tradition of natural law
that an unjust law is no law at all and that active, nonviolent resistance to
laws and customs which perpetuate segregation is not only morally
permissable but morally obligatory. Dr. King's letter shows the influence of
Mohandas Gandhi, the Indian leader who helped bring about India's
independence of British control, and Henry David Thoreau, whose "Essay on
Civil Disobedience," written in 1859, called upon citizens to refuse to pay
their taxes as a way of pressuring government to end slavery.

You express a great deal of anxiety over our willingness to break laws. This is
certainly a legitimate concern. Since we so diligently urge people to obey the
Supreme Court's decision of 1954 outlawing segregation in the public schools,
at first glance it may seem rather paradoxical for us consciously to break laws.
One may well ask: "How can you advocate breaking some laws and obeying
others?" The answer lies in the fact that there are two types of laws: just and
unjust. I would be the first to advocate obeying just laws. One has not only
a legal but a moral responsibility to obey just laws. Conversely, one has a
moral responsibility to disobey unjust laws. I would agree with St. Augustine
that "an unjust law is no law at all."

   Now, what is the difference between the two? How does one determine
whether a law is just or unjust? A just law is a man-made code that squares
with the moral law or the law of God. An unjust law is a code that is out of

harmony with the moral law. To put it in the terms of St. Thomas Aquinas: An unjust law is a human law that is not rooted in eternal law and natural law. Any law that uplifts human personality is just. Any law that degrades human personality is unjust. All segregation statutes are unjust because segregation distorts the soul and damages the personality. It gives the segregator a false sense of superiority and the segregated a false sense of inferiority. Segregation, to use the terminology of the Jewish philosopher Martin Buber, substitutes an "I—it" relationship for an "I—thou" relationship and ends up relegating persons to the status of things. Hence segregation is not only politically, economically and sociologically unsound, it is morally wrong and sinful. Paul Tillich has said that sin is separation. Is not segregation an existential expression of man's tragic separation, his awful estrangement, his terrible sinfulness? Thus it is that I can urge men to obey the 1954 decision of the Supreme Court, for it is morally right; and I can urge them to disobey segregation ordinances, for they are morally wrong.

Let us consider a more concrete example of just and unjust laws. An unjust law is a code that a numerical or power majority group compels a minority group to obey but does not make binding on itself. This is *difference* made legal. By the same token, a just law is a code that a majority compels a minority to follow and that it is willing to follow itself. This is *sameness* made legal.

Let me give another explanation. A law is unjust if it is inflicted on a minority that, as a result of being denied the right to vote, had no part in enacting or devising the law. Who can say that the legislature of Alabama which set up that state's segregation laws was democratically elected? Throughout Alabama all sorts of devious methods are used to prevent Negroes from becoming registered voters, and there are some counties in which, even though Negroes constitute a majority of the population, not a single Negro is registered. Can any law enacted under such circumstances be considered democratically structured?

Sometimes a law is just on its face and unjust in its application. For instance, I have been arrested on a charge of parading without a permit. Now, there is nothing wrong in having an ordinance which requires a permit for a parade. But such an ordinance becomes unjust when it is used to maintain segregation and to deny citizens the First-Amendment privilege of peaceful assembly and protest.

I hope you are able to see the distinction I am trying to point out. In no sense do I advocate evading or defying the law, as would the rabid segregationist. That would lead to anarchy. One who breaks an unjust law must do so openly, lovingly, and with a willingness to accept the penalty. I submit that an individual who breaks a law that conscience tells him is unjust, and who willingly accepts the penalty of imprisonment in order to arouse the conscience of the community over its injustice, is in reality expressing the highest respect for law.

Of course, there is nothing new about this kind of civil disobedience. It was evidenced sublimely in the refusal of Shadrach, Meshach and Abednego to obey the laws of Nebuchadnezzar, on the ground that a higher moral law was at stake. It was practiced superbly by the early Christians, who were willing to face hungry lions and the excruciating pain of chopping blocks rather than submit to certain unjust laws of the Roman Empire. To a degree, academic freedom is a reality today because Socrates practiced civil disobedience. In our own nation, the Boston Tea Party represented a massive act of civil disobedience.

We should never forget that everything Adolf Hitler did in Germany was "legal" and everything the Hungarian freedom fighters did in Hungary was "illegal." It was "illegal" to aid and comfort a Jew in Hitler's Germany. Even so, I am sure that, had I lived in Germany at the time, I would have aided and comforted my Jewish brothers. If today I lived in a Communist country where certain principles dear to the Christian faith are suppressed, I would openly advocate disobeying that country's antireligious laws.

I must make two honest confessions to you, my Christian and Jewish brothers. First, I must confess that over the past few years I have been gravely disappointed with the white moderate. I have almost reached the regrettable conclusion that the Negro's great stumbling block in his stride toward freedom is not the White Citizen's Counciler or the Ku Klux Klanner, but the white moderate, who is more devoted to "order" than to justice; who prefers a negative peace which is the absence of tension to a positive peace which is the presence of justice; who constantly says: "I agree with you in the goal you seek, but I cannot agree with your methods of direct action"; who paternalistically believes he can set the timetable for another man's freedom; who lives by a mythical concept of time and who constantly advises the Negro to wait for a "more convenient season." Shallow understanding from people of good will is more frustrating than absolute misunderstanding from people of ill will. Lukewarm acceptance is much more bewildering than outright rejection.

I had hoped that the white moderate would understand that law and order exist for the purpose of establishing justice and that when they fail in this purpose they become the dangerously structured dams that block the flow of social progress. I had hoped that the white moderate would understand that the present tension in the South is a necessary phase of the transition from an obnoxious negative peace, in which the Negro passively accepted his unjust plight, to a substantive and positive peace, in which all men will respect the dignity and worth of human personality. Actually, we who engage in nonviolent direct action are not the creators of tension. We merely bring to the surface the hidden tension that is already alive. We bring it out in the open, where it can be seen and dealt with. Like a boil that can never be cured so long as it is covered up but must be opened with all its ugliness to the natural medicines of air and light, injustice must be exposed, with all the tension its exposure creates, to the light of human conscience and the air of national opinion before it can be cured.

In your statement you assert that our actions, even though peaceful, must

be condemned because they precipitate violence. But is this a logical assertion? Isn't this like condemning a robbed man because his possession of money
precipitated the evil act of robbery? Isn't this like condemning Socrates because his unswerving commitment to truth and his philosophical inquiries
precipitated the act by the misguided populace in which they made him drink
hemlock? Isn't this like condemning Jesus because his unique God-
consciousness and never-ceasing devotion to God's will precipitated the evil
act of crucifixion? We must come to see that, as the federal courts have consistently affirmed, it is wrong to urge an individual to cease his efforts to gain
his basic constitutional rights because the quest may precipitate violence. Society must protect the robbed and punish the robber.

I had also hoped that the white moderate would reject the myth concerning time in relation to the struggle for freedom. I have just received a letter
from a white brother in Texas. He writes: "All Christians know that the colored people will receive equal rights eventually, but it is possible that you are
in too great a religious hurry. It has taken Christianity almost two thousand
years to accomplish what it has. The teachings of Christ take time to come to
earth." Such an attitude stems from a tragic misconception of time, from the
strangely irrational notion that there is something in the very flow of time that
will inevitably cure all ills. Actually, time itself is neutral; it can be used either
destructively or constructively. More and more I feel that the people of ill will
have used time much more effectively than have the people of good will. We
will have to repent in this generation not merely for the hateful words and
actions of the bad people but for the appalling silence of the good people.
Human progress never rolls in on wheels of inevitability; it comes through the
tireless efforts of men willing to be co-workers with God, and without this
hard work, time itself becomes an ally of the forces of social stagnation. We
must use time creatively, in the knowledge that the time is always ripe to do
right. Now is the time to make real the promise of democracy and transform
our pending national elegy into a creative psalm of brotherhood. Now is the
time to lift our national policy from the quicksand of racial injustice to the solid
rock of human dignity.

You speak of our activity in Birmingham as extreme. At first I was rather
disappointed that fellow clergymen would see my nonviolent efforts as those
of an extremist. I began thinking about the fact that I stand in the middle of
two opposing forces in the Negro community. One is a force of complacency,
made up in part of Negroes who, as a result of long years of oppression, are
so drained of self-respect and a sense of "somebodiness" that they have adjusted to segregation; and in part of a few middle-class Negroes who, because
of a degree of academic and economic security and because in some ways they
profit by segregation, have become insensitive to the problems of the masses.
The other force is one of bitterness and hatred, and it comes perilously close
to advocating violence. It is expressed in the various black nationalist groups
that are springing up across the nation, the largest and best-known being Elijah
Muhammad's Muslim movement. Nourished by the Negro's frustration over

the continued existence of racial discrimination, this movement is made up of people who have lost faith in America, who have absolutely repudiated Christianity, and who have concluded that the white man is an incorrigible "devil."

I have tried to stand between these two forces, saying that we need emulate neither the "do-nothingism" of the complacent nor the hatred and despair of the black nationalist. For there is the more excellent way of love and nonviolent protest. I am grateful to God that, through the influence of the Negro church, the way of nonviolence became an integral part of our struggle.

If this philosophy had not emerged, by now many streets of the South would, I am convinced, be flowing with blood. And I am further convinced that if our white brothers dismiss as "rabble-rousers" and "outside agitators" those of us who employ nonviolent direct action, and if they refuse to support our nonviolent efforts, millions of Negroes will, out of frustration and despair, seek solace and security in black-nationalist ideologies—a development that would inevitably lead to a frightening racial nightmare.

Oppressed people cannot remain oppressed forever. The yearning for freedom eventually manifests itself, and that is what has happened to the American Negro. Something within has reminded him of his birthright of freedom, and something without has reminded him that it can be gained. Consciously or unconsciously, he has been caught up by the *Zeitgeist*, and with his black brothers of Africa and his brown and yellow brothers of Asia, South America and the Caribbean, the United States Negro is moving with a sense of great urgency toward the promised land of racial justice. If one recognizes this vital urge that has engulfed the Negro community, one should readily understand why public demonstrations are taking place. The Negro has many pent-up resentments and latent frustrations, and he must release them. So let him march; let him make prayer pilgrimages to the city hall; let him go on freedom rides—and try to understand why he must do so. If his repressed emotions are not released in nonviolent ways, they will seek expression through violence; this is not a threat but a fact of history. So I have not said to my people: "Get rid of your discontent." Rather, I have tried to say that this normal and healthy discontent can be channeled into the creative outlet of nonviolent direct action. And now this approach is being termed extremist.

But though I was initially disappointed at being categorized as an extremist, as I continued to think about the matter I gradually gained a measure of satisfaction from the label. Was not Jesus an extremist for love: "Love your enemies, bless them that curse you, do good to them that hate you, and pray for them which despitefully use you, and persecute you." Was not Amos an extremist for justice: "Let justice roll down like waters and righteousness like an ever-flowing stream." Was not Paul an extremist for the Christian gospel: "I bear in my body the marks of the Lord Jesus." Was not Martin Luther an extremist: "Here I stand; I cannot do otherwise, so help me God." And John Bunyan: "I will stay in jail to the end of my days before I make a butchery of my conscience." And Abraham Lincoln: "This nation cannot survive half slave and half free." And Thomas Jefferson: "We hold these truths to be self-evident, that all men are created equal..." So the question is not whether we will be extremists, but what kind of extremists we will be. Will we be extremists for hate or for love? Will we be extremists for the preservation of injustice or for the extension of justice? In that dramatic scene on Calvary's hill three men were crucified. We must never forget that all three were crucified for the same crime—the crime of extremism. Two were extremists for immorality, and thus fell below their environment. The other, Jesus Christ, was an extremist for love, truth and goodness, and thereby rose above his environment. Perhaps the South, the nation and the world are in dire need of creative extremists.

I had hoped that the white moderate would see this need. Perhaps I was too optimistic; perhaps I expected too much. I suppose I should have realized that few members of the oppressor race can understand the deep groans and passionate yearnings of the oppressed race, and still fewer have the vision to see that injustice must be rooted out by strong, persistent and determined action. I am thankful, however, that some of our white brothers in the South have grasped the meaning of this social revolution and committed themselves to it. They are still all too few in quantity, but they are big in quality. Some—such as Ralph McGill, Lillian Smith, Harry Golden, James McBride Dabbs, Ann Braden and Sarah Patton Boyle—have written about our struggle in eloquent and prophetic terms. Others have marched with us down nameless streets of the South. They have languished in filthy, roach-infested jails, suffering the abuse and brutality of policemen who view them as "dirty niggerlovers." Unlike so many of their moderate brothers and sisters, they have recognized the urgency of the moment and sensed the need for powerful "action" antidotes to combat the disease of segregation.

STUDY QUESTIONS

√ 1. How, according to King, can one distinguish between a just law and an unjust law? Do you agree with him on this point?
  2. King says that one who wishes to violate an unjust law must be prepared to accept the legal penalty for his or her action. Why does King establish this condition? How does this condition help to illustrate the difference between a criminal and civil resister who acts out of conscience?
  3. What is the crux of King's criticism of white moderates?
  4. What was King's opinion of black nationalist groups?
√ 5. How does the fact that many blacks were denied the right to vote figure into King's justification of violations of law?

In Defense of Anarchism
Robert Paul Wolff

Robert Paul Wolff (1933–   ) is a professor of philosophy at the University of
Massachusetts. During his first year as a university professor, Wolff
announced to his students that he would solve the fundamental problem of
political philosophy. He writes: "I had no trouble formulating the problem—
roughly speaking, how the moral autonomy of the individual can be made
compatible with the legitimate authority of the state....But mid-way through
the semester, I was forced to go before my class, crestfallen and very
embarrassed, to announce that I had failed to discover the grand solution."
Eventually Wolff was led into the position of *political anarchism*—the view that
no State has legitimate authority over its citizens.

 Throughout history governments have ordered citizens into battle, and
most of the time the wars people have fought have been unnecessary and
immoral. Yet people usually submit to the demands of the State. Indeed,
most often, this submission is based on the simple admission that the State
has the right to command. This admission presents a dilemma: if the State has
the *right* to command, then I am obliged to obey, even if I disagree with its
orders. It makes no sense to say that someone has a *right* to do something,
unless there is a corresponding obligation to allow that activity. To say that I
have the right to free speech, for example, means that others have the
obligation to allow me to speak freely, even if they disagree with what I say.
Therefore, if I admit that the State has the right to command, that the State is
a legitimate authority, then I give up moral independence and allow myself to
be guided by the will of another. Wolff maintains that this forfeit of moral
autonomy is never legitimate, and this means that no State has legitimate
authority over its citizens. We, not the State, are the rightful arbiters of what
we ought to do.

The fundamental assumption of moral philosophy is that men are responsible
for their actions. From this assumption it follows necessarily, as Kant pointed
out, that men are metaphysically free, which is to say that in some sense they
are capable of choosing how they shall act. Being able to choose how he acts
makes a man responsible, but merely choosing is not in itself enough to constitute *taking* responsibility for one's actions. Taking responsibility involves
attempting to determine what one ought to do, and that, as philosophers since
Aristotle have recognized, lays upon one the additional burdens of gaining
knowledge, reflecting on motives, predicting outcomes, criticizing principles,
and so forth.

 The obligation to take responsibility for one's actions does not derive
from man's freedom of will alone, for more is required in taking responsibility
than freedom of choice. Only because man has the capacity to reason about

his choices can he be said to stand under a continuing obligation to take responsibility for them. It is quite appropriate that moral philosophers should group together children and madmen as beings not fully responsible for their actions, for as madmen are thought to lack freedom of choice, so children do not yet possess the power of reason in a developed form. It is even just that we should assign a greater degree of responsibility to children, for madmen, by virtue of their lack of free will, are completely without responsibility, while children, insofar as they possess reason in a partially developed form, can be held responsible (i.e., can be required to take responsibility) to a corresponding degree.

Every man who possesses both free will and reason has an obligation to take responsibility for his actions, even though he may not be actively engaged in a continuing process of reflection, investigation, and deliberation about how he ought to act. A man will sometimes announce his willingness to take responsibility for the consequences of his actions, even though he has not deliberated about them, or does not intend to do so in the future. Such a declaration is, of course, an advance over the refusal to take responsibility; it at least acknowledges the existence of the obligation. But it does not relieve the man of the duty to engage in the reflective process which he has thus far shunned. It goes without saying that a man may take responsibility for his actions and yet act wrongly. When we describe someone as a responsible individual, we do not imply that he always does what is right, but only that he does not neglect the duty of attempting to ascertain what is right.

The responsible man is not capricious or anarchic, for he does acknowledge himself bound by moral constraints. But he insists that he alone is the judge of those constraints. He may listen to the advice of others, but he makes it his own by determining for himself whether it is good advice. He may learn from others about his moral obligations, but only in the sense that a mathematician learns from other mathematicians—namely by hearing from them arguments whose validity he recognizes even though he did not think of them himself. He does not learn in the sense that one learns from an explorer, by accepting as true his accounts of things one cannot see for oneself.

Since the responsible man arrives at moral decisions which he expresses to himself in the form of imperatives, we may say that he gives laws to himself or is self-legislating. In short, he is *autonomous.* As Kant argued, moral autonomy is a combination of freedom and responsibility; it is a submission to laws which one has made for oneself. The autonomous man, insofar as he is autonomous, is not subject to the will of another. He may do what another tells him, but not *because* he has been told to do it. He is therefore, in the political sense of the word, *free.*

Since man's responsibility for his actions is a consequence of his capacity for choice, he cannot give it up or put it aside. He can refuse to acknowledge it, however, either deliberately or by simply failing to recognize his moral condition. All men refuse to take responsibility for their actions at some time or other during their lives, and some men so consistently shirk their duty that they present more the appearance of overgrown children than of adults. Inasmuch as moral autonomy is simply the condition of taking full responsibility for one's actions, it follows that men can forfeit their autonomy at will. That is to say, a man can decide to obey the commands of another without making any attempt to determine for himself whether what is commanded is good or wise.

This is an important point, and it should not be confused with the false assertion that a man can give up responsibility for his actions. Even after he has subjected himself to the will of another, an individual remains responsible for what he does. But by refusing to engage in moral deliberation, by accepting as final the commands of the others, he forfeits his autonomy. Rousseau is therefore right when he says that a man cannot become a slave even through his own choice, if he means that even slaves are morally responsible for their acts. But he is wrong if he means that men cannot place themselves voluntarily in a position of servitude and mindless obedience.

There are many forms and degrees of forfeiture of autonomy. A man can give up his independence of judgment with regard to a single question, or in respect of a single type of question. For example, when I place myself in the hands of my doctor, I commit myself to whatever course of treatment he prescribes, but only in regard to my health. I do not make him my legal counselor as well. A man may forfeit autonomy on some or all questions for a specific period of time, or during his entire life. He may submit himself to all commands, whatever they may be, save for some specified acts (such as killing) which he refuses to perform. From the example of the doctor, it is obvious that there are at least some situations in which it is reasonable to give up one's autonomy. Indeed, we may wonder whether, in a complex world of technical expertise, it is ever reasonable *not* to do so!

Since the concept of taking and forfeiting responsibility is central to the discussion which follows, it is worth devoting a bit more space to clarifying it. Taking responsibility for one's actions means making the final decisions about what one should do. For the autonomous man, there is no such thing, strictly speaking, as a *command*. If someone in my environment is issuing what are intended as commands, and if he or others expect those commands to be obeyed, that fact will be taken account of in my deliberations. I may decide that I ought to do what that person is commanding me to do, and it may even be that his issuing the command is the factor in the situation which makes it desirable for me to do so. For example, if I am on a sinking ship and the captain is giving orders for manning the lifeboats, and if everyone else is obeying the captain *because he is the captain,* I may decide that under the circumstances I had better do what he says, since the confusion caused by disobeying him would be generally harmful. But insofar as I make such a decision, I am not *obeying his command;* that is, I am not acknowledging him as having authority over me. I would make the same decision, for exactly the same reasons, if one of the passengers had started to issue "orders" and had, in the confusion, come to be obeyed.

In politics, as in life generally, men frequently forfeit their autonomy. There are a number of causes for this fact, and also a number of arguments which have been offered to justify it. Most men, as we have already noted, feel so strongly the force of tradition or bureaucracy that they accept unthinkingly the claims to authority which are made by their nominal rulers. It is the rare individual in the history of the race who rises even to the level of questioning the right of his masters to command and the duty of himself and his fellows to obey. Once the dangerous question has been started, however, a variety of arguments can be brought forward to demonstrate the authority of the rulers. Among the most ancient is Plato's assertion that men should submit to the authority of those with superior knowledge, wisdom, or insight. A sophisticated modern version has it that the educated portion of a democratic population is more likely to be politically active, and that it is just as well for the ill-informed segment of the electorate to remain passive, since its entrance into the political arena only supports the efforts of demagogues and extremists. A number of American political scientists have gone so far as to claim that the apathy of the American masses is a cause of stability and hence a good thing.

The moral condition demands that we acknowledge responsibility and achieve autonomy wherever and whenever possible. Sometimes this involves moral deliberation and reflection; at other times, the gathering of special, even technical, information. The contemporary American citizen, for example, has an obligation to master enough modern science to enable him to follow debates about nuclear policy and come to an independent conclusion.[1] There are great, perhaps insurmountable, obstacles to the achievement of a complete and rational autonomy in the modern world. Nevertheless, so long as we recognize our responsibility for our actions, and acknowledge the power of reason within us, we must acknowledge as well the continuing obligation to make ourselves the authors of such commands as we may obey. The paradox of man's condition in the modern world is that the more fully he recognizes his right and duty to be his own master, the more completely he becomes the passive object of a technology and bureaucracy whose complexities he cannot hope to understand. It is only several hundred years since a reasonably well-educated man could claim to understand the major issues of government as well as his king or parliament. Ironically, the high school graduate of today, who cannot master the issues of foreign and domestic policy on which he is asked to vote, could quite easily have grasped the problems of eighteenth-century statecraft.

The defining mark of the state is authority, the right to rule. The primary

---

[1] This is not quite so difficult as it sounds, since policy very rarely turns on disputes over technical or theoretical details. Still, the citizen who, for example, does not understand the nature of atomic radiation cannot even pretend to have an opinion on the feasibility of bomb shelters; and since the momentous choice between first-strike and second-strike nuclear strategies depends on the possibility of a successful shelter system, the uninformed citizen will be as completely at the mercy of his "representatives" as the lowliest slave.

obligation of man is autonomy, the refusal to be ruled. It would seem, then, that there can be no resolution of the conflict between the autonomy of the individual and the putative authority of the state. Insofar as a man fulfills his obligation to make himself the author of his decisions, he will resist the state's claim to have authority over him. That is to say, he will deny that he has a duty to obey the laws of the state *simply because they are the laws.* In that sense, it would seem that anarchism is the only political doctrine consistent with the virtue of autonomy.

Now, of course, an anarchist may grant the necessity of *complying* with the law under certain circumstances or for the time being. He may even doubt that there is any real prospect of eliminating the state as a human institution. But he will never view the commands of the state as *legitimate,* as having a binding moral force. In a sense, we might characterize the anarchist as a man without a country, for despite the ties which bind him to the land of his childhood, he stands in precisely the same moral relationship to "his" government as he does to the government of any other country in which he might happen to be staying for a time. When I take a vacation in Great Britain, I obey its laws, both because of prudential self-interest and because of the obvious moral considerations concerning the value of order, the general good consequences of preserving a system of property, and so forth. On my return to the United States, I have a sense of reentering *my* country, and if I think about the matter at all, I imagine myself to stand in a different and more intimate relation to American laws. They have been promulgated by *my* government, and I therefore have a special obligation to obey them. But the anarchist tells me that my feeling is purely sentimental and has no objective moral basis. All authority is equally illegitimate, although of course not therefore equally worthy or unworthy of support, and my obedience to American laws, if I am to be morally autonomous, must proceed from the same considerations which determine me abroad.

The dilemma which we have posed can be succinctly expressed in terms of the concept of a *de jure* state. If all men have a continuing obligation to achieve the highest degree of autonomy possible, then there would appear to be no state whose subjects have a moral obligation to obey its commands. Hence, the concept of a *de jure* legitimate state would appear to be vacuous, and philosophical anarchism would seem to be the only reasonable political belief for an enlightened man.

STUDY QUESTIONS

√ 1. What does Wolff mean by autonomy?

√ 2. How can a person forfeit his or her autonomy, according to Wolff?

√ 3. Why, according to Wolff, can you forfeit your autonomy but not your responsibility? Give examples of situations in which a person does this.

✓ **4.** Why, for an autonomous person, is there no such thing as a *command*, in Wolff's view?

5. Authority is legitimate power. Why, according to Wolff, can no government (state) ever possess authority to issue commands to its citizens?

6. If you and two friends agree to attend a movie which the majority of the group selects, and then the two friends select one which you prefer not to see, do you have a moral duty to go to the movie despite your disappointment? Would going to the movie compromise your autonomy?

7. "Wolff speaks about the 'obvious moral considerations concerning the value of order.' Now, if order is a moral good, and government is necessary to preserve order, and obedience to law is necessary to preserve government, then citizens have a moral duty to obey the law." How would Wolff respond? What is your position?

8. "That which is anarchic within me (which is very strong) tunes in strongly to the idea of a society in which people decide for themselves what taxes to pay, what rules to obey, when to cooperate and when not to cooperate with the civil authorities. But that which is reasonable within me, which I am glad to say most often prevails, recognizes that societies so structured do not exist and cannot exist" (William F. Buckley). How would Wolff respond to Buckley? Do you think Buckley is right?

Autonomy and Authority—
The Solution of Democracy
Carl Cohen

Carl Cohen (1931–   ) is professor of philosophy at the University of Michigan. In what follows, Cohen gives the standard reply of a supporter of democracy to the claim of philosophical anarchists that personal autonomy is incompatible with political authority. Democracy is government of, by, and for the people. It is the only form of government where people govern themselves. In a democracy, every adult citizen participates in the lawmaking process, directly or indirectly. When a citizen agrees to participate in this process, he or she implicitly agrees to accept the outcome, even though the individual disagrees with it on occasion. In this way the citizen's autonomy is preserved, according to Cohen, for the citizen is self-legislating. The citizen imposes the law upon himself or herself. When the commands of the State coincide with those citizens give themselves, there is no conflict between

.tonomy and authority. It is the democratic citizen's participation in making
.he laws that establishes the duty to obey them.

Cohen believes that a citizen has a weighty obligation to obey the law, but
not an absolute obligation. He speaks about the duty to obey the law as a
prima facie duty, that is, a qualified or conditional duty. While I have made a
promise to obey the laws which I help to make, exceptional circumstances
could arise wherein a more important moral duty takes precedence over my
duty to keep my promise. It is only in such cases, and not for the sake
merely of personal pleasure or convenience, that one is justified in refusing to
comply with the law.

1   ANARCHISM

By what right does government govern? Legislators, policemen, and judges
tell us what we must do and what we may not do. Who or what gives them
the authority to rule over us? What *justifies* any system of government?

Anarchists insist that *no* government can be justified. They reason as
follows. All governments compel obedience to their laws. All compulsion is
inconsistent with free, voluntary action by individual citizens. Free voluntary
action is presupposed by true morality. Every state, therefore, in enforcing its
laws, forces its citizens to forfeit their autonomy—and thus every state sub-
verts morality. States and governments are intrinsically coercive; they can be
powerful, but they cannot be moral.

By what right does government govern? By no right. The state is the
enemy of morality (the anarchist concludes), and all right-thinking people are
enemies of the state.

This conclusion is profoundly mistaken—and yet the argument seems
plausible. If morality presupposes individual autonomy, and every government denies that autonomy, then no government can be morally justified.
Where is the mistake?

2   AUTONOMY

Autonomy *is* the cornerstone of morality; the anarchist is not mistaken about
that. For an act to be moral in the fullest sense, the actor must do it out of
respect for a rule he imposes upon himself, not out of fear or habit. Two persons may act in ways that are on the surface indistinguishable, both (for example) returning lost property to its rightful owner. If one does so as an application of a self-imposed moral rule, while the other acts merely out of
prudence, we do not need the help of moral philosophers to see that the
former—the self-legislating, autonomous actor—is the more honorable.

Autonomy, although necessary for complete morality, is not sufficient
for it. Autonomous actors, even if well-meaning, may do wrong, like Robin
Hood and Pancho Villa. They may even be bad, like Stalin or Lady Macbeth.

Autonomy is not itself a virtue, but the requisite condition of virtue. If we know only that an act is self-legislated, we know nothing about *what* was done, but a great deal about *how* it was done. With autonomy conduct might not be right; without autonomy it cannot be fully moral. Full moral approval of an agent requires not only that the acts performed be in accordance with good rules, but also that the rules obeyed be truly self-imposed. That, as Kant taught, is part of our common rational understanding of morality.

The anarchist confronts us with this problem: How can moral autonomy be maintained in the face of governmental authority? When the commands of the state coincide with those a citizen gives himself, no conflict arises. But governments *enforce* laws; they make people do what otherwise they would not do. Not just tyrannical government (says the anarchist), but every government imposes laws upon its citizens from without. I may be obliged to stop at a stop sign, or wear a seat belt, even when I am convinced that safety does not require it. I may be obliged to pay a tax I think unfair. Can *state*-legislation be consistent with *self*-legislation? Yes, it can.

3   COMMITMENT AND DEMOCRACY

Autonomy does not consist in doing whatever one pleases. Autonomous action is legislated, although that legislation issues from one's self. Rules for conduct, even if they are one's own rules, entail constraints. These restraints are sometimes hardships. We are obliged, *because* we are self-legislating, to do sometimes what we might prefer not to do, or to refrain from doing what would please us.

Can such obligations be morally justified? Of course they can. They are justified by self-*commitment*. We are governed by our own rules because of the self-imposed obligation to keep our word.

That obligation is realized when we give our word to others. If I agree to pay a man five hundred dollars to paint my barn, and he does the job satisfactorily, I may not refuse to pay him because, after the agreement, I established a new rule for myself never to buy or sell labor. I may adopt that rule for the future, but doing so cannot cancel my debt to the man I hired. Part of my self-government is the restriction upon my own conduct arising from commitments I make deliberately. The promises I give, the contracts I entered upon, are among these.

In real life we make many commitments—to other people, to ourselves, and sometimes to institutions. Some commitments are made in writing, others orally or through our conduct; they differ in strength and importance. The web of commitments that we build provides the framework of our moral lives. Moral conflicts result from tangles in this web.

Some strong commitments are made between individuals and their governments; this explains the possibility of the moral justification of government. Although we are autonomous moral agents, we are constrained by our voluntary commitments to our fellow citizens, our community. These constraints may be expressed in laws—and such laws we have an obligation to obey. In obeying them we do not forfeit our autonomy. On the contrary, we would be untrue to ourselves if we did not respect them.

The anarchist's mistake is the failure to appreciate the obligations that flow from a self-commitment to obey the law. These obligations can arise under democratic governments only. Democratic governments alone are based upon participation. By participating in civic life, every citizen makes commitments to the community. That participation renders the authority of government legitimate; only participation in making the laws can justify the moral obligation to obey them.

In a democracy—but only in a democracy—each citizen has a right to a voice in the lawmaking process. Enjoyment of this right commits the citizen to respect the laws resulting from that process. The agreement to participate is not contingent upon getting one's own way. Each citizen knows, even before learning what issues will arise, that no one will always get his way. But believing the legislative process fair, each person is committed in advance to observe the rules that are its outcome. To that system, full consent is given. Governments derive their just powers from this consent of the governed.

Democracy alone—of all possible systems of government—can reconcile the autonomy of the citizen with the authority of the state. No aristocracy or despotism, however benevolent, can effect that reconciliation. Every authoritarian system must and will deny the moral autonomy of its citizens. Here lies the key to what democracy is, and why it alone is right: It is the way in which a group of people impose legislative restraints upon themselves.

Who gives democratic government the authority to rule over us? *We* do. Only we have that authority to give. The Preamble to the Constitution of the United States puts this crisply: "We the people of the United States...do ordain and establish this Constitution for the United States of America." When the laws of any government result from the deliberative participation of its citizens, all its citizens are rightly bound by them. Democracy is autonomy writ large.

4   MORAL DISOBEDIENCE

Is the duty to obey the laws of a democratic government absolute? No. In rare circumstances our self-imposed commitment to obey the laws may be overridden by other, more powerful obligations. The conscientious citizen may then face an agonizing dilemma, being obliged to break the law, not for pleasure or convenience (indeed, the punishment may be severe), but out of respect for his own highest personal principles.

When two moral principles conflict and cannot be reconciled, one must overrule the other. But the principle overruled remains a genuine component of the moral situation, and continues to deserve respect. If I promise to meet you for tea, but the compelling need of an injured neighbor obliges me to miss

what about not agreeing to "play"?

the date without any opportunity beforehand to tell you how things stand, I certainly act rightly in helping my neighbor. Such an obligation overrides my obligation to you in this case, but it does not erase my promise. I have a *prima facie* obligation to keep my promises; that obligation is general and weighty. If exceptional circumstances compel me to break a serious promise, I must justify the decision to subordinate (in those circumstances) my general obligation to do what I had committed myself to do.

The obligation to obey the laws of a democratic state is, like the general obligation to keep promises, *prima facie* and very powerful. Only rarely may it be overruled justifiably. The participating citizen in a democracy commits himself, autonomously, to respect the laws in general. He does not make himself slave to the state; he may remain responsive to truly exceptional circumstances. But the rules of his own government he is under weighty obligation to obey.

5   PARTICIPATION

How can the citizens of a democracy genuinely participate in lawmaking? Can they really govern themselves? Critics of democracy commonly contend that self-government is a delusionary ideal. In tiny groups it may be realized, say they, but in communities of thousands, or millions, it is an impossibility. In every state a few powerful people make the laws and enforce them; the rest accept them and obey. The self-government of the masses is a dangerous myth. At most (these critics conclude) the masses may hope to influence the lawmakers; they cannot hope to govern.

Not so, we answer. National self-government is difficult, but it is entirely feasible and in many cases genuine. The criticism arises from a misunderstanding of what self-government entails. It does not entail most citizens' involvement in making most community decisions. The bulk of day-to-day governing consists of technical decision making, applying rules to cases. The technical issues are often sophisticated, the rules complex, and the cases numerous. To do such work, special bodies are appointed, special officers employed. They make the run of administrative decisions, and their specific powers are carefully delegated to them by the people.

The officeholders who temporarily exercise those powers are ultimately controlled by the citizens of a democratic community. In setting policy, in making *directive* (as opposed to *administrative*) decisions, the people may truly govern themselves. Democracy is genuine when every citizen has the equal right to participate in that steering of the whole.

That equal right is realized and protected in some countries—but certainly not in all. In Sweden, in Israel, in Holland, in Great Britain, in the United States, in Canada, and in many other lands, citizens enjoy the right to participate in setting the direction of the whole. Like all democracies, these named have flaws—but there remains all the difference in the world between countries in which the people have a genuine voice in their government and coun-

tries in which they do not. No one who has experienced the oppression of
fascism, or of totalitarian communism, will call the right to participate in government a delusion. Self-government is precious just because, although sometimes real, it is very far from universal.

General participation is the essence of democratic government. It takes
many forms, of which voting is but one. It is difficult to measure, and it is
realized in varying degrees at different times and places. Democracy is always
a matter of degree; some communities are more democratic, some less. Some
states claim the name but do not deserve it. The critical question is easy to ask
but not so easy to answer: Do the members of the community have, in practice, the protected right to participate in making directive decisions for the
whole?

6   INDIRECT DEMOCRACY

Direct participation by the citizen in policy making is feasible where the community is small. In clubs or committees, in villages run on the town-hall model,
almost all may be heard, their participation being immediate and effective. In
a very large community, a referendum may occasionally give the individual
citizen direct voice on some issues. Direct democracy, where size and circumstances permit it, is ideal. But it is often not feasible.

Most democratic governments are indirect. The laws are made and policy issues deliberated upon and resolved by representatives of the people,
elected by the citizens to make decisions in their name. In choosing representatives, therefore, popular participation becomes most lively and most concrete. By participating in the election of persons who will act for them, for
limited terms and with limited powers, the people make, indirectly, the policy
decisions and laws that govern all.

7   VOTING

Voting is central to democracy. Although not the whole of citizen participation, it is its most evident and most decisive form. Fairness in the electoral
process is therefore critical; it requires, at a minimum, respect for certain *operating principles*, and the protection of certain *procedural rights*. Among the
essential rights, the most important are these:

- The right to run for office;
- The right to campaign freely, for one's self or another;
- The right of all to register to vote;
- The right to cast one's vote free of all coercion;
- The right to join with others to form parties, caucuses, movements; and
  in general the right to do whatever fair competition for election may
  require.

Among the essential operating principles, the most important are these:

- That the apportionment of voting constituencies be periodically adjusted to insure all voting citizens equal weight in the outcome;
- That the method of election (whether by geographical district, proportional representation, or some combination of these) be fair, and be itself chosen by the electorate;
- That money, essential for a political campaign of any size, not be allowed to corrupt the electoral competition;
- That the system for counting, recording, and appealing the votes cast be scrupulously honest and impartial, and the results completely public.

These procedural aspects of the electoral process make participation effective; they constitute the skeleton of a working democratic system. Safeguarding these rights, and realizing these principles concretely, with voting lists and machines, offices and officers, regulations and appeals, and so on, is a complicated and expensive affair. Electoral methods and their mechanical details, of which there is an unlimited variety, must be adjusted to the needs of the particular democracy and the preferences of its citizens. Improving the voting system will be a never-ending business in a healthy democracy.

Electoral devices are the bones of democracy; its muscle is the spirit of the electors, always inspecting, activating, and safe-guarding their instrument.

8 PAPER DEMOCRACY

No voting system, however technically perfect, can by itself insure democracy. Everyone is familiar with electoral systems that sound splendid on paper but are empty in practice. Paper democracy is of two kinds. The first results from fraud. Votes may be cast and representatives elected, all the forms given lip service—while the power to make important decisions remains in the hands of a few who really govern. The trappings of democracy are paraded and lauded, while the real will of the people is ignored. Much fuss is made about voting and the tabulation proudly announced, but there is no genuine opportunity for the citizens to choose their own representatives because nominations and elections are fully controlled by the powers that be—the land-owning oligarchies in some Latin American countries, the managers of the one dominant party in some Asian countries. The outcome is manipulated by permitting no serious opposition, or no opposition at all. Conflicting interests inevitably arise in large communities. Political parties reflect these conflicts of interest. Where there is but one party permitted, therefore, or where efforts to oppose established authority are punished, or where we learn that through some miracle a candidate has been elected by 99 percent of the vote, we may be sure that there is fraud afoot. Opposition and argument are essential in honest democratic politics; if they are missing, the rest is phony.

Paper democracy may also result from apathy. Self-government demands the energy of the selves concerned. The breadth and depth of interest will fluctuate with different issues and times, of course, but where the citizens do not bother to use the machinery of politics, the democracy rots from within. If the people are not interested enough to do what is necessary to govern themselves, there are always those who, with contempt and self-satisfaction, will gladly govern in their place. Either the people will direct themselves, or others will do the directing for them.

We democrats, therefore, have a heavy and continuing responsibility to make our government truly our own. We must serve as gadflies, evaluating skeptically the legislators and executives we elect—and the technicians they hire in our name. We must devote more time and energy to public matters than citizens under any other system of government, just because all that public business is our business, and we ignore it at our peril. What George Bernard Shaw said of socialism is certainly true of democracy: It consumes a great many evenings. Factual investigation, reflection upon public issues, expression of convictions to friends and representatives, political argument and lobbying— all that is involved in the laborious process of making policy—is our duty. Its fruits will be sour or luscious depending upon the vigor, the persistence, and the intelligence of our day-to-day political activity. That activity is the flesh of democracy. Without it, the rest is dry bones.

9 DEMOCRACY AS METHOD

So democracy is a process, a kind of governing. It is not socialism, capitalism, or any other economic system. It is not to be identified with the forms or institutions of any country—the United States, or Great Britain, or any other— although such countries do try to realize democracy. It is not just majority rule, or the competition for leadership, or the protection of minority rights, or any of those good things normally associated with it. Democracy is the general name for a *way* of conducting our common business. It is that way in which the business is conducted according to the people's wishes. No one can know in advance what the people of any community will wish. It follows that democracy, in itself, entails no particular conclusions in resolving controversy. It is not itself a solution to any particular problem, but an instrument with which solutions to many problems may be sought. This explains its very general applicability. In distinction from every specific plan for the preservation of peace, or the elimination of unemployment, or the improvement of human beings, democracy is a method by which a community's objectives are established and advanced.

Democrats may therefore be advocates of any goal or plan they believe appropriate—so long as they are prepared to accept as legislative what the people choose, and to protect the procedural rights of all in choosing. A commitment to democracy is a commitment, in John Dewey's classic phrase, to the supremacy of method.

Even good methods cannot guarantee good results. Can democracy, honestly pursued, yield bad outcomes? Yes. Genuinely democratic governments may make serious errors in economic or educational policy; they may adopt unwise or inequitable laws; they may wage unjust wars. That the people choose their own course gives no guarantee that the right course will be chosen. Just as individuals acting autonomously may act unwisely or unjustly, societies in which autonomy is writ large may do the same. Intelligence and goodness in the behavior of self-governing communities must flow from the intelligence and goodness its citizens manifest.

The fact that democracies err does not condemn them; no system of government is perfect. But which system makes the most mistakes? And which makes the worst ones? If the mistakes of the people are not to be borne, whose mistakes are to be preferred?

STUDY QUESTIONS

1. Why, according to Cohen, can autonomy be preserved in a democracy, but not in a dictatorship or any other form of government?
2. Cohen says that autonomy is a necessary but not a sufficient condition for morality. What does this mean?
3. Cohen builds his case upon the claim that rules for conduct, even if they are one's own, entail constraints upon oneself. What does he mean by this, and how does it figure into his argument?
4. Is Cohen correct in saying that in a democracy "each citizen has a right to a voice in the lawmaking process"?
5. If a person is deprived of the opportunity to vote, to run for office, or to participate in the lawmaking process in other ways, then, if one follows Cohen, would that person be under no duty to obey the law?

12

Classical Political Theories: Dictatorship, Democracy, and Communism

PROBLEM INTRODUCTION

Each of the more than 160 nations in the world today can be associated with a specific political theory—dictatorship,* democracy, or communism. To understand a nation thoroughly it is important to grasp the political theory which it embraces. Such a study is necessarily philosophical because political theories are tied to implicit or explicit views of man's nature, reality, the limits and content of knowledge, and morality. In this section of the book you will study contributors to each of the three classical political theories: Hobbes to dictatorship, Locke and Mill to democracy, and Engels to communism.

The first philosopher on record to espouse dictatorship as a superior political system was Plato in his dialogue entitled the *Republic.* One of Plato's motives for writing this discourse which describes an ideal political system was to provide guidance to those who wished to rebuild the city-state of Athens at a point when, in Plato's eyes, it was deteriorating rapidly. Athens had been defeated in the Peloponnesian War by Sparta, its traditional religious beliefs were on the decline, to the detriment of private and public morals, and political power seemed to be increasingly in the hands of self-interested and unenlightened individuals. In effect, Plato said to his contemporaries, if you wish to have the best possible political system, here is what you must do. The key to his proposals is to put citizens in specific roles for which they are suited by aptitude and training. Every individual, he says, has natural talents which qualify him or her to serve society in the capacity of ruler, soldier, or worker. The perfect society is one in which all citizens are channeled into one of these

---

*Dictatorship is any political system in which political power is held by a single all-powerful leader or small clique. Fascism is a twentieth-century brand of dictatorship, such as Mussolini's regime in Italy, which exalts race and nation and which glorifies war.

476

appropriate "classes," and each class carries out its appointed function efficiently. This results not merely in efficiency, but also in "harmony," *the* definitive feature of a truly "just" society in Plato's view.

The class of rulers in Plato's society would be composed of those few extraordinary individuals who can exercise power wisely and virtuously. To qualify intellectually they would be trained carefully so that eventually they could grasp ultimate reality—the realm of "forms," or essences, which are stable and unchanging, unlike the physical realm, which is in flux. To qualify morally they would be exposed to literally decades of moral training, with frequent testing, to assure that they are thoroughly devoted to public service. They would forfeit entirely the right to marry and raise children, and to own property or acquire wealth. The cultivation of their innate intellectual and moral aptitude would turn them into ideal political leaders; their superior knowledge and virtue entitle them to possess power exclusively. Members of the remaining classes, soldiers and workers, would not interfere with the ruling class in carrying out its duties, for they lack the qualifications to do so. They would be expected to obey and to revere the mortal gods who guide and direct the community.

If leaders are brilliant and selfless, and common people are dimwits, Plato's authoritarian and socially stratified society would seem to make sense. But are these assumptions warranted? A host of modern writers argue that knowledge is inherently subject to error, or "fallible," no matter the possessor, which seems to imply that it would be a mistake to grant power to any person or clique on the pretext that their knowledge is not subject to error, or "infallible." But, for the sake of argument, let us say that perhaps leaders can acquire knowledge which is highly probable, if not certain. Would this be sufficient to salvage the case for a ruling elite? Critics of dictatorship think not, and these are some of their arguments. In the first place, they say, it is naive to expect that a cadre of leaders can be trained who are models of virtue. Plato is trying to turn human beings into angels. History is simply too filled with examples of abuses of power by rulers for selfish purposes to warrant any hope that leaders with absolute power can wield it purely out of concern for the common good. Power itself corrupts; even if an individual were to begin a political career as a person of virtue, they suggest, it is highly unlikely that he or she would finish it that way. Democrats—supporters of democracy—say there is no such thing as a benevolent dictatorship. The common good will be served much better by limiting the power of any individual, through separation of powers in government and fixed terms, than through trusting a leader to be a latter-day Solomon.

Next, there is the issue of Plato's conception of common people. Democrats suggest that Plato's low opinion of the bulk of the population may have had some justification when he lived, some twenty five centuries ago, when formal education was available to only a few, but that it is out of place today. With the passage of time and the enrichment of experience, people are not the same today as they were ages ago. People are educable, they say, and the phenomenon of universal public education enables them to understand public issues and to vote intelligently and responsibly—to govern themselves. Also, common people sometimes exhibit more "common sense" than a Ph.D. For these reasons, democrats insist, government "of, by, and for the people"— Abraham Lincoln's definition of democracy—is practicable in the twentieth century.

Another and quite different approach to dictatorship was followed by Thomas Hobbes, a seventeenth-century British philosopher, whose *Leviathan* appears in part in our readings. Hobbes supported an all-powerful government despite the fact that he believed that all human beings, including would-be leaders, are self-interested. To appreciate his position we need to reflect on some historical, scientific, and philosophical considerations.

Hobbes lived through probably the most tumultuous days in modern British history. The Thirty Years' War, constant friction between monarchs and Parliament, and civil war combined to give Hobbes a first-hand look at society when law and order are tenuous, and when they collapse altogether. He became convinced that the supreme achievement of government is to establish and maintain *order*. In developing his political thought Hobbes was deeply influenced by contemporary scientific discoveries, particularly those of Galileo and Harvey. Galileo began his physics with the assumption that the behavior of every physical body could best be understood in terms of general laws of motion. One of these was the law of inertia, which asserts that a body in motion will stay in motion unless affected by an opposing force. Harvey's experiments in anatomy had revealed that the human body functioned like a complicated machine—the arteries, veins, nerves, and organs being biological gears and springs. Putting these ideas together, Hobbes conceived of the human person as a mechanical system of matter in motion, a machine whose behavior could be completely explained and predicted by physical principles. He became the consummate materialist: emotions, thoughts, sensations—all psychological states—were merely manifestations of matter in motion. As Hobbes observed the social and political upheaval around him, he took the behavior of contending individuals and factions struggling to extend their power to be an expression of human nature, rather than a local and temporary effect of the social climate. People were, he thought, naturally aggressive, hostile, self-serving, greedy, and proud. Instinctively they seek their own pleasure at the expense of others. Hobbes felt that he could explain this behavior by his materialism since, as the law of inertia had predicted, people are material systems preserving themselves in motion.

In such a tense and conflict-ridden atmosphere, how is survival possible? Hobbes recognized that to give perfect liberty to everyone is to invite anarchy— what he called the "state of nature," a state of affairs without government, where there is no way to keep people from attacking one another. Clearly, it is in each person's self-interest to cease this perpetual war and to gain a modicum of security. Yet people will not become gentle of their own free will. In order to bring about peace and mutual survival, a natural motive must be found for subduing aggressiveness. This motive is *fear*. There must be some overarching power, Hobbes argues, capable of restraining the natural violence of people by threatening to inflict harm upon them if they violate the law. The "sovereign" sees to it that crime does not pay—if you violate the law, he or she says, the pain you will suffer will far exceed the pleasure you reaped. This deters people from crime. Any attempt to divide political power, as in a democracy, is sure to unleash the natural ferocity of the individual. A dictatorship, then, is the sensible, the scientific, the ideal form of government.*

Critics of Hobbes accuse him of cynicism and bad sociology. He seems to take the worst in human nature as the norm, they say. The knowledge that people can be rapacious leads to the belief that they will be rapacious. This is not the case, however, due to institutional influences which shape us. Family, church, and school, among others, evoke not only tolerance, but sympathy, care, and love in abundance. They help to curb or sublimate egoistic tendencies and to cultivate social ones. Hobbes ignores these facts; he yanks human beings out of their actual social context and ends up with a distortion of human nature and therefore an artificial and contrived basis for government. Further, critics doubt the utility of deterrence in alleviating crime. There is no conclusive evidence, for instance, that the death penalty deters individuals from capital offenses such as murder.† Also, if you consider that only a small fraction of law-breakers are ever charged and indicted, let alone convicted, but that most people generally comply with the law, then it would appear that there are forces at work other than the threat of punishment by the State. If the threat of punishment were the only disincentive to crime, then crime statistics would soar. Also, both democrats and anarchists (those opposed in principle to any government) charge that government, especially unlimited government, can itself foster conflict and human destruction. In the twentieth century, for example, fascists such as Hitler and Mussolini perceive the State as an actual person, an organism, which will either grow or decay. Growth comes through flexing one's muscles and increasing one's power—through expansion and conquest. Decay comes through self-restraint. The result has been massive killing and butchery, all of it under the leadership and inspiration of power-crazed dictators who reveled in war. On the basis of the record, putting power in the hands of *Der Führer* or *Il Duce*, or some other would-be messiah, hardly nourishes political stability or mutual survival.

Whatever the strengths and weaknesses of Hobbes's political philosophy, his countrymen did not adopt it. In 1688 William of Orange was invited by Parliament to assume the British throne, but only if he granted important concessions which are landmarks in the development of "limited" government. Increasingly, notions such as individual rights, government by consent,

---

*The specific form of government which Hobbes actually preferred is a hereditary monarchy with a single all-powerful ruler. See his *Leviathan*, Chap. XIX.

†See Thorstein Sellin (ed.), *Capital Punishment* (New York: Harper & Row, 1967): also Bedau and Pierce (eds.), *Capital Punishment in the United States* (New York: AMS Press, 1976). For an opposite view, one which concludes that the death penalty is a deterrent to murder, see Isaac Ehrlich, "The Deterrent Effect of Capital Punishment: A Question of Life and Death," *American Economic Review*, vol. 60, no. 3, pp. 397–417, June 1975.

majority rule, and the separation of powers became commonplace in England.
The power of the monarchy has been reduced to where the monarch today is
a figurehead.

John Locke, who was born when Hobbes was forty-four years old, is an
important figure in the evolution of limited government. His political writings, including the *Second Treatise on Government*, which is excerpted in our
readings, provided the theoretical justification for the efforts of Parliament to
curtail the powers of the Crown, and for the bargain struck by Parliament and
William of Orange in 1688. In the *Second Treatise* Locke attempts to imagine
what society would be like in the absence of government. Even though there
is no government to make and enforce laws in this "state of nature," Locke
tells us, there is a Law of Nature and individuals are authorized to enforce it.
The Law of Nature, which can be discovered through reason, bestows upon
all human beings an entitlement to do whatever is necessary to develop or
fulfill their humanness. This means that all of us have "rights" to life, liberty,
and estate, or as Locke refers to them collectively, to "property" (from the
Latin *proprius,* meaning "one's own"). If an individual threatens your rights,
you may resist, punish, and take reparation from that individual. However,
individuals who abide by the Law of Nature find it impossible to protect themselves from those who do not; sounding much like Hobbes, Locke observes
that in the absence of government "the greater part of men are no strict observers of equity and justice." Unable to protect their rights in the state of
nature, people therefore establish government for that purpose. In doing so,
they delegate to government the authority to make and enforce laws, but they
stipulate that government must abide by the will of the majority. (Actually
Locke spoke not about the majority but the *lex majoris partis,* which means
literally "the law of the greater part," the precise meaning of which is most
difficult to determine; Locke, in fact, may have wanted it that way.)

Not all who favor limited government accept Locke's line of reasoning.
Like Hobbes he is charged with bad sociology. Mill, for example, says that a
pregovernmental society is a myth; wherever there are human beings, there
is government. The only real question in Mill's mind is which form of government is most *useful* in promoting the happiness, or pleasure, of the people.
To him there was little question that democracy is superior to other political
systems for this purpose. But democracy must not permit a new form of tyranny in modern society—the "tyranny of the majority."* If government seeks
to promote an individual's pleasure, it must understand that the one best suited
to know what is pleasurable or painful for an individual, *presuming that he or
she is an educated adult,* is the individual. Thus, government must be as tolerant
as possible, Mill says, interfering with individuals only when they threaten

---

*Mill was so fearful of the consequences of a newly enfranchised voting majority of uneducated
commoners that he favored practices such as a literacy test for voting, plural voting for the well-
educated, and guaranteed representation in government to various minorities. See his *Considerations on Representative Government* (Indianapolis: Bobbs-Merrill, 1958).

harm to others. Since Mill rejected Hobbes's pessimistic view of human nature, he did not believe that these intrusions would be frequent. A genuinely democratic government, guarding against the tyranny of the majority, will cultivate individuality by tolerating beliefs and life styles which are eccentric, unorthodox, and even bizarre. Not only would this benefit the individual, by allowing him or her to pursue pleasure and avoid pain with the fewest possible restrictions, but it would also benefit society by encouraging the growth of genius. Toleration, Mill says, is the "seedbed of genius," and the more geniuses we have, the more progress we make. Mill consistently attempted to show that personal liberties benefit the individual and society in valuable ways. You are entitled to think and act as you wish, not because it is your right in a Lockean sense, but because such activity is useful to you and to others.

But will we ensure the freedom and development of individuals if we erect a democratic government which welcomes diversity? Not as long as we have a capitalistic economic system—so said Karl Marx, "father of communism" and a contemporary of Mill. Marx saw the increasing regimentation of society in the nineteenth century as the necessary result of powerful and subtle historical forces which shaped and controlled consciousness itself. Society organizes itself in a certain way so as to provide for the material needs of its members. A ruling class arises which determines the ways the productive forces will be used, initiates and promotes certain ruling ideas, and erects a political state to secure its power. The only "freedom" cherished in modern capitalism, Marx argued, is freedom for producers to compete in a free market; this is freedom of owners to hire cheap labor, to fire whomever they wish, and to regulate prices and wages. The only "freedom" enjoyed by the working class is the freedom to be exploited. For evidence of this Marx pointed to the fourteen-hour work day, abuses of child labor, unsafe and unhealthful working conditions, subsistence wages, and a desperate craving for transport from this "vale of tears" into eternal bliss in the afterlife.

Thus, for Marx, if one genuinely wishes to liberate the individual, one must take control of the productive forces of society out of the hands of the few, and put it in the hands of the community. Under capitalism an enormous productive potential develops which is never fully tapped. This is because capitalists produce only when they feel assured of a profit. When the productive forces are in the hands of the community, under the administration of the workers' state, the criterion of production will shift from private profit to *public need*, resulting in a dramatic rise in the standard of living. This blend of democracy as a political system and socialism as an economic system is communism.

Marx did not expect communism to happen overnight. The *bourgeoisie*—the ascendant class—could hardly be expected to welcome their own demise, and the State, which marches to their drum, will no doubt come to their aid. Thus, the *proletariat*—the working class—should expect a long struggle which could take a violent turn. Marx did not relish violence, but he did not shrink from it either; sometimes power yields only to power, no matter how just the cause. Some of Marx's followers, including Lenin, were of the opinion that socialism would supplant capitalism only at the point of a gun. Lenin also insisted that the workers' revolution would succeed in the long run only if a dedicated cadre of leaders possessed sufficient power to plan and direct it, and to prepare the ground for full-scale communism in the postrevolutionary era. This postrevolutionary state, which most contemporary communist nations claim to be undergoing, is called the "dictatorship of the proletariat." However, Marx, his collaborator Engels, and Lenin anticipated that eventually the State as a coercive force, as a police officer, would "wither away" due to the fact that classes will cease to exist. Individuals will have equivalent power and status in the community, both politically and economically.*

Ironically, although Marx and his followers view the State as merely an appendage of the class in power, and expect it to disappear eventually, Marx came to his philosophical vision through the influence of Hegel, a German philosopher who applauded the State as humanity's greatest achievement. Hegel's view of the State is grounded in a complex philosophical perspective of reality as a single cosmic spirit which moves inexorably to ever higher stages of development amid conflicts of all sorts. Conflicts in history, Hegel says, are merely external reflections of the conflict of ideas in the cosmic spirit which are subsumed in a higher and more mature viewpoint. The nation-state is the historical counterpart to the full-scale development of spirit as a rational, self-conscious being. Marx overcame his youthful infatuation with Hegel's "idealism"—the view that reality is basically mind or consciousness, and adopted instead a "materialism"—the view that all existent things are forms of matter. But Marx retained Hegel's belief that conflict is essential to development, and that development is virtually assured with the passage of time. For Marx, though, it is human beings who evolve to ever higher stages amid conflicts among humans, and between humans and nature. Oddly enough, in this perspective capitalism becomes a necessary stage in man's progress—it creates the productive potential to satisfy all of humanity's needs; it shrinks the world through a world market and a world economy; and it creates its own "grave-diggers," the working class.

Critics of communism argue that democracy is compatible with capitalism, especially as its excesses are curbed through governmental intervention, labor unions, and moral pressures, or that democracy does indeed require socialism, but that this can be achieved without a bloody and violent revolution—through ballots instead of bullets. Many say that democratic ends require democratic means—revolutionary violence and a "temporary" dictatorship can hardly be expected to flower into brotherly love and self-government.

---

*Some contemporary Marxists deny that individuals will have equivalent power and status in full-scale communism. They see a need for a political elite to run the government on a day-to-day basis, as well as various strata of people along occupational lines with differing levels of prestige. For instance, see the Polish social theorist W. Wesolowski, *Classes, Strata, and Power* (London, Boston, and Henley: Routledge & Kegan Paul, 1979).

Actual communist governments seem to be ruthless and repressive, they observe, and it is naive or cruelly misleading to claim that an entrenched ruling elite will surrender its power on cue.

The writers in this section have helped to shape today's political landscape, fraught as it is with tension, conflict, and the terrifying, almost unthinkable possibility of a nuclear holocaust. If there is to be a future worth living, or a future at all, a necessary first step is understanding the conflicting political theories which are competing for allegiance—and power—in our world.

In Defense of Dictatorship

Thomas Hobbes

Thomas Hobbes (1588–1679) was the first philosopher to systematically apply
physical principles to ethics and social philosophy. Taking Galileo's new
physics as a model, Hobbes proposed to show that every change could be
understood as a change of matter in motion. Human beings were thought of
as mechanical systems of material particles, governed by the same physical
laws as other material bodies. Hobbes interpreted all psychological states as
physical in nature, and saw the most fundamental need of the human system
as the drive to preserve itself in motion. Physics, therefore, was the
foundation for natural aggressiveness. People are by nature devoid of any
feelings of kindliness or sympathy. In his usual way, Hobbes interpreted
feelings of sympathy as actually arising from the contemplation of ourselves
undergoing a painful fate.

   This psychological picture of human beings led Hobbes to certain political
conclusions. If left alone, people will attack one another with impunity as
long as there is some hope of gaining power over others. Political order
requires that power be placed in the hands of a single sovereign so that no
one could believe it possible to wrest it away. In Hobbes's own day, power
was divided between Parliament and the king, and this led to a civil war.
Parliament won the victory and Charles I was executed in 1649. Since Hobbes
had defended an absolute sovereign, he fled to France, believing that
Parliament would take reprisals against him. While in France, he was briefly
engaged to tutor the future Charles II, but his reputation as an atheist and
freethinker made his position in France untenable. He returned to England
after an exile of eleven years, and spent the rest of his days writing treatises
and books, and enjoying his reputation as the "father of atheists."

There be in animals, two sorts of *motions* peculiar to them: one called *vital*;
begun in generation, and continued without interruption through their whole
life; such as are the *course* of the *blood*, the *pulse*, the *breathing*, the *concoction*,
nutrition, *excretion*, etc. to which motions there needs no help of imagination:
the other is *animal motion*, otherwise called *voluntary motion*; as to *go*, to *speak*,
to *move* any of our limbs, in such manner as is first fancied in our minds. That
sense is motion in the organs and interior parts of man's body, caused by the
action of the things we see, hear, etc.; and that fancy is but the relics of the
same motion, remaining after sense, has been already said in the first and
second chapters. And because *going, speaking*, and the like voluntary motions,
depend always upon a precedent thought of *whither, which way*, and *what*; it
is evident, that the imagination is the first internal beginning of all voluntary
motion. And although unstudied men do not conceive any motion at all to be
there, where the thing moved is invisible; or the space it is moved in is, for the

From Thomas Hobbes, *Leviathan* and *Philosophical Rudiments*, from *The English Works of Thomas
Hobbes*, Vols. II and III, Sir William Molesworth, ed., London, 1839.

shortness of it, insensible; yet that doth not hinder, but that such motions are. . . .

As, in sense, that which is really within us, is, as I have said before, only motion, caused by the action of external objects, but in appearance; to the sight, light and colour; to the ear, sound; to the nostril, odour, etc.: so, when the action of the same object is continued from the eyes, ears, and other organs to the heart, the real effect there is nothing but motion, or endeavour; which consisteth in appetite, or aversion, to or from the object moving. But the appearance, or sense of that motion, is that we either call *delight*, or *trouble of mind*.

This motion, which is called appetite, and for the appearance of it *delight*, and *pleasure*, seemeth to be a corroboration of vital motion, and a help thereunto; and therefore such things as caused delight, were not improperly called *jacunda, á juvando*, from helping or fortifying; and the contrary, *molesta, offensive*, from hindering, and troubling the motion vital.

. . . Whatsoever is the object of any man's appetite or desire, that is it which he for his part calleth *good:* and the object of his hate and aversion, *evil;* and of his contempt, *vile* and *inconsiderable*. For these words of good, evil, and contemptible, are ever used with relation to the person that useth them: there being nothing simply and absolutely so; not any common rule of good and evil, to be taken from the nature of the objects themselves.

. . . In the nature of man, we find three principal causes of quarrel. First, competition; secondly, diffidence; thirdly, glory.

The first, maketh men invade for gain; the second, for safety; and the third, for reputation. The first use violence, to make themselves masters of other men's persons, wives, children, and cattle; the second, to defend them; the third, for trifles, as a word, a smile, a different opinion, and any other sign of undervalue, either direct in their persons, or by reflection in their kindred, their friends, their nation, their profession, or their name.

Hereby it is manifest, that during the time men live without a common power to keep them all in awe, they are in that condition which is called war; and such a war, as is of every man, against every man. For WAR, consisteth not in battle only, or the act of fighting; but in a tract of time, wherein the will to contend by battle is sufficiently known: and therefore the notion of *time*, is to be considered in the nature of war; as it is in the nature of weather. For as the nature of foul weather, lieth not in a shower or two of rain; but in an inclination thereto of many days together: so the nature of war, consisteth not in actual fighting; but in the known disposition thereto, during all the time there is no assurance to the contrary. All other time is PEACE.

Whatsoever therefore is consequent to a time of war, where every man is enemy to every man; the same is consequent to the time, wherein men live without other security, than what their own strength, and their own invention shall furnish them withal. In such condition, there is no place for industry; because the fruit thereof is uncertain: and consequently no culture of the earth; no navigation, nor use of the commodities that may be imported by sea; no commodious building; no instruments of moving, and removing, such things as require much force; no knowledge of the face of the earth; no account of time; no arts; no letters; no society; and which is worst of all, continual fear, and danger of violent death; and the life of man, solitary, poor, nasty, brutish, and short. . . .

All society therefore is either for gain, or for glory; that is, not so much for love of our fellows, as for the love of ourselves. But no society can be great or lasting, which begins from vain glory. Because that glory is like honour; if all men have it no man hath it, for they consist in comparison and precellence. Neither doth the society of others advance any whit the cause of my glorying in myself; for every man must account himself, such as he can make himself without the help of others. But though the benefits of this life may be much furthered by mutual help; since yet those may be better attained to by dominion than by the society of others, I hope no body will doubt, but that men would much more greedily be carried by nature, if all fear were removed, to obtain dominion, than to gain society. We must therefore resolve, that the original of all great and lasting societies consisted not in the mutual good will men had towards each other, but in the mutual fear they had of each other.

The cause of mutual fear consists partly in the natural equality of men, partly in their mutual will of hurting: whence it comes to pass, that we can neither expect from others, nor promise to ourselves the least security. For if we look on men full-grown, and consider how brittle the frame of our human body is, which perishing, all its strength, vigour, and wisdom itself perisheth with it; and how easy a matter it is, even for the weakest man to kill the strongest: there is no reason why any man, trusting to his own strength, should conceive himself made by nature above others. They are equals, who can do equal things one against the other; but they who can do the greatest things, namely, kill, can do equal things. All men therefore among themselves are by nature equal; the inequality we now discern, hath its spring from the civil law. . . .

Among so many dangers therefore, as the natural lusts of men do daily threaten each other withal, to have a care of one's self is so far from being a matter scornfully to be looked upon, that one has neither the power nor wish to have done otherwise. For every man is desirous of what is good for him, and shuns what is evil, but chiefly the chiefest of natural evils, which is death; and this he doth by a certain impulsion of nature, no less than that whereby a stone moves downward. It is therefore neither absurd nor reprehensible, neither against the dictates of true reason, for a man to use all his endeavours to preserve and defend his body and the members thereof from death and sorrows. But that which is not contrary to right reason, that all men account to be done justly, and with right. Neither by the word *right* is anything else signified, than that liberty which every man hath to make use of his natural faculties according to right reason. Therefore the first foundation of natural right is this, that *every man as much as in him lies endeavour to protect his life and members*. . . .

It may seem strange to some man, that has not well weighed these things; that nature should thus dissociate, and render men apt to invade, and destroy one another: and he may therefore, not trusting to this inference, made from the passions, desire perhaps to have the same confirmed by experience. Let him therefore consider with himself, when taking a journey, he arms himself, and seeks to go well accompanied; when going to sleep, he locks his doors; when even in his house he locks his chests; and this when he knows there be laws, and public officers, armed, to revenge all injuries shall be done him; what opinion he has of his fellow-subjects, when he rides armed; of his fellow citizens, when he locks his doors; and of his children, and servants, when he locks his chests. Does he not there as much accuse mankind by his actions, as I do by my words? But neither of us accuse man's nature in it. The desires, and other passions of man, are in themselves no sin. No more are the actions, that proceed from those passions, till they know a law that forbids them: which till laws be made they cannot know: nor can any law be made, till they have agreed upon the person that shall make it. . . .

To this war of every man, against every man, this also is consequent; that nothing can be unjust. The notions of right and wrong, justice and injustice have there no place. Where there is no common power, there is no law: where no law, no injustice. Force, and fraud, are in war the two cardinal virtues. Justice, and injustice are none of the faculties neither of the body, nor mind. If they were, they might be in a man that were alone in the world, as well as his senses, and passions. They are qualities, that relate to men in society, not in solitude. It is consequent also to the same condition, that there be no propriety, no dominion, no *mine* and *thine* distinct; but only that to be every man's, that he can get; and for so long, as he can keep it. And thus much for the ill condition, which man by mere nature is actually placed in; though with a possibility to come out of it, consisting partly in the passions, partly in his reason.

The passions that incline men to peace, are fear of death; desire of such things as are necessary to commodious living; and a hope by their industry to obtain them. And reason suggesteth convenient articles of peace, upon which men may be drawn to agreement. These articles, are they, which otherwise are called the Laws of Nature. . . .

A LAW OF NATURE, *lex naturalis*, is a precept or general rule, found out by reason, by which a man is forbidden to do that, which is destructive of his life, or taketh away the means of preserving the same; and to omit that, by which he thinketh it may be best preserved. For though they that speak of this subject, use to confound *jus*, and *lex, right* and *law*: yet they ought to be distinguished: because RIGHT, consisteth in liberty to do, or to forbear; whereas LAW, determineth, and bindeth to one of them: so that law, and right, differ as much, as obligation, and liberty; which in one and the same matter are inconsistent.

And because the condition of man, as hath been declared in the precedent chapter, is a condition of war of every one against every one: in which case every one is governed by his own reason; and there is nothing he can make use of, that may not be a help unto him, in preserving his life against his enemies; it followeth, that in such a condition, every man has a right to every thing; even to one another's body. And therefore, as long as this natural right of every man to every thing endureth, there can be no security to any man, how strong or wise soever he be, of living out the time, which nature ordinarily alloweth men to live. And consequently it is a precept, or general rule of reason, *that every man, ought to endeavour peace, as far as he has hope of obtaining it; and when he cannot obtain it, that he may seek, and use, all helps, and advantages of war.* The first branch of which rule, containeth the first, and fundamental law of nature; which is, *to seek peace, and follow it.* The second, the sum of the right of nature; which is, *by all means we can, to defend ourselves.*

From this fundamental law of nature, by which men are commanded to endeavour peace, is derived this second law; that *a man be willing, when others are so too, as far-forth, as for peace, and defence of himself he shall think it necessary, to lay down this right to all things; and be contented with so much liberty against other men, as he would allow other men against himself.* For as long as every man holdeth this right, of doing any thing he liketh; so long are all men in the condition of war. But if other men will not lay down their right, as well as he; then there is no reason for any one, to divest himself of his: for that were to expose himself to prey, which no man is bound to, rather than to dispose himself to peace....

From that law of nature, by which we are obliged to transfer to another, such rights, as being retained, hinder the peace of mankind, there followeth a third; which is this, *that men perform their covenants made:* without which, covenants are in vain, and but empty words; and the right of all men to all things remaining, we are still in the condition of war.

And in this law of nature, consisteth the fountain and original of .
For where no covenant hath preceded, there hath no right been transferred, and every man has right to every thing; and consequently, no action can be unjust. But when a covenant is made, then to break it is *unjust;* and the definition of *injustice,* is no other than *the not performance of covenant.* And whatsoever is not unjust, is *just.*

But because covenants of mutual trust, where there is a fear of not performance on either part...are invalid; though the original of justice be the making of covenants; yet injustice actually there can be none, till the cause of such fear be taken away; which while men are in the natural condition of war, cannot be done. Therefore before the names of just, and unjust can have place, there must be some coercive power, to compel men equally to the performance of their covenants, by the terror of some punishment, greater than the benefit they expect by the breach of their covenant; and to make good that propriety, which by mutual contract men acquire, in recompense of the universal right they abandon: and such power there is none before the erection of a commonwealth. And this is also to be gathered out of the ordinary definition of justice in the Schools: for they say, that *justice is the constant will of giving to every man his own.* And therefore where there is no *own,* that is no propriety, there is no injustice; and where there is no coercive power erected, that is, where there is no commonwealth, there is no propriety; all men having right to all things: therefore where there is no commonwealth, there nothing is unjust. So that the nature of justice, consisteth in keeping of valid covenants: but the validity of covenants begins not but with the constitution of a civil power, sufficient to compel men to keep them: and then it is also that propriety begins. . . .

The only way to erect such a common power, as may be able to defend them from the invasion of foreigners, and the injuries of one another, and thereby to secure them in such sort, as that by their own industry, and by the fruits of the earth, they may nourish themselves and live contentedly; is, to confer all their power and strength upon one man, or upon one assembly of men, that may reduce all their wills, by plurality of voices, unto one will: which is as much as to say, to appoint one man, or assembly of men, to bear their person; and every one to own, and acknowledge himself to be author of whatsoever he that so beareth their person, shall act, or cause to be acted, in those things which concern the common peace and safety; and therein to submit their wills, every one to his will, and their judgments, to his judgment. This is more than consent, or concord; it is a real unity of them all, on one and the same person, made by covenant of every man with every man, in such manner, as if every man should say to every man, *I authorise and give up my right of governing myself, to this man, or to this assembly of men, on this condition, that thou give up thy right to him and authorise all his actions in like manner.* This done, the multitude so united in one person, is called a COMMONWEALTH, in Latin CIVITAS. This is the generation of that great LEVIATHAN, or rather, to speak more reverently, of that MORTAL GOD, to which we owe under the IMMORTAL GOD, our peace and defence. For by this authority, given him by every particular man in the commonwealth, he hath the use of so much power and strength conferred on him, that by terror thereof, he is enabled to perform the wills of them all, to peace at home, and mutual aid against their enemies abroad. And in him consisteth the essence of the commonwealth; which, to define it, is *one person, of whose acts a great multitude, by mutual covenants one with another, have made themselves every one the author, to the end he may use the strength and means of them all, as he shall think expedient, for their peace and common defence.*

And he that carrieth this person, is called SOVEREIGN, and said to have *sovereign power;* and every one besides, his SUBJECT.

. . . I observe the *diseases* of a commonwealth, that proceed from the poison of seditious doctrines, whereof one is, *That every private man is judge of good and evil actions.* This is true in the condition of mere nature, where there are no civil laws; and also under civil government, in such cases as are not determined by the law. But otherwise, it is manifest, that the measure of good and evil actions, is the civil law; and the judge the legislator, who is always representative of the commonwealth. From this false doctrine, men are disposed to debate with themselves, and dispute the commands of the commonwealth; and afterwards to obey, or disobey them, as in their private judgments they shall think fit; whereby the commonwealth is distracted and *weakened*.

Another doctrine repugnant to civil society, is, that *whatsoever a man does against his conscience, is sin;* and it dependeth on the presumption of making himself judge of good and evil. For a man's conscience, and his judgment is the same thing, and as the judgment, so also the conscience may be errone-ous. Therefore, though he that is subject to no civil law, sinneth in all he does against his conscience, because he has no other rule to follow but his own reason; yet it is not so with him that lives in a commonwealth; because the law is the public conscience, by which he hath already undertaken to be guided. Otherwise in such diversity, as there is of private consciences, which are but private opinions, the commonwealth must needs be distracted, and no man dare to obey the sovereign power, further than it shall seem good in his own eyes.... There is [another] doctrine, plainly, and directly against the essence of a commonwealth; and it is this, *that the sovereign power may be divided.* For what is it to divide the power of a commonwealth, but to dissolve it; for pow-ers divided mutually destroy each other. And for these doctrines, men are chiefly beholding to some of those, that making profession of the laws, endeavour to make them depend upon their own learning, and not upon the legislative power....

A *commonwealth* is said to be *instituted,* when a *multitude* of men do agree, and *covenant, everyone, with every one,* that to whatsoever *man,* or *assembly of men,* shall be given by the major part, the *right* to *present* the person of them all, that is to say, to be their *representative;* every one, as well he that *voted for it,* as he that *voted against it,* shall *authorise* all the actions and judgments, of that man, or assembly of men, in the same manner, as if they were his own, to the end, to live peaceably amongst themselves, and be protected against other men.

From this institution of a commonwealth are derived all the *rights,* and *faculties* of him, or them, on whom sovereign power is conferred by the con-sent of the people assembled.

First, because they covenant, it is to be understood, they are not obliged by former covenant to anything repugnant hereunto. And consequently they that have already instituted a commonwealth, being thereby bound by cov-enant, to own the actions, and judgments of one, cannot lawfully make a new covenant, amongst themselves, to be obedient to any other, in any thing what-soever, without his permission. And therefore, they that are subjects to a mon-arch, cannot without his leave cast off monarchy, and return to the confusion of a disunited multitude; nor transfer their person from him that beareth it, to another man, or other assembly of men: for they are bound, every man to every man, to own, and be reputed author of all, that he that already is their sovereign, shall do, and judge fit to be done: so that any one man dissenting, all the rest should break their covenant made to that man, which is injustice: and they have also every man given the sovereignty to him that beareth their person; and therefore if they depose him, they take from him that which is his own, and so again it is injustice. Besides, if he that attempteth to depose his sovereign, be killed, or punished by him for such attempt, he is author of his own punishment, as being by the institution, author of all his sovereign shall do: and because it is injustice for a man to do anything, for which he may be punished by his own authority, he is also upon that title, unjust. And whereas some men have pretended for their disobedience to their sovereign, a new covenant, made, not with men, but with God; this also is unjust: for there is no covenant with God, but by mediation of somebody that representeth God's person; which none doth but God's lieutenant, who hath the sovereignty under God. But this pretence of covenant with God, is so evident a lie, even in the pretenders' own consciences, that it is not only an act of an unjust, but also of a vile, and unmanly disposition.

Secondly, because the right of bearing the person of them all, is given to him they make sovereign, by covenant only of one to another, and not of him to any of them; there can happen no breach of covenant on the part of the sovereign; and consequently none of his subjects, by any pretence of forfeiture, can be freed from his subjection. That he which is made sovereign maketh no covenant with his subjects beforehand, is manifest; because either he must make it with the whole multitude, as one party to the covenant; or he must make a several covenant with every man. With the whole, as one party, it is impossible; because as yet they are not one person: and if he make so many several covenants as there be men, those covenants after he hath the sovereignty are void; because what act soever can be pretended by any one of them for breach thereof, is the act both of himself, and of all the rest, because done in the person, and by the right of every one of them in particular....

...No man that hath sovereign power can justly be put to death, or otherwise in any manner by his subjects punished. For seeing every subject is author of the actions of his sovereign; he punisheth another for the actions committed by himself.

And because the end of this institution, is the peace and defence of them all; and whosoever has right to the end, has right to the means; it belongeth of right, to whatsoever man, or assembly that hath the sovereignty, to be judge both of the means of peace and defence, and also of the hindrances, and disturbances of the same; and to do whatsoever he shall think necessary to be done, both beforehand, for the preserving of peace and security, by prevention of discord at home, and hostility from abroad; and, when peace and security are lost, for the recovery of the same. And therefore,

...It is annexed to the sovereignty, to be judge of what opinions and doctrines are averse, and what conducing to peace; and consequently, on what occasions, how far, and what men are to be trusted withal, in speaking to multitudes of people; and who shall examine the doctrines of all books before they be published. For the actions of men proceed from their opinions; and in the well-governing of opinions, consisteth the well-governing of men's actions, in order to their peace, and concord. And though in matter of doctrine, nothing ought to be regarded but the truth; yet this is not repugnant to regulating the same by peace. For doctrine repugnant to peace, can no more be true, than peace and concord can be against the law of nature. It is true, that in a commonwealth, where by the negligence, or unskilfulness of governors, and teachers, false doctrines are by time generally received; the contrary truths may be generally offensive. Yet the most sudden, and rough bursting in of a new truth, that can be, does never break the peace, but only sometimes awake the war. For those men that are so remissly governed, that they dare take up arms to defend, or introduce an opinion, are still in war; and their condition not peace, but only a cessation of arms for fear of one another; and they live, as it were, in the precincts of battle continually. It belongeth therefore to him that hath the sovereign power, to be judge, or constitute all judges of opinions and doctrines, as a thing necessary to peace; thereby to prevent discord and civil war.

...It is annexed to the sovereignty, the whole power of prescribing the rules, whereby every man may know, what goods he may enjoy, and what actions he may do, without being molested by any of his fellow-subjects; and this is it men call *propriety*. For before constitution of sovereign power, as hath already been shown, all men had right to all things; which necessarily causeth war: and therefore this propriety, being necessary to peace, and depending on sovereign power, is the act of that power, in order to the public peace. These rules of propriety, or *meum* and *tuum*, and of *good, evil, lawful*, and *unlawful* in the actions of subjects, are the civil laws; that is to say, the laws of each commonwealth in particular; though the name of civil law be now restrained to the ancient civil laws of the city of Rome; which being the head of a great part of the world, her laws at that time were in these parts the civil law....

But a man may here object, that the condition of subjects is very miserable; as being obnoxious to the lusts, and other irregular passions of him, or them that have so unlimited a power in their hands. And commonly they that live under a monarch, think it the fault of monarchy; and they that live under the government of democracy, or other sovereign assembly, attribute all the inconvenience to that form of commonwealth; whereas the power in all forms, if they be perfect enough to protect them, is the same: not considering that the state of man can never be without some incommodity or other; and that the greatest, that in any form of government can possibly happen to the people in general, is scarce sensible, in respect of the miseries, and horrible calamities, that accompany a civil war, or that dissolute condition of masterless men, without subjection to laws, and a coercive power to tie their hands from rapine and revenge: nor considering that the greatest pressure of sovereign governors, proceedeth not from any delight, or profit they can expect in the damage or weakening of their subjects, in whose vigour, consisteth their own strength and glory; but in the restiveness of themselves, that unwillingly contributing to their own defence, make it necessary for their governors to draw from them what they can in time of peace, that they may have means on any emergent occasion, or sudden need, to resist, or take advantage on their enemies. For all men are by nature provided of notable multiplying glasses, that is their passions and self-love, through which, every little payment appeareth a great grievance; but are destitute of those prospective glasses, namely moral and civil science, to see afar off the miseries that hang over them, and cannot without such payments be avoided.

STUDY QUESTIONS

1. How does Hobbes define the word "good"? Could there be a common good for all persons?
2. Would Hobbes say that it is possible for someone to willingly give up his or her life? What would he say about martyrs and heroes?
3. "The trouble with Hobbes is that he bases his politics on people's worst impulses. Civil society should be organized so as to improve human nature—to bring out and cultivate the emotion of love, the feeling of interdependence, and acts of charity." How would Hobbes respond to this comment?
4. Hobbes argues that right and wrong, justice and injustice, would not exist prior to the founding of a commonwealth. Why is this? Do you agree?
5. Hobbes argues that the law takes precedence over conscience. Are there some cases where he cannot say this without inconsistency?
6. Evidently, Hobbes sees little danger of the sovereign using the position of power to attack his or her subjects. Assuming that Hobbes is essentially correct about human nature, could you convince a monarch to be strong but benevolent?
7. Why, according to Hobbes, can there be "no breach of the covenant" by the sovereign?
8. Hobbes insists that the sovereign is censor of all ideas and opinions on the ground that a "doctrine repugnant to peace, can no more be true, than peace and concord can be against the law of nature." Do you agree? Why or why not?

Limited Government: The Natural Rights Approach

John Locke

John Locke (1632–1704) made important contributions to the theory of knowledge and to political thought. He is a key source of the doctrines of government by consent, majority rule, natural rights, the separation of powers, and the legitimacy of revolution which were so important in the birth

Reprinted with permission of Macmillan Publishing Company from John Locke, *The Second Treatise of Government*, edited by Thomas P. Reardon. Copyright 1952 by the Bobbs-Merrill Company; renewed copyright © 1980 by Thomas P. Reardon.

of the United States. Locke is the antithesis of the ivory tower intellectual. In his personal life Locke aligned himself with the Whigs and other forces intent on circumscribing the traditional powers of the British monarchy. For many years Locke served as secretary to a prominent Whig politician, Anthony Ashley Cooper. He was also a commissioner with the Board of Trade and Plantations. His political theory, published anonymously and circulated widely, is generally regarded as the theoretical justification for the so-called Glorious Revolution of 1688, in which the powers of the king were reduced significantly. Locke wrote two political treatises, the first one attacking the doctrine of the divine right of kings, then being espoused by loyalists, and the second one stating his case for limited government.

The material which follows is taken from Locke's *Second Treatise of Government*, originally published in 1690. In this work Locke sets forth his theory of limited government. He sees government as originating in the consent of the governed to protect their natural rights to life, liberty, and estate, collectively referred to as property. Like Hobbes he refers to society without government as a State of Nature and society with government as Political Society or Civil Society. In the absence of government, he tells us, there are serious obstacles to the enjoyment of natural rights. Look for his reference to these "wants" as you read. Government, he tells us, is established through a social contract in which the citizens agree to be bound by law and the decrees of government as long as government abides by the will of the majority. Thus, it is the will of the majority and the rights of individual citizens which limit the powers of government.

Locke also argues that private property is acquired through laboring upon nature, a view which ironically found a sympathetic reception later by a number of theorists and reformers who argued that capitalism amounts to legalized stealing from workers by the wealthy, who own and control the means of production in society. Finally, in one of the most intriguing aspects of his theory, Locke tells us that although all individuals have natural rights, we "forfeit" them when we repudiate the rule of reason and act instead like "beasts."

Locke has drawn much criticism, even from those who favor limited government. For instance, some claim that he contradicts himself on pivotal elements in his theory, that he provides no way to avert massive economic inequities, and that his great attention to majority rule overlooked the prospect of tyranny of the majority over the minority. Keep these criticisms in mind as you read Locke.

DEFINITION OF POLITICAL POWER*

Political power, then, I take to be a right of making laws with penalties of death and, consequently, all less penalties for the regulating and preserving of property, and of employing the force of the community in the execution of

Editors' note: The editors have deviated from the original order of paragraphs in some cases and have provided the headings.

such laws and in the defense of the commonwealth from foreign injury; and all this only for the public good.

THE STATE OF NATURE

To understand political power right and derive it from its original, we must consider what state all men are naturally in, and that is a state of perfect freedom to order their actions and dispose of their possessions and persons as they think fit, within the bounds of the law of nature, without asking leave or depending upon the will of any other man.

A state also of equality, wherein all the power and jurisdiction is reciprocal, no one having more than another; there being nothing more evident than that creatures of the same species and rank, promiscuously born to all the same advantages of nature and the use of the same faculties, should also be equal one amongst another without subordination or subjection; unless the lord and master of them all should, by any manifest declaration of his will, set one above another, and confer on him by an evident and clear appointment an undoubted right to dominion and sovereignty. . . .

THE LAW OF NATURE AND RIGHTS

But though this be a state of liberty, yet it is not a state of license; though man in that state have an uncontrollable liberty to dispose of his person or possessions, yet he has not liberty to destroy himself, or so much as any creature in his possession, but where some nobler use than its bare preservation calls for it. The state of nature has a law of nature to govern it, which obliges every one; and reason, which is that law, teaches all mankind who will but consult it that, being all equal and independent, no one ought to harm another in his life, health, liberty, or possessions; for men being all the workmanship of one omnipotent and infinitely wise Maker—all the servants of one sovereign master, sent into the world by his order, and about his business—they are his property whose workmanship they are, made to last during his, not one another's pleasure; and being furnished with like faculties, sharing all in one community of nature, there cannot be supposed any such subordination among us that may authorize us to destroy another, as if we were made for one another's uses as the inferior ranks of creatures are for ours. Every one, as he is bound to preserve himself and not to quit his station willfully; so by the like reason, when his own preservation comes not in competition, ought he, as much as he can, to preserve the rest of mankind, and may not, unless it be to do justice to an offender, take away or impair the life, or what tends to the preservation of the life, the liberty, health, limb, or goods of another.

EXECUTIVE POWER OF THE LAW OF NATURE

And that all men may be restrained from invading others' rights and from doing hurt to one another, and the law of nature be observed, which wills the peace and preservation of all mankind, the execution of the law of nature is, in that state, put into every man's hands, whereby everyone has a right to punish the transgressors of that law to such a degree as may hinder its violation; for the law of nature would, as all other laws that concern men in this world, be in vain if there were nobody that in that state of nature had a power to execute that law and thereby preserve the innocent and restrain offenders. And if anyone in the state of nature may punish another for any evil he has done, everyone may do so; for in that state of perfect equality, where naturally there is no superiority or jurisdiction of one over another, what any may do in prosecution of that law, everyone must needs have a right to do....

THE STATE OF WAR

And hence it is that he who attempts to get another man into his absolute power does thereby put himself into a state of war with him, it being to be understood as a declaration of a design upon his life; for I have reason to conclude that he who would get me into his power without my consent would use me as he pleased when he got me there, and destroy me, too, when he had a fancy to it; for nobody can desire to have me in his absolute power unless it be to compel me by force to that which is against the right of my freedom, i.e., make me a slave. To be free from such force is the only security of my preservation; and reason bids me look on him as an enemy to my preservation who would take away that freedom which is the fence to it; so that he who makes an attempt to enslave me thereby puts himself into a state of war with me. He that, in the state of nature, would take away the freedom that belongs to any one in that state must necessarily be supposed to have a design to take away everything else, that freedom being the foundation of all the rest; as he that, in the state of society, would take away the freedom belonging to those of that society or commonwealth must be supposed to design to take away from them everything else, and so be looked on as in a state of war....

PROPERTY: PUBLIC AND PRIVATE

Whether we consider natural reason, which tells us that men, being once born, have a right to their preservation, and consequently to meat and drink and such other things as nature affords for their subsistence; or revelation, which gives us an account of those grants God made of the world to Adam, and to Noah and his sons; it is very clear that God, as King David says (Psalm CXV. 16), "has given the earth to the children of men," given it to mankind in common. But this being supposed, it seems to some a very great difficulty how any one should ever come to have a property in anything. I will not content myself to answer that if it be difficult to make out property upon a supposition that God gave the world to Adam in his posterity in common, it is impossible that any man but one universal monarch should have any property upon a supposition that God gave the world to Adam and his heirs in succession, exclusive of all the rest of his posterity. But I shall endeavor to show how men might come to have a property in several parts of that which God gave to mankind in common, and that without any express compact of all the commoners. . . .

Though the earth and all inferior creatures be common to all men, yet every man has a property in his own person; this nobody has any right to but himself. The labor of his body and the work of his hands, we may say, are properly his. Whatsoever then he removes out of the state that nature has provided and left it in, he has mixed his labor with, and joined to it something that is his own, and thereby makes it his property. It being by him removed from the common state nature has placed it in, it has by this labor something annexed to it that excludes the common right of other men. For this labor being the unquestionable property of the laborer, no man but he can have a right to what that is once joined to, at least where there is enough and as good left in common for others. . . .

LIMITS TO PROPERTY

It will perhaps be objected to this that "if gathering the acorns, or other fruits of the earth, etc., makes a right to them, then any one may engross as much as he will." To which I answer: not so. The same law of nature that does by this means give us property does also bound that property, too. "God has given us all things richly" (I Tim. vi. 17), is the voice of reason confirmed by inspiration. But how far has he given it us? To enjoy. As much as any one can make use of to any advantage of life before it spoils, so much he may by his labor fix a property in; whatever is beyond this is more than his share and belongs to others. Nothing was made by God for man to spoil or destroy. And thus considering the plenty of natural provisions there was a long time in the world, and the few spenders, and to how small a part of that provision the industry of one man could extend itself and engross it to the prejudice of others, especially keeping within the bounds set by reason of what might serve for his use, there could be then little room for quarrels or contentions about property so established. . . .

FLAWS IN SOCIETY WITHOUT GOVERNMENT

If man in the state of nature be so free, as has been said, if he be absolute lord of his own person and possessions, equal to the greatest, and subject to nobody, why will he part with his freedom, why will he give up his empire and subject himself to the dominion and control of any other power? To which it is obvious to answer that though in the state of nature he has such a right, yet the enjoyment of it is very uncertain and constantly exposed to the invasion of others; for all being kings as much as he, every man his equal, and the greater part no strict observers of equity and justice, the enjoyment of the property he has in this state is very unsafe, very unsecure. This makes him willing to quit a condition which, however free, is full of fears and continual dangers; and it is not without reason that he seeks out and is willing to join in society with others who are already united, or have a mind to unite, for the mutual preservation of their lives, liberties, and estates, which I call by the general name "property."

The great and chief end, therefore, of men's uniting into commonwealths and putting themselves under government is the preservation of their property. To which in the state of nature there are many things wanting:

First, there wants an established, settled, known law, received and allowed by common consent to be the standard of right and wrong and the common measure to decide all controversies between them; for though the law of nature be plain and intelligible to all rational creatures, yet men, being biased by their interest as well as ignorant for want of studying it, are not apt to allow of it as a law binding to them in the application of it to their particular cases.

Secondly, in the state of nature there wants a known and indifferent judge with authority to determine all differences according to the established law; for every one in that state being both judge and executioner of the law of nature, men being partial to themselves, passion and revenge is very apt to carry them too far and with too much heat in their own cases, as well as negligence and unconcernedness to make them too remiss in other men's.

Thirdly, in the state of nature there often wants power to back and support the sentence when right, and to give it due execution. They who by any injustice offend will seldom fail, where they are able, by force, to make good their injustice; such resistance many times makes the punishment dangerous and frequently destructive to those who attempt it.

Thus mankind, notwithstanding all the privileges of the state of nature, being but in an ill condition while they remain in it, are quickly driven into society. Hence it comes to pass that we seldom find any number of men live any time together in this state. The inconveniences that they are therein exposed to by the irregular and uncertain exercise of the power every man has of punishing the transgressions of others make them take sanctuary under the established laws of government and therein seek the preservation of their property. It is this makes them so willingly give up every one his single power of punishing, to be exercised by such alone as shall be appointed to it amongst them; and by such rules as the community, or those authorized by them to that purpose, shall agree on. And in this we have the original right of both the legislative and executive power, as well as of the governments and societies themselves....

THE SOCIAL CONTRACT AND MAJORITY RULE

Whenever, therefore, any number of men are so united into one society as to quit every one his executive power of the law of nature and to resign it to the public, there and there only is a political or civil society. And this is done wherever any number of men, in the state of nature, enter into society to make one people, one body politic, under one supreme government, or else when any one joins himself to, and incorporates with, any government already made; for hereby he authorizes the society or, which is all one, the legislative thereof to make laws for him as the public good of the society shall require, to the execution whereof his own assistance, as to his own decrees, is due. And this puts men out of a state of nature into that of a commonwealth by setting up a judge on earth, with authority to determine all the controversies and redress the injuries that may happen to any member of the commonwealth; which judge is the legislative, or magistrates appointed by it. And wherever there are any number of men, however associated, that have no such decisive power to appeal to, there they are still in the state of nature....

For when any number of men have, by the consent of every individual, made a community, they have thereby made that community one body, with a power to act as one body, which is only by the will and determination of the majority; for that which acts any community being only the consent of the individuals of it, and it being necessary to that which is one body to move one way, it is necessary the body should move that way whither the greater force carries it, which is the consent of the majority; or also it is impossible it should act or continue one body, one community, which the consent of every individual that united into it agreed that it should; and so every one is bound by that consent to be concluded by the majority. And therefore we see that in assemblies empowered to act by positive laws, where no number is set by that positive law which empowers them, the act of the majority passes for the act of the whole and, of course, determines, as having by the law of nature and reason the power of the whole....

But though men when they enter into society give up the equality, liberty, and executive power they had in the state of nature into the hands of the society, to be so far disposed of by the legislative as the good of the society shall require, yet it being only with an intention in every one the better to preserve himself, his liberty and property—for no rational creature can be supposed to change his condition with an intention to be worse—the power of the society, or legislative constituted by them, can never be supposed to extend farther than the common good, but is obliged to secure every one's property by providing against those three defects above-mentioned that made the state of nature so unsafe and uneasy. And so whoever has the legislative or supreme power of any commonwealth is bound to govern by established standing laws, promulgated and known to the people, and not by extemporary decrees; by indifferent and upright judges who are to decide controversies by those laws; and to employ the force of the community at home only in the execution of such laws, or abroad to prevent or redress foreign injuries, and secure the community from inroads and invasion. And all this to be directed to no other end but the peace, safety, and public good of the people. . . .

TYPES OF POWER

First, then, *paternal* or *parental power* is nothing but that which parents have over their children to govern them for the children's good till they come to the use of reason or a state of knowledge wherein they may be supposed capable to understand that rule, whether it be the law of nature or the municipal law of their country, they are to govern themselves by—capable, I say, to know it as well as several others who live as free-men under that law. The affection and tenderness which God has planted in the breast of parents toward their children makes it evident that this is not intended to be a severe arbitrary government, but only for the help, instruction, and preservation of their off-spring. But happen it as it will, there is, as I have proved, no reason why it should be thought to extend to life and death at any time over their children more than over anybody else; neither can there be any pretense why this pa-rental power should keep the child, when grown to a man, in subjection to the will of his parents any further than having received life and education from his parents obliges him to respect, honor, gratitude, assistance, and support all his life to both father and mother. And thus, it is true, the paternal is a natural government, but not at all extending itself to the ends and jurisdictions of that which is political. The power of the father does not reach at all to the property of the child, which is only in his own disposing.

Secondly, *political power* is that power which every man having in the state of nature has given up into the hands of the society and therein to the governors whom the society has set over itself, with this express or tacit trust that it shall be employed for their good and the preservation of their property. Now this power which every man has in the state of nature, and which he parts with to the society in all such cases where the society can secure him, is to use such means for the preserving of his own property as he thinks good and nature allows him, and to punish the breach of the law of nature in others so as, according to the best of his reason, may most conduce to the preser-vation of himself and the rest of mankind. So that the end and measure of this power, when in every man's hands in the state of nature, being the preser-vation of all of his society—that is, all mankind in general—it can have no other end or measure when in the hands of the magistrate but to preserve the members of that society in their lives, liberties, and possessions, and so cannot be an absolute arbitrary power over their lives and fortunes, which are as much as possible to be preserved, but a power to make laws, and annex such penalties to them as may tend to the preservation of the whole, by cutting off those parts, and those only, which are so corrupt that they threaten the sound and healthy, without which no severity is lawful. And this power has its original only from compact and agreement, and the mutual consent of those who make up the community.

Thirdly, *despotical power* is an absolute, arbitrary power one man has over another to take away his life whenever he pleases. This is a power which neither nature gives—for it has made no such distinction between one man and another—nor compact can convey, for man, not having such an arbitrary power over his own life, cannot give another man such a power over it; but it is the effect only of forfeiture which the aggressor makes of his own life when he puts himself into the state of war with another. For having quitted reason, which God has given to be the rule betwixt man and man and the common bond whereby human kind is united into one fellowship and society; and having renounced the way of peace which that teaches, and made use of the force of war to compass his unjust ends upon another where he has no right; and so revolting from his own kind to that of beasts by making force, which is theirs, to be his rule of right; he renders himself liable to be destroyed by the injured person and the rest of mankind that will join with him in the execution of justice, as any other wild beast or noxious brute with whom mankind can have neither society nor security. And thus captives, taken in a just and lawful war, and such only, are subject to a despotical power, which, as it arises not from compact, so neither is it capable of any, but is the state of war continued; for what compact can be made with a man that is not master of his own life? What condition can he perform? And if he be once allowed to be master of his own life, the despotical arbitrary power of his master ceases. He that is master of himself and his own life has a right, too, to the means of preserving it; so that, as soon as compact enters, slavery ceases, and he so far quits his absolute power and puts an end to the state of war who enters into conditions with his captive....

THE LEGITIMACY OF REVOLUTION

The reason why men enter into society is the preservation of their property; and the end why they choose and authorize a legislative is that there may be laws made and rules set as guards and fences to the properties of all the members of the society to limit the power and moderate the dominion of every part and member of the society; for since it can never be supposed to be the will of the society that the legislative should have a power to destroy that which every one designs to secure by entering into society, and for which the people submitted themselves to legislators of their own making. Whenever the legislators endeavor to take away and destroy the property of the people, or to reduce them to slavery under arbitrary power, they put themselves into a state of war with the people who are thereupon absolved from any further obedience, and are left to the common refuge which God has provided for all men against force and violence. Whensoever, therefore, the legislative shall transgress this fundamental rule of society, and either by ambition, fear, folly, or corruption, endeavor to grasp themselves, or put into the hands of any other, an absolute power over the lives, liberties, and estates of the people, by this breach of trust they forfeit the power the people had put into their hands for quite contrary ends, and it devolves to the people, who have a right to resume their original liberty and, by the establishment of a new legislative, such as they shall think fit, provide for their own safety and security, which is the end for which they are in society. What I have said here concerning the legislative in general holds true also concerning the supreme executor, who having a double trust put in him—both to have a part in the legislative and the supreme execution of the law—acts against both when he goes about to set up his own arbitrary will as the law of the society....

Here, it is like, the common question will be made: Who shall be judge whether the prince or legislative act contrary to their trust? This, perhaps, ill-affected and factious men may spread amongst the people, when the prince only makes use of his due prerogative. To this I reply: The people shall be judge; for who shall be judge whether his trustee or deputy acts well and according to the trust reposed in him but he who deputes him and must, by having deputed him, have still a power to discard him when he fails in his trust? If this be reasonable in particular cases of private men, why should it be otherwise in that of the greatest moment where the welfare of millions is concerned, and also where the evil, if not prevented, is greater and the redress very difficult, dear, and dangerous?

STUDY QUESTIONS

1. On what two grounds does Locke claim to base his theory of property?
2. What are the limits on private property which Locke establishes? Once money is introduced into the economy, do these limits become meaningless?
3. What is agreed to in the social contract? Is the idea of a social contract artificial? Do citizens today really enter into a social contract or give free consent to their government as Locke suggests?
4. Locke says that a person can forfeit his or her rights. When does this occur? Do you agree with him? Would he support the death penalty?
5. What does Locke mean by "majority"? Historically, how has Locke's "majority" been interpreted in the United States?
6. What are the three "wants" in the State of Nature which government is established to overcome?
7. Locke says that "the greater part [of men] are no strict observers of equity and justice," and therefore that life in the State of Nature is "very unsafe, very unsecure." Is this characterization of man really any different from Hobbes's? If not, why does Locke support limited government instead of dictatorship?
8. Could Locke ever support a socialistic economic system?

Limited Government:
The Utilitarian Approach
John Stuart Mill

In 1859 John Stuart Mill (see biographical sketch, p. 409) published what many consider the most important and persuasive defense of personal freedom and individuality in the English language. In this essay, *On Liberty*, Mill argued that society has no right to interfere in the affairs of the individual beyond what is required for the protection of others. Mill stood firmly on the side of freedom of the press, freedom of association, and freedom to think and act as one wishes. He reasoned that a limited government which promoted such freedom would enable individuals to fulfill their own nature and would spur the development of genius, which thrives in an atmosphere of toleration.

Mill was dubious about Locke's doctrine of rights and his alleged pregovernmental State of Nature. Though defending democracy, he rejected much of Locke's thought. Indeed, he pointed an accusing finger at Locke as a contributor to a new form of tyranny, the "tyranny of the majority," which, he said, was as devastating and repressive as tyranny by a single political sovereign. In his private life Mill spent a great deal of time with a married woman, Harriet Taylor, which caused both to suffer from gossip and rumors. Also, when he wrote in favor of women's rights in *The Subjection of Women*, he found that many of his friends deserted him, and that many women refused to speak out for themselves or were actively hostile to the suffrage movement. These personal experiences were proof that custom can create sentiments which stand in the way of the full development of individuals. He therefore challenged both the political *and* social expressions of tyranny.

The subject of this essay is not the so-called liberty of the will, so unfortunately opposed to the misnamed doctrine of philosophical necessity; but civil, or social liberty: the nature and limits of the power which can be legitimately exercised by society over the individual. A question seldom stated and hardly ever discussed in general terms, but which profoundly influences the practical controversies of the age by its latent presence, and is likely soon to make itself recognized as the vital question of the future. It is so far from being new, that, in a certain sense, it has divided mankind almost from the remotest ages; but in the stage of progress into which the more civilized portions of the species have now entered, it presents itself under new conditions, and requires a different and more fundamental treatment.

The struggle between liberty and authority is the most conspicuous feature in the portions of history with which we are earliest familiar, particularly in that of Greece, Rome, and England. But in old times this contest was between subjects, or some classes of subjects, and the government. By liberty,

From *On Liberty* by John Stuart Mill, first published in 1859. Many editions.

,eant protection against the tyranny of the political rulers. The rulers
conceived (except in some of the popular governments of Greece) as in
:cessarily antagonistic position to the people whom they ruled. They con-
,ted of a governing One, or a governing tribe or caste, who derived their
,uthority from inheritance or conquest, who, at all events, did not hold it at
the pleasure of the governed, and whose supremacy men did not venture,
perhaps did not desire, to contest, whatever precautions might be taken against
its oppressive exercise. Their power was regarded as necessary, but also as
highly dangerous; as a weapon which they would attempt to use against their
subjects, no less than against external enemies. To prevent the weaker members of the community from being preyed upon by innumerable vultures, it
was needful that there should be an animal of prey stronger than the rest,
commissioned to keep them down. But as the king of the vultures would be
no less bent upon preying on the flock than any of the minor harpies, it was
indispensable to be in a perpetual attitude of defense against his beak and
claws. The aim, therefore, of patriots was to set limits to the power which the
ruler should be suffered to exercise over the community; and this limitation
was what they meant by liberty. It was attempted in two ways. First, by obtaining a recognition of certain immunities, called political liberties or rights,
which it was to be regarded as a breach of duty in the ruler to infringe, and
which if he did infringe, specific resistance, or general rebellion, was held to
be justifiable. A second, and generally a later expedient, was the establishment of constitutional checks, by which the consent of the community, or of
a body of some sort, supposed to represent its interests, was made a necessary
condition to some of the more important acts of the governing power. To the
first of these modes of limitation, the ruling power, in most European countries, was compelled, more or less, to submit. It was not so with the second;
and, to attain this, or when already in some degree possessed, to attain it more
completely, became everywhere the principal object of the lovers of liberty.
And so long as mankind were content to combat one enemy by another, and
to be ruled by a master, on condition of being guaranteed more or less effi-
caciously against his tyranny, they did not carry their aspirations beyond this
point.

A time, however, came, in the progress of human affairs, when men
ceased to think it a necessity of nature that their governors should be an independent power, opposed in interest to themselves. It appeared to them
much better that the various magistrates of the State should be their tenants
or delegates, revocable at their pleasure. In that way alone, it seemed, could
they have complete security that the powers of government would never be
abused to their disadvantage. By degrees this new demand for elective and
temporary rulers became the prominent object of the exertions of the popular
party, wherever any such party existed; and superseded, to a considerable
extent, the previous efforts to limit the power of rulers. As the struggle proceeded for making the ruling power emanate from the periodical choice of the
ruled, some persons began to think that too much importance had been attached to the limitation of the power itself. *That* (it might seem) was a resource

against rulers whose interests were habitually opposed to those of the people. What was now wanted was, that the <u>rulers should be identified with the people; that their interest and will should be the interest and will of the nation.</u> The nation did not need to be protected against its own will. There was no fear of its tyrannizing over itself. Let the rulers be effectually responsible to it, promptly removable by it, and it could afford to trust them with power of which it could itself dictate the use to be made. Their power was but the nation's own power, concentrated, and in a form convenient for exercise. This mode of thought, or rather perhaps of feeling, was common among the last generation of European liberalism, in the Continental section of which it still apparently predominates. Those who admit any limit to what a government may do, except in the case of such governments as they think ought not to exist, stand out as brilliant exceptions among the political thinkers of the Continent. A similar tone of sentiment might by this time have been prevalent in our own country, if the circumstances which for a time encouraged it had continued unaltered.

But in political and philosophical theories, as well as in persons, success discloses faults and infirmities which failure might have concealed from observation. The notion that the people have no need to limit their power over themselves, might seem axiomatic when popular government was a thing only dreamed about, or read of as having existed at some distant period of the past. Neither was that notion necessarily disturbed by such temporary aberrations as those of the French Revolution, the worst of which were the work of a usurping few, and which, in any case, belonged not to the permanent working of popular institutions, but to a sudden and convulsive outbreak against monarchical and aristocratic despotism. In time, however, a democratic republic came to occupy a large portion of the earth's surface, and made itself felt as one of the most powerful members of the community of nations; and elective and responsible government became subject to the observations and criticism which wait upon a great existing fact. It was now perceived that such phrases as "self-government," and the "power of the people over themselves," do not express the true state of the case. The "people" who exercise the power are not always the same people with those over whom it is exercised; and the "self-government" spoken of is not the government of each by himself, but of each by all the rest. <u>The will of the people, moreover, practically means the will of the most numerous or the most active *part* of the people; the majority, or those who succeed in making themselves accepted as the majority:</u> the people, consequently *may* desire to oppress a part of their number, and precautions are as much needed against this as against any other abuse of power. The limitation, therefore, of the power of government over individuals loses none of its importance when the holders of power are regularly accountable to the community, that is, to the strongest party therein. This view of things, recommending itself equally to the intelligence of thinkers and to the inclination of those important classes in European society to whose real or supposed interests democracy is adverse, has had no difficulty in establishing itself; and in political speculations "<u>the tyranny of the majority</u>" is now generally included among the evils against which society requires to be on its guard.

Like other tyrannies, the tyranny of the majority was at first, and is still vulgarly, held in dread chiefly as operating through the acts of the public authorities. But reflecting persons perceived that when society is itself the tyrant—society collectively over the separate individuals who compose it—its means of tyrannizing are not restricted to the acts which it may do by the hands of its political functionaries. Society can and does execute its own mandates; and if it issues wrong mandates instead of right, or any mandates at all in things with which it ought not to meddle, it practices a social tyranny more formidable than many kinds of political oppression, since, though not usually upheld by such extreme penalties, it leaves fewer means of escape, penetrating much more deeply into the details of life, and enslaving the soul itself. Protection, therefore, against the tyranny of the magistrate is not enough: there needs protection also against the tyranny of the prevailing opinion and feeling; against the tendency of society to impose, by other means than civil penalties, its own ideas and practices as rules of conduct on those who dissent from them; to fetter the development, and if possible, prevent the formation, of any individuality not in harmony with its ways, and compels all characters to fashion themselves upon the model of its own. There is a limit to the legitimate interference of collective opinion with individual independence; and to find that limit, and maintain it against encroachment, is as indispensable to a good condition of human affairs, as protection against political despotism.

But though this proposition is not likely to be contested in general terms, the practical question, where to place the limit—how to make the fitting adjustment between individual independence and social control—is a subject on which nearly everything remains to be done. All that makes existence valuable to anyone, depends on the enforcement of restraints upon the actions of other people. Some rules of conduct, therefore, must be imposed, by law in the first place, and by opinion on many things which are not fit subjects for the operation of law. What these rules should be is the principal question in human affairs; but if we except a few of the most obvious cases, it is one of those which least progress has been made in resolving. No two ages, and scarcely any two countries, have decided it alike; and the decision of one age or country is a wonder to another. Yet the people of any given age and country no more suspect any difficulty in it, than if it were a subject on which mankind had always been agreed. The rules which obtain among themselves appear to them self-evident and self-justifying. This all but universal illusion is one of the examples of the magical influence of custom, which is not only, as the proverb says, a second nature, but is continually mistaken for the first. The effect of custom, in preventing any misgiving respecting the rules of conduct which mankind impose on one another, is all the more complete because the subject is one on which it is not generally considered necessary that reasons should be given, either by one person to others or by each to himself. People are accustomed to believe, and have been encouraged in the belief by some who aspire to the character of philosophers, that their feelings, on subjects of this nature, are better than reasons, and render reasons unnecessary. The practical principle which guides them to their opinions on the regulation of human conduct, is the feeling in each person's mind that everybody should be required to act as he, and those with whom he sympathizes, would like them to act. No one, indeed, acknowledges to himself that his standard of judgment is his own liking; but an opinion on a point of conduct, not supported by reasons, can only count as one person's preference; and if the reasons, when given, are a mere appeal to a similar preference felt by other people, it is still only many people's liking instead of one. To an ordinary man, however, his own preference, thus supported, is not only a perfectly satisfactory reason, but the only one he generally has for any of his notions of morality, taste, or propriety, which are not expressly written in his religious creed; and his chief guide in the interpretation even of that. Men's opinions, accordingly, on what is laudable or blamable, are affected by all the multifarious causes which influence their wishes in regard to the conduct of others, and which are as numerous as those which determine their wishes on any other subject. Sometimes their reason, at other times their prejudices or superstitions; often their social affections, not seldom their antisocial ones, their envy of jealousy, their arrogance or contemptuousness: but most commonly their desires or fears for themselves—their legitimate or illegitimate self-interest. Wherever there is an ascendant class, a large portion of the morality of the country emanates from its class interests, and its feelings of class superiority. The morality between Spartans and Helots, between planters and Negroes, between princes and subjects, between nobles and roturiers, between men and women, has been for the most part of the creation of these class interests and feelings; and the sentiments thus generated react in turn upon the moral feelings of the members of the ascendant class, in their relations among themselves. Where, on the other hand, a class, formerly ascendant, has lost its ascendancy, or where its ascendancy is unpopular, the prevailing moral sentiments frequently bear the impress of an impatient dislike of superiority. Another grand determining principle of the rules of conduct, both in act and forbearance, which have been enforced by law or opinion, has been the servility of mankind towards the supposed preferences or aversions of their temporal masters or of their gods. This servility, though essentially selfish, is not hypocrisy; it gives rise to perfectly genuine sentiments of abhorrence; it made men burn magicians and heretics. Among so many baser influences, the general and obvious interests of society have of course had a share, and a large one, in the direction of the moral sentiments; less, however, as a matter of reason, and on their own account, than as a consequence of the sympathies and antipathies which grew out of them; and sympathies and antipathies which had little or nothing to do with the interest of society, have made themselves felt in the establishment of moralities with quite as great force.

The likings and dislikings of society, or of some powerful portion of it, are thus the main thing which has practically determined the rules laid down for general observance, under the penalties of law or opinion. And in general, those who have been in advance of society in thought and feeling, have left this condition of things unassailed in principle, however they may have come into conflict with it in some of its details. They have occupied themselves rather in inquiring what things society ought to like or dislike, than in questioning whether its likings or dislikings should be a law to individuals. They preferred endeavoring to alter the feelings of mankind on the particular points on which they were themselves heretical, rather than make common cause in defense of freedom, with heretics generally....The great writers to whom the world owes what religious liberty it possesses, have mostly asserted freedom of conscience as an indefeasible right, and denied absolutely that a human being is accountable to others for his religious belief. Yet so natural to mankind is intolerance in whatever they really care about, that religious freedom has hardly anywhere been practically realized, except where religious indifference, which dislikes to have its peace disturbed by theological quarrels, has added its weight to the scale. In the minds of almost all religious persons, even in the most tolerant countries, the duty of toleration is admitted with tacit reserves. One person will bear with dissent in matters of church government, but not of dogma; another can tolerate everybody, short of a Papist or a Unitarian; another everyone who believes in revealed religion; a few extend their charity a little further, but stop at the belief in a God and in a future state. Wherever the sentiment of the majority is still genuine and intense, it is found to have abated little of its claim to be obeyed....

The object of this essay is to assert one very simple principle, as entitled to govern absolutely the dealings of society with the individual in the way of compulsion and control, whether the means used be physical force in the form of legal penalties, or the moral coercion of public opinion. That principle is, that the sole end for which mankind are warranted, individually or collectively, in interfering with the liberty of action of any of their number, is self-protection. That the only purpose for which power can be rightfully exercised over any member of a civilized community, against his will, is to prevent harm to others. His own good, either physical or moral, is not a sufficient warrant. He cannot rightfully be compelled to do or forbear because it will be better for him to do so, because it will make him happier, because, in the opinions of others, to do so would be wise, or even right. These are good reasons for remonstrating with him, or reasoning with him, or persuading him, or entreating him, but not for compelling him, or visiting him with any evil in case he do otherwise. To justify that, the conduct from which it is desired to deter him must be calculated to produce evil to someone else. The only part of the conduct of anyone, for which he is amenable to society, is that which concerns others. In the part which merely concerns himself, his independence is, of right, absolute. Over himself, over his own body and mind, the individual is sovereign.

It is perhaps hardly necessary to say that this doctrine is meant to apply only to human beings in the maturity of their faculties....Those who are still in a state to require being taken care of by others, must be protected against their own actions as well as against external injury. . . . Liberty, as a principle, has no application to any state of things anterior to the time when mankind have become capable of being improved by free and equal discussion. Until then, there is nothing for them but implicit obedience to an Akbar or a Charlemagne, if they are so fortunate as to find one. But as soon as mankind have attained the capacity of being guided to their own improvement by conviction or persuasion . . . , compulsion, either in the direct form or in that of pains and penalties for non-compliance, is no longer admissible as a means to their own good, and justifiable only for the security of others.

It is proper to state that I forego any advantage which could be derived to my argument from the idea of abstract right, as a thing independent of utility. I regard utility as the ultimate appeal on all ethical questions; but it must be utility in the largest sense, grounded on the permanent interests of man as a progressive being. Those interests, I contend, authorized the subjection of individual spontaneity to external control, only in respect to those actions of each which concern the interest of other people. If anyone does an act hurtful to others, there is a *prima facie* case for punishing him, by law, or, where legal penalties are not safely applicable, by general disapprobation. There are also many positive acts for the benefit of others, which he may rightfully be compelled to perform: such as to give evidence in a court of justice; to bear his fair share in the common defense, or in any other joint work necessary to the interest of the society of which he enjoys the protection; and to perform certain acts of individual beneficence, such as saving a fellow-creature's life, or interposing to protect the defenseless against ill-usage, things which whenever it is obviously a man's duty to do, he may rightfully be made responsible to society for not doing. A person may cause evil to others not only by his actions but by his inaction, and in either case he is justly accountable to them for the injury. The latter case, it is true, requires a much more cautious exercise of compulsion than the former. To make anyone answerable for doing evil to others is the rule; to make him answerable for not preventing evil is, comparatively speaking, the exception. Yet there are many cases clear enough and grave enough to justify that exception. In all things which regard the external relations of the individual, he is *de jure* amenable to those whose interests are concerned, and, if need be, to society as their protector. There are often good reasons for not holding him to the responsibility; but these reasons must arise from the special expediencies of the case; either because it is a kind of case in which he is on the whole likely to act better, when left to his own discretion, than when controlled in any way in which society have it in their power to control him; or because the attempt to exercise control would produce other evils, greater than those which it would prevent. When such reasons as these preclude the enforcement of responsibility, the conscience of the agent himself should step into the vacant judgment seat, and protect those interests of others which have no external protection; judging himself all the more rigidly, because the case does not admit of his being made accountable to the judgment of his fellow-creatures.

But there is a sphere of action in which society, as distinguished from the individual, has, if any, only an indirect interest; comprehending all that portion of a person's life and conduct which affects only himself, or if it also affects others, only with their free, voluntary, and undeceived consent and participation. When I say only himself, I mean directly, and in the first instance; for whatever affects himself, may affect others through himself; and the objection which may be grounded on this contingency, will receive consideration in the sequel. This, then, is the appropriate region of human liberty. It comprises, *first*, the inward domain of consciousness; demanding liberty of conscience in the most comprehensive sense; liberty of thought and feeling; absolute freedom of opinion and sentiment on all subjects, practical or speculative, scientific, moral, or theological. The liberty of expressing and publishing opinions may seem to fall under a different principle, since it belongs to that part of the conduct of an individual which concerns other people; but, being almost of as much importance as the liberty of thought itself, and resting in great part on the same reasons, is practically inseparable from it. *Secondly,* the principle requires liberty of tastes and pursuits; of framing the plan of our life to suit our own character; of doing as we like, subject to such consequences as may follow: without impediment from our fellow-creatures, so long as what we do does not harm them, even though they should think our conduct foolish, perverse, or wrong. *Thirdly,* from this liberty of each individual, follows the liberty, within the same limits, of combination among individuals; freedom to unite for any purpose not involving harm to others: the persons combining being supposed to be of full age, and not forced or deceived.

No society in which these liberties are not, on the whole, respected, is free, whatever may be its form of government; and none is completely free in which they do not exist absolute and unqualified. The only freedom which deserves the name, is that of pursuing our own good in our own way, so long as we do not attempt to deprive others of theirs, or impede their efforts to obtain it. Each is the proper guardian of his own health, whether bodily, or mental and spiritual. Mankind are greater gainers by suffering each other to live as seems good to themselves, than by compelling each to live as seems good to the rest....

The time, it is to be hoped, is gone by, when any defence would be necessary of the "liberty of the press" as one of the securities against corrupt or tyrannical government. No argument, we may suppose, can now be needed, against permitting a legislature or an executive, not identified in interest with the people, to prescribe opinions to them, and determine what doctrines or what arguments they shall be allowed to hear. This aspect of the question, besides, has been so often and so triumphantly enforced by preceding writers, that it need not be specially insisted on in this place. Though the law of England, on the subject of the press, is as servile to this day as it was in the time of the Tudors, there is little danger of its being actually put in force against political discussion, except during some temporary panic, when fear of insurrection drives ministers and judges from their propriety; and, speaking generally, it is not, in constitutional countries, to be apprehended, that the government, whether completely responsible to the people or not, will often attempt to control the expression of opinion, except when in doing so it makes itself the organ of the general intolerance of the public. Let us suppose, therefore, that the government is entirely at one with the people, and never thinks of exerting any power of coercion unless in agreement with what it conceives to be their voice. But I deny the right of the people to exercise such coercion, either by themselves or by their government. The power itself is illegitimate. The best government has no more title to it than the worst. It is as noxious, or more noxious, when exerted in accordance with public opinion, than when in opposition to it. If all mankind minus one, were of one opinion, and only one person were of the contrary opinion, mankind would be no more justified in silencing that one person, than he, if he had the power, would be justified in silencing mankind. Were an opinion a personal possession of no value except to the owner; if to be obstructed in the enjoyment of it were simply a private injury, it would make some difference whether the injury was inflicted only on a few persons or on many. But the peculiar evil of silencing the expression of an opinion is, that it is robbing the human race; posterity as well as the existing generation; those who dissent from the opinion, still more than those who hold it. If the opinion is right, they are deprived of the opportunity of exchanging error for truth: if wrong, they lose, what is almost as great a benefit, the clearer perception and livelier impression of truth, produced by its collision with error....

As it is useful that while mankind are imperfect there should be different opinions, so is it that there should be different experiments of living; that free scope should be given to varieties of character, short of injury to others; and that the worth of different modes of life should be proved practically, when any one thinks fit to try them. It is desirable, in short, that in things which do not primarily concern others, individuality should assert itself. Where, not the person's own character, but the traditions or customs of other people are the rule of conduct, there is wanting one of the principal ingredients of human happiness, and quite the chief ingredient of individual and social progress.

In maintaining this principle, the greatest difficulty to be encountered does not lie in the appreciation of means towards an acknowledged end, but in the indifference of persons in general to the end itself. If it were felt that the free development of individuality is one of the leading essentials of wellbeing; that it is not only a co-ordinate element with all like that is designated by the terms civilization, instruction, education, culture, but is itself a necessary part and condition of all those things; there would be no danger that liberty should be undervalued, and the adjustment of the boundaries between it and social control would present no extraordinary difficulty. But the evil is, that individual spontaneity is hardly recognized by the common modes of thinking, as having any intrinsic worth, or deserving any regard on its own account....

He who lets the world, or his own portion of it, choose his plan of life for him, has no need of any other faculty than the ape-like one of imitation.

He who chooses his plan for himself, employs all his faculties. He must use observation to see, reasoning and judgment to foresee, activity to gather materials for decision, discrimination to decide, and when he has decided, firmness and self-control to hold to his deliberate decision. And these qualities he requires and exercises exactly in proportion as the part of his conduct which he determines according to his own judgment and feelings is a large one. It is possible that he might be guided in some good path, and kept out of harm's way, without any of these things. But what will be his comparative worth as a human being? It really is of importance, not only what men do, but also what manner of men they are that do it. Among the works of man, which human life is rightly employed in perfecting and beautifying, the first in importance surely is man himself. Supposing it were possible to get houses built, corn grown, battles fought, causes tried, and even churches erected and prayers said, by machinery—by automatons in human form—it would be a considerable loss to exchange for these automatons even the men and women who at present inhabit the more civilized parts of the world, and who assuredly are but starved specimens of what nature can and will produce. Human nature is not a machine to be built after a model, and set to do exactly the work prescribed for it, but a tree, which requires to grow and develop itself on all sides, according to the tendency of the inward forces which make it a living thing. . . .

STUDY QUESTIONS

1. Why does Mill believe that the control of society over its members is more formidable than the political oppression of a dictatorship?
2. What is the sole justification for society interfering in the lives of its members? What are some illegitimate reasons?
3. Mill says that there are certain acts for the common good that society may demand of the individual. In effect he is saying that society may punish people for refusing to bring about some good, not only for doing harm. How does Mill justify this? Do you agree?
4. "It does me no injury for my neighbor to say there are twenty gods or no god. It neither picks my pocket nor breaks my leg" (Thomas Jefferson). But what if people believed that atheism weakened the moral fiber of society? Couldn't they use Mill's criterion of self-protection to suppress this opinion? What do you think Mill would say?
5. Some people in the United States practice polygamy. Some members of religious cults believe that handling poisonous snakes is an exercise of faith. Naturally, some of the faithful have died in such displays of religious fervor. Both of these practices are unlawful. Using Mill's criterion, can you tell whether such practices should be permitted?
6. Mill believes that individuality is one of the chief ingredients of human happiness. Do you agree? Why do so many people seem not to value it?

7. Mill says that the men and women of today "are but starved specimens of what nature can and will produce." Obviously he thinks that the people of the future will be more individualistic and, hence, better. But surely eccentricity and difference are not intrinsically valuable, and inasmuch as they prevent the achievement of social unity and cooperation, they appear to be positively harmful. How would you define *individualism* so as to make its increase a positive good?

8. Mill wrote: "It is not useful, but hurtful, that the constitution of the country should declare ignorance to be entitled to as much political power as knowledge." He called for plural voting whereby individuals with proven superior intelligence would have more than one vote in elections. Do you agree with Mill? Why or why not? Does his stance damage his credentials as a supporter of democracy?

9. Most nineteenth-century liberals such as Mill were suspicious of government and viewed it as a threat to individual freedom. One writer faults Mill on this account as follows: "[Mill] never really faced the problems of individual freedom that are peculiarly characteristic of an industrial society or the problems of freedom that press most heavily on wage earners in such a society" (George Sabine, *A History of Political Theory*, 3d ed. [New York: Holt, 1961], p. 711). What is your view? Is extensive governmental activity, in the form of legislation and regulation, necessary to foster individual freedom in an industrial society?

Communism

Friedrich Engels

Friedrich Engels (1820–1895) was the son of a wealthy German manufacturer. Engels turned aside the opportunity for a life of comfort and luxury in order to collaborate with Karl Marx; with Marx he came to see capitalism as a doomed economic system because of emerging economic and political forces which would lead to its demise. In addition to serving as Marx's literary and political collaborator, Engels helped Marx financially when he and his family were hard pressed in London. Engels helped in research and writing for some writings which carried Marx's signature, including several pieces published by the *New York Tribune*, for which Marx was a European correspondent. After Marx's death, Engels oversaw the editing and publication of two volumes of *Das Kapital*, Marx's major critique of capitalism. Though Engels was overshadowed by Marx, he made many important philosophical contributions to communist theory, and because his writing was

From Friedrich Engels, *Socialism: Utopian and Scientific*, the 1892 edition.

superior to Marx's in clarity and style, he was responsible for communicating the essence of communism to hundreds of thousands who found Marx inscrutable. From all indications the two men had deep respect and admiration for one another. Theirs was an unusually successful partnership.

The following is an excerpt from Engels's *Socialism: Utopian and Scientific.* Marx and Engels observed a variety of well-known authors—including Saint-Simon, Fourier, and Owen—put forward proposals to redistribute wealth and power in nineteenth-century Europe so that the many and not merely the few would prosper. Marx and Engels viewed these as pie-in-the-sky plans which would not work because they were not grounded, as was the theory of Marx and Engels, in a substantive analysis of the economic forces which shape history. They felt that they had discovered the laws of the development of matter and that these foreordained the eventual triumph of communism, a unique blend of democracy and socialism. In this selection Engels describes some of the most important concepts in communist theory. He emphasizes the all-importance of economic conditions in determining ideas and values, the origin of class conflict due to the division of labor, the contradictions inherent in capitalism, and the seizure of economic and political power by the working class as a prelude to communism. The State protects the interests of the ascendant economic class, and so the "bourgeois" State must give way to a "proletarian" one, with the latter eventually disappearing as a coercive force as classes themselves disappear. In communism there will be no classes, since the traditional division of labor will no longer exist, and the means of production will be under the control of the community at large, and not of individuals who can use it for private advantage.

As you read Engels, see if you can tell exactly what he means by a "class." Do such classes actually exist, and are they in conflict? If so, what class do you belong to—bourgeoisie or proletariat?

The materialist conception of history starts from the proposition that the production of the means to support human life and, next to production, the exchange of things produced, is the basis of all social structure; that in every society that has appeared in history, the manner in which wealth is distributed and society divided into classes or orders is dependent upon what is produced, how it is produced, and how the products are exchanged. From this point of view the final causes of all social changes and political revolutions are to be sought, not in men's brains, not in men's better insight into eternal truth and justice, but in changes in the modes of production and exchange. They are to be sought not in the *philosophy*, but in the *economics* of each particular epoch. The growing perception that existing social institutions are unreasonable and unjust, that reason has become unreason and right wrong,[1] is only proof that in the modes of production and exchange changes have silently taken place with which the social order, adapted to earlier economic conditions, is no longer in keeping. From this it also follows that the means of getting rid of the in-

---

[1] Mephistopheles, in Goethe's *Faust.*

congruities that have been brought to light must also be present, in a more or less developed condition, within the changed modes of production themselves. These means are not to be invented by deduction from fundamental principles, but are to be discovered in the stubborn facts of the existing system of production.

What is, then, the position of modern socialism in this connection?

The present structure of society—this is now pretty generally conceded— is the creation of the ruling class of today, of the bourgeoisie. The mode of production peculiar to the bourgeoisie, known, since Marx, as the capitalist mode of production, was incompatible with the feudal system, with the privileges it conferred upon individuals, entire social ranks and local corporations, as well as with the hereditary ties of subordination which constituted the framework of its social organization. The bourgeoisie broke up the feudal system and built upon its ruins the capitalist order of society, the kingdom of free competition, of personal liberty, of the equality, before the law, of all commodity owners, of all the rest of the capitalist blessings. Thenceforward the capitalist mode of production could develop in freedom. Since steam, machinery, and the making of machines by machinery transformed the older manufacture into modern industry, the productive forces evolved under the guidance of the bourgeoisie developed with a rapidity and in a degree unheard of before. But just as the older manufacture, in its time, and handicraft, becoming more developed under its influence, had come into collision with the feudal trammels of the guilds, so now modern industry, in its more complete development, comes into collision with the bounds within which the capitalistic mode of production holds it confined. The new productive forces have already outgrown the capitalistic mode of using them. And this conflict between productive forces and modes of production is not a conflict engendered in the mind of man, like that between original sin and divine justice. It exists, in fact, objectively, outside us, independently of the will and actions even of the men that have brought it on. Modern socialism is nothing but the reflex, in thought, of this conflict in fact; its ideal reflection in the minds, first, of the class directly suffering under it, the working class.

Now, in what does this conflict consist?

Before capitalistic production, i.e., in the Middle Ages, the system of petty industry obtained generally, based upon the private property of the labourers in their means of production; in the country, the agriculture of the small peasant, freeman or serf; in the towns, the handicrafts organized in guilds. The instruments of labour—land, agricultural implements, the workshop, the tool—were the instruments of labour of single individuals, adapted for the use of one worker, and, therefore, of necessity, small, dwarfish, circumscribed. But, for this very reason they belonged, as a rule, to the producer himself. To concentrate these scattered, limited means of production, to enlarge them, to turn them into the powerful levers of production of the present day—this was precisely the historic role of capitalist production and of its upholder, the bourgeoisie. In the fourth section of *Capital* Marx has explained in detail how since the fifteenth century this has been historically worked out through the three phases of simple co-operation, manufacture and modern industry. But the bourgeoisie, as is also shown there, could not transform these puny means of production into mighty productive forces without transforming them, at the same time, from means of production of the individual into *social* means of production only workable by a collectivity of men. The spinning-wheel, the hand-loom, the blacksmith's hammer, were replaced by the spinning-machine, the power-loom, the steam-hammer; the individual workshop, by the factory implying the co-operation of hundreds and thousands of workmen. In like manner, production itself changed from a series of individual into a series of social acts, and the products from individual to social products. The yarn, the cloth, the metal articles that now came out of the factory, were the joint product of many workers, through those hands they had successively to pass before they were ready. No one person could say of them: "I make that; this is *my* product...."

In the mediaeval stage of evolution of the production of commodities, the question as to the owner of the product of labour could not arise. The individual producer, as a rule, had, from raw material belonging to himself, and generally his own handiwork, produced it with his own tools, by the labour of his own hands or of his family. There was no need for him to appropriate the new product. It belonged wholly to him, as a matter of course. His property in the product was, therefore, based *upon his own labour*. Even where external help was used, this was, as a rule, of little importance, and very generally was compensated by something other than wages. The apprentices and journeymen of the guilds worked less for board and wages than for education, in order that they might become master craftsmen themselves.

Then came the concentration of the means of production and of the producers in large workshops and manufactories, their transformation into actual socialized means of production and socialized producers. But the socialized producers and means of production and their products were still treated, after this change, just as they had been before, i.e., as the means of production and the products of individuals. Hitherto, the owner of the instruments of labour had himself appropriated the product, because, as a rule, it was his own product and the assistance of others was the exception. Now the owner of the instruments of labour always appropriated to himself the product, although it was no longer *his* product but exclusively the product of the *labour of others*. Thus, the products now produced socially were not appropriated by those who had actually set in motion the means of production and actually produced the commodities, but by the *capitalists*. The means of production, and production itself, had become in essence socialized. But they were subjected to a form of appropriation which presupposes the private production of individuals, under which, therefore, everyone owns his own product and brings

it to market. The mode of production is subjected to this form of appropriation, although it abolishes the conditions upon which the latter rests.[2]

   This contradiction, which gives to the new mode of production its capitalistic character, *contains the germ of the whole of the social antagonisms of today.*
The greater the mastery obtained by the new mode of production over all
important fields of production and in all manufacturing countries, the more it
reduced individual production to an insignificant residuum, *the more clearly
was brought out the incompatibility of socialized production with capitalistic
appropriation....*

   But the perfecting of machinery is making human labour superfluous. If
the introduction and increase of machinery means the displacement of millions of manual by a few machine-workers, improvement in machinery means
the displacement of more and more of the machine-workers themselves. It
means, in the last instance, the production of a number of available wage-
workers in excess of the average needs of capital, the formation of a complete
industrial reserve army, as I called it in 1845, available at the times when industry is working at high pressure, to be cast out upon the street when the
inevitable crash comes, a constant dead weight upon the limbs of the working
class in its struggle for existence with capital, a regulator for the keeping of
wages down to the low level that suits the interests of capital. Thus it comes
about, to quote Marx, that machinery becomes the most powerful weapon in
the war of capital against the working class; that the instruments of labour
constantly tear the means of subsistence out of the hands of the labourer; that
the very product of the worker is turned into an instrument for his subjuga-
tion. Thus it comes about that the economizing of the instruments of labour
becomes at the same time, from the outset, the most reckless waste of labour
power, and robbery based upon the normal conditions under which labour
functions; that machinery, "the most powerful instrument for shortening labour
time, becomes the most unfailing means for placing every moment of the
labourer's time and that of his family at the disposal of the capitalist for the
purpose of expanding the value of his capital." (*Capital,* English edition, p.
406) Thus it comes about that the overwork of some becomes the preliminary
condition for the idleness of others, and that modern industry, which hunts
after new consumers over the whole world, forces the consumption of the
masses at home down to a starvation minimum, and in doing thus destroys
its own home market. "The law that always equilibrates the relative surplus

---

[2] It is hardly necessary in this connection to point out that, even if the form of appropriation
remains the same, the *character* of the appropriation is just as much revolutionised as production
is by the changes described above. It is, of course, a very different matter whether I appropriate
to myself my own product or that of another. Note in passing that wage-labour, which contains
the whole capitalistic mode of production in embryo, is very ancient: in a sporadic, scattered form
it existed for centuries alongside of slave-labour. But the embryo could duly develop into the
capitalistic mode of production only when the necessary historical preconditions had been furnished.

population, or industrial reserve army, to the extent and energy of accumulation, this law rivets the labourer to capital more firmly than the wedges of Vulcan did Prometheus to the rock. It establishes an accumulation of misery, corresponding with accumulation of capital. Accumulation of wealth at one pole is, therefore, at the same time, accumulation of misery, agony of toil, slavery, ignorance, brutality, mental degradation, at the opposite pole, i.e., on the side of the class that produces *its own product in the form of capital."* (*Capital*, p. 661) And to expect any other division of the products from the capitalistic mode of production is the same as expecting the electrodes of a battery not to decompose acidulated water, not to liberate oxygen at the positive, hydrogen at the negative pole, so long as they are connected with the battery....

Whilst the capitalist mode of production more and more completely transforms the great majority of the population into proletarians, it creates the power which, under penalty of its own destruction, is forced to accomplish this revolution. Whilst it forces on more and more the transformation of the vast means of production, already socialized, into state property, it shows itself the way to accomplishing this revolution. *The proletariat seizes political power and turns the means of production into state property.*

But, in doing this, it abolishes itself as proletariat, abolishes all class distinctions and class antagonisms, abolishes also the state as state. Society thus far, based upon class antagonisms, had need of the state. That is, of an organization of the particular class which was *pro tempore* the exploiting class, an organization for the purpose of preventing any interference from without with the existing conditions of production, and, therefore, especially, for the purpose of forcibly keeping the exploited classes in the condition of oppression corresponding with the given mode of production (slavery, serfdom, wage-labour). The state was the official representative of society as a whole; the gathering of it together into a visible embodiment. But it was this only in so far as it was the state of that class which itself represented, for the time being, society as a whole: in ancient times, the state of slaveowning citizens; in the Middle Ages, the feudal lords; in our own time, the bourgeoisie. When at last it becomes the real representative of the whole of society, it renders itself unnecessary. As soon as there is no longer any social class to be held in subjection; as soon as class rule, and the individual struggle for existence based upon our present anarchy in production, with the collisions and excesses arising from these, are removed, nothing more remains to be repressed, and a special repressive force, a state, is no longer necessary. The first act by virtue of which the state really constitutes itself the representative of the whole of society—this is, at the same time, its last independent act as a state. State interference in social relations becomes, in one domain after another, superfluous, and then dies out of itself; the government of persons is replaced by the administration of things, and by the conduct of processes of production. The state is not "abolished." It *dies out.* This gives the measure of the value of the phrase "*a free state,*" both as to its justifiable use at times by agitators, and as to its ultimate scientific insufficiency; and also of the demands of the so-called anarchists for the abolition of the state out of hand....

The socialized appropriation of the means of production does away, not only with the present artificial restrictions upon production, but also with the positive waste and devastation of productive forces and products that are at the present time the inevitable concomitants of production, and that reach their height in the crises. Further, it sets free for the community at large a mass of means of production and of products, by doing away with the senseless extravagance of the ruling classes of today and their political representatives. The possibility of securing for every member of society, by means of socialized production, an existence not only fully sufficient materially, and becoming day by day more full, but an existence guaranteeing to all the free development and exercise of their physical and mental faculties—this possibility is now for the first time here, but *it is here*.[3]

With the seizing of the means of production by society, production of commodities is done away with, and, simultaneously, the mastery of the product over the producer. Anarchy in social production is replaced by systematic, definite organization. The struggle for individual existence disappears. Then for the first time man, in a certain sense, is finally marked off from the rest of the animal kingdom, and emerges from mere animal conditions of existence into really human ones. The whole sphere of the conditions of life which environ man, and which have hitherto ruled man, now comes under the dominion and control of man, who for the first time becomes the real, conscious lord of Nature, because he has now become master of his own social organization. The laws of his own social action, hitherto standing face to face with man as laws of Nature foreign to, and dominating him, will then be used with full understanding, and so mastered by him. Man's own social organization, hitherto confronting him as a necessity imposed by Nature and history, now becomes the result of his own free action. The extraneous objective forces that have hitherto governed history pass under the control of man himself. Only from that time will man himself, more and more consciously, make his own history—only from that time will the social causes set in movement by him have, in the main and in a constantly growing measure, the results intended by him. It is the ascent of man from the kingdom of necessity to the kingdom of freedom.

---

[3]A few figures may serve to give an approximate idea of the enormous expansive force of the modern means of production, even under capitalistic pressure. According to Mr. Giffen, the total wealth of Great Britain and Ireland amounted, in round numbers, in

   1814 to £2,200,000,000.
   1865 to £6,100,000,000.
   1875 to £8,500,000,000.

   An an instance of the squandering of means of production and of products during a crisis, the total loss in the German iron industry alone, in the crisis 1873–1878, was given at the second German Industrial Congress (Berlin, February 21, 1878) as £22,750,000.

STUDY QUESTIONS

1. Why, according to Engels, are there classes, and why are they in conflict?
2. What does Engels mean by the "incompatibility of socialized production with capitalist appropriation"?
3. Engels sees capitalism as structurally flawed, as seen in inescapable, periodic economic crises, such as unemployment, overproduction, and even depression. Has capitalism changed to avoid such consequences?
4. John Dewey was once asked if he was a communist. He replied that it had taken him over thirty years to divest himself of one religion, and that he was not about to take up another. Do you agree with Dewey that communism, or Marxism, is a religion? What is the difference, if any, between embracing a political theory and affirming religious beliefs?
5. Some critics of communism describe the leaders of the Communist party in the Soviet Union, and elsewhere, as "surrogate bourgeoisie." What does that mean, and do you agree or disagree?
6. Are there any philosophical grounds, or practical grounds, on which we can have any confidence that the Soviet Union and the United States can survive and coexist?
7. "All political theories are butchered in practice" (Shipka's Law). Do you agree?
8. Why does Engels say that with communism, for the first time, human beings will make their own history? Do you agree?

SELECTED READINGS FOR PART FIVE

Useful anthologies are Robert Paul Wolff (ed.), *Political Man and Social Man* (New York: Random House, 1966), Carl Cohen (ed.), *Communism, Fascism, and Democracy* (New York: Random House, 1966); and Tibor R. Machan (ed.), *The Main Debate: Communism versus Capitalism* (New York: Random House, 1987). Two excellent histories of political thought are Strauss and Cropsey (eds.), *History of Political Philosophy* (Chicago: Rand McNally, 1963); and George H. Sabine, *A History of Political Theory* (New York: Holt, 1961). Besides Plato's *Crito*, you will want to read his *Republic* and *Laws* for an overview of his theory. Probably the best critique of Plato and Marx is Karl Popper, *The Open Society and Its Enemies* (Princeton, N.J.: Princeton, 1950). On the question of the individual and obedience to the State, there are several very important works, including Carl Cohen, *Civil Disobedience* (New York: Columbia, 1971); Abe Fortas, *Concerning Dissent and Civil Disobedience* (Cleveland: World Publishing, 1968), a book which argues in the tradition of Socrates in Plato's *Crito* and which was written during the height of resistance to the Vietnam War; and Martin Luther King, *Why We Can't Wait* (New York: Harper & Row, 1963), from which the excerpt in the text is taken. An excellent collection of writings on anarchism is L. I. Krimerman and L. Perry (eds.), *Patterns of Anarchy* (Garden City, N.Y.: Doubleday, 1966). One of America's best-known anarchists is Paul Goodman; for a sample of his writings, see *People or Personnel and Like a Conquered Province* (New York: Random House, 1968). To see the influence of Thoreau on Gandhi in his activities in South Africa and India, and Gandhi's doctrine of *satyagraha*, or love-force, see D. M. Datta, *The Philosophy of Mahatma Gandhi* (Madison: University of Wisconsin, 1953); and C. D. S. Devanesen, *The Making of the Mahatma* (New Delhi: Orient Longmans, 1969).

A readily available edition of Hobbes's major political treatise is *Leviathan, Parts I and II* (Indianapolis: Bobbs-Merrill, 1958); a good collection of critical essays on the *Leviathan* is B. H. Baumrin (ed.), *Hobbes's Leviathan: Interpretation and Criticism* (Belmont, Calif.: Wadsworth, 1969). For an excellent overview of Hobbes's life and philosophy, see Richard Peters, *Hobbes* (Baltimore: Penguin, 1967). One of the best collections of Locke's work in social and political philosophy is H. R. Penniman (ed.), *John Locke on Politics and Education* (New York: Van Nostrand, 1947). The excerpt in the text is taken from *John Locke, The Second Treatise of Government* (Indianapolis: Bobbs-Merrill, 1952). For Locke's theory of natural law as the basis of rights, see John Locke, *Essays on the Law of Nature* (London: Oxford, 1954). For an overview of Locke's philosophy, see Richard I. Aaron, *John Locke* (London: Oxford, 1955).

Mill's most important political writings are *Considerations on Representative Government* (Indianapolis: Bobbs-Merrill, 1958) and *On Liberty* (Indianapolis: Bobbs-Merrill, 1956). For Mill's powerful indictment of discrimination against women in British custom and law, see his *Subjection of Women* (Buffalo, N.Y.: Prometheus, 1986). This essay is a milestone in the struggle for women's rights. A good source of pro and con criticisms of Mill's political thought is David Spitz (ed.), *On Liberty* (New York: Norton, 1975). One of the best collections of Mill's writings is Marshall Cohen (ed.), *The Philosophy of John Stuart Mill* (New York: Modern Library, 1961). For Mill's life, see his *Autobiography* (Indianapolis: Bobbs-Merrill, 1957) and Michael St. James Packe, *The Life of John Stuart Mill* (New York: Capricorn Books, 1970). There are many good collections of the writings of Marx and Engels, including Robert C. Tucker (ed.), *The Marx-Engels Reader* (New York: Norton, 1972) and Lewis S. Feuer (ed.), *Marx and Engels* (Garden City, N.Y.: Doubleday and Co., 1959). Marx's major economic treatise is *Capital* (New York: Modern Library, 1906). A work which many scholars feel ties the early philosophical work of Marx together with his later economic writings is Karl Marx, *The Grundrisse* (New York: Harper & Row, 1971). A superb analysis of the relation of Marx's thought to Hegel is Sidney Hook, *From Hegel to Marx* (Ann Arbor: University of Michigan Press, 1962). Also, for a carefully argued and thorough criticism of Marx's political thought, written in a style and at a level accessible to students without extensive backgrounds in philosophy, see Hook's *Revolution, Reform, and Social Justice* (New York: New York University Press, 1975). There are many excellent interpretations and analyses of Marx; one of the most respected is M. M. Bober,

Karl Marx's Interpretation of History (New York: Norton, 1965). A classical, brief account of Marx's life and intellectual development is Isaiah Berlin, *Karl Marx: His Life and Environment* (London: Oxford, 1963). Probably the single best thorough treatment of Marx's life and thought in one volume is David McClellan, *Karl Marx: His Life and Thought* (New York: Harper & Row, 1973). A much briefer version of this work is David McClellan, *Karl Marx* (New York: Viking, 1975).

For a contemporary critique of Marx's attack on capitalism, see Kelso and Adler, *The Capitalist Manifesto* (Westport, Conn.: Greenwood Press, 1958). Herbert Marcuse argues that capitalism, particularly with the aid of modern advertising, continues to enslave the masses despite the general material prosperity in *One Dimensional Man* (Boston: Beacon Press, 1964). For a call to nonrevolutionary, reformist socialism as the cure to the excesses of corporate capitalism, see Eduard Bernstein, *Evolutionary Socialism* (New York: Schocken Books, 1961). This classic statement of democratic socialism can be read profitably with John Dewey, *Individualism Old and New* (New York: Capricorn Books, 1930) and Norman Thomas, *A Socialist's Faith* (Port Washington, N.Y.: Kennikat Press, 1971). Writings of socialist authors from around the world may be found in Erich Fromm (ed.), *Socialist Humanism* (Garden City, N.Y.: Doubleday, 1966). Advanced students will find fresh and illuminating appraisals of Marx in M. Cohen, T. Nagel, and T. Scanlon (eds.), *Marx, Justice, and History* (Princeton, N.J.: Princeton University Press, 1980).

Probably the two most widely read and discussed books in political philosophy in the recent past are John Rawls, *A Theory of Justice* (Cambridge, Mass.: Harvard, 1971), which presents the case for the welfare state, and Robert Nozick, *Anarchy, State, and Utopia* (New York: Basic Books, 1974), which presents the case for limited democratic (and capitalist) government. Rawls has received widespread attention both by philosophers and social scientists since the publication of *A Theory of Justice.* An excellent introduction to this work is Robert Paul Wolff, *Understanding Rawls* (Princeton, N.J.: Princeton University Press, 1977).

Judith A. Best, *The Mainstream of Western Political Thought* (New York and London: Human Sciences Press, 1980), has well-written summaries and comparisons of major ancient and modern Western political theorists.

Finally, the same basic reference books noted in the previous parts of the text can be consulted by students for a wealth of information about all the main personalities and issues in political philosophy. Those sources are Paul Edwards (ed.), *The Encyclopedia of Philosophy* (New York: Macmillan Free Press, 1967); Philip P. Wiener (ed.), *Dictionary of the History of Ideas* (New York: Scribner, 1974); and G. H. R. Parkinson (ed.), *The Handbook of Western Philosophy* (New York: Macmillan, 1988). The *Encyclopedia* is an eight-volume work; the index appears in volume 8. The *Dictionary* consists of four volumes plus an index. The *Handbook* is a single volume with a table of contents in the beginning and an index at the end.